Designing Games for Ethics:

Models, Techniques and Frameworks

Karen Schrier
Columbia University, USA

David Gibson
Arizona State University, USA

INFORMATION SCIENCE REFERENCE

Hershey · New York

Senior Editorial Director:	Kristin Klinger
Director of Book Publications:	Julia Mosemann
Editorial Director:	Lindsay Johnston
Acquisitions Editor:	Erika Carter
Development Editor:	Myla Harty
Production Coordinator:	Jamie Snavely
Typesetters:	Casey Conapitski & Deanna Zombro
Cover Design:	Nick Newcomer

Published in the United States of America by
Information Science Reference (an imprint of IGI Global)
701 E. Chocolate Avenue
Hershey PA 17033
Tel: 717-533-8845
Fax: 717-533-8661
E-mail: cust@igi-global.com
Web site: http://www.igi-global.com

Library of Congress Cataloging-in-Publication Data

Designing games for ethics : models, techniques and frameworks / Karen Schrier
and David Gibson, editors.
    p. cm.
  Includes bibliographical references and index.
  Summary: "This book brings together the diverse and growing community of
voices on ethics in gaming and begins to define the field, identify its
primary challenges and questions, and establish the current state of the
discipline"--Provided by publisher.

  ISBN 978-1-60960-120-1 (hardcover) -- ISBN 978-1-60960-122-5 (ebook) 1.
Video games--Moral and ethical aspects. 2. Video games--Design. 3. Computer
games--Moral and ethical aspects. 4. Computer games--Design. I. Schrier,
Karen. II. Gibson, David, 1950 Aug. 27-
  GV1469.34.S52D47 2011
  794.8--dc22
                              2010051813

British Cataloguing in Publication Data
A Cataloguing in Publication record for this book is available from the British Library.

Ethan Kennerly
Gary Stoner
Gene Koo
Hanno Hildman
Ian Schreiber
James Diamond
Jamey Stevenson
Jaroslav Svelch
Jennifer Groff
Jessica Bayliss
Jim Preston
Jon Melenson
Jose Zagal
Karen Schrier
Lance Vikaros
Lindsay Grace
Marina Bers
Mia Consalvo
Miguel Sicart
Mitu Khandaker
Nahil Sharkasi
Nathaniel Croce
Nathan Freier
Neha Khetrapal
Peter Rauch
Randy Kulman
Rania Hodhod
Ronah Harris
Ross Fitzgerald
Rudy McDaniel
Sam Gilbert
Scott Leutenegger
Seth Sivak
Sharman Siebenthal Adams
Stephen Balzac
Stephen Jacobs
Susanna Ruiz
Tobi Saulnier

Table of Contents

Section 1
Introducing Ethics and Games

Chapter 1
Mia Consalvo, Massachusetts Institute of Technology, USA
Greg Costikyan, Independent, USA
Drew Davidson, Carnegie Mellon University, USA
Nick Fortugno, Playmatics, USA
David Shaenfield, Columbia University, USA
Pete Vigeant, ESI Design, USA
Christopher Weaver, Massachusetts Institute of Technology and Founder, Bethesda
*   Softworks, USA*
Karen Schrier, Columbia University, USA

Chapter 2
Jose P. Zagal, DePaul University, USA

Chapter 3
Jamey Stevenson, Realtime Worlds, UK

Section 4
Designing for Learning and Development

Section 5
Designing for Social Change and Civic Engagement

Detailed Table of Contents

Section 1
Introducing Ethics and Games

Chapter 1
    Mia Consalvo, Massachusetts Institute of Technology, USA
    Greg Costikyan, Independent, USA
    Drew Davidson, Carnegie Mellon University, USA
    Nick Fortugno, Playmatics, USA
    David Shaenfield, Columbia University, USA
    Pete Vigeant, ESI Design, USA
    Christopher Weaver, Massachusetts Institute of Technology and Founder, Bethesda
        Softworks, USA
    Karen Schrier, Columbia University, USA

In this chapter, seven experts from the games industry and from academia discuss late-breaking and big picture trends in ethics and games. Rather than deep analyses of the issues, these brief perspectives introduce main ideas related to current problems in ethics and games. These quick takes open up discourse on timely topics and ask questions that will lead to new research streams. A microcosm of the entire book, these quick reflections telegraph the themes that will emerge in the rest of the book. First, Mia Consalvo will discusses decision making in Dragon Age; next Greg Costikyan talks about Diplomacy and how game mechanics support ethical behavior. Drew Davidson then provides a meditation on the value of games, Nick Fortugno talks about ethics and Farmville, and educator David Shaenfield looks at new ways to support citizenship skills through gaming. Finally, designer Pete Vigeant gives his personal take on Red Dead Redemption and Bethesda Softworks founder and MIT professor Christopher Weaver unpacks controversies surrounding games.

Chapter 2

Jose P. Zagal, DePaul University, USA

Ethically notable games are those that provide opportunities for encouraging ethical reasoning and reflection. This chapter examines how games can encourage rational and emotional responses. By examining ethically notable videogames, it illustrates a few of the different design choices that can be used to encourage these responses and the effects they have on players. It also identifies five challenges toward creating ethically notable games and examines each in the context of commercially released videogames. Each of these analyses serves as a framework not only for reflecting upon and understanding ethics and morality in games but also for outlining the design space for ethically notable games.

Chapter 3

Jamey Stevenson, Realtime Worlds, UK

For those seeking an entry point into the complex topic of ethical games, a framework for classification and criticism can be a helpful tool, if only to provide a more gentle and coherent introduction to the subject. This chapter provides one such framework, based on identifying the overarching trends in contemporary ethical game design. It provides descriptions and examples of three different categories of ethical games, each of which are then considered within the context of the most prevalent critical flashpoints currently being debated by ethical game designers and detractors alike. By understanding the distinctions between the primary types of ethical games, readers will gain the ability to more effectively delineate which design decisions are likely to make a particular game susceptible to each of the critical pitfalls outlined.

Section 2
Game Design Critiques

Chapter 4

Jonathan Melenson, Aptify, USA

Many games classify player decisions as either "good" or "evil." This ignores the full range of moral behavior exhibited in real life and creates a false dichotomy: morally gray actions are overlooked or forced into one category or the other. The way actions are assigned to each category is subjective and biased toward the developers' own moral beliefs. The result is a system that fails to capture ethical nuance and take morality seriously. This chapter examines how a good-and-evil moral framework compromises gameplay, and then proposes a solution.

This chapter discusses ethical dilemmas and their role in game design. The chapter first defines what ethical dilemmas are and then argues for why they are compelling in games. This argument will analyze the role of decisions in games, what makes for interesting decisions, and then address how avatars and the magic circle nature of games indulge several kinds of fun while still having players experience a sense of moral residue. Finally, the chapter will provide recommendations on how designers can incorporate and analyze ethical dilemmas into their own games, tying our recommendations to examples to show how ethical dilemmas can provide interesting gameplay.

Chapter 6

This chapter argues for a game design ethic for war game production and the development of games that produce a more realistic and conscientious critique of warfare, defined as antiwar and conscientious war games. Given the medium's preponderance toward narratives and simulations of military conflict, there are surprisingly few works that seriously examine its consequences. This chapter surveys and critiques several existing antiwar and conscientious war games and examines design problems associated with exploring antiwar narratives. It concludes with an exploration of areas in which both new antiwar games can be developed and existing war games can be modified to produce conscientious messages about war. Artists and designers should have a vested interest in producing antiwar games to both enrich the medium and improve society by inspiring audiences to seek alternatives to conflict.

In God of War, the protagonist Kratos seeks revenge against the Ares of Greek mythology. As Kratos, the player is called upon to act in a manner reminiscent of Nietzsche's "master morality," reveling in power unrestricted by concern for any "objective" moral code or sympathy for his fellow man. The structure of the action/adventure genre in which God of War operates is particularly well-suited to this kind of morality. With one hero amid a world of disposable non-player characters, punctuated by the occasional appearance of a "boss" figure that behaves more like Kratos, a stark distinction is made between the powerful and the weak. This dichotomy is at the heart of Nietzsche's master/slave distinction. Kratos and Ares seek to inspire fear; the hordes of disposable Athenians they both slaughter so carelessly seek only to avoid it. In allowing gamers to "play with" a moral worldview so starkly defined, God of War becomes a valuable tool for investigating and critiquing moral ideas in general.

Section 3
Design, Production, and Use of Games

This chapter demonstrates how legal concepts, accepted practices, and research in reverse engineering (a process of disassembling a system to understand how it works) can provide ethical and legal outlets for end-users. The game industry has influenced reverse engineering law and practice, challenging ethical practices in industry, academia, and with end-users. Although these communities supposedly rely on legal precedents, actual laws are often misunderstood, ignored, or just unknown. The communities continually struggle to balance the protection of intellectual property with consumer freedom, and reverse engineering demonstrates this conflict. We demonstrate how a variety of communities embrace reverse engineering through a series of case studies involving current commercial games and technology. The case studies include the modding community, massively-multiplayer online game community tools, digital preservation, and reverse engineering education. Although a clear ruling on legality eludes the field, we conclude with suggestions on dealing with ethical and legal aspects surrounding this issue.

This chapter introduces critical gameplay design as a technique for creating digital games that offer alternative play. Critical gameplay provides the opportunity to explore game ethics through the way games are designed to be played. Since game designers outline the rules of play, game designs outline designer's definitions of what is ethical and important. Taking the notion that design is a reflection of the designer's values, this chapter outlines methodologies for exposing the intrinsic values in play and creating gameplay models from alternative ethics and values. The chapter concludes with examples of critical gameplay games that have been demonstrated to international audience.

Novel kinesthetic and mimetic video game interfaces, such as the Wii Remote, PlayStation Move, and Microsoft Kinect, are seeing widespread mainstream appeal. However, with games ranging from the family-friendly Rock Band series, to the banned Manhunt 2, this chapter discusses the ethical implications of interfaces that seek to increase the verisimilitude of our game experiences, and offers a position from which to further consider the controller as an integral part of the overall game design.

Chapter 11

Adrienne Shaw, University of Pennsylvania, USA

Often, literature on the representation of marginalized groups in videogames focuses on how groups have been and should be portrayed in games. Taking a different focus, this chapter offers a broader ethical basis for the production and critique of games. It begins by outlining the issues surrounding the representation of marginalized groups (focusing on sexuality, gender and race) in digital games. It then addresses the ethical importance of representation in games as fictional play spaces. Moving from there, the writings on hospitality, recognition, and truthfulness are examined with regard to the representation of marginalized groups in games. It then uses these concepts to create an integrated ethical argument for diversity in videogames that takes into account gameplay, representation, and their relationship.

Section 4
Designing for Learning and Development

Chapter 12

Nathan G. Freier, Rensselaer Polytechnic Institute, USA
Emilie T. Saulnier, 1st Playable Productions, USA

This chapter discusses the significant role that virtual worlds, particularly massively multiplayer online games (MMOGs), such as Club Penguin and World of Warcraft, play in the social and moral development of children and adolescents. A central argument of the chapter is that MMOGs and other virtual worlds provide a new backyard within which children and adolescents engage in active social interaction and play out moral dilemmas. It discusses three important areas of development in the context of interactions in MMOGs. First, it explores the process of perspective-taking, which is an important factor in empathy and pro-social behavior. Second, it explores the impact that MMOGs might have on stereotyping behavior and the phenomenon of stereotype threat, a harmful outcome of stereotyping behavior. Finally, it considers the role of moral dilemmas in development and how MMOGs provide unique environments for social and moral problem solving.

Chapter 13

Randy Kulman, LearningWorks for Kids, USA
Gary Stoner, University of Rhode Island, USA
Louis Ruffolo, University of Rhode Island, USA
Stephanie Marshall, University of Rhode Island, USA
Jennifer Slater, University of Rhode Island, USA
Amanda Dyl, University of Rhode Island, USA
Alice Cheng, University of Rhode Island, USA

Numerous studies support the contention that videogames can be useful in developing specific attention and memory skills. Videogames and other digital technologies also require the practice of critical-thinking and executive-functioning skills, but there is little evidence that these skills, which lead to decision-making and problem-solving skills, can be generalized from the game to the real world. This chapter examines strategies that use videogames to enhance the development of these problem-solving and ethical decision-making skills. This chapter discusses the use of these strategies with a clinical population of children with Attention Deficit Hyperactivity Disorder (ADHD) and learning disabilities and considers methods for parents, teachers, and game publishers to make popular videogames a potent teaching tool for developing decision-making skills in children.

Chapter 14

Rania Hodhod, University of York, UK
Paul Cairns, University of York, UK
Daniel Kudenko, University of York, UK

Promoting ethical, responsible, and caring behavior in young people is a perennial aim of education. Schools are invited to include moral teaching in every possible curriculum. Efforts have been made to find non-traditional ways of teaching such as games or role play or engaging students in moral dilemmas. However, classroom environments need to consider time constraints, curriculum standards, and differing children's personalities. Computer systems can offer rich environments that detect and respond to student knowledge gaps, misconceptions, and variable affective states. This chapter presents AEINS, an adaptive narrative-based educational game that helps the teaching of basic ethical virtues to young children to promote character education. The central goal is to engage students in a dynamic narrative environment and to involve them in different moral dilemmas (teaching moments) that use the Socratic method as the predominant pedagogy. The authors argue that AEINS incorporates appropriate game design principles and successfully manages the interaction between the narrative level and the tutoring level to maximize student learning. Moreover, it is able to convey the moral skills to its users, as shown in the evaluation.

Chapter 15

Ross FitzGerald, Shady Hill School, USA
Jennifer Groff, Futurelab, UK

Ethical and moral development is a result of cognitive structures generated through experience in the pivotal stage of adolescence, during which formal education plays a critical role. Recent advancements in cognitive psychology have explored the very nature of moral development, as well as the critical role education plays in that development. Digital games are potentially powerful learning environments to shape moral development for students. This chapter describes two case studies of digital games used in a middle school classroom to enhance moral development. Finally, it reflects upon and analyzes these cases using the developmental theories of Robert Selman and others as a framework.

Section 5
Designing for Social Change and Civic Engagement

Chapter 16

Andrea Gunraj, The Metropolitan Action Committee on Violence Against Women and Children, Canada
Susana Ruiz, University of Southern California & Take Action Games, USA
Ashley York, University of Southern California & Take Action Games, USA

This chapter defines basic principles of anti-oppression and its ethical implications. Anti-oppression is a framework used in social work and community organizing that broadly challenges power imbalances between different groups of people in society. This chapter positions these principles in the realm of game creation and argue for their use—particularly in the development of social issue games that in one way or another seek to spotlight and challenge social power imbalances. While the chapter outlines some essential theory, it ultimately takes a practice-based perspective to make a case for and support the incorporation of anti-oppressive principles in game design and development. It features the work of five organizations from around the world about their strategies for implementing equity in game/interactive design and development, and closes with broad guidelines to support integration of anti-oppression principles in game creation.

Chapter 17

Nahil Sharkasi, University of Southern California, USA

In the field of fertility medicine, technology has vastly outpaced our ethical, legal, and social frameworks leaving us in a quagmire of gray morality. Seeds is a role-playing game and ethics simulation about Assisted Reproductive Technology and its effect on 21st century medical decisions. Players play the role of a fertility doctor and must make difficult ethical decisions through courses of treatment while balancing economic, emotional, and scientific concerns. With Seeds, the goal is to foster meaningful decision-making that may transfer from the game world into the real world through stimulating role-play and by creating a safe space for exploration of ethical issues. This chapter offers critical reflection on the design choices made in the process of creating this ethical exploration space on the subject of Assisted Reproductive Technology.

Chapter 18

Sharman Siebenthal Adams, University of Michigan-Flint, USA
Jeremiah Holden, InGlobal, USA

This chapter examines ethical ambiguities confronted by the design and play of serious games focused on civic engagement. Our findings derive from our examination of two educational simulation games that focus on contemporary issues related to social and political conflict. We believe game simulations are complex in nature and offer particularly rich environments for cognitive learning. Within the following chapter we examine the relationship between games and learning, specific approaches to game design, and the ability of games to encourage civic engagement. While we found that game participants gained knowledge of curricular content and practiced democratic skills during their experiences with the online simulations, there also occurred unintended consequences. In turn, we believe it is critical to analyze deeper ethical ambiguities related to the consequences of civic-minded game design and gameplay and support research efforts to further recognize and expand upon the development and research of serious games involving civic-minded educational online simulations.

While gaming technologies are typically leveraged for entertainment purposes, our experience and aspiration is to use them to encourage engagement with global, politically-sensitive issues. This chapter focuses on our game design concerning the struggle of Uganda, a design that allows players to experience the atrocities and inhumane conditions and, by illuminating such values as peace and justice, helps them more generally to appreciate the moral complexity of a humane intervention. Rather than theoretical constructs to be debated in the abstract, the ethical struggles involved in determining a humane intervention in the game setting are grounded in different Non-Player Characters' perspectives and operationalized within the underlying game dynamics. Beyond reporting on the designed game, the chapter draws the reader into the struggles of designing such an ethically contentious game.

Foreword

It is a great privilege to be able to write a few prefatory words about Designing Games for Ethics: Models, Techniques, and Frameworks. Games are one of the most powerful and durable new forms of popular culture for the information age. More and more, the challenging models of mastery, which are embodied in all games, are being explicitly applied to games for learning. What Karen Schrier and David Gibson have done in bringing these contributions together is asked us to think about the ethics of what it means to design games and to think of how we can design games that help us to explore and understand ethics.

Media theorist Henry Jenkins has addressed the dual challenges of encoding a moral vision into a game and developing moral frameworks around the experience of playing a game. He notes that "…the first requires an intervention on the level of design, or encouraging the people who make the games to take seriously their potential as a medium for exploring ethical issues. The second requires an intervention on the level of education, or fostering a mode of play that encourages players to use games to perform meaningful thought experiments and using them as a vehicle through which to explore and refine their own emerging ethical perspectives." This collection of articles expands upon the designer-educator theme and brings to readers the personal journeys of researchers, developers, and explorers.

The essays in this collection focus on the challenges Jenkins identifies, and also extend beyond those to other different, interlocking issues and questions. How do we design the best possible games for fostering ethical thinking in an urgent and timely manner? What theories help us understand the ethical imperatives of the stories, rules, systems, worlds, and images we design? Are there methodologies developed in other fields that we might appropriate for the study of the ethics of game design? How do we weigh the relative impact of images and narrative, and rules and systems, and what is the relationship of all of these to the actual experience of playing a game, including the mechanics and qualities that make a game exciting? Since both narrative and game rules are intertwined, what are the signs of effective integration? How do we measure "effectiveness" in ethical terms? What about the social aspects of play—how do the norms and values of an online world or offline peer group inform our experiences? What are the inherent dangers as well as potentials?

There are also specific cultural factors to be included. For example, how are marginalized groups served or harmed more by a game that focuses on their characteristic struggles? One ethical issue all game designers confront relates to violence in games. What is the line between realism and violence, especially when portraying those in economically-disadvantaged worlds? Is there a way for violence to be a subject of ethical inquiry for the game player without being exploitative? Why is the very notion of violence in games so controversial in our society?

Similarly, in what ways does gender factor into the discussion of ethics in gaming? A world without girls and women is hardly ethical, but how does one represent females in games in a way that is egalitarian and appropriate given the way that many forms of popular culture, including game culture, feature and sometimes exploit sexuality so flagrantly? Simply representing females without conventional beauty prescriptions circumvents one set of problems, while introducing equally problematic ethical concerns.

None of these are easy questions, and none of the answers are simple either. These essays often combine the scholarly with the experiential, and, in some cases, game designers learn lessons in the course of trying to teach ethics. More than one author, for example, sets out on the educational path, determined to "teach an ethical lesson" through a game, only to wind up learning a lesson instead. That experience helped them to add complexity and nuance to their original conceptions, and perhaps even to their early idea of what does or does not constitute an "ethical" game dilemma. What will their next game development idea involve as a result? Will they begin with an historical event or a situation where history will be made through peer-to-peer pedagogy? Other authors examine the impact of immersive reality on deciding among multiple perspectives. Such an experience can heighten the discomfort of leaving aside one's initial ethical positions, to accept the legitimacy of another's point of view. Does such an experience expand the definition and cultural value of a game?

We have entered a new era, with constantly evolving platforms for communication and learning, and we concomitantly innovative ways to think about game design, game play, game practice, and game mechanics. These essays lead the way, offering us many new possibilities in digital games and simulations. No one can predict what the games of the future will be. That's as it should be. Uncertainty, intrigue, problems, and challenges that require on-the-spot decision making are the heart of game mechanics and are also at the heart of this serious, thoughtful, imaginative, and challenging inquiry into Designing Games for Ethics.

Cathy N. Davidson
Ruth F. DeVarney Professor of English and John Hope Franklin Humanities Institute Professor of Interdisciplinary Studies
Duke University
www.hastac.org
www.dmlcompetition.net

Cathy N. Davidson *is the Ruth F. DeVarney Professor of English and the John Hope Franklin Humanities Institute Professor of Interdisciplinary Studies at Duke University. Her work for the last decade has focused on the role of technology in the twenty-first century. In 1999 she helped create ISIS (the program in Information Science + Information Studies) at Duke University and, in 2002, co-founded HASTAC (Humanities, Arts, Science, and Technology Advanced Collaboratory, pronounced "haystack"), an international network of networks with now over 4500 members. Her MacArthur research (with HASTAC co-founder David Theo Goldberg) was hosted on the interactive Institute for the Future of the Book website and then published as MacArthur report, The Future of Learning Institutions in a Digital Age (MIT Press). From 1998 until 2006, Davidson served as Vice Provost for Interdisciplinary Studies at Duke and she was a founding co-director of the John Hope Franklin Humanities Institute. Davidson is the author or editor of some twenty books on wide-ranging topics including technology, the history of reading and writing, literary studies, travel, Japan, Native American writing, electronic publishing, and the future of learning in a digital age. Her forthcoming book is Now You See It: The Science of Attention in the Classroom, at Work, and Everywhere Else (forthcoming, Viking Press, 2011). Davidson blogs regularly on new media and learning as Cat in the Stack at www.hastac.org.*

Preface

Designing Games for Ethics: Models, Techniques, and Frameworks is the second book in a two-volume series addressing an emerging field of study: ethics and games. It's only been nine months since finishing the first book in this two-part series, *Ethics and Game Design: Teaching Values through Play*, yet so much has changed. And as I give birth to the second book, I note that the questions we raised in the first volume have become even more urgent and timely: How do we better design and use games to foster ethical thinking and discourse? What are the theories and methodologies that will help us understand, model, and assess ethical thinking in and around games? What do games tell us about our ethics? What are the ethics surrounding the creation, deployment and use of games? How are cultural values and beliefs represented in games? How do we use games in classrooms and informal educational settings to support moral development? This publication is the first academic collection to address these questions.

Ethics is a system of choices and moral judgments that are thought to achieve the life of a good human being (Sicart, 2005), as well as an individual behavior; the process of making choices according to one's own conception of how to be a "good" person. Games, while highly varied in form and function, are rule-based systems with "variable and quantifiable outcomes; where different outcomes are assigned different values; where the players exert effort in order to influence the outcome ... and the consequences of the activity are optional and negotiable" (Juul, 2005). When we put the two together—ethics and games—the result is more than the sum of the parts. While there are many ways to explore the intersection of games and ethics, this book covers three key areas of the field: (1) how we can design and use games to better support ethical thinking, reasoning, empathy, and citizenship; (2) what are the ethics of creating games, including their production, development, and distribution; (3) how are values reflected and propagated through play, for example, through the cultural practices related to gaming, discourses surrounding gaming, or through interacting with individual games as texts, media or artifacts.

Ethical reasoning, reflection, and discourse have always been an essential component of nurturing a healthy, diverse citizenship. In fact, these skills are necessary for navigating our globally interconnected, rapidly evolving world. We need to be able to analyze, empathize, make decisions about values, identify biases, and reflect on one's beliefs, and assess other's perspectives as an engaged, informed citizenship within a diverse democracy such as our own. And, as new forms of cultural expression emerge and access expands to new participatory (and global) cultures, both young people and adults need to be adept at negotiating ethical dilemmas in ever-changing environments and communities. More and more young people are becoming media producers, as well as consumers, yet they may not understand how to manage and negotiate ethical dilemmas, or how to behave in participatory communities (Jenkins, 2006). With these cultural changes occurring, educators are struggling with how to teach these essential skills to their students and integrate them into curricula (Schrier and Kinzer, 2009).

Yet, today, the notion of games and ethics often sparks controversy over games themselves. For example, some scholarship today focuses on whether videogames are too violent, or if they too powerfully influence the creation of bad values—evoking similar reactions as film, comic books, television, rap, and rock music when they were introduced. In this book series, we seek to look beyond whether games are inherently good or bad, and instead think about how people negotiate values, and how play might foster reflection on one's own, society's or a particular game's ethics. The authors in this collection want to understand the potential for games to motivate and develop thought about ethics and values, and not how to use games to prescribe a dose of "proper values." After all, societal values evolve, norms change, and ethics differ from culture to culture. Simply indoctrinating citizens with good values for one specific moment and social context is not going to help them navigate complicated questions within other situations or circumstances. Social and global issues are complex and the answers are never clear. We need global citizens who can think deeply about choices, fully engage with complicated issues, reflect on their values, and decide what is right for them, their families, their societies and the world—today, tomorrow and yesterday.

This book is about developing engaged, informed citizens, not just by using games themselves, but through the study and practice of games and game cultures. As games become increasingly embedded into everyday life, understanding the ethics of their creation and use, as well as their potential for practicing ethical thinking, becomes more relevant. That means helping equip designers, developers, players, purchasers, writers of games with a deeper understanding of the ethics of gaming, game production, and distribution. For example, game publishers, parents, journalists, players, policy makers, and creators want to understand the ethical issues surrounding games and game play, such as the use of gaming hardware for other purposes, cheating in games, or the representation of violence, gender, race, and sex in games.

Moreover, commercial game developers are increasingly integrating moral choices into off-the-shelf games, such as the *Fable, Fallout* and *Mass Effect* series, enabling—with mixed results—players to grapple with real-world ethical issues within a fictional game world. The popularity and growing ethical complexity of newer games, such as *Heavy Rain, Red Dead Redemption* and *Dragon Age*, all released since the first book in this series, show that developers are seeking ways to incorporate ethical landscapes into their designs, and audiences are intrigued.

I wrote in the first book's preface that the notion that games can help people reflect on values is both innovative and as old as humankind. Play has always been a way to allow people to experiment with other perspectives, to reenact scenarios and possibilities, to practice collaborating and competing, and to try out different roles. One way to support play is through games. I argue that games may be particularly well-suited to the practice and development of ethical thinking, since, for example, the computationally rich media platform offers the ability to iterate and reflect on multiple possibilities and consequences (Schrier and Gibson, 2010). Games also provide a virtually authentic content within which to practice and experience ethical dilemmas and decision making. They enable players to reflect on their decisions and outcomes, and allow them to consider the implications of their choices, without many of the risks of real-world consequences (Schrier and Kinzer, 2009).

A few weeks ago, I had this extremely vivid dream. In it, I inhabited another person, who looked just like me, but had much different histories, experiences, beliefs and values than my own. I was a jewel thief, and at the moment I entered the dream, I was evading the police, deleting incriminating files off of my laptop, and then happily escaping with the expensive gems. I was embodying a totally different ethical and emotional system, one which led me to feel no remorse about stealing priceless heirlooms. My dream allowed me to experience a totally new perspective, one that I would never be able to (nor would want to) access in my everyday life. Luckily, I woke up from the dream without having to experience any of the consequences of stealing jewels, but I still can remember what it was like to inhabit a new ethical identity.

I feel that games have the potential to evoke this, and to engage the imagination in a way that you feel like you really are a jewel thief, or a renegade, or a paragon, or any of the millions of possibilities in between. Being able to access a diversity of ethical perspectives is perhaps even necessary for fully appreciating humanity, life, and beyond.

I observe that as we delve deeper into this new field of ethics and games, it ultimately invites us to reevaluate what it means to be human and gain insight into our own humanity. Through games, and play, we are seeking new ways to experience the world, to understand humankind, to reflect on our identities, our destinies, our pasts, and our mysteries. We may never fully answer these questions, but hopefully games will help us begin to approach them.

A major goal of this collection is to bring together the diverse and growing community of voices and begin to define the field, identify its primary challenges and questions, and establish the current state of the discipline. Such a rigorous, collaborative, and holistic foundation for the study of ethics and games is necessary to appropriately inform future games, policies, standards, and curricula. This new discipline invites, and even requires, a variety of different perspectives, frameworks, and critiques—from computer science, education, philosophy, law, game design, learning theory, media studies, management, cognitive science, psychology, and art history (Gibson and Baek, 2009).

Thus, each author in this volume uses a unique perspective to frame the problem: some implement cognitive or social psychology methodologies, others come from a design background, some focus on pedagogical theories, while others employ a philosophical angle. Some are game designers and practitioners, others are researchers, and still others theorists; many are hybrids of all three. We hope this multidisciplinary approach will serve readers who want to view ethics and games from other perspectives, and use those perspectives to inform their own research directions. The following is an overview of the chapters in this first volume of the collection:

In Chapter 1, *Quick Takes on Ethics and Games: Voices from Industry and Academia*, I curated a medley of reflections and perspectives in the field of ethics and games. The contributors—Mia Consalvo, Greg Costikyan, Drew Davidson, Nick Fortugno, David Shaenfield, Pete Vigeant, and Christopher Weaver—are experts in their fields, and each have a unique point of view on the major themes of this book. Rather than deep analyses of the issues, these are brief meditations on the main ideas related to current problems in ethics and games.

Chapter 2, Jose Zagal's *Ethical Reasoning and Reflection as Supported by Single-Player Videogames* sets the stage for thinking about how to better design and use games to foster ethical reasoning and reflection. The author, a professor at DePaul University, gives a broad overview of the theoretical frameworks on ethics and morality, focusing on what he calls "ethically notable videogames," or games that involve ethical decision making and story lines. He looks specifically at a few ethically notable commercial games, including *Ultima IV, Manhunt,* and *Fire Emblem: Radiant Dawn*.

In Chapter 3, Jamey Stevenson lays out a general framework for classifying and critiquing ethics games, to help practitioners and academics better navigate the topic of ethics and games. He uses this framework to then introduce and unpack some of the major issues and debates surrounding the design of games for ethics. He also uses this to recommend ways to make games more ethically engaging.

After setting the stage for the book's themes, the next chapters offer in-depth analyses of current games and gaming environments, and consider how ethical choices, morality and values are incorporated into a game's design and experience. In Chapter 4, Jonathan Melenson, in his *The Axis of Good and Evil*, offers a critique of current games, and their inclusion of ethical dilemmas and decision making. He argues that games need to expand to include choices that are more morally gray. To do this, he looks at games such *Fable II*, *Mass Effect*, and *Fallout III* as well as examples of other forms of popular culture, such as movies and books.

Chapter 5 complements Melenson's arguments. *Ethical Dilemmas in Gameplay: Choosing Between Right and Right*, Ian Schreiber, Bryan Cash, and Link Hughes discuss the state of ethics games today, and how to better innovate the ways ethical dilemmas are incorporated into games. They specifically look at games such as *BioShock*, *PeaceMaker*, *The Suffering*, *Silent Hill 2*, *Mass Effect*, *Splinter Cell: Pandora Tomorrow*, *Dragon Age*, and *Knights of the Old Republic*. They developed their recommendations when convening at Project Horseshoe, a conference that encouraged a mini-think tank on issues of gameplay and ethics.

In Chapter 6, *War and Play: Insensitivity and Humanity in the Realm of Pushbutton Warfare*, Devin Monnens argues for a more conscientious design of war in games. In investigating a variety of war games, including *Drop Zone 4*, *Cannon Fodder*, and *Metal Gear Solid 3: Snake Eater*, Monnens defines and critiques, what he calls, wargames and antiwar games. He also looks at approaches to antiwar games, such as *September 12th*, *Giant Tank*, and *Train*, and develops a set of recommendations for designers of war games.

Chapter 7, Peter Rauch's *God of War: What is it Good For? Nietzsche's "Master Morality" and the Single-Player Action/Adventure Genre*, takes a more philosophical approach to game design critique. In this chapter, Rauch provides a close reading of *God of War* using Nietzsche's "Master Morality" concept. He then broadens the scope by showing how this critique can be used to reflect on humanity, and to help us design better ethics games.

The next chapters hone in on the way that games are developed, used, and played, and the cultural, sociological and historical issues around gaming and game creation. In Chapter 8, *The Ethics of Reverse Engineering for Game Technology*, David Schwartz and Jessica Bayliss look into the legal concepts, cultural practices, and sociological issues surrounding the process of reverse engineering game systems to understand how it works, and to use it for a variety of purpose. They provide a series of case studies to elucidate the complex questions that reverse engineering raises, and posit suggestions on approaching these issues.

Chapter 9, Lindsay Grace's *Critical Gameplay: Design Techniques and Case Studies*, defines critical gameplay design techniques. This chapter raises important considerations and techniques when designing games for ethics, by considering the social, cultural and psychological aspects of game play. He provides a clear framework for reflecting on and evaluating a game's mechanics. His examples are supported using a number of well- and lesser-known games such as *The Sims*, *King of the Mountain*, *Levity*, and *I Wanna Be the Guy*.

Mitu Khandaker, in Chapter 10, *How Games Can Touch You: Ethics of the Video Game Controller*, expands our perspective on games by looking specific on the kinesthetic and mimetic videogame interfaces, such as the Wii Remote and *Guitar Hero* or *Rock Band* instruments. By looking at games such as *Manhunt 2* and *Rock Band*, she uncovers the ethical implications of these interfaces.

In Chapter 11, *Toward an Ethic of Representation: Ethics and the Representation of Marginalized Groups in Videogames*, Adrienne Shaw moves the question of how we should represent marginalized groups in videogames to more broadly addressing understanding the issues of representation in games. She creatively uses theories from hospitality, recognition and truthfulness to lay out her arguments.

In the next section, the contributors look at the question of how to better design games for learning and supporting ethical thinking, reasoning and reflection. In Chapter 12, Nathan Freier and Emilie Saulnier discuss the moral and social development of children and adolescents, particularly as it relates to virtual worlds and massively multiplayer online games (MMOGs). They specifically look at *Club Penguin* and *World of Warcraft*, and reflect specifically on ways they might affect perspective-taking skills, stereotyping behavior, and social and moral problem solving abilities.

Randy Kulman, Gary Stoner, Louis Ruffolo, Stephanie Marshall, Jennifer Slater, Amanda Dyl, and Alice Cheng collaborate in Chapter 13, *Teaching Executive Functions, Self-Management, and Ethical Decision-Making through Popular Video Game Play*. In this chapter, they look at the ways games might help support attention and memory skills, which can enhance ethical thinking and decision making skills, particularly for those who have Attention Deficit Hyperactivity Disorder (ADHD) and learning disabilities.

In Chapter 14, researchers Rania Hodhod, Paul Cairns and Daniel Kudenko, in *Fostering Character Education with Games and Interactive Story Generation*, investigate how their novel educational game, AEINS, may support the teaching of ethical virtues and promote character education. They discuss the theoretical framework underlying the game's creation, as well as their design process and results.

In Chapter 15, *Leveraging Digital Games for Moral Development in Education: A Practitioner's Reflection*, Ross FitzGerald and Jennifer Groff take a practical approach to use games to teach ethics. Using a moral and cognitive development perspective, they describe two case studies of in-classroom use of ethics games. They tested two games, *Diplomacy* and *Civilization IV: Colonization at the Shady Hill*, a pre-K to 8 grade school in Cambridge, Massachusetts.

Finally, in the last section, the contributors investigate how games might promote social change and citizenship skills. In Chapter 16, *Power to the People: Anti-Oppressive Game Design*, Andrea Gunraj, Susana Ruiz and Ashley York explain the principles of anti-oppression and how they could be incorporated into game design. To do this, they interview four organizations—Take Action Games, the Metropolitan Action Committee on Violence Against Women and Children, Values @ Play, Global Kids, and Molleindustria—and from this, develop a set of guidelines to support integration of anti-oppression principles.

In Chapter 17, *The Doctor Will Be You Now: A Case Study on Medical Ethics and Role Play*, Nahil Sharkasi describes her novel game, *Seeds*, and how it supports ethical decision making. *Seeds* is a role-playing game and ethics simulation about Assisted Reproductive Technology and its effect on 21st century medical decisions. In her chapter, she reflects on her design choices, and recommends future directions.

In Chapter 18, *Games, Ethics and Engagement: Potential Consequences of Civic-minded Game Design and Gameplay*, Sharman Siebenthal Adams and Jeremiah Holden examine the potential for games to support citizenship and civic engagement. To do this, they looked deeply into the ways players interacted with *The Arab Israeli Conflict* and *First Wind*, both web-based games.

To conclude the book, in Chapter 19, Sasha Barab, Tyler Dodge, Edward Gentry, Asmalina Saleh and Patrick Pettyjohn describe a novel game in *Uganda's Road to Peace May Run through the River of Forgiveness: Designing Playable Fictions to Teach Complex Values*. In this compelling chapter, they describe a game design focused on the struggle of Uganda, called *River of Justice*. They provide a close reflection on their design choices, and explicate a list of lessons learned and implications.

My hope is that this book collection will continue to inspire interdisciplinary dialogue and research, and further strengthen the ethics and games community, and more broadly, the global community.

Karen Schrier
Columbia University, USA

REFERENCES

Gibson, D., & Baek, Y. (Eds.). (2009). Digital simulations for improving education: Learning through artificial teaching environments. Hershey, PA: IGI Global.

Jenkins, H., Clinton, K., Purushotma, R., Robison, A., & Weigel, M. (2006). Confronting the challenges of participatory culture: Media education for the 21st century. Chicago, IL: MacArthur Foundation.

Juul, Jesper. (2006). Half-Real. Video games between real rules and fictional worlds. Cambridge, MA: MIT Press.

Schrier, K. and Gibson, D. (2010). Ethics and game design: Teaching values through play, Hershey, PA: IGI.

Schrier, K. and Kinzer, C. (2009) Using digital games to develop ethical teachers in D. Gibson (Ed). Digital simulations for improving education: Learning through artificial teaching environments, Hershey, PA: IGI.

Sicart, M. (2005). Game, player, ethics: A virtue ethics approach to computer games. International Review of Information Ethics, 5, 14-18.

Acknowledgment

It's not easy to pull together a cohesive, holistic collection of research to serve as a foundation for a new field of study. To do so, we need to bring together the appropriate voices, contextualize the relevant theories and methodologies, and frame the right questions. Such an effort must acknowledge the many complexities of the field, while also keeping the content accessible to a wide audience. Moreover, the study of ethics and games has additional challenges—it requires practitioners, researchers, and theorists from diverse disciplines to help define the field. Yet it is the very need for multidisciplinary lenses that makes the field of ethics and games so interesting and appealing. I believe this study—and the perspectives it brings—will truly innovate our thinking about what it means to be human in the 21st century.

Currently, there are numerous disparate centers, organizations, individuals, departments, consortia and labs that, despite their different origins, are working to better understand the question of how to use games to support ethical thinking and values discourse. I thank them for their groundbreaking efforts in approaching these complex questions. I am inspired by their enthusiasm, and motivated to continue to bring together this community. I am eager to see what they discover about ethics and games, and what it tells us about our humanity.

I want to thank my parents, Janet and Steven Schrier, and my brother and sister-in-law, David and Tracy Schrier, for providing endless encouragement, lots of love and humor, and moral support. My interest in games and ethics comes from the values and passions they continue to share with me. I would like to thank my grandparents, Anne and Bernard Berner, who were always happy to play card and board games with me.

I am continually encouraged by my husband-to-be, David Shaenfield. His passion for education, playfulness, and insight into the field inspire me each day. His support, advice, editing ability and knowledge have been invaluable throughout this book's development process. David emailed me last year after he heard about the first book in this series, Ethics and Game Design: Teaching Values through Play, and wanted to learn more about it. As a result, we started sharing our work, and getting to know each other better. Thus, this book series—and our shared interest in teaching ethical and citizenship skills—ultimately brought us together. My goal in editing the collection was to bring together disparate voices and perspectives, and to form a community that could share ideas about an essential new discipline. And although, when I was editing the first book, I did not realize that it would lead to such a joyous outcome, I did envision that it would encourage cross-disciplinary collaborations and serendipitous interactions. I hope this book series will bring readers those types of special partnerships, just as it has done for me.

I also want to thank my friends and colleagues in the games industry, including the members of the International Game Developers Association (IGDA), who continually reinvigorate my passion for developing, writing about, and playing games. Their insight and enthusiasm helps me remember why games are so meaningful to me. I especially thank the community for hosting a panel and party to celebrate Ethics and Game Design: Teaching Values through Play. Big thanks in particular to the panel participants: Nick Fortugno, David Langendoen, Colleen Macklin, Lance Vikaros, and IGDA head Wade Tinney.

A huge thank you to my co-editor, David Gibson, a leader in the field of ethics and games, who provided enormous help with everything from envisioning the book's themes, to shaping each author's contribution. Ever since he was editor of my first published chapter, he has provided a huge amount of support and encouragement. I would not have been able to conceive of and then accomplish this book without him.

I want to thank my past and present graduate advisors, who have helped shape my ideas and inspired me to continue to pursue this field of study. Henry Jenkins III, my mentor while I was a graduate student at MIT, who has been extremely supportive of this effort. Chris Dede, from the Harvard Graduate School of Education, has provided tons of encouragement and advice throughout the years. My current doctoral advisor, Charles Kinzer, at Columbia University, is extremely supportive of my endeavors in school and beyond. He served on the editorial board of this publication, and was my co-author on the chapter where I first began to imagine the possibilities for delving into the field of ethics and games.

I am very grateful to the editors and staff at IGI Global for their professionalism, encouragement and care. I truly enjoyed working with the editors, including Dave, Myla, Tyler, Jan, Christine, Kristin, and Katy. I especially want to thank the marketing department and particularly Greg Guenther for all of his help.

I would like to thank the members of the editorial advisory board—Mia Consalvo, Nathaniel Croce, Drew Davidson, Stephen Jacobs, Charles Kinzer, David Shaenfield and Jose Zagal. They helped immensely in judging and reviewing the contributions, and are themselves inspirational leaders in the field of games. Finally, I want to thank all the contributors to this volume, who each worked tirelessly to write thoughtful and unique chapters, and whose research will help to shape this exciting new field.

Karen Schrier
Columbia Universtiy, USA

Section 1
Introducing Ethics and Games

Chapter 1
Quick Takes on Ethics and Games:
Voices from Industry and Academia

Mia Consalvo
Massachusetts Institute of Technology, USA

Greg Costikyan
Independent, USA

Drew Davidson
Carnegie Mellon University, USA

Nick Fortugno
Playmatics, USA

David Shaenfield
Columbia University, USA

Pete Vigeant
ESI Design, USA

Christopher Weaver
*Massachusetts Institute of Technology and
Founder, Bethesda Softworks, USA*

Karen Schrier
Columbia University, USA

ABSTRACT

In this chapter, seven experts from the games industry and from academia discuss late-breaking and big picture trends in ethics and games. Rather than deep analyses of the issues, these brief perspectives introduce main ideas related to current problems in ethics and games. These quick takes open up discourse on timely topics and ask questions that will lead to new research streams. A microcosm of the entire book, these quick reflections telegraph the themes that will emerge in the rest of the book. First, Mia Consalvo will discusses decision making in Dragon Age; next Greg Costikyan talks about Diplomacy and how game mechanics support ethical behavior. Drew Davidson then provides a meditation on the value of games, Nick Fortugno talks about ethics and Farmville, and educator David Shaenfield looks at new ways to support citizenship skills through gaming. Finally, designer Pete Vigeant gives his personal take on Red Dead Redemption and Bethesda Softworks founder and MIT professor Christopher Weaver unpacks controversies surrounding games.

DOI: 10.4018/978-1-60960-120-1.ch001

INTRODUCTION

Karen Schrier

Game design practices evolve as new relationships, cultural norms, social behavior and technologies emerge. Likewise, theories, frameworks, and methodologies relevant to games research need to constantly grow as we develop new games, ideas, critiques, cultural practices, and values. To capture the spirit of the breadth of ethics and games today, I curated a selection of experts from industry and academia. Unlike the deeper analyses in the rest of the book, these pieces are shorter, more personal and more reflective visions of the past, present, and future of ethics and games. An *amuse-bouche* for the meal of the rest of the book, these pieces cover the three themes, or strands of study, that are represented in this book. These include: (1) how we can use games to better teach ethics, values and citizenship, and the design principles underlying teaching values through play; (2) developing a design ethic for games, and the ethics of creating games, including their production, development, and distribution; (3) cultural, historical, psychological, and sociological aspects, including the cultural practices related to gaming, discourses surrounding gaming, or how players interact with individual games as texts, media or artifacts. Games, as we will see, can be a window into our own humanity. While these strands interweave and overlap, each contributor defines his or her unique path, and what results is a just-in-time perspective on a timely topic.

First, Mia Consalvo, a visiting professor at MIT, discusses decision making in *Dragon Age*, giving an inside look at her own ethical choices and experiences playing the popular RPG game. Next famed indie game designer Greg Costikyan talks about his view on *Diplomacy* and uses it to show how game mechanics can support particular types of ethical behavior.

Director of the Entertainment Technology Center at Carnegie Mellon, Drew Davidson, then provides a meditation on the value of games by discussing insights from his edited collection, *Well Played 1.0*. Nick Fortugno, casual games expert and designer of games such as *Diner Dash*, compares *Farmville* to slot machines, and questions the ethics of particular game mechanics. Human development researcher and professor, David Shaenfield, looks at how games could support citizenship and ethical thinking skills, such as collaboration and argumentation.

Next, interaction designer Pete Vigeant provides a personal take on *Red Dead Redemption*, which at the time of this book's submission, has only been released for a few weeks. And finally, Chris Weaver—founder of Bethesda, which developed popular commercial games with ethical components such as *Fallout 3* and *Morrowind*—unpacks controversies surrounding games.

I hope this chapter serves as a useful introduction to the key issues and questions *in Designing Games for Ethics: Models, techniques and Framework*.

CONFESSIONS OF A GAMER: I ALWAYS PLAY THE NICE GAL

Mia Consalvo

It was just a bit annoying—Jowan was staring at me, waiting for my answer—would I help him or not? I couldn't decide. I felt there was something important about him that I'd forgotten, something that might come back to haunt me later if I made the wrong choice. And in Bioware's *Dragon Age* (2009)—an RPG featuring branching storylines and the ability to choose between multiple paths that offer selfless as well as selfish choices in order to complete quests—I'd learned to be a little cautious before acting. In replaying the game and starting over as a mage, my character began her training at the Circle Tower, the point of entry for any mage's origin story, and within the fiction of the game the place where all mages grow up and learn how to control magic (and are ostensibly controlled themselves). I remembered running into an NPC named Jowan in my prior play through of the game as a warrior, but I couldn't remember exactly what he had done—whether he was a traitorous mage poisoning a town's leader, or if he had become a blood mage and gone out of control in the Tower later in the storyline. The dilemma was this: should I help him escape the Circle and the possibility that the mages were going to turn him into a Tranquil—a process that would neuter him of all emotion—or should I instead report him for having an illegal romance with another mage, and thus ruin his chances of escape? In other words, should I do something that would make my "friend" happy (I was supposed to infer this friendship, having just been introduced to him in the game), or should I follow the rules of my training and insist on a greater good? I stared at the screen, trying to decide. I felt like I should turn him in, but I didn't want to be that person—the rat.

Dragon Age tells the story of the world of Ferelden, which has been overrun by forces of darkness called the Darkspawn. Its historic defensive force—the Gray Wardens—have been slandered and the remaining force is scattered across the world, leaving the world without a force for good. It's the job of the player as a Gray Warden to rally support from the various races (including humans, elves and dwarves), in order to bring an assault against both a traitorous leader as well as the Darkspawn. Players are given a large world to explore, with both broader and more specific goals to complete. How the player does so is their own choice, both in terms of the order of various tasks, as well as various ways to complete them. So while the game does use the typical "save the world" trope, it also features ways for players to tailor that task in ways that they would prefer.

I had first started playing *Dragon Age* intent on creating a character (my warrior) that was cold and somewhat selfish, yet ultimately intent on doing the right thing for the world of Ferelden. But,

as usual, I instead defaulted to a warm, generous character, graciously helping most everyone who asked me. I didn't give it another thought until a colleague announced he was going to play through *Mass Effect* (2007) as "the jerkiest jerk I can be" instead of the "nice guy" he always played in such games. Another colleague did the same with *Mass Effect 2* (2010), which piqued my curiosity. Did most people usually act as the "nice person" in role-playing games with ethical dilemmas, and does this reflect how they act in real life? Was there a larger pattern, or did I just happen to work in a place with very nice people?

When I first wrote about cheating in videogames, one of the benefits I mentioned about games was their open possibility space—in a game you can try out different play styles and options, experiment with the choices the game might offer, or that you might create for yourself (2007). At the time I was thinking mainly of cheating as a way to explore alternate play styles, but there are other interesting opportunities offered to players for experimentation—in particular different ethical decision-making choices, which game developers have been trying to make deeper and more complex over time.

For example, collaborative groups such as the game developers who gather annually at the Project Horseshoe think tank retreat argue that in relation to ethical choices, games should do more than offer players branching good/evil (i.e., a/b) pathways. Games that present only a dichotomous choice offer players no real surprises except for different endings and different skill-up trees to complete. This is exemplified in *Star Wars: Knights of the Old Republic* (2003) and its options for players to choose between the light side and the dark side of the force. Likewise, the Project Horseshoe group argues that games such as *Bioshock* (2007) do not offer true ethical dilemmas—the choice, for example, to harvest Little Sisters or not for their ADAM is based on purely selfish reasons. As they explain, "saving or harvesting is not a particularly difficult decision, especially once the player realizes they get more ADAM for doing the 'right' thing," which would be not killing the Little Sisters, resulting in an award of even more ADAM to the player than they would have received through killing them (Team HJ, 2009).

Similarly, game studies scholars explore how games provide ethical dilemmas embedded in gameplay mechanics, which can result in players trying to optimize their gameplay pathways, rather than experiencing truly meaningful moments in games (Mosberg Iversen, 2010; Sicart, 2009). Mosberg Iversen suggests that in such cases players can become frustrated at being offered choices without clear consequences, or feedback on how the choices will affect game play outcomes. In response, they then seek outside help to figure out how best to min-max their way to winning, or what they deem the best ending to a particular game, rather than explore what they think an interesting path might be (2010).

A notable exception that Zagal points to is the strategy RPG *Fire Emblem: Radiant Dawn* (2007), where players must control various groups of characters throughout different stages of the game. Late in the game, the system demands that the player fight against the forces she had earlier named, trained, and gotten to know. Zagal argues that the game is successful because it "creates a moral tension between the player's goals and those posed by both the narrative and the gameplay" (2009, p. 7). Such moments occur because, as Sicart explains, players are moral beings, and the most interesting games offer individuals an opportunity to explore "the relation between the values we have as players and how they relate to who we are outside the game" (2009, p. 105).

Going back to my initial example, *Dragon Age* offers players some fairly interesting choices, along with others that can seem like the traditional min-maxing approach. So while *Dragon Age* provides multiple decision points for players to grapple with, the changes resulting from those decisions are not always apparent to the player, at least immediately following the choice. Yet

your party members can approve or disapprove of your actions, and the same actions will generally please and displease different members of your party. Some may even turn on you or leave your group if they disagree with your actions or words strongly enough, giving you a real sense that there is no one "correct" answer for each decision. But of course, no matter what the player chooses, the larger storyline remains unchanged, with the final battle a test of the player's skills in battle and strategy. So, no matter whether I (or anyone else) played a hero or a bastard, or helped Jowan or not, I could still save the world and be renowned. But maybe the larger question is, just how differently are other people choosing to play this game, and similar games with these sorts of ethical systems?

In spring 2010, students in my class on cheating, ethics and games interviewed 21 individuals about their play styles in games that offered ethical choices through different character actions and dialogue options, basically good guy/bad guy configurations or alignments. What they found was intriguing—when playing games like *Fable 2* (2008), *Mass Effect* and *Knights of the Old Republic*, almost all individuals also chose to play—at least on their first play through—as the good guy. And for many, it was something that they commonly did when they played RPGs, with the option to play evil not considered an option for them. For example, one of the participants in the study, Apple (all names are pseudonyms), explains that in a game such as *Fallout 3* (2008) "I always seem to go good. I can go evil if I force myself to be evil—I really have to force myself to do it, it never comes naturally to me." Likewise, another participant, Chime, elaborates "I generally do good 'cause it's easier. 'Cause that's how I was raised. Like, for example, it's easier to be good, 'cause that's how you're trained. … [a]s a person, but you translate that into gamer world, almost innately."

Other players highlighted their difficulties in playing the evil path, with participant Deal explaining that while playing *Oblivion* (2006) "I was trying to do kind of 'evilish' things, but when I went into 'game autopilot' mode, I would naturally make the good guy choices. And I started to get 'renowned' back—good guy points, essentially—and I was like 'no, I don't want to do this! Stop it!'" For such players, choosing the route of good felt right or natural, almost as if it were the default way to play. This could be due to their upbringing, social pressure, or a sense of aligning a game avatar's personality with one's own, such that the avatar's actions would mirror the player's sense of right and wrong, as well as type of response, in the various situations encountered. On the other hand, other players didn't reference their own morality in making decisions in the game, but instead felt like the path of good offered the most rewards, and therefore was the logical choice for achieving the best game result. Thus, participant Journey plays the good path because "the good guy always wins, the bad guy never wins. It's the rules. If it's Batman versus Joker, Batman always wins."

Of course for a few players, the evil or selfish pathway beckoned or seemed the logical approach when starting a game. For example, participant Bloom generally chooses to play the bad guy because, "I like to kill things, and when you kill things you get bad karma." For him, second play throughs of a game might include an alternate pathway (of good), but, "you have to be more conscious, you can't just do anything you want. It's a pain in the butt, but it's a part of playing through in a different way." In other words, he liked playing the bad path because he didn't have to focus so much on acting appropriately well behaved in the game world. And participant Jello, another player who "pretty much always" plays evil, admitted that "eventually just being evil gets really boring" and what he actually prefers is "more than making my character evil I want to make him super unpredictable. … You just gotta mix it up sometimes so you never get bored."

And many players do also play through the game a second (or multiple) times, often choosing the bad/evil path, because as the gamer Fish explains "I go down every path to see every difference in the storyline." But overwhelmingly, players choose the path of good first, and evil for their second play through. Perhaps this means that most of us want to play the hero, or find it difficult to play against type. Thus, games with choices ranging from simply selfish to outright evil may try to push us against those perhaps unconsidered barriers in our own mind—different play throughs are encouraged through the addition of achievements, and even just the knowledge of multiple endings or storylines can motivate players to come back to a game for another play through, to see how alternate decisions might have changed the course of events, as well as how various characters reacted to my choices. That's what brought me back to *Dragon Age*.

Yet even these vaunted bad guy pathways in what one of my students called "moral alignment games," with all their flashy options and our reluctance to engage with them, aren't really that evil. Many just offer the player the more selfish route. For example, in *Dragon Age*, I don't have to help various dwarves find lost family members—but if I do I can gain some useful items as a reward. And if I choose not to help, nothing bad really happens.

But one recent game that does stand out in its insistence on going beyond selfishness as an expression of evil is *Modern Warfare 2* (2009) and its (in)famous 'No Russian' level. Here, the player (if s/he has chosen to play the optional level) takes part in an airport massacre, gunning down unarmed, innocent civilians, in hopes of gaining the trust of a group of terrorists. Yet in this instance, many players do actually object—some quite insistently—arguing that the level is offensive and not a valuable addition to the game. So, it would seem that as much as we want (or call for) more interesting ethical predicaments in games, there are certain choices with which we do not care to be confronted. While Sicart (2009) argues that games can help us explore the differences between our in-game actions and who we are outside the game, it seems our daily selves exert a strong pull on how we play—with many of us choosing to play the good guy, to be the hero, at least when given the option to do so.

DIPLOMACY, THE PRISONERS' DILEMMA, AND THE MECHANICS OF ETHICS

Greg Costikyan

How are ethics evoked in games?

Consider *Diplomacy* (Calhammer, 1959), a seven-player game played on a map of Europe with borders approximating those of 1914. Despite the setting, it is essentially an abstract strategy game. Moves are written, revealed simultaneously, and resolved. Each area of the board may contain one unit. The crux of the game is the "support order." A unit may "support" in moving or holding position in an adjacent area. Only if a moving unit has more support than the defender is the defender dislodged and does the attacker occupy the area.

Units may "support" moves by other units belonging to the same player—and may also support moves by other players' units. The opposing positions are of equal power; hence, no single player can triumph against any other single player. Only by forming alliances can you succeed. While the game allows for draws, the goal is to win by conquering more than half of the board. Consequently, in addition to *forming* alliances, *breaking* them is also critical; in most cases, it is essential for a player to backstab his ally at just the right moment to win. Because of the simultaneous movement nature of the game, you can never be quite certain that your ally will in fact do what he or she claims to be doing in the coming turn—or whether your ally is planning on turning on you.

Diplomacy is, therefore, a game that encourages lying, scheming, backstabbing, betrayal—and conscious, cold-hearted appraisal, at all moments, of where each of the other player's interests truly lie. Though there is certainly a strategic aspect to the game—like *Chess, Diplomacy* has spawned a literature devoted to the strategies of the game—victory more often goes to the calculating and effective liar than to the strategist.

Diplomacy is a game that can only exist because of "the Magic Circle" (Huizinga, 1938), the convention that events within a game have only endogenous meaning and that they are not to influence our behavior external to it. In other words, within the game, lying and betrayal are permissible, even admirable if performed elegantly, but

Figure 1. An image of the Diplomacy board game map

the anger and negativity usually associated with this kind of behavior is not supposed to translate back to the real world.

A classic statement of game play convention is "It's not whether you win or lose, but how you play the game." Except in *Diplomacy*, it *is* whether you win or lose, and any means necessary for victory are acceptable. Despite Magic Circle's convention that actions within the game are not to affect our relationships outside it, games of *Diplomacy* often lead to ill will. I have seen fist-fights break out during a game—quickly suppressed by the other players, of course, enforcing the convention of the Magic Circle.

Is *Diplomacy* an ethical game? An unethical game? Certainly the behaviors it inculcates in its magic circle are ones that, in normal life, we would consider unacceptable, though widespread. There are, however, useful ethical lessons to be drawn from *Diplomacy*—if only in terms of identifying pathological behavior and learning how to deal with it. And *Diplomacy* teaches lessons about the nature of *realpolitik* and the behavior of nations, as well.

From the standpoint of those interested in fostering ethical behavior in games, *Diplomacy* also has lessons to teach. Clearly, the mechanics of *Diplomacy*—specifically, simultaneously revealed moves, the support order, balanced positions with a defender advantage that produces a necessity for both alliance and betrayal—elicit one style of ethical behavior: that is, behavior that would be viewed outside the game as *un*ethical. It suggests that other game mechanics can be used to foster different systems of ethics.

The prisoners' dilemma (Flood, 1952) is illustrative here, as well. A classic problem in game theory, the prisoners' dilemma involves two players who are making a simultaneous decision (as in *Diplomacy)*. If neither testifies against the other, both receive small prison sentences. If both testify, both receive large prison sentences. If only one testifies, however, that player goes free, while the other receives the maximum sentence. Even though it would, from a Pareto-optimal standpoint, be best for neither to testify, both have a strong incentive toward betrayal, and both logic and psychological studies show that only mutual betrayal is sustainable.

If, however, a study is organized to provide repeated tests, then players have an incentive to engage in "tit for tat" behavior, punishing betrayal with a subsequent betrayal, and non-betrayal becomes the sustainable strategy (Axelrod, 1984). From a game design standpoint, this implies that the mechanics of a game— in this case, a simple matter of whether turns are iterated—determines the outcome, in terms of the ethics of player choices.

In short, both *Diplomacy* and the prisoners' dilemma demonstrate that to the degree that games foster ethical behavior, this is a consequence of the mechanics of the game. The theme or narrative frame of a game may predispose players in one direction or another, but actual outcomes derive from the mechanics.

Or to put it another way: the mechanic is the message.

THE VALUE OF GAMEPLAY

Drew Davidson

A good game can and should teach players what they need to know and do to succeed. Ideally, the very act of playing the game should enable players to master the gameplay mechanics so they can successfully meet the rising challenges and complete the experience. In a well-designed game, the experience is kept pleasurably frustrating; it's not too easy, nor is it too hard. The meaning of a game comes through a mastering of the gameplay mechanics across the experience of playing a game.

In *Well Played 1.0*, a book I edited, contributors performed in-depth close readings of video games to parse out the meaning they found in the experience of playing a game and how it can be "well played." Contributors analyze sequences in a variety of games in detail to illustrate and interpret how the various components of a game can come together to create a fulfilling playing experience unique to this medium.

To clarify, we used the term "well played" in two senses. On the one hand, well played is to games as well read is to books. So, a person who reads books a lot is "well read" and a person who plays games a lot is "well played." On the other hand, well played can also refer to well done, both created well and played in a good way. So, a job can be "well done" by a person, and a game can be "well played" by the development team. Together, an aesthetic is formed out of the game's design and the experience of playing through it.

If a game gets too hard, too easy, too confusing, or if it just is too long and seems never-ending, players most likely will not finish. For these reasons and more, players can reach a point where they lose their sense of engagement, becoming bored, frustrated and tired of playing the game. But if a game enables players to advance and continues to hold their attention, players will want to successfully complete the game experience.

Crawford (1984) refers to this as a smooth learning curve in which a player is enabled to successfully advance through the game. Csikszentmihalyi's (1991) notion of flow, in which a person achieves an optimal experience with a high degree of focus and enjoyment, is an apt method for discussing this process as well. And Gee (2004) notes that well designed games teach us how to play them through rhythmic, repeating structures that enable a player to master how to play the game. In terms of Bogost's (2007) unit operations, the units are being juxtaposed well so that the meaning and mastery builds as you play. I believe all these concepts show how games create an aesthetic experience unique to medium.

I think it is useful to consider games from these various perspectives. In doing so we can, as Marie-Laure Ryan (2001) notes, observe features that remain invisible from other perspectives. Engaging this medium of videogames, we tell our stories of the game as we relate the varied and visceral experience of the games we play. Noah Falstein (2004) discusses the "natural funativity" of games, how they are activities that help us live in the world. And stories are how we stitch together a continuity of our experiences. They are our "mystories," our stories that enable us to understand the world (Ulmer, 1989). Narratives are how we convey the perspective of our experiences (Meadows, 2002), or as Greg Costikyan (2001) states, "Play is how we learn; stories are how we integrate what we've learned, and how we teach others the things we've learned ourselves through play."

I believe that games are an interesting medium, because there are definite para-linguistic activities involved, meaning is conveyed through gesture, space, color, sound and activity and agency. These all can combine into engaging aesthetic experiences, and meaning unfolds as we engage and play games. Through the act of playing games, ethics and values are imparted; choices are made, consequences occur, and actions are explored. Overall, the goal is to help develop and define a literacy of games as well as a sense of their meaning and value as an experience. Video games are a complex medium that merits careful interpretation and insightful analysis.

ADDICTION AND THE ETHICS OF MECHANICS

Nick Fortugno

Slot machines occupy an interesting position in the study of games. Many game designers disdain slot machines, and our culture generally has an ambivalent at best relationship with these wildly popular and successful gambling devices. People who study games will often point to the pure randomness of the system of a slot machine or the lack of meaningful choice in the experience, but there are many games that are just as random (e.g., *Candyland, Chutes and Ladders*) that do not have the same visceral response. One could certainly argue that the money that slot machines take from people is the real problem, but all commercial games take money from people. So if slot players are enjoying their play experience, isn't it a wise use of their money to increase their general happiness?

Much of the language around slot machines (and gambling in general) references addiction, and correspondingly, the addictiveness of slot machines is their primary danger. Thus, the argument here is that users do not actually enjoy the experience of playing a slot machine; instead, something about the function of the slot machine leads people to compulsively play, despite the destructiveness of the game. Of course, the addiction trope is an odd choice on the surface. How could a machine that one chooses to play and that has no direct bodily or hormonal influence be truly addictive in the way we recognize chemicals to be?

The answer lies not as much in biology as in psychology, specifically the psychology of reinforcement and extinction of actions. The classic example of these effects is found in Skinner boxes. In these studies, rats were placed in a cage

Figure 2. Graph of the rats' behavior (Source: Wikipedia)

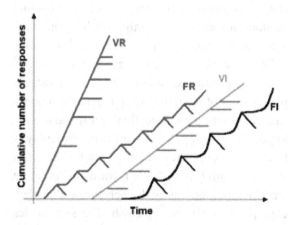

with a level that when pressed would occasionally dispense a food pellet. In different tests, the researchers would change the ratio of level pushes to pellets dispensed. There are two basic ways to set up the ratio: the level could dispense a pellet every X number of absolute pushes (called a ratio) or it could dispense a pellet every X number of pushes since the last push that successfully dispensed a pellet (called an interval). On top of this, the number of pushes is either case could be fixed or random (which a randomly determined range). Based on the results of these tests, there were clear changes in the rats' behavior simply based on which relationship between level push and pellet drop was implemented, as seen in Figure 2.

As Figure 2 clearly indicates, a successfully tuned variable reward ratio (where a pellet is dropped a random number of lever pulls within a range, independent of previous successful pulls) creates the greatest number of pulls by a large margin. The important thing to keep in mind here is that the rat's desire for food is the same in all cases. It is simply the reward system that is changing the behavior. What this proves is that for rats, it is possible to create compulsive behavior simply by tuning a system properly.

Of course, this does not only apply to rats. A slot machine is a device controlled by a variable reward ratio. Every X1-Xn number of pulls of the lever (literally a lever in traditional machines) the player is given a reward. And that's basically all there is to a slot machine. There are many kinds of bonuses and near-misses, but in the most basic sense, the system reduces to a reward every few pulls. The bare application of this system is striking; there is also no feedback about loss, even the feedback on minor wins is extremely muted, and the entire experience of playing a line takes no more than a few seconds. (The flashy rewards are reserved exclusively for the big pay-offs, and that is primarily feedback to attract spectators to also play.) A round on a slot machine is an extremely refined and focused application of a variable reward ratio.

And this is ultimately what we find unsettling about slot machines as a culture. We recognize that is illogical to play these games—both because the payout is not commensurate with the expense and because there is nothing particularly fun about pulling the lever—but we see people play them compulsively and at great loss. The idea that a carefully-tuned system of rewards can make people behave like rats, continuing to engage simply because of frequency of winning, is a disturbing thought, and slot machines are nothing but that system at work.

Slot machines are a relatively straightforward case, but what makes the question of variable reward rates interesting is that slot machines are not the only games that use systems like this. Games routinely use systems such as these to incent player action and provide motivation. Take the genre of role-playing games. An RPG mechanic centers around an achiever loop in which players fight opponents and receive rewards in terms of experience points and equipment to empower them to defeat larger opponents. However, the specific rewards offered by an encounter are not fixed, and the random distribution of the treasures can be used to motivate play. *World of Warcraft (WoW)*, for example, uses this structure with epic item drops as major quest rewards. The final encounter of a major-enough event will always drop an epic item, but the specific item dropped is randomly selected from a pre-determined set. As players are in different classes, this means that only one of that set of items will be valuable to any given player, so the instance can be seen as a kind of slot machine that produces the item the player needs on a variable ratio. This leads players to repeat the instance over and over in an attempt to claim their prize.

Of course, *WoW* is rarely thought of with the same kind of concern that slot machines are. This may have to do with the richness of the social play of the MMO, or the strategic landscape of *WoW*, which is deep and challenging enough that the game is fun independent of the epic rewards.

Whatever the specific reason, it is clear that there is a lot more going on in a typical RPG than the simple random number generator of a slot machine. RPGs can use variable reward ratios to motivate players, but that alone does not make them systems that produce compulsive behavior. Instead, reward ratios are just one of many tools that a designer can use to create a fun experience in a given game.

The real question then is the point at which a mechanic can move from a component of a greater fun game to an addictive exploit of human (or perhaps mammalian) psychology. The above example implies that there is a level of complexity of content and mechanic that makes a difference. If the game offers the reward structure as a single part of a larger mechanic, then the game as a whole has an effect on a user of which the reward structure is a relatively minor part. So when does a game cross the line?

The early crop of social networking games that has appeared on sites such as Facebook is an interesting case to examine. The earliest successful games on Facebook are games like *Mafia Wars* and *Mobsters*. These "mafia" games and the reskinned versions of the same mechanic (e.g., *Vampire Wars*) are sometimes called light RPGs. They resemble RPGs in that players have stats that they use to complete quests for rewards. However, in these light RPGs, the resolution of the quest is take care of with the press of a single button. The chance of completing a quest and getting a reward is based on the player's stats with some random noise, and the quality of the money reward itself is somewhat randomized. The games only permit players a certain amount of "energy" and players must spend energy to do quests. If players do not want to wait to regenerate energy over long periods of time, they can spend money to get more throws. So basically the gameplay is that the player pushes a button based on her stats and gets a slightly variable reward, spending an amount of resources with each throw that they can spend money to replenish. The similarities to a slot machine are quite close, and it is hard to imagine that the giant, cash-heavy companies that released these "mafia" games did not optimize the reward rates of their quests to maximize return play. Since this is the entirety of the mechanic of these games, does that make these kinds of Facebook games addictive in that same way slot machines are?

It is not simply the literal mechanic of these games that resembles the variable reward rates of Skinner boxes. To what extent does the coin dropping in other player's boards in a game such as Restaurant City or Café Town constitute of variable reward? Does the random distribution of gifts or treasures in a *Farmville* or *Treasure Isle* occur at a frequency that inspires compulsion? One could even argue that the timing of friends in visiting one's farm or otherwise participating in one's personal game could be a variable reward structure itself. After all, one knows that any friends who play the game will likely help out at some point, but it is never exactly clear when they will show up or what they will provide. All of these things could provide a psychological hook to keep players in the game. Do these games provide enough of an experience to have a more complex emotional response, or is this simply another case of the rat pulling the lever because the lever is programmed just right?

And of course variable reward rates are not the only kind of psychological trick that game designers use to create compulsive play behavior. Well-known phenomena such as cognitive dissonance can certainly be used by games to create loyalty and emotional involvement. Even something as basic as the achiever cycle I mentioned earlier—fight-earn-level-fight—could be seen as a kind of compulsive behavior. In fact, we could interpret all of grind mechanics as an exploit of the frailties of human thinking processes.

I am certainly not saying that any of these games are actually addictive or that any of them rely solely on an exploit of human brain chemistry. There is a clear difference in player perception

of and reaction to games such as slot machines and *WoW*. It is impossible to say exactly which components of a complex game are the key motivators and whether any single element of such a system could be taken in isolation. Also, the vast majority of games provide a fun experience for their players. But given that we know that these kinds of psychological exploits exist, and that we can see the destructive effects of a raw exploitative system such a slot machine, it seems to me a valid question to ask whether a mechanic can be used unethically. If an interactive system is nothing more than an exploitation of a flaw in mammalian brain structure, is it any different than a chemical structure that is designed to create an addiction? I am a firm believer in the aesthetic potential and the transformative power of games, but I think it is naïve not to look closely at how we make experiences addictive. We need to make sure we are not simply making rats who ignore their hunger in order to pull the lever one more time.

DEVELOPING COLLABORATIVE CITIZENS THROUGH GAME PLAY

David Shaenfield

As we enter the second decade of the 21st century, we see can observe two competing perspectives regarding the role of play in human development. On the one hand is the Vygotskian tradition of the importance of play to promoting cognitive and social developments such as self-regulation, co-operation, and empathy. This is complemented by more focused empirical studies from the learning sciences championing video game play to engage students and lead them to better learning outcomes.

However, on the other hand, the common perspective in many schools is that play is not central to human development, as evidenced by the amount of "play" time allotted during the school day (Miller & Almon, 2009). The learning sciences community must take responsibility for this perspective as well. Research from this community supports the development of early academic competence as a crucial foundation for later learning and development. Unfortunately, in practice, this has resulted in a movement away from time for play in the early childhood years, and toward a model of scripted direct instruction on academic skills.

I would like to propose a return to an appreciation of the affordances of engaging in play understood through a developmental perspective. This perspective does not simply acknowledge the role of play during the early childhood years, but suggests that engaging in play throughout the lifespan provides the opportunities for actualizing the potential for human development, including moral development and the skills associated with citizenship.

Educators and policy makers have been constructing lists of 21th century competencies and citizenship skills for decades. Most of these lists include some mention of developing collaborative skills that foster cooperation among people holding diverse perspectives. Thus, we should ask how we can encouragement the development of collaborative skills. In my own work with adolescents, I found that developing meta-level regulatory skills plays a crucial role in their ability to engage in and benefit from a collaborative activity designed to provide the opportunity to develop argumentative discourse skills (Shaenfield, in review; Kuhn, Goh, Iordanou & Shaenfield, 2008).

These meta-level regulatory processes fall under three distinct categories: 1) planning, 2) predicting, and 3) evaluating. Planning refers selecting and implementing a strategy. Predicting refers to the anticipated effect of a strategy either implemented by oneself or by a collaborator or opponent. Finally, evaluating refers to making judgments on the effectiveness of strategy use.

These aspects of collaborative activity were observed in audio recordings of the collaborating pairs I studied. In addition to recording the collaborative discourse, we can see how that discourse regulates the real-time decisions of the players. This allows for the dense collection of data, known as the microgenetic method (Siegler, 2006), that allows for a fuller picture of trajectories of development to emerge compared to standard pre- and post-testing (effects) testing that currently overwhelms much of educational psychology scholarship.

I believe that play, as supported by games, has the potential to support these skills. Such games include massively multiplayer roleplaying games like *World of Warcraft*, where guild members work together toward a common goal, and cooperative games such as the *Lego* series or *Super Mario Brothers Wii*. I hope to apply my analysis of collaborative discourse to gaming environments, and further investigate how games can support skills associated with ethical thinking and citizenship.

It is also important to understand the role of game play in developing collaborative skills from both within and outside the school walls. As youth spend an ever-increasing amount of time online and in gaming environments, researchers need to understand how skills develop in these informal contexts as well and how they relate to the skills we value academically. For example, how do the skills of resource and time allocation in a game like *Plants vs. Zombies* relate to decisions students make to allocate time and resources to academic study? Can playing resource management games such as *Plants vs. Zombie* help kids understand a complicated system of values or a complex social issue?

As younger and younger children are given more responsibility to make decisions on how to spend their time, many are choosing to play games. I have made the brief argument here that we should take these activities seriously as environments within which the skills for individual and societal development emerge. It is up to the developmental psychology community to expand their scope and include play as a focus of study, and it is up to educators to expand their scope and see play as an activity that leads to development.

RED DEAD ETHICS

Pete Vigeant

I get on my horse and ride. It's quiet. I'm not in any particular rush, nor interested in going anywhere specific. I keep pushing my horse to gallop. There's a path but I ignore it. Some coyotes make their presence known. I aim but miss. There will be more.

My name is John Marston and I'm an outlaw—rather, I was an outlaw. Or maybe I'm still an outlaw. I was brought to Armadillo to redeem myself; to bring a former friend to justice. Perhaps it's just revenge. I was left for dead.

I focus on my horse. He's getting tired and annoyed that I keep ramming him into rocks. It's dark and I'm in the brush. A light flickers ahead. Some camping travelers invite me for a sit. They talk about hard times and I zone out for a bit. There was a time that I wouldn't tolerate this pace. A group of off-guard cowboys sitting around the fire were target practice. I may be getting old.

I get up and decide to make my own fire, a distance away from the group. I'm tired and it's late. I look for a good spot when I hear gunfire in the distance. The hair on the back of my neck stands and I'm on my horse. My gun is ready, but I arm with a lasso.

The small town ahead of me is being terrorized by a group of bandits, celebrating the death of a man who is being dragged through the streets from a rope tied to a horse. The horse doesn't seem to notice, but it is likely distracted by the grizzly, filthy villain sitting on it's back, firing recklessly into the air. I hear women screaming and get off my horse. The fun is about to begin.

The first bandit doesn't notice the rope until he's hit the ground. I hogtie him while his buddies circle back, guns blazing. The remaining three are agitated. They don't stop to help their friend, instead chase me with their bullets. I'm grateful at their lousy shots. I take damage, but secure two more. The last can't seem to take a hint. I dodge

back and forth and drop him like the rest. They all struggle on the ground, cursing and swearing. And it's over.

The town becomes calm. No one seems to notice what has happened anymore, except a few hysterics heard still running and screaming in the distance. I walk by a woman who says a nice greeting. Strange, but I know she knows. I have a feeling of fame. And honor. I did the right thing.

My horse comes at my whistle. I ride back into the desert and find some coyotes howling and laughing. I draw my gun and aim. My finger drops from the trigger. There will always be more coyotes. I make a fire......and save my game.

Red Dead Redemption, developed by Rockstar San Diego and published by Rockstar Games, is an open-world 3rd person perspective western that pushes the boundaries of decision making in gaming. The traditional open-world shooter, such as *Grand Theft Auto IV* and *Just Cause 2*, allows and encourages the player to shoot everything and everyone. The penalties for wanton destruction are slight and do not change the gameplay. The users, therefore, do not necessarily have to think before shooting. The outcome will likely be the same and eventually the heat from the authorities will dissolve.

Rockstar's open-world adventure through the West offers a completely different experience. While one has the ability to shoot anyone or anything, the penalties for doing so can be significant. The plot of the story is built around a reformed character that is working with the law to capture some hardened criminals. Killing, robbing and destroying property will change the hero into a rogue outlaw—a man with the same mission, burdened by the added inconvenience of being pursued from multiple sides.

Being "good," however, is quite difficult. The game constantly rewards the player for finding opportunities to help others without spilling blood. Shooting wanted outlaws is fine, but capturing them alive gives a better Fame and Honor boost. These ratings open new missions and allow the character to buy discounted merchandise. The challenge is not getting killed while lassoing those wanted few. In general, the characters that a player is asked to catch are surrounded by henchmen that storm bullets over an unprotected lawman. The few seconds that it takes to hog-tie a single bandit is almost enough to completely evaporate a character's health. The simplest route by far is to switch over to a rifle and finish off each outlaw from a safe distance. Reputation, though, is key, regardless of personal peril.

Red Dead Redemption does not force a player to resort to fatal violence always, but there are moments that guns are required. Hunting, for instance, is a major side quest of the game. Some criminals are so surrounded by henchmen that the only way to successfully pursue is to thin out the group. This is a representation of the Old West—violence was a way of life. Most of the bad guys that a player hogties on behalf of the law are subsequently shot instead of being dragged through the judicial process. The non-playing characters live in a world of frontier justice that is hard to defy.

Pacifists can rejoice that the future of open world gaming is not necessarily dictated by unnecessary killing. The dynamic that makes open worlds appealing is the freedom of choice, and *Red Dead Redemption* has found a way to make shooting almost optional. Most players will actually have a moment of reflection on whether or not to pull the trigger—and that is a wonderful thing.

VIDEOGAME ETHICS 1.01

Christopher Weaver

ethics | ˈɛθɪks|
plural noun

1   *[usu. treated as pl.] moral principles that govern a person's or group's behavior: Judeo-Christian ethics. the moral cor-*

rectness of specified conduct: the ethics of euthanasia.

2   *[usu. treated as sing.] the branch of knowledge that deals with moral principles.*

When I started Bethesda Softworks in 1985, a discussion of ethics in games was virtually non-existent. PC games were rudimentary and the requirements of storytelling, game design and graphics, assuming there were any, did not take notice of the implications for the way people would experience the games we were designing. We were far more focused on getting something to work in realtime given the limitations of the CPUs, the operating systems and the toolsets then available. Function drove form. In the PC games world of 1985, we were creating the *incunabula* of the time.

Today, the processors and tool sets are far more powerful, the graphic capabilities are enormous, and the stories and storytelling much more complex. The "Art of Games" has evolved to a point where ethics, and other such important considerations, now play an important role in the overall design. It is with the present state of the Industry in mind that I pen this commentary.

In his book, *The Ethics of Computer Games*, Miguel Sicart provides a thoughtful, procedural approach to understanding the ethical considerations of creating virtual environments within which people engage. He argues that computer games are themselves ethical devices where game players are ethical agents, and that the ethics of computer games should be seen as a complex and interwoven amalgam of inherent moral duties, responsibilities and obligations. He observes that game construction of virtual worlds nevertheless requires real world moral decisions and ethical obligations.

While his treatise is somewhat academic, Sicart's view of game worlds as ethical systems sheds light on a core truth that seems to have escaped deep discussion and investigation within the games community. All too often, the designer puts game goals above any limiting mechanism for achieving those goals, in other words, "the ends justify the means." Considering that video-games have now emerged as an important cultural linchpin within the media framework, it is both puzzling and troubling that there is not a better understanding of the effect and mechanics of the way videogames teach, inform and influence.

A short time ago, a European company announced that it intended to introduce a game, *Office Massacre*. The object of the game was to win points by killing co-workers. I, along with some others in the industry, objected strenuously to its sale, citing the inappropriateness of such a game during a time when office shootings were increasing as evidenced by numerous articles of people "coping" with perceived injustice by invoking the ultimate form of violence as a replacement for social justice.

Recently, there were numerous references in Western media to a Japanese company that introduced a game, *RapeLay*, where the object was to rape young women and show the action in graphic detail. It is as if the game designers wished to provide a prurient opportunity to experience a rapist's sociopathic actions for the price of their game as nothing precludes or otherwise prevents the player from engaging in the most despicable of misogynistic acts.

Yet, as reprehensible as these examples may be, they are not isolated incidents. For example, the *Grand Theft Auto* (*GTA*) series is notorious for rewarding socially proscribed behavior and instead celebrates savage rape, theft, murder, and all forms of similar, antisocial mayhem. The series is one of the most popular of all time. What does this say about not just the designers but the players? Clearly there is social hunger for such antisocial outlets.

One might ask what possesses designers to believe that any ends are justified, regardless of potential for harm, to create a best seller that feeds some inappropriate psychological tendency or prurient interest on the part of the player. Others might have alternate readings of the relationship among game designers, culture, game artifact, and game players.

If we consider that games are not just mechanical systems of virtual experience and exploration, but ethical systems, with rules that create values of play, then what is appropriate within those rules? Drawing on concepts from philosophy and game studies, Sicart proposes a framework for analyzing the ethics of computer games as both designed objects and player experiences.

In their paper *The Ethics of Video Games: Mayhem, Death, and the Training of the Next Generation,* co-authors Donald Gotterbarn and James Moor make a strong case for reviewing the ethical dimensions of the way game design and development is taught:

There is however a significant ethical issue with video games that has not been discussed in the literature. Video games are treated by members of the game design and development community as a domain of software development that seems to lack clear ethical impacts beyond some minimal affect on the users of the software....

There is a family of video games based on rapid decisions which are related to the success of the gamer in that game. These include role playing games, real-time strategy games, games whose success is determined by the number killed, or to use the games euphemism 'the number K.O.ed" The Xbox and Game Boy generation of students raised on these games are being trained that decisions are all and only about themselves. (Gotterbarn, 2008).

Gotterbarn and Moor detail the strengths and weaknesses of the way a variety of game design and development curricula are taught and that the nature of these programs are limited by their lack of ethical and moral value models. While they defend videogames as a genre, citing some benefits such as surgical simulation, they nevertheless believe that designers and programmers are taught to look only for efficiency and speed—at the expense of ethical rules and ultimate impact on decisions beyond the player's character and the overall storyline.

The implications are clear and Gotterbarn warns, "We are training a generation to make decisions without any attention to the consequences for others of their actions" (Moor and Gotterbarn, 2009).

In the early days of programming, many computer scientists failed to consider the impacts of their work—a lack of professional responsibility to those affected by the systems being developed. Computer science has changed over the years, for example, there is now a required social component and ethics class required for CSAB accreditation. But, one of my concerns is that history is repeating itself in video game design. The interest during the early days was in one side of software development: data structures and algorithmic analysis. There was no mention of social consequences. The emphasis in new game curricula is in efficient engines and impressive graphics—not in the social or moral impact of the work.

While there is not, as yet, conclusive research pointing to absolute proportionality between videogames and violence or other similar antisocial behavior, it nevertheless behooves the industry to look more carefully at the impacts of its actions. How decisions are made is important. And few would question that how we learn to make those decisions, and what internal references we use to develop the internal perspective to weigh the consequences of our actions is important as well.

Joseph Wiezenbaum was one of the earliest scientists to raise the flag and question what we were missing when we did not consider the moral responsibility of what we were doing. His early work set the stage for computer and social scientists in the decades that followed.

If we are to apply the questioning of Weizenbaum and utilize the 18th Century adage propounded by Jeremy Bentham that, "It is the greatest good to the greatest number of people which is the measure of right and wrong," then the videogames industry owes itself a hard look in the social mirror. The industry is no longer the childhood curiosity of the few. It is the social pastime and teacher of the many and we need to learn from those who have walked this ground before.

REFERENCES

amby EmmaB. (2007, April 17). Violent video games – recent research. *Psychology and Crime News*. Retrieved April 30, 2009 from http://crime-psychblog.com/?p=1453

Anderson, C., & Bushman, B. (2001). Effects of violent video games on aggressive behavior, aggressive cognition, aggressive affect, physiological arousal, and prosocial behavior: A meta-analytic review of the scientific literature. *Psychological Science, 12*(5). doi:10.1111/1467-9280.00366

Apple Inc. (2009). *Version 2.1.2 (80.3) Apple Inc. dictionary*. Cupertino, CA: Apple Inc.

Axelrod, R. (1984). *The evolution of cooperation*. New York: Basic Books.

Bogost, I. (2007). *Persuasive games: The expressive power of videogames*. Cambridge, MA: MIT Press.

Calhammer, A. (1959). *Diplomacy*. Boston: Games Research, Inc.

Consalvo, M. (2007). *Cheating: Gaining advantage in videogames*. Cambridge, MA: The MIT Press.

Costikyan, G. (2001). *Where stories end and games begin*. Retrieved from http://www.costik.com/gamnstry.html

Crawford, C. (1984). *The art of computer game design*. Berkley, CA: McGraw Hill.

Csikszentmihalyi, M. (1991). *Flow: The psychology of optimal experience*. New York: Harper Collins.

Davidson, D. (2009). *Well played 1.0: Video games, value and meaning*. Pittsburgh, PA: ETC Press.

De Freitas, S. (2008). Emerging trends in serious games and virtual worlds. In *Emerging technologies for learning* (*Vol. 3*). Coventry, UK: Becta. [Research report]

Dodig-Crnkovic, G. (2006). On the importance of teaching professional ethics to computer science and engineering students. In Magnani, L. (Ed.), *Computing and Philosophy*. Pavia, Italy: Associated International Academic Publishers.

Falstein, N. (2004, November 10). Natural funativity. Retrieved from http://www.gamasutra.com/features/20041110/falstein_01.shtml

Flood, M. M. (1952). *Some experimental games. Research memorandum RM-789*. Santa Monica, CA: RAND Corporation.

Gee, J. P. (2004). *Learning by design: Games as learning machines*. Paper presented at the Game Developers Conference, San Jose CA. Retrieved from http://labweb.education.wisc.edu/room130/PDFs/GeeGameDevConf.doc

Gert, B. (1998). *Morality: Its nature and justification*. Oxford: Oxford University Press.

Gert, B. (1999). Common morality and computing. *Ethics and Information Technology*, *1*(1), 53–60. doi:10.1023/A:1010026827934

Gotterbarn, D. (2008). Video game ethics: Mayhem, death, and the training of the next generation. In *Proceedings of Ethicomp*. Mantova, Italy: Tipografia Commerciale.

Gotterbarn, D., & Moor, J. (2008). Virtual decisions: Just consequentialism, video game ethics, and ethics on the fly. *ACM SIGCAS Computers and Society, 39*(3).

Huizinga, J. (1950). *Homo ludens*. Boston: Beacon Press.

Johnson, D. (2001). *Computer ethics* (3rd ed.). Upper Saddle River, NJ: Prentice Hall.

Kuhn, D., Goh, W., Iordanou, K., & Shaenfield, D. (2008). Arguing on the computer: A microgenetic study of developing argument skills in a computer-supported environment. *Child Development*, *79*(5), 1311–1329. doi:10.1111/j.1467-8624.2008.01190.x

Manovich, L. (2001). *The language of new media*. Cambridge, MA: The MIT Press.

Meadows, M. (2002). *Pause & effect: The art of interactive narrative*. New York: New Riders.

Miller, E., & Almon, J. (2009). *Crisis in the kindergarten: Why children need to play in school*. College Park, MD: Alliance for Childhood.

Moor, J. (1985). What is computer ethics. *Metaphilosophy*, *16*, 266–275. doi:10.1111/j.1467-9973.1985.tb00173.x

Moor, J. (1998, March). Reason, relativity, and responsibility in computer ethics. *ACM SIGCAS Computers and Society*, *28*(1), 14–21. doi:10.1145/277351.277355

Moor, J. (1999). Just consequentialism and computing. *Ethics and Information Technology*, *1*, 65–69.

Mosberg Iversen, S. (2010). Between regulation and improvisation: Playing and analyzing games in the middle. Unpublished doctoral dissertation, IT-University Copenhagen. Retrieved from http://ncom.nordicom.gu.se/ncom/research/between_regulation_and_improvisation%28186467%29/

Rachels, J. (1999). *The elements of moral society: The elements of moral philosophy* (3rd ed., pp. 70–95). Boston: McGraw Hill.

Rawls, J. (1971). *A theory of justice*. Cambridge, MA: Harvard University Press.

Ryan, M. L. (2001). *Narrative as virtual reality*. Baltimore, MD: Johns Hopkins University Press.

Schank, R. (1995). *Tell me a story*. Chicago, IL: Northwestern University Press.

Shaenfield, D. (In review). Arguing with peers: Examining two kinds of discourse and their cognitive benefits. *Discourse Processes*.

Sicart, M. (2009). *The ethics of computer games*. Cambridge, MA: The MIT Press.

Siegler, R. (2006). Microgenetic studies of learning. In W. Damon & R. Lerner (Series Eds.), D. Kuhn & R. Siegler (Vol. Eds.), *Handbook of child psychology: Cognition, perception, and language* (Vol. 2, 6th ed.). Hoboken, NJ: Wiley.

Slim, H. (2008). *Killing civilians: Method, madness, and morality in war*. New York: Columbia University Press.

Tavinor, G. (2007). Towards an ethics of video gaming. Paper presented at FuturePlay, Toronto, Canada.

Team, H. J. (2009). Group report: Choosing between right and right: Creating meaningful ethical dilemmas in games. The Fourth Annual Game Design Think Tank, Project Horseshoe. Retrieved from http://www.projecthorseshoe. com/ph09/ph09r3.htm

Ulmer, G. (1989). *Teletheory*. New York: Routledge.

Waddington, D. (2007). Locating the wrongness in ultra-violent video games. *Ethics and Information Technology, 9*, 121–128. doi:10.1007/s10676-006-9126-y

Weizenbaum, J. (1986). *Computer power and human reason: From judgment to calculation*. San Francisco, CA: WH Freeman & Co.

Zagal, J. (2009, September). Ethically notable videogames: Moral dilemmas and gameplay. Paper presented at the *Breaking new ground: Innovation in games, play practice and theory* conference of the Digital Gameresearch Association, London, UK.

Chapter 2
Ethical Reasoning and Reflection as Supported by Single-Player Videogames

Jose P. Zagal
DePaul University, USA

ABSTRACT

Ethically notable games are those that provide opportunities for encouraging ethical reasoning and reflection. This chapter examines how games can encourage rational and emotional responses. By examining ethically notable videogames, it illustrates a few of the different design choices that can be used to encourage these responses and the effects they have on players. It also identifies five challenges toward creating ethically notable games and examines each in the context of commercially released videogames. Each of these analyses serves as a framework not only for reflecting upon and understanding ethics and morality in games but also for outlining the design space for ethically notable games.

INTRODUCTION

As recent work in moral psychology has shown, emotions (e.g. Greene, Sommerville, Nystrom, Darley & Cohen, 2001) as well as moral rules, each play a critical role in moral judgment (e.g. Nichols & Mallon, 2005). These findings echo, in some sense, the fundamental qualities of games: activities prescribed by rules to elicit and create emotionally meaningful experiences in their participants (Salen & Zimmerman, 2004). It would seem that games provide an ideal medium for providing players with experiences that make them reflect on their ethics and moral reasoning. In practice, this potential has been elusive.

Ethical reasoning is reasoning about right and wrong human conduct. It begins with the identification of a moral or ethical issue. A game that afforded ethical reflection would also, among other things, encourage players to assess their own ethical values, the social context of issues identified, and consider the ramifications of alternative actions. I call games that provide opportunities for encouraging ethical reasoning and reflection ethically notable. In this chapter, I aim to explore

DOI: 10.4018/978-1-60960-120-1.ch002

some of the ways in which games can be ethically notable as well as the challenges in achieving this.

In the first part of the chapter I discuss what I mean by games that encourage ethical reasoning and reflection. I focus principally on two aspects that I call the rationalized and emotional responses. Games that encourage rationalized responses typically engage players' critical thinking and problem-solving skills in moral contexts or situations. Games that elicit emotional responses often encourage players' investment in the narrative and fictive elements of a game while simultaneously facilitating their reflection on their in-game choices and decisions.

In the second part of the chapter, I closely examine three videogames I propose are ethically notable. First, I analyze the fantasy role-playing game *Ultima IV* (Garriott, 1985) and explore how it attempts to make the player feel personally invested or responsible for their in-game decisions. I also examine the ethical system it encodes and describe how it requires the player to learn and follow it in order to succeed. More specifically, I look at how it encourages rationalized responses by providing players with dilemmas or situations in which their understanding of the ethical system is challenged. Next, I analyze the controversial action/stealth game *Manhunt* (Rockstar North, 2003). I argue that different design elements in *Manhunt* create moral tension between the game's rewards structure and the motivations of the characters as defined by the narrative. Via an emotional response, *Manhunt's* design helps the player question the motivations behind their actions, especially when they run counter to the game's narrative. Finally, I examine tactical role-playing game *Fire Emblem: Radiant Dawn* (Intelligent Systems, 2007). In this game, by cleverly manipulating the way the narrative is presented and by forcing the player to control a variety of characters as its multi-faceted plot unfolds, the game helps create moral tension between the player's goals and those posed by both the narrative and the gameplay. The analysis of

each of these ethically notable games highlights some of the different ways that ethical reasoning and reflection can be encouraged through gaming environments.

In the final section, I shift focus from success stories to concentrate on the challenges faced when attempting to create ethically notable gameplay experiences. My analysis, grounded in examples from multiple games, identifies five challenges for creating ethically notable games. The first challenge lies in helping the player understand when, and why, certain actions or moments in a game are morally relevant. For example, if a game encodes a particular moral framework, the player should be able to understand why given actions are right or wrong and be able to deduce the moral consequences of his actions. The second challenge lies in achieving the proper focus of the moral tension. For instance, many games attempt to achieve an emotional response from their players, by showing characters troubled by moral situations. It is often the case, however, that the player becomes detached from the emotional impact of these moments because the focus of the moral tension is on the character, rather than the player. The player may simply be a witness to a moral situation and lack the agency to guide the decision made by the player's character. Third, I examine how games that challenge their players to make moral choices often see these goals subverted by gameplay. For example, a moral choice may be understood by the player as one of play style or choice of gameplay. Fourth, I ponder the desirability and possible ethical limitations in providing strong emotional responses in gameplay experiences. Finally, I wonder whether the design goal of providing meaningful consequences is, in fact, shared by players. I conclude with a discussion of the main issues presented. The discussion highlights how our analyses serve as a framework not only for reflecting upon and understanding ethics and morality in games but also for outlining the design space for ethically notable games.

Ethically Notable Games

Games can be an ideal medium for providing players with experiences that make them reflect on their ethics and moral reasoning by helping players identify moral or ethical issues, encourage them to assess their own ethical values and the social context of issues identified, and also consider the ramifications of alternative actions. Not all games encourage ethical reasoning and reflection. I call those that do ethically notable. I am not referring to those games that have been controversial or subject to extraordinary media attention. Nor do I mean those games with ethical frameworks that are consistent or complete (more on that later). Rather, by ethically notable I mean games that, using a variety of design elements including narrative, gameplay, and more, create opportunities for their players to think about ethics.

Ethical reflection can occur for a variety of reasons. These may be related to the game, or may simply occur due to the player's personal circumstances (e.g., an in-game scenario may remind the player of something unethical he did outside of the game). However, it can be productive to focus on two perspectives when exploring ethical reflection: the ethics of the activity of play and the ethics of actions in games as defined by the games themselves.

What does it mean to examine the ethics of play? Games create spaces that mediate our understanding of the ethics of players' actions. Therefore, actions considered unethical in an out-of-game context may be expected or even demanded while playing a game. A good player may be one that best exploits his opponent's weaknesses or deceives his fellow players most effectively. Is this behavior unethical? Similarly, what does it mean to play fairly? What are the values of good or bad sportsmanship? These are just a few examples of play issues that may lead to ethical reasoning. In fact, research has been done to explore some of these. For example, Taylor explores the importance that informal (or unwritten) rules have in supporting positive play experiences (Taylor, 2008). Consalvo, on the other hand, explores cheating, or how players negotiate how, when, and for what reasons to subvert a game's rules (Consalvo, 2007). Woods notes how board game players often negotiate the integrity of the social fabric during competitive game playing: oftentimes, such as when playing a learning game or when the enjoyment of the game by all participants is more important, not playing to win is the correct choice (Woods, 2009). More generally, the ethics of play is often an issue when examining the interaction between two or more players. Multiplayer games, such as alternate reality games, live action role-playing games, MMOs, social games, and board games, have design elements that often make them ethically notable. However, their analysis is beyond the scope of this chapter and left for future work.

What does it mean to examine the ethics of actions in games as defined by the games themselves? When playing games, players often engage rich narrative storylines and employ complex discursive practices and problem solving strategies in order to understand and master underlying game mechanics (Gee, 2003; Shaffer, 2006). In practice, the narratives, symbols, and rules that make up a game constitute an ideological framework (Frasca, 2004). The player participates in a simulated environment with its own rules and narratives. What happens when some of these rules are normative? In videogames, certain behaviors and actions are often rewarded while others are not. Those behaviors that are encouraged can be considered desirable or good while the opposite holds for those that are discouraged. By coupling the evaluation of in-game actions with the narrative framework that contextualizes them, a videogame can both represent as well as enact an ethical framework. For example, in the first person shooter *Unreal*, the player was often rewarded for not shooting the benevolent aliens called Nali. If a player helped and protected them, they often led the player to secret areas with valuable supplies.

Consider also the fantasy role-playing videogame *Fable* whose ethical system is one of its core elements of gameplay (Molyneux, 2004). In *Fable*, some of the actions performed by the player are categorized by the game's narrative as good while others are evil. Actions are assigned points that determine the characters alignment. This, in turn, determines the player character's physical appearance and how non-player characters will respond. The player, by learning and understanding which (and when) actions are considered good or evil, can begin to understand the ethical framework that is procedurally encoded in the game, and also reflect on ethics more generally.

These two perspectives, the ethics of play and the ethics of in-game actions, work together in helping players reflect on ethical issues. However, it is also useful to consider the perspective of the player regarding such reflection. After all, players should also assess their own ethical values as they play. What kinds of responses do players have with respect to ethical issues of play or in-game actions? In the next section, we examine some of these responses.

Emotional Responses: Guilt, Shame, and Moral Dilemmas

Much research has been conducted to explore player's emotional responses as they play games. Players are often asked to self-report their emotional responses, defined in terms of joy, pleasant relaxation, anger, fear, depressed feeling, and sense of presence (Ermi & Mayra, 2005; Ravaja et al., 2004). Physiological responses such as heart rate or skin conductance, are also often measured directly while players play a game (Ravaja, Saari, Laarni, Kallinen & Salminen, 2005). These measures, and the sense we make of them, are valuable for understanding the experience of gameplay. For the purposes of this chapter, our focus will be somewhat broader as I will be referring to emotions like guilt, shame, and embarrassment that

are not usually measured and are perhaps more challenging to observe in laboratory settings.

Emotional responses that are ethically motivated, so to speak, are usually triggered when the player realizes that they have, or are about to, violate a moral standard. For instance, a player may feel shame or guilt for something they did in a game such as shooting an innocent alien in Unreal. In the case of shame, the objectionable in-game behavior is seen as reflecting, more generally, an objectionable self ("I did a bad thing, therefore I am a bad person"). The case of guilt is similar, although the focus is on the thing that was done, rather than the individual (Tangney, Miller, Flicker, & Barlow, 1996). Games that encourage emotional responses often encourage players to become invested in their narrative and fictive elements of a game while simultaneously highlighting the role that the player has in guiding the choices and decisions made in a game. Sometimes, like in *Chrono Trigger*, the player is not aware that choices he makes in the game are interpreted by the game as a reflection of his values and ethics. Early in the game Crono, the player-controlled character is falsely accused of kidnapping and taken to a courtroom to face trial. The trial's outcome depends on a series of seemingly irrelevant actions and interactions that Crono may (or may not) have had earlier in the game during a town festival. If Crono picked up an unattended package of food, its rightful owner appears at the trial. "Him! He ate my lunch right off the table!" he accuses. On the other hand, doing the right thing leads to witnesses testifying in Crono's favor. "This nice man.... He brought me my kitty. Thank you for being so kind!" says a little girl whose cat was recovered. Each of the witnesses comments on Crono's morality as reflected by his actions. As the trial unfolds, the player is often shocked to realize that the things he did earlier reflect his moral character. Sicart describes a similar example from *Metal Gear Solid 3: Snake Eater*, when during a trip up a river, the player is reminded of all the needless deaths he has caused. If the player hasn't killed more than those required to progress in the game, he faces few ghosts and the trip is short. If he killed soldiers who needn't have died, the trip is much longer and tortuous (Sicart, 2009).

It is also sometimes the case that misunderstandings can lead to powerful emotional responses. In the following example, interactive fiction author Emily Short has been playing *Fable II* with a female character when she meets a male non-player character:

"I saw the symbol of a ring on the meter of how much he liked me. I reasoned that this meant, if I made him like me more, he'd give me a ring. So I spent a little time with him, doing dances and falling over afterward, because he seemed to get a big kick out of this buffoonery. I made faces. I gave him the thumbs-up sign. I flirted a little, just to butter him up.

But when he'd fallen in love with me and wanted to get married, I was startled and not at all pleased. I realized what the ring on his meter indicated then, when it was too late and I'd led him on. I had no intention to get married, but when he started to follow me around (a mistake thanks to more confused socialization on my part), I let him.

I let him follow me out into the wild, and when we were set upon by bandits I didn't give him a second thought, just assumed he'd look out for himself or have the sense to hide behind a rock. My dog never got killed, after all. But then the battle ended and he wasn't following me anymore.

I actually couldn't tell what had just happened: did he run away? Or — it seemed more likely — did he fight and die because I was too absent-minded to attend to him? I felt guilty about that. It was the first thing in the game that made me feel like I'd

done something wrong. [...] I'd cold-bloodedly ignored some guy, toyed with his affections and then led him to his death. That felt culpable." (Short, 2009)

Emotional responses can also be triggered through the use of moral dilemmas. Moral dilemmas occupy an important part of our history both as a central topic of philosophical discussion as well as the substance of much of our creative and expressive work. The power of drama, as witnessed in theatre, literature, and film, often relies on placing characters in seemingly irresolvable moral situations. Using a variety of rhetorical devices and strategies, the spectator, reader, and viewer not only witness the emotional turmoil of the characters but are captivated by it. We empathize with the characters and share their pain and turmoil. Computers, however, allow their users to play equivalent roles to both the drama performer as well as the audience member (Laurel, 1991). Pohl (2008) argues that it is the emotional involvement that characterizes computer games. She distinguishes two forms of emotional involvement: the instantaneous (we play because we want to win) and the spontaneous (we continue to play because we identify with and care about the story). The narrative frame draws us in and makes us care about the game character's fate. We feel for him, we identify with his concerns and want to know how the story turns out for him and for us (Pohl, 2008). Theatre, film, literature and games can all present troubled characters facing moral dilemmas and, hopefully, emotionally involve the spectator, reader, or player. However, games are particularly well-suited to directly present the player with a moral dilemma. This is not the same as presenting the player with a dilemma faced by a character. I call this the distinction between the character's dilemma and the player's dilemma. The dilemma faced by the character is, by definition, one step removed and thus potentially less powerful or effective for eliciting ethical reflection. Our case studies in the following sections illustrate various forms of moral dilemmas observed in videogames.

Rational Response: Puzzles and Simulations

Games that encourage rationalized responses typically engage players' critical thinking and problem-solving skills in moral contexts or situations. In these instances, moral situations are perceived as problems or puzzles to be explored and solved. It is often the case that figuring out the morally "optimal" solution is part of the fun. For instance, in the PC game *Star Trek: Starfleet Academy*, the player must face a scenario called the Kobayashi Maru. This scenario is well-known in *Star Trek* canon as a test given to Star Fleet Academy cadets. It is a no-win scenario designed to test a cadet's character in the face of impossible odds. In the videogame, the player is given the choice to reprogram the simulator (to cheat) prior to the test. Three different cheating options are provided. Players well-versed in *Star Trek* lore would presumably recognize the scenario and try to determine what the correct course of action should be. Should they cheat in the same way as Captain Kirk from the original TV show did, by reprogramming the simulator so that the enemy captains fear and respect the player? Or, should they honor the spirit of the test and try to do their best? Perhaps the best situation is to cheat at the test in a novel way? In this case, meta-knowledge of the *Star Trek* universe creates an interesting ethical situation in which the player must try to figure out the "ideal" solution.

In other cases a player may want to explore the limits of the ethical system. What sorts of actions are morally significant in the game and which ones aren't? How are certain actions evaluated? Someone playing *The Sims* may want to see how damaging certain actions are to the relationships between characters in the game. Is it possible to abuse a Sim-guest so much that they commit suicide? Will a Sim character try to prevent an-other from causing harm? What kinds of amorous relationships can Sims enter into? The designer of *The Sims*, Will Wright, notes how: "In some sense, when you're playing the game you're trying to reverse-engineer the simulation in your head (quoted in Sieberg, 2000)." In essence, players exploring these situations are crafting experimental situations to test both the limits of the game's encoded ethical framework as well as the design space of the game.

Games also encourage rational responses when they present procedurally encoded ethical systems such that playing a game can be seen as a means of engaging with a particular ethical perspective. In these cases, players often "experiment with ethics" as a sandbox in which they may examine the consequences of certain kinds of behavior as well as the reasons for those consequences. Games that allow players to play as "good" or "evil" often encourage these kinds of responses. In this case, the ethical choices don't determine overall success at the game (you can "beat the game" regardless of whether you played as an evil or good character). For example, PC role-playing game *Baldur's Gate* has an alignment system that reflects in-game character's morality using two axes (good/evil and lawfulness/chaos). Depending on your character's alignment (and also their reputation), other characters may choose to join (or leave) your party, you may receive greater discounts or markups in stores or temples, and certain gameplay options become available. Playing an "evil" character is usually not all that different in terms of how the game's storyline unfolds compared to that of the "good" character. In the context of the game both are considered valid.

CASE STUDIES

Earlier I discussed what I mean by games that encourage ethical reasoning and reflection. I examined two lenses for considering ethics in games: the ethics of play and the ethics of in-game actions. I then examined two types of responses players often have when reflecting in ethical issues in games: the rationalized and emotional responses. Games that encourage rationalized responses typically engage players' critical thinking and problem-solving skills in moral contexts or situations. Games that elicit emotional responses often encourage players' investment in the narrative and fictive elements of a game while simultaneously facilitating their reflection on their in-game choices and decisions. In the following sections I will analyze three games focusing on their narrative, gameplay, the interaction between them, and ultimately how they are perceived and understood by the player. Each of these examples provides a case study for ethically notable games.

The Virtues of *Ultima IV*

Ultima IV: The Quest of the Avatar (*UIV*) is perhaps the earliest videogame to explicitly encode an ethical system and require its players to discover, learn, and adhere to it to win the game. *UIV* was designed by Richard Garriott and was released in 1985 for the Apple II computer (Garriott, 1985). After creating the first three *Ultima* games, Garriott noted how the narratives of computer RPG games were simplistic and player actions were mostly devoid of consequences. The storyline of these games was essentially "here's some money, here's some weapons, here's some monsters, go kill them and you win." (Spector & Tyler, 1999) *UIV* was different. It attempted to use gameplay as a means to build a story and a message with philosophical and ethical implications (Mäyrä, 2008). In doing so, it helped develop the computer role-playing game genre to another level of maturity by emphasizing social and cultural conflict over "hack 'n' slash" (Barton, 2008; CGW, 1996; Halford & Halford, 2001). Garriott explained how "the idea I'm trying to put forth is more philosophical than religious—that in a society where people have to interact with each other, there are certain kinds of rules whose rationale you should be able to

understand." (Addams, 1990) Scorpia's review of *UIV* explains the goal of the game:

You, an ordinary person, are called upon to make the long and arduous journey that will culminate in your becoming an Avatar, a perfect mortal. There is no central evil to defeat here; no Mondain, no Minax, no Exodus awaits you [Note: Scorpia refers to the villains in the earlier games in the series]. Rather, this is a quest where you seek to perfect your inner being, to become enlightened in the eight virtues of Compassion, Valor, Honor, Justice, Humility, Sacrifice, Spirituality, and Honesty. (Scorpia, 1986)

Success in *UIV* required players to learn about, and adhere to, the eight virtues listed above. Failure to follow the requirements for each virtue resulted in a setback. In gameplay terms, acting in a virtuous manner would result in positive progress toward achieving enlightenment in a particular virtue. For example the virtues of compassion and sacrifice could be "increased" by donating gold to beggars and blood to healers respectively (Addams, 1990). Conversely, fleeing from combat would result in a loss of progress toward valor. Also, what mattered was the net effect over a multitude of independent actions. It was not enough to do one good deed; you had to do enough of them.

Garriott felt it was important that *UIV*'s players feel a degree of personal and social responsibility toward their actions in the game. His reasoning was that "in most of these games you are the puppeteer running this puppet around the world. If this puppet is doing bad things, it's not you, it's the puppet." (Spector & Tyler, 1999) So, rather than create a character by choosing from available options or using random dice-rolls, the character in *UIV* was supposed to be "the essence of you as an individual." (Spector & Tyler, 1999) In the introductory sequence of the game the player meets a gypsy woman who asks the player to answer seven questions:

On the table before you lie two cards, one representing the virtue of Valor, the other representing the virtue of Justice. As though from a distance, the gypsy's voice floats across to you, saying: 'Consider this: Thou halt been sent to secure a needed treaty with a distant lord. Thy host is agreeable to the proposal, but insults thy country at dinner. Dost thou: a) Valiantly bear the slurs or b) Justly rise and demand an apology?' (Scorpia, 1986)

Each question posed a moral dilemma with two possible answers. Since each response represented a particular virtue in the game, answering the dilemma was interpreted as favoring one virtue over the other. In the example above, answering "a) Valiantly bear the slurs" meant favoring the virtue of valor over that of justice (option "b" in example above). The purpose of this sequence of dilemmas was to determine which of the eight virtues was favored by the player. Since each of the professions embodied a specific virtue, the player's character would thus, in some way, represent their values in the game. Garriott describes how, anecdotally, when people were asked to rank the eight virtues in order of importance, their responses were almost exactly the same as what was determined by the game (Spector & Tyler, 1999). The character used in the game was thus determined by the players' personal ethics, rather than simply choosing, or randomly generating, a character at will. (Scorpia, 1986) The character creation process encourages a rationalized response from the player that invites them to reflect on their personal ethics and establishing priorities between different virtues.

UIV's use of moral dilemmas was a novel approach to character creation. It was not, however, the only time players faced them. One of Garriot's design goals was to make sure the game was full of ethical tests (Massey, 2007). He describes one of the tests as follows:

One of the things that I was very proud of in Ultima IV is a room I had created in the final dungeon and the room included a lever in middle of the floor and when you threw the lever it opened the gates on some cages that were in the corners of the room and the cages were full of children. The children were in fact really monsters, because that is all they could be at that level of technology, and the children would attack you in the center of the screen next to the lever. You'd be surrounded by these children who were attacking you and since you were the Avatar at this point and you were at the very end of the game, I knew—or I hoped—that players would be very worried about what to do about the situation. They wouldn't want to kill the children because they'd be in fear of losing their compassion or their honor or a wide variety of other metrics that the game really was watching. I assumed players would struggle over what to do in this room. (Massey, 2007)

The goal of the "children's room" in *UIV*, as explained above, was to elicit an emotional response, make the player uncomfortable and question the game. Is the game really asking me to slaughter children? What should I do? The dilemma is twofold. First, the game apparently requires an action that is morally repugnant in the real world. Second, the game appears to require the player to do something that contradicts the stated goals of the game. Virtuous people do not kill children. Fortunately, there were multiple ways around the dilemma. Player's could cast a sleeping spell, force them to run away, and so on. While there is no formal evidence of the effectiveness of the "children's room" in promoting ethical reasoning, issues with its design did come up during playtesting.

A few weeks prior to us publishing Ultima IV, my brother [Robert Garriott] came into my office with a letter that he'd received from one of our QA testers and the letter basically read: 'I refuse to work for a company that so clearly supports child abuse.' And they referred to this room as a game design that encouraged child abuse because I had forced the players into harming these children in this room. My brother came to me up in arms and going like, 'Oh my god Richard, how could you have included such a horrible thing in your game?' To which I responded and said, 'First of all, the fact that someone would take it that seriously and be so emotionally moved by this incredibly simple thing that I put in this game, I find is a statement of success'. (Massey, 2007)

While the QA tester's reaction was perhaps unwarranted (after all, there was a way to solve the dilemma), it serves to illustrate how games can make players feel personally invested or responsible for the decisions they make in a game. Thus, I argue that *Ultima IV* is an ethically notable game because:

- It attempts to make the player feel personally invested or responsible for the decisions they make in the game. (emotional response)
- It encodes an ethical system and requires the player to learn it and follow it to succeed. (rational response)
- It provides players with dilemmas or situations in which their understanding of the ethical system is challenged. (rational and emotional)

MANHUNT: THE DILEMMA OF VIOLENCE

Manhunt is a videogame developed by Rockstar North and originally released for the Playstation 2 in 2003 (Rockstar North, 2003). In the game, the player controls the character James Earl Cash, a death row criminal who is rescued from his execution and coerced into starring in his kidnapper's snuff film productions. The kidnapper, known as "The Director," witnesses and records Cash's carnage though a network of security cameras. The Director also goads, threatens and provides instructions via an earpiece worn by Cash. The player controls Cash in a third-person perspective

and the gameplay is best described as requiring both elements of action and stealth. Cash is outnumbered and must carefully and quietly make his way through a gauntlet of dilapidated environments to surprise and execute his victims using a variety of items including plastic bags, shards of glass, bats, and other weapons.

Manhunt is in many ways the opposite of *UIV*. The player-controlled character, through the game's mechanics and narrative context, is not encouraged to be good or carry out good actions. It actively encourages the opposite. As I will show, however, the game is also capable of creating an emotional experience in the player.

Manhunt created a media controversy when it was released due to the graphic nature of the violence it depicted. The most notorious element of violence in the game is the execution system. Executions are perhaps the most effective way to eliminate opponents and are, on occasion, required to progress in the game. The player, however, is responsible for deciding how brutal an execution should be. For example, let's say Cash sneaks up behind a gang member with a plastic bag. Pressing the attack button will result in Cash yanking the bag over the victims head and suffocating him. If the player holds down the button for a few seconds, the execution is more violent and Cash might punch the victim in the face in addition to suffocating him. The third, and most brutal, type of execution is carried out by holding down the attack button even longer.

The premise and violence in *Manhunt* are undeniably gory and brutal. From an ethical perspective, however, this game is not notable due to the violence of the executions. It is notable because of the position in which the game places the player. As mentioned, the brutality of an execution is a choice made by the player. *Manhunt* forces the player to question and evaluate her actions and motivations for how to play the game. The player is forced to examine the role of successful play as a moral dilemma itself. There are no intrinsic (in-game) benefits for carrying out executions in the most brutal way. Extrinsically, players are rated at the end of each area and, by obtaining high ratings (three or five stars, depending on the difficulty level), they can unlock bonus features and codes. This only applies to five of the twenty areas and there is no discernible benefit for getting five stars in all the areas (Rodoy, 2003). So, why should the player choose to execute Cash's opponents in the most brutal way possible? The player is tasked with reflecting on how far they are willing to go in carrying out the executions. Not only are the executions brutal and sickening, but they are also unpleasant to watch.

Manhunt's player-based (rather than character-based) moral dilemma is made all the more intense through the use of a USB headset. Using the headset allows the player to use his voice to distract enemies in the game. It also enables the player to hear The Director's instructions directly via the earpiece. Both elements narrow the cognitive and emotional distance between the player and the grotesque world of *Manhunt*. The microphone does this by allowing a more direct form of agency while the headset heightens the tension by channeling The Director's wishes and desires directly to the player's ear. In this way, The Director assumes the role of the "evil conscience." As a player, you hear him inside your head. His voice goads, taunts, and cheers you on when you cave in to his desires. There is nothing more sickening and disturbing than hearing The Director cackle maniacally as Cash murders a gang member. As expected, The Director derives more pleasure from the more gruesome executions.

Let us examine the narrative and gameplay context the player is provided with when deciding if he should execute gruesome executions instead of "regular" ones? Can the player shift his moral responsibility by placing it on the character whose role he is simply playing? The answer, from the position of the narrative, is no. Cash is a convicted death row criminal and it is reasonable to assume that, when placed in a kill or be killed situation, Cash would not hesitate to kill. The Director wants Cash to be as brutal as possible since his illegal snuff-film operation demands it. Cash, however,

has no motivation to perform the most brutal types of executions. The Director is the antagonist, what reason would Cash have to want help him? Also, executions are risky to execute. While the player keeps the attack button pressed, Cash is exposed and vulnerable to attack. We might expect Cash to reason that a solution to his predicament might be to kill as few enemies as possible and to do so in the least gruesome way (thus not allowing himself to further The Director's desires). From the context of the narrative, the player has no reason or motivation to opt for greater brutality in executions. Role-playing Cash does not exculpate the player from Cash's actions.

From a game design perspective, the context for deciding the dilemma is the opposite. In a macabre twist, the player is awarded "extra points" for completing more gruesome executions. As mentioned, higher ratings serve no function or purpose within the context of the game. The player is not rewarded with anything that makes playing the game any easier. The non-player characters don't know or care that the player got a five-star rating in the previous area. The only purpose of the rating system seems to be to tempt the player. To force the player to question how much he really values a meaningless measure of achievement. How far would you go for the five-star rating? As a game player, how do you value your competitiveness and achievements as a player (get the most points and unlock the most extras) versus doing the right thing in the context of the narrative? The juxtaposition of the games' reward structure and its narrative highlights the true moral dilemma of *Manhunt*. I argue that *Manhunt* is an ethically notable game because:

- It creates moral tension between gameplay rewards structure and the motivations of the characters as defined by the narrative. (emotional response)
- It encourages players to assess their own ethical values with respect to both the gameplay and narrative contexts of the game.

FIRE EMBLEM: RADIANT DAWN

While *UIV* encodes a virtue ethics framework that is arguably positive, it would seem that everything about *Manhunt* is negative. Is it possible to create a player's dilemma without a salient ethical framework or morally repugnant gameworld?

Fire Emblem: *Radiant Dawn* (*FE:RD*) is a tactical role-playing game for the Nintendo Wii console (Intelligent Systems, 2007). It features a multi-faceted storyline in which the player follows (and controls) characters from different factions that occasionally intersect. It is at these intersections that the game becomes ethically notable.

FE: *RD* is divided into four sections. In the first section, the player controls a group of characters led by a character called Micaiah. In section two, the player controls two different groups of characters from earlier versions of the game. In the game's third section, the player controls each of the three groups separately. In the final chapter of the third section, the player controls a group of characters led by Ike who faces an enemy force led by Micaiah. Micaiah's force includes many characters the player has, until recently, been controlling and improving. Totilo describes how in this chapter:

[The goal] was to annihilate every character on the other side. Was I reading this right? I had to slaughter all of the enemies? All of Micaiah's forces? [...] I could not believe what the game was asking me to do. I sat dumbfounded. Really? I have to destroy all of those characters I spent all that time improving? Zihark, and all the rest, had to bite the bullet? (Totilo, 2008)

Faced with the dilemma and his unwillingness to blindly accept the missions' goals, Totilo ventured online to see if there was a way out. He discovered that instead of annihilating enemies he cared about, he "only" needed to ensure that 80 enemy combatants perished. Totilo's solution to the dilemma was to ensure that the characters he cared about remained as far from each other as possible, regardless of whether or not they were labeled by the game as "the enemy."

And as soon as I did it, I felt a bit sick. Video games always require you to value some characters' lives over others. Goombas' lives don't matter. Mario's does. But here I was deciding that some of my enemies should die and that others shouldn't. It got more twisted. After a few turns of action I noticed that the kill-counter in the upper right hand corner of the screen was counting deaths of enemy soldiers and unnamed partner soldiers who were fighting alongside Ike as part of the same total. That meant I could reach my goal of 80 battlefield deaths not just through the slaughter of certain enemies but through the death of my own allies.

Is it creepy that I took this as good news? This meant the mission would end sooner, that my chosen people on both sides would be out of harm's way faster. I began to root for my 'enemy' Zihark when he strode out into the battlefield again and started chopping down my allies. (Totilo, 2008)

Totilo realizes that he is subverting not only the game's narrative, but also the established game goals. Micaiah views Ike as the enemy and the gameplay goal is consistent with that. Why should he not do as instructed? Totilo was clearly uncomfortable with the dilemma and how he responded.

I had made quite a judgment of gameplay-based morality. I had decided that some characters, some who were with me and some who were against me, deserved to live. I'd judged that others, some with me and some against me, were better off dead. I'd chosen favorites. Essentially, the characters with names, the ones I had trained—they deserved life. The unnamed grunts both helping and harming me? Expendable. I'd cheered for the deaths of supposed friends and allies and was relieved when they failed to kill enemies I had once trained. I refused to assist some allies in need. I'd transgressed traditional battle lines. Like I said above, I felt a twist in my gut. What kind of battlefield general had this game made me? What kind of commander of men and women? (Totilo, 2008)

We could argue that Totilo's solution to his dilemma was an unethical one. However, that would miss the point: Totilo was emotionally invested to such a degree that he was willing to forgo the context of both narrative and gameplay. Unlike *UIV* and *Manhunt*, he faced an ethical dilemma that, while intended by the game's designers, wasn't about a particular in-game ethical framework. Thus, I argue that *FE:RD* is an ethically notable game because:

- It creates a moral tension between the player's goals and those posed by both the narrative and the gameplay.
- It encourages players to assess their own ethical values with respect to the narrative context of the game.

DISCUSSION

In this chapter, I argued that an ethically notable game is one that provides opportunities for encouraging ethical reasoning and reflection. I have also shown how games can achieve this by creating different kinds of moral tension. By examining three games, I have shown different ways that games can accomplish this. However, it can also be valuable to consider the following questions to analyze and better understand the ethical reasoning potential of a particular game.

Is the Ethical Framework Discernible and Consistent?

The effort that goes in to creating an ethical framework in a game will ultimately be for naught if the player is not able to discern right from wrong (according to the game's values). More importantly, the player should understand why given actions are right or wrong and be able to deduce the moral consequences of his actions. Ethical systems that are opaque to their players risk becoming perceived as morally irrelevant: if there is no way to understand, why bother. Ethical systems that are inconsistent face an even greater risk: confusing the player. Confusion subverts the efforts of establishing an ethical framework by making the evaluation seem arbitrary. I note that it is not necessary for the framework to be both comprehensive (consider all actions in the game as ethical in some sense) and complete (ethically consider all possible intentions and/or goals behind player actions). Rather, the ethical rules must apply when the player expects them to, and when they do not it must be possible for the player to understand why. For example, in many adventure games players steal or loot objects with no apparent consequences; it does not matter if the object came from a treasure chest found in the woods or if it came from a chest located inside the house of a friendly neighbor. Other games discriminate if the item was from an urban location (e.g., the rule that it's not okay to steal from a villager's home) or from the wilderness (e.g., the rule that it's okay to loot a chest in the woods). Rauch notes how *Fable* can often seem inconsistent "since 'examine' and 'take' use the same key, I have often found myself 'stealing' items by accident. At moments like these, the rules of both Albion and Fable itself can seem alarmingly random, and this randomness interferes with player experience by frustrating both the ability to grasp the intricacies of the rule system and the ability to maintain suspension of disbelief and become emotionally involved in the narrative." (Rauch, 2007)

Who Faces the Moral Dilemma?

The power of moral dilemmas in games is that they can require the player to participate (rather than simply to be a spectator). However, it is easy to fall into the trap of assuming that simply because there is a moral dilemma in the game, the player will become personally invested. Many games, especially those with well-developed storylines, involve characters in moral situations. It is often the case that the player is merely a witness to the moral situation and lacks the agency to guide the decision made by the player's character. Earlier, I referred to these cases as character-based moral dilemmas and now I will describe a few examples. One of the most-often remembered and discussed moments in *Final Fantasy VII* (Square, 1997) is the death of the character Aeris (Edge, 2007; Lopez & Theobald, 2004). Aeris, who is at certain times a player-controllable character, chooses to sacrifice herself to save the planet. Her decision is one that is made by the game's designers. It's a dilemma the character faced and was troubled by, although the player had no real say in the matter. Similarly, in the third person-shooter game *Max Payne* (Remedy Entertainment, 2001), although the character Max is depicted as troubled by his situation and many of the decisions he makes, the player does not participate in any of those choices. Should Max ally with a known criminal to gain equipment and resources that will let him take out another mob boss? Max decides, not the player.

Is the Dilemma Moral?

Difficult decisions are not always moral decisions. A player wracked by the decision of how to spend a limited number of points on character upgrades is arguably more concerned with gameplay than ethics. It is not hard to realize that these situations are not moral dilemmas. The danger lies when dilemmas are presented as moral but, for some reason or another, are not regarded as such by players. In the first-person shooter game *Star Wars Jedi Knight: Dark Forces II* (JK) (LucasArts, 1997), the player controls Kyle Katarn. The game follows Katarn as he journeys to confront his father's murderers, while simultaneously

discovering (and developing) his latent abilities in The Force (a metaphysical power in the *Star Wars* universe). Over the course of the game, the player earns points that can be used to increase a variety of (Force) abilities categorized into three groups: dark, light, and neutral. The player can, for the most part, spend the points on any of the abilities he fancies. Once the player is approximately two-thirds of the way through the game, "Kyle finally decides on the light or dark side of the Force, and acts accordingly. (This decision is determined both by the powers you've taken, and how you've treated civilians throughout the first parts of the game)" (Thomas, 2004). The decision to embrace evil (or not) is arguably one that should not be taken lightly. However, two things conspire against considering this a moral dilemma. First, the player is not allowed to make the decision at that specific moment in the game. This is because the result (join the Dark/Light side of the force) happens as the result of an accumulation of many decisions that have been made over hours of gameplay. Second, and perhaps more importantly, there are no real consequences to the decision. As Dulin noted in a review, "many [players] will also be disappointed to learn that the distinction between the Light and Dark sides, once the choice has been made, is not as striking as one would hope" (Dulin, 1997). Dulin continues, noting that "The Light Side is obviously the path you are supposed to take—you get more cut-scenes and more narration throughout the last few levels. But apart from this and the different Force powers at your disposal, choosing the Dark Side only leads to one really shocking plot element, a slightly altered level, and a completely different ending (which is, in many ways, far more satisfying)." (Dulin, 1997) When faced with what is perhaps the game's key moral dilemma, the player must choose between light and dark side based on what content they want to experience and what force powers they would like to use for the rest of the game. Evil and good are understood by the player at a procedural level, a state in the machine, rather than at a semantic one (Sicart, 2008, 2009).

Is There a Need for Emotional Distance?

I have argued for the importance of creating emotional responses, such as guilt, for encouraging ethical reflection. However, should we assume that players do, in fact, desire and value these kinds of experiences? Dow, et al. (2008) studied player's reactions to an augmented reality version of the interactive drama Façade. In this version of the game, players interact by walking around a physical stage modeled after the 3-D world of the desktop-based version of Façade (Mateas & Stern, 2003). Players interact with the game by wearing a video-see-through pair of goggles, and speaking directly to the characters (Dow et al., 2008). The game's narrative revolves around a social situation where the player has been invited by a couple to a dinner party only to quickly realize that their "marriage is falling apart, and the couple is looking to the player to help them settle their grievances" (Dow, 2009). Dow notes that many players exhibited genuine emotional reactions during their experience, however, many of those players preferred the desktop version of the game (Dow, 2009). This was "because being in the same space with an arguing couple was too physical and intense. The less immersive interface of the desktop version allowed players to feel free to 'goof off,' 'decide how they wanted to feel,' and enjoy the experience from a safe distance rather than constantly feeling 'on the spot'" (Dow, 2009). So, if we create games designed to make players feel awkward, guilty, or generally uncomfortable, how do we know that players will, once the experience has concluded, actually get something positive out it? Perhaps more importantly, and this was not an issue with Dow's experience, what are the ethical limitations we face as game designers and creators? Is it ethical to create a situation designed to make

a player feel bad about him or herself? What are the potential (negative) long-term effects?

How Meaningful Should In-Game Consequences Be?

The designers of the *Fable* videogame series have prided themselves on the role that moral choices play in the game. *Fable*'s ad-copy promised "For every choice, a consequence," while *Fable II* refined this idea ensuring that choices and consequences were especially meaningful. Sometimes, this was not possible. For example, early in the game there is a quest in which the player needs to decide whether to give warrants to a criminal to dispose of, or turn them over to a guard. In an interview with Simon Carless, *Fable II*'s lead designer Peter Molyneux noted how "there was 'a big mistake that we made' to not convey that this small task had very significant meaning for your good or evil status later in the game. As Molyneux said: 'If you don't tell people... the significance of the choice that they are making, you can run into trouble'" (Carless, 2009). At other times, the game was successful in creating meaningful consequences. At the end of the game, players must make a difficult decision. They have to decide whether to choose the needs of the many (resurrect thousands of characters), the needs of the few (resurrect their slain dog, sister, and family), or the needs of the one (obtain a massive monetary reward). After the game was released, "Molyneux said that he 'did have hate mail from people' who could not bring themselves to sacrifice the multitudes, and chose the other path [the few]" (Carless, 2009). They were angry because they could not choose to save the many and at the same time save their dog, an in-game companion that joins the player early in the game and follows them around for the duration. These players were closely attached to their canine companion and were not willing to accept the consequence of their choice. "Apparently these complaints 'got to such a furor' that the first *Fable*

II downloadable content pack was changed to enable the return of the dog, a particularly faithful companion [this was apparently implemented in the 2nd downloadable content pack rather than the first]. But, quipped Molyneux: 'Don't expect us to be as merciful as that in the future'" (Carless, 2009). Similarly, in *Fallout 3*, the player could gain an animal follower (a dog called Dogmeat) who was not replaceable once deceased. The downloadable expansion *Broken Steel* allowed for a workaround by providing an in-game perk called "Puppies!" By choosing this perk players can regain a canine companion, explained by the game's narrative as one of Dogmeat's puppies (Huijboom, 2009). These examples highlight a tension between the desire for games to provide ethically meaningful choices and consequences, and our willingness as players to live with those choices. Players seem to want it both ways.

CONCLUSION

Delwiche argues that videogames have affordances that can shape attitude and behavior (Delwiche, 2007), Bogost argues they can persuade (Bogost, 2007), and Gee holds that games can provide valuable opportunities for learning (Gee, 2003). Does this mean we can use games to make moral demands of players by encouraging them to reflect on ethical issues? I have shown how games can achieve this. Specifically, my analyses of *Ultima IV*, *Manhunt*, and *Fire Emblem: Radiant Dawn* highlight a variety of ways games can make the player feel personally invested or responsible for the decisions they make in the game. They can also encode an ethical system and require the player to learn it and follow it to succeed. Sometimes games may present players with dilemmas or situations in which their understanding of an ethical system is challenged. We can also create moral tension between the player's goals and those posed by both the narrative and the gameplay. But there is still much work to be done to

fully explore the potential for ethical reasoning and reflection through gaming. As recent work in moral psychology has shown, both emotions (e.g. Greene, et al., 2001) as well as moral rules play a critical role in moral judgment (e.g. Nichols & Mallon, 2005). If ever there was a perfect testbed for helping people learning about ethics and ethical reasoning, games would be it. After all, these findings from moral psychology echo, in some sense, the fundamental qualities of games: activities proscribed by rules to elicit and create emotionally meaningful experiences in their participants (Salen & Zimmerman, 2004). I believe that the medium has only just begun to scratch the surface and we wonder what other mechanisms we can develop to foster ethical thinking. In what additional ways can we use games to help explore ethical questions?

REFERENCES

Addams, S. (1990). *The official book of Ultima*. Radnor, PA: COMPUTE! Books.

Barton, M. (2008). *Dungeons and desktops*. Wellesley, MA: A K Peters.

Bogost, I. (2007). *Persuasive games*. Cambridge, MA: The MIT Press.

Carless, S. (2009). In-depth: Peter Molyneux on the importance of choice. Retrieved February 12, 2010, from http://www.gamesetwatch.com/2009/08/indepth_peter_molyneux_on_the.php

CGW. (1996). *150 best games of all time* (pp. 64–80). Computer Gaming World.

Consalvo, M. (2007). *Cheating: Gaining advantage in videogames*. Cambridge, MA: MIT Press.

Delwiche, A. (2007). From the Green Berets to America's Army: Video games as a vehicle for political propaganda. In Williams, J. P., & Heide Smith, J. (Eds.), *The players' realm* (pp. 91–107). London: McFarland and Company.

Dow, S. (2009, June). Damn it Jim, I'm a gamer not a therapist. *Ambidextrous*.

Dow, S., MacIntyre, B., & Mateas, M. (2008). *Styles of play in immersive and interactive story: Case studies from a gallery installation of AR Façade*. Paper presented at the ACM SIGCHI Conference on Advances in Computer Entertainment (ACE'08).

Dulin, R. (1997). Jedi Knight: Dark Forces II: Review. Retrieved March 17, 2009, from http://uk.gamespot.com/pc/action/jediknightdark-forces2/review.html

Edge. (2007). Final Frontiers. *Edge Magazine, 177*, 72-79.

Ermi, L., & Mayra, F. (2005). *Challenges for pervasive mobile game design: Examining players' emotional responses*. Paper presented at the Proceedings of the 2005 ACM SIGCHI International Conference on Advances in computer entertainment technology.

Frasca, G. (2004). Videogames of the oppressed: Critical thinking, education, tolerance, and other trivial issues. In Wardrip-Fruin, N., & Harrigan, P. (Eds.), *First person: New media as story, performance, and game* (pp. 85–94). Cambridge, MA: MIT Press.

Garriott, R. (1985). *Ultima IV: Quest of the Avatar*. Austin, TX: Origin Systems.

Gee, J. P. (2003). *What video games have to teach us about learning and literacy*. New York: Palgrave-McMillan.

Greene, J. D., Sommerville, R. B., Nystrom, L. E., Darley, J. M., & Cohen, J. (2001). An fMRI investigation of emotional engagement in moral judgment. *Science, 293*(5537), 2105–2108. doi:10.1126/science.1062872

Halford, N., & Halford, J. (2001). *Swords and circuitry: A designer's guide to computer role-playing games*. Roseville, CA: Prima Publishing.

Huijboom, S. (2009). Fallout 3: Broken Steel: Broken Steel Walkthrough version 1.01. Retrieved February 12, 2010, from http://www.gamefaqs.com/console/xbox360/file/959299/56480

Intelligent Systems. (2007). *Fire Emblem: Radiant Dawn*. Redmond, WA: Nintendo.

Laurel, B. (1991). *Computers as theatre*. Reading, MA: Addison-Wesley Publishing.

Lopez, M., & Theobald, P. (2004). Case file 28: Is Square Enix milking the Final Fantasy VII franchise? Retrieved March 12, 2009, from http://www.gamespy.com/articles/551/551742p2.html

LucasArts. (1997). *Star Wars Jedi Knight: Dark Forces II*. San Francisco, CA: LucasArts.

Massey, D. (2007). Richard Garriott Interview, Part 2. Retrieved March 2, 2009, from http://www.warcry.com/articles/view/interviews/1436-Richard-Garriott-Interview-Part-2

Mateas, M., & Stern, A. (2003). *Facade: An experiment in building a fully-realized interactive drama*. Paper presented at the Game Developer's Conference, Game Design Track, San Jose, CA.

Mäyrä, F. (2008). *An introduction to game studies: Games in culture*. London: SAGE.

Molyneux, P. (2004). *Fable*. Guildford, UK: Lionhead Studios.

Nichols, S., & Mallon, R. (2005). Moral dilemmas and moral rules. *Cognition, 100*(3), 530–542. doi:10.1016/j.cognition.2005.07.005

Pohl, K. (2008). Ethical reflection and involvement in computer games. In S. Günzel, M. Liebe & D. Mersch (Eds.), *Conference proceedings of the philosophy of computer games 2008* (pp. 92-107). Potsdam, Germany: Potsdam University Press.

Rauch, P. E. (2007). *Playing with good and evil: Videogames and moral philosophy*. Boston: Massachusetts Institute of Technology.

Ravaja, N., Saari, T., Laarni, J., Kallinen, K., & Salminen, M. (2005). *The psychophysiology of video gaming: Phasic emotional responses to game events*. Paper presented at the Changing Views: Worlds in Play, DIGRA.

Ravaja, N., Salminen, M., Holopainen, J., Saari, T., Laarni, J., & Jarvinen, A. (2004). *Emotional response patterns and sense of presence during video games: potential criterion variables for game design*. Paper presented at the Proceedings of the third Nordic conference on Human-computer interaction.

Remedy Entertainment. (2001). *Max Payne*. Espoo, Finland: Gathering of Developers.

Rockstar North. (2003). *Manhunt*. New York: Rockstar Games.

Rodoy, D. (2003). Manhunt: Hardcore 5-Star Level FAQ. Retrieved April 2, 2009, from http://www.gamefaqs.com/console/ps2/file/915100/27381

Salen, K., & Zimmerman, E. (2004). *Rules of play: Game design fundamentals*. Cambridge, MA: The MIT Press.

Scorpia. (1986, Jan-Feb). Ultima IV: Quest of the Avatar. *Computer Gaming World,* pp. 12-14.

Shaffer, D. W. (2006). *How computer games help children learn*. New York: Palgrave Macmillan. doi:10.1057/9780230601994

Short, E. (2009). Homer in Silicon: Communicating character. Retrieved February 1, 2010, from http://www.gamesetwatch.com/2009/10/column_homer_in_silicon_commun.php

Sicart, M. (2008). *The banality of simulated evil*. Paper presented at the iEnter.

Sicart, M. (2009). *The ethics of computer games*. Boston: MIT Press.

Sieberg, D. (2000). The world according to Will. Retrieved May 25, 2010, from http://www.salon.com/technology/feature/2000/02/17/wright/print.html

Spector, C., & Tyler, M. (1999). Interview with Richard Garriott. In McCubbin, C., & Ladyman, D. (Eds.), *Ultima IX Ascension: Prima's official strategy guide* (pp. 246–297). Rocklin, CA: Prima Publishing.

Square. (1997). *Final Fantasy VII*. Foster City, CA: Sony.

Tangney, J. P., Miller, R. S., Flicker, L., & Barlow, D. H. (1996). Are shame, guilt, and embarrassment distinct emotions? *Journal of Personality and Social Psychology, 70*(6), 1256–1269. doi:10.1037/0022-3514.70.6.1256

Taylor, L. N. (2008). Gaming ethics, rules, etiquette and learning. In Ferdig, R. E. (Ed.), *Handbook of research on effective electronic gaming in education*. Hersheyp, PA: Information Science Reference.

Thomas, D. (2004). Jedi Knight: Dark Forces II FAQ. Retrieved March 17, 2009, from http://www.gamefaqs.com/computer/doswin/file/24354/18837

Totilo, S. (2008). An ethical dilemma like I've never played before — "Fire Emblem" beats "BioShock" at its own game? Retrieved March 19, 2009, from http://multiplayerblog.mtv.com/2008/02/05/an-ethical-dilemma-like-ive-never-played-before-fire-emblem-beats-bioshock-at-its-own-game/

Woods, S. J. (2009). (Play) ground rules: The social contract and the magic circle. *Observatorio (OBS*). Journal, 3*(1), 204–222.

Chapter 3
A Framework for Classification and Criticism of Ethical Games

Jamey Stevenson
Realtime Worlds, UK

ABSTRACT

For those seeking an entry point into the complex topic of ethical games, a framework for classification and criticism can be a helpful tool, if only to provide a more gentle and coherent introduction to the subject. This chapter provides one such framework, based on identifying the overarching trends in contemporary ethical game design. It provides descriptions and examples of three different categories of ethical games, each of which are then considered within the context of the most prevalent critical flashpoints currently being debated by ethical game designers and detractors alike. By understanding the distinctions between the primary types of ethical games, readers will gain the ability to more effectively delineate which design decisions are likely to make a particular game susceptible to each of the critical pitfalls outlined.

INTRODUCTION

This is a discussion of ethics and game design, and as such, it is only fitting to begin by invoking a higher authority: namely Shigeru Miyamoto, the game designer responsible for *Super Mario Bros.* (Miyamoto, 1985) and *The Legend of Zelda* (Miyamoto, 1986). With regard to the distinctive qualities of adulthood, Miyamoto stated that "an adult is a child that has more ethics and morals, that's all" (Sheff, 1993, p. 51). At the time that Miyamoto made this claim, the target audience for

digital games was primarily comprised of younger players, but we are currently in the midst of a sea change. The same children who spent their misbegotten youths being captivated by digital games have retained a seemingly insatiable appetite for the medium as they have grown older, and consequently there has been an increasing demand for the games themselves to mature, to expand their thematic and conceptual boundaries to remain relevant to an increasingly sophisticated player base.

As independent game creator Jonathan Blow (2006) has remarked, an important next step in the evolution of digital games is the creation of

DOI: 10.4018/978-1-60960-120-1.ch003

interactive experiences that speak to the human condition. Miyamoto's premise, provided we accept it, would seem to indicate that incorporating ethical concepts into our designs is a potentially viable technique for creating games that resonate with this rapidly expanding contingent of adult players. It is perhaps unsurprising, then, that games that facilitate ethical exploration on the part of players are currently a subject of great interest within both academic and commercial domains.

In many ways, this interest in ethical games is a natural progression of the view of game design as a form of expression. There is ample precedent for the practice of using our available modes of expression to illuminate ethical concepts, whether in the form of linear media, such as Ursula K. Le Guin's (1975) use of concrete literary description to formulate a theoretical critique of utilitarianism in *The Ones Who Walk Away from Omelas*, or in more playful forms such as the traditional "Parable of the Long Spoons" folk riddle, which seeks to impart the values of altruism and cooperation by encapsulating them within the revelatory "eureka!" moment that accompanies the realization of a puzzle solution (Landers, 1995).

Yet even among those who consider ethical game design a worthy avenue of pursuit, there is little consensus regarding how to best utilize the innate potential of digital games to provide a compelling context wherein players can engage in ethical exploration. While certain techniques are gradually beginning to gain support, it is safe to say that contemporary approaches to incorporating ethical ideas within digital games remain in a nascent phase, and while the resultant atmosphere of experimentation is exciting, it can also be bewildering for those who are merely seeking a basic primer regarding the current ethical game development landscape. This presents a challenge both for ethical game designers who are attempting to formulate their own methodologies, as well as for educators who are attempting to structure a curriculum that includes a thorough examination of current ethical games.

This essay attempts to alleviate this problem by introducing a framework for classifying ethical games into three types—static, adaptive, and systemic—based on a coarse set of essential high-level design properties common to the games found in each individual group. These categories are not intended to be either definitive or mutually exclusive, but rather to serve the more pragmatic purpose of providing an anchor point for readers as they attempt to glean further insights regarding the most crucial design tradeoffs endemic to ethical games.

The presentation of the framework itself is organized into three sections:

The first section, *Three Types of Ethical Games*, describes the aforementioned typology of ethical games and provides examples of games that are representative of each category. This overview serves as the lynchpin of the framework, and all other topics discussed are considered within the context of these primary groupings. Some of the most crucial questions posed in this section include: What prevailing distinctions can be used to separate and categorize existing approaches to ethical games? What are some examples from games that help clarify these distinctions?

The second section, *Debating Ethical Design: Key Issues and Critical Perspectives*, examines some of the most divisive and recurrent issues surrounding the design of ethical games. Understanding these issues not only yields a greatly enhanced comprehension of the current state of ethical games, it also confers upon readers the ability to perform honest, unsparing appraisals of how effectively each of the approaches outlined in the first section actually manages to involve players in thinking about ethical concepts. Questions considered in this section include: What are some of the more frequently cited criticisms and sources of contention with regard to current ethical games? Of the categories identified in the first section, which are most likely to be susceptible to each of the criticisms discussed?

In the final section, *Choose Your Own Quagmire: Deepening Ethical Engagement,* I conclude by briefly discussing some examples of additional techniques employed by game designers who have attempted to refine, synthesize, and even outright circumvent the categories defined in the first section. Having outlined some of the most substantial challenges and opportunities faced by each of these categories in the previous section, I will conclude with a brief attempt to elucidate what the future may hold, including suggestions for potentially fruitful avenues of expansion. Questions posed include: What further techniques for ethical engagement in games exist outside of the categories in this framework? How else might the more central, defining criticisms of ethical games be addressed, subverted, or refuted?

Next, I will begin the discussion by defining the three primary categories of ethical games that comprise the basis of my framework.

THREE TYPES OF ETHICAL GAMES

Attempts to utilize games for the purpose of engaging players in ethical thought are nothing new. The practice dates back at least at far as the early commercial board game *The Mansion of Happiness* (Abbott, 1843), which dealt explicitly with moral themes and sought to convey values such as honesty, temperance, and gratitude to players (Hofer, 2003). Nevertheless, the potential for using digital games in this capacity is currently in the midst of a Renaissance, having sparked the imagination of a number of prominent game designers including Peter Molyneux, Ken Levine, and Clint Hocking, among many others. There has been a recent surge of interest within the digital game development community in creating games that engage players in the act of ethical exploration.

Yet despite, or perhaps because of, the heightened level of attention that is currently being directed toward this subject, there remains a great deal of disagreement regarding exactly how the singular potential of digital games can be most effectively leveraged to achieve such lofty goals as fostering empathy, critical thinking, experimentation, and self-reflection on the part of players. The diversity of current approaches to ethical game design, while ultimately beneficial, can have the adverse effect of causing the topic to initially appear daunting to newcomers who are attempting to study, analyze, and ultimately contribute to the work that is currently being done in this area.

This section attempts to provide an entry point into understanding the expansive array of techniques employed by ethical game designers. This is achieved by organizing the vast and active ecosystem of ethical games into a simplified taxonomy of three overarching types—static, adaptive, and systemic—and providing examples of games that embody the unique qualities of each individual category. The methodology used to formulate these types consisted of studying a wide range of games and identifying persistent tropes and trends in how they each attempted to involve players with ethical ideas and themes. The distinctions used to classify the types have been chosen to emphasize functional delineations that can serve as a solid, practical basis for further inquiry. The types themselves will serve as a foundation for the examination of ethical game criticisms found in the next section.

Ethical Game Types

At the highest level, there are three major types of games that attempt to incorporate ethical ideas. I will begin by providing a brief definition for all three types, before moving on to look at each one individually in further detail:

1. **Static** ethical games are games that incorporate ethical themes via fixed goals and progression, in which the player does not directly make any ethical decisions.
2. **Adaptive** ethical games are games in which ethical decisions are made directly by the

player, but the game system does not associate any overt formal, quantifiable outcome, such as a numerical reward or penalty, with these decisions.

3. **Systemic** ethical games are games in which ethical decisions are made directly by the player, and are tied to the formal game simulation via changes in statistics or other quantifiable metrics.

Having presented the basic definitions, I will now consider each of the types more thoroughly, along with example games that serve to highlight the distinctions between them.

Static

Static ethical games incorporate ethical themes via fixed goals and progression, in which the player does not directly make any ethical decisions. Out of all three ethical game types, the static approach is closest to that of traditional media in the way ethical themes are addressed; any such themes within ethical games that favor this approach are presented in a purely linear manner via a static narrative. As a result, the actual exploration aspect of the ethical concepts presented is left more as a thought exercise for the player to undertake at a meta-level, outside of the main action of the game itself.

An example of an ethical game that could be classified as static is *Shadow of the Colossus* (Ueda, 2005). In the game, the only way to achieve the goal is to guide the protagonist to hunt down and slaughter a number of giant creatures, none of which have caused any direct harm to the player prior to being forced to defend themselves. The game encourages players to question the ethics surrounding the protagonist's motivations by portraying the majority of the colossi as docile and peaceful, possessed of a quiet grace and beauty which the player must disrupt via a series of violent and intrusive acts of aggression. However, despite being invited to disapprove of these actions and

to reconsider the motives that inspire the game's protagonist to undertake them, players are not provided with any alternative aside from slaying all of the colossi if they wish to complete the game.

A recurring technique in static ethical games is to frame the game goals as being assigned to the player by an entity that is later revealed to possess dubious motives. In *Shadow of the Colossus* this role is filled by Dormin, but there are many examples from other games, such as Atlas in *BioShock* (Levine, 2007) and the government official in *Opera Omnia* (Lavelle, 2009). In some cases, this is accomplished via a form of dramatic irony, wherein the player is led to be suspicious but remains powerless to alter the events taking place. In other cases, the player is kept in the dark to allow for a sudden narrative swerve or reveal that serves to recontextualize prior events.

It is important to note that just because a game's treatment of ethical themes is static does not necessitate that it is unsubtle or didactic, any more than in the case of linear media that deals with ethical subject matter. In the instance of *Shadow of the Colossus,* the static portrayal allows the game to present a highly effective context for ethical engagement without resorting to sermonizing or being openly reproachful toward the player for their complicity in what occurs. By forcing the player to directly enact a seemingly unethical task, *Shadow* confronts them with an ethical scenario of intense immediacy, while also placing them within a structure that accurately reflects the myopic mindset of the game's solipsistic protagonist, who emphatically refuses to be dissuaded from the messy work at hand. Based on the benefits *Shadow* derives from its static treatment of ethics, it would be reasonable to argue that attempting to fit the game into one of the other ethical game categories would have resulted in a less compelling experience.

The most common criticism of this type of game, which I will revisit in greater detail in the next section, is that it is not an effective use of the characteristic qualities of the medium. Since games thrive on player choice, conveying an ethical concept by relegating the player to following a static progression begs the question of whether the same message could just as easily, if not more easily, have been conveyed via linear media.

Adaptive

In adaptive ethical games, ethical decisions are made directly by the player, but the game system does not associate any overt formal, quantifiable outcome, such as a numerical reward or penalty, with these decisions. In such games, players typically have the ability to dynamically reconfigure or navigate their own unique path through a larger mesh of static content nodes. The most common example of this is branching narrative, in which players can alter the sequence of events and gain access to different sets of static content by choosing between various actions or dialogue options.

Adventure games and interactive fiction are two closely related genres that often employ some permutation of adaptive methods, with just a few examples being *Fahrenheit* (Cage, 2005), *Shadow of Memories* (Kawano, 2001), *Blade Runner* (Castle, 1997), and *The Pandora Directive* (Jones, 1996). However, the prominence of the ethical component within the decisions made by players in these games varies from case to case and can often be considered arguable or ambiguous. Even in an adventure game with an explicitly ethical motif, such as *Seven Games of the Soul* (Fructus, 1999), most of the actual ethical considerations are relegated to static narrative; the significant ethical choices in which the player can actively participate remain scant in comparison to the amount of time spent on traditional adventure game activities such as puzzle solving and scavenging for important items. Although the game does utilize adaptive methods, it does so in the service of strategic and logical challenges rather than ethical exploration. Thus, in terms of ethical engagement the game would more likely fall into the static category.

In some ways, this aforementioned ambiguity regarding what actually constitutes an ethical decision is emblematic of the more qualitative nature of the adaptive approach. This tendency is not necessarily a drawback, however, as it can be leveraged by designers to enhance the depth of the ethical scenarios presented to players. One such example is the role-playing game *The Witcher* (Kiciński, 2007), in which players are presented with various short-term decisions that often end up having unforeseen long-term ramifications. While the initial choice might be made purely on either strategic or ethical grounds, the ways in which these choices ripple outward prompts the player to reflect on the other aspects they may not have considered when making their original decision. As long as the chain of causality defined by the designer remains feasible, this technique can be an effective tool for encouraging players to question their own moral certitudes, as their initial confidence in a decision gradually wavers and shifts toward ambivalence.

Another potential benefit of the qualitative ambiguity inherent in the adaptive method is that it allows designers the opportunity to craft an authorial tone that is most suitable to facilitating their desired form of ethical exploration. For example, in the interactive fiction *The Baron,* author Victor Gijsbers (2006) intentionally adopts a staunchly neutral tone in presenting players with a fascinating inquiry into the nature of abuse, and how abusers attempt to justify their actions. By refusing to depict any outcome or choice as preferable to another, Gijsbers provides players with the space to consider many alternative viewpoints, accepting or refuting each one based on their own interpretations of the scenario being presented. Further ambiguity is introduced by allowing players to continually revisit their initial ethical stance within varying contexts. The resultant experience is one of undiluted ethical exploration, in which the insights are ultimately supplied by the player rather than the author.

The question of tone and its impact upon the perception of events reflects a common criticism of adaptive ethical games. Since the outcome of each decision is typically defined in a static fashion by the author, some consider it inevitable that the system of choice and consequence in such games will be subjugated to the authorial bias and whims of the designer. If the designer's subjective judgment strongly influences the structure of the causal links and ethical affordances available to players, adaptive games run the risk of shifting away from an exploratory tenor and into more sententious territory. This problem is of course not unique to adaptive ethical games, but is perhaps most pronounced in this category of games due to the perceived gap between player intent and designed outcome. This issue can be mitigated by ensuring that any narrative branches at least satisfy the baseline criteria of plausibility, but reconciling the problem of bias entirely in far from trivial. I will revisit this criticism in further detail in the next section.

Another frequently cited criticism of using branching narrative in an ethical context is that committing unethical acts within a game will never succeed in evoking genuine feelings of guilt or remorse from players due to the inherent unreality of the game space. This difficulty is compounded if the game has a fixed goal, as pragmatism is often a much more compelling concern than humanity within the magic circle that defines a game. As with the question of bias, I will return to these concerns in the next section, when I examine criticisms of ethical games more closely.

Finally, there is also a more practical concern regarding adaptive ethical games: the difficulty of managing the combinatorial increase in static content needed to create truly robust branching narratives. Since introducing branching narrative can drastically increase the scope of a game, many developers attempt to reduce the associated complexity by limiting the narrative branches to multiple endings, often based solely on a handful of crucial, catalyzing decisions that act like simplified "if/then" rules in determining the final outcome. To imbue the other decisions the player makes with significance and make the world seem more responsive, this technique is often supplemented with more localized reactions for choices that are deemed to have less bearing on the overall plot, such as optional side quests in role-playing games.

Systemic

In systemic ethical games, ethical decisions are made directly by the player and are tied to the formal game simulation via changes in statistics or other quantifiable metrics. Occasionally these metrics are purely descriptive, acting simply as an ethical "score," but typically they will have some effect on the simulated behavior of other game entities toward the player, or the access the player has to different portions of the game environment. Often the metrics will influence progression via functional rewards or penalties applied to the player's avatar, or take the form of aesthetic alterations to the avatar's outward appearance that serve as a reflection of their internal character.

The most common manifestation of a systemic approach within current ethical games is the presence of an "alignment" statistic, with a frequently cited example being the single variable light/dark continuum used in *Star Wars: Knights of the Old Republic* (Hudson, 2003). Having a single, omnipresent ethical metric that is increased by performing designer-defined benevolent deeds and decreased via malevolence or selfishness has become increasingly popular in modern games, and similar systems can be found in the karma mechanics of *inFAMOUS* (Fox, 2009) and *Fallout* (Cain, 1997), the reputation systems of *Black & White* (Molyneux, 2001), *Fable* (Molyneux, 2004), *Ogre Battle* (Matsuno, 1993), and *Galactic Civilizations* (Wardell, 2003), and various other games spanning a wide array of genres including *The Suffering* (Rouse, 2004), *Oddworld: Munch's Oddysee* (Lanning, 2001), *Real Lives* (Runyan,

2010), and *Vampire: The Masquerade* (Reign-Hagen, 1991).

Interestingly, these single variable representations of ethical data are actually *less* structurally complex than their predecessors, such as the multivariate good/evil and lawful/chaotic alignment system of *Dungeons & Dragons* (Arneson & Gygax, 1974) and many *D&D*-derived digital games such as *Baldur's Gate* (Ohlen, 1998) and *Planescape: Torment* (Avellone, 1999), or the eightfold virtue system of *Ultima IV: Quest of the Avatar* (Garriott, 1985). With only a few notable exceptions, such as the independently tracked paragon and renegade statistics used in *Mass Effect* (Hudson, 2007), the overall trend in modern ethical simulation seems to be toward simplicity, at least on a formal level.

Perhaps the most popular alternative to having a universal morality meter in systemic ethical games is modeling interpersonal relationships between game characters or factions via a trust or friendship mechanic, which is typically altered based on whether a particular entity approves or disapproves of the player's actions. These systemic ethical relationships are typically modeled at a societal level in strategy games that involve diplomacy or geopolitical maneuvering, such as *Sid Meier's Alpha Centauri* (Reynolds, 1998), *Balance of Power* (Crawford, 1985), and *Hidden Agenda* (Gasperini, 1988). Other games, like *The Thing* (Curtis, 2002), *Real Lives*, and *Façade* (Mateas & Stern, 2005), take a more fine-grained approach by modeling these relationships on a more personal level. By making the ethical measurements relative rather than absolute, designers can help to make the simulations in systemic ethical games seem a bit less dogmatic. Introducing concepts such as personal vendettas, grudges, and debts into the model also causes an ethical simulation to feel slightly less ethereal, bringing it closer to the realm of applied rather than theoretical ethics.

A common middle ground between the aforementioned methods is the "quest" style of systemic ethical gameplay, in which players can choose to fulfill missions for different factions that represent conflicting interests and philosophies. This can allow the player to achieve a simple form of ethical exploration, by allying themselves with different groups and learning more about that group's perspective. Examples of games that utilize this type of structure include the *Deus Ex* (Smith & Spector, 2000) series, *Splinter Cell: Double Agent* (Ferland, 2006), and *Way of the Samurai* (Nakanishi, 2002).

The primary criticism directed at games of this type is that attaching a quantifiable result to moral decisions drains the ethical dimension from these choices, forcing players to focus on the numerically expedient minimax solutions that will yield the best strategic result. Essentially, the argument is that emphasizing logical concerns inevitably precludes (or at least tends to overshadow) any possible ethical considerations on the part of the player. These criticisms will be examined in greater detail in *The Fallacy of Ethical Immersion* and *Game Goals as Intrinsic Goods* in the next section.

Another criticism of systemic ethical games is that the abstractions typically used to model ethics in most current instances, such as the rather stark notions of good and evil, lack any semblance of the ambiguity found in real world ethical dilemmas. This is often further compounded by the designer's attempts to reduce confusion and allow for intentionality in player choice, which is most intuitively accomplished by clearly delimiting the good and evil choices in a blatantly obvious fashion. As many critics of this method have noted, once the designer has gone so far as to unequivocally label one action right and another action wrong, the extent of player ethical exploration is reduced to the exceedingly staid and shallow initial choice of "do I want to be a hero or villain?"

Summary

In this section, I have classified ethical games into three distinct categories based on the methods with which they attempt to engage players in ethical thought. *Static* ethical games incorporate ethical themes via fixed goals and progression, in which the player does not directly make any ethical decisions. In *adaptive* ethical games, ethical decisions are made directly by the player, but the game system does not associate any overt formal, quantifiable outcome, such as a numerical reward or penalty, with these decisions. In *systemic* ethical games, ethical decisions are made directly by the player, and are tied to the formal game simulation via changes in statistics or other quantifiable metrics.

This is admittedly an extremely coarse typology, and the categories are by necessity designed to be neither definitive nor mutually exclusive; nevertheless, they provide a useful vantage point for organizing our thoughts regarding ethical games. In the next section, I look at some of the most prominent criticisms of ethical games, examining how differing viewpoints on a number of polarizing issues relate to the classifications I have described.

DEBATING ETHICAL DESIGN: KEY ISSUES AND CRITICAL PERSPECTIVES

Being able to classify ethical games is a step toward achieving a broader understanding of the field, but this primarily constrains us to analyzing the work that has already been done in the area. Because ethical engagement is a moving target, the reality is that the categories presented in the first section are more flexible than they might initially appear. The techniques employed by ethical game designers are constantly being critiqued and refined within the greater development community, and to grasp the larger tectonic shifts that are occurring beneath our placid surface structure we need to examine some of the discussions that are currently taking place regarding ethical design.

In this section, I survey the current atmosphere surrounding ethical game design and pick out four

of the most contentious issues related to ethical games that are currently being debated by both commercial developers and academics. Not all of these issues are equally relevant to every one of the three types of ethical games outlined in the previous section, so my discussion will also make certain to explicate which of the ethical game categories are most susceptible to the pitfalls with which each critical issue is associated. After completing this section, readers will possess the ability to dive headfirst into the midst of the ethical design debate, confident in their understanding of the core issues that define the field.

The first topic, *The Fallacy of Ethical Immersion*, considers whether digital games have the capacity to truly evoke responses such as guilt and contrition on the part of players. The next topic, *Instruction vs. Exploration*, concerns the fundamental purpose behind ethical game design: should the designer's goal be to communicate a specific ethical lesson to the player, or rather to simply confront players with various ethical concepts and questions? The view of *Game Goals as Intrinsic Goods* is next discussed, in which I seek to clarify the differences between goal-oriented and freeform play with regard to ethical games. Finally, I look at how designers can address the matter of personal bias while creating an ethical game in *Design and Bias*.

The Fallacy of Ethical Immersion

I think the problem is that if you need to tell players about a questionable moral choice through words or a meter, you've sort of missed the point. We've all done things in our lives that probably wasn't morally entirely up to snuff, and there's a primal feeling that happens when you do that.

(Ken Levine, quoted in Edge, 2006, p.47).

A defining feature of games and simulation lies in their capacity to create a space of interaction that is divorced from reality, and thus devoid of real world consequences. A common criticism of ethical games is that, to be effective, they are perceived by some as being reliant upon making the player feel guilty or remorseful for undertaking actions that do not possess any actual moral significance. To some degree, this argument is simply an extension of the ongoing "immersion vs. remediation" discussion regarding new media that has been taking place for a long time, recast within the purview of ethical games. Frank Lantz has coined the term "the immersive fallacy" as a derisive descriptor for what he feels is the mistaken yet widespread belief that games are approaching a convergence point of representational verisimilitude that will one day cause them to be indistinguishable from reality (Salen & Zimmerman, 2003, pp. 450-455), and he has also been critical of ethical games that attempt to capitalize on player guilt to embellish their presentation of ethical choices (Sirlin, 2007).

This notion of the futility of relying on immersion is more complex than mere graphical fidelity, but rather applies to the fundamental relationship between simulation and the actual subject it targets. An example of a game that illustrates this idea can be found in *Execution*, an experimental game by independent developer Jesse Venbrux (2008). In the game, the player can choose to either shoot a graphically simplistic character that is helplessly tied to a pole, or they can press escape to exit and, in essence, win the game by deciding not to play. If the player chooses to shoot the character, subsequently reloading the game will result in the character remaining dead—even uninstalling and reinstalling the game will not revive the character. The game achieves this effect by storing a value within the registry of the user's computer, an area of memory that is typically reserved for more persistent data such as crucial operating system information.

While *Execution* is successful in presenting a more realistic simulation of death, critics of ethical immersion would contend that this increased fidelity does not actually provide any additional moral depth to the player's actions. The player may be initially surprised that reloading the game has failed to reset the state of the character, but the fundamental unreality of the scenario remains at the forefront of the player's knowledge, preventing them from feeling truly remorseful about pulling the trigger on their simulated victim. Venbrux himself eventually conceded that these limitations remained a hindrance, after performing a thorough appraisal of whether the game was truly successful in achieving the goal of affecting others in an instinctive manner (Venbrux, 2008). Interestingly, with regard to the moral ramifications of *Execution*, initial responses from players yielded at least as much discussion surrounding the ethics of writing a value in the registry of the player's computer without permission as the amount of discussion it fostered regarding the ethics of shooting the game character (Burch, 2008).

An alternative view holds Lantz's criticisms of immersion to be valid, but also considers this supposed weakness of ethical games to be liberating rather than discouraging. If we accept that attempting to evoke the "primal feeling" referred to by Levine is not the most promising technique available to us, we can use this as the impetus to pursue other methods of ethical exploration by refocusing our efforts on less visceral designs that are not reliant on the arguably fruitless pursuit of the mythical ideals of pure simulation. This can also be problematic, however, as without the presence of this primal intuition that is normally supplied by our conscience when performing genuine moral actions, it becomes difficult to determine exactly what constitutes an ethical choice. Lacking the compass of conscience to guide us, the line can become quite hazy with regard to precisely what distinguishes an ethical choice from, for instance, a purely strategic game decision.

Systemic ethical designs might provide an opportunity to circumvent this issue, since they do not depend as heavily upon an immersive narrative context, tending instead to be oriented more toward a Brechtian approach of critical distancing and logical evaluation. However, designers of ethical games that are pitched more toward a narrative focus, such as static and adaptive types, may wish to be wary and take these considerations into account when constructing their ethical scenarios.

There is an additional consideration that arises from this critique of immersive consequences in ethical games: what is to prevent the player from resorting to the most interesting option in all cases, or simply choosing the most entertaining path available? Is this sort of experimentation still a valid form of ethical exploration, or is there a different attitude that we wish to foster within our players to increase the likelihood that they are thinking critically about the concepts presented? If the player is naturally obdurate, or simply isn't in an especially empathetic or open-minded mood while playing our game, is there really anything we as designers can do to compel them to feel otherwise?

Next, I look at different stances on instructional and exploratory design as it pertains to ethical games.

Instruction vs. Exploration

I wasn't really trying to say we should make games that impart values. I was trying to say we should make games that allow the player to explore himself. [...] There's a risk that, even more than with literature, games can become didactic if we do that. To try and teach someone a specific set of values in games is trickier because what games ought to do, in my opinion, is present the entire space of the problem. Instead of saying, "You should be honest," it should say, "This is what honesty means" through the mechanics. This is what happens when you tell the truth or you tell a lie--instead of trying to make a game that says

"Lying is bad and honesty is good" (Clint Hocking, quoted in Ruberg, 2007, p.3).

Perhaps the most fundamental disagreement among creators of ethical games relates to intent. Are we building these ethical experiences for the purpose of imparting a specific set of beliefs, or are we merely providing a moral "playground," an environment for experimentation that encourages players to consider ethical concepts or questions from multiple viewpoints? Stated roughly, is our primary goal instruction or exploration?

Clint Hocking's quote above summarizes the exploration stance quite clearly. This preference appears to be a rather prevalent one among game developers:

Videogames should seek to ask questions, not make statements. Traditional media is simply better at making statements than games are. If you want to express your point of view, make a movie or write a book, but if you want to get someone to ponder, if you want to present to them with a question to explore, make a game (Portnow, 2008).

All things considered, the audience was probably right on target in suggesting that the ethical dimension of a game is brought about by raising questions, not by providing answers (Kreimeier, 2000, p.2).

Far from the narrator dictating the 'moral' of a story, emergent game consequences allow gamers to explore, with varying degrees of verisimilitude, the result of "what happens if I do this?". The replay element of interactive media may encourage an open and experimental stance toward consequences and ethical decision making. The virtual nature of interactive media, along with the ability of players to try again and see how consequences differ, mean that media become a space of active engagement where choice and consequence can be explored. [...] The deeper the complexity of these systems, the more potential there is for ethical exploration (Beattie, 2007, p.4).

Beattie's quote is especially relevant, as he presents it within the context of an argument against what he characterizes as the unquestioned assumptions of Australian game censors, who tend to evaluate games based on the belief that "the player's status is subservient to the intentions of the author and the reward framework embedded in the code by the author" (Beattie, 2007, p.1). Beattie notes that these views often extend beyond the mere premise of games as tools of instruction, treating game rewards as a form of operant conditioning. In stark contrast to the exploration model, these instruction-based perspectives function under the belief that "interactivity can only be measured as compliance or interference with the 'true' ethical framework of the text" (Beattie, 2007, p.1).

To some extent, the emphasis on raising questions rather than providing clear-cut answers fits in with the larger notion of "abdication of authorship" that has been circulating within various sectors of the game development community in recent years (Gaynor, 2008). This same view often equates open-ended scenarios and non-linear game structures with the notion of exploration. But is this truly a valid association? As mentioned in the previous section, just because an ethical game adopts a static treatment does not inherently make it overbearing or preachy. It is also worth reiterating that instructional lessons can just as easily be present in the underlying subtext of a branching narrative as they can in a more static presentation. If a designer of an adaptive ethical game wishes to communicate a personal belief that dropping out of school inevitably leads to a life of crime, they need only configure the relationships between player choices and corresponding narrative outcomes such that this specious causal link is borne out by the game.

As far as systemic ethical games are concerned, the design of the systems can still be utilized to impart moral lessons, albeit ones that are typically communicated less directly. This indirection may cause systemic ethical games to be perceived as less prescriptive, but there is still the possibility for a designer to embed ideological rhetoric within a system. As Gonzalo Frasca (2003, p.227) notes, "the simauthor always has the final word: she will be able to decide the frequency and degree of events that are beyond the player's control." Even if we choose to adopt an exploration-based approach, the challenges in actually realizing this goal are considerable. At least one of these challenges actually arises from the inherent properties of games themselves: namely, the inclusion of goals.

Game Goals as Intrinsic Goods

The creation of a final goal creates a new value for every action performed by the player. Now everything that the player does or does not will be measured in relationship to how close or far it placed her from the final goal. Creating a ludus creates a moral set of rules, defining what is right and wrong. [...] This binary logic is usually translated to the actions of the player. If killing the gatekeeper will allow the player to enter the castle and therefore to win, then killing is right and not killing the gatekeeper is wrong, at least by the game standards (Frasca, 2001).

In a truly freeform exploration of ethics, the question of what constitutes an intrinsic good would ideally remain open to debate. Yet Frasca's quote illustrates a crucial contradiction in ethical experiences that conform to the traditional games model: in such games, the goal is arbitrarily defined by the designer and is not subject to negotiation. In ethical terms, only the goal of the game has intrinsic worth, and the ethical quality of any given game action can only be assessed in terms of that action's instrumental value relative to this predefined goal.

Various games have attempted to circumvent this problem in a number of ways, most notably via moving away from the traditional games model by actively subverting the sacrosanct status of goals. This can either be done in a conservative manner by providing multiple goals from which players can select their preferred option, or in a more radical fashion by abolishing the concept of goals entirely.

While this is perhaps a necessary step toward increasing our capacity to provide unbounded ethical exploration, it is worth noting that eliminating goals altogether means giving up one of our most effective design tools for creating intuitive play experiences. Sacrificing goals moves us away from traditional games and closer to the realm of simulation, and runs the risk of putting the player in murkier waters with regard to meaningful interaction. However, it can also provide substantial benefits, allowing designers to create more diverse expressive contexts that challenge players to evaluate, experiment, and formulate a more personal approach within an unfettered environment.

When there is a clear goal, players are more or less forced to focus on optimizing their strategies, but this may run counter to what players want to do. [...] If the classical game model forces players to optimize their strategies and, to some extent, ignore the aesthetic value of the game pieces, removing or weakening the game goal accommodates a wider range of player types and game experiences. In such games, the player can choose to buy a nice couch rather than an optimal couch (Juul, 2005, p.199).

In certain cases, the benefits of relaxing and subverting goal structures can outweigh the drawbacks. Instead of generating meaning via clearly discernable player states as in the traditional games model, ethical games that abandon goals are instead free to focus on more realistic depictions of ethical quandaries. In the case of the earlier example of *The Baron*, the author discards clear goals in favor of ambiguity expressed through the juxtaposition of concrete, functional player actions with constantly shifting representational metaphors. The result is compelling, but it also cannot really be classified as a game in the strictest sense. Of course, there are many games that adopt a compromise position, retaining the concept of goals but opting to utilize them in non-traditional ways. The resultant designs arguably have the potential to achieve a much more nuanced depiction of everyday ethical scenarios.

The choice between paidia and ludus structures is ideologically essential for a simauthor because both carry different agendas. The simulated world in ludus games seems more coherent because the player's goals are clear: you must do X in order to reach Y and therefore become a winner. This implies that Y is a desired objective and therefore it is morally charged. Ludus is the simulational structure of choice for modernist simauthors: these designers have moral certitudes (Mario is good, the monsters are bad). Clearly defined goals do not generally leave much room neither for doubts nor for contesting that particular objective. [...] Based on this, it would seem that paidia is a less modernist technique aimed at designers who have more doubts than certitudes (Frasca, 2003, pp.230-231).

Because it arises from the fundamental structure of traditional games, the concept of the game goal as an intrinsic good pertains equally to all types of ethical games. However, each category of ethical game also presents unique opportunities for tweaking the traditional game structure. For instance, static ethical games can borrow techniques from linear narrative such as unreliable narrators and imperfect information to cause players to reconsider whether the goal of the game is actually worth achieving. Some of the most effective examples of ethical engagement in games, including many of the example games cited in this paper, arose from designers who possessed the courage to embrace a more iconoclastic approach to game structure.

While goals play a vital role in shaping the ethical scenarios depicted within our games, there are many other subtle ways in which our own assumptions can creep in and influence our designs. This does not necessarily preclude us from supporting ethical exploration, but it can nevertheless hinder our attempts if we fail to properly identify our own ingrained preferences and prejudices when we are designing an ethical system. In the next section, I examine this relationship between bias and design in further detail.

Design and Bias

But, if we walk that road, it is much much more important that we are aware of our own biases. Making games that allow the player to explore some aspect of themselves or their opinions has to be done in good faith. If this is done falsely it presents a more insidious threat than modern propaganda games will ever be (Portnow, 2008).

Through the design process, values and beliefs become embedded in games whether designers intend them to or not (Flanagan, Nissenbaum, Belman & Diamond, 2007, p.1).

In their work, system designers necessarily impart social and moral values. Yet how? What values? Whose values? For if human values – such as freedom of speech, rights to property, account-ability, privacy, and autonomy – are controversial, then on what basis do some values override others in the design of, say, hardware, algorithms, and databases (Friedman, 1997, p.1)?

Not only is bias unavoidable in design, but to the extent that design relies upon the imposition of arbitrary constraints, design quite literally *is* bias. A common complaint leveled at ethical games is that their systems are not actually flexible enough to allow players to express their own values, but are instead limited to the rigid classifications defined by the designers.

At first glance, this would appear to be an intractable problem. Without imposing any constraints at all, we lose the ability to provide even a simulation, much less a game. Yet any constraint we create will inevitably reflect our own imperfect, limited understanding of the phenomenon we are attempting to simulate. This problem is even more pronounced when we are designing ethical systems, which are substantially more ethereal and subjective than, for example, a physics simulation.

Sources of technical bias can be found in several aspects of the design process, including limitations of computer tools such as hardware, software, and peripherals; the process of ascribing social meaning to algorithms developed out of context; imperfections in pseudo-random number genera-tion; and the attempt to make human constructs amenable to computers, when we quantify the qualitative, discretize the continuous, or formal-ize the nonformal (Friedman & Nissenbaum, 1997, p.25).

However, this does not inhibit us from finding a suitable balance that seeks to at least mitigate systemic bias while still allowing us to create a context for meaningful exploration. The important thing to realize is that just because our formaliza-tions are not definitive, this does not mean that they cannot still be useful.

Suchman is right in noting that "once encapsulated and reduced to the homogeneous black circles and arrows of the diagram, the 'conversation' is findable anywhere." But she is wrong in saying that "specific occasions of conversation are no longer open to investigation, or at least not in any other terms." This is like saying that once Laban invented and applied a systematic dance notation, "specific occasions of dance are no longer open to investigation, or at least not in any other terms." Only the most narrowminded application of such a tool would blind one to further investigations and dimensions of the phenomena (Winograd, 1997, p.109).

Provided that we acknowledge the inevitability of bias, how might we reconcile this admission with our desire to provide ethical exploration? A pragmatic approach would be to focus on conveying the underlying thought processes behind our ethical constructs and typologies to our players. Accomplishing this entails allowing a greater degree of transparency into our design process than we might ordinarily be comfortable providing, and treating players more like collaborators rather than patrons. Thankfully, there is ample precedent for such an approach, whether we take our cues from the flourishing open source software community or from the proliferation of digital games that support and encourage player modifications. By providing players with the tools to stretch, warp, improve, and configure our systems in order to suit their own purposes, we are taking a step toward reducing the imposition of bias.

Structure is not an imposition of control for authoritarian motives, but a necessity of continued operation. The question is not whether to impose standardized regimes, but how to do so appropriately (Winograd, 1997, p.111).

Ideally, we would always strive to provide players with as much control over our ethical systems as possible by exposing key systemic leverage points. But in reality, the best method of providing these sorts of hooks can be elusive, and actually building them into our systems is often time consuming. The idea that players will have the capacity to fully customize our ethical models

is unrealistic at best, misleading at worst. Simply put, we have a need in system design to standardize, to formalize, and to hold certain assumptions as fixed, constant, or axiomatic. As a result, it is essential for ethical game designers to properly document not only their final systems, but also the process through which those systems came to fruition. When designing ethical systems, it is necessary to communicate to users not just the composition of the system itself, but the mindset out of which the system arose.

Decisions about game mechanics, which dictate how players may and may not function in a game world, and narrative content, which sets the rule system within a coherent framework, may reflect designers' conscious and unconscious considerations of values and their beliefs about "how the world works," even when that world is fictional. We are arguing that these issues should be surfaced regularly as developers—particularly those who are engaged in the design of activist games and "games for change"—create games in order to reflect on the values that have been embodied in the game and the features that enable players to experience and understand them (Flanagan, Nissenbaum, Belman & Diamond, 2007, p.6).

The issue of bias affects designers regardless of which type of ethical game they are creating. The primary difference is that in systemic ethical games, the clandestine assumptions made by the designer are often less obvious and therefore possess even greater potential for deception than bias associated with the other ethical categories. Therefore, while it is important for all designers to be open and honest regarding their own inclinations, it is especially crucial for creators of systemic ethical games to be forthcoming regarding any personal bias that might not otherwise be readily apparent to players.

Summary

In this section, I have examined four of the most formative, polarizing issues pertaining to ethical game design. First, I looked at the inherent difficulty of attempting to evoke actual feelings of compunction in players as a result of unethical game actions. Next, I investigated the preferences of designers toward either exploratory or instructional styles of communication in ethical games. I then discussed the relationship between game goals and moral certitude, and presented some alternatives to the traditional game model that can serve as avenues of inspiration for ethical game designers. Finally, I sought out techniques to mitigate the problem of bias in design, and to communicate the underlying assumptions of a game system in cases where bias can not be completely excised.

Having concluded the general overview of the classifications and criticisms of ethical games, I will finish with a brief look at some outlying examples of design techniques that exist within the margins of my original classifications.

CHOOSE YOUR OWN QUAGMIRE: DEEPENING ETHICAL ENGAGEMENT

As with any system of classification, the three ethical game types outlined previously are not infallible. Some ethical games fit comfortably into the categories of static, adaptive, and systemic, while others are not so easily pigeonholed. Perhaps unsurprisingly, the examples that defy simple classification also offer some of the most intriguing instances of current ethical game design. I will conclude the discussion with a brief look at some additional trends in ethical games that fall somewhere outside the purview of my system of classification.

- **Formal reward imbalances favoring evil actions.** Certain games attempt to equate doing good deeds with the notion of sacrifice by introducing formal reward imbalances that favor unethical actions, thus forcing the player to forgo a potential strategic advantage in order to retain the moral high ground. The most commonly cited example of this technique is found in *BioShock*, which offers players the choice of whether to "harvest" or "rescue" characters known as Little Sisters, a decision which ostensibly involves a tradeoff between strategic and ethical concerns. As discussed in *The Fallacy of Ethical Immersion* and *Game Goals as Intrinsic Goods*, this can be a hard sell as it is only natural for strategic concerns to override ethical ones in games with fixed goals. Another recurring problem with such scenarios is the need to preserve game balance, which often leads designers to undermine these reward incongruities by making both the good and evil paths ultimately orthogonal, as in the aforementioned *BioShock* example, where observant players discovered that the main difference was simply delayed gratification for those who opted to play the hero rather than the villain. The *Fable* series deals with this problem in a different way, by making the consequences of ethical choices largely cosmetic rather than functional.

- **Expression of ethical messages via the difficulty of accomplishing certain tasks.** This is similar to the previous item, but also includes "message" games such as *Nuclear War* (Malewicki, 1965), in which the odds are deliberately stacked in favor of a certain outcome (all players lose) in order to satirically express the futility and terror of nuclear proliferation and the arms race. While difficulty can be a valuable tool for conveying meaning within system design, using this technique can easily lead away from ethical exploration and toward a more domineering form of instruction. One possible way to mitigate this is to document the assumptions behind the game's difficulty curve, as discussed previously in the *Design and Bias* section.

- **Simulation of a moral "economy" through manipulation of ethical currency or interactive distribution of scarce resources.** This technique is rarely seen in digital games, and is more often found in thought experiments from other subjects closer to the fringes of moral philosophy, with perhaps the most famous example being the prisoner's dilemma from game theory. One existing digital game that deserves to be mentioned in relation to this concept is *Afterlife* (Stemmle, 1996). In the game, players use an interface reminiscent of *SimCity* (Wright, 1989) in order to construct and manage efficient versions of heaven and hell. These realms are occupied by simulated souls that exhibit different behavior depending on their personal belief structures. Another game that arguably fits into this mold is *Karma Tycoon* (Scheer, 2007), in which players take charge of the operations of a nonprofit organization tasked with earning "karma points" by performing good deeds within the community.

- **Lethal vs. non-lethal tactics.** This technique is often seen in games that incorporate stealth action, such as the *Metal Gear Solid*, *Splinter Cell*, and *Deus Ex* series. Playing through the game by neutralizing enemies in a non-lethal manner is typically presented as a preferable alternative for skillful players, but also a more difficult undertaking. One interesting inversion of this is found in the boss fight against "The Sorrow" in *Metal Gear Solid 3: Snake Eater* (Kojima, 2004). In

this battle, the player must dodge spectral figures representing the enemies they have killed throughout the game – the more enemies that have been dispatched using lethal means, the more ghosts will hinder the player's movements. In a sense, the conscience of the game's protagonist is manifested within a formal representation for this challenge.

- **Personality tests.** Certain ethical decisions are provided solely as a method of codifying the player's own ethical outlook, in essence providing a personality litmus test that is often subsequently reflected in the player's avatar. Classic examples are found in games such as *Ultima IV: Quest of the Avatar* and *Ogre Battle*, which present a series of ethical dilemmas to the player as part of the character creation process. Peter Molyneux, a key figure behind the creation of the *Fable* series, has heralded this method as a highly effective use of digital games for the purpose of facilitating ethical exploration, as it makes use of their interactive nature in order to encourage players to more closely examine their own moral views and presuppositions (Palmer, 2004). Some games, such as *Alter Ego* (Favaro, 1986) and *Timothy Leary's Mind Mirror* (Leary, 1985), take this concept even further by basing the entire experience around the concept of guided self-reflection. Other games take a more lighthearted approach, for example *Scruples: The Game of Moral Dilemmas* (Makow, 1984), a party game which uses ethical quandaries as a sort of social icebreaker.

Summary

These trends reflect just a few of the multifarious ways in which the classifications and criticisms presented in this essay can be circumvented, subverted, and transcended by those who have gleaned a superior understanding of ethical game design. Having comprehended the distinctions between static, adaptive, and systemic ethical games and the pitfalls associated with each category, readers are hereby invited to choose their own quagmire, to treat the classifications described in the prior sections as mutable rather than rigid, to move beyond the framework presented here and begin to envision new and inventive approaches to seemingly insoluble problems.

CONCLUSION

In this essay, I have outlined a framework for classification of ethical games into three types: static, adaptive, and systemic. I have considered these types both on their own and in relation to some of the most contentious and seminal criticisms levied at ethical games as a whole. I have also contrasted these categories with some additional trends found in ethical games that do not directly fit the mold of my framework. Based on the classifications and criticisms discussed, we can begin to identify some of the most important considerations that ethical game designers must take into account when structuring their games. Having obtained a broader understanding of the existing landscape of ethical games, readers are encouraged to utilize the framework presented here as a launching point for further inquiry and analysis into the field.

REFERENCES

Abbott, A. (1843). *The mansion of happiness: An instructive moral and entertaining amusement* [Board game]. Salem, MA: W. & S. B. Ives.

Arneson, D., & Gygax, G. (1974). *Dungeons & Dragons* [Role-playing game]. Lake Geneva, WI: TSR.

Avellone, C. (Lead Designer). (1999). *Planescape: Torment* [Computer game]. Beverly Hills, CA: Interplay Entertainment.

Beattie, S. (2007). *Sam Fischer versus Immanuel Kant: The ethics of interactive media*. Paper presented at the 4th Australasian conference on Interactive entertainment, Melbourne, Australia.

Blow, J. (2006). *Game design rant 2006: "There's not enough innovation in games!"*. Retrieved May 1, 2009, from http://number-none.com/blow/slides/rant_2006.html

Burch, A. (2008). *Indie nation #19: Execution*. Retrieved April 15, 2010, from http://www.destructoid.com/indie-nation-19-execution-87257.phtml

Cage, D. (Designer). (2005). *Fahrenheit* [Computer game]. New York: Atari.

Cain, T. (Producer). (1997). *Fallout* [Computer game]. Beverly Hills, CA: Interplay Entertainment.

Castle, L. (Executive Producer). (1997). *Blade Runner* [Computer game]. London, United Kingdom: Virgin Interactive Entertainment.

Crawford, C. (1985). *Balance of Power* [Computer game]. Novato, CA: Mindscape.

Curtis, A. (2002). *The Thing* [Computer game]. Los Angeles, CA: Vivendi Games.

Favaro, P. J. (1986). *Alter Ego* [Computer game]. Santa Monica, CA: Activision.

Ferland, M. (Producer). (2006). *Splinter Cell: Double Agent* [Computer game]. Montreuil-sous-Bois, France: Ubisoft.

Flanagan, M., Nissenbaum, H., Belman, J., & Diamond, J. (2007). A method for discovering values in digital games. Paper presented at the *Situated Play DiGRA 07 Conference,* Tokyo, Japan.

Fox, N. (Director). (2009). *inFAMOUS* [Computer game]. Tokyo, Japan: Sony Computer Entertainment.

Frasca, G. (2001). *Videogames of the oppressed: Videogames as a means for critical thinking and debate.* Retrieved May 1, 2009, from http://www.ludology.org/articles/thesis/

Frasca, G. (2003). Simulation versus narrative: Introduction to ludology. In Wolf, M. J. P., & Perron, B. (Eds.), *The video game theory reader* (pp. 221–235). New York: Routledge.

Friedman, B. (1997). Introduction. In Friedman, B. (Ed.), *Human values and the design of computer technology* (pp. 1–18). New York: CSLI Publications.

Friedman, B., & Nissenbaum, H. (1997). Bias in Computer Systems. In Friedman, B. (Ed.), *Human values and the design of computer technology* (pp. 21–40). New York: CSLI Publications.

Fructus, N. (Original designer). (1999). *Seven Games of the Soul* [Computer game]. Paris, France: Cryo Interactive Entertainment.

Garriott, R. (Designer). (1985). *Ultima IV: Quest of the Avatar* [Computer game]. Austin, TX: Origin Systems.

Gasperini, J. (1988). *Hidden Agenda* [Computer game]. Minneapolis, MN: Springboard Software.

Gaynor, S. (2008). *The immersion model of meaning.* Retrieved April 15, 2010, from http://fullbright.blogspot.com/2008/11/immersion-model-of-meaning.html

Gijsbers, V. (2006). *The Baron* [Computer game].

Hofer, M. (2003). *The games we played: The golden age of board and table games.* Princeton, NJ: Princeton Architectural Press.

Hudson, C. (Producer). (2003). *Star Wars: Knights of the Old Republic* [Computer game]. San Francisco, CA: LucasArts.

Hudson, C. (Director). (2007). *Mass Effect* [Computer game]. Redmond, WA: Microsoft Game Studios.

Jones, C. (Designer). (1996). *The Pandora Directive* [Computer game]. Salt Lake City, UT: Access Software.

Juul, J. (2005). *Half-real: Video games between real rules and fictional worlds.* Cambridge, MA: The MIT Press.

Kawano, J. (Producer). (2001). *Shadow of Memories* [Computer game]. Tokyo, Japan: Konami.

Kiciński, M. (Game Vision). (2007). *The Witcher* [Computer game]. Warsaw, Poland: CD Projekt.

Kojima, H. (Designer). (2004). *Metal Gear Solid 3: Snake Eater* [Computer game]. Tokyo, Japan: Konami.

Kreimeier, B. (2000). *Puzzled at GDC 2000: A peek into game design.* Retrieved May 1, 2009, from http://www.gamasutra.com/features/20000413/kreimeier_01.htm

Landers, A. (1995). Heaven and hell – The real difference. In Canfield, J., & Hansen, M. V. (Eds.), *A 2nd helping of chicken soup for the soul: 101 more stories to open the heart and rekindle the spirit* (p. 55). Deerfield Beach, FL: Health Communications.

Lanning, L. (Director). (2001). *Oddworld: Munch's Oddysee* [Computer game]. Redmond, WA: Microsoft Game Studios.

Lavelle, S. (2009). *Opera Omnia* [Computer game]. UK: increpare games.

Le Guin, U. K. (1975). *The wind's twelve quarters: Short stories.* New York: Harper & Row.

Leary, T. (1985). *Timothy Leary's Mind Mirror* [Computer game]. Redwood City, CA: Electronic Arts.

Levine, K. (Writer). (2007). *BioShock* [Computer game]. Novato, CA: 2K Games.

Makow, H. (1984). *Scruples: The game of moral dilemmas* [Board game]. Winnipeg, Canada: High Game Enterprises.

Malewicki, D. (Designer). (1965). *Nuclear war* [Card game]. Scottsdale, AZ: Flying Buffalo.

Mateas, M., & Stern, A. (2005). *Façade* [Computer game]. Procedural Arts.

Matsuno, Y. (Designer). (1993). *Ogre Battle: The March of the Black Queen* [Computer game]. Tokyo, Japan: Quest Corporation.

Miyamoto, S. (Designer). (1985). *Super Mario Bros.* [Computer game]. Kyoto, Japan: Nintendo.

Miyamoto, S. (Designer). (1986). *The Legend of Zelda* [Computer game]. Kyoto, Japan: Nintendo.

Molyneux, P. (Designer). (2001). *Black & White* [Computer game]. Redwood City, CA: Electronic Arts.

Molyneux, P. (Designer). (2004). *Fable* [Computer game]. Redmond, WA: Microsoft Game Studios.

Nakanishi, K. (Director). (2002). *Way of the Samurai* [Computer game]. Tokyo, Japan: Spike.

Ohlen, J. (1998). *(Lead Designer). Baldur's Gate* [Computer game]. Beverly Hills, CA: Interplay Entertainment.

Palmer, G. (Producer). (2004). *The video game revolution* [Television program]. Seattle, WA: KCTS Television.

Portnow, J. (2008). *The ethics of persuasive games*. Retrieved May 1, 2009 from http://www.edge-online.com/blogs/the-ethics-persuasive-games

Reign-Hagen, M. (Designer). (1991). *Vampire: The masquerade* [Role-playing game]. Stone Mountain, GA: White Wolf.

Reynolds, B. (Lead Designer). (1998). *Sid Meier's Alpha Centauri* [Computer game]. Redwood City, CA: Electronic Arts.

Rouse, R., III. (Writer). (2004). *The Suffering* [Computer game]. Chicago, IL: Midway Games.

Ruberg, B. (2007). *Clint Hocking speaks out on the virtues of exploration*. Retrieved May 1, 2009, from http://www.gamasutra.com/features/20070514/ruberg_01.shtml

Runyan, B. (Designer). (2010). *Real Lives* [Computer game]. Marysville, CA: Educational Simulations.

Salen, K., & Zimmerman, E. (2004). *Rules of play: Game design fundamentals*. Cambridge, MA: The MIT Press.

Scheer, K. (Director). (2007). *Karma Tycoon* [Computer game]. New York: DoSomething.org.

Sheff, D. (1993). *Game over: Nintendo's battle to dominate an industry*. London: Hodder & Stoughton.

Sirlin, D. (2007). *Can games teach ethics?* Retrieved April 15, 2010, from http://web.archive.org/web/20080525080934/http://www.sirlin.net/archive/can-games-teach-ethics/

Smith, H., & Spector, W. (Designers). (2000). *Deus Ex* [Computer game]. London, United Kingdom: Eidos Interactive.

Staff, E. (2006, October). The lurking deep. *Edge, 169*, 44–49.

Stemmle, M. (Designer). (1996). *Afterlife* [Computer game]. San Francisco, CA: LucasArts.

Ueda, F. (Director). (2005). *Shadow of the Colossus* [Computer game]. Tokyo, Japan: Sony Computer Entertainment.

Venbrux, J. (2008). *Execution* [Computer game].

Venbrux, J. (2008). *Execution, a postmortem (heh)*. Retrieved April 15, 2010, from http://www.venbrux.com/blog/?p=23

Wardell, B. (Designer). (2003). *Galactic Civilizations* [Computer game]. Montreal, Canada: Strategy First.

Winograd, T. (1997). Categories, disciplines, and social coordination. In Friedman, B. (Ed.), *Human values and the design of computer technology* (pp. 107–113). New York: CSLI Publications.

Wright, W. (Designer). (1989). *SimCity* [Computer game]. Emeryville, CA: Maxis.

Section 2
Game Design Critiques

Chapter 4
The Axis of Good and Evil

Jonathan Melenson
Aptify, USA

ABSTRACT

Many games classify player decisions as either "good" or "evil." This ignores the full range of moral behavior exhibited in real life and creates a false dichotomy: morally gray actions are overlooked or forced into one category or the other. The way actions are assigned to each category is subjective and biased toward the developers' own moral beliefs. The result is a system that fails to capture ethical nuance and take morality seriously. This chapter examines how a good-and-evil moral framework compromises gameplay, and then proposes a solution.

INTRODUCTION

Q: *What do newspapers, 1950s television, and video games have in common?*

A: *They all present the world in black and white.*

Decades have passed since computer screens were limited to white text on a black background, so when I use the term black and white to describe video games, I'm referring to the way games today convey ethical choices. Consider: game developers are now capable of generating entire worlds filled with lush forests, azure rivers, and characters so detailed you can count the freckles on their cheeks. When it comes to creating complex ethical dilemmas and choices, however, developers are still painting with a two-toned palette. Rather than presenting ethical situations using nuances and shades of moral gray, many role-playing games (RPGs) classify strategic decisions, such as whether to attack a guard or sneak past him, into one of two categories: good or evil. Sneaking is good. Killing is evil. Benevolent actions earn the player "good points" and malevolent actions net "evil points" with each type of point counter-acting the other. The results of this zero-sum game are often represented by what I call a "moral axis," which serves as a visual representation of the player character's ethical composition.

DOI: 10.4018/978-1-60960-120-1.ch004

Before continuing further, I feel it is important to discuss the term "ethics." While much has been written on the nature of ethics and what constitutes right and wrong, such specific definitions and investigations are beyond the scope of this chapter. Numerous philosophers have debated the word, devising complicated theories and systems, hoping to arrive at an adequate explanation of what is good and how to achieve it. Because it is a question unlikely to be resolved, I will instead use "ethics" in the broadest sense of the word: the behavior and thought processes that lead us towards producing the greatest good for the greatest number of people while still respecting the rights of the individual. For a more thorough discussion of the topic, I recommend reading David Simkins' chapter, Playing with Ethics: Experiencing New Ways of Being in RPGs, in the first volume of this series.

Moving along, let's take a look at a sample moral axis:

Many games use a moral axis to show the player his "moral alignment" in the game. Whenever the player receives good or evil points, the axis's needle moves closer to either the good or evil end of the spectrum. This metric is then used to determine many Non-Player Character (NPC) reactions to the player. For example, it wouldn't make sense for the local sheriff to greet you with a smile if you've spent the game stealing candy from babies. Conversely, the thieves' guild shouldn't want to accept you into their group if you've got a reputation as a righteous kitten protector.

In effect, a moral axis is a tool that is used to simulate authentic ethical relationships to immerse the player in the game. Just as luxurious graphics seek to draw the player in visually, a moral axis attempts to create meaningful character and story interactions by allowing the player to make ethical decisions that impact the game world and play possibilities. Increasing the game's range of responses to ethical behavior and increasing players' freedom to behave in a manner of their choosing only makes a game more interesting and enjoyable (Simkins, 2010).

Unfortunately, although the moral axis was designed to help simulate ethical interactions and dilemmas, in practice it oversimplifies morality. In this chapter I will discuss four major problems with the moral axis as a moral framework:

1. The moral axis creates a *false dichotomy* by classifying all moral actions as either good, or evil. This ignores the entire spectrum of morally gray behavior.
2. The moral axis treats morality as a *zero-sum* game. Good points cancel out evil points, and vice versa.
3. The moral axis's *judgments are subjective* and determined by the game designers. The developers may feel that stealing from the rich to give to the poor is moral. The player may not.
4. The moral axis *cannot assess a player's intentions*. Any action that yields a bad result awards evil points, regardless of the player's goals or motivations.

These four problems, in turn, disrupt the sense of immersion the moral interactions were intended to provide. (I'll discuss a notable exception to item number two— BioWare's *Mass Effect*—in more detail later on.)

MORAL AXIS PROBLEM #1: A FALSE DICHOTOMY

Day and night. East and West. The New York Yankees and the Boston Red Sox. It's easy to cleave the world into diametrical opposites, but it's also a mistake—which brings us to the first problem with the moral axis: its framework rests on the fundamentally incorrect assumption that all actions can be categorized as either good or evil. Real life contains shades of moral gray, where the right choice isn't always clear, if such

Figure 1. A sample moral axis

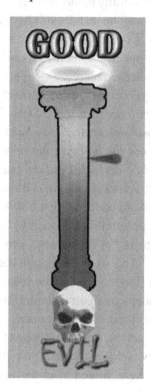

a choice exists at all. In games that use the moral axis, players are presented with black and white decision points: either rescue the orphan trapped in the well, or bake him into a cake. There is no middle ground.

In this sense, players are not given a choice as to *how* to behave ethically but *whether* to behave ethically. This all-or-nothing mentality fails to take morality seriously and promotes a Disneyesque world view. Will you play as the handsome young hero, or the cackling, mustache-twirling villain? Lionhead Studios' *Fable II* embraces this cliché to an extreme—as characters commit good or evil deeds they take on a more angelic or demonic appearance, even going so far as to grow horns or earn a halo. This cartoonish representation, although in-line with the games artwork and style, makes it difficult to take the notions of good and evil seriously.

Ethical decisions should be opportunities to challenge the player's moral code by forcing him

to make tough calls in no-win situations (Staines, 2010). But because the choices are constrained to one of two options, they amount to little more than contrived exercises where the player decides which game experience he would prefer. The "R" in RPG could just as well stand for "rail" since the player is inexorably stuck on one of two pre-determined paths. This practice also promotes backwards-thinking. Instead of generating realistic approaches to a problem based on the particular conflict, developers are encouraged to design along moral lines when creating player options; each game scenario must include good and evil "solutions."

Why do game developers choose this frame-work? One answer is that it is simple and convenient to implement. Players are given an alternate game-experience while the developers need only invest minimal time and effort creating the two sets of choices. But this shoehorning of moral choice-making creates as many problems as it solves. Consider BioWare's *Knights of the Old Republic*. In it, players may choose to walk the righteous path of the Jedi by aligning themselves with the light side of the force, or succumb to the temptations of the dark side and grow sinister. Players, of course, can perform both good and bad actions, thereby remaining "neutral" and hovering near the middle of the moral axis, but there is no advantage to moral limbo. The game rewards only extreme behavior—players receive increasing bonuses to their light-side powers as they climb the moral axis while suffering greater penalties to dark-side powers. The reverse holds true for those who choose evil. Most games that use a moral axis follow a similar pattern, with items, quests, or rewards becoming available only for players who have opted for a specific path. There is little incentive to choose the middle option.

This problem of the excluded middle is sometimes referred to in gaming circles as The "Han Solo Problem," named for the eponymous Star Wars protagonist. Han Solo is commonly considered a morally gray character, shooting first and asking questions later, all while risking his life to save the damsel in distress. Players following in the footsteps of Han Solo are likely to end up with a neutral value on the moral axis and, consequently, an unsatisfying and limited gaming experience.

Several games have confronted this exact issue. Bethesda's *Fallout 3*, set in a post-apocalyptic nuclear wasteland, and the third installment in a series known for its three dimensional characters and intricate story lines, is one such game. But even its developers admit that resolving the Han Solo problem is complicated. The following is an interview Todd Howard, the Executive Producer of *Fallout 3*, gave MTV Multiplayer (Totilo, 2008):

Todd Howard, executive producer, "Fallout 3": *We actually support you with [playable paths of] good, evil and even neutral — who are people who do good things and bad things.*

Multiplayer: *Do you get anything for playing as "neutral"?*

Howard: *Yeah.*

Multiplayer: *Usually you don't get anything.*

Howard: *Well, realized [sic] we who were playing it, a lot of us were neutral. You get certain followers who will want to come with you. Certain followers will only come with you if you're evil. Some only if you're good. And there are Achievements you will only get if you're neutral.*

Multiplayer: *And these are cool things? Because, again, you're calling it "neutral." It already sounds like something not to be proud of. Yet I know it's the one I'm going to wind up being...*

Howard: *Some of [things you get] are very cool. And some of them are avoiding a negative that comes with being evil. If you're evil some people will come after you. If you're neutral they won't. If you're good some people will come after you. If you're neutral they won't.*

This interview suggests that the neutral path, rather than having its own quests and benefits, merely doesn't have the typical penalties normally associated with a good or evil alignment. Aside from being able to recruit a few specific characters

to his party, a morally neutral player doesn't have any advantages—he just doesn't have any disadvantages. This could be addressed by including more neutral-specific content, but regrettably the problem is more extensive:

Multiplayer: *Everybody loves Han Solo, right? They like him more than Luke Skywalker, who's the goody two-shoes. And Han Solo is the guy who — he's not the bad guy, but he will murder people in cold blood. He's got that mixture.*

Howard: *I can't say we've conquered that.*

Here, Howard concedes that *Fallout 3*'s game design can't account for "good guys" who sometimes engage in "evil" actions, also known as "antiheroes." And so, even though the Bethesda team made efforts to resolve the issue by including the concept of neutral karma and specific consequences for it, they were unable to address it to their satisfaction. So what stopped them? Why couldn't they conquer the Han Solo problem?

The answer is hinted at in the beginning of the interview:

Todd Howard, executive producer, "Fallout 3": *We actually support you with [playable paths of] good, evil and even neutral —**who are people who do good things and bad things.** [emphasis added] (Totilo, 2008)

Here, Todd Howard reveals an underlying misconception regarding the nature of good, evil and neutral moral alignments. Individuals who perform both good and evil actions aren't necessarily neutral; they may be antiheroes, self-ish—yet non-malicious cowards, or even villains who engage in the occasional act of mercy. The neutral path serves as little more than a third rail; a nebulous catch-all for behavior that cannot be tagged as purely good or evil.

Thus, we can see now that the true problem with the moral axis's dichotomy isn't that there aren't enough rewards for players taking the neutral path—it's that individuals cannot be neatly summarized with one convenient label. Human behavior is more complex than that, as each of us make ethical decisions not based on a clear set of principles or identity, but based on multiple factors, such as our situation, personalities, and background (Jones, 2008). Furthermore, many actions do not neatly conform to the good and evil definitions, and, rather than being appropriately labeled as "ambiguous," are instead classified as "neutral"—a bold assumption that anything not good or evil must lie between the two on an invisible continuum.

This interpretation of morality leaves much to be desired, as complex three-dimensional characters are flattened to fit the moral axis's mold. Han Solo isn't straddling the line between good and evil; he's a reluctant hero, the archetypal rebel with a heart of gold. But because his many indiscretions whittle away at his heroic gestures, he gets stuck with a neutral alignment. Likewise, *Superman*'s Lex Luthor might donate millions to charity, but he also performs malevolent acts behind the scenes. Such a character, despite being clearly associated with the side of evil, ends up in the same place as Han Solo. This leads us to the second problem with the moral axis.

MORAL AXIS PROBLEM #2: MORALITY IS A ZERO-SUM GAME

Everyone loves a redemption story. At the climax of *Star Wars: Return of the Jedi*, the evil Darth Vader overthrows the Emperor and returns to the light side after years of ruling with an iron fist. These depictions of change and salvation make for great movies and literature because they treat morality seriously. Vader's transformation was powerful not because it happened suddenly (it didn't), but because it wasn't easy. His change came only after witnessing his son dying at the hands of the Emperor. Games that use the moral axis haven't yet grasped this concept; instead they treat morality as a zero-sum game, where good deeds and evil actions nullify each other. In this respect, the moral axis, rather than being swayed by emotional, compelling decisions and events,

more closely resembles the sale of indulgences. Because good points and evil points cancel each other, a player finding himself too far down the road of evil need only balance the scales by performing a few petty favors. Do you want to steal that powerful sword from the blacksmith without angering the king? No problem—go ahead and loot the item, then pay off your sins by tossing a few gold pieces to charity. The king will never know the difference. Money can't buy you love, but apparently it can buy forgiveness.

Simply put, a zero-sum view of morality leads to inauthentic moral transactions in games. In *Fable II*, it's possible to atone for crimes as heinous as murder by dancing a jig for the townspeople, while in *Fallout 3* stealing items can net a karmic profit. The chart below shows how various player actions influence karma in *Fallout 3*:

In *Fallout 3*, stealing an item costs five karma (good points), but because donating caps (money) to a church earns one karma per cap, all the player needs to do is pilfer an item that sells for more than five caps to play Robin Hood. Also note that a point-based system leads to strange moral equivalencies. A hero who risks his life to kill a Very Evil Character is on the same footing as one who donates 100 caps to a church. Similarly, the thief who leads a life of crime but never kills is no better than the villain who murders a shopkeeper in cold blood.

A zero-sum system strips the emotional content from ethical decisions and packages them as points. Consequently, players are not concerned with their character's moral fiber as much as their moral axis value and how it affects NPC behavior. The king and blacksmith are no longer characters in a narrative, but instead have been reduced to pawns in the player's quest for in-game success. By allowing players to alter their moral identity at will, ethical decisions and actions become just another gameplay mechanic to be exploited (Staines, 2010).

Is this really what morality amounts to? A series of debits and credits to an ethical account? Can any good deed or donation to charity, no matter how large, atone for the murder of an innocent? Most people would agree that some sins cannot be paid for with "blood money" but this is exactly what developers rule when they assign specific amounts of positive or negative karma for actions.

BioWare tried to address this problem in *Mass Effect*, by tracking the player's Paragon (lawful) and Renegade (antihero) actions on separate axes. Receiving either type of point has no bearing on the points previously earned, which prevents players from simply erasing the mistakes of the past. This, too, avoids punishing the occasional antihero action or act of mercy. Regrettably, the solution falls short as the end result tends to be the same as that of a single-axis system. By design, any axis-based system, whether it uses one, or two—remains point-based and additive. Many small indiscretions are still converted into points and totaled, which unfairly equates them with larger, more egregious sins. And because there are two axes, the developers must decide which one to give priority when determining NPC responses. How should a player with similar Paragon and Renegade values be treated? There's no obvious answer to this question.

A point-based system of morality forces developers to assign moral values to every player action, and inject their own moral beliefs into the game. If you revisit *Fallout 3*'s karmic chart, you'll note that the system doesn't penalize players for stealing from evil characters, which passively presents a moral judgment that it's okay to rob bad people. This brings up the third problem with the moral axis: its valuations are inherently subjective.

MORAL AXIS PROBLEM #3: MORAL AXIS VALUATIONS ARE SUBJECTIVE

Is Robin Hood a champion of the people or a scoundrel? Is Batman a lawless vigilante, or a public defender? Is Donkey Kong a rapacious ape, or just lonely? Objective moral truth is hard to come by, as every individual has his own unique beliefs about what is right and what is wrong (Bailey, 2006).

Consider the classic runaway-trolley thought experiment: a runaway trolley is on a collision course for a group of five innocent people and will assuredly kill them. You are given the option of flipping a switch to change the trolley to another track where it will only hit one hapless bystander (Foot, 1967). You can assume for the sake of the thought experiment that all lives are of equal value. Most people, when presented with this problem, exchange the one life for the five and minimize the harm caused. Their decision changes, however, when the situation is framed slightly differently. Instead of flipping a switch, the person must shove an obese man into the path of the oncoming trolley to slow it down and prevent the deaths (Thompson, 1976). The choices and outcomes are the same, sacrificing one person who would otherwise not be killed to save many, but the perception of the problem has changed as people are now more hesitant to make the trade.

The trolley scenario demonstrates a simple point: our moral beliefs are fluid and subjective, dependent on the way problems are framed, as well as our backgrounds, experience, and unique value judgments (Jones, 2008). Different people can look at the trolley problem and come to contrasting, yet reasonable conclusions about the "right" decision. Consequently, the moral axis's valuations depend solely on the developer's moral opinions as they alone decide whether an act is good or evil.

It is important to note here that not all developer bias stems from a moral axis framework, nor is it necessarily detrimental. Creating fictional game worlds requires that developers make numerous decisions, many of which involve imagining the consequences for each of the player's actions. In this light, the very actions the game restricts and allows are themselves a form of bias. *Fallout 3*, for instance, doesn't allow the player to kill children but allows the killing of many other types of innocents, a subjective value judgment that a child's life is worth more than an adult's (Parkin, 2008). These design choices shape the theme and tone of a game, and it would be impossible to create a game from a truly neutral view point. Asking a developer to remove this implicit bias would be akin to asking Disney to rewrite *Aladdin* to account for Jafar's point of view. In cases like these, the term "bias" should be replaced with the term "perspective."

So, what distinguishes developer bias from a design decision? Why is the moral axis the former, and not the latter? The answer is that the moral axis was never intended to advance an agenda. Quite the opposite, it originates as a mode of player choice; a method for creating alternate gameplay experiences. Unfortunately, every time a developer assigns a karmic value to an action, they are announcing their opinion of the player. These judgments feel frustrating because rather than giving players the freedom to cut their own moral path, they pigeonhole them into conforming or rebelling against the developer's subjective proscriptions of morality.

The "Tenpenny Tower" quest encountered in *Fallout 3* exemplifies developer subjectivity. Here, the player meets a ghoul (a disfigured and mutated human) named Roy Phillips who announces his plans to murder all the residents of Tenpenny Tower, a luxury hotel inhabited by humans who are severely bigoted against ghouls. The ghouls initially tried to negotiate with the residents so that they, too, could live in the tower, but were attacked by them. "We tried playing nice," Roy explains, "but they shot at us" (Fallout 3, Bethesda Softworks, 2008). Roy then asks the player for help in his plot, but the residents of the tower, fearing an oncoming assault, have a proposal of their own: preemptively eliminate Roy and his fellow ghouls.

To complete the quest, the player is given a total of three options:

1. Assist Roy in murdering the residents. This results in a loss of karma.
2. Side with the residents by helping them assassinate the ghouls. This also results in negative karma.
3. Broker a peaceful solution between the two groups for positive karma. This involves convincing the sadistic proprietor of Tenpenny Tower, Allistair Tenpenny (who is fond of taking pot shots at people from the top of the tower with his sniper rifle) to allow the ghouls to move in. If the player does this, things initially work out, but upon returning to the tower later, the player learns that Roy decided to slaughter all of the inhabitants anyway, looting their corpses and dumping them in the basement.

Here, Bethesda has created an ethically ambiguous situation that combines notions of ownership, bigotry, vengeance, and justice. Neither party has a clear conscience, and to make matters worse, the "right" decision yields a bad result. Unfortunately, the moral axis demands the developers pick a side, and, as a result, each decision point and player action must be arbitrarily assigned positive or negative karma. If the player kills Roy after he has massacred the residents, for instance, he is penalized with a loss of karma. Is killing Roy, a bloodthirsty psychopath, immoral? Or is it closer to justice, because it prevents the villain from killing again? The ethical case is far from open and shut—the developers could just as easily have awarded positive karma. But no matter which side they come down on, their bias is unavoidable. In fact, it's a core component of the moral axis framework as every game decision must be viewed through a moral lens.

Take one last look at the karmic chart, as seen in Figure 2.

Notice that killing a Very Evil Character awards 100 karma. But who decides if killing evil is a good thing? If it is, then how much karma is it worth? For that matter, how does one distinguish

Figure 2. Karma Affecting Actions in Fallout 3 (Planet Fallout Wiki, 2009)

Fallout 3 Karma Affecting Actions	
Action	**Karma Consequence**
Kill a Very Evil Character	+100
Kill an Evil Character	—
Murder a Neutral/Good Creature	-25
Murder a Neutral/Good Character	-100
Steal from a Neutral/Good Character	-5 (per item)
Donate caps to a church	+(x) (Depends on amount)
Do something good in Freeform Quests	+50 Karma or more
Do something evil in Freeform Quests	-50 Karma or more

between "Very Evil" and just plain "Evil?" Both Allistair Tenpenny and Roy Phillips can be considered evil, so why is it that killing Allistair, under any circumstance, rewards the player with positive karma, while killing the murderous Roy Phillips results in a loss of karma?

These types of moral judgments serve only to frustrate players as they are neither rewarded nor punished according to their acts within a context, but according to the developer's unwavering moral code. As Jaroslav Švelch notes in The Good, The Bad, and The Player: The Challenges to Moral Engagement in Single-Player Avatar-Based Video Games, in the first volume of this series, "This sort of arbitrariness demasks the system and reveals that the consequences come not from the fictional world, but from the designers."

And so we are now faced with the fourth major problem with the moral axis: it cannot assess a player's intentions.

MORAL AXIS PROBLEM #4: THE MORAL AXIS CANNOT ASSESS INTENTIONS

Which is worse: inadvertently running over your neighbor's dog, or deliberately swerving to hit him? Even though the outcomes are the same, there is an underlying difference between the two. One act is accidental, and has no bearing on one's moral character. The other act is evidence of a deranged mind, a sign the individual should be locked away or given treatment.

The above scenario, although simple in presentation, proves a powerful point: intentions matter when determining moral reprehensibility (Parker, 1984). Intuition tells us that the consequences of any act must be considered along with a person's intentions (Bell, 2009). The moral axis, however, only cares about the former, relying entirely on prima facie observations. Context, rationale, and motivations are all irrelevant as far as the axis is concerned; if Lex Luthor donates to charity to win the mayor's good graces, the axis sees only the charity and declares the act benevolent.

Developers of games that use a moral axis are not unaware of this problem. In *Knights of the Old Republic*, BioWare added descriptive tags to dialogue options to differentiate between good and bad intentions. In one scenario, for example, the player is confronted by a group of aliens he had betrayed prior to the events of the game, and is presented with the following conversation options:

[Persuade] I am a servant of the light now. I want to make amends for the mistakes of the past.

[Persuade/Lie] I regret the mistakes of my past. I want to make amends. (BioWare, 2003)

The first choice represents sincerity and a genuine desire to reform; the second indicates a devious lie. The tags are needed to clarify the player's motivations. Does the player really think he's reformed, or is he just manipulating the hapless group to serve his own ends?

The solution appears effective at first, but regrettably becomes cumbersome in the face of more complex situations, as Peter Rauch documents in his thesis: Playing with Good and Evil: Videogames and Moral Philosophy (2007). He writes of *Fable*, developed by Lionhead Studios and Peter Molyneux:

...a woman complains of her philandering husband, and asks the protagonist to find out where he is and what he's doing. Sure enough, the player finds the man engaged in an amorous embrace with another woman—upon discovery, he offers the protagonist a coin to keep quiet. (The game warns the player that rumors travel fast in the village, and people will know he took the bribe.) If the player takes the bribe, he or she receives two "evil" points and gets the coin, although he or she can balance those points out by breaking his promise to the adulterous husband and telling his wife the truth (Rauch, 2007, p. 34).

...the game as it currently exists can respond to play actions, but not player intent. The importance of intent in morality is hotly debated of course, and intent is coded into Fable by the designers. However, the player has no role in deciding this intent...If the player's intent for a given action differs from that which the designers scripted, the result can be quite jarring (Rauch, 2007, p. 36).

Here, Rauch makes a very astute observation: It can be quite frustrating for a player to initiate an action expecting one result only to have the game interpret the action completely differently. This is because all the player's actions come with assumed intentions—they are hard-coded into the game and the player has no way of clarifying his underlying reasons. If the player takes the bribe, and doesn't

tell the wife, the axis presumes the player meant to selfishly exploit the wife's misfortune. This interpretation overlooks the possibility that the player may take the bribe to punish the husband and didn't tell the wife because he thought it might be better for her not to know. Rauch writes:

The wife clearly suspects her husband, and seems to be bothered more by his continued absence (and consequent inability to help with the household) than by his infidelity. However, it could still be argued that the wife would be happier not knowing the truth about her husband's activities, and the husband would certainly prefer this outcome. He prefers it so much, in fact, that he's willing to pay for it. Under these assumptions, taking the bribe and staying quiet could be seen as the most moral solution. If we assume that the wife would, in fact, prefer to know, the issue is still not resolved....doesn't a man who attempts to bribe a child to deceive his wife deserve to lose the money he offers? An option to accept the bribe, tell the truth, and then return the bribe to the wife (who will, presumably, use it more responsibly) might produce an even better result (Rauch, 2007, p. 52).

Given the plethora of possible player motivations, it would be nearly impossible for developers to anticipate every single one and then create the game content for it. Even if they could identify the most likely intentions, each decision point would be cluttered by a lengthy list of actions and descriptions. Imagine how the choices would appear for this scenario:

Refuse the bribe to punish the husband because he shouldn't be allowed to get away with his crime.

Accept the bribe to punish the husband as he deserves to lose his money for being a no-good louse.

Accept the bribe out of selfishness because you don't care what the husband has done, only that you are being offered a chance to make a profit.

Accept the bribe because you really need the money, but feel guilty about it. After all, you need to buy medicine for your sick grandmother.

The permutations of choices and reasons for each choice quickly become overwhelming both in number and in scope. There's no way to enumerate all the possible options, and these are but a few of them. Given both time and technological constraints, the developers are forced to simplify the number of decisions, listing only the most common moral archetypes.

But wait, the problem gets worse. Tagging actions within explicit decision points only addresses the intentions problem within a narrow context; the moral axis would be unable to discover the player's motivations for all other game actions. In *Fallout 3*, a player could gun down Allistair Tenpenny for profit before knowing he was malicious, yet would still be awarded good points because Tenpenny happened to be classified as evil. Only the act itself is being judged, not the player's motivation; the player is presumed to have killed Tenpenny for righteous reasons.

TRANSCENDING THE MORAL AXIS: BEYOND GOOD AND EVIL

Considering time and budget constraints as well as artificial intelligence hurdles, it's no surprise that the moral axis has become entrenched as a gaming convention. Good and evil are often assumed to be the best, or at least, most convenient template for creating and responding to player decisions. But this two-dimensional, cookie-cutter approach to gameplay overlooks many other avenues. In real life, people react to others based not only on their moral behavior, but according to a variety of factors, such as their age, race, gender, clothing, job title, social status, physical attractiveness, and personality. A person's moral character is often his least visible characteristic, a small part of a complicated social equation.

Properly addressing morality in games requires a fundamental shift in thinking as the notion of measuring morality has mistakenly become intertwined with the concept of both player choice and NPC behavior. Fortunately, some developers have already recognized this and taken steps towards creating a solution. NPCs in the *Fallout* games will occasionally treat you differently if you are playing as a woman, characters in Bethesda's *Oblivion* will only judge the player based on what they could reasonably know upon first meeting the person, and games such as *Vampire: The Masquerade—Bloodlines* have very different game experiences for each vampire clan that the player may play as. And kudos must be given to the game *The Witcher* for creating delayed and unforeseen consequences for many of the player's actions. This muddies the moral waters and more closely mirrors real life, where individuals cannot always know the long-term effects of their choices.

These solutions, although steps in the right direction, remain incomplete so long as games aspire to objectively quantify the player's morality. The labels of good and evil should be cast aside, karma points forgotten, developer judgments eliminated, and intentions legitimately considered. Morality must cease to be a gameplay mechanic and instead become a storytelling device.

Fable II, despite using a moral axis, recognized this to an extent. Below is an excerpt from an interview with Peter Molyneux, again courtesy of MTV Multiplayer (Klepek, 2008):

Don't think that being good or evil will unlock different parts of the game that will allow you to be more powerful...Don't think that you're going down these paths that lead you to completely different content in either one. You're not. You're just doing it to be who you want to be. You're going to have the same choices at the end of the game, whether you play good or evil.

This, however, may be too much of an over-correction. While Molyneux pays greater respect to the idea that players should behave morally for the sake of character immersion and not because it will unlock quests or rewards, he fails to acknowledge the extent to which individuals' decisions affect how people respond to them, and subsequently, their future choices.

So how can developers better represent morality in games? What can be done so that players are free to make moral choices that more accurately reflect those found in the real world? When considering this question we must remember the reason games began to measure morality in the first place: to allow NPCs to better respond to player actions. Games don't need objective methods for quantifying morality; they need ways of creating realistic NPCs whose actions are believable. Measuring morality for its own sake accomplishes nothing.

To get NPCs to behave more appropriately as characters, we must begin to look at them as their name suggests: as *characters* in a narrative, not informational kiosks or karmic opportunities. They must be brought to life and become more than the person a player visits to purchase potions. What do characters have? Why, they have personalities, and backstories, and *values*.

The days of slapping a name on the blacksmith, giving him a Scottish accent, and calling him a character must come to an end. Rather, every NPC should be given his own artificial conscience—a unique moral code by which he can judge the player. How does *he* perceive the player's morality? BioWare's most recent *RPG, Dragon Age: Origins*, has already implemented some of this solution by abolishing the moral axis and allowing the player's party members to react to specific player actions according to their own values. In this sense, the moral axis, instead of existing as a global, all-seeing eye, has been replaced by localized, individual NPC assessments of the player's persona. Does the NPC approve of stealing from the king, but not the town's shopkeeper? Is he okay with murdering ghouls, but not humans?

Because NPCs don't claim to be omniscient like the axis, it's okay for them to make assumptions and mistakes. Part of creating more realistic, believable characters is by making them flawed. It doesn't matter if Roy Phillips is good or evil, or if the player kills him for selfish or altruistic reasons—Roy's cronies will always perceive it as an offense. The action's true moral value, if it even has one, is inconsequential.

And so, ironically, solving the problem of morality in games lies not in seeking objective truth but in embracing subjectivity. Being condemned by an omniscient axis is frustrating because it acts as a transparent proxy for developer opinions. But being judged by an NPC within the context of the NPC's personality and motivations seems legitimate because the NPCs are not assumed to have any moral authority. Their verdicts are just another opinion based on their fictional interests. Continuing this line of reasoning, an NPC's moral conscience need not be restricted to moral criteria when evaluating player behavior. In this regard, an NPC's artificial conscience could be supplemented or replaced by a list of preferences, expanding an NPC's ability to react beyond the moral domain.

This approach creates more natural and believable conflicts. Two people reaching for the last slice of pizza is not an example of a moral struggle—it's a conflict of interests and preferences. Good and evil never enter the equation; the situation is simply one person versus another. This isn't to say that good and evil can't exist, merely that they can be better modeled using a larger umbrella of preferences.

What might such preferences include? On a more macro level, preferences could be used to create in-group and out-group dynamics, which is one way of looking at how people treat others (Castillo, 2010). NPCs could be programmed to prefer members of certain groups over members of others. So far, most games have used these alignments to keep track of whether the player has decided to side with one in-game faction or another, but there's no reason such groupings couldn't be used to address issues such as nationality, race, or gender. Removing morality as the primary means of determining NPC reactions and replacing it with individual preferences frees NPCs to make judgments based on nearly anything.

How might such a preference system work? Consider the Tenpenny Tower example. Allistair Tenpenny could be programmed to like humans and hate ghouls. Under the hood, this would translate to a high preference for any action that helps a human, and a low preference for an action that harms a human. Conversely, Allistair would have a high preference for killing, stealing, or otherwise harming ghouls and a low preference for actions that help them. In game terms, Allistair might reproach the player for killing a human while encouraging the player to attack ghouls. Moreover, Allistair could respond to the player positively or negatively based on whether the player shares his preferences—in this case, his bigotry towards ghouls. This could be done by looking to the player's past actions, such as whether he's killed a high number of ghouls or has made anti-ghoul statements.

So what happens when an NPC encounters a situation where he has conflicting preferences? For example, suppose an NPC has a low preference for stealing, but also a high preference for the player because the player saved the NPC's village. How would he react if he witnessed the player stealing an item? One way of resolving this apparent conflict would be to simply weigh the preferences based on the strength of each conviction. If the NPC has only a marginal dislike of stealing he might be able to ignore the crime. Alternately, this could be used as an opportunity to give depth to NPCs, who may comment that they are grateful to the player, but disagree with the player's methods.

Another possible solution would be to borrow the concept of mortal and venial sins from the Catholic Church. According to Catholic doctrine,

venial sins are "forgivable" and can never add up to a mortal sin, which is usually a more severe crime such as murder. The NPC could then look to his own list of forgivable and unforgivable sins to differentiate the mercurial thief from a ruthless assassin. (*Fallout 1* and *2* did this to an extent by bestowing a permanent "childkiller" reputation to a player who killed a child, even if it was by accident. Any future interactions with certain NPCs would then be influenced by this reputation.)

Finally, this system of NPC preferences could also be used to determine how NPCs interact with other NPCs. This may lead to more interesting emergent behavior, which is behavior that arises from the interplay between the game's rules and is not hard-coded by the developers. For example, relationships could be set up between NPCs by determining their degree of like for one another. Members of a family would have a very high preference for each other, while NPCs who disliked each other would have low preference values. If an action harms an NPC, the other NPCs could approve or disapprove of the act based on their preference for that NPC along with their other values. An NPC who hates another NPC might sanction the player stealing from him, while one who only marginally dislikes him may still report the player to the authorities based on a dislike of stealing. This system of preferences could be further enhanced by giving each NPC a Maslovian hierarchy of needs for things such as food, health, or property. Any action that lowered an NPCs value of these resources could be interpreted as harm based on their degree of preference for each.

FURTHER DIRECTIONS: DESIGN CONSIDERATIONS FOR ETHICAL INTERACTIONS

In this chapter I've outlined just a few possible solutions in the vast sea of alternatives to the moral axis. Yes, the moral axis is convenient, but it also fails to offer players a legitimate ethical experience. To have games that realistically simulate NPC reactions to ethical decisions and behavior, the moral axis as an omnipresent, absolute arbiter of objective morality must be discarded. Players know the character they're trying to play and don't need to be told how naughty or nice they are—especially not based on the developer's particular notion of morality. Where can games go from here? Below are some questions developers should consider when designing player choices and NPC interactions.

- What types of conflicts lead to player choices that do not neatly fall under the good and evil classifications? Do all conflicts have to pit good against evil?
- How can we better model relationships between the player and NPCs? What criteria would best create more meaningful NPC responses?
- How can the types of interactions with NPCs be expanded? Most RPGs allow only three types of interactions: kill the NPC, steal from the NPC, or engage in a conversation with predetermined paths.

Whatever the answers to these questions, one thing remains clear: the moral axis and its stale caricature of morality are obsolete. Developers must move beyond good and evil when presenting moral scenarios because it compromises their ability to create authentic NPC interactions and immersive gameplay. By imbuing NPCs with their own set of values and preferences, NPCs are better able to interpret and respond to their surroundings, thus enhancing the storytelling and allowing increasingly complex gameplay possibilities. Designers can then take the first step to achieving more engaging narratives and transporting players into a lifelike ethical world—which is one place the moral axis will never be able to take us.

REFERENCES

Bailey, R. (2006). Morality on the brain: Cerebral scans for right and wrong. *Reason Magazine*. Retrieved April 14, 2010, from http://reason.com/news/show/35014.html

Bell, V. (2009). Experimental philosophy of others' intentions. *Mind Hacks*. Retrieved April 14, 2010, from http://www.mindhacks.com/blog/2009/02/experimental_philoso.html

Castillo, J. J. (2010) Sherif's Robbers Cave experiment: Realistic conflict theory. *The scientific method, science, research and experiments*. Retrieved June 13, 2010 from http://www.experiment-resources.com/robbers-cave-experiment.html

Foot, P. (1967). The problem of abortion and the doctrine of the double effect. *Oxford Review, 5*, 5–15.

Jones, D. (2008). The emerging moral psychology. *Prospect Magazine*. Retrieved April 14, 2010, from http://www.prospect-magazine.co.uk/article_details.php?id=10126

Klepek, P. (2008). Peter Molyneux believes 'Fable II' solves the 'Han Solo Problem'. *MTV Multiplayer*. Retrieved April 14, 2010, from http://multiplayerblog.mtv.com/2008/09/16/molyneux-fable-ii-han-solo/

Parker, R. (1984). Blame, punishment, and the role of result. In Feinberg, J., & Gross, H. (Eds.), *Philosophy of law* (4th ed.). Belmont, CA: Wadsworth Publishing Company.

Parkin, S. (2008). Opinion: 'Fallout 3—I kill children'. *Gamasutra*. Retrieved April 14, 2010, from http://www.gamasutra.com/php-bin/news_index.php?story=20908

Planet Fallout Wiki. (2009). *Fallout 3 Karma*. Retrieved June 10, 2010, from http://planetfallout.gamespy.com/wiki/Fallout_3_Karma

Rauch, P. (2007). *Playing with good and evil: Videogames and moral philosophy*. Unpublished master's thesis, Massachusetts Institute of Technology. Retrieved April 14, 2010, from http://cms.mit.edu/research/theses/PeterRauch2007.pdf

Simkins, D. (2010). Playing with ethics: Experiencing new ways of being in RPGs. In Schrier, D. K., & Gibson, D. (Eds.), *Ethics and game design: Teaching values through play* (pp. 69–85). Hershey, PA: IGI Global.

Staines, D. (2010). Videogames and moral pedagogy: A neo-Kohlbergian approach. In Schrier, D. K., & Gibson, D. (Eds.), *Ethics and game design: Teaching values through play* (pp. 35–51). Hershey, PA: IGI Global.

Švelch, J. (2010). The good, the bad, and the player: The challenges to moral engagement in single-player avatar-based video games. In Schrier, D. K., & Gibson, D. (Eds.), *Ethics and game design: Teaching values through play* (pp. 52–68). Hershey, PA: IGI Global.

Thompson, J. J. (1976). Killing, letting die, and the trolley problem. *The Monist, 59*, 204–217.

Thompson, J. J. (1985). The trolley problem. *The Yale Law Journal, 94*, 1395–1415. doi:10.2307/796133

Totilo, S. (2008). 'Fallout 3' developer tackles, fails to conquer Han Solo problem. *MTV Multiplayer*. Retrieved April 14, 2010, from http://multiplayerblog.mtv.com/2008/07/28/fallout-3-and-the-han-solo-problem/

ADDITIONAL READING

Abbott, M. (2008, November 18). Second thoughts. *The Brainy Gamer: Thoughtful conversation about video games*. Retrieved June 10, 2010, from http://www.brainygamer.com/the_brainy_gamer/2008/11/second-thoughts-on-emergent-narrative.html

Abbott, M. (2009, February 13). Fallout 3 [Review]. *PopMatters*. Retrieved June 10, 2010, from http://www.popmatters.com/pm/review/70438-fallout-3/

Avellone, C. (2002). Fallout Bible 9. *The Vault, the Fallout Wiki*. Retrieved April 14, 2010, from http://fallout.wikia.com/wiki/Fallout_Bible_9

Chris. (2005). Moral psychology I: Where is morality in the brain? *Mixing memory*. Retrieved April 14, 2010, from http://mixingmemory.blogspot.com/2005/07/moral-psychology-i-where-is-morality.html

Chris. (2005). Moral psychology II: The life and death of moral rationalism. *Mixing memory*. Retrieved April 14, 2010, from http://mixingmemory.blogspot.com/2005/08/moral-psychology-ii-life-and-death-of.html

Clarkson, M. (2009, July 17). Critical compilation: Fallout 3. *Critical Distance* [Blog]. Retrieved June 10, 2010, from http://www.critical-distance.com/2009/07/17/fallout-3/

Dean, J. (2007) War, peace and the role of power in Sherif's Robbers Cave experiment. *PsyBlog - Understand your mind with the science of psychology*. Retrieved April 14, 2010, from http://www.spring.org.uk/2007/09/war-peace-and-role-of-power-in-sherifs.php

Farr, D. (2009, August 13). Hum-drum morality. *Vorpal Bunny Ranch* [Blog]. Retrieved June 10, 2010, from http://vorpalbunnyranch.blogspot.com/2009/08/hum-drum-morality.html

Furman, T. (2009). Blameworthiness. *MSU Philosophy Club* [Blog]. Retrieved April 14, 2010, from http://msuphilosophyclub.blogspot.com/2009/02/blameworthiness.html

Goldstein, H. (2008). Fable II: Saint or sinner. *IGN Xbox 360: Games, cheats, news, reviews, and previews*. Retrieved April 14, 2010, from http://xbox360.ign.com/articles/921/921312p1.html

Jenkins, H. (2007). Fable and other moral tales: A study in game ethics (Part One). *Confessions of an Aca-Fan: The official weblog of Henry Jenkins*. Retrieved April 14, 2010, from http://henryjenkins.org/2007/08/games_and_ethics.html

Jenkins, H. (2007). Fable and other moral tales: A study in game ethics (Part Two). *Confessions of an Aca-Fan: The official weblog of Henry Jenkins*. Retrieved April 14, 2010, from http://henryjenkins.org/2007/08/fable_and_other_moral_tales_a.html

Krpata, M. (2009, January 5). Falling in and out of love, part 1. *Insult swordfighting, where everyone fights like a dairy farmer* [Blog]. Retrieved June 10, 2010, from http://insultswordfighting.blogspot.com/2009/01/falling-in-and-out-of-love-part-1.html

Maciak, L. G. (2009, July 31). Fallout 3: Side quest rant. *Terminally Incoherent: Utterly random, incoherent, and disjointed rants and ramblings* [Blog]. Retrieved June 10, 2010, from http://www.terminally-incoherent.com/blog/2009/07/

MacRae, F. (2007). Disney's villains 'give children negative images of the elderly'. *Mail Online*. Retrieved April 14, 2010, from http://www.dailymail.co.uk/news/article-458808/Disneys-villains-children-negative-images-elderly.html

Nieborg, D. (2008). Morality and "gamer guilt" in Fable 2. *Valuable Games*. Retrieved April 14, 2010, from http://blogs.law.harvard.edu/games/2008/11/19/morality-and-gamer-guilt-in-fable-2/

Riley, D. (2008, November 17). What about the oasis? *The New Gamer* [Blog]. Retrieved June 10, 2010, from http://thenewgamer.com/content/archives/what_about_oasis%3F

Sternberg, R. J. (1998). *1995). In search of the human mind* (2nd ed., pp. 444–448). Orlando, FL: Harcourt Brace & Company.

Tuhus-Dubrow, R. (2009). Can organic produce and natural shampoo turn you into a heartless jerk? *Slate*. Retrieved April 14, 2010, from http://www.slate.com/id/2237674/

Chapter 5
Ethical Dilemmas in Gameplay:
Choosing Between Right and Right

Ian Schreiber
Independent, USA

Bryan Cash
Schell Games, USA

Link Hughes
CCP Games, USA

ABSTRACT

This chapter discusses ethical dilemmas and their role in game design. The chapter first defines what ethical dilemmas are and then argues for why they are compelling in games. This argument will analyze the role of decisions in games, what makes for interesting decisions, and then address how avatars and the magic circle nature of games indulge several kinds of fun while still having players experience a sense of moral residue. Finally, the chapter will provide recommendations on how designers can incorporate and analyze ethical dilemmas into their own games, tying our recommendations to examples to show how ethical dilemmas can provide interesting gameplay.

INTRODUCTION

Computer game designers have attempted to incorporate ethics into their games for quite some time now. One of the earliest examples of this was with *Ultima IV* (Origin Systems, 1985) where Richard Garriott attempted to create a game about "the player's personal virtues" (Computer Gaming World, 1986). Since then, other games have played with ethics and ethical decision making, in some cases using it as one of the primary selling points of their games. Lionhead's *Fable* (2004) used the tagline of "For Every Choice, a Consequence." BioWare's *Knights of the Old Republic* (2003), abbreviated *KOTOR*, asked, "Can you master the awesome power of the Force on your quest to save the Republic? Or will you fall to the lure of the dark side?"

DOI: 10.4018/978-1-60960-120-1.ch005

KOTOR and *Fable*, while lauded for their attempts to tackle morality and ethical issues, were still heavily criticized. *KOTOR* was viewed as not about ethical decisions, but instead about optimizing towards one of the extremes of light or dark side (Hocking, 2004). The explicit binary choices that the player had to make were largely heavy-handed and obvious in their implications with virtually no middle ground or ambiguity to decisions. Players could choose to either provide money to a begger (light) or threaten the beggar with physical harm (dark). The designers for *Fable* "put very little effort into deciding why given actions are right or wrong" with "few clear principles … defined to guide … decisions" (Rauch, 2007). As such, players were often given seemingly contradictory feedback as a result of their actions, or were punished/rewarded with no regard for the potential intent of the player. In critiquing these games, it should be said that there is nothing inherently wrong with either games' approach, and both managed to be financial and critical successes. However, in terms of providing an ethically meaningful game (that is to say, a game that approaches the subject of ethics in a manner that encourages deep reflection and thought in their player), both left something to be desired.

One concept that has been pointed out to be a characteristic of particularly ethically notable games is the ethical dilemma (Zagal, 2009). In this chapter, we will define what an ethical dilemma is, and then argue for why they can create compelling gameplay by analyzing the emotions they illicit and examining the potential role of games as ethical sandboxes.

DEFINITIONS AND VOCABULARY

In this chapter, ethics refers to the study of systems of rules which are used to distinguish "right" actions—those which are ethical, moral, and valuable—from "wrong" actions. These systems are referred to as ethical systems, while specific rules that comprise an ethical system are called ethical principles.

Ethical dilemmas are situations where an agent has a number of different options, each of which they have a moral obligation to select, but they cannot select all of them (McConnell, 2006).

A commonly-cited example is that there is a young man in World War II-era France. He is his elderly mother's sole means of support, yet he feels an obligation to leave to fight in the war to defend his homeland. The young man's ethical system judges both options as morally good, yet they are mutually exclusive. He is forced to select which is more important to him (Sartre, 1957).

From this definition, it becomes clear why the situations presented in *KOTOR* were largely not ethical dilemmas. There, the conflicts involved a player selecting which ethical system (light side or dark side) they followed, rather than having to select between options that were conflicting moral imperatives to their side. Other games such as *Fable* and *Mass Effect* work similarly.

One key characteristic of ethical dilemmas involves the sensation an agent has after making a decision. Recall that the agent has a moral obligation to select all options, but cannot. Having failed to select all options, the agent has morally failed. The sensations of guilt and remorse at not having selected the other option(s) is called moral residue (McConnell, 2006). Consider the example of Sartre's student mentioned above. It would be entirely appropriate for the young man to feel guilt after abandoning his mother. Likewise it would be expected that he feel remorse at not helping his country. Note that these feelings do not mean that the agent believes they have performed the 'wrong' action as all actions should be considered 'right.' With an ethical dilemma, the agent should feel a genuine need to perform all options, and regret when they ultimately cannot.

The difficulty of ethical dilemmas and the phenomena of moral residue are part of what make these situations compelling and meaningful in for games.

ETHICAL DILEMMAS IN GAMES

Before specifically analyzing why ethical dilemmas are compelling, it is useful to first describe some of the qualities of a game. One definition of games is that they are "problem solving activities, approached with a playful attitude," with play being defined as "manipulation that satisfies curiosity" (Schell, 2008).

One of the first points that comes from this definition is the notion of problem solving. Ethical dilemmas are most certainly problems that must be solved. The format of most hypothetical dilemmas is often phrased where the agent is presented the problem and a list of potential solutions, and then must select between them. Dilemmas certainly seem to fit under that part of the definition of a game, but are they compelling? Sid Meier famously said a good game is a "series of interesting choices" (Rollings and Morris, 2000), and while it is clear that ethical dilemmas are *choices*, one might ask how they are *interesting*.

Inherent Interest and Projection

Jesse Schell proposed three major components of interest (Inherent Interest, Poetry of Presentation, and Projection). We will consider two of these, inherent interest and projection. Inherent interest is the quality of events that are simply more interesting than others. These are events that appeal to base and higher instincts, with dramatic change or anticipation of dramatic change. Projection is the extent to which a player is compelled to use their powers of empathy and imagination to put themselves into an experience (Schell 2008).

In terms of inherent interest, ethical dilemmas are one of the most vital components in a dramatist's toolbox. Drama feeds on difficult conflicts with high stakes. Dostoevsky's *Crime and Punishment* wrestled with the question of if murdering and stealing from a cruel rich woman to allow a man to go to school was justified. Shakespeare's *Hamlet* involved a prince wrestling with his need

to be morally upstanding and his baser desire to avenge his father's murder. These situations require characters to struggle with everything they believe in to pick what they believe is most right. The potential for dramatic change is huge, and the situations hold tremendous interest.

Drama also benefits from the interest of projection. The audience placing themselves in the characters' shoes is part of the appeal of ethical dilemmas in a dramatic piece. While the protagonist of *Crime and Punishment* wrestles with their ethical dilemma, the audience is asking themselves the same questions on what they would do and feel in that situation.

Ethical dilemmas in games have projection interest similar to dramas, with ethical dilemmas being posed to the player's avatar in the game. However, games go one step farther, ultimately leaving the final choice of an ethical dilemma to the player. Here we need to delve into the player's relationship with their avatar, and the importance this gives ethical dilemmas in games.

Player Motivations and Reactions

When dealing with ethical dilemmas in a game, how do players react? Since there are so few examples of ethical dilemmas in games, no research has yet been done on this, but we can take an educated guess based on the motivations players have to play a game at all. Player motivations include:

1. Competition, either against others or against one's own best performance
2. Control, for example over one's self, others, or one's environment
3. Immersion, losing one's self in the game world
4. Novelty, seeking out new experiences
5. Realism, seeing the game behave and respond in a believable manner
6. Self-reactive, an internal psychological reward for meeting personal or social standards (Shaw *et al.*, 2005)

From these, we can construct a corresponding set of likely responses and reactions when an ethical dilemma is encountered in a game:

1. **Competition:** a player who is playing to "win" or "beat the game" would ignore the ethical dimensions of the decision and treat it purely as a gameplay decision. Labels of "good" or "evil" do not matter as much as the in-game rewards for each choice, such as access to new skills, allies, or combat bonuses.

2. **Control:** a player who wants to control the situation may feel frustrated that an unfair situation is being forced on them; no matter what they choose, they lose something dear to them, thus reminding the player that they are *not* in complete control of the game. On the other hand, such a player can recognize that they are the ones in control of the outcome of such a critical situation, and they are likely to take the choice seriously.

3. **Immersion:** a player who is engaged with the game's storyline may choose a persona for their character (distinct from their own real-world personality) which they will then role-play through the choices in the game. This player would consider how their chosen character would approach the ethical dilemma, rather than what they personally feel is "more right."

4. **Novelty:** a player who is looking for new experiences would likely play the game multiple times, trying a variety of decisions to see how the game reacts to each one. Such a player would be more concerned with the game reacting differently to each choice so that each playthrough was unique.

5. **Realism:** a player who wants a realistic play experience will be paying the most attention to how the game responds to their choice, no matter what choice they make. If the gameplay effects seem arbitrary or if the consequences do not logically follow from the actions, this player will be disappointed.

6. **Self-reactive:** a player who wants to feel good about themselves ethically will approach an in-game dilemma directly, deciding what they would personally do in the situation. This player will feel the greatest degree of moral residue, since they are emotionally invested in the outcome of the decision.

Note that these are not mutually exclusive. An individual may have several motivations for playing a game, and may therefore approach an ethical dilemma from several points of view before making a binding decision. In some cases, a player may therefore have to make two decisions when faced with an ethical dilemma in a game: first they must decide *how they are going to decide* (do they choose based on their own personal standards, based on what they think their character would do, or based on the likely in-game consequences?) and then they must face the dilemma itself. This kind of layered decision-making is difficult, non-obvious, and therefore *interesting* (as posited by Sid Meier).

The Magic Circle

The pleasures that ethical dilemmas can elicit seem to contrast with the subject of moral residue that we discussed earlier. We covered how players should feel a sense of guilt, or remorse, or regret after having dealt with an ethical dilemma. Games are sometimes described as "magic circles," self-contained worlds with their own unique sets of rules and constructs (Huizinga 1955). The actions of a player and the results of those actions are safely contained within the scope of the game, and this makes moral residue a very important aspect of ethical dilemmas in games.

Because the situations presented in a game are largely hypothetical (as they exist within the fictional magic circle), the stakes are not as high as they would be in real life. Given a situation where a person must choose only one of their children to live, there is significance in whether the person is a character in a novel, an avatar controlled by a player, or an individual in real life needing to make that choice.

However, in the case of the ethical dilemma in a game, the player will still have a small sense of the moral residue associated with that choice. Just as roller-coasters give a sense of danger within a safe context, so too does an ethical dilemma in a game give a player a bit of the moral residue of if they were to actually make that choice. This is important and desired, because part of the enjoyment of hypothetical ethical dilemmas comes from that learning experience (Hocking, 2004). Even in the case of those who treat a game purely as an ethical "sandbox" to try out a variety of styles, the player still wants a sense of the consequences and the results because that's part of the pleasure and the appeal of these dilemmas.

Ethical dilemmas in games are compelling because they tug and touch at emotions that players normally don't experience except in very uncomfortable situations in real life. These dilemmas have tremendous inherent interest in terms of narrative, and in the scope of a game allow players to project themselves into a magic circle where they may try out several ethical positions within a safe space.

RECOMMENDATIONS FOR DESIGNING ETHICAL DILEMMAS

Having covered why ethical dilemmas can provide for compelling gameplay, we begin to look into just what factors game designers need to take into account when incorporating them into games. While this is still largely unexplored territory and this chapter cannot claim to be exhaustive, the following recommendations can provide a starting point for designers.

1. Remember the Definition of an Ethical Dilemma

Remember that a dilemma involves two or more competing ethical principles where the agent (in this case, the player) cannot select all of them. As the decision is framed in the narrative, ask yourself if it actually is an ethical *dilemma*, or some other kind of ethical decision-making.

An oft-cited example of ethical decision-making is the central decision in *BioShock* (2K Games, 2007). In this game, the player encounters brainwashed young girls that are referred to as Little Sisters, and they are given the option of either "saving" them (removing their brainwashed state) or "harvesting" them (a euphemism for mercilessly killing them). There is a gameplay consequence to the decision, in that the player gets a different amount of a special resource called ADAM that is used to power up their avatar.

Note that this situation is not actually a dilemma. There are few if any moral systems where gaining some extra power for an individual would be balanced with dozens of innocent lives. While this is an ethical choice between doing what is right (saving the girls) and what is selfish (killing the girls to help yourself), there is no ethical system where the player would be compelled to do both due to competing ethical principles.

Could this situation be turned into a dilemma? To do that, one would have to balance the ethical weights of the two choices, either by lessening the ethical imperative to save the girls, or increasing the importance of harvesting them (or both). Here are some examples of how this might have been accomplished:

- Perhaps "saving" the girls would have a side effect, where it might not always work, the girls might die anyway, and in fact they might die an excruciatingly painful death. Meanwhile, "harvesting" might be changed so that it was a certain but painless death.

- Perhaps the player has a greater purpose. In the actual game, the player's only goal is escape—that is, to save their own life. Suppose instead that an entire adult population of a city were held hostage, only the player could save them, and it would be easier to rescue the adults if the player gained extra power from harvesting the Little Sisters. In this case, the player would have to ethically balance the lives of the girls against the lives of adults.
- Perhaps one of the Little Sisters holds inside of her a dangerous power, something that could ultimately take hundreds or thousands of innocent lives. The player may have no way of knowing which particular girl is so dangerous, so their options are to let them all live, slaughter all of them just to be sure, or kill a percentage of them and take a gamble. Consider how the situation would further change if that one Little Sister was not innocent, but was in fact intentionally working towards a mass-murder scheme (even if all of the *other* Little Sisters are just innocent girls).

While none of these hypothetical scenarios were in the original game—and this may have been an intentional design decision, to include an ethical choice but not an ethical dilemma—these examples show how to turn a choice into an ethical dilemma, if this is the game designer's goal.

2. Offer Multiple, Suboptimal Choices

Related to the previous point, ethical dilemmas are easiest to design if you strive to give the player several ways to accomplish a particular goal, where none of the choices is optimal and each choice has its own problems.

An example that demonstrates this technique is *PeaceMaker* (ImpactGames, 2007). In this game, the player takes the role of either the Israeli or Palestinian Prime Minister and must govern,

negotiate, and manage their state until peace with the other side can be reached. At any given time, the player has an extensive list of actions available, each of which can solve some problems but at the risk of causing other problems.

As an example, playing the Palestinian Prime Minister, the player may want to improve the mood of the Palestinians and gain their support and approval. They may do this by giving speeches, which might be received well but they run the risk of being seen as political hot air that actually has the reverse effect of causing the people to lose faith in their government. A stronger option, speaking out vehemently against Israel, will certainly unite the people, and it might prevent third-party groups from performing violent acts, thus buying the player time to accomplish something... but it will also anger the Israeli government and push the agenda further from the peace that the player is ultimately hoping to achieve. As with the real-world conflict that the game models, there are no optimal moves and no obviously "right" answers; the player must consider a number of factors before making a suboptimal choice.

3. Provide Permanence to the Player's Decisions

In *KOTOR*, while the player's light/dark side alignment does have an effect during the game (in terms of giving bonuses to the player's abilities and opening some optional sidequests), it doesn't affect the main storyline or the ending. Instead, the player is given one final choice at the very end to either redeem themselves or submit completely to evil, and the player can choose either path. Many games that work on some kind of alignment system work similarly (Heir, 2010).

The difficulty with this method is that the player is able to save near the end and experience both endings by making a single choice. By putting so much weight on a single end decision, the designers remove a lot of significance from the many earlier decisions that the player has made throughout the course of the game. The player can simply reload their last save game to see the results of each choice. As a result, the player's choices are not permanent. This reduces the moral residue of a dilemma; the player is able to experience the benefits of each choice individually, thus not feeling as guilty that they have given up something. After all, they did not actually lose anything—the saved game lets them do whatever they want!

One hypothetical (if powerful) solution to this problem, for certain key decisions, would be to save information in such a way that *even if* the player reloads an earlier save, the game will remember their decision and not allow the player to change it (Heir, 2010). Giving such weight to a decision would raise both the inherent interest and projection of the player, as their decision is now more significant than they are used to in most games, and they are forced to consider their options carefully.

Another less drastic solution is to create long-term effects to the player's decisions. The player may make a choice early in the game, only to confront the results of that choice 20 or 30 hours later. This is what BioWare did with *Dragon Age: Origins* (2009). Throughout the game, the player makes a number of key decisions, and each one affects the flow of the final battle at the end. Additional choices that the player makes throughout the game affect the ending sequence. Even if the player keeps an earlier saved game before each choice, they would still need to play through virtually the entire game to see the full effects of their alternate choices. This adds more weight to each decision as the player encounters it, knowing that they will not be able to choose again unless they start over with a fresh playthrough.

Another solution, particularly for choosing among alternate endings, is to make the ending the result of the player's *collective* choices throughout the game, rather than a single choice at the end. As an example of this, in *The Suffering* (Surreal Software, 2004), the amnesic main character is filling in their backstory based on their in-game actions. One of the player's combat abilities is to turn into an extremely powerful monster, but doing so too often increases the chance that at the end of the game, the character realizes he killed his wife in a blind rage.

4. Give Feedback

When the player is faced with an ethical dilemma and they make a choice, especially if the choice has long-term consequences, the player may not know the exact effects of their choice for some time. However, the player should at least know that *something* has happened, that an important choice has been made, and that the game has recognized their choice as significant.

Looking again at *The Suffering*, the player is not told of the effects of turning into a monster, in terms of how it will affect the game's ending. While the ending may make sense to the player in retrospect, it could also be seen as not playing fair; the player was not aware that they were making an ethical decision until after the fact.

In this example, the game designers could have occasionally included very brief cut scenes after the player took on their monster form, perhaps a flashback image of the main character shouting at his wife or striking her in anger. If the player finishes a particularly difficult combat *without* using their monster powers, perhaps they could be treated to a flashback image of the main character remembering some positive qualities or interactions with his wife when she was alive. Short encounters such as this could serve as both a feedback mechanism, and foreshadowing of the ending.

5. Align the Mechanics with the Game Narrative

The game *Silent Hill 2* (Konami, 2001) used a similar method to *The Suffering* to determine its ending: it would build a kind of personality profile of the player by tracking certain actions throughout the game, and then providing the appropriate ending based on the player's in-game choices. For example, if the player spent considerable time injured when they were capable of healing themselves, the game would interpret that as the main character being suicidal, and the player would receive what was arguably the "worst" ending.

To use a term coined by Clint Hocking, this is an example of **ludonarrative dissonance**. The mechanics of the game are not in line with the story. A player may have good reason not to use healing items; the items may be scarce, and the player may feel the need to conserve them. In this case, the player is actually acting in a very *non-suicidal* manner. They are trying to optimize their chance of survival by saving the healing items until using them is absolutely necessary. Yet, this runs counter to the game's interpretation. The player is punished in a way that feels arbitrary, because the player's intentional use of the game mechanics is not responded to appropriately. It doesn't help that the player is not informed that their behavior is tracked in this way by the game, making the ending feel even more arbitrary. Compare this to the ending of *The Suffering*, where there may have been a lack of information, but the ending narrative at least makes sense in the context of the gameplay.

6. Consider the Gameplay Consequences

With any game action (ethical or not), the designer must decide on the outcome of that decision. For ethical dilemmas, are they framed within the game's systems, or are they merely choices that affect the interactive narrative of the game? That is, does the player get additional money, items, or special abilities in the game as a direct outcome of their choice, or do they just get to see a different ending cinematic? There are potential hazards either way.

If there is a gameplay consequence, this can reduce the emotional impact of the ethical decision,

because the player may make the choice based on game mechanics ("min-maxing") and not ethics. This will be particularly true of players whose primary play motivation is competition—playing to "win." If the decision is framed in terms of gameplay (get a big monetary payoff by helping a crime lord, or get a unique item by working with the sheriff), the player may see the decision as a gameplay decision with ethical narrative trappings, rather than treating it as a purely ethical decision. To quote Raph Koster describing *Grand Theft Auto III*: "This is why gamers are dismissive of the ethical implications of games—they don't see 'get a blowjob from a hooker then run her over.' They see a power-up" (Koster, 2005).

A second issue with gameplay consequences is that they create an implicit value statement. The relative *gameplay* value of each choice of a dilemma acts as a moral weight. This can be overt, as with *BioShock*, where saving the Little Sisters gives nearly as much ADAM over the course of the game as harvesting them, and also gives the player some unique items (Ajar, 2007). The player is rewarded for doing the right thing, and as a result the designers make a clear judgment of what they feel the "right" way to play the game is.

On the other hand, if there is no gameplay consequence at all, that can also reduce the emotional impact, because the choice ultimately does not change the game's outcome. An example of this would be an ethical dilemma presented in *Mass Effect* (BioWare, 2007), where the player is given an order to exterminate the last of an alien race that had caused much death and destruction in the past. The alien begs for its life, insisting that it has learned from the lessons of the past, and that it can and will exist peacefully. While this initially seems like a powerful moment in the story, the drama is lessened by the end of the game, when the player realizes that their choice did not have an effect on either the gameplay or the narrative (Heir, 2010).

7. Consider the Narrative Consequences

Based on the significant use that ethical dilemmas have had in drama, it is worthwhile for designers to spend time developing their narrative consequences. However, this is more than just providing an additional layer of feedback for the player, and actually taps into some aspects of player motivation and moral residue. Often, games are satisfied with showing the direct result of a player's action, ignoring the indirect narrative results that can come from *not* selecting an option. Those indirect results can be incredibly rewarding to the experience of some players.

Part of the pleasure of a game comes from imagining how a character reacts to different inputs. Incorporating the positive and negative ramifications of a character's choice can provide more creative fodder for a player motivated by immersion or novelty, allowing them to have a more fully realized sense of their avatar's story.

In *Splinter Cell: Pandora Tomorrow* (Ubisoft, 2004), the player is sent to rendezvous with another agent. That agent guides the player through the level to a secret enemy location. Upon arriving in the elevator, the player receives a message from their commanding officer telling them to kill the other agent immediately. Here the player has two simple options—obey and kill the agent, or disobey and do nothing. The developers designed it such that selecting either option would leave tremendous questions up in the air about the option that was not selected. Not killing her leaves the character around for some time to arouse suspicion in the player. Killing her leaves all question of her motivation and actual allegiance hidden. This situation allowed players to really dwell on the ramifications of their actions, building up the story of their character thoughts and motivations.

Players interested in realism can appreciate being given a sense that all that they do (and all that they do not do) has an effect on the world.

This emphasizes the complexity of the game world and their actions within it.

In the earlier *Mass Effect* example, once a player has decided to exterminate the last of an alien race, they should certainly be treated to vignettes of the galaxy celebrating the eradication of the threat. However, they might also come across artifacts or histories that hint at more complexity and motivation to the now-extinct alien race, and a few people who look down on the character for enacting a one-man genocide. The player made a difficult and arguably good choice, but some knowledge of the other path can be very interesting.

Note that narrative consequence does not need to slap the player over the head with a guilt trip. A bit of ambiguity (not revealing information in *Pandora Tomorrow*, only hinting at the motivations in *Mass Effect*) can do a great deal in letting a player feel that they made the best choice they could, while still referencing the missed opportunities of the other options.

CONCLUSION

In this chapter, we have described what ethical dilemmas are and why they are worth pursuing for designers. They provide unique challenges, allow players to feel a closer connection to their characters and the game, and bring up difficult emotions that are meaningful in ways with which players are unfamiliar. We have also provided some recommendations for designing ethical dilemmas in games, referencing examples from a variety of games that have tried (with varying degrees of success) to do this in the past.

Ethical dilemmas are a powerful tool that designers can use to create new and interesting experiences for their players. Dilemmas are by no means a simple matter to implement, but they can be incredibly compelling. At this time, there is still a significant amount of unexplored territory in the field of ethical dilemmas in games. While we have analyzed why they are interesting and provided a few points to keep in mind, there is still a great deal of work to be done. As more ethical dilemmas in games are implemented, iterated, playtested, and critiqued, we look forward to additional research on the kinds of dilemmas that players find most meaningful, and how best to create them.

REFERENCES

Ajar. (2007). *BioShock spoiler thread* [Online posting]. The Escapist Forums, Gaming Discussion. Retrieved June 1, 2010 from http://www.escapistmagazine.com/forums/read/9.48000-BioShock-Spoiler-Thread#318863

Computer Gaming World. (1986). *Inside Ultima IV*. Anaheim, CA: Golden Empire Publications.

Heir, M. (2010). *Designing ethical dilemmas*. Paper presented at Games+Learning+Society conference, Madison, WI.

Hocking, C. (2004, September). *Ethical decision making in Splinter Cell*. Paper presented at IGDA Chapter meetingMontreal, Canada.

Huizinga, J. (1955). *Homo Ludens: A study of the play-element in culture*. Boston, MA: Beacon Press.

Koster, R. (2005). *A theory of fun for game design*. Scottsdale, AZ: Paraglyph Press.

McConnell, T. (2006). *Moral dilemmas*. Retrieved June 1, 2010, from http://plato.stanford.edu/entries/moral-dilemmas/

Rauch, P. (2007). *Playing with good and evil: Videogames and moral philosophy*. Boston, MA: Massachusetts Institute of Technology. Retrieved June 1, 2010, from http://cms.mit.edu/research/theses/PeterRauch2007.pdf

Rollings, A., & Morris, D. (2000). *Game architecture and design*. Scottsdale, AZ: Coriolis Group Books.

Sartre, J. P. (1957). Existentialism is a humanism. In Kaufmann, W. (Ed.), *Existentialism from Dostoevsky to Sartre* (Mairet, P., Trans.). New York: Meridian.

Schell, J. (2008). *The art of game design: A book of lenses*. Burlington, MA: Morgan Kaufmann.

Schreiber, I., Seifert, C., Pineda, C., Preston, J., Hughes, L., Cash, B., & Robertson, T. (2009). *Choosing between right and right: Creating meaningful ethical dilemmas in games*. Paper presented at Project Horseshoe conference, San Antonio, TX. Retrieved June 1, 2010, from http://www.projecthorseshoe.com/ph09/ph09r3.htm

Shaw, P., Ward, J. G., & Weber, R. (2005). *Player types and game qualities: A model to predict video game playing*. Paper presented at FuturePlay conference, Ann Arbor, MI.

Zagal, J. (2009). *Ethically notable videogames: Moral dilemmas and gameplay*. Retrieved June 1, 2010, from http://www.digra.org/dl/db/09287.13336.pdf

APPENDIX

Ultima IV (Origin Systems, 1985)

Grand Theft Auto III (Rockstar Games, 2001)

Silent Hill 2 (Konami, 2001)

Knights of the Old Republic (BioWare, 2003)

Fable (Lionhead Studios, 2004)

Splinter Cell: Pandora Tomorrow (Ubisoft, 2004)

The Suffering (Surreal Software, 2004)

Bioshock (2K Games, 2007)

Mass Effect (BioWare, 2007)

PeaceMaker (ImpactGames, 2007)

Dragon Age: Origins (BioWare, 2009)

Chapter 6
War and Play:
Insensitivity and Humanity in the Realm of Pushbutton Warfare

Devin Monnens
International Game Developers Association Game Preservation Special Interest Group, USA

ABSTRACT

This chapter argues for a game design ethic for war game production and the development of games that produce a more realistic and conscientious critique of warfare, defined as antiwar and conscientious war games. Given the medium's preponderance toward narratives and simulations of military conflict, there are surprisingly few works that seriously examine its consequences. This chapter surveys and critiques several existing antiwar and conscientious war games and examines design problems associated with exploring antiwar narratives. It concludes with an exploration of areas in which both new antiwar games can be developed and existing war games can be modified to produce conscientious messages about war. Artists and designers should have a vested interest in producing antiwar games to both enrich the medium and improve society by inspiring audiences to seek alternatives to conflict.

INTRODUCTION

Ludic wars are black and white—1s and 0s. They shallowly depict war as a necessary and normalized struggle (King & Leonard, 2010, p.102) between good and evil without questioning the nature of that depiction or the mechanism that communicates it. The presence of such narratives becomes problematic due to lack of dialectic— voices countering or questioning this overarching

statement and its monolithic moral system are rare, particularly when compared with propagandistic recruitment tools such as *America's Army* (2002). Whereas film's John Rambo has his *Full Metal Jacket* (1987), videogames have no voice to put the pain of soldiers and tears of widows into context. How can we hope to investigate these problems in games of pushbutton warfare where the basic underlying mechanics enforce military objectives enacted by firepower and strategy? How can the value of human life be calculated and the gravity

DOI: 10.4018/978-1-60960-120-1.ch006

of one's actions understood when the only two outcomes are win and lose, 1 and 0?

Miguel Sicart (2009) defines games as ethical because they contain values embedded in their systems either by accident or design that affect player experience. It is therefore important for designers to understand the effects of decisions made during the design process. Such a philosophy is concerned with how users interact with a system, whether by limiting a game's number of save slots to one on a *Pokemon* cartridge or how a game's rules, or mechanics, define how its moral and ethical systems are framed for players. The purpose of design ethics is therefore to consider user experience and the effects of decisions made. Thus, an ethics of design for war games involves the awareness of the effects design decisions have on the models, interpretations, and moral systems of war that players encounter and generate through play experience.

It is ethically important for game designers to consider such issues because as creators of products that may be consumed by audiences measured in the millions, designers control the moral structure of works that have the potential to positively or negatively influence player perceptions about warfare. War is prevalent in games because conflict is both inherent to games (Crawford, 2003; Salen & Zimmerman, 2004), and violent conflict is easy to depict (Crawford, 2003). War games—that is, games depicting war—are important morally because their value systems shape how audiences understand and frame military conflict. This in turn may influence how audiences understand real-world conflicts and react to new conflicts developing in contested spaces.

We should establish a design ethics for war games by developing antiwar games and reflecting their lessons in war game design. Doing so will help designers express their values regarding war and present players with opportunities to enact constructive and reflective dialogue within those systems.

This chapter investigates the ethical systems of games about war and how they may be restructured as a dialectic and human response to military conflict. Through a historical comparison and analysis of representations of war in games with those of conscientious and antiwar games, this chapter seeks to define methods for integrating antiwar messages to provide a more complete image of war that remains compelling enough to engage players while addressing problems in antiwar rhetoric.

WAR GAMES

Games have depicted war for centuries in nearly every genre from the combat vehicle simulator (*Army Battlezone*, 1981) to card games (*Echelons of Fire,* 1995). They may be specifically about war, as in a military first-person shooter (FPS) such as *Medal of Honor* (1999) or like Chess may only abstractly represent conflict. War games may depict historical wars, speculative future wars, fictional wars, or the wars of fantasy and science fiction; the wars may be abstract or naturalistic. Even a game of Tic-Tac-Toe can be considered a fierce battle of territorial control and all the militarist and colonialist narratives it implies. With the invention of *kriegspeil* in the early 19th Century, games have also been used as simulations and training for warriors, and most recently as recruitment tools, a history concisely described by Ed Halter (2005).

War games present simplified artificial warfare in a safe environment for the sake of entertainment or simulation. Their rules, or mechanics, are usually limited to operating a weapon, battlefield strategy, and logistics of resource management. From Checkers to *Call of Duty,* war games enable participation in fictional combat and little else, presenting false or over-simplified representations of warfare that paradoxically conflict with reality while simultaneously advertising realism. Identifying these characteristics, even if not in an exhaustive list, will frame a perspective from which to analyze antiwar games. While some of these characteristics are present in games as a whole, their emphasis in war games introduces unique opportunities for critique.

Limited Experiences of Soldiers and Combat

From a narrative standpoint, player experience is usually limited to soldiers rather than civilians. This narrowly represents the experience of war as that of the soldier, due in large part to the familiarity and popularity of those narratives, as well as military conflict's ease of representation. Additionally, because of this focus on soldiering as conflict, the experience of war—commonly described as 99% boredom and 1% abject terror—is understandably reversed, suggesting war is in fact solely about fighting rather than marching, labor, and endless waiting.

Civilians are Absent

War games also fail to depict civilians within the combat zone. Unlike real warfare, ludic battles are simplistic affairs between belligerents, with civilians absent from the Middle Eastern streets of *Call of Duty: Modern Warfare* (2007) (King & Leonard, 2010, p. 91) and cities unaffected by collateral damage from the dogfights of *Ace Combat 6: Fires of Liberation* (2006). Civilian casualties, if portrayed, usually only illustrate the barbarity of the enemy, such as Orc raids on Human settlements in *WarCraft III: Reign of Chaos* (2002), or conversely, a Human raid on an Orcish settlement in *N3: Ninety-Nine Nights* (2006).

Goals are Not Questioned

In a war game, goals also take a different perspective. Games valorize goals, presenting their attainment as both desirable and socially rewarded (Juul, 2005, p. 40). As a result, players are culturally discouraged from questioning their goals, which creates paradoxical histories in some war games. In the case of *Battlefield 1942* (2002), where players may play as both Axis and Allies, motive has been effectively divorced from historical context: players do not fight to win as the Nazis or Japanese because they believe in those ideals but because they want to beat their opponents. This focus on objective over context illustrates a moral paradox inherent to some war games.

Life is Devalued

War games place little value on human life: whether it takes five casualties or five hundred to accomplish a mission in a game such as *StarCraft* (1998) does not matter, so long as the mission is accomplished. Casualties are unfortunate but necessary consequences of warfare and indeed expected—if you want to play soldier, someone will have to play the corpse. Battle in turn becomes spectacle, an effect taken to the fullest in the detailed graphics of modern videogames.

Death is Not Realistic

Finally, despite war games' focus on realistic detail of weapons and uniforms, death in war games such as *Call of Duty: World at War* (2008) is a far cry from the long and obscene deaths in films such as *Saving Private Ryan* (1998). Even *Medal of Honor: Pacific Assault* (2004), which depicts debilitating wounds, reduces death throes to low groans rather than the shrieks and howls recorded in firsthand accounts. Additionally, corpses gradually disappear from the battlefield, leaving the scene of carnage clean and aseptic. Though done to maintain game performance, it is disconcerting to witness dead soldiers disappear, especially when players are responsible for their lives, as in *Brothers in Arms: Road to Hill 30* (2005). Such representations reinforce mythologies of combat death as quick and mostly painless.

A Need for Antiwar Games

As the above examples illustrate, traditional war game design decisions result in games that fail to depict war in a more serious or realistic tone, presenting skewed ethical systems. War games may render a soldier's weapon realistically or simulate the movement and combat of troops on a battlefield with a high degree of accuracy, but are ultimately limited in scope and abstraction. This myopic perspective erases many aspects of war and affects a game's moral system. War games aren't about critiquing war: they are about playing soldier. In doing so, they suggest that all a soldier does is fight without asking why or what it means and how it affects him or her and the people left at home.

If game design ethics is concerned with the effects of design decisions, then the images and suggestions produced by the mechanics of war games are important because they help generate perspectives by which audiences understand military conflict. Given that most war games produce these same messages, their imagery presents audiences with a monolithic and simplified view of war. Antiwar games are thus required in order to establish alternative perspectives on warfare and present a more complicated picture of military conflict that can help broaden player horizons regarding culture and humanity.

DEFINING ANTIWAR GAMES

An antiwar game is a game, digital or otherwise, which seeks to produce an antiwar message. The antiwar message may be an opposition to a particular war, whether past, present, or potential, or it may be opposition to war in general. Antiwar media may employ ethical and logical arguments against war or images of the horrors of war and their effects on individuals, society, and the environment.

Note that antiwar philosophy is separate from, but may at times intersect with, philosophies of pro-peace, pacifism, and antimilitarism. Pro-peace initiatives search for non-violent solutions to conflict, urban or military. Pacifism is opposition to all violence, military or otherwise. Antimilitarism is opposition towards the establishment of a military body and its glorification. Thus, an individual's antiwar philosophy might not be pro-peace, pacifistic, or anti-military, or it may be all, and such ethical systems may also be present within an antiwar game.

The most successful antiwar works are those that succinctly communicate antiwar rhetoric as their central message. This differentiates them from other works with small antiwar messages as part of the piece but not central to it. For example, *Red Cliff* (2009), dramatizing the titular Chinese battle from the early third century AD, presents a well-intentioned but half-hearted antiwar statement at the film's conclusion as the survivors survey the carnage of battle. Despite this conscientious message, the film's focus is not on the horrendous losses incurred on both sides but on the heroics of the Han soldiers and their generals, serving more as a memorial to their sacrifices than as a condemnation of war. To be successful, the true antiwar work must wholly embrace its message and employ this rhetoric to the fullest extent.

CONSCIENTIOUS WAR GAMES: FROM *DROP ZONE 4* TO *HAZE*

Before examining examples of antiwar games, it is important to first discuss games that integrate an antiwar message into their gameplay and narrative but do not have the antiwar message central to their ethical system. Such games produce a more complex image of war and examine its moral properties. They will be referred to here as conscientious war games, a term derived from both "conscientious objector," someone who refuses to fight on religious or moral grounds, and "conscientious," something done with conscience or care.

Conscientious war games are fairly scarce. Games have traditionally been interpreted as a means of entertainment rather than as systems of meaning capable of employing narrative and metaphor. With the rise of commercial board games in the 19th Century, several games were created specifically with moral and instructive purposes. *The Landlord's Game* (1904) and *The Checkered Game of Life* (1860) demonstrated that even simple board games could produce messages about such topics as the land rent system and mortality (Lepore, 2007). However, commercial games remained largely entertainment-oriented into the 20th Century, and it was only through several works such as Alberto Giacomettie's *On ne Joue Plus* (No More Play, 1932), Yoko Ono's *Play it by Trust* (1966), and the New Games Movement that antiwar messages were produced. Where war was concerned, games were designed as entertainment and military training tools, often with the goal of accurately simulating historical combat statistically and later visually (Halter, 2006). Generally, commercial games about war concentrate on the mechanics of action and tactics, focusing little on war's impact, with several notable exceptions.

The conscientious war games described below illustrate means by which designers of commercial games have previously applied antiwar messages to their games to change players' perspectives on war and present possible design strategies towards the production of antiwar games.

Drop Zone 4

The earliest example of an antiwar videogame is *Drop Zone 4* (1975) by Meadows Games. In this arcade game, an aircraft drops bombs on a fleet of ships. The game's designer, David Main, then actively involved in antiwar activities, felt morally obligated to add a rule that would give players a free play if they dropped all their bombs

without hitting a single ship. However, he also made playing by this rule a challenge: "[I]t was actually more difficult to win a free game by dropping all bombs and missing all the crudely graphic 'ships' than to hit at least one" (Monnens, 2008a). *Drop Zone 4* is not explicitly an antiwar game, and The Pacifist Option, as Main calls the strategy, was never printed in the game's instructions: Meadows Games deemed it too controversial, calling it "a special bonus for novice players" (Monnens, 2008a). Significantly, Main's design also demonstrates that game expression is not limited by technology. Though *Drop Zone IV* was not as influential as contemporary titles, it introduced a new mode of play that was both challenging and supportive of Main's philosophies while still allowing players to play using a more traditional system, demonstrating that it is possible to build an ethical design that can support multiple audiences.

The *Metal Gear Solid* Series and *Metal Gear Solid 3: Snake Eater*

Metal Gear Solid, based on the tagline, "Tactical Espionage Action," depicts the adventures of Solid Snake, who protects the world from nuclear holocaust threatened by Metal Gear, a bipedal tank with nuclear launch capabilities. The games contain antiwar undertones, such as Snake's reluctance to fight and kill, as well as rewriting historical narratives on nuclear weapons (Higgin, 2010). The series, with its origins in *Metal Gear* (1987), was produced in response to designer Hideo Kojima's concerns about games' focus on shooting and killing to earn a high score, and reinforced this concern through game mechanics. Kojima became interested in methods of forcing players to see the results of their actions and take responsibility for them: "I want players to think, even if it's just a little, about what violence and war are" (Fear, 2008). Kojima thus sees presenting the consequences of violence and warfare accurately as a goal to his work, if not an ethical responsibility.

In *Metal Gear Solid*, players are encouraged to avoid encounters with the enemy, to sneak around bases while eluding detection: shooting everything in sight will result in the arrival of more soldiers who will quickly overpower the player. Later games employed nonlethal gameplay strategies, such as a tranquilizer gun. These mechanics have influenced other commercial works, such as Looking Glass Studio's *Thief II: The Metal Age* (2000), where it is possible to complete the game without killing anyone (Au, 2000).

Metal Gear Solid's strongest antiwar message appears in *Metal Gear Solid 3: Snake Eater* (2004), where an earlier incarnation of Snake confronts the ghost of a long-dead psychic called The Sorrow. The Sorrow transports Snake to a haunted river where he confronts the vengeful spirits of everything he has killed, from small animals to the ghastly spirits of dead soldiers, each bearing the grisly wounds Snake inflicted. Snake is unable to attack the ghosts and must instead avoid them while struggling upstream through the fast-flowing river. The player confronts the consequences of each life he took and is forced to look upon the agonized faces and twisted bodies of his victims. The more people Snake has killed, the longer the river, with a player who kills indiscriminately staying for twenty minutes or more.

While Kojima may consciously seek to present a negative portrayal of war, his games are ultimately about action and empowerment, and though his games give players the option of choosing to avoid violence, this is not their central mechanic. However, the series' origins as an ethical response, at least in part, to military combat games allowed Kojima to produce a novel genre that is still influential today.

Cannon Fodder

One game that takes a more direct approach to criticizing war is *Cannon Fodder* (1993). *Cannon Fodder*'s quirky, satirical look at war begins with its title sequence where a red corn poppy, symbolizing remembrance for the war dead, is accompanied by the bizarre pop song "War Has Never Been So Much Fun." Full of biting satire, such as the manual's dark humor ("Don't try this at home, kids!") and ironic mission titles ("The Sensible Initiation"), the game demonstrates the stupidity of war through dark humor and the dynamics of recruitment and combat.

In *Cannon Fodder*, each soldier is given a unique name, even though he is merely an interchangeable cog in the war machine, easily replaceable by the next victim. When a soldier survives a mission, he is promoted, gaining greater accuracy, speed, and attack range, making veterans more valuable than raw recruits and building the player's personal attachment and feeling of ownership. Players are thus encouraged to send raw recruits into unexplored territory to locate enemy forces, implicating the logic of cannon fodder: as explained by Falstaff to Prince Henry in Shakespeare's *Henry IV*, "[T]hey'll fill a pit as well as better [men]" (p. 447). Players are reminded of the names of casualties in the mission results screen, with soldiers receiving their own gravestone on "Boot Hill" outside of the recruitment office, courtesy of the "High Scoring Heroes Bureau." As Boot Hill steadily fills with gravestones, the long line of civilians eagerly awaiting their turn in the "Slaughter Zone" becomes more ironic. This message is subtle, its meaning gradually revealed as the game progresses.

However, the effectiveness of *Cannon Fodder*'s moral system is questionable because its central mechanics involve locating and destroying enemy soldiers and their bases. Aside from the dynamics of recruitment and death, most of the game's satirical rhetoric is communicated through superficial visual and textual design. Due to this disconnect, the game was criticized by both the British press and the Royal British Legion, whose knee-jerk response was to consider *Cannon Fodder* an insult to the honor of the army and its veterans, particularly those of the First World War (AP2, n.d.). Whether players also understood the game's message is another point of contention, given most reviews' focus on how well the game plays and its dark humor.

Haze

With reactions to current conflicts in the Middle East, the past decade has seen a push for new commercial games integrating antiwar messages in narrative and gameplay, such as *Blacksite: Area 51* and David Jaffe's canceled PSP title, *Heartland* (Van Zelfden, 2008). The most notable of these is *Haze* (2008). The game's narrative and mechanics focus on Nectar, a drug that increases soldiers' fighting abilities and aggressiveness but also produces hallucinogenic side effects. Nectar prevents soldiers from seeing the real battlefield, replacing it with an idyllic environment free of blood and corpses. The game follows the career of Shane Carpenter, a Mantel soldier fighting against the resistance group The Promise Hand in the jungles of South America. The narrative serves as a mirror to the War on Drugs, where Mantel seeks to control the plants that produce Nectar to benefit pharmaceutical companies. As Carpenter is gradually exposed to the atrocities of Mantel, he "goes native," joining The Promise Hand.

Though flawed in execution, *Haze* demonstrates some potential for antiwar games through interactive scripted sequences. In one such sequence, Carpenter follows his squad through an abandoned factory while the platoon jokes about how they massacred its workers. Suddenly, Carpenter's Nectar flow is disrupted, revealing dozens of corpses littering the room, a jolting scene that recalls as much the survival horror genre as it does war atrocities. This sequence is more powerful than a non-interactive cutscene precisely because the player experiences it rather than watches it happen.

A similar sequence lies in the game's final mission. The Promise Hand decides to assault Mantel's base after first disrupting their Nectar supply, rendering them helpless. Carpenter first protests the assault, but eventually concedes. Inside the base, Mantel soldiers lie sick against the walls, hallucinating or pleading, rocking helplessly back and forth in pain. Because players have the opportunity to shoot them, they are presented an ethical choice, ultimately becoming complicit in atrocities of war committed by The Promise Hand against their former tormentors.

Though *Haze* is at its core a shooter, and antiwar messages are mostly presented through the vehicle of narrative rather than play mechanics, its interactive sequences increase immersion by allowing players to make ethical choice in real-time, demonstrating the potentials of games to present powerful messages through gameplay.

THE EFFECTIVENESS AND AMBIGUITY OF ANTIWAR MESSAGES

While games like *Drop Zone 4, Metal Gear Solid 3, Cannon Fodder,* and *Haze* produce conscientious statements about war, the effectiveness of their ethical systems seems questionable. For instance, if players continually rate a game like *Cannon Fodder* based on its solid play control and dark humor while failing to mention its antiwar commentary, are players really affected by the game's antiwar rhetoric?

While these games contain conscientious antiwar messages, they are not explicitly antiwar because their rhetoric is not consistently and strongly applied throughout. The games' mechanics may also make the player complicit: while their narratives decry war, military conflict is in fact perpetuated through continued play, reducing that message to ambiguity. While on the one hand, the games' messages were communicated to large audiences, they appealed to audiences who appreciated their military action content—war, in fact, has never been so much fun.

These problems of ambiguity and effectiveness are part of antiwar media as a whole. One of the biggest dangers is that antiwar messages can be undermined by the very same material used to illustrate the horrors of war. Some audiences are, in fact, drawn to antiwar films and literature primarily for the spectacle of combat. One such case is the famous helicopter attack from *Apocalypse Now* (1979) where psychotic Col. Kilgore raids a Vietnamese village, Wagner's "Flight of the Valkyries" blaring over the loudspeakers, under the pretense of letting the platoon's pro-surfer show off his skills. This sequence illustrates the absurdity of the Vietnam War while tying it to historical narratives of American colonial domination (Westwell, 2006, pp. 66-68). However, when the film is shown to the Marines in *Jarhead* just before the First Gulf War, the soldiers are ecstatic. This interpretation is made possible by the audience's desire to see combat. As *Jarhead*'s director, Sam Mendes, argues in the film's commentary, "All antiwar movies are basically pro-war movies when you play them to Marines."

One solution is to focus on the results of combat, omitting the violence itself. Such a narrative is presented in Dalton Trumbo's *Johnny Got His Gun* (1939). Here, the protagonist has lost his face and limbs to a shell in World War I. He is confined to a hospital bed for the rest of his life, horribly disfigured and unable to move, see, hear, or speak—only reflect. The narrative is divided between two periods: what happens to Johnny in his hospital bed and what happened to him before he was drafted. He longs for things he once took for granted: the ability to see, to hear, to run, to hug, to kiss, to love, to be with his family and friends—and his lover. The losses of these basic needs are shared by all casualties of war: once readers experience this loss through Johnny's eyes, they realize war's full impact.

Trumbo accomplishes this in large part because he does not focus on combat sequences, which would only serve as a distraction to his message. *Johnny Got His Gun* thus has more effective anti-

war rhetoric because Trumbo spends so little time on the war and nearly all of it on Johnny, his life, and his loss. The novel is about *people*, not about *action*, specifically the kind of violent action that has the danger of overpowering antiwar narratives.

This is in turn problematic because games are defined by actions (Galloway, 2006). To engage in ethical design, designers must consider not only new types of actions players can perform but also reconsider the meaning of traditional game mechanics they choose. War game designers must either diverge from relying on combat as their games' central mechanic, critique those mechanics, or develop new ones that more fully explore the ethical value systems of war. Games able to accomplish this might be called true antiwar games.

APPROACHES TO ANTIWAR GAME DESIGN

Artists and designers have historically taken many approaches to building antiwar games. However, most antiwar games were developed only over the past decade, with early works limited mostly to gallery exhibitions of ludic media, or game-like, art such as John Klima's *Serbian Skylight* (1999) and Tamiko Thiel and Zara Houshmand's *Beyond Manzanar* (2000). This was largely due to the high technical barrier of entry required to build digital games and a lack of effective distribution networks, which changed at the start of the 21st Century when game technology became more accessible. Artists and designers such as Ruth Catlow (*3 Player Chess*, 2003) could now build their work using cheap, powerful platforms such as Java, Flash, and the Unreal Engine, and distribute their work through Internet venues. This environment, in conjunction with public response to 9/11 and the wars in Afghanistan and Iraq, lead to the production of the modern antiwar game, and accompanying it, new philosophies of game design.

"Is It Barbaric to Design Videogames after Auschwitz?"

Among the first designers of the modern antiwar game was Gonzalo Frasca, then a student at Georgia Institute of Technology. His work explored representations of serious topics in games, asking the central question of whether it would be barbaric to design a game after Auschwitz (Frasca, 2000). This question was modified from the philosopher Theodore Adorno, who posited it would be improper to write poetry about the Holocaust. Such a question is crucial for both Frasca and antiwar games because it asks whether an interactive medium is capable of respectfully addressing serious topics such as genocide, whereas graphic novels and comedic film have already done so. In his essay, Frasca analyzed central aspects of games and their relationship with non-interactive narratives, primarily how consequences to player choice can be negated by simply reloading the game. Frasca also critiqued games' win-lose logic and concept of an achievable victory condition where in real life there might be none.

In response to this analysis, Frasca designed games that addressed the reversibility of player action by removing scoring systems, treating goals as answers to questions rather than ends to means. His antiwar games, *Kabul Kaboom* (2001), *September 12th* (2003), and *Madrid* (2003) demonstrate this logic by limiting player agency within unwinnable scenarios to make players consider the games' rhetorical messages.

Kabul Kaboom

Kabul Kaboom is a critique of the United States' simultaneous and inconsistent strategies of aggression and relief during the War in Afghanistan. While dropping bombs aimed at military targets, the United States Air Force dropped similarly-colored relief packages, casually dismissing civilian deaths from their "smart bombs" as regrettable but necessary (Lee, 2003). In *Kabul Kaboom*, the player controls a wailing mother who must catch hamburgers dropping from the sky while avoiding the rain of bombs. Inevitably, she will hit a bomb and be mercilessly blown to pieces. Shuenshing Lee describes the game as a tragic message about survival, reinforced by the game's intense difficulty and mechanics inspired by the 1983 Activision game *Kaboom!*: "[I]n a no-exit space with endless warfare...the civilian victim chases and dodges, receives and rejects simultaneously, doomed to perish indignantly within moments."

The image of the woman is from Picasso's *Guernica* (1937), which depicts the bombing of the Spanish city by Nazi planes on April 27, 1937. The game's background is a photograph of a nighttime missile strike on Kabul. By juxtaposing imagery from *Guernica* with the Afghan War, Frasca carries the message of the original painting to contemporary warfare: civilians are always casualties, and there is fundamentally little difference between the bombing of Guernica and the bombing of civilians in the Afghan War. Thus, Frasca critiques the naivety of the strategy employed by the Air Force and their insensitivity to civilian deaths while producing a level of immediacy and empathy for the victims through identification. By communicating a message through failure, Frasca demonstrates ethical values inherent to traditional game rules: where victory has meaning, so does defeat.

September 12th

September 12th (2003), Frasca's most famous game, is a critique on United States foreign policy regarding the war on terror. In *September 12th*, the player is offered to fire guided missiles at terrorists wandering a Middle Eastern village. In this "toy world," missiles are slow and inaccurate: by the time the missile reaches its target, the terrorist may have already left the area and civilians wandered in. Civilians encountering their dead compatriots will wail in grief and rage before becoming terrorists out of anger for the loss of their friends and family. As a result, *September 12th* is unwinnable. Through this futility, *September 12th* argues that the United States' strategy of bombing terrorists from a distance will only serve to produce more terrorists in a never-ending cycle of revenge and retaliation. As Frasca states, "Terrorism is a terrible problem and we think it should be fought in a more intelligent way" (Newsgaming, 2003). Thus, while *Kabul Kaboom!* presents a no-win scenario, the only way to win *September 12th* is not to play.

Madrid

Frasca's third game, *Madrid* (2004), is a memorial for victims of the March 11, 2004 terrorist attack in Spain, and by extension, all terror victims. *Madrid* presents the player with a candlelight vigil composed of people from all over the world and all walks of life, each with a shirt with the name of a city that has suffered a terrorist attack. Players click the memorial candles to keep the flames brightly lit before the wind blows them out, signifying that remembrance requires continued renewal. In contrast with Frasca's previous works, *Madrid* also presents players with an achievable, though difficult, goal, demonstrating that memorials can succeed through vigilance, perseverance, and renewal. As a result, *Madrid* also presents a more positive image, a rally for peace and hope rather than opposition and despair.

Other game designers responded to the Wars in Iraq and Afghanistan by producing antiwar games protesting American foreign policy. These include *Wolfengitmo* (2006), a mod of *Wolfenstein 3D* (1992) criticizing the treatment of prisoners in Guantanamo Bay Prison, and *Antiwargame* (2003), which explores the politics of managing the economy, media, and military during war. However, these games' subject matter is restricted politically and ideologically to current wars in the Middle East and might therefore be read as critiques against current military policies rather than war as an institution. In contrast to both

these and Frasca's earlier work, *Madrid* seems timeless through the extension of its memorial to all terrorist victims.

Giant Tank

As another approach to solving this problem of liberating the antiwar message from specific conflicts, I developed the antiwar game *Giant Tank* (2008). *Giant Tank* portrays a battle between a tank and a lone soldier armed with only a rifle. The player is not the tank. The game is unwinnable because players are not given the tools required to accomplish their mission. Their superiors are indifferent, presenting hollow propaganda that "It will take many bullets to win!" By constraining play space and limiting player action, I sought to confront players with the hopelessness of the situation and the casualness with which their lives have been thrown away.

Giant Tank presents a scene from a battle that has occurred many times—and recurs to this day: mechanized warfare against ill-equipped foot soldiers. Though the character designs are products of modern warfare, they are not specific to a particular conflict or nationality. The tank is an abstraction of the brutal machine of war, the soldier a helpless, frightened individual sent to the front to fight on the losing end of this battle of unequal force.

Though *Giant Tank* attempts to divorce itself from the politics of current wars, it is more directly a critique of current interpretations of World War II, where American victory has been used to justify support of the wars in Iraq and Afghanistan. This waving of the bloody shirt ignores the terrible cost of war and its dehumanizing effects: there is nothing great about a soldier being crushed by a tank. Miring the antiwar message in contemporary politics makes it easier for audiences to ignore this fact, presenting opposition to only certain wars rather than war in general. If games can demonstrate a broad antiwar philosophy, even a little, designers can impact those to whom the language of games speaks.

Carry: A Game about War

One game that suggests new directions to accomplishing this is Nathan Paoletta's *carry: a game about war.* (2007), a tabletop role-playing game set in Vietnam. The central mechanic of *carry* is character interaction—how soldiers' reactions in wartime are defined by the emotional burdens they bring with them. War gives these burdens power, adding to their weight and serving as motivational factors for how the characters will react. This revelation helps players understand the decisions people make in war and how those decisions affect them psychologically as well as physically.

Though Paoletta drew on antiwar media about Vietnam (*The Things They Carried* (1990), *Full Metal Jacket,* and *Platoon* (1986)), he notes that his game is not an antiwar game—though it might be played as such (Paoletta, 2010). (Note that subversive gaming for antiwar protests is a topic explored in *Velvet Strike* (2001) and *dead-in-iraq* (2006), but is beyond the scope of this chapter.) Further, *carry* is not about the Vietnam War itself, but rather "the fiction American culture has created about Vietnam" (Paoletta, 2006). *carry* is thus a reflection of this fiction through the filter of perceptions about the war, for in the end, it is impossible to really find Vietnam through individuals' fragmented experiences mythologized by popular culture, history, and circumstance.

Despite *carry*'s ambiguity, it is important to note that Paoletta wrote explicit rules asking players to treat the game's subject matter seriously and to discuss the game after its completion. These rules are enforced by the dynamic relationships between players, and their violation will spoil the game and break with its spirit. *carry* can more easily discuss psychological reactions to war because it is mediated through interpersonal communication rather than human-computer interaction and enforced by players. Such explicit rules

seem another possible solution to the quandary regarding consequence and game outcome, and certainly deserve deeper investigation.

Train

Further exploring the nature of consequence and rules to communicate antiwar messages is Brenda Brathwaite's board game, *Train* (2008). Almost in direct response to Frasca's (2000) earlier question, "Is it barbaric to design... games after Auschwitz?" *Train* puts players in the role of a conductor transporting Jewish prisoners to Nazi death camps. Because this fact is usually not revealed until the first train reaches its terminus, players are blindly absorbed with the intense strategies of how to get there most efficiently. Thus, *Train* challenges players' cultural willingness to follow rules and valorize game goals without question. This meaning is communicated via the concept of "the mechanic is the message," wherein games communicate meaning through mechanics. *Train* accomplishes this through two central mechanics: tactility and player interactions with rule ambiguity.

The tactility in *Train* centers on the manipulation of tokens representing Jewish prisoners. These tokens are initially lined in neat, orderly rows before being knocked over and disrupted when players casually grasp the pieces. This suggests the destruction of the Jewish community after *Kristallnacht*, an event that can be reenacted by symbolically breaking the glass panes composing the game board. Prisoners are then loaded onto flimsy boxcars with narrow doorways that force players to shove them inside like cattle. These surprisingly violent mechanics of hand-grasping-piece and round peg in a square hole make the player complicit in the act of dehumanization and genocide due to their physicality—players cannot help but get their hands dirty (see more about *Train* in the first volume of *Ethics and Game Design* (2010)).

Much of *Train*'s meaning is also derived from player interpretation of the game's purposefully ambiguous rules. In order for any game to be played, all players must agree on the meaning of its rules and clarify ambiguities by consensus (Sniderman, 1999). This means *Train*'s ambiguous rules allow players to generate their own interpretations of the game system. For instance, *Train*'s derail rule, which returns half the passengers on a train to the start and causes the other half to "refuse to reboard" is ambiguous because it does not indicate what happens to those passengers afterward: were they executed, simply left beside the tracks, or did they escape to Denmark? These interpretations permit multiple ways of playing *Train,* including the potential of saving everyone.

Note that none of these interpretations are suggested explicitly by the game's rules; rather, they result from the emergent dynamics of rule systems. By moving the mechanic beyond explicit rules and into the realm of player interaction, Brathwaite suggests alternative strategies for expression that lie with the player.

RECOMMENDATIONS

Based on my analyses of the mechanics and ethical systems of the above games, the following are recommendations for creating games that express antiwar value systems. While there is much more research needed in this area, these recommendations provide insight into ethical considerations for designers of war games.

Allow for Mechanics beyond Violence

Games should examine other aspects of military life beyond combat, such as caring for a wounded comrade and dealing with the weather, fellow soldiers, and post-traumatic stress. The results could affect how the soldiers interact with each other and serve as compelling character building scenarios.

Portray Death and Combat Wounds More Realistically

Dead bodies should remain on-screen until the player leaves the area, altering gameplay systems such as enemy respawn accordingly. Designers should also not fear portraying wounded and dying soldiers in agony—but should give players the opportunity to treat those injuries and alleviate the pain. These new play experiences will not significantly alter war games, but rather give them more depth and realism.

Diversify Player Roles

Antiwar games present opportunities to expand player roles beyond that of the solider. *Darfur is Dying* (2006) placed players in the role of children gathering water from a well while avoiding capture and death from the Janjaweed militia, providing a powerful experience of fear and hopelessness. Other games suggest further roles players can take, such as mothers in a battlefield (*Hush,* 2008), combat medics (*WWI Medic,* 2004), or journalists (*Beyond Good and Evil,* 2003).

Encourage Reflection

Antiwar games can allow opportunities for players to consider the moral implications of their actions and the game's ethical value systems. One example lies in Lindsay Grace's first person shooter, *Bang! You're Dead* (2009). When players kill another solider, they are presented with a "long interruptive experience" in which the victim's life is recounted in a two-minute long photo montage (Grace, 2009, p. 17). By chronicling a fictional character's history using found images of real soldiers, Grace allows players to reflect on the consequences of killing an enemy soldier, an act that occurs hundreds of times in commercial war games.

Investigate Games of Conflict Avoidance

If games can simulate waging war, they can also simulate ending or preventing war. Two approaches to this genre of "peacefare" (Adams, 2006) or "unwar games" (Crawford, 2003, pp. 282-284) are Chris Crawford's *Balance of Power* (1985), a strategy game about the Cold War, and ImpactGames' *PeaceMaker* (2006), about ending conflict between Israel and Palestine. Though in both games the outbreak of war is instant failure, both contain conflict. Crawford framed the Cold War as an extension of geopolitical struggles, and *PeaceMaker* players must balance popular opinion of both the local government and the opposition. While *Balance of Power* cynically illustrates the political maneuvering of global superpowers, *PeaceMaker* provides a sense of immediacy by using real news footage and basing outcomes on actual events. Both games simulate possible solutions to the conflicts they simulate and help players understand the complex political undercurrents preventing their easy resolution, stressing moderation over extremism. Further, by allowing players to play both sides, *Balance of Power* and *PeaceMaker* let players gain understanding of the nature of the conflict and empathy for the people on each side. Thus, *Balance of Power* and *PeaceMaker* suggest new directions for antiwar game design and a promise of the positive impact such games can have.

These are just a few ideas artists and designers could implement in the creation of antiwar games. As more games are produced which explore the human condition and designers' expressive vocabulary expands, a renaissance of expression within the medium shall surely open.

NEXT STEPS

The ethics of war game design demonstrate both great need and great opportunity to expand the messages of war beyond the abstracted experiences of combat and tactics that games most often depict. These can be explored not only through narrative but also through action, simulation, player experience, and choice. Further, producing games with rules and structure as well as visual and narrative components that explore these themes is central not only to antiwar game design but to expressive game design in general.

While antiwar games can use the rhetoric of illustrating the horror of war and its psychological effects, this approach is clearly hazardous through possible ambiguity. Further, while portraying the results of combat without depicting its causes can create a stronger and more direct effect, doing so requires a radical approach to game design. There is also the possibility for games that demand a call to action, to change foreign policy and strategy, to end current conflicts and prevent future conflicts from occurring, a strategy of mitigation and prevention.

To seriously think about antiwar games requires that we as critics and designers redefine current definitions of games. The more we understand this medium, the better we will be able to create games that can express empathy, sensitivity, and reflection. To do so, we must believe in the capabilities of the medium of the game, that anything is possible so long as there is someone willing to try. We must do this because it will ultimately enrich our culture to develop these expressive potentials and explore serious, culturally relevant topics using a medium that speaks to many people.

Antiwar games will help us better understand and develop the medium of the game while simultaneously producing messages about war and society, about man and conflict and its terrible toll on human life, society, the environment, and the mind. By producing more games that critique war and forward antiwar values, we can inspire players to seek means of ending current conflicts and preventing future conflicts as they arise. In doing so, we can help produce a world that is safer and in which we better understand and appreciate life and the world around us.

REFERENCES

AP2. (n.d.) Poppy game insult to our war dead. *The Complete AP2*. Retrieved from http://dspace.dial.pipex.com/ap2/dissent/poppy.html

Adams, E. (2006). The designer's notebook: Asymmetric peacefare. *Gamasutra*. Retrieved from http://www.gamasutra.com/features/20070131/adams_01.shtml

Au, W. (2000, June 20). Game over. *Salon*. Retrieved from http://www.salon.com/technology/feature/2000/06/20/dark_glass

Bogost, I. (2006). *Unit operations*. Cambridge, MA: The MIT Press.

Bogost, I. (2007). *Persuasive games: The expressive power of videogames*. Cambridge, MA: The MIT Press.

Coppola, F. F. (Producer) & Coppola, F. F. (Director). (1979). *Apocalypse now* [Motion picture]. United States: United Artists.

Crawford, C. (1985). *Balance of power* [Macintosh software]. Novato, CA: Mindscape.

Crawford, C. (2003). *Chris Crawford on game design*. Boston, MA: New Riders.

Fear, E. (2008, January 3). Jade Raymond interviews Hideo Kojima. *Develop*. Retrieved from http://www.develop-online.net/news/29006/Jade-Raymond-interviews-Hideo-Kojima

Frasca, G. (2000). Ephemeral games: Is it barbaric to design a game after Auschwitz? *Ludology.org*. Retrieved from http://www.ludology.org/articles/ephemeralFRASCA.pdf

Frasca, G. (2001). *Kabul Kaboom* [Videogame, Flash software]. United States: Ludology.org.

Free Radical Design. (2008). *Haze* [PlayStation 3 software]. Montreal, Quebec: Ubisoft, Inc.

Grace, L. (Designer). (2009). *Bang! You're Dead* [Windows software]. United States: L. Grace.

Grace, L. (2009). Critical gameplay. Unpublsihed MFA thesis, University of Illinois, Chicago. Retrieved from http://www.evl.uic.edu/files/events/Critical_Gameplay_Thesis.pdf

Halter, E. (2006). *For Sun Tzu to Xbox: War and video games*. New York: Thunder's Mouth Press.

Higgin, T. (2010). 'Turn the game console off right now!': War, subjectivity, and control in *Metal Gear Solid 2*. In Huntemann, N. B., & Payne, M. T. (Eds.), *Joystick soldiers* (pp. 252–271). New York: Routledge.

ImpactGames. (2007). *PeaceMaker* [Windows software]. Pittsburgh, PA: ImpactGames.

Juul, J. (2005). *Half-real*. Cambridge, MA: The MIT Press.

King, C., & Leonard, D. (2010). Wargames as a new frontier—Securing American empire in virtual space. In Huntemann, N. B., & Payne, M. T. (Eds.), *Joystick soldiers* (pp. 91–105). New York: Routledge.

Konami Computer Entertainment Japan, Inc. (1998). *Metal gear solid* [PlayStation software]. El Segundo, CA: Konami Digital Entertainment, Inc.

Konami Computer Entertainment Japan, Inc. (2004). *Metal gear solid 3: Snake eater* [PlayStation 2 software]. El Segundo, CA: Konami Digital Entertainment, Inc.

Lee, S. (2003). 'I lose, therefore I think': A search for contemplation amid wars of push-button glare. *Game Studies, 3*(2). Retrieved from http://gamestudies.org/0302/lee/

Lepore, J. (2007, May 21). The meaning of life. *The New Yorker*.

Main, D. (1975). *Drop Zone 4* [Arcade software]. United States: Meadows Games.

Mendes, S. (Director), Wick, D., & Fisher, L. (Producers). (2006). *Jarhead* [Motion picture]. United States: Universal Studios.

Monnens, D. (2008a, April 12). An 'interview' with David Main. Message posted to http://deserthat.wordpress.com/2008/04/12/an-interview-with-david-main/

Monnens, D. (2008b). *Giant tank* [Scratch software]. Denver, CO: Desert Hat.

Monnens, D. (2008c). *War and play: Insensitivity and humanity in the realm of pushbutton warfare*. Unpublished master's thesis, University of Denver, CO. Retrieved from http://www.deserthat.com/media/critical_game_theory/game_studies/WarAndPlay.pdf

Newsgaming. (2003). *September 12th, A toy world: Political videogame about the war on terror*. Retrieved from http://www.newsgaming.com/press092903.htm

Newsgaming. (2003). *September 12th* [Flash Software]. Uruguay: Newsgaming.

Newsgaming. (2004). *Madrid* [Flash Software]. Uruguay: Newsgaming.

Paoletta, N. D. (2006, July 21). Literacy. *Hamsterprophecy: Prevision*. Message posted to http://hamsterprophet.wordpress.com/2006/07/21/literacy/

Paoletta, N. D. (2007). *Carry. A game about war*. Carol Stream, IL: Hamsterprophet Productions.

Paoletta, N. D. (2010). Personal correspondence. January 29, 2010.

Penn, G., & Root Associates. (1993). Cannon Fodder instruction manual (p. 18). Retrieved from http://files.the-underdogs.info//games/c/cannon/files/cannon.pdf

Salen, K., & Zimmerman, E. (2004). *Rules of play*. Cambridge, MA: The MIT Press.

Sensible Software. (1993). *Cannon fodder* [Amiga software]. London: Virgin Interactive Entertainment (Europe) Ltd.

Shakespeare, W. (1975). *King Henry IV—First Part*. In *The Complete Works of William Shakespeare* (pp. 424-454). New York: Avenel Books.

Sicart, M. (2009). *The ethics of game design*. Cambridge, MA: The MIT Press.

Sniderman, S. (1999). Unwritten rules. *The Life of Games 1*. Retrieved from http://www.gamepuzzles.com/tlog/tlog2.htm

Solid States. (2007)... *Edge, 173*, 54–61.

Trumbo, D. (1971). *Johnny got his gun*. New York: Bantam Books.

Van Zelfden, N. (2008). Inside David Jaffe's Heartland. *The Escapist, 146*. Retrieved from http://www.escapistmagazine.com/articles/view/issues/issue_146/4817-Inside-David-Jaffes-Heartland

Westell, G. (2006). *War cinema: Hollywood on the front line*. London: Wallflower.

Woo, J. (Director), & Woo, J., Chang, T., & Sanping, H. (Producers). (2008). *Red cliff* [Motion picture]. United States: Summit Entertainment.

ADDITIONAL READING

Bogost, I. (2007). *Persuasive games: The expressive power of videogames*. Cambridge, MA: The MIT Press.

Halter, E. (2006). *From Sun Tzu to XBox*. New York: Thunder's Mouth Press.

Huntemann, N. B., & Payne, M. T. (Eds.). (2010). *Joystick soliders*. New York: Routledge.

Chapter 7

God of War:
What is it Good For?
Nietzsche's "Master Morality" and the
Single–Player Action/Adventure Genre

Peter Rauch
Massachusetts Institute of Technology, USA

ABSTRACT

In God of War, the protagonist Kratos seeks revenge against the Ares of Greek mythology. As Kratos, the player is called upon to act in a manner reminiscent of Nietzsche's "master morality," reveling in power unrestricted by concern for any "objective" moral code or sympathy for his fellow man. The structure of the action/adventure genre in which God of War operates is particularly well-suited to this kind of morality. With one hero amid a world of disposable non-player characters, punctuated by the occasional appearance of a "boss" figure that behaves more like Kratos, a stark distinction is made between the powerful and the weak. This dichotomy is at the heart of Nietzsche's master/slave distinction. Kratos and Ares seek to inspire fear; the hordes of disposable Athenians they both slaughter so carelessly seek only to avoid it. In allowing gamers to "play with" a moral worldview so starkly defined, God of War becomes a valuable tool for investigating and critiquing moral ideas in general.

INTRODUCTION

Of the gods we believe, and of men we know, that by a necessary law of their nature they rule wherever they can. And it is not as if we were the first to make this law, or to act upon it when made: we found it existing before us, and shall leave it to exist for ever after us; all we do is to make use of it, knowing that you and everybody else, having the same power as we have, would do the same as we do (Thucydides)

While adventure games may take players to fantastic and disparate worlds, the morality therein remains quite familiar: a confused, often contradictory mish-mash of moral ideas, running the gamut from self-interest to personal virtue to the

DOI: 10.4018/978-1-60960-120-1.ch007

aggregate happiness of society. In *The Legend of Zelda: Twilight Princess,* for example, Link's own happiness, the happiness of Hyrule's inhabitants, and the means with which he pursues his goals are generally in accordance with every moral philosophy yet imagined, as there is near-universal agreement on the morality of actions like Link's in the situations presented by the game. Consequently, whether Link (or the game's writer) were an admirer of Kant's categorical imperative or Rand's ethical egoism, it would have no effect on the storyline or gameplay, despite the radical opposition of those two philosophies. *Fable*, on the other hand, allows a character to be nominally "good" or "evil," although the results are often inconsistent, silly, and largely irrelevant to play: a player may literally "pay off" their sins by donating to a temple, or save money by eating tofu.

Standing in contrast to this bland moral confusion is *God of War*, a single-player action/adventure game published in 2005, which aligns the player with a protagonist whose morality is as foreign to the modern mind as the mythological milieu that he inhabits. It is my argument that this nihilistic morality, closely resembling certain elements of Nietzsche's philosophy, is inherently consistent with the conventions of the single-player action/adventure genre. To that end, I will situate *God of War* in the conditions of its own medium and genre, compare and contrast it with games and conventions from related genres, and describe how the game allows and encourages players to enact the edicts of a Nietzschean morality. Set in the age of Greek mythology, *God of War* is an action/adventure game that depicts the life, death, and deification of Kratos, a Spartan warrior on a mission to assassinate Ares. In playing as Kratos, the player is called upon to act in a manner reminiscent of Nietzsche's "master morality," reveling in power unrestricted by concern for any *a priori* moral code or sympathy for his fellow man. Kratos' quest is motivated, from beginning to end, purely by vengeance, and any "good" done on behalf of the lesser inhabitants of his world, or

to abstract ideals of justice, is purely incidental. The revenge Kratos seeks is not reliant on any "higher" celestial or deontological authority: Kratos does not invoke a rule against which Ares can be said to have trespassed. Like Nietzsche's "nobles," Kratos is "value-determining," in that he determines that harming Kratos is bad (not to be confused with wrong) in general because it is bad for Kratos. God of War chronicles Kratos' attempts to challenge the gods to normativize his own values.

The structure of the genre (action/adventure) and mode (single-player) in which *God of War* operates are particularly well-suited to this kind of morality. One "hero" is pitted against a world of disposable non-player characters (NPCs), punctuated by an occasional appearance by a "boss" figure, who behaves more like Kratos, establishing a stark dichotomy between the powerful and the weak. This is the dichotomy at the heart of Nietzsche's master/slave distinction, which I will discuss in detail in terms of *God of War*. Kratos and Ares seek to inspire fear; the hordes of disposable Athenians they both carelessly slaughter seek, fruitlessly, to avoid it. In allowing us to "play with" a Nietzschean moral worldview so starkly defined, God of War becomes a valuable tool for investigating and critiquing that worldview. To explore such applications of this text, I will first elucidate the expressive structure of the videogame medium, then review Nietzsche's master morality and through it investigate the action/adventure genre in general and God of War in particular.

BACKGROUND

Frasca (2000, p.223) defines simulation as a "model [of] a (source) system through a different system maintains (for somebody) some of the behaviors of the original system." By this definition, nearly any videogame can be accurately described as a simulation. Contrasting simulation with representation (an expressive technique associated with media such as literature, theater or film), Frasca suggests that videogames can go beyond merely depicting ideas, and actually model them in greater detail than purely representative media might permit. "For the first time in history, humanity has found in the computer this natural medium for modeling reality and fiction. Simulation [...] provides a different—not necessarily better—environment for expressing the way we see the world" (Frasca, 2000, p. 233). In gamer parlance, "simulation" (or "sim") is more commonly employed as a distinction between games than as a constitutive element of the videogame medium itself. Specifically, the "sim" designation tends to denote games that are "realistic" in subject matter and play mechanics, such as flight sims or driving sims. Frasca's more expansive conception of simulation is as a means of "modeling reality and fiction," suggesting not only that can simulation be applied to the fantastic as well as the realistic, but that the two can be integrated into a virtual world in which players can experiment, and learn, the same way they do in the real world.

Frasca's ideas about videogames as a simulative medium suggest that a videogame is something that is experienced, iteratively, not exclusively as a series of ordered events but also as a possibility space. That possibility space is shaped and constrained by three "ideological levels" (Frasca, 2000, p. 232). The first is conventional narrative, the "story" around which the game events are organized. The second is that of "goal rules," and the third is that of "manipulation rules." Manipulation rules comprise all actions available to the player, while goal rules concern only those actions required to "win" a given game. For example, *Fable* allows the player to gamble in taverns. While it can be helpful to earn some extra money, gambling isn't a particularly reliable way to accomplish even this feat, and gambling is generally not helpful in terms of finishing the game. The rules concerning the player's ability to gamble, and the mechanics of the tavern game, are manipulation rules. The opposition between goal

and manipulation rules highlights a fundamental tension in the gameplay itself: the necessity of abstract rule systems to provide order and motivation, known as the *ludus,* and the tendency toward improvisation and "free play," known as *paidia* (Caillois, 2006, p. 141).

I have written here of the "player" and the "protagonist." I have not chosen these terms accidentally, nor are they interchangeable. Player and protagonist are two facets of the avatar, the entity that symbolically situates the player in the gameworld, i.e., "the guy you control." In *God of War,* the differences between the player and the protagonist are substantial, as each possesses information that is either hidden from, or inherently alien to, the other. Specifically, the protagonist Kratos knows his own past, whereas the player begins the game largely in the dark: from the opening cut-scene, the player can determine that Kratos is a sort of mercenary for the gods of Olympus, that he is seeking liberation from his own tortured memories, and that he will eventually (at the prophesized conclusion of the story) attempt suicide. However, the player does not know which events Kratos so dearly yearns to forget. These memories are parceled out to the player through flashbacks as Kratos progresses through the game.

Just as there are matters about which the player is more ignorant than the protagonist, there are also matters about which the protagonist is more ignorant than the player. Kratos does not seem to know that he cannot, in a traditional sense, die; nor does he know that there are specific "checkpoints" littered throughout the world that will resurrect him more conveniently. Players may begin a new game file as often as they like, but Kratos always experiences the events of the game in the present. There is no reason to suspect that Kratos understands why it would be important that he kill his foes with lengthy combination attacks, long strings of blows issued with only the smallest respite for specific defensive techniques, as opposed to more ordinary hacking and slashing. The player must use these combos as much as possible to maximize the number of red orbs released from each kill. These red orbs are used to upgrade Kratos' weapons and magic (he is exceedingly unlikely to accomplish his goals without them), but there is no evidence that "red orbs" hold any meaning for Kratos: they are not mentioned in any of his conversations, and the player learns about them from text windows relayed directly to her, seemingly without Kratos' knowledge or intention. The red orbs seem to be a purely extra-diegetic play mechanic, like "respawning" after a diegetic death, or references to the functions of the PlayStation controller. They impinge on Kratos' awareness, motives and actions no more than does the fact that he is a fictional character in a videogame.

Just as there is a disparity of knowledge between the player and the protagonist, there is also a disparity of motivation. After all, if the protagonist can be thought of as a person, one who knows things that the player does not, it stands to reason that the protagonist might also want things that the player does not. Furthermore, due to their differences in information and motivation, the player and protagonist might want the same things, but for different reasons. The avatar, being both player and protagonist, incorporates both of their interests and perspectives, essentially projecting the player "into" the protagonist whose values might not be entirely consistent with her own. The process of "playing in" an alien value system can be an emotional one, as James Paul Gee recounts:

This sort of thing really takes hold in the first God of War [...] when to progress you (the God of War) must place a caged prisoner in a fire—it is a horrible moment—and there is no choice here—you absolutely do not want to do it—for one stark moment the amalgam of character-player is broken and the game says both that you have to realize that this is what the God of War would do and see if there is any shred of your soul that will live with it (and, alas, there is, at least in

my case), and thus you meld again—uncomfortably—with the God of War—an amazing narrative moment that no book or film could do (personal communication, May 28, 2008).

As Frasca implies in his ordering of simulation's three ideological levels, narrative conventions—such as plot, character, and theme—both shape and constrain *ludus* and *paidia*. The interaction of all three ideological levels is what gives videogames their sense of immersion and embodiment, what makes them work. Gee writes of videogames as incorporating a process of identification with a character, and (conditionally) accepting their goals as your own. This process of identification is succinctly described by Gee's young son, on having begun a game of *Sonic Adventure 2 Battle* as the "bad" protagonist: "the bad guy [is] the good guy" (Gee, 2007, p. 147).

THE SYNTHETIC AVATAR

The dual nature of the avatar complicates any notion of choice on the part of player or protagonist. Certainly, the ergodic nature of the videogame medium necessitates that the player makes decisions, and that the game responds in accordance with those decisions. The actual consequences of those decisions, however, are funneled into a binary outcome: if 0, the system "resets" and the player attempts the level again; if 1, the story continues. Because the action/adventure genre emphasizes *ludus*, the player is rewarded for following the rules of the game, which in this case are also the "rules" of the story. A comparison with another medium is apt: while readers may condemn Humbert Humbert for his actions in Lolita, they cannot actively change them. Certain schools of literary theory notwithstanding, the book's narrative has already happened, even if the reader experiences it in the present. Similarly, we cannot assume that Kratos' range of options is as limited as ours. If we can find only one course of action, it might be that Kratos has already ruled out the alternatives for us.

Gamers, of course, are a varied and chaotic breed, and play games in different ways. However, any game that incorporates the *ludus* principle must necessarily have a way (or a range of ways) in which it is intended to be played. In the context of an action-adventure game, this generally involves "beating the game" by playing the game to completion; in *God of War*, it involves guiding the protagonist Kratos through the game's various trials and tribulations, which culminate in a climactic battle with Ares. There is a set of guiding principles a player must learn and internalize to play the game this way, and I refer to these principles as the game's "ethics." While goal rules determine what *must* be done and manipulation rules determine what *can* be done, gameplay ethics concern what *should* be done: the tactics and techniques most likely to make the goals attainable. However, regardless of the player's personal motives for playing the game the way the designer intended or expected it to be played, the protagonist has his own motives, dictated by the narrative. I use the term "ethics" to denote a set of rules that are conditionally imposed upon the acceptance of a role, rules that may or may not be at variance with "general morality." A doctor's morality might be determined by logic, religion or moral sentiment, but his ethics, specifically his medical ethics, are proscribed by his profession. In *God of War*, one of the player's roles is that of Kratos himself, and playing the game "correctly" (or ethically) necessitates playing "in character," and pursuing Kratos' interests as if they were her own. The player does not need to accept Kratos as a moral entity, or accept his actions as "good," but the fact remains that she isn't going to complete the game if she insists on substituting her own ideals for those of Kratos.

Kratos clearly *is* the kind of person/god who would unblinkingly burn an innocent person to death to get what he wants. The narrative gives us no reason to suspect that this is a difficult decision for Kratos, and the game provides no alternatives to allow the player to "act out" her internal conflict. Yet, theoretically, the designers could have allowed this possibility: in *Metal Gear Solid 2 (MGS2)*, the avatar is required to grab an entomophobic woman from behind, and drag her (entirely against her will, as might be implied by the context) through a room infested with insects. The morally questionable actions required in the *MGS2* scenario are far more sympathetic than those of the aforementioned scenario in *God of War*, but the player is nonetheless given some choices on how to "project" their discomfort onto the protagonist. Since the insects pose no real danger to her, her refusal to cross the room is fundamentally irrational—and stands in the way of the protagonist completing his mission and, effectively, saving the world—it is quite easy to take a "lesser of two evils" perspective and simply drag her across the floor without hesitation. Alternatively, the player may look, fruitlessly, for another way to solve the problem. In my own experience playing *MGS2*, I was highly disturbed by what it seemed I was being asked to do, and pestered one of the supplementary characters for alternative options until he lost patience with me and demanded I drag her across the damn floor already. Playing "in character" obviously requires the player to adapt her perspective to that of the protagonist, but in some games, the protagonist will *himself* be adapting his perspective to that of the gameworld, to the perspective that the "simauthor" intends him to adopt and the player must dutifully follow along.

Ultimately, I argue, the ideals that matter most are those of neither the player nor the protagonist, but of the gameworld itself. Frasca notes that the rules of any given game are inevitably biased toward certain behaviors and results. While Frasca's example of what?, a game about labor rights called *Strikeman*, describes the inherent biases in perspective that would crop up in any simulation of a real-life phenomenon, even an openly fictional universe cannot represent causes and effects in an entirely "neutral" way. Although few would describe *God of War* as a simulation in its colloquial sense, I argue that by Frasca's definition, *God of War* can be accurately described as a simulation of the narrative conventions of the Greek epic. What does this mean in terms of the relationship between player and protagonist that synthetically constructs the avatar? That the role the player takes on is not, strictly speaking, that of Kratos, although it includes Kratos. Rather, the player is taking on the role of an actor playing Kratos, working from a script that allows for some degree of improvisation. (One can imagine the player, having missed a crucial cue, abashedly yelling "Line!" shortly before Kratos' broken body is swallowed and digested by the Hydra.)

POWER, NOBILITY AND GENRE

The story enacted in *God of War*, written by the designers and enacted, with limited freedom, by the player, falls within the conventions of the action-adventure genre. In this genre, games generally pit the protagonist against seemingly insurmountable odds: while there is only one Solid Snake (*MGS*), just how many soldiers are patrolling Shadow Moses at any given time? It would be pointless to count the number of individual "enemies" in any action or adventure game, not only because they're so numerous, but because in many cases they are functionally infinite. In many early arcade games, minor antagonists were simply spawned, on the fly, to fill the vacuum created by their predecessor's elimination, and modern games usually retain some variant of this concept. The protagonist (and thus, the player) triumph over these odds with the aid of two nearly universal gameplay conventions. The first is the protagonist's miraculous (and usually extra-diegetic) tendency toward resurrection, formerly via a set number of "lives" to be lived consecutively, and more recently via specific save/restore points to which a defeated avatar may infinitely return. The second

is that the minor antagonists are overwhelmingly inferior to the protagonist. In some games they are stupid, in others they are comparatively weak and frail, and in most games they are both. The major antagonists, the so-called "bosses," are not as obviously and uniformly inferior. Rather, major antagonists are often depicted as unstoppable, aside from an utterly fatal Achilles' heel that the player is intended to discover.

In cooperative multiplayer games— there is more than one protagonist, but the aforementioned conventions remain. In competitive multiplayer games, the protagonist/antagonist binary is problematized, as players and their avatars must compete as equals. Put succinctly, in competitive play, every fight is a "boss fight," in that both parties are expected to be competent and adaptable, and cannot be dismissed like so many non-player characters (NPCs). The gameplay mechanics of *God of War*, if transposed into a competitive multiplayer game, would most closely resemble a fighting game. (In fact, one of *God of War*'s more notable imitators is *Mortal Kombat: Shaolin Monks*, which adapted the mythos of the *Mortal Kombat* series of one-on-one fighting games into a cooperative adventure game, complete with a hidden competitive "versus" mode.) Many massively multiplayer online games (MMOGs), or games that combine the two elements, populating their servers with hordes of both human players (of widely varying power) and disposable, endlessly resurrecting NPC "mobs," as well as the occasional civilian NPC to relay narrative exposition. MMOGs often further subdivide the competitive-cooperative angle into Player-versus-Environment (PvE) and Player-versus-Player (PvP) modes.

Mortal Kombat, an archetypal "fighter," provides players (and their opponents, real or virtual) with a small number of characters who are all, in the hands of a suitably skilled player, highly competent, each with their own backstories and relationships with other characters. In fact, one of the key goals to fighting game design is to ensure that the bulk of these characters are "balanced" against one another, so that no character will have an overwhelming advantage over any other during a contest between two equally skilled players. With the exception of "boss" characters (disproportionately powerful) and "joke" characters (disproportionately weak), none of these characters can be treated as disposable. Moreover, these games are fundamentally designed to be played by humans—sentient beings capable of abstract thought and adaptive strategy—against *other humans;* the AI only functions to mimic the behavior of a human player, within the capabilities of the designers, when a real-world opponent is not present. In the single-player adventure, there is nobody else "like" the protagonist. These games take place in a world that is populated by two distinct groups, the heroically strong (the protagonist, whose greatness is enabled by his player, and the major antagonists) and the miserably weak (everyone else). This binary is a constitutive element of the genre and mode. Similarly, the honor given to others is proportional to their strength. The civilian NPCs and minor adversaries are non-entities, deprived of personhood, forgotten as quickly as they appear. The major adversaries, the so-called "bosses," are not so easily dismissed, narratively or martially. They are designed to be more memorable, the narrative acknowledges their existence, and their appearance usually signals a climactic event. In short, they matter more than the nameless, faceless drones that precede them

GENRE AND MORALITY

In *Beyond Good and Evil,* Friedrich Nietzsche attempts to explain the origin of human morality by referring to a similar dichotomy. "There are *master morality* and *slave morality* [....] The moral discrimination of values has originated either among a ruling group whose consciousness of its difference from the ruled group was accompanied by delight—or among the ruled, the slaves and dependents of every degree" (Nietzsche, 2000, p.

394). The noble man, the master, *makes* morality, not *ex nihilio* but through his actions. The slave reacts—retaliates—by inverting morality and turning it against those who made it. The key difference, the point on which this inversion pivots, is the master's and slave's antithetical perspectives on fear: "Here is the place for the origin of that famous opposition of 'good' and 'evil': into evil one's feelings project power and dangerousness, a certain terribleness, subtlety, and strength that does not permit contempt to develop. According to slave morality, those who are 'evil' thus inspire fear; according to master morality it is precisely those who are 'good' that inspire, and wish to inspire, fear, while the 'bad' are felt to be contemptible" (Nietzsche, 2000, p. 397).

The inspiration of fear, Nietzsche argues, is a pleasure with which our protagonist is not at all unfamiliar. Kratos is a Spartan warrior, feared by his allies and enemies alike. In one of title's earliest scenes, he comes upon a prisoner trapped aboard a sinking ship; the prisoner chooses certain death by the sea rather than risk being "freed" by an entity as fearsome as Kratos. In another, later, scene, a woman flees from Kratos even when he pleads for her to stay—not for her own safety, but for Kratos' own ease in acquiring the key around her neck. Nonetheless, he seems to wish her no particular harm, and the same cannot be said of the animated corpses with which Ares has filled her home. In her terror of the so-called Ghost of Sparta, she (intentionally or accidentally) falls to her death.

Even to the extent that the player can be said to "be" Kratos, through their synthesis in the avatar, these examples do not necessarily say anything about what behaviors are (conditionally) valorized within the world of a particular game. Even if this fear is inspired by Kratos' actions, the bulk of these actions can be assumed to have taken place long before the player was ever invited to participate in Kratos' story in the game's opening level. To be certain, the player, as Kratos, kills hundreds of Ares' minor minions during the course of the game, in the extraordinarily violent and dramatic ways that have become the hallmark of the action and adventure genres. Even absent any direct, synchronic violence directed at living, mortal humans, it would be narratively appropriate for Kratos to inspire fear in all he meets simply because he's *very, very good at killing*. The narrative alludes to this fact in flashbacks concerning Kratos' military career before his deal with Ares, and the subsequent deaths of his wife and child. One could almost feel pity for Kratos, feared by his fellow man merely for his dedication to, and competence in, an unpleasant but necessary profession. This conception of the warrior is very "modern," which is to say it is profoundly out of step with the rest of the world presented in *God of War*. Nietzsche would mock this claim; Kratos would be appalled by it. Consequently, the narrative takes care to prevent the player from arriving at this rather absurd reading, and the player is thus invited (perhaps forced) to participate in the kinds of actions that earned Kratos this fearsome reputation in the first place.

"BEING" KRATOS

At one point, killing his way through Ares' siege of Athens, the player, as Kratos finds that he must cross a gap between rooftops. A bridge has been built for this purpose, but it has been withdrawn, held in its useless place by the limited might of a terrified Athenian. On seeing this unfortunate missing word, Kratos commands the Athenian to release the bridge; the man refuses, claiming that if he were to allow the bridge to extend, all manner of monstrous creature might walk across it and harm him. It is a matter of interpretation whether Kratos himself qualifies as one such monstrous creature in the Athenian's mind, but the Spartan deals with the problem coldly and effectively. From the player's perspective, this is simply a puzzle to be solved, and that puzzle is ultimately expressed in the question, "how can I get across that gap?"

Absent an ethical imperative to take the Athenian civilian's happiness, autonomy or existence into consideration, the civilian is eminently disposable, and whatever pity the player (or Kratos) might feel is more than balanced by the concordant frustration at being unable to progress. Thus this puzzle is revealed to be a simple question of exploration.

Elsewhere in the level, Kratos is given (by a manifestation of Zeus) the ability to throw bolts of lightning, and upon returning to the rooftop, he uses this gift to promptly execute the Athenian, releasing the bridge and allowing him to pass. In contrast to the caged soldier in Gee's example, the Athenian at the bridge is actively responsible for the circumstances that lead Kratos to kill him. Kratos would happily kill the monsters the bridge keeper so fears, if only he could get across the bridge to do so. Conversely, Kratos doesn't care about him very much, and would happily let him alone if he'd lower the bridge. In his fear, the Athenian is not thinking clearly, and makes a fatally stupid decision. The responsibility borne by the Athenian discourages the player from pitying him, just as his extra-diegetic role as an obstacle to the player's progress encourages the player to be annoyed by his stubbornness. Might there be more humane alternatives? Almost certainly, but the game does not make them available. More importantly, could the player, as Kratos have found a way to spare the frightened Athenian? Very likely, but he doesn't seem to try. Like electricity itself, he's seeking the shortest route, and the violent solution the game allows can be inferred to be Kratos' first choice. Players might not feel satisfaction when they electrocute the Athenian, but most will feel some sense of relief that the path is open, and perhaps some pleasure that their new weapon is so simple, so practical, so powerful. And with this relief, and this pleasure, the player has met Nietzsche's "master" halfway. The master "feels contempt for the cowardly, the anxious, the petty, those intent on narrow utility; also for the suspicious with their unfree glances, those who humble themselves, the doglike people who allow themselves to be mistreated" (Nietzsche, 2000, pp. 394-395). The weak, by virtue of their feeble, fearful values, have made themselves into objects of scorn, and the strong should have no reservations about exploiting them as they see fit.

If Kratos' ultimate goal is his own serenity, the protection of Athens is a proximate goal he must pursue, with all his ferocity, to achieve. This is a common enough narrative device in action-adventure games. What is most notable about Kratos' brand of heroism is that, though he may risk his life again and again to protect Athens, he feels no compunction whatsoever to protect *Athenians*. In one memorable scene, the player faces off against several minotaurs in an Athenian public square. Upon his arrival, Kratos finds the minotaurs killing Athenians, who are running haphazardly about in terror. The minotaurs soon turn their clubs on him, and a comparatively lengthy battle ensues, one of the more challenging yet seen at that point in the game. The Athenian civilians are numerous, and their paths often take them into harm's way. In endeavoring to take down the minotaurs, the player might find herself killing a few civilians by accident; the player might even find herself killing a few intentionally. This possibility does not, in itself, speak significantly of the game's ideology. As Frasca notes in reference to the similarly vulnerable NPC prostitutes in the *Grand Theft Auto* series, "[r]hetorically, a game where you may kill sexworkers is very different from a game in where you must kill them in order to win" (2000, p. 232). In this particular scene, when Kratos kills a civilian, blue orbs are released, which allow the player to use magical attacks more frequently. Since this makes the battle considerably easier, the game rules are effectively encouraging the player to kill civilians, as needed, to augment her supply of magical munitions. No rule states that the player *must* kill them, but if she's serious about giving Kratos his revenge against Ares, she *should* kill them. The player is thus rewarded for treating the Athenians as disposable, as Kratos seems designed to. Beyond the self-satisfaction

of having triumphed in the face of intentionally inflated difficulty, no such reward is given for respecting the value of their lives.

In fact, there are relatively few "rewards" to be found in *God of War,* beyond the obvious and necessary reward of being able to move to new locations and advance the story, and the equally necessary but largely extra-diegetic reward of upgrading weapons and magic to facilitate the primary reward. There are no rewards for performing meritorious deeds along the way, as is common in other single-player action games. Players trying to convince themselves that Kratos is really, at heart, a "good" person in the traditional sense (Christian, humanist, utilitarian, etc.) will find little support for this claim in the text, even the portions of the text in which they exert some control. While Kratos' essential burden is fundamentally one of inconsolable grief for the deaths of his wife and child, it would be erroneous to claim that he seeks any kind of atonement, because he accepts no responsibility for their deaths. It was Ares who pointed Kratos toward the Athenian shrine in which they were to meet their ends, and Ares who opted to conceal this information from his elect assassin. While Kratos is the instrument of their deaths, he considers Ares to be the cause. Whatever guilt he might feel exacerbates, rather than mitigates, his desire for revenge.

Kratos kills to gain power, and the player seeks power so that Kratos may more effectively kill. There seems no "greater good" to which he appeals. It is thus clear that, for Kratos, the salvation of Athens is purely a means to an end. There is no equilibrium that he seeks to restore, and he seems unconcerned about the political or theological consequences of deicide. Kratos is driven to kill Ares, no doubt, but not because Ares has transgressed his sacred role as a son of Zeus and Hera, or because he has violated some deontological ideal of justice. Ares has clearly wronged many people; as a god, it might well be considered his right to do so. In Kratos' mind, however, Ares must be killed for one reason and one reason only, *because he has wronged Kratos.* This too is consistent with Nietzsche's master morality: "The noble type of man experiences itself as determining values; it does not need approval; it judges, 'what is harmful to me is harmful in itself'; it knows itself to be that which first accords honor to things; it is value-creating" (2000, p. 395). While there exist other fine reasons for killing Ares, such as the possibility of rewards from the other gods, they can concern Kratos only when they are seen in the proper context, as developing from this first rule.

In examining the action/adventure genre, we find a series of nested challenges for which a player's skill is rewarded. In short, we find a game. To make the avatar/protagonist more in line with conventional heroes, a non-specific altruistic morality is often retrofitted onto the player's actions, resulting in vague and problematic moral ideas. The Nietzschean morality present in the *God of War* universe differs from this tradition in the sense that it does not clash with the essential conventions of the genre, but rather seems to naturally develop from them. In the next section, I will discuss the implications of this idea for future game design.

FURTHER RESEARCH DIRECTIONS

Nietzsche's claim of this "first" morality, built upon the raw assertions of the noble, strong and cruel, is historically to be supplanted by its antithesis, slave morality. Nietzsche identifies "Rome against Judaea, Judaea against Rome" as the archetypal form of this clash, but he identifies numerous other examples. In that Rome, "the strong and noble" (Nietzsche, 2000, p. 489) will eventually (in "real" history, at least) dominate Kratos' Greece and seize its cultural icons for itself, it seems worth wondering what ludic consequences might be wrought from a similar "slave rebellion in morals" in the *God of War* universe (Nietzsche, 2000, p. 298). The conclusion of *God of War* is careful to note that Kratos remains on what once

was Ares' throne "forever," and the events of the sequel (the aptly named *God of War II*) suggest that Kratos will eventually annihilate the remaining Olympian deities. Milton wrote of the Greek pantheon symbolically ceding its existence to the imminent arrival of Christ; more recently, the plots of *Xena: Warrior Princess* and *Battlestar Galactica* similarly concerned the annihilation and replacement of deities.

How exactly this "re-sentiment," or inversion of values, would take place is as unclear as it is unlikely. We can be certain, however, that the genre conventions of the single-player action game—violently individualistic and hierarchical, with no external values against which to ascertain "goodness"—would be wildly ill-suited to the task. One could argue that the rise of MMOs that encourage complex coordination among large groups signals a shift away from the pure individualism in gameplay associated with single-player gaming. However, this comparatively large-scale cooperation—such as "raids" involving twenty players—is only partially encouraged by the games' internal ethics; to understand *World of Warcraft* as a rule system, it would also be necessary to develop an interpretive theory that problematizes the rules of behavior developed, instituted and enforced by players, with little to no help from the designers. Even were such a theory developed, it is presently unclear whether or not the behavior enacted by players or avatars actually differs significantly from the aforementioned multiplayer models which keep the master/slave binary largely intact. PvE (Player versus Environment) play teams the strong against the weak, PvP (Player versus Player) play pits the strong against the strong, and team PvP play pits teams of the strong against teams of the strong. It is difficult to imagine a game that actually valorizes the weak and places their experience as the moral ideal. Perhaps the valorization of power is endemic not only to game design, but the human condition itself: Christian theologian Reinhold Niebuhr suggests that, where large groups are concerned, our goal should be "only to make the forces of nature [specifically, selfishness and violence] the servants of the human spirit and the instruments of the moral ideal" (1960, p. 256).

CONCLUSION

God of War does not attempt to deal with these ideas, but it does give players a unique perspective from which to consider them. *God of War*'s play mechanics are not significantly different from many other titles; it stands out as an object of study for what it lacks. *God of War* does not attempt to justify the genre's valorization of strategic brutality, nor does it attempt to mitigate its marginalization of those who are not, by virtue of their ability to assert morality through violence, "noble." Rather, it lays out a popular genre in what seems to be its purest form, with a narrative that incorporates only its constitutive elements, and tells us that master morality *fits* the action-adventure game more closely than any comparable moral system. Attempts to model more altruistic moral systems in action/adventure games invariably create internal conflicts, but Kratos demonstrates a moral consistency that is as refreshing as it is terrifying. If Kratos is a hero, he is a hero few of us would aspire to be, and one none of us would hope to meet. Sharing in his exploits is, and should be, a disturbing experience. His saving grace, when viewed from the safe distance of a monitor, is that he makes us wonder why his more classically "heroic" counterparts should be any less disturbing.

REFERENCES

Caillois, R. (2006). The classification of games. In Salen, K., & Zimmerman, E. (Eds.), *The game design reader: A rules of play anthology* (pp. 129–147). Cambridge, MA: MIT Press.

ESA v. Blagojevich. (2006). 469 F.3d 641 (7th Cir.).

Frasca, G. (2000). Simulation versus narrative: Introduction to ludology. In Wolf, M. J. P., & Perron, B. (Eds.), *The video game theory reader* (pp. 221–236). New York, NY: Routledge.

Gee, J. P. (2007). *What video games have to teach us about learning and literacy*. New York: Palgrave MacMillan.

King, G., & Krzywinska, T. (2002). *Introduction. Screenplay: Cinema/videogames/interfaces* (pp. 1–32). London: Wallflower.

Konami. (2001). *Metal Gear Solid 2: Sons of Liberty* [Playstation 2].

Midway. (2005). *Mortal Kombat: Shaolin Monks* [Playstation 2].

Niebuhr, R. (1960). *Moral man and immoral society*. New York: Scribner's.

Nietzsche, F. (2000/1886) *Beyond good and evil.* In *Basic writings of Nietzsche* (W. Kaufman, Trans., pp. 179-436). New York: Modern Library. (Original work published 1886)

Nietzsche, F. (2000/1887) *On the genealogy of morals.* In *Basic writings of Nietzsche* (W. Kaufman, Trans., pp. 437-600). New York: Modern Library. (Original work published 1887)

Rauch, P. (2007). Playing with good and evil: Videogames and moral philosophy. Unpublished master's thesis, Massachusetts Institute of Technology. Retrieved from http://cms.mit.edu/research/theses/PeterRauch2007.pdf

Rauch, P. (2008, March 23). Guns, germs and steel: Ethics and genre shift." In *Undisciplined.* Retrieved from http://undisciplinedtheory.blogspot.com/2008/03/guns-germs-and-steel-ethics-and-genre.html

SCEA. (2005). *God of war* [Playstation 2].

Section 3
Design, Production, and Use of Games

Chapter 8
The Ethics of Reverse Engineering for Game Technology

David I. Schwartz
Rochester Institute of Technology, USA

Jessica D. Bayliss
Rochester Institute of Technology, USA

ABSTRACT

This chapter demonstrates how legal concepts, accepted practices, and research in reverse engineering (a process of disassembling a system to understand how it works) can provide ethical and legal outlets for end-users. The game industry has influenced reverse engineering law and practice, challenging ethical practices in industry, academia, and with end-users. Although these communities supposedly rely on legal precedents, actual laws are often misunderstood, ignored, or just unknown. The communities continually struggle to balance the protection of intellectual property with consumer freedom, and reverse engineering demonstrates this conflict. We demonstrate how a variety of communities embrace reverse engineering through a series of case studies involving current commercial games and technology. The case studies include the modding community, massively-multiplayer online game community tools, digital preservation, and reverse engineering education. Although a clear ruling on legality eludes the field, we conclude with suggestions on dealing with ethical and legal aspects surrounding this issue.

INTRODUCTION

Reverse engineering (RE) is a process by which any commercially-available system is disas-

sembled to learn how it works (Raja & Fernandes, 2008). For example, RE might mean learning how to customize Microsoft's Xbox™ gaming console (Huang, 2003) or studying mechanical design by taking apart small household appliances (Wu, 2008). Anytime a person inspects something

DOI: 10.4018/978-1-60960-120-1.ch008

(which does not include just mechanical devices) and asks, "I wonder how this works?" they engage in RE. But, RE isn't always so innocent. To explain how the issues of RE can become complex, we will first enlist the help of a hypothetical end-user that we have named "Mitchell Ketchup." In the Background section, we delve deeper into RE's legal history and terminology to set up four case studies that explore how various groups have addressed legal and ethical aspects.

Mitchell Ketchup's Dilemma

Mitchell Ketchup likes to play old arcade games on his even older gaming console. But, one day his console breaks! All of his old games cannot play on the gaming console anymore, and he cannot replace it because consoles like his are rare and expensive, especially since companies no longer produce them. However, Mitchell discovers a website that has an emulator for his gaming console. Better yet (at least for him), he learns that he can download the emulator, as well as all of his old games! He can even download games he never owned—including new games created by a community of programmers passionate about the old console. Mitchell even found software tools to increase his game performance, e.g., custom software that interacts with a game (usually MMOs) to automatically play a particular character. But, he also learns that it is illegal to download "cracked" (i.e., decoded) games and/ or tools that play them.

So, what should Mitchell do?

Ethical Questions

Mitchell's dilemma suggests several key questions:

- If the emulator and downloadable games were constructed through illegal RE, is Mitchell engaging in illegal activity? Is he being unethical?

- Is it ethical to create new works for an emulator that RE helped to create?
- Should Mitchell download only the games he already owns? Is he "allowed" to download others?
- Are the tools that improve Mitchell's performance on the games ethical for single player games? What about multi-player games?

Mitchell's dilemma—and the corresponding questions—are common in today's gaming culture. RE is a well-known process in all kinds of industries, especially where competitors strive to understand competing designs and technologies. But, end-users and academics (both faculty and students) also engage in RE for a variety of other purposes, which include the following artifacts of gaming culture, academia, and industry:

- A website called *ROM World Emulators*.
- A book called *Hacking the Xbox: an Introduction to Reverse Engineering* (Huang, 2003).
- A college course on alternative game interfaces/controllers in which students disassemble controllers, learn how they work, and make their own based on that technology (Doctorow, 2009).
- A client-side "mod" for a massively-multiplayer online game that filters incoming network traffic before it displays in the game to filter out real money trading spam (Aion Source, 2010).

Some of these resources are legal (at least in the USA), some are not, and some have vague legal standing —yet, they exist, right, wrong, and "in between." Better yet, do "right" and "wrong" imply ethics and/or legality? To help clarify the analysis, we need to define two criteria:

- **Legal:** An action or artifact that does not violate a government's law. In general, we will refer to federal law in the USA, but occasionally we will expand the geographic scope.

- **Ethical:** Moral acceptability regardless of legal status.

The case studies later in this chapter will address each of the above artifacts with respect to legality and ethics. As discussed below, end-users consist of a multitude of people, which include gamers, students, academics, and more. For example, later we introduce Makers, who are end-users that invent and share their work, which often includes game technology. All of these end-users will likely espouse the legality and ethics for any of the above artifacts. But, how do we evaluate the extent to which they have the *right* to use them, legally, and/or ethically? And what of the "Mitchells" that simply want to access games and other technology that they had already bought?

BACKGROUND

To delve into the implications of Mitchell's dilemma and subsequent ethical questions, we provide a background for the field of RE. This section explains its history, the process of RE, and the legal implications. We also address the people engaged in, and affected by, RE to frame the discussion and our case studies in the chapter.

Reverse Engineering

Reverse Engineering (RE) is "the process of duplicating an existing part, subassembly, or product, without drawings, documentation, or a computer model" (Raja & Fernandes, 2008, pg. 2). Note that RE indeed includes hardware and other processes, despite a tendency to focus on software and other digital artifacts. In 1974, the United States Supreme Court stated that

...a trade secret does not offer protection against discovery by fair and honest means, such as by independent invention, accidental disclosure, or by so-called reverse engineering, that is by starting with a known product and working backward to divine the process which aided in its development or manufacture (Raja & Fernandes, 2008, pg. 198).

Ibrahim (2010) describes modern RE tools for games that include debuggers, disassemblers, and network protocol analyzers (i.e., packet sniffers). These tools are also extensively used outside of RE. Debuggers can help analyze why a program crashes, disassemblers can help programmers optimize their programs, and network protocol analyzers can help game developers to determine problems with network transmission. These tools can also crack software programs for the hacking community for illegal distribution. Although the tools themselves are not "wrong," their uses can be.

Legal Precedents

One fascinating aspect of the game industry's history is how the development of commercial games actually led to a variety of landmark decisions. For example, Zieminski (2008) gives a detailed account of company negotiations between Atari Games and Nintendo in 1992, in which Nintendo's president apparently dozed off while talking with an Atari executive during a dinner party—all the while Atari employees were actively attempting to reverse engineer Nintendo's technology.

The cases of *Atari Games v. Nintendo* (1992), *Sega v. Accolade* (1992), and *Sony v. Connectix* (2000) provide frequently cited decisions in which the court essentially supported the application of RE. Below, we summarize the findings documented in detail in Zieminski (2008) and Raja & Fernandes (2008):

- **Sega v. Accolade (1992):** Accolade could disassemble code unprotected by copyright.

- **Atari Games v. Nintendo (1992):** Atari could legitimately make "intermediate" copies of certain Nintendo software for RE.
- **Sega v. Accolade (1992):** "Connectix's intermediate copying and use of Sony's copyrighted BIOS was a fair use for the purpose of gaining access to the unprotected elements of Sony's software" (Raja & Fernandes, 2008). In other words, unauthorized emulation is legal.

However, recent cases have begun to tighten previous decisions. For example, in Blizzard v. MDY (Siy, 2008), the district court has currently ruled that MDY cannot legally copy Blizzard's *World of Warcraft™* (WoW) game into memory so that their software "Glider" can play the game on autopilot (also known as "botting"—players can let their bots "autogrind," which many players find wrong). This case has been appealed, triggering a question of whether players actually *own* the games that they buy, or if they just *license* the game. Blizzard claims that players only license the game and that players may not determine how they use the game. Moreover, these cases suggest an important concept—fair use—which we discuss below.

Fair Use and Legal Protections

The United States legal definition of Fair Use (i.e., whether or not someone is free to use someone else's copyrighted work) suggests four factors: the purpose and character of the use, the nature of the copyrighted work, the amount and kind of copying, and the effect of the use on the market/value of the original work. Even the government's definition, however, is deliberately vague, stating that the "…distinction between fair use and infringement may be unclear and not easily defined…." (U.S. Copyright Office, 2010).

In the game industry legal cases above, the courts needed to decide whether the companies charged with illegal activity had fairly—or unfairly—reverse engineered a competitor's product. In each case, the United State Supreme Court upheld some aspect of Fair Use with respect to a company who disassembled part of another company's source code. For additional examples, Zieminski (2008) indicates several cases in which the Court denied claims of wrong doing due to an appropriate application of fair use.

The legal cases presented in the above section also address copyright, which includes software as well traditional written works. Thus, we need even more legal definitions to clarify the discussion. Below, we summarize definitions and concepts introduced in Ibrahim (2000) and Chilling Effects Clearinghouse (2010), supplemented by the U.S. Copyright Office (2010) and international definitions where possible.

- **Intellectual property:** "creations of the mind: inventions, literary and artistic works, and symbols, names, images, and designs used in commerce" (World Intellectual Property Organization, 2010).
- **Copyright:** "artistic creations" that are fixed in a medium (that includes code) (World Intellectual Property Organization, 2010; Ibrahim, 2010).
- **Patent:** essentially, protection for "inventions" or processes (U. S. Patent and Trademark Office, 2010).
- **Digital Millennium Copyright Act (DMCA):** "The anti-circumvention provision of the DMCA, 17 U.S.C. 1201, prohibits the circumvention of any technological measures that control access to any part of the work" (Ibrahim, 2010).
- **First sale doctrine (or exhaustion doctrine):** "you bought it, you own it" (Von Lohmann, 2007). The first sale doctrine actually dates back to "common-law doctrine against restraints on alienation of chattels"

(Stern, 2008; Zieminski, 2008).

These dizzying and often conflicting principles and legal precedents try to balance an end-user's right to copy/dissect the original owner's work with the rights of the creator. To explain how all of these principles affect RE, we start with hardware. Based on the "you bought it, you own it" principle (Von Lohmann, 2007), companies already engaged in RE with products long before software existed. In fact, many readers may have tried taking apart a toy as a child just to see how it works.

But with respect to software, the issue becomes murky, especially with DMCA and EULAs (end-user license agreements). As Ibrahim (2010) indicates,

The anti-circumvention provision of the DMCA, 17 U.S.C. 1201, prohibits the circumvention of any technological measures that control access to any part of the work. It also prevents the distribution of software that enables circumvention of an access control (Ibrahim, 2010).

Yet academic courses and publications continue to study software RE (e.g., Case Four later in the chapter). Legal cases also ensue, as organizations like the Electronic Frontier Foundation (EFF) struggle with these sorts of restrictions, especially in regard to the original intent of the first sale doctrine.

The introduction of DMCA has further complicated the issue as shown in the recent case of *Blizzard v. BnetD* (Electronic Freedom Foundation, 2010). In this case, a group of three software programmers created a program that interoperated with Blizzard's video game software, enabling individuals to play on servers other than those offered by Blizzard's Battle.net service. The 8th Circuit Court of Appeals ruled that RE of the Blizzard game circumvented technological measures controlling access to the game and also violated their End User License Agreement in several ways.

The case forced the domain name bnetd.org to be given to Blizzard.

This ruling has been widely criticized as it appears to prevent creating new programs that interoperate with older ones and potentially allows companies to outlaw competing products that may interact with their own. Interestingly enough, the ruling has not stopped the distribution of BnetD or its derivative software PvPGN. The software is open source, with a variety of individuals contributing to it, and the software is now distributed from websites in countries that do not have anti-circumvention legislation. The open source community behind the continued construction and maintenance of this software clearly believes in allowing players to participate in games not running on Blizzard's servers.

Makers

Besides the notion of protection, we need to clarify *who* needs (or drives the need for) protection and might seek to weaken (or threaten) said protection. The main participants are the game industry, gamers, and academics. Although the term "hacker" may apply to malicious computer programmers (e.g., trying to crack a password), it is frequently misapplied. Hacking may simply mean extended periods of any kind of programming. Moreover, the notion of hacking seems to ignore the other kind of RE—exploring and dissecting all kinds of hardware.

Instead, in this chapter we will focus on another particular kind of end-user, the *Maker*, or the modern-day inventor. In fact, some extend the notion of inventor to *outlaw inventor* (Flowers, 2006; Schulz & Wagner, 2008). Since the word "outlaw" implies malicious intent, this chapter focuses on Makers, which are a growing community of do-it-yourself hobbyists who often use games and/or game technology to create new products to share with others (Doctorow, 2009). They embrace a variety of forms of tinkering, often disassembling and adapting existing products for their own uses, such as making new games. For example, a variety of magazines and forums provide collaborative outlets and discussion for their software and hardware designs (e.g., Instructables.com, 2009).

Makers deserve a special focus in this chapter for two main reasons:

- Makers generally do not have malicious intent. Although both groups will use RE to dissect a product, a Maker seeks invention, whereby a "hacker" (or more appropriately, "cracker") seeks disruption.
- Makers often dissect games and game technology (e.g., Carless, 2004; Huang, 2003).

What about end-users with malicious intent? Although attempts to eliminate criminals have yet to succeed in all aspects of life, we believe that in the particular case of the game industry and its passionate end-users, we can diffuse many negative behaviors by creating positive outlets. These ideas are indeed subjective, and so, we will frame our judgments of the practices surrounding RE.

The Ethics of RE

Throughout this chapter, we attempt to stay descriptive of RE practices and cases, although the reader might have noted various subjective statements so far. For example, consider our statements about an end-user's goal in weakening or threatening protections against RE. In a way, we have polarized end-users, lumping them into "positive gamers" and "malicious hackers." Realistically, people do not easily divide into binary camps. Rather than identify whether someone is more of a hacker, Maker, or other kind of end-user, we seek to understand how various people interpret, apply, or redefine legal "standards," which, by their own legal documents, are vague and sometimes contradictory.

In essence, the attempt to define, defend, and/or counteract RE in court cases represents the struggle between the protection of intellectual property and freedom of its use. Even in academia, researchers note the threat of RE (Gibson, 2009; Genov, 2008; McLoughlin, 2008). As Ibrahim (2010) points out for software, "…the practice of reverse engineering has come under assault over the past several years." Whether one agrees that RE is indeed "under assault," these sources indicate that end-users (and often the industry itself) worry and/or disagree with the current state of RE.

How do we define ethics with respect to RE and the struggle between protecting intellectual property and providing fair use? Zieminski (2008) suggests three aspects of this issue, which we adapt below as questions to resolve:

- Should RE law revert to the initial precedents set by the game industry itself (e.g., drop DMCA)?
- Can economic cost-benefit analysis objectively highlight RE's actual effects?
- Will changes to RE law balance protection and freedom?

Three more questions may help to flesh out the ethical framework in which to address RE, as follows:

- Can end-users gain access to abandonware?
- Can end-users have constructive outlets?
- Can the entire community further the state of game research?

To demonstrate how the practice of RE relates to these ethical questions, we return to Mitchell Ketchup with specific examples in the game industry and community.

An Industry Viewpoint

Nintendo almost directly answers Mitchell Ketchup's dilemma. Consider Nintendo's various responses in their corporate legal FAQ (Nintendo, 2010). For example, in response to Nintendo's view of *emulators* (software that simulates official game hardware) and *ROMs* (read-only memory chips that can store games) as tools to promote and increase sales, they say,

Distribution of an emulator developed to play illegally copied Nintendo software hurts Nintendo's goodwill, the millions of dollars invested in research & development and marketing by Nintendo and its licensees. Substantial damages are caused to Nintendo and its licensees. It is irrelevant whether or not someone profits from the distribution of an emulator. The emulator promotes the play of illegal, NOT authentic games. Thus, not only does it not lead to more sales, it has the opposite effect and purpose (Nintendo, 2010).

The complete FAQ has many other responses to "plain-speak" questions, often phrased as many end-users might ask, just like the following:

People Making Nintendo Emulators and Nintendo ROMs are Helping Publishers by Making Old Games Available that are No Longer Being Sold by the Copyright Owner. This Does Not Hurt Anyone and Allows Gamers to Play Old Favorites. What's the Problem? (Nintendo, 2010).

In response, Nintendo (2010) states, "The problem is that it's illegal…" and continues from there, including many other related questions and responses. This response provides a major example of how the game industry can perceive and react to RE. Though Nintendo does not present the sole (and final) view on legal and moral challenges, they do present a clear stance on this issue without legalese—thus clearly targeting Makers, distributors, and other end-users. Although their FAQ will likely adapt in time, it does demonstrate how the game industry may interpret and respond to Makers and others.

A Gamer Viewpoint

Mitchell Ketchup wants access to games no longer supported or available anymore. Games (and other software) no longer supported and/or available are called *abandonware*. For example, the Abandonware Ring's (2002) FAQ addresses their stance on preserving abandoned software, presented verbatim below:

…A good example of the problems this is already causing is going on right now in the movie industry. Decaying nitrate-based film from the early days of motion pictures may not be restored because Moviecraft and other companies that restore and reissue these movies can't do so because they can't identify the copyright holders and the movies seem to never pass into the public domain. Preservation activities in general, and particularly digital preservation activities, are made more difficult when material never enters the public domain…. This is why we have abandonware…. (Abandonware Ring, 2002).

Even if the group simply posts abandonware online to provide free access to the game, the above viewpoint illustrates a common justification seen throughout the Maker/gamer world—if something's abandoned, isn't a user helping by keeping it "alive?" In fact, later in this chapter, Case Study Three presents one solution to abandonware, but the challenge has a larger scope than just access to games.

Bridging the Divide

At their core, the above statements from Nintendo and the Abandonware Ring both discuss RE. They each take a strong stance, either pro- or anti-RE. Various other industry and non-industry groups, however, do not share the same opinions concerning the distribution and, in many cases, the dissection/replication of games and game technology. For example, ROMs that illegally decode and transfer pirated games often provide technology to create and distribute completely original games. Even academics have gotten involved with RE—a GameBoy™ development site has at least one academic program using the GameBoy to teach assembly programming (e.g., ECE238Spr08, 2008).

In fact, many games already ship with software deliberately aimed at players to serve as co-creators. *Modding* is the process of creating new games using tool sets provided along with commercial computer games. Mods may actually create games that are very popular—*Counter-Strike*™ was originally a mod of *Half Life*™, later bought by Valve.

These examples of RE have demonstrated successful collaborations, and others may be acceptable. In this chapter, we seek to address a way to "bridge the divide," providing legal and ethical solutions that protect intellectual property and still satiate an end-user's desire to access unavailable games and/or tinker with them. In the next section, we will frame four case studies with which we can demonstrate ways to resolve the struggle between protection of IP and freedom of its use.

CASE STUDIES

Mitchell Ketchup's dilemma has several different questions and potential solutions. RE supported by industry and academia can provide a legal and ethical means to assuage the concerns of other industry and the needs of end-users. Why should the game industry worry about excessive restrictions? Besides the typical end-user argument of building goodwill with consumers, the nature of the products themselves tend to involve gamers. By their very design, games involve engagement and a degree of tinkering, especially in various genres that involve exploration. A player often needs to experiment with a game to play it—by "poking" and "prodding," the player hopefully learns the

game (Koster, 2004). This process is akin to RE, at least in terms of a game as a system.

Below, we explore four case studies that demonstrate the success of communities "bridging the divide" between protection of IP and freedom of its use with respect to RE:

- **Case 1:** Consumers as co-developers—how industry-sponsored tools/products, like modding and the hosting of user-generated content, demonstrates how industry already provides productive outlets for end-user creativity and interest.
- **Case 2:** MMO add-ons—end-user created tools in MMOs can aid players and prevent spam in the games.
- **Case 3:** Preserving virtual worlds—work in preserving virtual worlds, an ongoing project, can collect (via emulators and other means) significant game artifacts. Providing universal and free access can reduce the need for illegal copying.
- **Case 4:** RE in academia—academic courses in which students dissect and rebuild existing products (especially with hardware) have demonstrated success in motivating students and providing constructive outlets.

In each case study, we explain how RE is a core practice that contributes to a product and/or project's success and addresses aspects of the ethical questions that we raised earlier in the chapter.

Case 1: Consumers as Co-developers

When end-users mod a game and release it to the world, they engage in more than modding—they belong to a *convergence culture*, which involves consumers and products merging across several forms of media (Jenkins, 2008). In an era when media crosses multiple formats, consumers receive multiple inputs that capture their attention and invite their participation. However, with forums, product reviews, video postings, and more, consumers can greatly affect a product's perception, and more. Convergence culture describes the idea that the consumer is an active *co-developer*, and not just a passive participant (Deuze, 2009; Apperley, 2007; Jeppesen & Molin, 2003).

For example, when a company releases a computer game with modding tools, end-users can share their work, essentially expanding the scope of the original game, if not changing the design entirely. Thus, the company essentially employs an "army" of free workers, happily creating additional content. User-generated content follows similar reasoning—when users upload creatures for *Spore™* or levels for *LittleBigPlanet™*, players of these games now have access to additional content.

This "army" is akin to related ideas:

- *Citizen science*, in which the community at large tackles complex/tedious problems by individuals solving smaller pieces (Citizen Science Project, 2010).
- *Open source software*, in which a community of programmers share and adapt code.

But unlike the above areas, game co-developers, who are also end-users, generate content that often spurs on sales of the original IP. This effort contributes to the industry who still owns the original intellectual property.

How do modding and user-generated content relate to RE? Except in cases in which game companies give away engine and/or game source code, the mod/content tools do provide a sort of internal access. The co-developer learns how to make content/levels/games built upon a supplied (and hidden) code base. RE also happens for game design, which is indeed another system. Thus, the end-user has a compromise—enough access to create custom work but enough protection to prevent illegal viewing of source code. Moreover, the opportunity for modding can provide a produc-

tive outlet to channel urges to reverse engineer the original product. Gains in community innovation and essentially free labor might far outweigh losses by malicious hacking, thus addressing the ethical dilemma of balance.

Case 2: Massively Multiplayer Online Game Add-Ons

It has become more and more common to reverse engineer aspects of massively multiplayer online (MMO) games to provide tools (add-ons) to players. Web portals, like Curse Network, have built their businesses around the existence of such tools. Whereas WoW specifically allows the creation of player tools, many MMO companies prohibit such activities in their license agreements. For example, the NCSoft title Aion™ has a user agreement that specifically states,

You acknowledge that you do not have the right to create, publish, distribute, create derivative works from or use any software programs, utilities, applications, emulators or tools derived from or created for the Game except that you may use the Software to the extent expressly permitted by this Agreement (NCSoft Corporation, 2009).

As one can expect, the agreement does not cover player tools or add-ons. However, some tools are passively allowed by the game company, such as Aion's player-created damage meters and a global chat channel spam filter.

Damage meters enable players to gauge their damage per second (DPS) when grouped in the game and killing monsters. Aion currently lacks a damage meter within the game, and so players "discovered" that they could output combat data to a file parsed by a program external to the game. In turn, players can essentially enhance the Aion interface with this data, which the game company passively allows. Given that the game supervisors do not currently ban such users, it seems that some external programs and RE are acceptable, whereas others are not.

The spam filter exists as a separate program that runs in the background while playing Aion, and it directly interacts with the network traffic for the game (Aion Source, 2010). When the game initially released, spammers flooded public chat channels, preventing players from communicating. The primary reason for the spam appears to be that network traffic for those channels is sent in plain text to and from the game client, and thus, players could easily insert text onto those channels for all to see. Non-spamming players solved the problem by creating a spam filter on the client side via a separate program (add-on). The game company passively allowed the spam program and then later adopted a similar method of filtering spam within their client.

The game company, NCSoft, consistently banned attempts by real money traders and yet the company still allowed the spam filtering program. In essence, the company made an ethical choice that reverse engineering the networking protocol for the game is OK when it greatly benefits players—but it is not allowed when harming the players.

Investigating programs that automate gameplay in some fashion illustrate a thorny issue concerning RE and MMOs. Programs called *bots* within MMOs handle a repetitive and/or boring task that yields reward for the character in the game over long periods of time. User agreements for games typically disallow bots. The main legal case mentioned in any discussion of botting is the *Blizzard v. Glider* case, which we introduced earlier (Siy, 2008). Glider is a software program that allows users to automate playing within WoW. Blizzard claimed Glider violated Blizzard's copyright through loading WoW into Glider's RAM (thus, copying it) and that they harmed Blizzard through enabling or encouraging users to violate WoW's terms of service. Blizzard appears to have won this case currently, although the ethics of automating game playing remains an open question.

The acceptability of bots and botting seems to relate directly to whether the bots are used for overall player harm or player help. On the other hand, the following uses of botting appear to cause player harm in the game and are considered unethical by players:

- Using bots to gather and sell quantities of items when other players don't get to bot and have to collect materials manually.
- Using bots to "farm gold" and sell it for real money to players.
- Using bots to level players automatically when regular players cannot level automatically.

Players share a strong opinion that game developers should disallow bots from being part of their game since they believe it leads to unfair game play. Players tend to believe that everyone should start the game equally and that they should be judged based on their skills in playing the game. However, input devices that allow extensive key macros enter MMO games with an advantage. Recently, MMO games have attempted to overcome this through either the use of allowed extensive player macros (*Aion™*) or even providing bots to players so that everybody has one (*Jade Dynasty™*). Although players may actually try to create custom controllers (as we discuss later), the fact that online games do allow some customization does demonstrate a kind of supported—and fair—RE.

Thus, MMOs offer a mixed message with respect to RE and ethics. Although some may use RE to cheat the game or serve out-of-game uses, players and even some companies accept RE. In fact, end-user projects may positively influence a game. However, recent rulings and tightening regulations may limit future uses of RE by end-users, thus limiting innovations and player interest.

Case 3: Preserving Virtual Worlds

An ongoing and rather important archiving and research project called *Preserving Virtual Worlds* attempts to legally address the need to archive games (Preserving Virtual Worlds, 2010). Not so coincidentally, the preservation and archiving aspects of the project should seem strikingly familiar to Mitchell Ketchup's dilemma and the various abandonware sites.

In the project site, they do indicate that they are beholden to intellectual property law—part of the archiving is "dependent on resolution of IP and technical issues" (Preserving Virtual Worlds, 2010). Although they do not explicitly claim, "let's legitimize abandonware sites!" the project seems to imply that future Mitchell Ketchups might one day legally access games via the library system.

How does RE factor in? The project involves trying to learn how to preserve game artifacts and play experiences primarily through two overall approaches: emulation and migration, as discussed below:

...With respect to virtual worlds, emulation requires the simulation of the original operating system and environment for which the game was originally designed, using contemporary hardware and software, while migration requires one to translate digital objects, relationships, and behaviors into an alternative hardware- and software-dependent format, in order to free it from the constraint of having to exist within the environment for which it was originally designed (Preserving Virtual Worlds, 2010).

According to this quote, the Preserving Virtual Worlds project does appear to embrace emulators, which are a form of RE. In fact, the project shows support from the government, industry, and academia. Even with the game industry disparaging illegal emulators, the International Game Developers Association (IGDA) (populated mostly by game industry professionals) supports a "Game Preservation Special Interest Group" (IGDA, 2010). This group deliberately links to the Vintage Game Preservation Society (Chappel, 2008)—which, in turn, points to the same illegal abandonware sites that Mitchell Ketchup wants to use!

The ethical issue at hand, though, reaches beyond Mitchell and the illegal distribution. The entire community has expressed fear that future generations will lose an important historical link, which is how games forged in this generation gave rise to future works. And so, we see a cultural benefit. Although this project is indeed ongoing and still must resolve IP and technical issues, it does demonstrate that the entire game community strongly realizes the importance of RE as a way to address a cultural and ethical issue. At the core, the project seems an attempt to provide a legitimate, legal, and industry-accepted resource for the same material posted in abandonware sites. Although it is unclear that the project will subsume sites for illegal distribution, the process by which the project has evolved indicates ways to balance IP protection and freedom.

Case 4: RE in Academia

Not only do academics often encourage RE, but they teach it—sometimes in ways that government and industry fund. Although many resources refer to RE education with respect to software (Costa-Soria et al, 2009; Ali, 2005), hardware-oriented courses exist. As of 2008, about 30 universities have incorporated RE (Wu, 2008). For example, Drexel University students routinely disassembled a broad assortment of store-bought devices in a course funded by a National Science Foundation education grant (Wu, 2008). These courses involve the "other" RE: disassembling and reassembling hardware to learn how it works. Engineering programs have found numerous benefits for students, including exposure to physical devices and learning about design. For example,

...Tim Simpson, a mechanical and industrial engineering professor and director of the Learning Factory at Pennsylvania State University, has his students take apart families of products, such as coffeemakers and single-use cameras. The students are often surprised to see that the products are very similar inside—the same basic structure with different features added (Wu, 2008).

Physical devices do offer some natural "obfuscation," which helps to address the kinds of thorny issues arising with software RE:

...Besides, taking something apart doesn't provide all the information needed to recreate it. "We can measure a part and see what the final fabricated dimensions are, but we don't know what the tolerances are... [We] can take a guess at what the material is, but we don't know exactly" (Wu, 2008).

But when Mitchell Ketchup wants to improve his gaming experience, does he turn to hardware? For example, as noted in Case Two, some MMO players seek refined interfaces to improve play. Moreover, people with disabilities might require customized controllers. One major example of Maker culture and distribution is Instructables (2010), which has a multitude of game hardware "hacks." Also, we refer again to Carless (2004) and Huang (2003) for game hardware examples. Following the first sale doctrine (either knowingly or not), the Makers and other end-users try to improve their playing.

These improvements sometimes get adopted by the industry, perhaps by perusing the same websites or a confluence of good ideas. For example, a popular and fan-led electronic drumming website had numerous posts in their forums about the possibility of connecting *Guitar Hero™* and *Rock Band™* to "real" electronic drum sets. Within about two years, industry endorsed hardware appeared on the market. The collective tinkering of Makers appears to drive innovation, industry growth, and development of desired products.

Hardware-oriented RE shows up outside of traditional engineering programs in art, design, and games programs. For example, *physical computing* and *tangible computing* courses typically involve students developing custom hardware and software composed of other devices (Igoe & O'Sullivan, 2004). Although these courses do not necessarily teach RE, the students often disassemble and reassemble physical devices to create unique experiences. These courses offer numerous benefits:

- Providing tangible experiences for students who have tended to just work with software.
- Embracing technology to create new and culturally significant experiences.
- Tackling sustainability issues (Dampere, 2009).

An example of RE applied to directly to game hardware happened at the Rochester Institute of Technology in 2009 with an experimental seminar on "alternative game interfaces." Just as established RE courses have students disassemble existing devices, the seminar had students examine game controllers and try to apply them to unique applications. Bringing "Making" into the classroom with game hardware and following similar engineering courses provides a legal and motivating experience to students who typically study just software. One of the course projects, a banjo-style controller recreated from a *Rock Band™* guitar controller, received accolades at the Game Developers Conference (Doctorow, 2009). This praise suggests that industry accepted this example of RE, perhaps given the student team's motivation and project's innovative quality.

In a way, Case Four demonstrates that RE has come "full circle" by returning to the notion of hardware. Although cracking of software continues to prove confusing, the first sale doctrine and support of government-funded RE education demonstrates the acceptability of hardware RE.

Because of interest in new interfaces, the game industry may greatly benefit from students' work in entertainment technology programs.

FUTURE RESEARCH DIRECTIONS

Although we have demonstrated several strong connections with RE and ethics, much work remains. Simply trying to decipher RE regulations is an arduous task, and one cannot just claim, "Well, I hereby declare I'm protected by Fair Use!" After all, what Mitchell Ketchup believes may not stand up in a court of law. Future work needs to clarify the morass of confusing legislation, while considering its practical application. To start, we believe that a variety of areas show tremendous promise in the ethics of RE.

"Game Law"

Given the game industry's influence with core RE laws and precedents, collaborations between legal and game researchers in academia might help governments clarify the rampant legal confusion. Game researchers, professionals, and end-users can provide a tremendous resource to legal scholars, though it seems such collaborations are still very infrequent. With numerous academic programs in games still growing, one outlet for students and faculty might be in the area of "Game Law," in which this research can occur.

International law

Given that games and game companies are "everywhere," how will researchers address international law? RE regulation in the United States is already confusing—but, how does it apply in other countries? With Nintendo's stance (Nintendo, 2010) and MMOs tending toward international audiences, we have at least provided an initial viewpoint, but much work remains.

Accessibility

The unethical use of bots and other ways to automate playing MMO games has perhaps clouded the fact that there is a substantial, ethical reason to use such automation: player handicaps. A wide variety of users cannot use a regular keyboard and mouse interface and may need some automation to enjoy playing a game. A single switch interface does not properly allow a user to play at a reasonable speed without automating some features of the game. Along with the work in Case Four, further collaborations for accessibility offer strong backing for continuing adoption of RE processes and tools.

Quantitative Studies

Throughout this chapter, we tended to focus on the Maker and the case of Mitchell Ketchup. Although we may have manipulated the argument somewhat, malicious and illegal end-users will continue to pursue their goals. Is there a need for malicious hacking? Can any "good" come out of it? This chapter presented a variety of cases that show ethical considerations through qualitative discourse. However, we believe that neutral party research (if possible) would help to direct funding to address the different *kinds* of illegal activities.

Citizen Science

Our focus on Makers hints at another fascinating area that strongly connects to RE processes: *citizen science* (Citizen Science Projects, 2010). In a convergence culture, other kinds of co-developers have emerged, though not in games. For example, *Galaxy Zoo* provides access to a multitude of end-users who essentially act as human "visualization sub-processors," tackling the immense problem of celestial identification. We believe that outlaw inventors and Makers engage in a kind of citizen science akin to the open source movement. It seems that research that unifies this emerging culture of co-development could help to write the next generation of RE law.

CONCLUSION

In this chapter, we provided a high-level summary of differing views of ethical and legal concerns with respect to the producers of games (the industry) and the consumers of games (Makers and gamers). As our case studies demonstrated, the game industry does seem to want to permit a degree of RE despite tightening regulations. A simple perusal of various corporate and fan-sites demonstrates deeply divided views. In fact, the game industry essentially caused core legal precedents in RE. Using case studies throughout industry and academia, this chapter addressed ways that RE benefits several aspects of game industry, end-users, and academic research. Through collaboration, the entire community has developed ways to balance the need for protection with the urge for free access, and as a result, has embraced RE.

Nevertheless, for readers seeking guidance on what they can—and cannot do—legally and ethically, much remains uncertain, at least until the suggested work above happens. With respect to hardware, "you bought it, you own it" seems to apply universally. However, the legality of software RE has proved rather murky, and the rule of thumb continues to be seeking permission ahead of time. While the court system continues to wrangle with fair use and RE, many organizations send mixed messages. Ultimately, many companies won't want to enforce RE laws potentially because it's simply bad business. Just as the appeal of open source software, people want to feel like co-creators of their media properties—companies that enable RE may thrive, while others may whither.

Can we balance protection with freedom? As shown above, what is legal may not necessarily be ethical and vice versa. Games provide an excellent means by which to explore these nebulous areas given the passion gamers have for the products. But, legal and ethical issues can be broached—the case studies above that illustrate clear situations in which industry, government, and academia actually support RE.

By *collaborating*, academics, industry, and end-users (and various combinations) seem to have resolved their legal and ethical differences. For example, MMOs that can adopt user-developed or third-party tools have documented success. In other cases, academic courses provide constructive outlets. Although it might seem too pat to say "hey, let's all work together," it does appear that collaboration in all of these areas has greatly reduced the controversial aspects of RE. We believe academia, especially with RE research/education, can offer a "truce" of sorts, providing a legal sandbox to satisfy many end-users while protecting industry IP. This aspect of RE already has widely adopted and approved support for hardware—we might do the same for software, as seen in the open source movement.

So, how do we answer our hypothetical question concerning Mitchell Ketchup's dilemma? We argue that Mitchell should understand the ethical dilemma, attempt to buy the missing hardware and software, reflect on the risks if he pursues "other means," and then seek ways to contribute to the evolving collaboration with all of the communities. It is not a perfect solution, but it is important to be aware of the potential ethics involved in reverse engineering–especially for the Mitchells of the world.

REFERENCES

Abondonware Ring. (2002). Abandonware: The official ring. Retrieved February 22, 2010, from http://www.abandonwarering.com

Aion Source. (2010). Spam Filter–Block Goldspam. Retrieved February 22, 2010, from http://www.aionsource.com/forum/aion-discussion/73017-spam-filter-block-goldspam.html.

Ali, M. R. (2005). Why teach reverse engineering? *ACM SIGSOFT Software Engineering Notes, 30*(4), 1–4. doi:10.1145/1082983.1083004

Apperley, T. (2007). Citizenship and consumption: Convergence culture, transmedia narratives and the digital divide. In *Proceedings of the 4th Australasian conference on Interactive entertainment*. New York: ACM.

Carless, S. (2004). *Gaming hacks: 100 industrial-strength tips & tools*. Boston: O'Reilly.

Chappel, L. (2008). The vintage game preservation society. *The Escapist*. Retrieved February 22, 2010, from http://www.escapistmagazine.com/articles/view/issues/issue_177/5502-The-Vintage-Game-Preservation-Society

Chilling Effects Clearinghouse. (2010). Chilling effects. Retrieved February 22, 2010, from http://www.chillingeffects.org

Citizen Science Projects. (2010). Citizen science projects. Retrieved February 22, 2010, from http://citizensci.com

Costa-Soria, C., Llavador, M., & Penadés, M. D. C. (2009). An approach for teaching software engineering through reverse engineering. In *European Association for Education in Electrical and Information Engineering Council Annual Conference Proceedings* (pp. 1-6). Valencia, Spain: European Association for Education in Electrical and Information Engineering Council.

Dempere, L. A. (2009). Reverse engineering as an educational tool for sustainability. In *International Symposium on Sustainable Systems and Technology* (pp. 1-3). Washington, DC: IEEE.

Deuze, M. (2009). Media industries, work and life. *European Journal of Communication, 24*(4), 467–480. doi:10.1177/0267323109345523

Doctorow, C. (2009). Homebrew banjo game-controller by RIT students. Retrieved February 22, 2010, from http://boingboing.net/2009/03/26/homebrew-banjo-gamec.html

Doctorow, C. (2009). *Makers*. New York: Tor Books.

ECE238Spr08. (2008). Assembly language programming. Retrieved February 22, 2010, from http://cratel.wichita.edu/cratel/ECE238Spr08

Electonic Freedom Foundation. (2010). Blizzard v. BNETD. Retrieved February 22, 2010, from http://www.eff.org/cases/blizzard-v-bnetd

Flowers, S. (2006). Harnessing the hackers: The emergence and exploitation of outlaw innovation. Retrieved February 22, 2010, from www.sussex.ac.uk/spru/documents/flowers-paper.pdf

Genov, E. (2008). Designing robust copy protection for software products. In *International Conference on Computer Systems and Technologies* (pp. IIIB 14.1-14.6). New York: ACM.

Gibson, J. P. (2009). Software use and plagiarism: A code of practice. In *Proceedings of the 14th annual ACM SIGCSE conference on Innovation and technology in computer science education* (pp. 55-99). New York: ACM.

Huang, A. (2003). *Hacking the Xbox: An introduction to reverse engineering*. San Francisco, CA: No Starch Press.

Humphreys, S. (2008). The challenges of intellectual property for users of social networking sites: A case study of *Ravelry*. In *Proceedings of the 12th international conference on Entertainment and media in the ubiquitous era* (pp. 125-130). New York: ACM.

Ibrahim, M. (2010). Analysis: Reverse engineering and you. *Gamasutra*. Retrieved February 22, 2010, from http://www.gamasutra.com/view/news/26845/Analysis_Reverse_Engineering_and_ You.php

IGDA. (2010). Game preservation SIG. Retrieved February 22, 2010, from http://wiki.igda.org/Game_Preservation_SIG.

Igoe, T., & O'Sullivan, D. (2004). *Physical computing: Sensing and controlling the physical world with computers*. Florence, KY: Course Technology PTR.

Instructables. (2009). Instructables. Retrieved February 22, 2010, from http://www.instructables.com

Jenkins, H. (2008). *Convergence culture: Where old and new media collide* (revised ed.). New York: NYU Press.

Jeppesen, L. B., & Molin, M. (2003). Consumers as co-developers: Learning and innovation outside the firm. *Technology Analysis and Strategic Management, 15*(3), 363–383. doi:10.1080/0953 7320310001601531

Koster, R. (2004). *Theory of fun for game design*. Scottsdale, AZ: Paraglyph Press.

McLoughlin, I. (2008). Secure embedded systems: The threat of reverse engineering. In *14th IEEE International Conference on Parallel and Distributed Systems* (pp. 729-736). Washington, DC: IEEE.

NCSoft Corporation. (2009). Aion user agreement. Retrieved February 22, 2010, from http://us.ncsoft.com/en/legal/user-agreements/aion-user-agreement.html

Nintendo. (2010). Legal information (copyrights, emulators, ROMs, etc.). Retrieved February 22, 2010, from http://www.nintendo.com/corp/legal.jsp

Preserving Virtual Worlds. (2010). Preserving virtual worlds. Retrieved February 22, 2010, from http://pvw.illinois.edu/pvw

Raja, V., & Fernandes, K. J. (2008). *Reverse engineering: An industrial perspective*. New York: Springer.

Schulz, C., & Wagner, S. (2008). Outlaw community innovations. Retrieved February 22, 2010, from http://epub.ub.uni-muenchen.de

Siy, S. (2008). MDY v. Blizzard: Cheating at WoW may be bad, but it's not copyright infringement. *Public Knowledge*. Retrieved February 22, 2010, from http://www.publicknowledge.org/node/1546

Stern, R. H. (2008). Quanta Computer Inc v LGE Electronics Inc: Comments on the reaffirmance of the exhaustion doctrine in the United States. Retrieved February 22, 2010, from http://docs.law.gwu.edu/facweb/claw/EIPR%27Quanta.pdf

U. S. Copyright Office. (2010). Copyright: Fair use. Retrieved February 22, 2010, from http://www.copyright.gov/fls/fl102.html

U. S. Patent and Trademark Office. (2010). Glossary. Retrieved February 22, 2010, from http://www.uspto.gov/main/glossary/index.html

Van Deusen, A., & Burd, E. (2005). Software reverse engineering. *Journal of Systems and Software, 77*(3), 209–211. doi:10.1016/j.jss.2004.03.031

Von Lohmann, F. (2007). You bought it, you own it: Quanta v. LG Electronics. *Electronic Freedom Foundation*. Retrieved February 22, 2010, from http://www.eff.org/deeplinks/2007/11/you-bought-it-you-own-it-part-iv-quanta-v-lg-electronics

World Emulators, R. O. M. (2009). Retrieved February 22, 2010, from http://www.rom-world.com/emulators.php

World Intellectual Property Organization. (2010). What is intellectual property? Retrieved February 22, 2010, from http://www.wipo.int/about-ip/en

Wu, C. (2008). Some disassembly required. *PRISM October 2008*. New York: ASEE. Retrieved February 22, 2010, from http://www.prism-magazine.org/oct08/tt_01.cfm

Zieminski, C. (2008). Game over for reverse engineering?: How the DMCA and contracts have affected innovation. *Journal of Technology Law & Policy*, 13(2), 289–339.

ADDITIONAL READING

Adams, E. A. (2010). *Fundamentals of game design* (2nd ed.). New York: New Riders.

Bidanda, B., & Bártolo, P. (in press). *Reverse engineering for medical, manufacturing and security applications*. New York: Springer.

Brown, G., Howe, T., Ihbe, M., Prakash, A., & Borders, K. (2008). Social networks and context-aware spam. In *Proceedings of the 2008 ACM conference on Computer supported cooperative work* (pp. 403-412). New York: ACM.

Chikofsky, E. J., & Cross, J. H. II. (1990). Reverse engineering and design recovery: A taxonomy. *Software*, 7(1), 13–17. doi:10.1109/52.43044

Conti, G. (2005, March). Why computer scientists should attend hacker conferences. *Communications of the ACM*, 48(3), 23–24. doi:10.1145/1047671.1047694

Cowley, B., Charles, D., Black, M., & Hickey, R. (2008). Toward and understanding of flow in video games. *ACM Computers in Entertainment*, 6(20).

Cummings, A. H. (2007). The evolution of game controllers and control schemes and their effect on their games. In *The 17th Annual University of Southhampton Multimedia Systems Conference*. Retrieved February 22, 2010, from http://users.ecs.soton.ac.uk/ahc08r/mms.pdf

Eilam, E. (2005). *Reversing: Secrets of reverse engineering*. New York: Wiley.

Erikson, J. (2008). *Hacking: The art of exploitation* (2nd ed.). San Francisco, CA: No Starch Press.

Favre, L. (2010). *Model driven architecture for reverse engineering technologies: Strategic directions and system evolution*. Hershey, PA: Engineering Science Reference.

Hardnett, C. R. (2008). Gaming for middle school students: Building virtual worlds. In *Proceedings of the 3rd international conference on Game development in computer science education* (pp. 21-25). New York: ACM.

Ingle, K. A. (1994). *Reverse engineering*. New York: McGraw-Hill Professional Publishing.

Jenkins, H. (2009). *Confronting the challenges of participatory culture: Media education for the 21st Century (John D. and Catherine T. MacArthur Foundation Reports on Digital Media and Learning)*. Boston: The MIT Press.

Kapp, K. M. (2007). *Gadgets, games, and gizmos for learning: Tools and techniques for transferring know-how from boomers to gamers*. San Francisco, CA: Wiley.

Kirkpatrick, G. (2009). Controller, hand, screen: Aesthetic form in the computer game. *Games and Culture*, 4(2), 127–143. doi:10.1177/1555412008325484

Lyons, C. (2010). Video games: Evolving from a simple pastime to one of the most influential industries in the world. *Undergraduate Research Journal at UCCS*, 3(1), 10–17.

McJohn, S. M., & Davis, M. H. (2007). *Intellectual property: Examples & explanations* (3rd ed.). Amsterdam, Netherlands: Wolters Kluwer Law & Business.

Miller, A. R. (2007). *Intellectual property—Patents, trademarks and copyright in a nutshell* (4th ed.). New York: Thomson West.

Miller, F. P., Vandome, A. F., & McBrewster, J. (2009). *Abandonware: Computer software, copyright, office suite, public domain, list of commercial video games released as freeware, orphan works*. Beau Bassin, Mauritius: Alphascript Publishing.

Miller, F. P., Vandome, A. F., & McBrewster, J. (2009). *First-sale doctrine: Copyright, Supreme Court of the United States, Copyright Act of 1976, copyright infringement, exhaustion doctrine, restrictive covenant, digital rights management*. Beau Bassin, Mauritius: Alphascript Publishing.

Parks, B. (2005). *Makers: All kinds of people making amazing things in garages, basements, and backyards*. Boston: O'Reilly.

Platt, C. (2009). *Make: Electronics: learning by discovery*. Boston: O'Reilly.

Raymond, E. S. (2001). *The cathedral & the bazaar: Musings on Linux and open source by an accidental revolutionary*. Boston: O'Reilly Media.

Sock Master's Game Console Controller Family Tree. (2010). Retrieved February, 22, 2010, from http://www.axess.com/twilight/console

Steinkuehler, C., & Chmiel, M. (2006). Fostering scientific habits of mind in the context of online play. In *Proceedings of the 7th international conference on learning sciences* (pp. 723-729). New York: ACM.

Tilley, S. R., Muller, H. A., Storey, M.-A., Wong, K., Jhanke, J. H., & Smith, D. B. (2000). Reverse engineering: A roadmap. In Finkelstein, A. (Ed.), *The future of software engineering*. New York: ACM.

Webb, S. D., & Soh, S. (2007). Cheating in networked computer games—a review. In *Proceedings of the 2nd international conference on digital interactive media in entertainment and arts* (pp. 105-112). New York: ACM.

Weber, S. (2005). *The success of open source*. Boston: Harvard University Press.

Yang, J., & Hu, G. (2009). A physics simulation engine for modeling autonomous motion through reverse engineering of soda constructor. In *IEEE/ACS International Conference on Computer Systems and Applications* (pp. 287-292). Washington, DC: IEEE.

Chapter 9
Critical Gameplay:
Design Techniques and Case Studies

Lindsay Grace
Miami University, USA

ABSTRACT

This chapter introduces critical gameplay design as a technique for creating digital games that offer alternative play. Critical gameplay provides the opportunity to explore game ethics through the way games are designed to be played. Since game designers outline the rules of play, game designs outline designer's definitions of what is ethical and important. Taking the notion that design is a reflection of the designer's values, this chapter outlines methodologies for exposing the intrinsic values in play and creating gameplay models from alternative ethics and values. The chapter concludes with examples of critical gameplay games that have been demonstrated to international audience.

INTRODUCTION

In his keynote to the participants of the International Game Developer's Association's (IGDA) Global 2010 Game Jam, Ste Curran spoke of the wilderness outside the space of traditional game design. He claims in his address that "gaming is this giant creative space, surrounded by a frontier, and beyond that frontier there are so many countries left to explore" (Curran, 2010). This chapter suggests outlines one approach to exploring that frontier, where many game designers see an ever

more rich set of possibilities. It is the space of undiscovered processes, or game play mechanics beyond our dreams. It is also the space of alternate ethics and morality. We are just beginning to map the discipline of software studies; likewise, game design is only starting to explore the ways in which game mechanics are in themselves ethical prescriptions.

One need only consider the conventional models of play to identify the edge of this frontier. It can be found in the prevalence of absolute assumptions in game design. Some examples include the following: collection of objects is good, elimination of obstacles is the best way to

DOI: 10.4018/978-1-60960-120-1.ch009

handle them, and that tools always offer benefits to us, never complicating our relationship with the challenges we face. This "wilderness" is also expressed in the host of assumptions we make and accept about the ways games are to be played and the expectations that enshroud them.

Critical gameplay is the study and production of computer and video games that seek to explore alternative ways to play. These play models are derived from critical reflection on the standards of gameplay and the culture that exists around them. As a three-step process, critical gameplay is created by observing a set of standard assumptions, deconstructing the assumptions in that standard, and reorienting that set of assumptions through the production of an alternate model of play.

By introduction the concept of critical gameplay design, this chapter will explore and enhance opportunities for critical evaluation of conventional game mechanics to create a clearer vision of the contours and boundaries of game design.

Such study is not part of the established practice of understanding how shooting game characters may or may not encourage violent behavior (Kutner & Olson, 2008), for example. It is not merely about understanding game scenarios and identifying their ethical underpinnings. It is more critical and more philosophical. It is no longer enough to ask about whether or not games train us into new patterns (Squire, 2003). Instead, this new area of study, calls for the inverse. It addresses questions about the rules in games. These questions may be about how games reinforce specific rationales or how designs bias toward specific ethics.

The proposed method for exploration of games delivers the potential to offer different paradigms for both the way we design game and the way we play them. Discovering alternative ways to play offers benefits in games for entertainment, education, and persuasion. The application of this methodology to digital game technology offers benefits to education, business, and societal study.

Just as explorers benefited from accepting that the world is not flat, game design can benefit from

the understanding and acceptance that games are not merely a reflection of social values, but they actually prescribe models of ethics (Barr, Noble, & Biddle, 2007). These ethics are transmitted more deeply than through the superficial monologues of non-player characters, or in the story-driven decisions a player makes. They are an integral part of the gameplay, surfacing in the actually mechanics of play. Yet, the evaluation and creation of alternate game mechanics still remains an unchartered wilderness.

BACKGROUND

Any understanding of the integration and necessity for play in society typically begins with a reference to J. Huzinga's *Homo Ludens* (1955). Much like the requisite attract screen of an arcade game, or a magic potion in a role-playing game, Huizinga's text serves as a lure. It brings the uninitiated into an academic understanding of games and society and the nearly omnipotent and certainly pervasive power of play.

Like good game design, this writing will not disappoint by glossing over this seminal text, but like good game design, its purpose is not to replay what has already been experienced. Instead, consider Huizinga as a foundational prerequisite. Many of the phrases and brilliant quotes of the text are unlike the focus of this chapter, familiar and often reproduced. Just as a player assumes multiple lives or the value of manna, you as reader can begin reading under the specter of *Homo Ludens*. But like the alternative play this chapter champions, a healthy critical distance to the often-referenced text will afford new potential. For the reader Huzinga exists as traditional game design, and this chapter seeks to address the non-traditional.

Consider only one small quote from Huzinga's book, "play creates order, is order. Play demands order absolute and supreme" (1955). If play is order, than an analysis of the unexplored spaces in play could begin with the fundamental question, what order is being designed? If play demands order absolute and supreme, how does the play we design demand players' adherence to its order? Does it reapply its rules via persistence, simply encouraging players to learn recitations of the same play over and over? Does it declare that there is but one way to play, when it demands order absolute and supreme? Does it judge or dismiss players who fail to play by its order? Are its demands polemical, propagandist, or even self-serving? Most importantly, what other order exists outside play's order?

Whereas a ball and all derivations of play involving the ball are restricted by the properties of the ball, a ball in a digital game world enjoys very few restrictions. The virtual world of a computer game, for example, need not adhere to real world physics, finite amount or fixed states. Instead computer and video game play, herein referred to as digital games, is very much limited by the properties of the cultural and development environment in which their play is constructed. Why, for example, do so many game engines employ object collision as an important basis for game implementation? What types of digital games could be created if design divorced itself from the standard object-oriented metaphors of development? This is where critical questions meet critical design to create critical gameplay.

The first step in critical gameplay design is observation. These observations are lead by asking critical questions. Critical questions are not difficult to formulate. They are constructed by looking past assumption toward the logical trajectory of the game as a medium. They begin by asking how games function. What types of order are employed or even enforced? What precipitates from such inquiry is a list of very broad questions that include:

- What happens if the game experience is shifted from from interactive entertainment to interactive learning experience?

- What if one basic assumption of the logical relationship of game elements is removed?
- How can the existing dynamics be used to create a very different experience?
- Are specific perspectives being left out of the roles designed into games?

The questions can precipitate from a systematic analysis of a single game and this rule or from patterns witness in a collection of games.

Second, these questions are used to deconstruct assumptions about play. If, for example, we consider removing score as an assumed element of a game, new questions arise. The first questions might be how can progress be communicated without score or how can score be made less numerical? Those are valid questions, but they are not deconstructive nor are they very critical. Instead, critical questions might read:

- If score indicates progress, is communicating progress essential to digital gameplay?
- What is the antithesis of score and does that add value to the play experience?

Not every question should yield an answer. Instead they should yield more questions that encourage exploration towards spaces that are unfamiliar.

The third step is to convert those critical questions into products that illustrate, answer, or further interrogate those same critical questions. This is the domain of critical design. Practiced most notably at the Royal College of Art, its first explorers are the design duo Dunne and Raby. Their products are, in their own declaration, anti-affirmative design. In their terms, affirmative design is the trajectory to which most design subscribes. It is an affirmation, acceptance, and furtherance of existing design models. It is, as Tim Brown describes in his TED Talk on the past trends of design: "what passed for design wasn't all that important—making things more attractive, making them a bit easier to use, making them more marketable … and not having much of an impact."

The fundamental critique of affirmative design is that it simply fails to ask important social questions. It fails to ask questions about the ethics of design practices and designed products. It fails to reevaluate its own practices. Instead, it trudges forward without critical reflection. Critical design is not concerned with trudging forward; it is only concerned with producing that which poses critical questions. This is evident in Dunne and Raby's *Huggable Atomic Mushroom Cloud*, an ironic object of comfort (Dunne & Raby, Projects, 2005). Their collectible *Evidence Dolls*, designed as a DNA hope chest for the modern young woman (Dunne & Raby, Projects, 2005). These objects serve as artifacts of critical questions about social interactions. A variety of other designer's work that pursues similarly critical design is outlined in their book, *Design Noir: The Secret Life of Electronic Objects* (Dunne & Raby, Design noir: the secret life of electronic objects, 2001). Importantly, it should be understood that these designs are most engaging in their ability to raise ethical intellectual questions rather than their ability to raise profits.

An earlier incarnation of critical design concerned itself with the process of map making. Maps, in themselves have a remarkable effect on perspective and social relationships. The mapping process of critical cartographers involved exposing the inadequacies of conventional maps. Many of these maps sought to expose the biases in popular mapping conventions. A critical cartograph might be as simple as choosing which continent to center in a world map or as complicated as resolving the many ways to accurately project the mathematics of a round world in flat, 2D space. The most controversial of these is the Peters Projection World Map which from its mathematic basis, claims area accuracy (Crampton, 1994). The more commonly used, Mercator projection map employs a process which inflates specific regions, depicting, for example, Greenland as larger than Africa, when in reality Africa is much larger than Greenland.

This balance of value (fidelity to the shape of the earth versus fidelity to land mass size) voices itself in two different depictions of the same subject.

In terms of game design, critical cartography demonstrates how slight changes in a designer's value system *project* themselves into finished products. By asking critical questions about the ethical fidelity of a land mass agnostic design, a designer was able to incite awareness. By making the alternate projection map, the designer demonstrated inadequacy. Consider how many types of agnosticisms may exist in games. What perspectives have been left out of game playing experiences, for example? What do those omissions indicate about the order inherent in the design of play in digital games?

This combination of critical question-asking and critical design practices creates critical gameplay. Games designed through critical gameplay techniques are not a panacea for ethical dilemmas, unsolved educational challenges or perfect designs. Just as the Peter's projection met with much negative critique, critical gameplay games ask for the same critical evaluation they apply to more traditional games.

The remainder of this chapter seeks to illuminate a more detailed process for designing critical gameplay games, providing examples of critical gameplay games, and offering some demonstration of its potential in practice.

DESIGNING CRITICAL GAMEPLAY: OVERVIEW

In teaching game design I have routinely heard students throw up their arms in frustration and say, we can't do anything new, it's all been done before. My typical response reminds them of the musical composer, who knowing that all the notes and chords exist, accepts the responsibility of finding new combinations of those notes to make new music. Simply, if the notes have already been played, then the designer's responsibility is to find new arrangements.

This analogy is somewhat true, but it ignores two fundamental truths. First it assumes that the notes we have defined are the only ones. Musical scholars would note that while there is a general range of frequencies the human ear can hear, all of these pitches are not defined by the limited notes and chords of the western musical tradition. Instead, a C-sharp or B-flat is a convention in a standard prescription of music composition.

For game design, there are these same silos. There is the shoot mechanic, there is the take mechanic. There is a fairly long list of game interactions that fit somewhat neatly into a canon. These are the conventional game mechanics, which like a 15th century harpsichord are played either masterfully or poorly. There are games that ask us to shoot beautifully and others that are horrible at it. But that range of digital game mechanics is fundamentally limited. It is likely a combination of historical successes and translating conventional game board mechanics. This canon is largely packed with game verbs. Our verbs are move, take, leave, jump, etc. These are not far from the same verbs we have been using since text adventures asked us to articulate those verbs in monochromatic text.

As affirmative design suggests, the simplest innovation in gameplay mechanics is to use that packed canon of game verbs, spilling them into game environments and listing it as an improvement. This approach subscribes to what is marketed, that it is more enjoyable to the player to be given more verbs and more nouns with which to use those verbs. Shoot plasma cannon, shoot frag grenade, shoot m16. Those same marketers would claim a better game is a game with more verbs, not necessarily new ones. To return to the music analogy, this is as comical as implying that more notes make a better song. What Chris Crawford wrote in 1982 hold true today, "A very common mistake many designers make is to pile too many game features onto the game structure" (Crawford).

Players are routinely marketed an increase in game verbs as an improvement to a game. In this thinking, a game design that not only lets you drive and turn a car is less fun than one that lets you skid, crash, jump, etc. Yet, game critics would agree that plenty of games that have increased their verb count, have not increased the enjoyment of their experience. Driv3r, for example, added both swimming and jumping to an already successful franchise with proven game verbs, yet reviews did not praise these additions as improvements to the experience (Atari, 2004).

The second weakness in the musical note analogy of game design is that it fails to look critically at what it means to compose play. It does not ask why or how, it only takes what is convention and seeks to compose music from that convention. It accepts good as *good*, and fails to update its perspective on convention. Good music in 1962 is not necessarily good music in 1992, nor is it good **to** every population or for every population. It fails to ask if there are other ways to compose or other standards for playing. In musical terms, the affirmative design standard leaves little room for jazz improvisation, heavy metal performance, DJ samples, or chip tunes because those musical styles do not fit into the criteria for classically good work.

This second weakness supports the first. If there are no critical questions remaining about what is good, then all that's left is more of the same goodness. Like a conservative cultural loop, failing to ask critical questions about design results in a deep, but not necessarily diverse collection of artifacts. If we do not consistently interrogate the foundation elements, musical note systems, we do not open opportunities for music that expresses itself using previously undefined notes. If we do not look critically at the composition systems, we miss the opportunity to compose and play what the existing system does not support. Historically, this type of critical reflection has yielded innovations in seemingly stagnant creative endeavors. It has lead to the growth of world music, the cross-pollination of design, science and art practices. It can be argued that electronic music is the result of adopting alternative composition and performance systems for example.

If you ask critical questions about the dominant game verbs in game design, you begin to see patterns in ethics and values. Adapting the play centric techniques of Tracy Fullerton (2008), you begin to also unearth the primary perspective of gameplay. It is intrinsically player focused. The verbs in games are primarily focus on the player as a singular, world-centric concept. Consider the mechanics of most games. The player dies, the world ends. Even in MMORPG or other play communities, the world ends not when one player leaves it, but when all (or all but one) leaves it. This is not fundamentally true in the world in which we live, but the ethic certainly emphasizes one clear set of values. The player is the center of the world.

Consider how few games ever retreat from this fundamental value. In discussing this observation of games, you will even find that some consider it an unfair criticism. The claim reads that as a person in the world, I, the player, have always understood the world from my own perspective and through my own senses. The world is necessarily player-centric, because we are simulating the universal experience of being. If this is an accurate representation, then why do real people do anything for subsequent generations? Why do people bother thinking about what happens when you die? Aren't there cultures that understand the world beyond a simple one-time around life-death cycle? This particular argument for player centric design is one that lacks critical reflection. It is short answer, to a complicated question.

Now consider that for years, the only element of change in a game world was the player. The player elicited change, to which the world responded. Non-player characters respond to players, while two players in competition respond to each other.

Historically, there had been no game before the player and no game after the player. In terms of critical mapmaking, the player's worldview is centered on one thing, themselves. What are the ethical ramifications of a self centered world? Is there but one good, one goal, or one need?

Consider the relative desert of games that encourage altruism. Consider how few historical games ask the player to move the play lens from their play perspective to another's. Save for preserving the player's management of the world, perspective rarely shifts. Now consider how many hours under that particular perspective a game is played. Rarely do you find a game which asks the player to balance two opposing goals at the cost of reaching either. Few digital games ask the player to be arbitrator, for example.

These observations on digital game interactions are enormous, integral and often difficult to decant from the many other game play mechanics piled on top of them to make a complete game. But, critical question asking at least offers some awareness and awareness can potentially birth new perspectives.

THE CRITICAL GAMEPLAY QUESTIONS

What are the critical questions that produce critical gameplay games? They are questions born from the social sciences and art. They begin by asking about the standards, and then moving toward another convention. Just as a ship follows the coast to chart its beaches, the critical questions arise from following the line of logic that defined the convention.

Consider the collect mechanic. As a convention it has been a part of computer and video gameplay for years. The obvious goal, as it goes, is to collect more of whatever you seek. The more coins, gold rings, manna, health, and energy you collect, the better. Yet, a simple extraction of logic asks some very important critical questions. Logically, how does that ethic translate? Is perpetual, unbounded desire for more a positive ethic? In contemporary parlance, some people suggest that it should instead be a *sustainable* desire. It is not reasonable to allow your desire for energy to exceed the resources that are available. In some cultures, we consider that greed, an ethically corrupt basis for motivation.

If it is not greed, we can ask the practical questions. Are there situations under which collecting more is a problem? Certainly, collecting more guilt, more nightmares, more sadness are all bad things in many western cultures. In these cases, we may seek a way to allow them to dissipate into the ether of everyday living. Why then, have we not seen a preponderance of leaving games? Where is the collection of reverse *Pac-man* games, for example, games where we must leave our guilt behind, lest the ghosts of our past catch up with us and ultimately destroy us. Where are the games where we are unburdened by our un-collecting?

Let us return to the practicalities of everyday living and the ethics of greed. In the most basic moral tales of the western storytelling tradition, the character whose collecting exceeds their capacity ends their story in pain or loss. It is as short as the child who ate so much they were made sick, or the king who exercised too much authority on their subjects and lost their kingdom via tyranny. In these cases, there is an ethical limit. There is a sense of cultural value, where it is fine to collect, until you have collected too much. In games, the most conventional mechanic is to simply prevent the player from collecting any more. There is no substantial cost in over collecting, only in failing to have the right collection at the right time.

It may also be that we must ask questions beyond our local culture and towards our larger social culture. In a capitalist society, is it simply that collecting makes the most immediate sense to us? Is it that we are simply using the intrinsic understanding that having more is good (as in wealth) to inform the gameplay experience? If so, why don't we ask the obvious questions about other

cultures? Why don't we ask about the Buddhist ethic of detachment, in its many forms?

The critical questions precipitate from examined explorations into what we understand to be a convention. As an explorer who sees two borders, but seeks to define the space between them, critical questions come from identifying that there is a space that needs to be defined. This definition through exploration serves the minimum benefit of orientation. It helps to locate game designs in a much larger societal landscape.

IDENTIFYING THE INVISIBLE MECHANICS: PLAYER PERSPECTIVE

The first step in understanding the design of critical gameplay is in identifying the seemingly invisible mechanics. The spaces that game design ignores are often revealed through analogy, considered thought, or versions of cultural anthropology. Each moment of discovery, as expressed through the production of a game, or through the critique of games, demarcates a point in the logical space in game design.

To understand the process of revealing a seemingly invisible mechanic, trace the intellectual deconstruction and exploration of player-centric design that follows. It is not an attack on player-centric design, as critical design does not attach affirmative design. It is provided only as a demonstration of revealing ethical bias in mechanics.

Player-centric design is so commonly assumed and taught in game design, that it becomes an invisible assumption. It is so ingrained that it ceases to be ethical and instead becomes factual. For some designers, it is no longer a choice in game play design; it is the only way to design games. Even in the grandest plan for new gameplay, many designers forget how many mechanics remain invisible to them in the design of a game.

Consider that as far as player-centric designs go, games in the realm of Sid Meier's *Civilization*,

Spore and *The Sims* succeed in moving away from player centric gameplay, toward a community centric design. They are games whose ethical decisions are based not solely on the needs of the player, as the player does not necessarily have a single avatar or agent to manage. They focus instead on larger social need. The needs of several Sims must be balanced, and those Sims may be active even if they are not in worldview. The player's needs are given to them, constantly changing, and in some ways out of their control. These are not games about saving princesses, destroying enemies, or annihilating alternate races. Instead they are about maintaining a local culture. These games are based more on the preservation of local community than the Machiavelli's self-preservation. They are player-centric, but they have at least expanded the sense of player. If many games ask the player to manage the self-centered needs of a single character, these other games more closely echo the experience of a parent, and incorporate the challenge of managing your child's needs.

Now consider a game in which the player is a secondary role. Just as we consider the actors in a theatrical production at play, so too games could employ the same complexity of play structures and roles. Game designs can move from player-centric, to supporting-role centric. This role does exist for game players in the self-constructed scenarios of cooperative missions and campaigns, as players organize themselves into self-sacrificing groups or assist in maneuvers such as cover fire or flanking. Yet, very few games employ such a mechanic as the central goal in a game. A game of assistance or supporting role, although quite logical, is quite rare. Instead, assistance more often takes the perspective of player centric address, posting the player as the last of a race, the only one capable of reversing the tide, or other situations in which a seemingly supporting role is converted to a key role.

Even in the very easy conversion of team sports, such as football or baseball, there is a bias towards player-centric design in digital games.

Many digital version of American football have the player switch roles in the middle of a play session, taking the responsibilities of coach, blocker, and quarterback. In soccer, as the ball is passed, the player takes control of the possessing non-player character. Even in situations where there is a clear standard for non-player centric design, the simulation is steered player-centric design. To return to the theater reference, what was once an ensemble performance is converted to a one-performer show.

By following similar intellectual paths, it is conceivable to map the ethics of existing and potential games. The following section lists the standard means for constructing conceptual maps of gameplay mechanics and their underlying values. These approaches include identifying the invisible values in games, ethics creep in game design, and omissions by the game designer. These approaches are not set forth as prescription for improving play as much as they are offered to encourage diversifying play and critical reflection.

IDENTIFYING THE INVISIBLE VALUES

Just as some mechanics may not be immediately apparent to players or designers, their requisite ethics remain under the surface. There remains a collection of values that are as obscured as the mechanic to which they are attached. Consider simply the ethic attached to the playground game, *King of the Mountain*. Children push and shove each other to maintain their position at the top of a hill or snow mound. The mechanic is simple, do anything that you are capable of without letting anyone else stay or arrive at the top. The most successful player understands their own limitations and strengths and how to exploit the weakness of others. The game is played with one eye on the upper limit of what is allowed. A hard push down the hill is okay, a direct punch might get you in trouble with teachers.

The game would be played very differently if your goal was to get someone else to the top of the mountain. Instead of worrying about how you can maneuver yourself, you are looking for ways to maneuver the other person's chances of success. It is not simply a point of support, but you must change your entire goal orientation. You are not worried about ever achieving dominance, instead you accept that you will never be *King of the Mountain*, and instead seek to help someone who has the chance to keep it. The ethic transitions from player centered goals, to a supporting role, with very little change in the game experience.

The more common version of *King of the Mountain* employs what some would consider a rat-race ethic. It is an all-out volley for power, for which there is but one winner. The values are clear. The second version maintains a similar set of values, but it relocates the locus of power. In the second version, the locus of power is moved to those who help maintain the position of power. The role of the person at the top diminishes, as their potential is limited like the king in *Chess*. They are central to the goal, but an ancillary means to accomplishing the goal. The *King of the Mountain* is preserved, but their abilities are far more limited than those actors that support them.

Now consider that the playground version of *King of the Mountain* is quite mutable. Children can adapt the game and make new rules, alliances, and define the order. Yet, within the confines of many digital games, play is not mutable. The player cannot change their abilities, save for systems that allow players to elect for additional challenge by limiting abilities or making the player more vulnerable. The values in games remain, and as is fundamental to most digital games, there is a *play to stay* system. If the player does not play as directed, the game typically quits, booting the player out of the experience until they choose to follow the rules. Change direction in a racing game, and you will be realigned. Get off the track and you will be brought back to the track. Choose to be a pacifist in a first person shooter, and your

game won't last long. Digital games rarely afford for alternate ways to play them. Even the best sandbox games impose rules which realign play toward the order prescribed by the game. Shoot too many people in a *Grand Theft Auto* game, and the police will chase you (Rockstar North, 2002).

Now consider that these ethics are enforced, through this play to stay standard. This quality is in itself a game mechanic. It is a way in which goals are not only accomplished in the game, they are enforced. Run off the track and the computer will return you to the track so that you can pursue the only true goal of any value, crossing the finish line. Combine that basic mechanic with any other commonly used mechanics and you begin to identify an enforced set of ethics. Collect a specific number of items to continue to the next level or earn extra playtime. Destroy a prescribed number of threats to continue play. These things are so fundamental to game play in digital spaces that they are ultimately invisible.

More interestingly, a prerequisite to game design is game playing. What is produced is informed by what was experienced, and ultimately what was accepted. Being subjected to the pay to stay experience is so integral that few look critically at reversing it. What results is a kind of ethic-value creep, where foundational values are merely expanded into more complicated systems, instead of being reevaluated and reconstructed.

IDENTIFYING ETHICS CREEP

As mentioned, ethics creep is the common situation under which a foundation set of values inhering in games is affirmed and expanded into more complicated systems of value. However, in the expansion of a fundamental ethic, which seeps into other cultures consuming the games we produce, we are in fact encouraging them toward that ethic. In analogy, we, as game designers are not seeking to assimilate the culture of that which we explore, we merely ask them to assimilate our culture. In exploration terms, we as designers are in a kind of manifest destiny. We are only seeking to see our artifacts abound, instead of asking about the native artifacts to which we may not be accustomed.

To understand these cultural impositions, consider the experience of a new game player. New game players are often shamed for not understanding the conventions of a game. They might not understand that moving an avatar onto something collects it, for example. But it is important to be critical of the gameplay mechanic itself. Why does moving on to something collect it? Why does it not destroy it, as in walking on a piece of food destroys its value. Why does walking on something not bury it or discard it?

The un-initiated player is a wonderful resource for identifying ethics creep. Those players who are unfamiliar with the standards of gameplay, although often dismissed, are sometimes touchstones for the transparent values in games. They can serve as un-indoctrinated critics. If we simply fail to be critical of our conventional gameplay mechanics, we fail to discover the potential in the ignored. This failure is a weakness, as it encourages us to accept things that only pollute our designs. The acceptance of a few standard sets of gameplay mechanics offers the benefits of clarity, at the cost of variety. It is true that if there is one set of values and one path toward those values, then the world is simpler, but it is clearly less rich. More important to the task of design, it lacks variety in solutions.

IDENTIFYING OMISSIONS

In her 2005 review of key questions in games and ethics, Mia Consalvo mentions that there are two groups who ask the question, is this a good game or bad game (2005). She claims there are merely game players and game critics. This is no longer true. The third and exceptionally important group to ask this question is the game designer. The game designer is either critic and player, or neither. The

game designer makes the decisions of both critic and player, but in the end, it is their decisions, which produce what the former groups evaluate.

This oversight is not from an unscholarly failure to understand the entirety of the problem but from a society-wide dismissal of the designer as source of ethic. Those who analyze games sometimes fail to critically analyze the fundamental source in the way we routinely analyze literature or film. Perhaps it is because games study is a relatively new media field or because games have had such a substantially clear relationship to commercial industries. Games are full of assumptions and full of omissions as much as they are full of presumptions and additions. Simply, it is important to remember that game designers are not just creating experiences; they are also removing certain experiences from the games we play.

One part of the design of critical gameplay games is to highlight those removed experiences to initiate a dialogue about why they simply don't exist. It is not enough to say that these types of gameplay are clearly positive or negative, it is more critical to ask why they have been omitted. While it is not the role of critical gameplay games to answer these questions, it is their responsibility to expose these alter-play experiences in an effort to offer more material to critique. In essence, critical gameplay games at least map the unexplored places, allowing game players and game critics to figure out whether or not they want to experience what had previously been ignored.

For this reason it is important to also discuss games created under a critical gameplay design process. The following section outlines a few of these games.

CRITICAL GAMEPLAY GAMES

In my first explorations into critical gameplay, I picked a few of the most common gameplay mechanics. I put these in a list and tried to address them very singularly. The first of these critical gameplay prototype games sought to expose the possibility, in the same way that an explorer might seek to prove an unchartered island's existence. There are still whole continents of game design to be discovered and explored.

I can deconstruct a few of these games, their design process, and their goals to outline the topography of critical gameplay. The following sections outline a few critical gameplay games. These games have been displayed internationally at the ACM Conference on Human Factors in Computing Systems, the International Digital Media and Art Association's Annual conference, the International Conference on Advances in Computer Entertainment Technology, the Annual Symposium of the Special Commission of Games and Digital Entertainment in Brazil, and in a solo exhibition named Critical Gameplay in Chicago, Illinois, USA. Documentation for each game is available at CriticalGameplay.com.

CRITICAL GAMEPLAY QUESTION: STEREOTYPE BY APPEARANCE

Stereotype is an ethical dilemma. It is sometimes an effective way to protect ourselves, as in all snakes are dangerous. Or it is a world limiting experience, as in the many beautiful, innocuous creatures seem we avoid because they look like snakes. Games are full of stereotypes. Perhaps as a remnant of once simple computer systems, games often rely on clearly defined, non-ambiguous types. In the oldest games, a non-player character might be a distinguished by color or shape. In modern games, the characters are more richly illustrated, even if their relationship to the player character is not. In general, a character's role is either enemy or not, and more often than not, it is distinguished by their appearance.

In its simplest dichotomy, a game character can be considered either a threat or a non-threat. As such, Black/White seeks to frustrate that distinction. First, the game does not allow the player to distinguish threats and non-threats by basic appearance. In the game, every character looks the same. The player character, non-player character threats and player character non-threats all share the same animation and images. In the game, the player's goal is conventional, move from one side of a level to the next avoiding or squashing threats. If the player squashes a non-threat, they are forced to restart the level. The player must balance their judgment to successfully traverse the level. The challenge arises in that the gameplay does not rely on the conventional binary cue of threats having one appearance, and non-threats having another. Instead of judging threats and non-threats by appearance, they must be judged by behavior. Threats act aggressively, lurching at the player as they approach. Non-threats, act passively, smiling as they pass the player. If the player makes contact with a threat, they die and must restart the level. If the player makes contact with a non-threat, nothing changes. The game seeks to explore alter-stereotype mechanics. The new value focus is designed to emphasize behavior over appearance.

To further emphasize the theme of its critique, the game is constructed in binary sets, with two levels, two types of characters, each animated in two frames, within two colors. There are several layers of binary aesthetic and technical implementation decisions.

CRITICAL GAMEPLAY QUESTION: THE COST OF SUBSCRIBING TO CHARACTER FICTIONS

When designing narratives for digital game experiences it is common to incorporate back-story into the non-player characters. This approach is expected to enrich the experience by making the fiction of the game world more believable. In a first person shooter, for example, the player is supposed to believe in the lives of their computer-controlled squad-mates or the enemies that they destroy. The critical question is why, when we pull the trigger, does that life end without circumstance and without remorse? If that fiction is so important, why not remind us of it?

Bang! is a critical gameplay game designed around this reflection. It provides the player with a traditional first person shooter situation. Explosions resound as the force shakes the player. Soldiers creep through the woods, viewed through the simulated night vision goggles of the player-soldier. When the player successfully shoots a skulking soldier, the game audio is silenced. The 3D graphics cut to black. A slow running, photographic slideshow of the victim's life plays in reverse. The player watches the victim with their friends, their wedding, their first kiss, their childhood birthday parties, and their baby pictures. The goal is an unnerving reminder of the duplicity of value. The critical observation is that it is both important to believe the character fiction and dismiss it.

CRITICAL GAMEPLAY QUESTION: THE DRAWBACKS TO COLLECTING

Levity is one the simplest Critical Gameplay games. Responding to the previously discussed mechanic of collecting, *Levity* reverses the mechanic. The player is afforded the ability to run and jump to traverse the platform-scrolling level. In their movement across the level, they are presented with rotating gold coins. If they collect the gold coins, their movements are slowed and their ability to jump lessons. Each coin they collect retards their movement, and lowers the height of their jump. In its first level, the player must figure out a way to avoid collecting anything in order to successfully traverse the level.

In subsequent levels, the player has the ability to give away what they've collected to regain some of their abilities. They can do so by donating their collected items to non-player characters in the level. These non-player characters jump at the

coins, but are unable to reach them. Their jumping interferes with the player's ability to jump, so it is to the player's advantage to placate the non-player characters by giving them anything they have collected. The primary concept behind the games is that the things the players collect weigh them down. Like many Critical Gameplay games, it is a prototype of teaching an alternate value system through the mechanics of gameplay. It asks the basic question, what if the habit of collecting was discouraged? What if players were encouraged to enjoy the freedom of lack?

CRITICAL GAMEPLAY QUESTION: CAN NON-ACTION BE ENGAGING

Wait is a response to the dominant belief that good game play comes from acting on a world. One of the most commonly exhibited games in the Critical Gameplay collection, Wait is designed to discourage the player from acting on the world. It entices the player with an animated grassy field with stone hills in the distance. The grass moves slowly in the wind, as the sounds of a forest fade into audibility. While the player peers into the field, elements of a forest fade into view. The trees reveal themselves, flying creatures begin to float between the trees, flowers show their blooms, and more. Yet as the player moves toward the scene, the elements fade back away.

Wait employs a game mechanic based on a rarely used game verb, waiting. The player's action is to wait and observe. To return to more typical expectations of a game the experience affords a scoring system. If a new object appears in the viewing frustum of the player, then they receive points for their observation. The points are awarded as a distinct tone upon each period of new observation. Likewise, if the player waits too long, the game falls back on the pay-to-stay mechanic by fading the entire world out of view and presenting the player with their final score. The idea is to balance observation with movement. It functions metaphorically as an experience in life philosophy. Instead of championing an end-goal oriented race through experience, it emphasizes the worth in balancing experience with careful reflection. It is designed as a reminder of the play present in a walk through the forest.

OTHER CRITICAL GAMEPLAY GAMES

The aforementioned list is not the only set of critical gameplay games. Those games were merely an early collection of games to be exhibited as critical gameplay. One of the most engaging critical gameplay experiences is a game that did not endeavor toward addressing the ethical issues in critical gameplay. Instead the game endeavored to demonstrate challenge and how challenge is derived. Kayin's Nasaki's *I Wanna Be the Guy* (Nasaki, 2007) is a game whose challenges rely on the standards of existing games. The game serves as critique for the standard cannon of gameplay mechanics, reminding players that walking into swords is dangerous (instead of a way to pick them up) and larger than life fruit may be threatening. The game functions as a détournement, emphasizing the logical problems with standard 2D gameplay assumptions through an exceptionally challenging experience. Released in 2007 the game met with a brief fan following, as people were enthralled with its seemingly impossible expectations. Yet, the very power of this game design is in the fact that the challenge rests largely on the expectations of experienced players. The game actively critiques common gameplay mechanics by demonstrating how they can be turned upside down.

CONCLUSION

This chapter seeks to outline the process of critical gameplay design as an alter-ethic producing methodology. In the last few years critical gameplay games have been exhibited and distributed through a variety of venues including academic conferences, the Games for Change festival, and independent game design communities. Their growing popularity and attention seem to predict an awareness of the potential for such approaches. Such approaches to play are distinctly increasing in activist and art game design communities.

These few case studies are provided as evidence of the possibilities in critical gameplay design. Each demonstrates a fundamental approach to deriving critical gameplay. As a three-step process, these are observation of the standard, deconstruction of the assumed value, and reorientation of assumptions.

This chapter sought to define critical gameplay and expose the process of designing a critical gameplay game. It did so by identifying the patterns of design, which include identifying the invisible mechanics, identifying the invisible values, identifying ethics creep, and identifying omissions. It also described the relationship of critical gameplay to other critical design practices, discerning the focus of critical game designers from other types of designers. In support of these observations, it provided several case studies addressing specific critical design questions in ethics and values.

As a relatively new approach to game design, Critical Gameplay offers an opportunity to explore the ethical foundations of gameplay standards. This chapter is not meant as an exhaustive resource, but merely as an orientation for the beginning explorer. Much like mapmaking, it has tried to identify a few key aspects of the topography of critical gameplay design. The hope is that the reader uses this information to further more exploration in this new area.

REFERENCES

Atari, (2004, June). Driv3R [Xbox].

Barr, P., Noble, J., & Biddle, R. (2007). *Video game values: Human–computer interaction and games* (pp. 180–195). HCI Issues in Computer Games.

Bogost, I. (2009, June 30). Persuasive games: Gestures as meaning. *Gamasutra*. Retrieved February 5, 2010, from http://www.gamasutra.com/view/feature/4064/persuasive_games_gestures_as_.php?print=1

Brown, T. (2009, September). Tim Brown urges designers to think big. *TED: Ideas worth spreading*. Retrieved January 15, 2010, from http://www.ted.com/talks/tim_brown_urges_designers_to_think_big.html

Consalvo, M. (2005, December). Rule sets, cheating, and magic circles: Studying games and ethics. *International Review of Information Ethics*, pp. 11-12.

Crampton, J. (1994). Cartography's defining moment: The Peters projection controversy, 1974–1990. *Cartographica: The International Journal for Geographic Information and Geovisualization, 31*(4), 13–32. doi:10.3138/1821-6811-L372-345P

Crawford, C. (1984). *The art of computer game design*. Berkeley, CA: Osborne/McGraw-Hill.

Curran, S. (Producer), Curran, S. (Writer), & Susan, G. (Director). (2010). *Global game jam keynote* [Video]. Global Game Jam.

Dunne, A., & Raby, F. (2001). *Design noir: The secret life of electronic objects*. Basel, Switzerland: Birkhäuser.

Dunne, A., & Raby, F. (2005). Projects. *Dunne and Raby*. Retrieved January 15, 2009, from http://www.dunneandraby.co.uk/content/projects/

Fuller, M. (2008). *Software studies: A lexicon.* Boston: MIT Press.

Fullerton, T. (2008). *Game design workshop: A playcentric approach to creating innovative games*. Oxford, UK: Elsevier.

Grace, L. (2010, April 10). The games. *Critical gameplay*. Retrieved April 10, 2010, from http://www.CriticalGameplay.com

Kutner, L., & Olson, C. K. (2008). *Grand Theft Childhood: The surprising truth about violent video games and what parents can do*. New York: Simon & Schuster.

Manovic, L. (2008). *Software takes command.* San Diego, CA: UCSD Software Studies Initiative. Retrieved from http://softwarestudies.com/softbook/manovich_softbook_11_20_2008.pdf

Mary, F., & Anna, L. (2009). *Anxiety, openness, and activist games: A case study for critical play. Breaking new ground: Innovation in games, play, practice and theory.* London: Digital Games Research Association.

Nasaki, K. (2007). *I Wanna be the guy* [Game]. Retrieved December 23, 2009, from http://kayin.pyoko.org/iwbtg/downloads.php

Rockstar North. (2002, May). Grand Theft Auto III [Playstation 2].

Squire, K. (2003). Video games in education. *International Journal of Intelligent Simulations, 2*(1), 49–62.

Chapter 10

How Games Can Touch You:
Ethics of the Videogame Controller

Mitu Khandaker
University of Portsmouth, UK

ABSTRACT

Novel kinesthetic and mimetic video game interfaces, such as the Wii Remote, PlayStation Move, and Microsoft Kinect, are seeing widespread mainstream appeal. However, with games ranging from the family-friendly Rock Band series, to the banned Manhunt 2, this chapter discusses the ethical implications of interfaces that seek to increase the verisimilitude of our game experiences, and offers a position from which to further consider the controller as an integral part of the overall game design.

INTRODUCTION

In 2007, the British Board of Film Classification (responsible for regulating films and videogames in the UK) issued a statement banning Rockstar's *Manhunt 2* ("BBFC Rejects Video Game Manhunt 2," 2007); this was the first game since 1997 to be thusly rejected. The statement claimed that the game "constantly encourages visceral killing with exceptionally little alleviation or distancing." Additionally, four United States Senators at that time also wrote a letter to the Entertainment Software Rating Board (ESRB) to suggest it reconsider its ratings system in light of *Manhunt 2*. Notably,

their concerns specifically addressed the fact that the game was available for the Nintendo Wii. The senators wrote (Tapper, 2007):

[The Wii] system permits children to act out each of the many graphic torture scenes and murders in Manhunt 2 rather than simply manipulating a game pad. This led one clinical psychologist to state that the realistic motions used with the Wii mean that 'You're basically teaching a child the behavioral sequencing of killing'. ...we do believe that the ESRB should take the Wii Remote controller, and future advances in game controllers, which create more realistic gaming environments, into consideration.

DOI: 10.4018/978-1-60960-120-1.ch010

These assertions are exemplary of the "moral panic" demonstrated by the "common media argument," as observed by Sicart, "that games lead to violent behavior and desensitization in the face of violence" (2009). Of course, in the case of *Manhunt 2* as above, it is seemingly the kinesthetic mimicry of the motion-sensing Wii Remote controller that raises ethical questions about the game. That is, the way in which the violent actions occurring onscreen must be physically *acted out* by the player, using the Wii Remote. The game provides a close mapping between the player's real-world action, and the in-game action. We can therefore question whether the game would garner the same kind of controversy had it been developed solely for a classic, non-motion based controller, in which the player's actions (pressing buttons) are abstracted from the character's actions on-screen.

Of course, such "moral panic" regarding new technology is not new; Janet Murray, in her seminal text *Hamlet on the Holodeck* (1997), describes the cultural history of such adverse reactions and the "fear with which we have greeted every new powerful representational technology." (1997, p. 21) For example, Huxley's *Brave New World* (1932) described a dystopian vision of the future, triggered by the advent of cinema, in which audiences could enjoy 'feelies': movies which pervade our bodily senses, and feature realistic, somatic representations of "arresting helicopter views, lots of sex, and characters who are constantly bursting into song." (Murray, 1997, p. 20) Murray states that "for Huxley and Bradbury, the more persuasive the medium, the more dangerous it is... as soon as we open ourselves to these illusory environments, we surrender our reason and join with the undifferentiated masses, slavishly wiring ourselves into the stimulation machine at the cost of our very humanity." (1997, p. 21)

This chapter will explore the ethics of videogame controllers, the physical hardware interfaces by which a player may interact with a videogame system. I will explore how interfaces which in-

creasingly map a player's real-life-body to the game system may increase the verisimilitude of "illusory environments." If this does indeed create experiences which are more "persuasive," I will explore the potential ethical implications of this, how much ethical responsibility lies with the player, and the designer respectively. An interdisciplinary approach, combining philosophy and interaction design, will inform this analysis. Where possible, empirical evidence will be referenced in this discussion; otherwise it will be made explicit that the statement is a hypothesis motivated by theory and/or experience as opposed to rigorous empirical observation.

The central thesis of this chapter is that as this verisimilitude of experiences within games increases with innovations in controller technology, from a virtue ethics perspective, there may be potential for misuse by a non-virtuous player. Furthermore, it is proposed that abstract games and simulations lay on opposite ends along a spectrum. As controller technology evolves to more accurately accommodate our bodily inputs, the player's game experience moves away from abstraction and toward simulation instead. It is argued that whilst in certain circumstances (such as training applications) this may be desirable, the sense of aesthetic distance required to critically evaluate one's actions within the game may be lost. Therefore, in terms of games designed for entertainment, any games which do not conform to what we would consider "ethical" in the real world, may have ethical implications if a non-virtuous person were to play them.

In this chapter, I will first define establish terms. I will look at what is meant by the 'controller', and, importantly what is meant in this context by "ethics" and "ethical implications" in this context. I will also discuss the ethical framework to be used throughout this analysis.

Next, I will examine the notion of aesthetic distance, a concept central to this thesis; the way in which a degree of separation is required for a player to be able to appreciate a game as 'art.'

This will be discussed within the context of the cybernetic relationship between the player and the game. I will argue that games are defined by their capacity for interactivity, of which the control interface is a crucial component dictating the possibilities for physical action. I will also extensively discuss the notion of embodiment in order to highlight the possibilities narrowing the gap between the player and the game, and what this means when simulating games with unethical themes. Finally, I will use this analysis in order to draw conclusions about the ethical responsibilities of both the player and the designer as innovations in controller technology move forward.

This analysis will thus begin with by defining key terms: what is the controller, and what do we mean by ethics in this context?

Defining the Controller

The controller is a player's crucial link to the game world and is a part of the game experience itself; it is the only component that is physical. These controllers may take the form of gamepads, joysticks, keyboards, computer mice, steering wheels, plastic instruments, dance mats, and so on. Interfaces which are kinesthetic or gestural (those which allow for movement or gestures respectively, such as the Nintendo Wii, Microsoft's Kinect, and Sony's PlayStation Move), mimetic interfaces (those which closely resemble their real-life counterparts in appearance and/or their use, such as the Rock Band or Guitar Hero series), or indeed, the classic controller (the traditional joystick-and-buttons gamepad) are all, nonetheless, notable for the physicality of the interaction they offer. It is only videogames that have maintained such obvious physical reliance on a ubiquitous mechanical controller, separating them from non-digital games (Myers, 2009). Gestural and kinesthetic control mechanisms, such as the Nintendo Wii, Microsoft's Kinect, and Sony's PlayStation Move, have become increasingly notable for their commercial popularity.

While the concept of gestural interfaces is not at all new (earlier examples include the *Nintendo Power Glove*, the *Sega Activator*, and so on), these previous examples were generally commercial failures. However, due to improvements in sensor technology being able to more accurately reflect a player's real-life bodily input within a game, novel interfaces of all types are becoming more prevalent. Such a paradigm is termed by Slater & Usoh (1994) as "Body Centered Interaction," and they empirically show that a user's sense of being there within a virtual environment is maximized with interaction techniques that match bodily proprioceptive (our sense of the different parts of our body in relation to one another) and sensory data.

An Ethical Approach

In beginning this line of inquiry, it is useful to first define what is meant by ethics and ethical in this context. The discussion in this chapter takes place within the frameworks of normative ethics; that is, a consideration for the rules, or norms, for our moral behavior, and the way we assess what is right and wrong, in everyday life (Stewart, 2009). Normative ethics breaks every action down into three components, and three types of normative theory, or moral philosophies, are concerned with each of these: utilitarianism concerns itself with the consequences, deontological theories are concerned with the action itself, and their motives, and virtue ethics concerns itself with the agent, or doer. This *applied* approach offered by normative ethics, and each of these three moral philosophies, are useful tools in examining our always-physical component of our interaction with videogames.

This chapter considers the ethics of games, with respect to the controller, to consist of tree ethical objects, to be explored throughout, using normative theories of ethics. These are thus:

1.   The designed system of the game itself (including the controller) as a set of procedures,

affordances, and mappings. Thus, from a consequential ethical approach (such as that considered by the mainstream media argument), the game may be deemed to have a certain "ethical potential" for consequences. This will be referred to hereafter as the game-object.

2.   The role, from a deontological perspective, of the game designer in the "distributed responsibility," as those that have given rise to a game with such "ethical potential."

3.   The ethical subject of the player themselves, and the ethical actuality of their experiences, as informed by virtue ethics, and the framework proposed by Sicart (2009). This will be referred to hereafter as the player-subject.

In this section, I will discuss what each of these ethical objects mean in terms of the central argument of this chapter. Embarking upon this examination, we are initially faced with the same questions asked by Sicart in *The Ethics of Computer Games* (2009): "Is it the ethics of the game, or the ethics of playing the game? Is there such a difference?" and "do game designers have moral responsibilities?" (2009, p. 3).

Sicart (2009) defines an ethical game experience as one "in which the player, a body-subject that exists and experiences the game system, can interact with that system as a moral agent"; that is, that they are a being capable of reflecting on what is right and wrong. Thus, an ethical game is "an experience that allows for the player's ethical behavior, interpretation, and, in the best possible case, contribution to the value system of the game experience" (p. 145). Furthermore, unethical content is posited as "the actions that are designed to simulate what we would consider unethical behavior outside the game, but also simulations that in themselves, can be considered unethical" (p. 191).

In line with this, the analysis in this chapter will also place importance on this phenomenology of playing, due to the aforementioned physicality

of interactions with controllers, a concept that will be further explored. Indeed, rather than being "a semantic quality of the game," [ethics] have much more to do with "the ontological nature of the game, as well as with the phenomenological experience of games." (Sicart, 2009)

This player-centric ethical framework uses virtue ethics to inform this approach, due to its concern with the agent, or doer. Virtue ethics is a moral philosophy assuming that what is ethical is defined not only by what "conventional morality requires," but also by "what a virtuous person," or in this case, a virtuous *player*, would do. This perhaps echoes Aristotle's virtues as related to "what the man of practical wisdom would determine." Thus, Sicart asserts that "the virtue ethics approach is essentially player-centered. It defines players as virtuous beings who make game play choices informed by their practical wisdom, guided by the presence (or absence) of a number of player-specific virtues." Therefore, virtuous players are able to cognitively distance themselves from a game experience, in order to step back and critically reflect upon their actions; this will, in the context of this chapter, be discussed alongside the notion of the 'aesthetic distance' of a given game and controller.

Additionally, the notion of "distributed responsibility" (Sicart, 2009) should be considered, referring to the fact that "in the game experience, there are a number of elements that share in non-proportional ways the responsibility for the game's ethical content." While we will use virtue ethics to inform our approach of the players in their experience of playing the game, a non-consequential, deontological perspective (one that is more concerned with intentions rather than consequences) will inform the consideration of the designer's responsibility.

This is an approach more concerned with the *intentions* associated with the creation of ethically questionable games, rather than on its consequences. Arguably, such a consequentialist approach is taken by the aforementioned "common media argument," purporting that games such as *Manhunt 2* lead to unintended behavior modification; for example, as the US senators stated, "teaching a child the behavioral sequencing of killing." However, these frameworks of virtue ethics, (concerned with the player-subject) and deontological theory (concerned with the designer's intentions) allow for discussion beyond the common media argument.

Considering these three ethical objects will inform the line of exploration in this chapter, which is the extent to which the innovations in controller technology increase the verisimilitude of experience within games, and what implications this may have.

In the next section, I will discuss the notion of aesthetic distance, and, as we consider how improvements in controller technology may move a game experience from one of abstraction to one of simulation, why this notion is required for artistic appreciation of a game. I will also discuss the relationship between the player and the game, as mediated by the controller, and thus highlight the primacy of interactivity within games, and how such improvements in technology lead to an increased sense of player embodiment, as elicited by the controller itself.

FROM ABSTRACTION, TOWARD SIMULATION

Aesthetic Distance

Game designer Greg Costikyan in advocates that, in one perspective, "games are a form of art in which [players] make decisions in order to manage resources through game tokens in the pursuit of a goal." (2002) If we note this definition of games as a form of art, then we can propose that the concept of "aesthetic distance" should apply here. This is a literary term, defined by *Encyclopedia Britannica* as "the frame of reference that an artist creates by the use of technical devices in and around the work of art to differentiate it psychologically from reality" (Encyclopædia Britannica, 2010). Indeed, the term was coined by Edward Bullough to refer to the perspective with which one should contemplate a work of art. Bullough wrote:

Distance... is obtained by separating the object and its appeal from one's own self, by putting it out of gear with practical needs and ends. Thereby the 'contemplation' of the object becomes alone possible. But it does not mean that the relation between the self and the object is broken to the extent of becoming 'impersonal' (Bullough, 1912).

This notion of aesthetic distance is in line with German playwright Brecht's techniques to alienate the play, reminding the spectators that they were experiencing a representation. This arose from his criticism of Aristotelian theatre, which he saw as keeping the audience immersed without giving them a chance to take a step back and critically think about what is happening on stage. In contrast to this, Brecht forced them to think about what they were watching. Blackman (1998) describes similar critiques made by interactive artists, in which the user's expectations were deliberately played around with by introducing into the electronic art works bugs and malfunctions, to disturb the choice offered to the user; these attempt to force the user to reflect upon their own preconceived expectations and desires within virtual space.

Therefore, the use of the virtue ethics perspective is appropriate here, as there is otherwise a tendency to think of the player as a passive, "guilty victim," who is "abandoned by her moral intuitions in a labyrinth demiurgically created by the game developers" (Sicart, 2009). Instead, we may consider a virtuous player, who is one who willingly and knowingly engages in the game; a moral user capable of reflecting ethically on the experiences they encounter in the game, and how it shapes their own values both within and outside of the game world. Therefore, the virtuous player is someone who is able to critically reflect upon their experience; this is comparable to the effect of enforcing a sense of aesthetic distance within an artistic experience, such as a game.

In this section, I will examine how the player relates the game, as mediated by the controller, and will also define and argue the concept of controller-evoked phenomenological embodiment as a mechanism by which the aesthetic distance is narrowed. By using philosophical and theoretical game design perspectives, I will argue that games played using classic controllers (such as the gamepad and keyboard) actually enforce a sense of aesthetic distance, allowing them to be more abstract experiences, which can be appreciated and evaluated as art by an ethically virtuous player. However, it is suggested that as controller technology evolves, and a sense of embodiment increases, the aesthetic distance actually *narrows*. This means that the player's experience of the game moves away from abstraction, and instead toward simulation. What this means, and the ethical implications of this, will be discussed.

The Embodied Player

Throughout history, there has been a prevalent belief in the Cartesian duality of mind and body; that is, that the notion that the mind exists separately from our physical selves. Increasingly, however, philosophers, psychologists, scientists, and even interaction designers alike are conceding that our bodily perceptions are the "ultimate foundation of our knowledge about ourselves and the world." As noted by Klemmer, "direct physical interaction with the world is a key constituting factor of cognitive development during childhood" (2006). Further, the neuroscientist Damasio states that "the body contributes more than life support; it also contributes a *content* that is part and parcel of the workings of the normal mind" (1994, p. 226). In short, human experience is shaped by our very physicality and our presence in the world;

we recognize the world through our ability to physically act within it.

The concept of embodiment is rooted in the phenomenological philosophies of the early 20th century. Phenomenology is a branch of philosophy that concerns itself with lived experience and has its roots in the work of philosophers such as Husserl, Heiddegger, and Merleau-Ponty. Merleau-Ponty describes the task of phenomenology as unveiling the pre-theoretical layer of human experience. That is, it is the study of how we each experience things. Dourish, in his seminal text "Where the Action Is" (2001), advocates the idea of embodiment as a sense of phenomenological presence, comparable to Biocca, who defines phenomenological embodiment as "being able to act through one's technologically enhanced body" (Biocca, 1997).

Steven Poole, author of *Trigger Happy*, a book about the aesthetics of videogames, states that "the videogame is not simply a cerebral or visual experience; just as importantly it is a physical involvement—the tactile success or otherwise of the human-machine interface" (2000, p. 73), and describes this relationship between a player and game as a "cybernetic thing." Westecott acknowledges that the classic controller presents a sense of abstraction between the physical actions of pressing the button and the visual happenings on-screen, thus it is tempting to equate the classic controller with a sense of Cartesian dualism; that the physical and the mental are separate (2008).

However, even with a classic controller, there is still a sense of spatial compliance; moving an avatar left, for example, also generally involves pressing the thumb stick or directional pad to the left side. Thus, the space of play, including the body, has always been implicated in the game experience to some degree; in this way, perhaps, the classic controller does not, as discussed above, break the "relation between the [player] and the object... to the extent of becoming impersonal." Simultaneously, Poole theorizes that the "distant mapping" of the classic controller enforces a sense of alienation from the game world, which he terms as "cybernetic dissonance" (2000); we can thus equate this to the notion of aesthetic distance. It is argued, then, that the verisimilitude of experiences offered by the classic controller are at the abstract end of the spectrum, enforcing a sense of aesthetic distance required for a virtuous player to be aware of their actions.

Of course, we do not play *with* the controller, but rather with "representations of objects arbitrarily assigned to various controller buttons and sequences." Of course, this assignment is not necessarily arbitrary, but rather a design decision (for a broad overview of this, see the text *Game Feel* by Steve Swink (2009)). For example, the closeness of this mapping between controller-and-game is variable, as is the nature of the mapping. This is a design decision, which varies from game to game. This concept of 'closeness' in interaction refers to how far an action on the controller relates to real-world action. For example, whilst using the drum peripheral to play *Rock Band* exhibits very close mapping to playing real drums (i.e. the action of drumming in Rock Band is the same as the action of drumming in real life), using a NES gamepad to play *Street Fighter* does not closely map to real fighting (i.e. pressing buttons is not the same as real life kicking or really performing a Dragon Punch). Gregersen & Grodal assert that the extent to which an embodied sense of agency, ownership, and personal efficacy is fostered is very much a question of overall design including interface design, and note how games may be designed to selectively target and activate the auditory, visual, and proprioceptive systems (2009). Such design decisions also dictate the verisimilitude of the game, dictating where along the abstraction-simulation spectrum a game experience may lay.

Sicart notes that phenomenological experience of the game is what Salen & Zimmerman define as interaction, and asserts that to interact with a system is to create meaning (2003). If interaction is the phenomenological experience of the game, then it follows that changing the nature of the interaction by altering the interface also changes the nature of the player's phenomenological experience.

Controller-Evoked Phenomenological Embodiment

In aiding our thinking about the cybernetic connection of playing videogames, and phenomenological embodiment, we may consider the technological degree to which a player's physical self is mapped to a game, via the controller. We can define this hereafter as its cybernetic bandwidth. The cybernetic bandwidth is formed of information channels (such as tangibility, kinesthetic movement, and force feedback) and the varying resolutions of these channels (i.e., how accurate it is). Therefore, the classic controller, while tangible, has one input modality, and thus would have low cybernetic bandwidth (unless there is also a *Rumble Pak*), whereas the Wii Remote that affords tangibility and kinesthetic movement has higher cybernetic bandwidth. Conversely, Microsoft's *Project Natal* control mechanism, which may have a higher resolution of kinesthetic movement (e.g., greater accuracy and more information sampled), does not afford tangibility, so has a different cybernetic bandwidth. This concept of the cybernetic bandwidth is therefore an abstract model, helpful in thinking about the degree of verisimilitude of the mapping between a player's physical actions, and the resulting in-game output.

However, increasingly physical interfaces (with a higher cybernetic bandwidth), move us beyond the abstraction of the keyboard or classic controller, and bring a sense of phenomenological embodiment back to the game experience, via the very physicality of the interface. For example, in a game such as *Boom Blox* (on the Nintendo Wii), although the player is disembodied in the sense of lacking any kind of avatar representation, the Wiimote helps to evoke a sense of phenomenological embodiment by being able to manipulate objects at hand naturally, by either using the grab tool (and being able to maneuver blocks as expected), or throwing the ball. Thus, the sense of embodiment and being able to act through one's technologically enhanced body is strong, despite the lack of visual representation. The embodiment is elicited through a sense of kinesthetic and tactile agency via the particular designed mapping between the Wii Remote and the game.

Therefore, a higher cybernetic bandwidth, arguably leads to his increased sense of phenomenological embodiment. However, as this verisimilitude of experience continues to increase, the game experience becomes one of simulation; this may lead to problems where the game features ethically questionable content.

Narrowing Gaps in Embodiment, Narrowing Aesthetic Distance

When a real life physical action is performed, such as hitting an object with a stick, this will translate into "easily felt force dynamics"; the enactor will feel the effect on their muscle tension, as well as the dynamics of posture and touch. However, such crucial sensory inputs are missing when using an interface such as Wii Remote, Sony Eye, or indeed, Natal, to hit a virtual representation of the same object in a virtual space.

Therefore, the cybernetic dissonance (i.e., the disjoint between the player's physical action and the action that occurs in the game) remains, though somewhat narrowed by increasingly real interfaces. A lack of total phenomenological mapping every sensory sense may still, as mentioned by Gregersen & Grodal, yield a dissociation of sensory experience (2009); that is, there still remains a gap in the phenomenological embodiment granted by the interface. Even though the Wii Remote has some advantage over Natal in this capacity, as it is not only gestural but also tactile, there are still shortfalls in physical feedback.

Therefore, as asserted by Gregersen & Grodal (2009), this yields an incongruent motor realism—which essentially translates to "what you

feel and what you see do not add up." The sense of ownership of the real body is high in such a scenario because body schema processes are activated, as opposed to when than when simply pressing a button on a classic controller, yet there is no visceral feedback to accompany this.

Indeed, empirical research has shown multimodal interfaces are potentially instrumental in reducing the problems associated with this incongruent motor realism (Barthelmess & Oviatt, 2009; Cohen et al., 1989); if a device such as the Wii Remote were, for example, augmented with a force feedback device, then during a tennis serve in Wii Sports, this could be activated, allowing for a greater sense of motor congruence than is currently elicited. There is thus a closer mapping between the player's expectations, and the actual feedback granted by the game system, granting a greater sense of real-world validity to the system, important if we are to design interfaces which are truly mimetic.

Of course, this becomes increasingly problematic as we consider a violent gestural game such as *Manhunt 2*; if ecological validity through the addition of force feedback were applied to the interface of a game such as *Manhunt 2*, allowing a player to feel the physical, visceral sense of stabbing a human being, we may posit that the controversy surrounding this would be greatly heightened.

In the next section, I will explore the way in which, from a virtue ethics perspective, the issue of multi-modal interfaces is a potent one, for both the designer and the player-subject; narrowing the gaps in embodiment lead to a closer mapping between reality and the game. By contrast, I will discuss the way in which classic control mechanisms, with their proposed sense of cybernetic dissonance, do not carry the same weight of ethical implications due to the aesthetic distance they necessarily afford.

Simulating Unethical Themes

The ethical implications of narrowing the embodiment gap become clearer once we apply this to a more morally questionable narrative, such as *Manhunt 2*.

We may, then, consider the ethics of employing a multi-modal interface in order to purposely heighten the sense of visceral violence in the game. It was asserted that some advanced type of force feedback technology could be employed in order to allow the player to feel the real, visceral sense of stabbing another human being.

Indeed, Slater & Usoh define interaction as "the ability of the participant to move through and change the world" (1994) and divide this into two further categories: the mundane and magical. They assert that "mundane interaction is that which attempts to faithfully reproduce a corresponding interaction in everyday reality," whereas "magical interaction involves actions that are only imaginable in everyday reality" (Slater & Usoh, 1994). We can further extend this to mean interactions which are exaggerated or have an oversimplified sequencing.

A hypothetical version of *Manhunt 2* as described above, which offers feedback corresponding to reality, would aspire to mundane rather than magical interaction in order to understand the reprehensible nature of these actions; creating an interface that is fully mimetic in order to more accurately reflect real-life outcomes. Such increased embodiment and agency may in fact heighten the artistic expression intended by a game; however, such a game would also be immensely ethically questionable from a virtue ethics perspective, and would strongly rely upon Sicart's notion of a "virtuous player," that is, "those player-subjects who have actually developed their ethical reasoning" (2009). Further to this, as the aesthetic distance would have narrowed in such a situation, one may posit that the virtuous player themselves must be relied upon to cognitively distance themselves.

Certainly, Bogost, in discussing *Manhunt 2* in a column entitled "Gestures as Meaning," also claims, "the game's coupling of gestures to violent acts makes them more, not less repugnant by implicating the player in their commitment" (2009). He asserts that "in *Manhunt 2*, we are meant to feel the power of Daniel Lamb's psychopathy alongside our own disgust at it. It is a game that helps us see how thin the line can be between madness and reason by making us perform abuse" (Bogost, 2009). This line of argument, however, relies upon the assertion by Salen & Zimmerman that the way in which games create meaning for players is via a mechanism of "double-consciousness," a "multilayered experience" that is "something separate from, but connected to the real world" (2003). In this sense, the player is fully aware of their game character (where appropriate) as an artificial construct. This constant transfer of identity, which Steve Swink in Game Feel (2009) describes as "capricious," is part of what makes games fun and engaging. However, the capricious flow of identity means that this extension can be "withdrawn" at an instant. Swink suggests that in this way, players avoid blame, but maintain engagement, "getting back to the pleasurable sensations of control more quickly" (2009).

The capricious sense of embodiment and cybernetic dissonance elicited by traditional interfaces can be thought of as offering a similar sense of alienation to German playwright Brecht's application in theatre, as described earlier in this chapter.

In this context, one can consider the relationship between the player and the character within a game as one of a puppeteer-and-puppet; however, with an increase in controller-evoked phenomenological embodiment, this increasingly becomes a relationship of direct identification. Indeed, such a scenario, especially when taken to full technological extremes (full spatial immersion), would perhaps seem the ultimate realization of the 'common media argument' of a "murder simulator." Thus, such a move away from cybernetic dissonance, and the aesthetic distance this grants, seems simultaneously powerful and problematic. Whilst an increased sense of embodiment may strengthen the rhetoric of a game seeking to highlight the reprehensible nature of violent action, it simultaneously creates a dangerous sense of close identification for those who would seek to misuse such an experience.

However, if we note that the games designer may selectively design a system to target and activate the auditory, visual, somatosensory, and proprioceptive systems, we can also consider that the feedback from such an action does not necessarily have to correspond to reality. If we consider instead that a multi-modal interface for *Manhunt 2* may instead aspire to 'magical' interaction, we can note the potential ethical implications for such a game which does not "differentiate [itself] psychologically from reality" (Encyclopædia Britannica, 2010), and yet is not intended for a player to understand the reprehensible nature of their actions. Such a hypothetical game would again, require not only an ethically virtuous player, but also one may consider the deontological intentions of the game designer, too. The latter concept is further explored in the next section.

Bogost asserts in *Persuasive Games* (2007), that "videogames have a unique persuasive power," as they provide a systemic view of the world which can promote a certain mental model (Bogost, 2007). He defines procedural rhetoric as "the art of persuasion through rule-based representations and interactions," and "the act of using processes persuasively" (Bogost, 2007); this can, arguably, be extended to the nature of the controller. An increased sense of phenomenological embodiment, it is asserted, also allows for kind of procedural rhetoric that is perhaps more visceral and powerful, by committing the 'forced actions' of the player to their real-world, physical embodiment.

Indeed, in the context of virtue ethics, Sicart asks, "does the act of playing games reinforce moral desensitization?" (2009). While this is a perspective often reflected in the "common media

argument," it can be argued that the greater the sense of phenomenological embodiment, the more the notion of the "virtuous player" must be relied upon, as we will further examine.

However, the player-subject is not the only ethical object that must be relied upon; the following case study of a particularly morally reprehensible game, *RapeLay*, will highlight the need for considering the deontological intentions of the games designer too, and include the designer as an ethical object who has a part of the distributed responsibility of the ethics of games.

RapeLay: A Case Study in Unethical Simulation

The PC game *RapeLay* (2006) has garnered much controversy for its content, which would rightfully fit Sicart's definition of 'unethical'; that is, "actions that are designed to simulate what we would consider unethical behaviour outside the game, but also simulations that in themselves, can be considered unethical." Indeed, the game is described thus:

In RapeLay, gamers direct a character to sexually assault a mother and her two young daughters at an underground station, before raping any of a selection of female characters ... RapeLay, which was released in 2006, encourages players to force the virtual woman they rape to have an abortion. If they are allowed to give birth the woman throws the player's character under a train, according to reviews of the game. It also has a feature allowing several players to team up against individual women. (Moore).

Despite the clearly morally reprehensible theme, a common supporting argument for *RapeLay* is equating the game with other media tackling similar themes. For example, if rape may be addressed in (once-banned) films such as *A Clockwork Orange*, then surely videogames, a medium rightfully striving to show its ability to handle mature and complex themes, should also be able to portray this. In *A Clockwork Orange*, however, the audience is meant to feel repugnance at the protagonist Alex's actions; we can equate this to Bogost's assertions about our own disgust at Daniel's actions in *Manhunt 2* (2007). Of course, these claims, as examined, remain valid as long as the player maintains a sense of double-consciousness, and if the player is virtuous.

It is, however, outside of the scope of this chapter to discuss the ethics of games in respect to their content, though we can see that comparing *RapePlay* to *A Clockwork Orange* in this way however becomes blurrier when the interface is altered, creating a sense of increased embodiment. *RapePlay* is currently designed for a classic keyboard-and-mouse interface, though can claims of 'artistic merit' be maintained if the game were released, or modified, to be played via a kinesthetic interface, such as the *Wii Remote*, or even *Natal*, so that the game could be kinesthetically acted out? This therefore ventures further into the territory of a full rape simulator, with very real potentials for misuse by a non-virtuous player. Would the undoubted public outcry that would ensue be justified in such a case? Again, we may refer to Sicart's assertion that "a designer is responsible for the object, but the players and their communities are ultimately responsible for the experience" (2009), though also acknowledges that "designers also play a role, due to their duties in the distributed responsibility network" (Sicart, 2009).

Furthermore, we can assert that it would be unethical, and non-virtuous for a game portraying rape with a kinesthetic interface to be purposely designed thus. Whilst such an assertion may depend on nuances of the game beyond the potential for interactivity and action, from a virtue ethics perspective, this is unethical to design or play such a game. Authorial intent is important here, and we thus consider the deontological perspective of the game designer's decision process in creating games which may allow for this kind of interaction. As Sicart states, "a player has to have

ludic maturity to understand the reasons behind the simulation and the fact that she is interacting with a game world specifically designed to produce a ludic experience" (2009).

In the next section, we discuss another facet of the potential for misuse of the powers of simulation; one that is the ethical responsibility of the game designer-object. This is the power to *misrepresent* simulation, and grant a mistaken sense of virtuosity to players.

MISREPRESENTING SIMULATION

The Problem with Magical vs. Mundane Mimicry

Rock Band is often criticized for replacing teen's interest in real instruments, and certainly Harmonix CEO Alex Rigopoulos is often questioned about this (Dubner, 2009). However, a study by Youth Music in the UK (2007) concluded that such games have in fact yielded more of an interest in "real" music among young people as a result. The report noted that focus group participants in the study were "forthright in their view that how closely a game's interface resembled a 'real' instrument was a vital part of its credibility, both in their eyes, and the eyes of their parents" (Youth Music in the UK, 2007). It's been noted of course, that games with instrument interfaces currently have a long way to go to make this leap—excepting, of course, the Rock Band drums and microphone, which exhibit the highest degree of mapping between the game interface and the real instrument. It does however remain to be seen whether players continue to be interested if they do not achieve the same level of success with real instruments as their simulated counterparts.

Jarvinen, (2009) analyses the emotional experience afforded by such music games, noting how pleasure is derived according to Kubovy's notion of virtuosity; that is, from one's own performance and ability. Juul (2009) suggests that players engaging with games such as *Guitar Hero*, *Rock Band*, *Dance Dance Revolution*, and *Singstar* are performing a choreographed scene, rather than playing music. These games support the display of virtuosity and creativity through specific motor and auditory skills; an example of something Slater and Usoh's (1994) notion of 'magical interaction'.

The real ethical issues however, perhaps rise in the lack of clarity presented to players about which of their embodied interactions are intended to be mundane, and to reflect reality, and which are exaggerated, magical interactions; and furthermore, the misconceptions in the media about this. For example, Wii Fit has effectively marketed itself as not a game, but as a utility for exercise. It follows then, that many consumers expect this as a replacement for gym membership or other exercise. However, empirical studies found that Wii Fit produced "underwhelming results," in terms of exercise intensity, and in all cases, performing an actual exercise activity rather than Wii Fit's virtual approximation resulted in "significantly higher" caloric expenditure. The Rhythm Boxing activity, in particular, burned one-third of the calories expended per minute of traditional boxing, although overall, Wii Fit burns twice as many calories as a sedentary videogame (Cowan, 2009).

As a subset of considering the designer's distributed responsibility as an ethical object, an additional question of business ethics is thus raised here; just because it is conceded that Wii Fit is more efficient at burning calories than classic, sedentary interfaces, is it ethical to not make the game's magical interaction explicit, given the activities within Wii Fit are not suitable replacements for real activity?

This chapter has largely discussed the potential for ethical problems which may arise when playing and designing games which offer an increased verisimilitude of experience due to the control mechanism. Of course, when played by a virtuous player-subject, such games, akin to simulation, have the potential for benefits, too;

the most notable of example of this is in training applications for military and/or healthcare. Indeed, a study of 33 laparoscopic surgeons found that those who played videogames were 27 percent faster at advanced surgical procedures and made 37 percent fewer errors compared to those who did not play videogames. Indeed, advanced videogame skill and experience are said to be "significant predictors of suturing capabilities, even after controlling for sex, years of medical training and number of laparoscopic surgeries performed" (Association, 2008). Additionally, a second study of 303 laparoscopic surgeons (82 percent men; 18 percent women) also showed that surgeons who played videogames requiring spatial skills and hand dexterity and then performed a drill testing these skills were significantly faster at their first attempt and across all 10 trials than the surgeons who did not the play videogames first (Association, 2008).

Sicart asserts that "game designers are ethically responsible for the ways they have created the formal system of rules; that is, according to the behaviors they want to encourage in players" (2009). For the purposes of this chapter, this formal system includes, of course, the control mechanism. He further states that "games force behaviors by rules: the meaning of those behaviors, as communicated through the game world to the player, constitutes the ethics of computer games as designed objects" (Sicart, 2009). With respect to controllers with higher cybernetic bandwidth, often these behaviors are kinesthetic and gestural, such as in the example of *Manhunt 2*.

TOWARD A CYBERNETIC HEGEMONY

Poole theorizes that "in general, cybernetic developments [that is, innovations in controller technology] will always increase the possibilities of closer and more pleasurable interaction with a video game." However, he also goes onto question how far this notion remains relevant as interfaces further evolve: "Will [total immersion], then become the dominant means of video game control? Perhaps; but if so, the spirit of Heidegger will rise again to warn that such cybernetic hegemony will necessarily narrow the field of possibilities" (Poole, 2000).

He suggests that "the perfect videogame feel requires the ever-increasing imaginative and physical involvement of the player to stop somewhere short of full bodily immersion" (Poole, 2008). Thus, the ethical game-object, and how it relates to the experience of the player-subject *requires* a boundary.

Such an assertion is in line with Salen & Zimmerman's concept of the immersive fallacy, which refers to the widely held, but seldom examined idea among gamers and developers alike that "the pleasure of a media experience lies in its ability to sensually transport the participant into an illusory, simulated reality" (2003, p. 450). We can see the widespread nature of this immersive fallacy manifest itself in countless commercial games which promise more and more realistic graphics, and thus, greater immersion. This notion is something that "takes over all our attention, our whole perceptual apparatus" (Murray, 1997). As Salen & Zimmerman point out, the danger of immersive fallacy "is that it misrepresents how play functions… and game design can suffer as a result" (2003). In other words, the immersive fallacy is the mistaken idea that the more realistic a game, the better, or more worthwhile it is; the way in which games create meaning for players is not through an abundance of technologically-delivered sensory information that aspires to reality, but, as Salen & Zimmerman suggest, via a mechanism of "double-consciousness"; that is, it is "something separate from, but connected to the real world" (2003).

This idea of a boundary between the player and the game is also one that is explored in the 1999 David Cronenberg movie, *eXistenZ*. In an analysis of this, Keane says that "much of the distinctive-ness of the film lays in its deliberate resistance to similarities with prior videogame and virtual reality films. Part of that distinctiveness is exactly the fact that Cronenberg concentrates so much on the physical interface between player and game" (2002). Keane cites Cronenberg speaking of the movie: "It seemed to me that what people are really doing in computer and video games is trying to get closer and closer to fusing themselves with the game... So I went that little bit further – if I want to be the game, the game will also want to be me" (David Cronenberg quoted in Keane, 2002).

Indeed, *eXistenZ* presents three kinds of control systems: the first one that the viewer is introduced to are *Meta-Flesh Game Pods*, which are connected via an *UmbyCord* into a *bioport* (an opening in the player's spinal cord). This highly invasive interface paradigm is further exacerbated in the game-within-the-game by the *MicroPod*, which disappears into the player's spinal cord completely. Finally, at the end of the film, the non-invasive VR system worn by the players is revealed. Therefore, from VR system, to plugging into spines, to pods disappearing completely into spines, Cronenberg increasingly *"fuses"* the player with the game, making the technology used to do so more invisible, and more intrusive, each time. Indeed, one of the movie's most iconic lines is its last, in which the protagonists ask: "Tell me the truth: Are *we still* in the game?", thus suggesting the blurring of the boundaries; a warning, perhaps, about the dangers of virtual reality and simulation.

Of course, we may equate this to Janet Murray's review of the early concerns about cinema and television, as mentioned in the introduction o this chapter; the ethics of becoming absorbed in a passive technical medium manifested themselves in the cultural media of the time through works such as *Huxley's Brave New World* (1932). Indeed, cultural theorist Steven Shaviro notes that "Each time we extend ourselves technologically, some part of the real gives way to the virtual. This is why every cultural innovation is attended by an ambivalent sense of loss" (2003, p. 104). This idea of extending ourselves technologically, akin to the idea of phenomenological embodiment as already discussed, is also presented by Marshall McLuhan. Shaviro cites McLuhan's assertion that "every technology is an extension of ourselves," although "in each instance of technological change... we misrecognize the very extensions that we have created and see them as forces alien to ourselves" (2003, p. 104).

Shaviro presents this notion of technological extension to being a cyborg, stating "I become a cyborg when some part of my actual body is taken over by the virtual. My sensory apparatuses, and my organs, are always being replaced or extended by technological devices. This process is coextensive with the whole of human culture" (2003, p. 103), and he notes that the distinction lies particularly in the use of "electromechanical devices" (2003). Therefore, "perhaps just wearing glasses doesn't quite make [one] a cyborg, but watching television certainly does" (Shaviro, 2003, p. 104).

Therefore, Shaviro presents a possible counter-argument to the central thesis of this chapter; if we have always been cyborgs to some extent, as he suggests, then are concerns over the ethical implications of increased fidelity of simulation unwarranted? If the boundary (the aesthetic distance) between ourselves and the game are minimized, is this cause for concern about non-virtuous players? Or can this be equated to early dystopian concerns about cinema, as in *Brave New World*?

However, as we have discussed, games are defined by their capacity for interactivity, differentiating them from other mediums. Indeed, as Sicart argues, "there are some specific ontological properties of computer games that raise unique ethical challenges" (2009), namely the primacy of interactivity. Therefore, it is argued that games can potentially offer an enhanced sense of verisimilitude to reality, given a controller with a high cybernetic bandwidth. Therefore, whilst we can place other mediums on the 'abstraction' end of

our proposed abstraction-simulation spectrum, games offer an unparalleled potential for simulation, greater than other forms of media.

Such an idea is akin to the notion of the aesthetic distance required to appreciate a game as a game, and thus for a virtuous player-subject to be able to critically evaluate their actions within a game. Thus, it is posited that an increased sense of aesthetic distance from a game, created by the controller, provides the player-subject with an abstract experience; it is suggested that such an abstract experience is required for players to be able to critically evaluate their actions as art. This is particularly salient when considering games which may feature "unethical content," as examined earlier in this chapter.

CONCLUSION

In this chapter, I have argued that increasingly accurate controller input modalities strengthen the prosthetic cyborgian relationship between a player and a game. In other words, as controllers get closer and closer to mapping a player's real-life, physical body, into a game, more and more parts of our experience are essentially replaced with this prosthetic relationship. Therefore, the experience no longer has as many mediating factors (e.g. abstraction from classic controllers) to help "differentiate it psychologically from reality" (Encyclopædia Britannica, 2010). This therefore, decreases the player's sense of aesthetic distance required for the player to critically evaluate a game experience as art.

Perhaps the only way in which we may be certain of the capricious transfer of identity may be to maintain cybernetic dissonance, so one may argue this is appropriate for the aesthetic distance required for tackling controversial themes. Conversely, as pointed out, in order to portray the reprehensibility of certain themes, one may assert that an increased sense of embodiment as granted by kinesthetic, mimetic interfaces is useful, when aspiring to mundane rather than magical interaction.

However, this increased verisimilitude means that rather than being appreciating an experience *as a game*, the game moves along the spectrum from abstraction toward simulation. This does not have as many ethical implications if we hold the notion of the virtuous player, who is able to "understand the reasons behind the simulation and the fact that she is interacting with a game world specifically designed to produce a ludic experience" (Sicart, 2009). However, if a non-virtuous player were to play the same game, this may be ethically problematic, as discussed in the analysis of *RapeLay*.

Sicart states that "games are powerful simulation tools that convey worldviews, messages, and values" (2009), and this power becomes even more prevalent with increased controller-evoked embodiment. Sicart continues that "Emptying games of ethical reflection in their design and using unethical content for its shock value as a marketing resource means not only devaluing the possibilities of games as a means of expression, but also making products that are unethical objects" (2009).

In the case of *RapeLay*, or indeed, *Manhunt 2*, we may also place ethical responsibility upon a designer not to create games which could be misused by an non-virtuous player, though simultaneously, we may also consider whether ethical concerns over the embodiment elicited in a game such as *Manhunt 2* may be reactionary and sensationalist in a current cultural context.

However, as videogame technology continues to evolve, including, but not limited to, the controllers, graphical fidelity, and other factors increasing the verisimilitude of game experiences, we can see this as an ongoing march toward the concept of the "Holy Grail" of the *Holodeck*; a notion addressed by Salen and Zimmerman (2003) as the immersive fallacy. Such a concept is explored by *eXistenZ* in the tradition of dystopian media regarding new technology, though

can be considered a specific warning against control mechanisms and games which are unable to "differentiate [themselves] psychologically from reality" (Encyclopædia Britannica, 2010), if we are to consider the Bullough's definition of aesthetic distance. Indeed, Cronenberg seems, in *eXistenZ* to present a dystopian scenario in which there is no boundary at all between the game and the player; a cybernetic hegemony. As stated by Cronenberg "it seemed to me that what people are really doing in computer and videogames is trying to get closer and closer to fusing themselves with the game," (Keene, 2002) and *eXistenZ* is the ultimate extrapolation of this trend, in which any boundaries between the player and the game, and thus, any aesthetic distance, is eliminated.

Cultural theorist Jean Baudrillard states that "a possible definition of the real is: that for which it is possible to find an equivalent representation" (2003). He asserts that "abstraction today is no longer that of the map, the double, the mirror, or the concept. Simulation is no longer that of a territory, a referential being or a substance. It is the generation by models of a real without origin or reality: a hyper-real which is henceforth sheltered from the imaginary, and from any distinction between the real and the imaginary" (1988). Indeed, game designer Harvey Smith suggests that "we might, paradoxically, have a truer experience swimming together through simulacra; an experience almost exclusively focused on the things that make us human, on the things that separate us from bacteria, shrubs or insects" (Smith, 2010); that is, it is perhaps the abstract experiences which have the most to teach us.

It may also be argued that dystopian media, such as the movie *eXistenZ* is typical of the "describes the fear with which we have greeted every new powerful representational technology" (Murray, 1999) and revisit Shaviro's assertion that "every cultural innovation is attended by an ambivalent sense of loss." It may also be argued that the philosophical and theoretical game design perspective undertaken in the analysis in this chapter has yet to be empirically proven. However, at the same time, in summing up the concerns and ethical implications highlighted within this paper, we may keep in mind this from Shaviro (2003):

You may say that all this is merely science fiction. None of it is happening, not now, not here, not yet. But science fiction does not claim to be reportage, just as it does not claim to be prophetic. It does not actually represent the present, just as it does not really predict the future. Rather, it involves both the present and the future, while being reducible to neither. For science fiction is about the shadow that the future casts upon the present. It shows us how profoundly we are haunted by the ghosts of what has not yet happened.

These epiphenomenal overviews of the ethical impact of the videogame control mechanism raise much uncertainty, and further questions as control mechanisms continue to evolve and mature. It is the ethical responsibility of game designers to explore the ethical issues raised by the decision to use a particular interface type in a game, and how the game uses the possibility space afforded by that interface. Indeed, Perron & Wolf (2009) question whether, as control mechanisms evolve, and new controllers and peripherals appear, there are universal statements and claims about interactivity that will hold up in the light of such future innovations. With this evolution, the scope of what games are able to achieve are also broadened. From this uncertainty, one conclusion can be drawn – the unethical course of action is then, perhaps, to not thoroughly consider the implications of the choice of technology and interface for games moving forward.

REFERENCES

Baudrillard, J. (1988). Simulacra and simulations. In Poster, M. (Ed.), *Selected writings* (pp. 166–184). Stanford, CA: Stanford University Press.

Baudrillard, J. (2003). The Hyper-realism of simulation. In Harrison, C., & Wood, P. (Eds.), *Art in theory 1900-2000: An anthology of changing ideas* (pp. 1018–1020). Malden, MA: Blackwell.

Biocca, F. (1997). The cyborg's dilemma: Progressive embodiment in virtual environments. *Journal of Computer-Mediated Communication, 3*(2).

Bogost, I. (2007). *Persuasive games*. Cambridge, MA: MIT Press.

Bogost, I. (2009). Persuasive games: Gestures as meaning. *Gamasutra*. Retrieved from http://www.gamasutra.com/view/feature/4064/persuasive_games_gestures_as_.php

Bullough, E. (1912). *Psychical distance' as a factor in art and as an aesthetic principle.*

Costikyan, G. (2002). I have no words and I must design: Towards a critical vocabulary for games. Retrieved from http://www.costik.com/nowords2002.pdf

Cowan, D. (2009). American Council on Exercise charts 'underwhelming' health benefits. *Gamasutra*. Retrieved from http://www.gamasutra.com/php-bin/news_index.php?story=26016

Damasio, A. (1994). *Descartes' error: Emotion, reason, and the human brain*. New York: G.P. Putnam.

Dourish, P. (2001). *Where the action is: The foundations of embodied interaction*. Cambridge, MA: The MIT Press.

Dubner, S. (2009). The 'Guitar Hero' answers your questions. *The New York Times*. Retrieved from http://freakonomics.blogs.nytimes.com/2009/01/13/the-guitar-hero-answers-your-questions/

Encyclopædia Britannica. (2010). Aesthetic distance. *Encyclopædia Britannica Online*. Retrieved June 10, 2010, from http://www.britannica.com/EBchecked/topic/7465/aesthetic-distance

Gregersen, A., & Grodal, T. (2009). Embodiment and interface. In Perron, B., & Wolf, M. J. P. (Eds.), *The video game theory reader 2* (pp. 65–83). New York: Routledge.

Jarvinen, A. (2009). Understanding video games as emotional experiences. In Perron, B., & Wolf, M. J. P. (Eds.), *The video game theory reader 2*. Cambridge, MA: MIT Press.

Kaptelinin, V., & Nardi, B. (2006). *Acting with technology: Activity theory and interaction design*. Cambridge: MIT Press.

Keane, S. (2002). From hardware to fleshware: Plugging into David Cronenberg's eXistenZ. In King, G., & Krzywinska, T. (Eds.), *ScreenPlay: Cinema, videogames, interfaces* (pp. 154–165). London, New York: Wallflower Press.

Klemmer, S. R., Hartmann, B., & Takayama, L. (2006). How bodies matter: Five themes for interaction design. Paper presented at the 6th conference on Designing Interactive Systems, University Park, PA.

Moore, M. (2009, February 13). Rapelay virtual rape game banned by Amazon. *The Telegraph*. Retrieved from http://www.telegraph.co.uk/technology/4611161/Rapelay-virtual-rape-game-banned-by-Amazon.html

Murray, J. H. (1997). *Hamlet on the holodeck: The future of narrative in cyberspace*. New York: The Free Press.

Myers, D. (2009). The video game aesthetic. In Perron, B., & Wolf, M. J. P. (Eds.), *The video game theory reader 2*. New York: Routledge.

Perron, B., & Wolf, M. J. P. (Eds.). (2009). *The video game theory reader 2*. New York: Routledge.

Poole, S. (2000). *Trigger happy: The inner life of videogames*. London: Fourth Estate.

Rejects Video Game Manhunt, B. B. F. C. 2. (2007). Retrieved March, 2009, from http://www.bbfc.co.uk/news/press/20070619.html

Salen, K., & Zimmerman, E. (2003). *Rules of play*. Cambridge, MA: MIT Press.

Shaviro, S. (2003). *Connected, or, what it means to live in the network society*. Minneapolis, MN: University of Minnesota Press.

Sicart, M. (2005). The ethics of computer game design. Paper presented at the Digital Games Research Association, Vancouver, Canada.

Sicart, M. (2009). *The ethics of computer games*. Cambridge, MA: The MIT Press.

Slater, M., & Usoh, M. (1994). Body centered interaction in immersive virtual environments. In Magnenat Thalmann, N., & Thalmann, D. (Eds.), *Artificial life and virtual reality* (pp. 125–148). Chichester, UK: John Wiley and Sons.

Smith, H. (2010). Jean Baudrillard. Retrieved from http://www.witchboy.net/2010/02/20/jean-baudrillard/

Stewart, N. (2009). *Ethics: An introduction to moral philosophy*. Cambridge: Polity Press.

Swink, S. (2009). *Game feel*. Cambridge, MA: MIT Press.

Tapper, J. (2007). *Hillary and Manhunt 2*. Retrieved from http://blogs.abcnews.com/political-punch/2007/11/hillary-and-man.html

Westecott, E. (2008). *Bringing the body back into play*. Paper presented at the [player] conference, IT University of Copenhagen.

Chapter 11

Toward an Ethic of Representation:
Ethics and the Representation of Marginalized Groups in Videogames

Adrienne Shaw
University of Pennsylvania, USA

ABSTRACT

Often, literature on the representation of marginalized groups in videogames focuses on how groups have been and should be portrayed in games. Taking a different focus, this chapter offers a broader ethical basis for the production and critique of games. It begins by outlining the issues surrounding the representation of marginalized groups (focusing on sexuality, gender and race) in digital games. It then addresses the ethical importance of representation in games as fictional play spaces. Moving from there, the writings on hospitality, recognition, and truthfulness are examined with regard to the representation of marginalized groups in games. It then uses these concepts to create an integrated ethical argument for diversity in videogames that takes into account gameplay, representation, and their relationship.

INTRODUCTION

How groups, specifically marginalized ones, are represented in digital games has been the subject of increasing attention in recent years (see Barton, 2004; Beasley & Collins Standley, 2002; Cassell & Jenkins, 2000; Chan, 2005; Consalvo, 2003a, 2003b; Delp, 1997; Dietz, 1998; Glaubke, 2002; Graner Ray, 2004; Haggin, 2009; Huntemann, 2002; Kafai, Heeter, Denner, & Sun, 2008; King & Krzywinska, 2006; Leonard, 2004, 2006a, 2006b; Machin & Suleiman, 2006; Miller, 2006; Scharrer, 2004; Sisler, 2006). Representation here refers to how particular identities are marked and deployed within a game. Much of this work focuses on videogame portrayals of women and other marginalized groups that, while they may not always be statistical minorities in a given context,

DOI: 10.4018/978-1-60960-120-1.ch011

are characterized by being under- or mis-represented in mainstream media. While the chapter will briefly outline these concerns, the goal is not to make claims about how these groups should be portrayed. Rather it is to make an ethics-based argument for the importance of diversity in game texts. Most research on representation in media implies that producers *should* be concerned with representation by stressing the ideological implications of misrepresentation (reviewed in Hermes, 2005, pp. 1-13). These approaches have not led to developing a framework that can serve as the basis of production ethics. By drawing together threads from three philosophical perspectives, recognition, hospitality and truthfulness, this chapter offers a starting point for such an ethic. Echoing Couldry, "[b]y *ethics*, I mean neither a specific ethical code…nor an agreed list of specific, and narrowly circumscribed, 'virtues'… but rather an open-ended process of reflecting on how we need to act so that we live well, both individually and collectively" (Couldry, 2006, p. 102). This is not an argument for how games should be designed, but rather an assertion of what must be ethically considered in the design process. For the purposes of this chapter, the author focuses on videogames which visually represent human-like characters and does not encompass online persistent worlds like those described in Castranova (2005) and Taylor (2006).

The chapter begins by looking at literature on the representation of marginalized groups in videogames, as well as literature that argues that producers should be concerned with proper representation. Similar concerns are discussed in relation to other media, but in the interest of space only representation in videogames are discussed here. While earlier research offers ideological critiques of representation in games, they do not necessarily offer an ethics based argument for diversity in videogames; that is the task of this chapter. One might argue, as interviewees in the author's past research have, that these are "just games" and thus issues of representation should

not be an issue (Shaw, 2007, 2009a, 2010). In response to such claims, however, this chapter demonstrates that there is still an ethical case to make for representation even in fictional realms. More specifically, three ethical perspectives are useful for making an argument for diversity in videogames.

We might discuss issues of representation through the lens of hospitality, as discussed in Ricoeur (2007), or recognition, as in Honneth (2007) or Taylor (1994). A Levinasian perspective (2001, 1996) on recognition usefully connects both recognition and hospitality. Recognition and hospitality, however, are not quite enough to make a complete argument for the importance of representation in games. Thus, truthfulness is discussed as an added consideration in an ethical approach to representation in videogames. We must also consider some of the particularities of videogames as a medium when addressing the issue of representation. Gameplay is arguably one of the main characteristics that makes videogames different from other media: "[g]ames are different, in that what matters is not just *representation* but also the active process of gameplay" (King & Krzywinska, 2006, p. 186). Thus in the final section the implications of these three philosophical perspectives are discussed in relation to the visual representation in games, gameplay, and the relationship between the two. In concluding, this chapter makes an ethical argument for the importance of representation in games by stressing reflexivity in the way videogames are constructed, as well as the ethical obligation of game designers to recognize and make videogame spaces hospitable to a diversity of identities at the level of representation and gameplay.

BACKROUND

This chapter discusses representation, or the way in which groups are portrayed in videogame texts, from the perspective of ethical theory. Generally, however, work on the importance of media representation does not necessarily call upon ethics as a philosophic discipline. Usually this type of research emphasizes what producers ought to do by describing what they have traditionally done as ideologically problematic and potentially damaging. They start with the assertion, as Dyer explains, that "[h]ow we are seen determines in part how we are treated; how we treat others is based on how we see them; such seeing comes from representation" (2002, p. 1; a similar formulation is given by Morley & Robins, 1995, p. 134). Media representations can have both "beneficial" or "negative" social implications, though the explication of these terms largely depends on one's point of view and politics as Gross and Woods argue (1999, p. 20). Looking at videogames specifically, various authors, as explored below, have expounded upon problems of underrepresentation and stereotypical representation of women, people of color, and members of the gay, lesbian, bisexual, transgender and queer community (LGBTQ).

It is outside of the scope of this chapter to address the many methodological challenges of quantifying the representation of marginalized groups in videogames, not the least of which is the fact that increasingly many games allow players to create their own avatars. It has, however, been established by some researchers that there are disparities between who is represented in games and who is not. Williams and colleagues (2009), for example, find that whites, men and adults were systematically overrepresented in games, while women, Hispanics, Native Americans, children and the elderly were greatly underrepresented. Some authors have also addressed these issues in online gaming (Haggin, 2009; Taylor, 2006). Outside of quantifying amounts of representation, we can use game journalist/blogger Jane Pinckard's (2003) description of the "Four Aspects of 'Genderspace'" to analyze any group's representation in games: marketing of the character outside of the game and intertextual use; the appearance

of the character; the character's abilities and reactions; and interactions between avatars in multiplayer environments. Most analyses of the representation of marginalized groups in games focus on sexuality, gender and race. While these are certainly not the only forms of marginalization individuals experience (e.g. religion, disabilities, age, nationality, etc.), and are not mutually exclusive categories, they are useful illustrative examples from the literature.

The author's previous work has focused on the representation of sexuality in videogames (Shaw, 2009). Though there are exceptions, often when sexuality is used in game content, games rely on heterosexual narratives (Consalvo, 2003a, p. 172). Similarly, there are few games that allow for a choice of gender beyond the male-female dichotomy (a counter-example would be the prototype CD-Rom *Runaways*, Kinder, 2000). Transgender characters are almost never present and when they are they are they are typically used as comical additions, like Birdo a character in *Super Mario Bros. 2* (Nintendo, 1988) who "who wears a pretty ribbon because he thinks he's a girl" (Kohler, 2008). In addition to specific characters that might be analyzed for embodying positive or negative stereotypes, unlike other media some videogames offer one additional form of representation: optional homo- (or bi-) sexuality. In the games like *Mass Effect* (Bioware, 2007), *Dragon Age* (Bioware, 2009), *Bully* (Rockstar, 2006), *Fable* (Microsoft Game Studios, 2004), *the Sims* (Electronic Arts, 2000-present), *The Temple of Elemental Evil* (Atari, 2003) and *Fallout 1* and *2* (Interplay Productions, 1997, 1998), players have some options for engaging in homosexual or even bisexual relationships (Barton, 2004; Consalvo, 2003a, 2003b; Ochalla, 2006; Thompson, 2004). Generally speaking, however, there is little representation of non-normative genders and sexualities in games. The ethical obligation of producers to create these portrayals, however, has not been explored.

Work on the representation of women in videogames tends to focus on the relationship between how women have been represented in games and the impact this has on women becoming gamers. According to Hayes for example, "[t]he highly sexualized representations of women in games, along with the predominance of fighting as a central game feature, have been the primary focus of concern as barriers to women gamers and a negative influence on (and reflection of) male behavior" (2007, p. 24). She goes on to explain that the response to this under and mis-representation of women was to develop a genre of girls' games, based on psychological generalizations of gendered play (p. 25). A great deal of research on gender in gaming focuses on how (and if) female gamers play, rather than game content as such (e.g. Cassell & Jenkins, 2000; Graner Ray, 2004; Lucas & Sherry, 2004). Who plays games is a necessary consideration, however, as this has important implications for what groups are represented and how they are portrayed as the cultural production literature has demonstrated (Becker, 2006; D'Acci, 1994; Henderson, 1999). When the content of games and not the makeup of the videogame audience is a focus, the overwhelming consensus is that when women are present in games they are highly sexualized and rarely central characters (e.g. Hayes, 2007; Graner Ray 2004). While this literature emphasizes the lack of representation of women in games as well as the gaming audience is a problem, it has not been grounded in an ethical argument; which is the task of this chapter.

Work on race and ethnicity in videogames tends to focus on stereotypes and the misrepresentation of people who are not of White/Anglo descent. Articles on the representation of Arabs in videogames, for example, are based on comparative analysis of images of Arabs in U.S. produced videogames to those in games produced in the Middle East (Machin & Suleiman, 2006; Sisler, 2006). The consensus in these pieces is that games produced outside of the Middle East rely on flat representations of an Arab "Other" while games produced within the region offer more nuanced portrayals. David Leonard's (Leonard, 2004, 2006a, 2006b) work on race looks at the relegation of African-American to sports and crime games. For example, he points out that eight out of ten black male videogame characters are sports competitors. He also argues that because both designers and players are predominately white, such play recalls the history of minstrelsy, a phenomena dubbed "high tech blackface." Chan (2005) examines several examples of the problems of racialized representations in videogames. In war games, for example, problematic representations of racial "others" are done under the thin guise of historical authenticity. In action adventure and true crime games, racial and ethnic minorities may be depicted, but often if these are the main characters in the game the rest of the characters in the game are primarily minorities as well. This is continually described as a problem among games studies theorists who address the politics of representation. It is rarely, however, discussed within the context of the philosophic literature on ethics.

Arguing that what producers have done is ideologically problematic is not the same as making an argument for why they are obliged to do otherwise. Ideological approaches to representation tend to imply the media representation have an impact on the lives of those who are members of groups being represented as well as those who view those representations. Whether such an impact exists is an empirical question, but one which need not necessarily be answered in order to make an ethical case of the importance of representation. There is a rich tradition of ethical theory which offers a firmer ground for arguing that producers are obliged to include a diversity of representation in videogames; specifically recognition, hospitality and truthfulness. In conjunction with this engagement with philosophic texts, this chapter draws on interviews conducted in previous studies. The author has conducted several research projects over the past four years interviewing and conducting participant observation with videogame players who have been marginalized in some way, including LGBTQ, Arab, Finnish, female and American born non-White/Anglo individuals, as well as game designers (Shaw, 2007, 2009a, 2009b, 2010a, 2010b). Themes from these interviews are integrated within the remainder of this discussion.

One dominant theme in particular has been the recurring assertion by interviewees that games are play spaces, fictional environments, in which realistic concerns such as diversity in representation have no place. Thus, before addressing the ethical arguments for diversity in representation an argument must be made for diversity in videogames being important in the first place. In the following section I review this argument against representation and demonstrate that we can still argue for the importance of representation even in fictional realms such as videogames.

JUST A GAME?

Before turning to the philosophical argument we must ask: are the arguments for diverse representations in videogames as equally powerful as those for representation in the news media (see for example: Christians, Ferrâe & Fackler, 1993; Couldry, 2006; Pinchevski, 2005; Ward, 2009)? As play spaces, where the goal (sometimes) is to take on new roles, to be someone else, we might argue that representation is less important. It is argued that online and game environments treat "identity as a set of roles that can be mixed and matched, whose diverse demands need to be negotiated" (Turkle, 1995, p. 180). Videogames and digital environments, some theorists argue, "enable us… to manipulate our 'selves' and to multiply them indefinitely" (Filiciak, 2003, p. 88). Of virtual cross-dressing Leonard asks: "[w]hat does it mean…when virtual reality provides space and ability to transcend one's spatial confinement and one's own identity to enter foreign lands and

othered bodies?" (2006a, p. 87). This type of playfulness is often, if not always, tethered to the very nature of videogames as a medium. Silverstone (2007) follows a similar train of thought with regard to play. He argues that "there is a difference between trust in a narrative or a report, that is trust in factual accuracy, and trust in the media's enabling structures, where accuracy might take second place…to aesthetics and to the authority of genre" (p. 126). Does the playfulness of games, though certainly games and play are not the same thing, trump the importance of representation in these texts?

Are producers obliged to create games in particular types of ways? Often the excuse for not dealing with issues of representation are based in the idea that these are fantasy worlds and should not be encumbered with reality or that they represent the reality of the fictional worlds they create. Of course *Grand Theft Auto* is violent, misogynistic and racist; It is a gangster fantasy, how could it be otherwise? That was indeed a claim made by interviewees in DeVane and Squire (2008). In war games, Chan (2005) asserts that problematic representations of groups are often couched in authenticity claims, particularly when games reference historical events. That Asians or Arabs tend to be enemies in reenactments of particular wars is dismissed by reliance on the historical record. Interestingly, arguments for representations of minorities rely on making the games more realistic. Interviewees in the author's previous research often said that diverse representations in games makes games better reflections of the world. Arguments against representation as a goal emphasize fantasy. In either case, however, there is an assumption that recognition requires a reference to reality while fiction is immune from recognition requirements.

Videogames are often fantasy based, and thus perhaps the need to properly represent reality can be suspended. As a previous interviewee asserted: "Once I'm in my fantasy environment, I want it to maintain that sense of fantasy. Let the debate roar outside the game" (Shaw, 2007). An interviewee in a different project argued against the importance of representation in media more generally: "Like for example, *Friends*, New York City with very few black people, that sort of thing. I don't care. I have no problem distinguishing reality from fiction" (Shaw, 2010). In both cases, the individuals draw on the notion of a "magic circle" of play, of fiction as separate from reality, which cordons off these texts from concerns about realistic representation. This notion of a magic circle of play as something distinctive and separate from reality draws from Huizinga's (1955) work on play, though Caillois (1961) argues that this concept may be a more accurate description of games than playfulness generally. It is also an issue which has been much debated in contemporary game studies (for discussions of this see Consalvo, 2009; Malaby, 2007; Salen & Zimmerman, 2003).

Even work that emphasizes the ideological implications of the mis- or under-representation of marginalized groups in videogames tends to rely on the real/fictional distinction. Chan argues that "[s]ince in-game representations do not circulate in a ludological vacuum, there are broader social consequences to consider" (2005, p. 29). In a chapter on *Grand Theft Auto*, for example, Leonard concludes by saying that:

[A] ghettocentric virtual reality matters because racism kills- the celebrations and demonizations of blackness jointly facilitate the hegemony of new racism.... It matters because social justice- the ability of all people to live their lives free of oppressions based on race, class, gender, sexuality, and ideology is a goal that U.S. society has long forgone for profit at any cost. It has never been 'just a game.' It has always been lives, livelihoods, injustice, and a desire for much, much more (Leonard, 2006b, p. 68).

This can be extended to online play as well. Turkle argues that online or digital worlds allow individuals to obtain a greater understanding of themselves, only when the significance of cyberspace is understood. "Some are tempted to think of life in cyberspace as insignificant, as escape or meaningless diversion. It is not. Our experiences there are serious play" (1995, p. 269). Beyond this, it should be emphasized, that much as play theorist Brian Sutton-Smith (1997) has argued, play and reality are not mutually exclusive arenas. As Silverstone says, "[t]he literal and the playful overlay and complicate the relationship between the factual and the fictional" (2007, p. 126). Indeed, Levinas addresses the gravity of play, though briefly, in *Essence and Disinterestedness*: "Being is play…. But is play free of interest?…. Does not disinterestedness … indicate an extreme gravity and not the fallacious frivolity of play?" (1996, p. 112). As many game studies theorists have argued, we can, and should, be critical of the ideological implications of game design. All of this, however, is an ideological critique, not an ethical argument. Arguing that we should not do one thing is not the same as arguing for the obligation not to do it; this is a task for ethical theory.

The benefit of an argument for representation that is based in ethical theory is that it means we ultimately do not have to be concerned with whether fictional texts should be concerned with realistic representations. Indeed an ethical perspective argues that producers should approach the design process in a particular way rather than creating a list of what they should or should not do. This approach, which here includes the notions of recognition, hospitality and truthfulness, can be applied as readily to a life-simulation videogame such as *The Sims*, a zombie shooter such as *Left 4 Dead* (Valve, 2008) or a fantasy such as *Grim Fandango* (Lucas Arts, 1998).

In the next two sections, I outline three different philosophic perspectives that can provide a basis for an ethical argument for the importance of diversity in representation: hospitality, recognition, and truthfulness. The first two, are the ethical grounding for much of the perspectives on media representation reviewed above though they are rarely referenced directly.

HOSPITALITY AND RECOGNITION

While not discussed directly, implicit in the above calls for diversity in media representation are arguments for recognition and hospitality. Larry Gross, for example, offers two ethical perspectives with regard to media representation that draw on the language, if not the literature, of hospitality and recognition. First, that "groups should be allowed to speak for themselves" (1988, p. 191); that is to say, media environments should be made hospitable. Second, that "[t]he power of the media should be used to equalize and not to skew further the radically unequal distribution of material and symbolic resources in our society" (1988, p. 192). Those who tend to be marginalized ought to be recognized. Both perspectives do have grounding in ethical theory, however. Here Ricoeur's work on hospitality and recognition, as discussed by Taylor, Honneth and Levinas, are reviewed as both concepts are useful in developing an ethnical argument for producer's obligations to present diverse representations in videogames.

The notion of hospitality is stressed in Ricoeur's work on translation, in which he argues that translation is necessary "not in the sense of a constraining obligation, but in the sense of something to be done if human action is to continue" (2007, p. 112). Hospitality, as described here, refers to creating the space for others to speak or in the case of videogames allowing individuals to feel able to engage with games on their own terms. One example might be the space made available in open-narrative, simulation, and role-playing games such as *Bully* and *The Sims* and *Fallout* series which allow the enactment of various sexualities. *Mass Effect* (Bioware, 2007), while certainly not alone, allows players to customize their avatar in terms of both physical and personality characteristics as they can make speech

choices that move their character in either direction on the renegade-paladin spectrum. Another example might be the translation and localization of games for different markets. Sports, music, children's and domestic-based games like *The Sims*, are games in which people might reasonably expect to participate in their native languages, or more general local cultural sensibilities. As an interviewee from a project conducted in Finland asserted, games like *The Sims* are "so much tied to your everyday culture and not like the videogame culture but your everyday culture.... It just feels more natural" (Shaw, 2009a). These are the games in which it is most obvious, most felt, that you are being forced to participate in another cultural sphere if they are not translated. These then are the games in which game designers have already learned the economic value of hospitality.

When Ricoeur discusses hospitality in terms of translation he says that it is important because "to translate is to do justice to a foreign intelligence. Your language is as important as mine. This is the formula for equity-equality, the formula for recognized diversity" (p. 31). Appiah makes a similar argument about language and minorities.

[T]here are two ways to bring full citizenship to minority-language communities. One is to make their language one of the political languages, and entitle them to access to official communications in it.... The other way is to teach them the political language, while allowing them, if they choose, to maintain their own (Appiah, 2005, p. 104).

Hospitality, making the public sphere (including media texts) open to a diversity of individuals, cannot work without recognition but what it calls for is more than recognition. It requires that individuals are given the space to participate in, not just be acknowledged in the public sphere. Sometimes that may mean giving them the language to speak within the public sphere as it is already defined, and at other times the public dialogue is opened up to include their language as well. In terms of games, this requires that games not presume that all players will come to a game from the same cultural perspective. Furthermore, one of the persistent problems in representation is that there is no one-size-fits-all model for "good" and "bad" representation. Ricoeur's discussion of translation helps us work through this. "[E]quivalence can only be sought for, worked out, presumed. And the only way to criticize a translation…is to propose another one presumed, or claimed, to be better or different" (2007, p. 114). "Good" and "bad" representation are relative terms, the relativity of which can only be worked out, never agreed upon. Translation must always be an ongoing process, as full translation is always impossible. The most one can achieve is equivalence not equality of meaning (p. 114). Making games texts open to such a process is step one in an ethical approach to representation in videogames.

Turning now to recognition, this is perhaps the ethical corollary to ideological claims about the importance of representation. Recognition, in the sense used by Taylor (1994) and Honneth (2007), is imperative to justice. Honneth argues that while different types of recognition are linked with different moral positions, what is common to all the traditions is the importance of recognition in protecting "our personal integrity as human beings" (p. 142). This is elaborated in Taylor's work as well. He states that the politics of recognition rests on the thesis that

[O]ur identity is partly shaped by recognition or its absence, often by the misrecognition of others, and so a person or group of people can suffer real damage, real distortion, if the people or society around them mirror back to them a confining or demeaning or contemptible picture of themselves (Taylor, 1994, p. 25).

A recognition-based argument, might, for example praise the game *Diner Dash*, in which the player works against the clock to serve hungry customers, while making certain cash quotas, for having the "business woman customer" appear as an African-American even though all other characters appear white. As Fraser (2005) asserts, however, "[b]y equating the politics of recognition with identity politics, it encourages both the reification of group identities and the displacement of redistribution" (p. 245). Recognition is not the same as redistribution. The African-American business woman in *Diner Dash* might be counter-stereotypical, but it does not call into question larger racial disparities in society. Recognition, and in turn representation, remain important nevertheless, as Valdivia (2002) describes in her review of the work of bell hooks, a feminist and critical race theorist who looks at the intersection of gender, race, and other identifiers in relation to overlapping systems of oppression including media representation. Representation and recognition are both indicative of and help to perpetuate differential access to resources, Valdiva argues.

Valdiva also discusses the importance of considering both who is represented and who are the presumed audiences for media when addressing issues of recognition. Chan presents a similar argument. Though he does not draw on ethical theory he does make an argument for recognition as the basis of a production ethic. Chan argues that "[a]n ethical critical awareness…hinges on the consideration of cultural inequities and interrogates the complicity of these e-games in reinforcing hegemonic notions of power, privilege and inequality" (p. 25). In making the argument in this way, his analysis implies that videogames makers are ethically obligated to recognize others (those who do not fall into the normative heterosexual, white/Anglo, male categories) in a particular way. In this sense he is arguing, much as Honneth (2007) does, that recognition is essential to justice. Chan goes on to describe the work of Leonard and Greenfield who argue that videogames often reinscribe unequal power relationship and rely on the fetishized commodification of minorities. He emphasizes, moreover, that it is not just the mis-representation of marginal groups that is the problem. We must also be critical of the fact that these groups are distinctly disadvantaged in the realm of play and pleasure; "These tropes are symptomatic of the ways in which racial otherness is configured paradoxically as both a source of anxiety and pleasure" (pp. 25-26). We get pleasure out of playing as the Other, and in doing so distance ourselves from that Other. Recognition in this sense is not just a matter of representation in texts, but also forces us to consider what audiences are being recognized by producers.

In addition to these perspectives, a Levinasian approach to recognition could also be productive in constructing an argument for representation (Levinas' work is developed further by Hofmeyr, 2009; Pinchevski, 2005). According to Levinas we only exist as individuals through the existence of the Other, and thus our very being is tied to our recognition of the Other. The Other for Levinas is not a specific group but anyone who is not us. It is only in recognizing the distinction from the Other that we can see ourselves as unique (this is distinct from the notion of a "mirror stage" as developed by Lacan in psychoanalysis). As Levinas puts it "[w]here is my uniqueness? At the moment when I am responsible for the other I am unique" (Levinas & Poirie, 2001, p. 66). Accordingly, our primary obligation is to the Other. This enhances the argument for representation and recognition based on justice frame, in that it does not insist that videogame producers recognize specific groups, but rather that they approach game development in a way which does not presume that their own perspectives will necessarily be shared by all players.

We should also take seriously Levinas's claim that we can never really know the Other. While, we generally talk about specific groups to be represented many of the problems of representation stem from presenting marginal identities as isolated and knowable. As Butler argues "personification sometimes performs its own dehumanization" (2004, p. 141). That is to say, an effort to be inclusive in game design can often result in a reification of

stereotypes. While both *Fable* games offer the option of same-sex marriage, in the second of the series non-player characters (NPCs) were labeled as straight, bisexual, lesbian, gay and celibate (in the first game whether or not a NPC was attracted to your avatar was less explicitly coded from the outset). Interestingly, in the author's play-throughs of the game, nearly all of the bisexual characters are thugs or prostitutes. In some ways, the effort to encode more explicit inclusivity into the game resulted in a reliance on specific stereotypes of sexuality. While stereotypes are not all inherently negative, reliance upon them is not the same as offering recognition or hospitality. Achieving diverse representation is difficult, but we should embrace this difficulty. Butler says that "[f]or representation to convey the human, then, representation must not only fail, but it must *show* its failure. There is something unrepresentable that we nevertheless seek to represent, and that paradox must be retained in the representation we give" (2004, p. 144). In videogames this need is even greater, as their ability to represent any identities is often limited by the mechanics of the medium itself (Shaw, 2009). We can also look at this in terms of truthfulness, as discussed in the next section.

TRUTHFULNESS

While recognition and hospitality offer useful starting points for an ethics-based discussion of representation in videogames, here truthfulness is developed as a way of extending upon both of these perspectives. Often, when lack of representation is critiqued or addressed in any medium, the answer to the problem is either the addition of more of characters of an underrepresented group or the subtraction of negative portrayals of a group. This, for instance, is the road down which hospitality or recognition might take us. However, "[t]he addition or subtraction approach to game design practice does not adequately provide a grounded ethical basis for understanding and confronting the social, symbolic and ideological dimensions of in-game representational politics" (Chan, 2005, p. 29). The problem is not just the quantifiable aspects of representation, but the much less explicable obligation to make game spaces open, hospitable, to all sorts of identities. Even when games cannot make all options available, however, they can be called upon to be truthful and reflexive upon their construction.

Turning an ideological critique into an ethical one, perhaps designers and researchers can think about representation in terms of truthfulness. In the case of *The Sims*, for example, there is a claim made by the game that you can create worlds any way you want. Biases, or at least unquestioned norms, do place limits on what that creation is allowed to entail however. This is one of the main reasons international releases of *The Sims* must be translated both in terms of language and content, as the U.S. norms do not always sell on the global market. By drawing on truthfulness, the concern is not so much with the truthfulness of a given representation. Those kinds of arguments tend to focus on stereotypes and their inherent problems. As Dyer has demonstrated this is not necessarily the best way to critique stereotypes. In his famous essay on the topic he distinguishes between "types... which indicate those who live by the rules of society (social types) and those whom the rules are designed to exclude (stereotypes)" (1999, pp. 298-299). Stereotypes are used as disciplinary forces by clearly demarcating those that belong and those that are peripheral. Rather than talking about whether stereotypes are true or offensive, it is better to ask what purpose they serve in the text.

The concern about truthfulness when making an ethical argument for representation in the videogames is how games are constructed as places of play and freedom. We can make comparisons between games and work on reality television in this regard. Andrejevic, for example, describes the myth of reality TV as "[t]he myth... that audience members gain meaningful control over the content of television programming when that programming becomes 'real'" (2004, p. 104). The problem here is two-fold. First, what is presented in the program is constructed as "reality," though it is packaged by producers to appeal to audiences in certain ways. Second, these shows are marketed via a notion of audience participation that hides the exploitation of audiences upon which the shows are dependent. While games are constructed as play spaces though they often contain references to reality, reality television is constructed as representing "reality" in spite of having been produced and packaged. Similarly, like Andrejevic's critique of reality television, Charles (2009) argues that games in general provide only the illusion of agency, and that "in appearing to satisfy its audience's desire for agency, in fact sublimates and dilutes this desire" (p. 289). While Charles' critique is perhaps harsh, that both videogames as a medium and certain reality television genres rely upon audience work and an illusion of either reality or fantasy to maintain audience engagement and distance the texts from certain types of critiques makes the construction of both less truthful. Couldry (2005) sums up Williams' (2002) argument that "it is never enough to pretend to tell the truth," which reality television often does. Similarly, the problem with videogames is that they encourage a playfulness that masks the ways in which the games limit the availability of particular identities. Playfulness is often used to distance games from critiques of how they have been constructed. One grounded example is the way in which *NHL 2K5* (Kush Games, 2004) allows players to control every aspect of their self made players and teams *except* for gender and race. The ability to create an avatar hides the limitations placed on that creation, limitations which in turn are accounted for via authenticity claims about who typically plays ice hockey.

We can also make a useful comparison between reality television and videogames because the unreality of reality television is excused by many of a show's game-like qualities. As Brenton and Cohen (2003) describe, "[t]hese pocket worlds are playgrounds for selves immersed in the retrenched, apolitical apparatus of a selfhood of first-persons; real persons, but in their contrived location so much easier to watch than real selves in the real world" (p. 53). Representation is constructed as only mattering in reality or representations of reality; fictional game worlds are immune. This kind of discourse masks the ways in which these worlds are constructed to privilege certain fantasies and not others. Similarly, game studies theorists also help to construct games as free spaces. Filiciak (2003), for instance, asserts that videogames provide new ways of constructing identity outside of oppressive structures: "The possibility to negotiate our 'self' minimizes the control that social institutions wield over human beings.... Avatars are not an escape from our 'self,' they are, rather, a longed-for chance of expressing ourselves beyond physical limitations" (p. 100). This freedom, however, is potentially much more like the freedom Rose (1996) describes: "[f]ree-dom is the name we give today to a kind of power one brings to bear upon themselves" (p. 96). We accept the limits the games have set upon us as necessary for our enjoyment of the games. T. L. Taylor (2006) describes this in terms of women who play the online game *EverQuest* and have to "bracket" their dissatisfaction with how women are represented to enjoy the game. Game makers can be more or less truthful, or transparent, about the demands they place upon players in this regard.

In videogames, every aspect of an "identity" must be accounted for and attributed to a video-game character, thus making clear the way it has been constructed. Game makers must be truthful and reflexive upon the decision to include certain identities and not others, however. The author's previous interviews with game designers indicate that producers believe that representations of minorities must always be made relevant in some way. Representations of sexuality, for example, must be relevant to the way the game is played

or inclusion of homosexuals runs the danger of either being stereotypical or seen as tokenism (Shaw, 2009). This is perhaps why all unmarked identities tend to reflect the dominant heterosexual, white male norm of many videogames. This can be examined by looking at the role of difference in how non-player characters are presented, as Chan (2005) and Leonard (2006b) describe. We might also analyze the role players are being asked to take in first-person perspective games (shooters or otherwise). In these games, identity markers matter little in the actual playing of these games, however "the white male is usually privileged by whatever markers of identity are supplied" (King & Krzywinska, 2006, p. 185). Using truthfulness as the basis of the argument, we could say that such games are evidence of the fact that there is more than game mechanics behind the privileging of certain identities over others. Two counter-examples are useful in furthering the point that videogames tend to privilege white, male (often heterosexual) characters. In the first-person per-spective game *Portal* (Valve Corporation, 2007) the main character/avatar is a woman. Unlike most first-person games, however, *Portal* is a puzzle game, rather than a shooting or fighting game. This perhaps makes the choice to make the character a woman slightly less transgressive. In a different case, in the first-person game *Mirror's Edge* (Electronic Arts, 2008) the character/avatar is also female. Though this is more of an action game than *Portal*, it was distinctly not a first-person shooter and was heralded for its unique gameplay aspects. While both games are valuable in their breaking away from the norms of game design, they demonstrate that the creative process requires critical reflection on when such norms are transgressed.

Even if the reasons for certain identities be-ing dominant are not malicious, the discourse surrounding it offer incomplete explanations that are misleading, which calls into question their commitment to truthfulness as described in Williams (2002).

Doubtless people will continue to make sense of the world in terms that help them to survive in it. But the question is how truthful those terms can be, and how far they can sustain the more ambitious ideals of truthfulness that we possess, together with institutions that both help to make those ideals effective and can themselves be sustained in knowledge of the truth (Williams, 2002, p. 268).

In sum, in contrast to reality television, which is asserted to be a true representation of reality despite being actually constructed by producers, games are constructed as fantasy in a way which hides the real world concerns and biases which shape their production. Certainly, games are always reductions of reality. They cannot offer all options to all players. They can, however, be more or less truthful about their construction. Focusing on truthfulness, that is, questioning how game designers are selectively concerned with the reality they represent, the extent of fiction in their fictional worlds, and the extent of sincerity in their construction as "free" play, extends our critique of videogame design choices and expands upon the ethical framework developed in hospitality and recognition. In the next section I discuss, how all three (hospitality, recognition and truthfulness) create a more useful ethical argument for the importance of representation in videogames.

GAME DESIGN ETHICS

This section will attempt to sketch some of the possibilities for an ethical argument for representation in videogames. First, however, it is necessary to review the trajectory of arguments made above. Typically, the representation of marginalized groups in videogames is analyzed via ideological critique. While this is a valuable intellectual tool, it does not help us develop an argument for what videogame makers. Two authors who have addressed this issue from an ethical angle are Brey

(1999) and Chan (2005). Both, however, tend to focus on realism.

Chan argues that when war games present negative portrayals of the enemy nations it is defended by arguments that those groups were viewed that way in those particular wars. Game designers, however, make decisions all the time about how "real" portrayals of war scenes are. "In the end these predeterminations belie the utterly constructed nature of the game-worlds...as well as the ideological dimensions of realist narratives" (p. 27). Taking a slightly different position, in his piece on ethics and virtual reality, Brey argues that unlike board games and other forms of play, there is greater resemblance between relity and virtual reality environments (in which he includes games). He goes on to apply Kantian duty ethics to virtual reality media, arguing that both moral development and the danger of psychological harm to those mis- or poorly represented in VR must be taken into consideration when designing virtual environments. He then distinguishes between the responsibility to avoid misrepresentation and the responsibility to avoid biased representation. The former "entails...proper precautions to ensure modeling mistakes do not occur" (p. 13), while the latter "can be derived from the general responsibility of engineers (and other professionals) to use their knowledge and skill for the enhancement of human welfare" (p. 13). This Brey states must be a conscious concern, and thus avoided, in an ethical design process. As discussed previously, however, this emphasis on "reality" to which a duty ethic obliges a creator can be problematic; other philosophical perspectives, including hospitality, recognition and truthfulness, offer useful ways of addressing this issue. Brey and Chan, however, both point towards three important concerns with analyzing games from an ethical perspective. They assert that such an analysis requires looking at gameplay, representation, and their relationship. Here this is done through the combined lenses of hospitality, recognition and truthfulness.

In terms of gameplay, ethically speaking is a game structured in a way which privileges one form of play over another? Do game designers create environments hospitable to certain types of play and not others? Are they truthful, both in terms of being reflexive and transparent, about these design choices? King and Kryzwinska argue that "the moment any choices are made about what material to include, how to treat it, and what kinds of activities are required of players in order to succeed, particular meanings are created" (2006, p. 172). Even when game designers offer and provide options to gamers to create their own in game experiences and representation still shape game texts in ways which privilege some identities over others. Consalvo (2003a), for example, points out that in *The Sims* game manual, only heterosexual pairings are depicted. This occurs despite the fact that the game has been heralded as one of the first to offer players the opportunity to play as homo- or bi-sexual avatars. Moreover, "when the dialog box for creating an individual Sim first appears … the default image of the hegemonic white male showing up first [reinforces] the traditional notion of white men being the 'norm' in American society, from which all others then deviate" (p. 185). Games are constructed as particular types of play spaces where certain types of identities and forms of play are valued over others. Certainly there are a variety of considerations that go into and stakeholders involved in creating videogames as reviewed in Shaw (2009b). These questions, however, can be asked of all members of the production chain whether that be in commercial or independent game design.

In addition to the ethical implications of gameplay, Brey and Chan also argue that we must take into consideration the ethics of representation. As argued in this chapter, however, it is best to analyze this in terms of recognition, hospitality and truthfulness. Games should recognize marginalized groups. As Levinas discusses, however, this need not be done in a way which marks the Other as "Other." Our obligation to the Other (those that

are not us in Levinas' use), means that the Other does not need to explain themself, but rather the impetus is on us to recognize the Other. It is the persistent marking of Others in games, by making their presence exceptional, which is the problem. Game designers often argue that their inability to develop thick descriptions of characters results in the lack of portrayals of marginal groups (Shaw, 2009). That is to say exposition is necessary to explain the non-hegemonic (the homosexual, the African-American, the female character). Others must always be explained, or must always explain themselves. But we can never really know the Other, however, so representations of others do not have to require more development than representations of dominant groups. Explaining a character is gay requires no more back-story than explaining that a character is straight. Do designers reflect truthfully upon the inclusion of some groups and not others in a given game? When Samus Aran, the main character in *Metroid* (Nintendo, 1986), was revealed to be a woman at the end of the game, was this done to transgress gender norms in game design or was it to reward the (assumed) male audience with a bikini-clad "trophy" upon completing the game? The former offers recognition and perhaps hospitability, the latter does not, but the deciding factor requires that the designers be truthful, both via reflection and transparency, about the design choice.

The relationship between the gameplay and representation requires making sense of how a game is structured in a way which shapes audiences' relationship to representations of different groups/identities. According to Franz Mayra, we can distinguish between core gameplay and representation when looking at games, but we must recognize the dialectical relationship between the two (2008, p. 18). Following from Newman's (2002) work, representation must be relevant to gameplay to provide valuable recognition of minorities. Many games, like *Fallout 3* (Bethesda Game Studios, 2008) and *Mass Effect*, offer players the option of customizing their characters in

Table 1. This table shows what the three philosophical perspectives encourage in terms of gameplay, representation, and the relationship between both

	Gameplay	Representation	Gameplay and Representation
Recognition		"Others" must be recognized (represented) in game texts.	Recognition must be relevant to how the game is played.
Hospitality	Allowing for a variety of play options		Creating space for various forms of representation (e.g. avatar creation).
Truthfulness	Reflection upon how games are structured to promote some kinds of play and not others.	Reflection upon why certain groups are represented in certain texts.	Reflection upon the relationship of certain forms of representation to certain forms of play.

a variety of ways, but aside from moral choices during the game, avatar creation becomes largely aesthetic. This means that these games are hospitable to non-dominate identities, but whether they offer recognition is variable. These kinds of games can be more or less truthful, moreover, about the extent to which choices made available to the player are structured. How games are structured to value certain identities in game mechanics is one concern. Another consideration is if a game is written so as to make sense using one type of character, but allows the player to create any character they want. This often results in making it clear to the player that while the game attempted to be hospitable it did not do so truthfully and it offered incomplete recognition.

As seen in Table 1, hospitality, recognition and truthfulness stress different concerns in consideration to gameplay and representation and the relationship between the two. Recognition alone does not necessitate making gamespaces open to the enactment of different visual representations or narrative options. Hospitality addresses these concerns, but does not encompass the ethical obligation to recognize the Other, particularly in the way Levinas describes it. Saying that a game is merely inhospitable or that it does not provide recognition might be dismissed by claims that such concerns are not relevant to a particular game text. Stressing truthfulness, then, in terms of how games are constructed to limit or promote certain types of representation over others offers

another critical ethical option. Truthfulness alone, however, could not address the twin concerns of hospitality and recognition. A combination of perspectives offers a more thorough grounding for a game production ethic.

Such an ethic can be applied to not only the game text itself, but also to the creative and consumptive ends of the media production process. As Valdiva says "[q]uestions of access also apply to the consumption of media in terms of what audiences can understand and afford" (2002, p. 435). Who is represented in *and* who the presumed audience of videogames are both important in addressing the moral problems related to representation. In addition, who is given space to create games is a concern as well. That is not to say that people who are members of marginalized groups are the only ones concerned with or capable of representing those groups. The author has argued elsewhere that a great failing of such an approach to representation assumes that individuals only want to see people "like them" in the media they consume (Shaw, 2010). This type of argument further marginalizes non-dominant groups. An ethical obligation as outlined here asserts that active reflection of who is given space to speak, who is spoken of, and the extent of truthfulness that limits the space in which things are spoken is necessary for a ethical game development process. This is true at all stages of the producer-text-audience process.

CONCLUSION

As discussed throughout this chapter, it is not enough to critique how groups are represented or make claims about how they should be represented. An ethically grounded theory allows us to develop an argument for why producers are obliged to display diversity in media texts. Drawing on ethical perspectives, it is argued here that game makers are ethically obligated to be hospitable to and recognize those that are not typically presented in these texts as well as Others, to use Levinas' term, in a more general sense to insist that game designers consider that their world views may not be held by everyone. We can question the truthfulness of games that rely on fiction to hide the limits they impose on players (and in this sense beyond the limits to be expected in the game rules). Truthfulness in this sense refers to both transparency as well as reflexivity, both of which are obligations of ethically oriented media makers. Recognition, hospitality and truthfulness can be applied both to the representation of identities in games as well as gameplay, audiences as well as industries.

This chapter does not offer specific guidelines for the representation of marginalized groups, for the specific reason that to do so is unnecessarily proscriptive. Ethics is about reflection much more than it is a list of rules. It is about providing a framework within which one decides how to act, rather than dictating how one should act. Moreover, this argument has been developed from the perspective that, as explored above, there are problems in arguing for particular forms of representation. Rather, than asserting a quota system for the representation of marginalized groups, this chapter asserts that game designers who wish to act ethically must actively reflect on their choices regarding gameplay and representation choices, as well as the relationship between the two. This is more useful than a simple appeal to diversity, as it encourages game designers to think more critically about the types of decisions they are already making during the design process. The considerations outlined here can, in future articulations, be explored in relation to games that do not include human representations as well as online play spaces, as well as investigations of how the videogame audience is constructed and the industry is structured. Though this is a sketch of the ethical considerations of developing games, it is hopefully a gesture in the right direction.

REFERENCES

Andrejevic, M. (2004). *Reality TV: The work of being watched*. Lanham, MD: Rowman & Littlefield Publishers.

Appiah, K. A. (2005). *The ethics of identity*. Princeton, NJ: Princeton University Press.

Barton, M. D. (2004, March 17). Gay characters in videogames. *Armchair arcade*. Retrieved April 1, 2006, from http://www.armchairarcade.com/aamain/content.php?article.27

Beasley, B., & Collins Standley, T. (2002). Shirts vs skins: Clothing as an indicator of gender role stereotyping in videogames. *Mass Communication & Society*, *5*(3), 279–293. doi:10.1207/S15327825MCS0503_3

Becker, R. (2006). *Gay TV and straight America*. New Brunswick, NJ: Rutgers University Press.

Brenton, S., & Cohen, R. (2003). *Shooting people: Adventures in reality TV*. New York: Verso.

Brey, P. (1999). The ethics of representation and action in virutal reality. *Ethics and Information Technology*, *1*(1), 5–14. doi:10.1023/A:1010069907461

Butler, J. (2004). *Precarious life: The powers of mourning and violence*. New York: Verso.

Caillois, R. (1961). *Man, play, and games* (Barash, M., Trans.). New York, NY: Free Press of Glencoe.

Cassell, J., & Jenkins, H. (2000). *From Barbie to Mortal Kombat: Gender and computer games.* Cambridge, MA: The MIT Press.

Castronova, E. (2005). *Synthetic worlds: The business and culture of online games.* Chicago, IL: University of Chicago Press.

Chan, D. (2005). Playing with race: The ethics of racialized representations in e-games. *IRIE, 4,* 24–30.

Charles, A. (2009). Playing with one's self: Notions of subjectivity and agency in digital games. *Eludamos, 3*(2), 281–294.

Christians, C. G., Ferrâe, J. P., & Fackler, M. (1993). *Good news: Social ethics and the press.* New York: Oxford University Press.

Consalvo, M. (2003a). Hot dates and fairy-tale romances: Studying sexuality in videogames. In Wolf, M. J. P., & Perron, B. (Eds.), *The videogame theory reader* (pp. 171–194). New York: Routledge.

Consalvo, M. (2003b). *It's a queer world after all: Studying the Sims and sexuality.* New York: GLAAD Center for the Study of Media & Society.

Consalvo, M. (2009). There is no magic circle. *Games and Culture, 4*(4), 408–417. doi:10.1177/1555412009343575

Couldry, N. (2005, March 4-5). Media and the ethics of 'reality' construction. *Media and Belief.* Retrieved from http://www.lse.ac.uk/collections/media@lse/Word%20docs/media_and_ethics_of_reality_construction.doc

Couldry, N. (2006). *Listening beyond the echoes: Media, ethics, and agency in an uncertain world.* Boulder, CO: Paradigm Publishers.

D'Acci, J. (1994). *Defining women: Television and the case of Cagney & Lacey.* Chapel Hill, NC: The University of North Carolina Press.

Delp, C. A. (1997). *Boy toys: The construction of gendered and racialized identities in videogames.* Greenville, NC: East Carolina University.

DeVane, B., & Squire, K. D. (2008). The meaning of race and violence in Grand Theft Auto: San Andreas. *Games and Culture, 3*(3-4), 264–285. doi:10.1177/1555412008317308

Dietz, T. L. (1998). An examination of violence and gender role portrayals in videogames: Implications for gender socialization and aggressive behavior. *Sex Roles, 38*(5-6), 425–442. doi:10.1023/A:1018709905920

Dyer, R. (1999). Stereotyping. In Gross, L., & Woods, J. D. (Eds.), *The Columbia reader on lesbians & gay men in media, society & politics.* New York: Columbia University Press.

Dyer, R. (2002). *The matter of images: Essays on representation* (2nd ed.). New York: Routledge.

Filiciak, M. (2003). Hyperidentities: Postmodern identity patterns in massively multiplayer online role-playing games. In Wolf, M. J. P., & Perron, B. (Eds.), *The videogame theory reader.* New York: Routledge.

Fraser, N. (2005). Rethinking recognition. In Leistyna, P. (Ed.), *Cultural studies: From theory to action.* Malden, MA: Blackwell.

Glaubke, C. R., & Children Now. (2002). *Fair play?: Violence, gender and race in videogames.* Oakland, CA: Children Now.

Graner Ray, S. (2004). *Gender inclusive game design: Expanding the market.* Hingham, MA: Charles River Media.

Gross, L. (1988). The ethics of (mis)representation. In Gross, L., Katz, J. S., & Ruby, J. (Eds.), *Image ethics: The moral rights of subjects in photographs, film and television.* New York: Oxford University Press.

Gross, L. P. (2001). *Up from invisibility: Lesbians, gay men, and the media in America.* New York: Columbia University Press.

Gross, L. P., & Woods, J. D. (1999). *The Columbia reader on lesbians and gay men in media, society, and politics.* New York: Columbia University Press.

Haggin, T. (2009). Blackless fantasy: The disapperance of race in massively multiplayer online role-playing games. *Games and Culture, 4*(3), 3–26.

Hayes, E. (2007). Gendered identities at play: Case studies of two women playing Morrowind. *Games and Culture, 2*(1), 23–48. doi:10.1177/1555412006294768

Henderson, L. (1999). Storyline and the multicultural middlebrow: Reading women's culture on National Public Radio. *Critical Studies in Mass Communication, 16*(3), 329–346. doi:10.1080/15295039909367099

Hermes, J. (2005). *Re-reading popular culture.* Malden, MA: Blackwell Publishing. doi:10.1002/9780470776568

Hofmeyr, B. (2009). *Radical passivity: Rethinking ethical agency in Levinas.* London: Springer.

Honneth, A. (2007). *Disrespect: The normative foundations of critical theory.* Cambridge: Polity Press.

Huizinga, J. (1955). *Homo ludens: A study of the play-element in culture.* Boston, MA: Beacon Press.

Huntemann, N., & Media Education Foundation. (2002). *Game over: Gender, race & violence in videogames.* Northhampton, MA: Media Education Foundation.

Kafai, Y. B., Heeter, C., Denner, J., & Sun, J. Y. (Eds.). (2008). *Beyond Barbie and Mortal Kombat: New perspectives on gender and gaming.* Cambridge, MA: The MIT Press.

Kinder, M. (2000). An interview with Marsha Kinder. In Jenkins, H., & Cassell, J. (Eds.), *From Barbie to Mortal Kombat: Gender and computer games* (pp. 214–228). Cambridge, MA: MIT Press.

King, G., & Krzywinska, T. (2006). *Tomb Raiders & Space Invaders: Videogame forms & contexts.* New York: I.B. Tauris.

Kohler, C. (2008, August 28). Captain Rainbow: Birdo's gender crisis. *Game Life* Retrieved May 5, 2009, from http://www.wired.com/gamelife/2008/08/captain-rainb-1/

Leonard, D. J. (2004). High tech blackface: Race, sports, videogames and becoming the other [Electronic version]. *Intelligent Agent, 4*(4). Retrieved from http://www.intelligentagent.com/archive/IA4_4gamingleonard.pdf

Leonard, D. J. (2006a). Not a hater, just keepin' it real: The importance of race- and gender-based game studies. *Games and Culture, 1*(1), 83–88. doi:10.1177/1555412005281910

Leonard, D. J. (2006b). Virtual gangstas, coming to a suburban house near you: Demonization, commodification, and policing blackness. In Garrelts, N. (Ed.), *The meaning and culture of Grand Theft Auto.* Jefferson, NC: McFarland and Company.

Levinas, E. (1996). *Emmanuel Levinas: Basic philosophical writings.* Bloomington, IN: Indiana University Press.

Levinas, E., & Poirie, F. (2001). Interview with Francois Poirie. In Robbins, J. (Ed.), *Is it righteous to be? Interviews with Emmanuel Levinas* (pp. 23–83). Stanford, CA: Stanford University Press.

Lucas, K., & Sherry, J. L. (2004). Sex differences in videogame play: A communication-based explanation. *Communication Research, 31*(5), 499–523. doi:10.1177/0093650204267930

Machin, D., & Suleiman, U. (2006). Arab and American computer war games: The influence of global technology on discourse. *Critical Discourse Studies, 3*(1), 1–22. doi:10.1080/17405900600591362

Malaby, T. (2007). Beyond play. *Games and Culture, 2*(2), 95–113. doi:10.1177/1555412007299434

Mayra, F. (2008). *An introduction to game studies: Game in culture*. London: Sage.

Miller, P. (2006). You got your race in my videogame [Electronic version]. *Escapist, 56*. Retrieved from http://www.escapistmagazine.com/issue/56

Morley, D., & Robins, K. (1995). *Spaces of identity: Global media, electronic landscapes and cultural boundaries*. New York: Routledge. doi:10.4324/9780203422977

Newman, J. (2002). The myth of the ergodic videogame: Some thoughts on player-character relationships in videogames. *Game Studies, 2*(1).

Ochalla, B. (2006, December 8). Boy on boy action: Is gay content on the rise? *Gamasutra*. Retrieved from http://www.gamasutra.com/features/20061208/ochalla_01.shtml

Pinchevski, A. (2005). *By way of interruption: Levinas and the ethics of communication*. Pittsburgh, PA: Duquesne University Press.

Pinckard. (2003). Gender play: Successes and failures in character designs for videogames. Retrieved April 16, 2005, from http://www.gamegirladvance.com/archives/2003/04/16/genderplay_successes_and_failures_in_character_designs_for_videogames.html

Ricoeur, P. (2007). *Reflections on the just*. Chicago, IL: University of Chicago Press.

Rose, N. S. (1999). *Powers of freedom: Reframing political thought*. New York: Cambridge University Press. doi:10.1017/CBO9780511488856

Salen, K., & Zimmerman, E. (2003). *Rules of play: Game design fundamentals*. Cambridge, MA: MIT Press.

Scharrer, E. (2004). Virtual violence: Gender aggression in videogame advertisements. *Mass Communication & Society, 7*(4), 393–412. doi:10.1207/s15327825mcs0704_2

Shaw, A. (2007, September 15-18). *In-gayme representation?* Paper presented at the The 7th International Digital Arts and Culture Conference: The Future of Digital Media Culture, Perth, Australia.

Shaw, A. (2009a, June). Peliharrastaja, or what gaming in Finland can tell us about gaming in general. Paper presented at Under the Mask: Perspectives on the Gamer, University of Bedfordshire, Luton, UK.

Shaw, A. (2009b). Putting the gay in game: Cultural roduction and GLBT content in videogames. *Games and Culture, 4*, 228–253. doi:10.1177/1555412009339729

Shaw, A. (2010a). Beyond Comparison: Reframing analysis of videogames produced in the Middle East. *Global Media Journal, 9*(16). Retrieved from http://lass.calumet.purdue.edu/cca/gmj/sp10/graduate/gmj-sp10-grad-article-shaw.htm

Shaw, A. (2010b, April). "Nice when it happens": An audience-based approach to the representation of marginalized groups in videogames. Paper presented at Now Conference, Madrid.

Silverstone, R. (2007). *Media and morality: On the rise of the mediapolis*. Malden, MA: Polity Press.

Sisler, V. (2006). Representation and self-representation: Arabs and Muslims in digital games. In Santoineous, M., & Dimitriadi, N. (Eds.), *Gaming realities: A challenge for digital culture* (pp. 85–92). Athens: Fournos.

Sutton-Smith, B. (1997). *The ambiguity of play*. Cambridge, MA: Harvard University Press.

Taylor, C. (1994). *Multiculturalism: Examining the politics of recognition*. Princeton, NJ: Princeton University Press.

Taylor, T. L. (2006). *Play between worlds: Exploring online game culture*. Cambridge, MA: MIT Press.

Thompson, C. (2004, April 7). The game of wife. *Slate*. Retrieved April 1, 2006, from http://www.slate.com/id/2098406/

Turkle, S. (1995). *Life on the screen: Iidentity in the age of the Internet*. New York: Simon & Schuster.

Valdivia, A. N. (2002). bell hooks: Ethics from the margins. *Qualitative Inquiry, 8*(4), 429–447. doi:10.1177/10778004008004003

Ward, S. (2009). Journalism ethics. In Wahl-Jorgensen, K., & Hanitzch, T. (Eds.), *The handbook of journalism studies* (pp. 295–309). New York: Routledge.

Williams, B. A. O. (2002). *Truth & truthfulness: An essay in genealogy*. Princeton, NJ: Princeton University Press.

Williams, D., Martins, N., Consalvo, M., & Ivory, J. D. (2009). The virtual census: Representations of gender, race and age in videogames. *New Media & Society, 11*(5), 815–834. doi:10.1177/1461444809105354

Section 4
Designing for Learning and Development

Chapter 12
The New Backyard:
Social and Moral Development in Virtual Worlds

Nathan G. Freier
Rensselaer Polytechnic Institute, USA

Emilie T. Saulnier
1st Playable Productions, USA

ABSTRACT

This chapter discusses the significant role that virtual worlds, particularly massively multiplayer online games (MMOGs), such as Club Penguin and World of Warcraft, play in the social and moral development of children and adolescents. A central argument of the chapter is that MMOGs and other virtual worlds provide a new backyard within which children and adolescents engage in active social interaction and play out moral dilemmas. It discusses three important areas of development in the context of interactions in MMOGs. First, it explores the process of perspective-taking, which is an important factor in empathy and pro-social behavior. Second, it explores the impact that MMOGs might have on stereotyping behavior and the phenomenon of stereotype threat, a harmful outcome of stereotyping behavior. Finally, it considers the role of moral dilemmas in development and how MMOGs provide unique environments for social and moral problem solving.

INTRODUCTION

Children are coming of age in a rapidly changing world. No longer are children limited to equilibrating the many factors of their social and physical environments—a challenging task in

and of itself—they must now come to understand and integrate the features of their technological environments (Freier & Kahn, 2009). For children who come of age with the new generation of technology already a part of their lives, they likely do not see this task as anything unusual. The technology is simply another part of their reality. But the experiences that children and adolescents

DOI: 10.4018/978-1-60960-120-1.ch012

have in multiplayer virtual worlds contrast to the experiences that they have in real life and to the experiences that prior generations of children and adolescents had before the development of these technologies. The virtual world provides limited physical feedback, abstracted social context, provide a surrogate extension of self, and require technical versatility to access. These clear and substantive differences may have implications for social and moral development.

In this chapter, we discuss the significant role that virtual worlds, particularly massively multiplayer online games (MMOGs) such as Club Penguin and *World of Warcraft*, are starting to play in the social and moral development of children and adolescents. The popularity of MMOGs is rapidly increasing, and there appears to be no slow down in this progress. In 2006, for example, the revenues accrued through MMOGs exceeded $1 billion (Harding-Rolls, 2007). By 2013, analysts expect MMOG subscriptions to top $2 billion in consumer spending (Carless, 2009). Beyond the consumer experience, MMOGs and virtual worlds, such as *Second Life*, a virtual world developed by Linden Lab, are being used in numerous educational contexts, supplementing a variety of core curricula. With these online experiences becoming widely accessible and increasingly mainstream, what were once niche communities of adult players are now being joined by children at earlier and earlier ages. Therefore, it is critical to assess the developmental implications for children.

In this chapter, our discussion will be informed both by direct experience of game play and anecdotal observation of children's game play. We also call upon existing interdisciplinary theoretical and empirical literature to buttress our discussion from areas of research including child development, game and virtual world studies, and human-computer interaction (HCI). We provide references to empirical evidence to support our claims whenever possible—and when not possible, we will make explicit that the statement is a hypothesis motivated by theory and/or experience as opposed to rigorous empirical observation.

One of our central arguments in this paper is that MMOGs and other virtual worlds provide a new "safe" environment (assuming the informed awareness of a parent or guardian) within which children and adolescents can engage in active social interaction and play out rich moral dilemmas. These virtual worlds may already be replacing real life environments in which children are perceived to be at a greater danger of physical harm and as a result have fewer unmanaged experiences (e.g., neighborhood backyards, parks or shopping malls). So, while the real world appears to offer increasingly less opportunity for experimentation and mistakes from which to learn, virtual worlds might offer an increasingly realistic array of analogous experiences with fewer perceived boundaries. It is the new backyard.

There are, of course, costs and benefits to such a replacement. This chapter attempts to identify and describe a few of the significant implications that MMOGs have for children's and adolescent's social and moral development. We discuss three topics that are central to social and moral development: perspective-taking, stereotyping, and engagement in moral dilemmas. Other developmental and technological topics will be discussed as appropriate to contextualize these three foci.

However, before discussing the developmental implications of coming of age interacting with MMOGs, let us consider a specific event that occurred on a *World of Warcraft* server. This event provides a concrete example, even if it is not a prototypical one, of the sorts of social and moral challenges that children and adolescents may face when interacting socially in these virtual spaces.

THE FUNERAL RAID

On March 4, 2006, roughly 40 people gathered together in tribute to a friend that had recently passed away. As the congregants mourned their loss, a group of young activists gathered nearby, out of sight. Announced days earlier, the tribute to a fallen comrade was to be used by this group of activists as a chance to make a statement. After careful planning and organization, the activists approached the mourners, and attacked. Within minutes, no mourner stood alive. The massacre had been enacted to perfection. And the entire event was recorded and made available for all to see. The video was posted on YouTube and includes contextual information regarding the announcement of the memorial and the response that individuals had to the raid. (Hollingsworth, 2006). The moral and social implications of this event would have sparked an outcry in any context. What makes this particularly unique is that it occurred online.

The individuals who had gathered virtually to mourn the loss of their friend were outraged. Playing and socializing in *World of Warcraft (WoW)* had been a favorite activity of the deceased. Her friends and family had decided to gather on a specific server in the *World of Warcraft* game in which player-versus-player (PvP) combat is tacitly agreed to as acceptable to players. People playing on PvP servers are assumed to have agreed to be attacked, and a Wild West mentality governs these virtual worlds—might makes right. The activist group, a player guild that called itself Serenity Now, was concerned that the PvP aspect of WoW was being undermined. They wanted to make a statement regarding the legitimacy of PvP. So, when they heard about the funeral, they planned the massacre of the characters that gathered virtually but represented people mourning in real-life (*irl*). However, the mourners may have been trying to make the point that, although they were in a PvP situation, overriding moral standards should still apply.

At the end of the funeral raid as shown in the video on YouTube, one of the players who led the raid ran up to the avatar of the deceased and stated in-game, "She loved fishing and snow and pvp[sic]." This expression suggests that the raiders

had known the deceased and her interests, and were acting in a way that they felt was aligned with her desires (i.e., they believed that she enjoyed the PvP attack aspects of the game). The video then ended with white text on a black screen stating, "Sorry for your loss," and "Yes, we know we are assholes:D." The disclaimer indicates that the raiders were aware of the potential negative reaction that their behaviors could have on those who were attending the funeral in mourning. Those who raided the funeral might have been engaged in a critical, self-reflective, perspective-taking activity that coordinated their own interests with both considerations for the deceased as well as an awareness of the potential psychological and emotional impact of their actions on others. The raid superficially appeared as an act antithetical to a notion of pro-social behavior, and instead it may have been an act that illustrated the complex nature of social and moral reasoning, both online and *irl*.

Reported in trade magazines and discussed in online forums ("Slaughter at the magic funeral (VIDEO)," 2006), the massacre was denounced by some as a disgraceful act against humanity. Others believed Serenity Now had done exactly what ought to be done in a virtual world designed for playing out warfare. No rules abide except those laid down by the designers and players in the virtual world and, in this case, the designers had specifically identified this world (hosted on a particular server) as open for PvP attacks, meaning ambushes and other aggressive behavior was considered normal gameplay.

For those who felt the act was reasonable and without negative outcomes, the boundary between the real and the virtual is assumed to be impermeable. From this perspective, one might believe that actions in the virtual world have little if any affect on the real world. The physical, psychological, and moral coordinates of the virtual space are independent of, perhaps even orthogonal to, their *irl* counterpart coordinates. But for those who chose to mourn the loss of this young woman in-game, the only coordinates that were independent were the physical. The psychological and moral coordinates of the virtual world could have been indistinguishable from the real world. While this type of debate has commonly occurred when cultures have come into conflict (e.g., the morality of conflict tactics between Native Americans and European settlers; or the morality of conflict tactics in Gaza today), it does not appear to be the case that differences in culture explain the polarization of views as to social and moral implications in the virtual world. Both the mourners and activists are presumed to be from the same broader consumer culture.

Given this opportunity for dramatic social and moral polarization, what are the repercussions, particularly from a developmental perspective, of children engaging in these types of rich social and moral dilemmas? We will address this question later in the chapter. First, however, we will discuss the relationship between technology design and developmental psychology.

Technology Design and Developmental Psychology

Freier (2009) argues that technology design for children, if it is to be successful in supporting rather than undermining healthy psychological development, must account for the many facets of children's developmental experiences. He outlines six facets that are of particular importance: embodiment, situatedness, dynamism, intentionality, sociality and morality. These facets derive from a constructivist perspective on child development and are informed heavily by social-cognitive domain theory, which states that children construct knowledge within conceptual domains that align with their experiences (Turiel, 1983; Turiel & Davidson, 1986; Turiel, Killen & Helwig, 1987). Developmental psychologists have shown evidence that children as young as three years of age can and do distinguish knowledge of various domains (e.g., conventional rules and

laws as differentiated from moral principles) (Smetana, 2006). Children routinely coordinate the various conflicts that occur between these differing domains of experience in their normal course of everyday experience (e.g., a child will often coordinate a personal interest in eating cookies with the conventional rule given by parents that there is no eating of sweets before dinner).

The coordination of conflicting internal concepts and external sensory information is one of the central mechanisms for developmental change within the constructivist mind (e.g., Piaget's assimilation, accommodation, and (dis) equilibration processes (see Piaget, 1985)). The same processes of coordination must play out in all areas of children's experience, including interactions in virtual worlds. However, virtual worlds and MMOGs tend to provide sensory information that is distributed differently among the various domains of knowledge. For example, when interacting through computer-mediated modalities, children quickly learn that they do not need to concern themselves with physical safety when acting online. Similarly, as has been shown many times over, the technological mediation reduces, or in some cases removes altogether, the social repercussions of a given action, possibly as a result of this perceived sense of physical separation (Kayany, 1998; Kiesler, Seigel & McGuire, 1988). The differential distribution has important implications for the development of children who come of age spending increasingly more time in these virtual worlds. With a reduction in the various forces that require coordination, the normal activity of coordinating concepts and sense information, needed to reason and act, is fundamentally changed.

In the following sections, we discuss three important areas of development in the context of interactions in MMOGs. First, we explore the process of perspective-taking, which is an important factor for such activities as empathy and pro-social behavior. Second, we discuss the potential impact that MMOGs might have on stereotyping behavior and the phenomenon of stereotype threat, a harmful outcome of stereotyping behavior. Finally, we consider the role of moral dilemmas in development, and how MMOGs may provide unique opportunities for children to engage in important social and moral problem solving in safe environments. Continued interaction in virtual worlds during critical periods of development may have both positive and negative implications for each of these areas of development, among many others, and we hope that our discussion that follows elucidates some of these important opportunities for further research.

Perspective-Taking

We begin with an important developmental issue, that of perspective-taking, which is a skill that develops throughout childhood and matures most often between the ages of 12 and 15 (Selman, 1971). Perspective-taking can be experienced in at least two distinct ways according to Bateson, Early, & Salvarani (1997). One approach is to imagine how another person feels as a method for understanding or empathizing with that person. A second approach is to imagine how you would feel if you were to experience what the other person is experiencing (i.e., put yourself in the other person's shoes). Bateson et al. showed that these two approaches differ in the amount of personal distress an individual feels as the result of the perspective-taking act, the latter producing distress and thus promoting both an empathetic response as well as an attention to one's self interests. This effect is important to consider when discussing perspective-taking in the context of interactions in MMOGs.

Traditional backyard play includes numerous activities that motivate children to practice perspective-taking including co-play and role-playing (Fein, 1981). When children co-play with peers, the two children become reciprocally aware of each other's state of mind through processes of shared knowledge construction (for detailed accounts of these processes see Baldwin, 1899/1973; Kohlberg, 1969; Vygotsky, 1980). The constructive process that occurs in peer play often results in a natural ability to take the perspective of the other. This outcome of perspective-taking that results from rich contact is also considered a means for reducing intergroup conflict as described in the contact hypothesis literature (Allport, 1954; Amir, 1969). Role-playing is also an important part of the development of perspective-taking. For example, when children engage in fantasy play, taking up fictional roles as homemakers, doctors, or explorers, they are practicing a sort of perspective-taking that includes placing themselves into other roles.

Perspective-taking as a general practice is indicative of healthy social and moral development. Research suggests, for example, that perspective-taking results in a reduction in negative stereotypic thought patterns (Galinsky & Moskowitz, 2000). Importantly, the lack of a perspective-taking ability can be associated with antisocial behavior and delinquency in adolescents and adults, as discussed by Chandler (1973). In this study, Chandler found that a program that improved the perspective-taking (and, specifically, role-playing) skills of chronically delinquent boys resulted in a significant reduction in delinquency after the intervention. Thus, it appears that perspective-taking is a central mechanism in pro-social cognition and behavior (Underwood & Moore, 1982; Denham, 1986).

Virtual worlds provide unique contexts of social interaction and role-playing, and though there is an abundance of research regarding perspective-taking taking *irl*, there is comparatively little research investigating whether the skill of perspective-taking that develops in offline interactions generalizes to online interactions, or vice-versa. There are plausible arguments that both support and undermine the positive potential for perspective-taking in MMOGs. One positive argument suggests that MMOGs provide explicit and effective scaffolding for the role-playing experience, and that this role-playing online is akin to the role-playing done in child and adolescent play, ultimately resulting in a similar development of perspective-taking abilities. Others take an even stronger position, arguing that MMOGs are better than real-world experiences at providing a rich role-playing experience, and thus may result in increased perspective-taking abilities. For example, Yee and Bailenson (2006) provide some preliminary evidence that the activity of taking on the identity of an elderly individual in a virtual space has a significant positive effect on people's attitudes toward the elderly. Reflecting growing acceptance of this technology by educators, virtual worlds, such as *Second Life*, and MMOGs are being used in numerous educational contexts, in part because of the demonstrated ease of presenting alternative perspectives and allowing for individuals to take on new identities (Delwiche, 2006; Holmberg & Huvila, 2008).

We can also make a number of counter arguments that attempt to undermine the notion that role-playing in MMOGs results in positive perspective-taking outcomes. For example, one counter argument that applies only to those MMOGs that include violence is that the promotion of violence in-game undermines any progress toward perspective-taking and prosocial behavior (e.g., Anderson & Bushman, 2001). Others might argue that the lack of any significant social repercussions for antisocial online behavior removes the natural check and balance that occurs as a result of real-world outcomes (e.g., pull a dog's tail and the dog barks, or worse, bites back) (cited from Foo & Koivisto, 2004). Another counter argument is that such role-playing in MMOGs that do not offer sufficient feedback to antisocial behavior may promote a sort of impoverished empathy, one that reflects the self's interests and emotions over those of others. In other words, akin to the Bateson, Early, & Salvarani (1997) work mentioned above, without a sufficiently balanced feedback mechanism individuals might be more inclined to consider their own self-interests due to the distress they experience in the role-playing activity. Thus

they identify their personal experience as a primary source of reference for empathetic activity, which then takes primacy over, or supplants altogether, the perceived experiences of others.

There is no clear definitive answer regarding whether MMOGs, in general, support or undermine the development of perspective-taking skills. However, MMOG designers can consider some of the implications for their design work in light of the knowledge that exists about perspective-taking processes. For example, MMOG designers might provide reputation mechanisms in-game that motivate analogies to real world repercussions for anti-social behavior (for a detailed discussion of reputation systems in games, see Sellers, 2008). MMOG designers also can focus on the production of balanced, intricate, and diversified storylines across character races that show a respect for the multiple perspectives portrayed in the MMOG world. The recent hit video game, *Dragon Age: Origins* by Bioware, though not an MMOG, shows how an investment in detailed, rich background (or origin) stories can create a positive model for perspective-taking. Modeling perspective taking within the game design itself by having non-player characters portray positive perspective-taking behavior and designing the storyline such that it promotes such perspective-taking behavior can result in positive reinforcement for players.

The role-playing that is inherent to most MMOGs creates a veil of anonymity that can have both positive and negative outcomes for perspective-taking skill development, as we discussed above. This veil of anonymity has implications for other areas of social and moral development, as well. For example, as we discuss in the next section, role-playing and anonymity might have important positive outcomes for stereotyping behavior and the negative effects of such behavior.

Stereotyping

Stereotyping, as a psychological phenomenon, is complicated and multi-faceted. Most psychologists see the general act of stereotyping as a necessary cognitive mechanism for filtering through the enormity of divergent sensory information (Spears & Haslam, 1997). However, many also consider a class of social stereotyping behaviors to be undesirable and damaging. This class of stereotyping behavior relies upon negative and often incorrect assumptions about specific individuals within general social groups (e.g., women, African-Americans, geeks, etc.) (Zanna & Olson, 1993). Such stereotyping behaviors can seem benign to the individual engaged in the stereotyping activity, but the negative effects can have dramatic outcomes for the stereotyped individual and group. Stereotype threat is a label often associated with the negative impact of stereotypes on individuals (Steele, 1997).

Stereotype threat is described as a phenomenon in which an individual's performance on a given task is hindered as a result of a particular negative stereotype made salient by a constellation of contextual factors. Steele and his colleagues have shown that this phenomenon occurs across a breadth of contexts and for a breadth of individuals and social groups. For example, in one study Steele shows that women's performance on a math exam is negatively affected by increasing women's awareness of the stereotype that women are not as strong in mathematics as men (Spencer, Steele & Quinn, 1999). Another study showed that both Caucasian and African-American men performed significantly worse on athletic tasks when the task was framed as diagnostic of "natural athletic ability" and "sports intelligence," respectively, suggesting that the stereotype threat phenomenon is not limited to traditionally stigmatized groups (Stone, Lynch, Sjomeling & Darley, 1999). Thus, when negative social stereotypes are activated proximate to an engagement in a domain-specific task, individual performance decreases and the individual's self-identification with that domain is undermined as a result (Steele, 1997).

Acting on the stereotype belief or being threatened by social stereotypes relevant to a given individual task are outcomes dependent on the shared awareness of social identity. The shared awareness of people's social identity *irl* is relatively hard to mitigate. However, virtual worlds, MMOGs and other online interactions anonymize identity by default. MMOGs use avatars as a method of representing the body in the virtual world. A game like *World of Warcraft* provides character-leveling mechanisms that function as both control variables for the difficulty of game play and as social indicators for experience in the game world. The avatar and the character level, among a number of other features, are the only accessible indicators (aside from direct social dialog) for inferring the age, gender, race or ethnicity, and general socioeconomic status of the person playing the character. So regardless of an individual's status in the game, it is very difficult to discover if a group member who "ninja looted" the treasure is a seven year old with low inhibitory control or a rude forty year old. (A "ninja loot" is a label given to an act in which a group member grabs treasure before waiting for the group as a whole to decide the best approach for distributing the discovered items.)

A benefit of allowing a player control of her own game "age" and appearance is that her real life appearance does not impact her social opportunities. In particular, access to social opportunities that might normally be restricted by the stereotyping of those individuals acting as gatekeepers controlling access to the opportunity. Thus, one of the potential benefits for child and adolescent development of MMOG interaction is that a given individual's judgments of social and moral character about others are likely informed more by a collection of actions contextualized in the game play then by superficial appearances. Others have posited such a hypothesis before (see, for example, Kolko, Nakamura & Rodman, 2000, for a collection of essays on the matter). Of course, this assumes that individuals are not stereotyping simply on the basis of other avatars' appearances, which can and does happen such as in the case of "gnome-killers" in *WoW*, where players target other avatars who have taken a gnome form in-game. These complicated issues of stereotyping play out in a unique online context and further understanding of the role of design in relation to the development of stereotyping behavior is necessary.

In addition to reducing the propensity for individuals to engage in stereotyping behavior, the ability to reconstruct one's identity in an online space also has potential implications for the stereotype threat phenomenon. In masking certain personal features, individuals are able to navigate a social space without making salient to others the threats to social identity that are common *irl*. One obvious outcome of this could be the lack of a reduction in task performance. In addition, individuals might find a decrease in personal anxiety that is commonly associated with stereotype threat conditions (Osborne, 2007). These hypotheses call for empirical validation.

Moral and Social Problem Solving

By increasing contact with individuals from diverse social groups, MMOGs may also act as neutral zones in which the process of reconciliation and relationship construction can play out (Amichai-Hamburger & McKenna, 2006), akin to the work of Cassell (2002) on the Junior Summit in which teenagers had opportunity to engage in dialogue through an online forum on topics of conflict (e.g., the Israel-Palestine conflict). By creating intrinsic motivation for active dialogue in the midst of problem-solving social and moral dilemmas, virtual worlds and MMOGs are potentially facilitating the development of moral reasoning. In this section, we discuss the role that moral dilemmas play in social and moral development, and how MMOGs can be not only the new backyard, but also the new classroom in which hypothetical moral dilemmas are enacted and addressed collaboratively.

Numerous child psychologists have explored the role of moral dilemmas in children's social and moral development. Psychologists and educators have come to understand that a child's active participation in the construction of and reasoning about solutions to specific, concrete moral dilemmas can produce generalizable skills useful for dilemmas faced in the real world (Kohlberg, 1980; Nucci, 2001). Consider the following dilemma as an example, borrowed from Kohlberg (1969, 379):

In Europe, a woman was near death from cancer. One drug might save her, a form of radium that a druggist in the same town had recently discovered. The druggist was charging $2,000, ten times what the drug cost him to make. The sick woman's husband, Heinz, went to everyone he knew to borrow the money, but he could only get together about half of what it cost. He told the druggist that his wife was dying and asked him to sell it cheaper or let him pay later. But the druggist said, "No." The husband got desperate and broke into the man's store to steal the drug for his wife. Should the husband have done that? Why?

The evaluation of this dilemma, that the husband either should have or should not have stolen the drugs, is not the primary concern of psychologists and educators. Instead, the emphasis is placed on the reasoning (and subsequent dialog) that supports one evaluative position over another. Traditionally, such dilemmas have been included as curriculum in a classroom—and such curriculum, if exercised properly, can be useful in promoting improved reasoning about moral issues.

However, these hypothetical dilemmas do not provide opportunity for moral action as can be found in other contexts of childhood development, particularly peer play. Problem solving and experimentation related to handling moral dilemmas are typically a theme throughout childhood play and children's interactions with their peers (Piaget, 1932/1969; Vygotsky, 1967). Children at play regularly establish games related to play-acting transgressions and enforcement of moral principles, and older teens regularly navigate issues of loyalty and morality as they develop and extend their friendships. The actions taken in these play contexts in conjunction with the shared reasoning amongst peer groups promote the association between reason and action. Contexts of activity in which both reasoning and action can be exercised are important for promoting moral development.

The comprehension and production of narrative around moral dilemmas is also considered an important factor in moral development (Freeman, 1991). Moral dilemmas are a highlight of popular children's literature (e.g., *Nancy Drew, Hardy Boys, Little House on the Prairie, Thoroughbred Club, Harry Potter*). Good fictional narratives promote the reader's identification with story characters, and by placing those characters into salient moral dilemmas, children are faced with the challenge of comprehending the often complex coordination of multiple social and moral factors.

If we consider the many facets of moral development in children and the activities that promote this development (e.g., the scaffolding of reasoning, the intimate relationship between reasoning and action, and the importance of narrative to provide meaning to experience), and the affordances of MMOGs with regard to these activities, it seems natural to make the argument that MMOGs provide a uniquely rich, multi-faceted context of activity that intrinsically support children's moral development.

Virtual worlds and MMOGs may not be designed specifically for the purpose of supporting moral development by providing opportunity for the enactment and resolution of moral dilemmas. However, the interactions of children in online role-playing and in deciding important questions about group membership are seen to be mimicking developmental experiences they have in real life. For instance a child playing in *World of Warcraft* might be faced with the conventional dilemma of choosing which friend to play with, or, if their best

friend moves to a different guild or server, whether they should move, too. Additionally, choices are made regarding the exclusion or inclusion of peers in quest groups based upon multiple social and, potentially, moral factors. Even simple dilemmas involving whether to show up at an agreed upon time to play with a friend test children's reasoning about the consequences of not keeping their word. We differentiate these ad hoc activities from the dilemmas presented in the game story, which often have moral relevance but which can go unrecognized by players, young and old, due to the amount of reading required or the common tendency to have the story merely serve as bookends that do not affect play. The game story has the potential to further increase this impact for those that attend to it.

Thus, MMOGs provide a unique context in which children are intrinsically motivated to engage in solving moral dilemmas that are contextualized in a broader social and fictional narrative. This is true not just for the designed experiences of game play, such as would be the case in many video games, but in MMOGs there is dramatic opportunity for social interaction to result in ad-hoc moral dilemmas, which in turn contribute much more salient, rich and accessible narratives for children to create, contribute to, and explore.

Implications for MMOG Design

In exploring these three areas of social and moral development, we recognize numerous implications for the design of virtual worlds and MMOGs. As we discussed, empirical observation and theoretical insight suggests that the skill of perspective-taking *irl* is often gained through a series of interactions and missteps with both peers and older members of society. The literature shows that there are destructive outcomes of stereotyping behavior on task performance and identification with the task domain (e.g., group leadership). Moreover, the active engagement and role-playing of moral dilemmas promotes critical reasoning skills that can be used for problem solving in the face of complicated social and moral challenges. How can MMOG design support these important processes?

Developmental Achievements in Game

Today's children and future generations of children will spend an increasing amount of their socialization time in online games and online chats. The development of social rules in children's games such as *Club Penguin*, or the rules enforced by guilds in *WoW*, illustrate early efforts to define norms that facilitate the protection of others. Game masters and moderators are faced with behavioral coaching without the benefit of being able to guess the developmental age of the transgressor, so are faced with daily choices as to how to enforce rules equitably. Perhaps, as a solution, MMOG designers have an opportunity to create technical scaffolding that supports peer stewardship (e.g., being a Secret Agent in *Club Penguin*, an individual dedicated to and recognized technically as someone capable of helping other penguins). Providing mechanisms by which individual players can earn achievements or titles in game that reflect their developmental success would simultaneously provide a goal for gamers to aspire to and support peer interaction promoting a sort of Vygotskian zone of proximal development.

Implementing Incremental Repercussions

In-game chat channels, guilds, and the ability to group or ignore other players provide both implicit and explicit feedback mechanisms through which children learn behavior. If a virtual world or an MMOG does not have enough of these mechanisms then antisocial behavior goes unchecked, until it reaches the point at which players may be banned. We discussed above the possibility

of creating explicit reputation systems, forms of which have been implemented in games previously. Going further, a game like Club Penguin provides mechanisms for moderators to take a parental/teacher role in eliminating the most extreme behavior, balanced by giving children "Agent" status to support finer-tuned community and peer scaffolding of social interactions. There may be additional opportunities to create a spectrum of constructs that systematize even more consequences, such as a penalty box, jail, or time out corner for the younger players.

Children's MMOG's already often utilize punitive approaches to manage transgressions such as banishment from a server or game. A more flexible approach that mirrors the natural and logical consequences of real life behavior might provide incremental developmental feedback that could work better over time. For instance, a player who is using inappropriate language could lose their chat ability for a period of time. Such incremental repercussions allow for experimentation and facilitate learning while continuing to enforce behavioral policies that allow for a shared enjoyment of the game.

Promoting the Construction of Moral Dilemmas

Finally, virtual worlds and MMOGs have an opportunity to allow for the co-construction of moral dilemmas through fictional narratives. Often, games such as *World of Warcraft* create detailed narratives that are intended to push the players along through their game play experience. However, these narratives can often feel like window dressing and more often it is the character leveling and collection of equipment and achievements that motivate many players to continue questing. Ad hoc dilemmas develop through the social interaction inherent to MMOGs, but there may be additional mechanisms to put into place that support the player creation of narratives (e.g., in-game stage and theatre production with the ability to move set pieces and direct NPCs actions). A number of games already have spaces that invite role playing, whether the Theatre in Club Penguin or an empty furnished shop in *World of Warcraft*.

CONCLUSION

In this chapter, we have argued that virtual worlds and MMOGs will play a role as the new backyard for child development and the design of these technologies will influence at least three areas of social and moral development. Virtual worlds and MMOGs may (1) impact, for better or worse, the development of perspective-taking skills, (2) inhibit the enactment of negative stereotyping behavior and the harmful outcomes of stereotype threat, and (3) develop moral and social problem solving through providing multi-faceted contexts for moral dilemmas which can be explored, reasoned about with peers, and addressed through action. In this discussion, we provided a brief analysis of the social and moral developmental implications of children's and adolescents' play in MMOGs, and how specific decisions for game design can result in specific developmental benefits and harms. In surveying these areas of development, we argue for the increased attention of game and virtual world designers to these important factors as they design compelling online experiences.

Gamers and technologists around the world are designing the new backyard of child development. In these virtual worlds, children are coming of age interacting with peers, playing out fictional narratives, and exploring complex social and moral spaces. The question becomes how we, as a community of researchers, gamers, educators, parents, and technologists, can build the most robust virtual backyards that will support our children's social and moral development without reducing the overall entertainment value. In answering this question, we are taking action to explicitly and proactively design the contexts in which our children and their children will construct their own

knowledge. In acknowledging the link between virtual and real world moral and social contexts events such as the Funeral Raid presented at the beginning of the chapter become a rich opportunity for defining and debating social mores. This is a wonderful and important opportunity for us all, and we should not shy away from the challenge of pushing these technologies as far as possible to enrich and support what we already know about child development.

REFERENCES

Allport, G. W. (1954). *The nature of prejudice*. Cambridge, MA: Perseus Books.

Amichai-Hamburger, Y., & McKenna, K. Y. A. (2006). The contact hypothesis reconsidered: Interacting via the Internet. *Journal of Computer-Mediated Communication, 11*(3), article 7. Retrieved from http://jcmc.indiana.edu/vol11/issue3/amichai-hamburger.html

Amir, Y. (1969). Contact hypothesis in ethnic relations. *Psychological Bulletin, 71*(5), 319–342. doi:10.1037/h0027352

Anderson, C. A., & Bushman, B. J. (2001). Effects of violent video games on aggressive behavior, aggressive cognition, aggressive affect, physiological arousal, and prosocial behavior: A meta-analytic review of the scientific literature. *Psychological Science, 12*(5), 353–359. doi:10.1111/1467-9280.00366

Baldwin, J. M. (1973). *Social and ethical interpretations in mental development*. New York: Arno. (Original work published 1899)

Bateson, C. D., Early, S., & Salvarani, G. (1997). Perspective taking: Imagining how another feels versus imagining how you would feel. *Personality and Social Psychology Bulletin, 23*(7), 751–758. doi:10.1177/0146167297237008

Carless, S. (2009, April 2). Interview: Screen digest on subscription MMO growth, Blizzard's next. *Gamasutra*. Retrieved from http://www.gamasutra.com/view/news/23003/Interview_Screen_Digest_On_Subscription_MMO_Growth_Blizzards_Next.php

Cassell, J. (2002). "We have these rules inside": The effects of exercising voice in a children's online forum. In *Children in the Digital Age: Influences of Electronic Media on Development*. Westport, CT: Praeger.

Chandler, M. J. (1973). Egocentrism and antisocial behavior: The assessment and training of social perspective-taking skills. *Developmental Psychology, 9*(3), 326–332. doi:10.1037/h0034974

Delwiche, A. (2006). Massively multiplayer online games (MMOs) in the new media classroom. *Journal of Educational Technology & Society, 9*(3), 160–172.

Denham, S. (1986). Social cognition, prosocial behavior, and emotion in preschoolers: Contextual validation. *Child Development, 57*(1), 194–201. doi:10.2307/1130651

Fein, G. (1981, December). Pretend play in childhood: An integrative review. *Child Development, 52*(4), 1095–1118. doi:10.2307/1129497

Foo, C. Y., & Koivisto, E. M. I. (2004). Defining grief play in MMORPGs: Player and developer perceptions. In *Proceedings of the 2004 ACM SIGCHI International Conference on Advances in Computer Entertainment Technology.* (pp. 245-250). New York: ACM.

Freeman, M. (1991). Rewriting the self: Development as moral practice. *New Directions for Child and Adolescent Development, 54*, 83–102. doi:10.1002/cd.23219915407

Freier, N. G. (2009). Accounting for the child in the design of technological environments: A review of constructivist theory. *Children, Youth and Environments, 19*(1). To be available online from http://www.colorado.edu/journals/cye

Freier, N. G., & Kahn, P. H., Jr. (2009). The fast-paced change of children's technological environments. *Children, Youth and Environments, 19*(1). To be available online from http://www.colorado.edu/journals/cye

Galinsky, A. D., & Moskowitz, G. B. (2000). Perspective-taking: Decreasing stereotype expression, stereotype accessibility, and in-group favoritism. *Journal of Personality and Social Psychology, 78*(4), 708–724. doi:10.1037/0022-3514.78.4.708

Harding-Rolls, P. (2007). Western world MMOG market: 2006 review and forecasts to 2011. *Screen Digest* [London]. Retrieved April 13, 2009, from http://www.screendigest.com/reports/07westworldmmog/NSMH-6ZFF9N/sample.pdf

Hollingsworth, J. (2006, March 19). Serenity Now bombs a World of Warcraft funeral. Retrieved from http://www.youtube.com/watch?v=IHJVolaC8pw

Holmberg, K., & Huvila, I. (2008). Learning together apart: Distance education in a virtual world. *First Monday, 13*(10). Retrieved from http://firstmonday.org/htbin/cgiwrap/bin/ojs/index.php/fm/article/viewArticle/2178/2033.

Kayany, J. M. (1998). Contexts of uninhibited online behavior: Flaming in social newsgroups on Usenet. *Journal of the American Society for Information Science American Society for Information Science, 49*(12), 1135–1141. doi:10.1002/(SICI)1097-4571(1998)49:12<1135::AID-ASI8>3.0.CO;2-W

Kiesler, S., Siegel, J., & McGuire, T. W. (1988). Social psychological aspects of computer-mediated communication. In Greif, I. (Ed.), *Computer support cooperative work: A book of readings* (pp. 657–682). San Mateo, CA: Morgan-Kaufmann.

Kohlberg, L. (1969). Stage and sequence: The cognitive-developmental approach to socialization. In Goslin, D. A. (Ed.), *Handbook of socialization: Theory in research* (pp. 347–480). Boston: Houghton-Mifflin.

Kohlberg, L. (1980). High school democracy and educating for a just society. In Mosher, R. L. (Ed.), *Moral education: A first generation of research* (pp. 20–57). New York: Praeger.

Kolko, B., Nakamura, L., & Rodman, G. B. (2000). *Race in cyberspace*. New York: Routledge.

Nucci, L. (2001). *Education in the moral domain*. New York: Cambridge University Press. doi:10.1017/CBO9780511605987

Osborne, J. W. (2007). Linking stereotype threat and anxiety. *Educational Psychology, 27*(1), 135–154. doi:10.1080/01443410601069929

Piaget, J. (1932/1969). *The moral judgment of the child*. Glencoe, IL: Free Press.

Piaget, J. (1985). *The equilibration of cognitive structures: The central problem of intellectual development*. Chicago, IL: University of Chicago Press.

Sellers, M. (2008). Otello: A next-generation reputation system for humans and NPCs. In C. Darken & M. Mateas (Eds.), *Proceedings of the Fourth Artificial Intelligence and Interactive Digital Entertainment Conference*, Stanford, CA (pp. 149-154). Menlo Park, CA: AAAI Press.

Selman, R. L. (1971). Taking another's perspective: Role-taking development in early childhood. *Child Development, 42*, 1721–1734. doi:10.2307/1127580

Slaughter at the magic funeral [Video]. (2006, May 4). Blog post on *Inane Asylum: Feeds of sound and fury signifying nothing*. Retrieved April 13, 2009, from http://www.hiphopmusic.com/inane/archives/2006/05/slaughter_at_th.html

Smetana, J. (2006). Social-cognitive domain theory: Consistencies and variations in children's moral judgments. In Killen, M., & Smetana, J. (Eds.), *Handbook of moral development* (pp. 119–154). Mahwah, NJ: Lawrence Erlbaum Associates.

Spears, R., & Haslam, S. A. (1997). Stereotyping and the burden of cognitive load. In Spears, R., Ellemers, N., Oakes, P. J., & Haslam, S. A. (Eds.), *The social psychology of stereotyping and group life* (pp. 171–207). Oxford, UK: Wiley.

Spencer, S. J., Steele, C. M., & Quinn, D. M. (1999). Stereotype threat and women's math performance. *Journal of Experimental Social Psychology, 35*(1), 4–28. doi:10.1006/jesp.1998.1373

Steele, C. M. (1997). A threat in the air: How stereotypes shape intellectual identity and performance. *The American Psychologist, 52*(6), 613–629. doi:10.1037/0003-066X.52.6.613

Stone, J., Lynch, C. I., Sjomeling, M., & Darley, J. M. (1999). Stereotype threat effects on black and white athletic performance. *Journal of Personality and Social Psychology, 77*(6), 1213–1227. doi:10.1037/0022-3514.77.6.1213

Turiel, E. (1983). *The development of social knowledge*. Cambridge: Cambridge University Press.

Turiel, E., & Davidson, P. (1986). Heterogeneity, inconsistency, and asynchrony in the development of cognitive structures. In Levin, I. (Ed.), *Stage and structure: Reopening the debate* (pp. 106–143). Norwood, NJ: Ablex.

Turiel, E., Killen, M., & Helwig, C. C. (1987). Morality: Its structure, functions and vagaries. In Kagan, J., & Lamb, S. (Eds.), *The emergence of morality in young children* (pp. 155–244). Chicago, IL: University of Chicago Press.

Underwood, B., & Moore, B. (1982). Perspective-taking and altruism. *Psychological Bulletin, 91*(1), 143–173. doi:10.1037/0033-2909.91.1.143

Vygotsky, L. S. (1967). Play and its role in the mental development of the child. *Social Psychology, 5*(3), 6–18.

Vygotsky, L. S. (1980). *Mind in society: The development of higher psychological processes.* Cambridge, MA: Harvard University Press.

Yee, N., & Bailenson, J. (2006). Walk a mile in digital shoes: The impact of embodied perspective-taking on the reduction of negative stereotyping in immersive virtual environments. In *Proceedings of PRESENCE* (pp. 24-26).

Zanna, M. P., & Olson, J. M. (1993). *The psychology of prejudice: The Ontario symposium (Vol. 7).* Hillsdale, NJ: Lawrence Erlbaum.

Chapter 13
Teaching Executive Functions, Self-Management, and Ethical Decision-Making through Popular Videogame Play

Randy Kulman
LearningWorks for Kids, USA

Gary Stoner
University of Rhode Island, USA

Louis Ruffolo
University of Rhode Island, USA

Stephanie Marshall
University of Rhode Island, USA

Jennifer Slater
University of Rhode Island, USA

Amanda Dyl
University of Rhode Island, USA

Alice Cheng
University of Rhode Island, USA

ABSTRACT

Numerous studies support the contention that videogames can be useful in developing specific attention and memory skills. Videogames and other digital technologies also require the practice of critical-thinking and executive-functioning skills, but there is little evidence that these skills, which lead to decision-making and problem-solving skills, can be generalized from the game to the real world. This chapter examines strategies that use videogames to enhance the development of these problem-solving and ethical decision-making skills. This chapter discusses the use of these strategies with a clinical population of children with Attention Deficit Hyperactivity Disorder (ADHD) and learning disabilities and considers methods for parents, teachers, and game publishers to make popular videogames a potent teaching tool for developing decision-making skills in children.

DOI: 10.4018/978-1-60960-120-1.ch013

INTRODUCTION

Videogames are increasingly considered a legitimate learning tool at home and in the classroom (Tapscott, 2009). Given that children ages 8 to 18 are involved with digital media an average of 7 hours 38 minutes per day (Rideout, Foehr, & Roberts, 2010), it is logical to employ the popular games and technologies being used to teach children useful, real life skills. Drawing an analogy to a healthy food diet may be pertinent to this discussion. That is, we need to find ways to take children's time and engagement with media and videogames and make it more "digitally nutritious." By this, we mean tapping the potential of videogames to promote children's healthy development. Taking this analogy one step further, videogame play should only be a part of a balanced "play diet" that also includes opportunity for social, physical, unstructured and mastery play. When appropriately used, though, digital play can provide many possibilities for learning. The cognitive demands of watching complex television shows, playing multi-leveled videogames and programming a cell-phone have been described by Johnson (2006) as making people more intelligent as measured by intellectual testing across generations. Educators are recognizing that we can use digital media to teach and learn academic content, and there is a great opportunity for using videogames and other digital technologies for the development of problem-solving, critical-thinking, and ethical decision-making skills.

Taking children's involvement with popular videogame play and making it an opportunity for learning thinking skills is an important and worthwhile goal. This is particularly true for children who struggle to learn with standard instruction in traditional school and home settings (DuPaul and Stoner, 2003), such as children with Attention Deficit Hyperactivity Disorder. The fact that many children with learning, attention, and social/emotional difficulties are so engaged by digital technologies makes this goal even more important (Brown, 2005). Taking advantage of every learning opportunity with these children and finding ways to make their involvement with videogames and other digital technologies more useful is imperative. This is the case especially if these technologies are going to help children learn effective problem solving skills in the context of academic and social demands and learning, and by extension, ethical decision-making skills. In the field of psychology, such skills have come to be known as executive functions or executive functioning skills.

Many popular videogames require the use of critical thinking skills or what psychologists refer to as executive functions to play and win the game (Gee, 2007). Learning to use these skills in a facile manner is important for all children, but particularly important for youngsters who experience learning, attention, and processing difficulties (Meltzer, 2007). However, current research indicates that while gamers practice these executive-functioning skills in gameplay, the skills are not easily transferred (or generalized) to daily activities. For example, platformer games often require shifting strategies or the executive function of flexibility, in order to be successful in game play. This chapter explores strategies that use the games that youngsters are playing as a tool for teaching them executive-functioning and ethical decision-making skills. We examine how these strategies can be used with a large sub-population of children (approximately 15 to 20%) who have attention, learning, and processing difficulties and also how similar strategies can be applied for the normative population.

To do this, we will first explore the role of children's play in learning and how videogame or digital play has become a major component of their daily activities. Then we will examine the concept of executive functions and how they play a large role in every day problem solving, and how they are utilized to play and beat commercial "off the shelf" videogames. Then we explain how these executive functions are a core component of knowledgeable and ethical decision making. Finally we examine a number of strategies that help in using videogames as a tool for transferring these skills from the game to the real world.

Play, Games, and Learning

In general, the work described herein lies in the realm of play and its contributions to children's development. The importance of play has been examined by a number of prominent psychologists and researchers (Elkind, 2006; Brown & Vaughan, 2009). Children learn from engaging in play. Play teaches children to follow rules, learn about relationships, imitate adults, and handle disappointment and success. It assists children in developing such skills as imagination and creativity, and to practice planning, prioritizing, and thinking about the future (Elkind, 2006).

Definitions of common types of play typically include fantasy, unstructured or pretend play, social, physical, artistic, rule-based, nature-oriented, solitary, mastery, and constructive play. Additionally, in today's world, play often involves interactions with digital technologies such as computers, videogames, cell-phones, or iPods. In the same way as traditional play, digital play also provides many opportunities for learning.

In recent years, videogames have been shown to provide excellent opportunities for learning and exploration. They can improve the development of real-world skills such as visual attention (Green & Bevalier, 2003), attention span (Rueda et al., 2005), and working-memory capacities (Klingberg, 2005, 2007). Videogame play also has been demonstrated to be an effective teacher for specific academic content (Shaffer, 2007). In addition, leading theorists such as James Paul Gee (2007) describe how videogame play enhances present learning, prepares an individual for further learning, and in turn can lead to better problem-solving and decision-making.

There is substantial evidence that many popular videogames provide gamers with an opportunity to practice a range of problem-solving, decision-making, and critical-thinking skills that can lead to ethical and responsible decision-making. These game-based skills, referred to by psychologists as executive functions, include planning, working memory, organization, cognitive flexibility, metacognition, and self-management, and are core skills required for success in many popular videogames. These skills are readily observed in game play. However, there are limited data demonstrating the transfer or generalization of these game-based skills to the real world (Lawrence et al., 2002; Wegerif, 2002).

Using videogame-based learning as a tool for promoting and strengthening executive functioning skills in real world tasks is challenging work however. Initial research in this vein is described later in this chapter. First though, we will discuss the importance of executive functioning skills for ethical decision-making.

Executive Functions and Ethical Decision-Making

There are several prominent theories of executive functioning (Barkley, 2003; Brown, 2006; Dawson & Guare, 2004) that have varying components in their definitions. For example, Dawson and Guare (2004) describe the importance of planning and organizational skills in a child's school performance and goal-setting. Most of these theories share a few major points that are critical to the relationship of executive functions to ethical decision-making. Each theory shares a component of self-regulation, or the ability to inhibit one's behaviors through a thoughtful consideration of a situation, and one's options for action or operating in that situation. For example, Barkley (2006) describes behavioral inhibition as playing an important role in the capacity to analyze and synthesize behavior and control one's motor responses. Each theory posits a need for cognitive flexibility, or the capacity to learn from one's actions. They all examine the concept of planning and organizational skills in

Table 1. Executive functions and their applications. (Adapted from Dawson and Guare, 2004)

Executive Functions	Definition	Potential Applications
Flexibility	The capacity to improvise, shift approaches, and be adaptable	Manages transitions Learns from mistakes
Goal-directed persistence	The ability to sustain ongoing effort and attention to complete a goal	Completes tasks such as chores and homework efficiently and without interruption
Metacognition	The ability to self-monitor and observe one's behavior	Explains sequence and rationale for decision-making
Organization	The capacity to arrange elements into a functioning whole	Readily finds materials for homework or studying
Planning	The ability to develop a roadmap or set of strategies to accomplish a goal	Saves money to buy a computer or video-game console
Regulation of affect	The ability to manage one's feelings effectively to make decisions	Accepts criticism without becoming overly angry or defensive
Response inhibition	The ability to delay or stop an action and use reflective, rather than impulsive, behavior	Shows appropriate caution while engaging in activities such as riding a bike or crossing a street
Social thinking	The ability to label and understand the needs of others and take their perspective	Motivates others through the use of understanding and leadership skills
Sustained attention	The ability to maintain one's focus and attention in the presence of distractions	Maintains attention to tasks that may be boring such as a chore or homework
Take initiation	The ability to initiate an activity without procrastination	Able to develop strategies when beginning or playing a game or activity
Time management	The ability to respond to things in a timely fashion	Prioritizes activities such as choosing to do homework prior to going out with friends
Working Memory	The ability to remember something and perform an activity using this memory	Follows complex and multi-step directions

decision making. The concept of working memory, or the capacity to hold a thought in mind while actively learning, also is considered a core executive function across theories(Barkley, 2003, Brown, 2006). Many also describe the process of metacognition, or the capacity to reflect on one's thinking. Goldberg (2001) describes how metacognition plays a core role in the capacity for humans to be civilized. In short, each of these theories presents a different conceptualization of what is commonly known as thinking skills. Specific executive functions and their applications in day to day tasks are summarized in Table 1.

Executive functions are thought to help us learn from past experiences or to keep information in mind when doing something (working memory), or to change our approach when our previous methods of doing something are no longer work-

ing (cognitive flexibility). Executive functions help a child find and complete their homework (organization), or walk through the steps of completing a long-term science project (planning). In videogame play, executive functions help a player to change strategies (cognitive flexibility) when a previously successful strategy no longer works on a more complex level of the game, or to be able to look ahead and anticipate the moves or strategies one might use to successfully beat a game (planning). The reflective thinking (metacognition) that helps a player to be thoughtful and deliberate in their approach to game play is a core characteristic of complex videogame play.

The original theories and research on executive functioning examined patients who had damage to the prefrontal cortex of their brains. These individuals displayed basic capacities of speech, long-term memory, and other signs of intellectual abilities. However, they often displayed a complete lack of decision-making capacity. Individuals lacking executive functioning skills as a result of damage to the prefrontal cortex could not consider the consequences of their behavior, were able to think only in the present, and were unable to reflect and learn from their actions. They were described as losing their sense of self or personality and the capacity for any degree of self-regulation or self-management (Brown, 2006).

Capacities for ethical decision-making and problem-solving skills are clearly seen within the confines of executive functions (Dawson and Guare, 2004). To make a thoughtful and ethical decision, individuals need the capacity for self-regulation, the ability to consider the consequences of their actions, and skills of planning and adaptability (Barkley, 2003). For example, children are considered civil and socially adept when they take turns in a game and share toys in play. Both of these activities require self-regulation and social thinking skills. Utilizing children's involvement in popular game play to help them develop and improve these skills and be able to transfer them to their daily activities thus can be seen as a natural part of parents' and teachers' agendas.

Practicing Game-Based Executive Functions

At their basic nature, most games, whether board games or videogames, require choices and decisions. While there are games of simple chance, such as the card game *War*, and those in which decisions are a matter of response to a stimulus, most compelling games require choices and active decision-making. Games with complexity and challenge, which are generally the most frequently played games, often require more thinking, decision-making, and choices throughout the game.

Videogame play requires choices and decision-making. While some games require rapid hand-eye coordination to shoot at a target or learning a sequence of moves to go from one level to another, many games require far more intensive, strategic approaches. Many popular and complex videogames require skills such as planning, organization, working memory, cognitive flexibility, and metacognition. These games require the player to make decisions, evaluate the impact of these decisions, and learn from the consequences of their actions.

For example, the skill of organization is used in a game like *World of Warcraft*. *World of Warcraft* is a Massive Multiplayer Online Role Playing Game (MMORPG) in which players create a character in their quest to become a great adventurer and can choose either to join the Fearsome Horde or the Noble Alliance. Players can complete thousands of quests, raid dungeons, or hunt for rare monsters or items. In addition, they must manage inventories of up to hundreds of different items and skills, and make decisions about items' relative importance, which items and powers to pair together, and which items to keep and which to sell. Games like *Batman: Arkham Asylum* or the *Street Fighter* series use working memory skills when they rely on the player memorizing multiple unique sequences of buttons to win fights. In *Street Fighter*, players choose a unique character that has a specific fighting style and set of moves that are easy to learn but hard to master. Players need to learn and remember their character's strengths, as well as those of their opponents and often remember specific counter-moves. Working memory skills are utilized when the player is keeping their past maneuvers in mind as they are acting in the present. Also, many platformer games like the *Super Mario Brothers* series challenge players to negotiate unchanging lines of obstacles. When players fails to negotiate an obstacle they die, and the only way for to succeed is to constantly remember each obstacle from a previous attempt, so that they can respond to it appropriately. Tower defense games, such as *Plants vs. Zombies* or *Fieldrunners*, require cognitive flexibility, where players are given a set of defensive tools (e.g. "towers") that they must set up to defend against increasingly difficult and evolving onslaughts of enemies. Each new onslaught of enemies will have different powers and abilities, which constantly force players to adjust their tools and strategies to meet the new challenges. If players are cognitively inflexible and do not adjust strategies within the game, they will quickly lose.

Generalizing Game-Based Executive Functions and Decision-Making to the Real World

There are many "serious games" designed to help in developing ethical behaviors and decision-making. Many of these games are specific to particular content, whether the focus is on understanding issues of energy conservation (*Enercities*) or on developing a sense of political involvement (*Darfur is Dying*). These games may provide situated learning in which a child learns to apply specific game-taught skills and values to a particular area. Some of the "serious" games may provide a closer approximation to situated learning (Brown, Collins, Duguid, 1989), in that the game content is more closely connected to a real world context. A number of more popular serious videogames such as Civilization III, present opportunities for learning about content and developing shared values (Shaffer, Squire, Halverson, and Gee, 2005).

Serious games may also serve to enhance a player's sensitivity to other, broader community and social issues. As most of these games often have a limited audience and represent only a very small portion of the games that children actually play, they are likely to have a limited impact upon teaching ethical decision-making to the larger audience of videogame players. A broader audience can be reached, however, through active teaching in the context of popular videogames.

Developing methods and materials that use popular videogames to strengthen children's executive functioning and ethical decision-making skills is of central importance to contemporary parenting and education. The rationale for using these games, in this manner, is quite simple. By definition, popular games are highly engaging to children, easily accessible, and engender the repeated practice of skills that lead to learning. The children are already there, thoroughly engaged in playing popular games. From an educational point of view, it is easy to see how a child's intense focus and engagement with videogames can be used as a tool for teaching these skills.

Game play provides an engaging format within which players can develop and practice these executive-functioning skills. However, questions remain as to whether this type of game play represents context specific learning, where the gamer is able to apply these skills only in a specific game or in similar games. In contrast, it is important to know to what extent the skills learned and practiced are transferable to real-world situations (Gee, 2005; Shaffer, Squire, Halverson & Gee, 2004). For the most part, it appears that popular videogame play without active reflection may not encourage the generalization of these skills to the real world (Wright, 2009) and, in turn, does not help in developing the executive-functioning skills that can lead to better ethical decision-making and problem-solving on the part of children and adolescents.

It appears that players do not generally, in the absence of coaching, detect how they are using these executive-functioning skills in game play, nor do they reflect upon how they might use these same skills in other places in the real world. In light of the massive amount of time and energy children devote to digital media, the authors of this chapter believe it is the responsibility of parents, educators, and game publishers to promote the generalization of game-based executive skills to real-world problem-solving. Using children's attention, motivation, and immersion in these games as tools to help them develop ethical decision-making skills through adjunctive teaching and game-based, self-directed strategies is a highly worthwhile goal. In the following sections, we present our initial work on developing methods and research to address this goal.

PILOT STUDIES

Videogames can be designed or used in a manner that helps children to learn executive-functioning skills, particularly those children who do not learn them as readily as others through typical teaching formats and settings. Many of these children are identified as having Learning Disabilities, Attention Deficit Hyperactivity Disorder, or processing difficulties. There is compelling data that these children learn reading and math skills much more readily with digital technologies when compared to traditional teacher directed, classroom teaching methods (Clarfield & Stoner, 2004; Ota & DuPaul, 2002). Moreover, many researchers have observed how ADHD and LD children are engaged by videogame play (Brown, 2006; Klingberg, 2009).

Children with attention and learning difficulties are characterized by problems in their capacity to generalize learning from one situation to another (Barkley, 2005). They tend to benefit from instruction containing the following elements: (a) using strategic thinking principles that help them to understand what they are about to learn, (b) observing models that demonstrate the learning process, (c) having support and practice opportunities while learning, and (d) having direct training in the transfer of skills from one place to another. Many of these youngsters struggle in traditional learning models, where materials are presented verbally, need to be read, or require written production in order to display competency. A large proportion of these children learn better when provided with multi-modal learning experiences that are able to sustain their attention, improve their engagement, and provide them with repeated practice opportunities. These are exactly the qualities that many videogames provide as a learning tool.

In this section, we describe a series of pilot studies conducted to explore the use of popular videogames for teaching executive functioning skills. As noted earlier, this research has been completed primarily with a clinical population of children who have learning and attention issues. While this is a fairly large portion of the population (estimates indicate the incidence of Learning Disabilities to be between 8 and 10 percent and of Attention Deficit Hyperactivity Disorder to be between 3 and 9 percent, with some overlap amongst these populations), there are also many other children who have these difficulties or other types of processing disorders at a sub-clinical level.

There is reason to believe that these students will also experience more difficulty in generalizing game-based learning to the real world. The difficulty of generalization is in fact a defining feature of children with Attention Deficit Hyperactivity Disorder and Learning Disabilities. Developing methods that help these children to be able to generalize from game-based learning to the real world is likely to be even more powerful with youngsters who *do not* have such difficulties.

The Concept of Using Videogames as a Teaching Tool

The basic premise of all of our work is that children are frequently easily engaged, highly attentive, and, as a result, receptive learners while playing popular videogames. By capturing children when they are in this highly receptive state, we amplify the opportunity for learning executive functioning skills.

At this point, very few popular games have embedded strategies that assist children in taking game-based skills and applying them directly to the real world. However, there are a few games in which feedback and questions may be asked that might stimulate children to think about real-world applications (*Roller Coaster Tycoon, Zoo Tycoon, The Sims*). Due to the paucity of games that actually connect game-based activities to real world problem solving, the primary approach in our studies is to use videogames as a teaching tool, where supplementary educational materials make this connection. We have developed strategies for parents, teachers, and kids to take what they are doing in a videogame and generalize those skills to the real world, by creating game-related and game-linked learning opportunities, facilitated by written materials, discussions, and practice activities as described next.

Strategic Teaching Strategies in These Studies

A number of strategic teaching skills are at the core of this approach. Again, while in our approach these strategic thinking skills are being applied externally to the game by teachers, parents, or learning modules, ideally they would be embedded into games without changing the very nature of the games (i.e., making the games into onerous learning games). These strategies include:

1. Making the learning goals explicit
2. Developing a partnership with children for learning executive skills that are in the game
3. Encouraging children to practice these skills in an interesting and reinforcing manner (playing the videogames)
4. Previewing strategies to help children recognize how they will use these executive-functioning skills in game play
5. Prompting metacognitive strategies that encourage children to reflect on their use of executive functioning skills in a game and possible uses in their daily activities
6. Employing generalization and point-of-performance strategies that link executive functions used with digital technologies to real-world experience

These strategic thinking skills are employed through a series of online "Playbooks" that provide parents and teachers with an understanding of the executive functioning skills that are used in the game. They include talking points to discuss how the skills help children in the game and a section called "Making It Real," which helps parents and teachers find ways for children to connect game-based skills to the real world.

In our latest studies, the children were also presented with e-learning modules called "Pre-Plays" and "RePlays" that helped them learn about game-based executive functions and how these functions might apply in the real world. The e-learning modules help the children go through a three-step process, which we refer to as "detect," "reflect," and "connect"; that is, detect, reflect, and connect the problem solving and decision-making skills used in the game, and consider their uses in outside the game situations. This three-step process helps children to identify (detect) when they are using an executive skill in a game, consider (reflect on) how the executive skill helped them in the game, and consider places where they could apply (connect) that skill in their daily routines.

In the following sections, initial research, conducted in four pilot studies, on the effectiveness and use of these strategies is described. These studies are summarized in Table 2.

Brain Training Study

Our first study used a pair of traditional brain-training games, along with our parent-training program, to teach real-world executive skills. Six children participated in this pilot study, in which neuropsychological data were collected prior to and after the completion of the study. The children were assigned a highly structured, intensive program of game play over the course of six weeks. Fifteen mini-games including *Pathfinder*, *Sound Bites*, *Missing Link*, *Coin-parison*, *Matchmaker* and *Calculations x 20* were chosen from *Brain Age* and *Big Brain Academy*. These games were chosen by trained game reviewers for their capacity to provide practice in the executive functions of planning, working memory, sustained attention,

Table 2. Pilot studies on teaching executive functions through popular videogame play

Study	Question(s)	Participants	Activities	Findings	Issues/Concerns
Brain training pilot	Does videogame play promote the development of executive functions (EF's)?	6 children, ages 8-11, with Learning Disabilities and/or Attention Deficit Hyperactivity Disorder	Played selected mini-games from Big Brain Academy and Brain Age 45 minutes per day, 3 days per week, for 6 weeks	Improvements over baseline performance in time management, and processing speed as measured by neuropsychological testing	Difficult to sustain child interest over time; correct dosage of game play; small sample
Tailoring game play to specific executive functions	Can prescribed game play, matched to EF weaknesses, improve these specific EF's?	10 children, ages 8-11, with Learning Disabilities and/or Attention Deficit Hyperactivity Disorder	Played online and Nintendo DS games prescribed to strengthen measured EF weaknesses, 45 minutes per day, 3 days per week, for 6 weeks; supplemented by materials to facilitate parent instruction	Targeted skills improved; non-targeted skills did not	Need for further study with matched controls; integrity/dosage of parent involvement
Social validity with parents	How do parents see themselves being involved with children's videogame play?	17 parents of children with learning difficulties and/or attentional problems	Interviewed parents individually about their current activities and perspectives	Majority of parents did not play or interact with children during videogame play; also reported little or no knowledge of how to teach in the context of videogame play, with the exception of game selection and length of time prohibitions	Small clinical sample—need to expand
Social validity with teachers	What are elementary and middle-school teachers' perspectives on the usefulness of a curriculum to teach executive skills using videogame play?	Six classrooms in a school for students with learning and behavior challenges, including approximately 40 students and 8 teachers	Teachers and students interacted around online videogames such as Tanks, guided by the LearningWorks for Kids instructional materials	Teachers reported the videogames and materials created teaching/learning opportunities; students were observed by teachers to independently discuss the use of Efs outside the context of game play	Student reading skill level sometimes a challenge; need more formal assessment of student behavior

and time management/processing speed. The children were required to play each of these mini-games three times a day, four days a week. The intensity of the practice of playing these games as a prerequisite for real-world improvement is seen in a series of studies conducted using videogame based working-memory training (Klingberg, 2005, 2007).

In addition to the game play, parents were provided with Playbooks that assisted them in using the child's game play as a teaching tool. Playbooks are essentially online teaching manuals to guide a parent or teacher's discussion of how executive functions are used in game play and related daily activities. The Playbooks contained a set of discussion points to help parents talk with their children specifically about executive functions used in game play. These Playbooks were designed to help children identify when they use executive skills in a game, reflect on how these skills assist them in beating the game, and connect these executive skills to the real world. Parents also had the "Making It Real" section of their Playbooks, which provided them with practice opportunities to reinforce the use of game-based executive skills in the child's day-to-day activities.

Only three of the original six participants completed the study. This appeared to be a reflection of the intensity and duration of the game play. Parents of children who did not complete the study reported that their children did not sustain their interest in repeatedly playing the games over the course of six weeks.

While the sample size was small, the resulting data that indicated children's improvement were compelling. Most notable were improvements in time-management and processing-speed strategies. Children displayed improvement on the Process Assessment of the Learner-II (PALS-II) Writing Test, a measure of writing speed, and significant improvement on the Test of Word Reading Efficiency (TOWRE) Sight Word Subtest, which measures how quickly children can read a set of words. Improvement also was seen on the children's capacity to do math minutes—that is, accurately and quickly complete grade appropriate math problems.

Parents' qualitative reports of observed changes in their children were even more encouraging. One parent described her son as displaying much improvement in school, to the point where he had received some grades of 100% on tests and quizzes, in contrast to never having received these types of grades in the past. Improved planning skills were also noted with this child, as he independently packed his backpack for a Boy Scout camping trip, which he had never able to do before. Increased persistence in practicing the piano and taking his papers to and from school was also observed. Another parent described her child as "flying through" math minutes at school and displaying enhanced persistence and responsibility at home. She attributed this to her child having developed a sense of success at practicing and playing videogames that he initially found to be frustrating and, with encouragement, was able to see gains that he made in the course of the study.

Significant improvement was also found on a measure of response inhibition, the Stroop Color and Word test t(2)= 7.77, p= 0.16 and the subtest of Sight word Efficiency on Test for Word Reading Efficiency (TOWER-SWE) was also significant

t(2)= -5.89, p= .028. Math Calculation test was also significant at the p<.o5 level (t(2)= -6.047, p= 026). On the Continuous Performance Task which measures an individual's sustained and selective attention and impulsivity, children also showed improvement. Finally, PAL copying Task B, a measure of writing speed, also showed significant change t(2)= -4.88, p= .039.

Together, these results from a small sample of children suggest that children who are difficult-to-teach, and have difficulty with self-regulation, experienced improvements on laboratory based tasks of attention, working memory and processing speed, as a function of structured play with videogames. Perhaps more importantly, they also demonstrated improvement on real world skills including math work, reading, organization, and in school performance.

TIP Study

In a second study the group's work took a different approach to the use of popular games to improve executive functioning skills. This study, titled the "Tailored Intervention Program (TIP)," used neuropsychological pre-testing to determine the areas in which participants displayed executive functioning weaknesses. A set of individualized prescriptions, using specific Internet and console games that practice areas of executive functioning weakness, were given to each child, along with parent Playbooks for each of the skills. In addition, parents were given psycho-educational instructional materials such as readings about executive functions, along with some basic training in the theory of executive functions. As in the previous study, parent Playbooks provided the parents with specific talking points to help their children identify and reflect on their use of executive skills in game play and a Making It Real section that helped them to connect and practice game-based skills in the real world.

Ten children participated in the TIP study. Parents again reported that there was some difficulty in getting the children to sustain their effort over the course of the study. Of the ten children who participated, seven were able to play the games and to record their participation at an acceptable level. The children appeared to be more likely to sustain their participation in the study as we relied more on Internet-based games and Nintendo DS games that allowed for practice of planning and time management. These games included *Harvest Moon* and *Animal Crossing,* which were individually prescribed and varied for each child over the course of the six-week participation.

Results of this study again supported a conclusion that using videogames can improve executive functioning skills. An important outcome of this work was that analysis of the data indicates that significantly more improvement was seen in the executive functioning skills that were practiced by the participants than those that were not practiced. In other words, we saw more improvement on game-based executive skills that were targeted in our prescriptions than we did in executive skills that were not targeted. In addition, the improvement of these skills from pre-test to post-test was clinically significant, as well. These results suggest that specific target executive function skills can be responsive to targeted instruction, using videogames.

A School-Based Curriculum Study

One additional study and one pilot program have also been implemented by the same research team. A school-based curriculum using popular videogames to teach executive-functioning skills was piloted at Mount Pleasant Academy in Providence, Rhode Island, across six classroom settings during November and December of 2009. This study was qualitative and developmental in nature. In this study, teachers, rather than parents, served as coaches in their use of Playbooks to help children transfer game-based executive functioning skills into the real world, classroom based activities and demands. This study also included supplementary

online and paper and pencil materials for the students to complete to learn about executive functions, set goals for improvement of their executive skills, and assist them in making the connection between game-based skills and the real world.

Interviews with teachers and students indicate that the children were extremely excited and active participants in the program, and the teachers found the skills being practiced to be relevant to classroom learning for their students. There were many reports of children talking about their use of executive skills. In this case, curricula were used to improve executive functions of sustained attention, working memory, and planning. Did teachers report improvements in classroom behavior and/ or academic performance? Difficulties included problems in reading for many of the younger children and the difficulty of some of the younger children understanding these concepts. The results of this study show that, in school/classroom settings, videogame based learning can be made relevant and useful for teachers and students.

Parent Perspectives

A fourth study was an interview study conducted with the parents of 17 children with attention and learning difficulties. Here the focus was to explore how parents interact with their children around the children's use of videogames. The findings are consistent with previous reports such as from the Pew Internet studies (2007) that indicate that approximately 30% of parents play videogames with their children. However, our data are particularly interesting, in that that parents consistently reported they did not know how to implement teaching strategies with videogames as they might with common daily activities involving parents and children, such as how to deal with playing and/or losing a game or discussing the need to practice to get better at playing a musical instrument. These results suggest the need to develop materials and strategies for parents, which can help guide their parenting interactions around videogames to produce intentional learning outcomes.

In summary then, these initial studies suggest (a) children can learn executive functions through videogame play, (b) in teaching executive functions through videogame play, targeted skills that are specifically taught are likely to improve more than skills practiced in the game but not specifically taught, (c) videogame based teaching of executive functions can result in improvements in school related skills, (d) teaching using videogames is judged to be a reasonable in school activity by teachers and students, and (e) parents could/would benefit from explicit instruction and materials on how to engage in parenting around children's use of videogames—especially when it involves trying to teach and strengthen specific skills that are embedded in the games. While each of these conclusions will benefit from further evidence through carefully controlled research, these initial findings provide the impetus for further work embedding parent and teacher facilitated teaching into the context of children's videogame play. The implications of this work are discussed next.

CONCLUSION AND RECOMMENDATIONS

To summarize, our research to date suggests the following:

1. Brain-training videogames have promise for developing decision-making and executive functioning skills, particularly if they are played repetitively and for an adequate duration.
2. Targeting particular areas of problem-solving or executive function weaknesses with videogames that practice these skills can result in measurable improvements in these areas.
3. Using videogames to teach these skills to youngsters with learning and attention problems can be effective. This would suggest that

applying the same practices to a population of normative learners would have an even greater chance for success.

4. Parents and teachers need to be educated about how to use popular videogames to enhance ethical decision-making and executive functioning skills in children.

Future research will need to explore the issue of generalizability of videogame-based learning to real world applications. This work should incorporate the use of video and non-videogame controls, and explore the benefits of game play with and without parent and teacher participation. Further assessment of the use of differentiated instructional or targeted strategies for youngsters as compared to a one-size-fits-all strategy will be useful. Comparison of game-based to traditional interventions for teaching executive skills for children with and without learning and attentional problems will also be important.

As a first step, it becomes imperative that parents and teachers begin to connect with children about their digital/electronic interests and use of videogames and other technologies. Rather than viewing children's interest in videogames as something that only kids do, parents will need to play the games themselves, learn about what makes them so interesting and engaging, and improve communication about game play. That is, it is important to do more than simply monitor and set limits on these videogames and digital technologies. Guidance for parents and teachers about suitable games and activities is currently available at websites such as whattheyplay.com and commonsensemedia.org. Further, instructions on how parents and teachers can identify and use specific videogames and technologies to develop executive skills can be found at learningworks-forkids.com. LearningWorks for Kids is a group of psychologists and educators dedicated to using digital technologies to teach critical thinking and self-regulatory skills to children.

Game publishers will need to embrace the concept that "videogames are good for you," by developing methods that make the games more digitally healthy. Embedding strategies for connecting game-based skills to the real world, acquiring "points" and "tokens" that promote generalization of skills, and the development of short previews or materials that encourage real-world learning are suggested. These suggestions are not an attempt to make commercial, off the shelf videogames into "learning games," but more akin to adding a bit of calcium to one's orange juice to add to the original health benefits provided.

Game play that teaches metacognition or reflection, develops skills for inhibiting responses and planning, and improves one's cognitive flexibility provides the basis for developing improved decision making and ethical thinking skills. Ethical decision-making is seen as partly a function of what the child learns from his parents, community, and other learning opportunities. Thus, given the ubiquitous nature of videogame play, it is imperative that we explore and develop evidence-based research to guide our policies, practices and decision-making about children's videogame play. In the same way that politicians have made policies about other popular technologies (cell phones, movie ratings, and videogame ratings) there is also a need to consider how these tools can be used in a positive fashion or children's healthy growth and development. Based on these conclusions, then, we end with the following recommendations.

Recommendation Summary

Based upon our research findings, we have developed a set of recommendations and considerations for using popular videogames to teach executive-functioning, self-management, and ethical decision-making skills.

1. **Use videogames to teach executive functions.** Identify popular, commercial, off-the-shelf videogames that practice executive-functioning skills.

2. **Demonstrate how videogames can practice executive functions.** Educate parents and teachers that videogames can teach important problem-solving and decision-making skills and provide general strategies for using games in this manner.

3. **Use the games kids are already playing.** Develop specific supplementary materials designed to teach executive-functioning skills that accompany individual popular videogames.

4. **Incorporate teaching executive skills into new games.** Educate and work with game publishers about how games can practice executive-functioning skills.

5. **Encourage parents to play videogames with their kids.** Educate parents about the importance of playing videogames with their children and the need to understand the skills that they children are practicing in these games.

6. **Connect game-based skills to the real world.** Educate parents, teachers, kids, and game publishers about the importance of generalizing game skills and knowledge to daily activities.

7. **Conduct large scale, controlled research on videogames and decision making.** Expand research activities to examine the effects of videogames on developing specific executive-functioning skills such as time management, planning, organization, and sustained attention that are keys to academic success.

8. **Increase the use of videogames for teaching alternative learners.** Expand research with a clinical population of children with attention and learning problems for a better use of their engagement with videogames to learn executive and academic skills.

REFERENCES

Barkley, R. (2005). *Attention-deficit hyperactivity disorder: A handbook for diagnosis and treatment* (3rd ed.). New York: Guilford Press.

Brown, J. S., Collins, A., & Duguid, P. (1989). Situated cognition and the culture of learning. *Educational Researcher, 18*(1), 32–34.

Brown, S., & Vaughan, C. (2009). *Play: How it shapes the brain, opens the imagination, and invigorates the soul.* New York: Penguin Group.

Brown, T. (2006). *Attention deficit disorder: The unfocused mind in children and adults.* New Haven, CT: Yale University Press.

Clarfield, J., & Stoner, G. (2005). Research brief: The effects of computerized reading instruction on the academic performance of students identified with ADHD. *School Psychology Review, 34*(2), 246–254.

Dawson, P., & Guare, R. (2004). *Executive skills in children and adolescents.* New York: The Guilford Press.

Dawson, P., & Guare, R. (2009). *Smart but scattered: The revolutionary "executive skills" approach to helping kids reach their potential.* New York: The Guilford Press.

DuPaul, G., & Stoner, G. (2003). *ADHD in the school: Assessment and intervention strategies* (2nd ed.). New York: Guilford Press.

Elkind, D. (2007). *The power of play: How spontaneous imaginative activities lead to happier, healthier children.* Cambridge, MA: Da Capo Press.

Gee, J. P. (2004). *Game-like learning: An example of situated learning and implications for opportunity to learn.* Retrieved from http://www.academiccolab.org/resources/documents/Game-Like%20Learning.rev.pdf

Gee, J. P. (2005). *Why videogames are good for your soul: Pleasure and learning.* Melbourne, Australia: Common Ground.

Gee, J. P. (2007). *What videogames have to teach us about learning and literacy* (Rev. ed.). New York: Palgrave MacMillan.

Goldberg, E. (2001). *The executive brain: Frontal lobes and the civilized mind.* New York: The Oxford University Press.

Green, C. S., & Bavelier, D. (2003). Action videogame modifies visual selective attention. *Letters to Nature, 42*(3), 534–537. doi:10.1038/nature01647

Johnson, S. (2005). *Everything bad is good for you: How today's popular culture is actually making us smarter.* New York: Penguin Group.

Klingberg, T. (2009). *The overflowing brain.* New York: Oxford University Press.

Klingberg, T., Fernell, E., Olesen, P., Johnson, M., Gustafsson, P., & Dahlström, K. (2005). Computerized training of working memory in children with ADHD – A randomized, controlled, trial. *Journal of the American Academy of Child and Adolescent Psychiatry, 44*(2), 177–186. doi:10.1097/00004583-200502000-00010

Lawrence, V., Houghton, S., Tannock, R., Douglas, G., Durkin, K., & Whiting, K. (2002). ADHD outside the laboratory: Boys' executive function performance on tasks in videogame play and on a visit to the zoo. *Journal of Abnormal Child Psychology, 30*, 447–462. doi:10.1023/A:1019812829706

Macgill, A. (2007). *Is video gaming becoming the next family bonding activity?* Retrieved from http://www.pewinternet.org/Commentary/2007/November/Is-video-gaming-becoming-the-next-family-bonding-activity.aspx

Meltzer, L. (Ed.). (2007). *Executive function in education: From theory to practice.* New York: Guilford Press.

Prensky, M. (2007). *Digital game-based learning*. New York: Paragon House Publishers.

Rideout, V. J., Foehr, U. G., & Roberts, D. F. (2010). *Generation M2 media in the lives of 8- to 18-year-olds*. Retrieved from http://www.kff.org/entmedia/mh012010pkg.cfm

Rideout, V. J., Foehr, U. G., & Roberts, D. F. (2010). *Daily media use among children and teens up dramatically from five years ago*. Retrieved from http://www.kff.org/entmedia/entmedia012010nr.cfm

Rueda, M. R., Rothbart, M. K., McCandliss, B. D., Saccomanno, L., & Posner, M. L. (2005). Training, maturation, and genetic influences on the development of executive attention. *Proceedings of the National Academy of Sciences of the United States of America, 102*(41), 14931–14936. doi:10.1073/pnas.0506897102

Shaffer, D. W. (2006). *How computer games help children learn*. New York: Palgrave Macmillan. doi:10.1057/9780230601994

Shaffer, D. W., Squire, K. R., Halverson, R., & Gee, J. P. (2004). *Videogames and the future of learning*. Retrieved from http://www.academic-colab.org/resources/gappspaper1.pdf

Tapscott, D. (2009). *Grown up digital: How the next generation is changing your world*. New York: McGraw Hill.

Wegerif, R. (2002). *Thinking skills, technology and learning*. Retrieved from http://futurelab.org.uk/resources/publications-reports-articles/literature-reviews/Literature-Review394

Wright, P. (2009). Trainee teachers' e-learning experiences of computer play. *Innovate, 5*(4). Retrieved from http://www.innovateonline.info/pdf/vol5_issue4/Trainee_Teachers'_e-Learning_Experiences_of_Computer_Play.pdf

Chapter 14
Fostering Character Education with Games and Interactive Story Generation

Rania Hodhod
University of York, UK

Paul Cairns
University of York, UK

Daniel Kudenko
University of York, UK

ABSTRACT

Promoting ethical, responsible, and caring behavior in young people is a perennial aim of education. Schools are invited to include moral teaching in every possible curriculum. Efforts have been made to find non-traditional ways of teaching such as games or role play or engaging students in moral dilemmas. However, classroom environments need to consider time constraints, curriculum standards, and differing children's personalities. Computer systems can offer rich environments that detect and respond to student knowledge gaps, misconceptions, and variable affective states. This chapter presents AEINS, an adaptive narrative-based educational game that helps the teaching of basic ethical virtues to young children to promote character education. The central goal is to engage students in a dynamic narrative environment and to involve them in different moral dilemmas (teaching moments) that use the Socratic method as the predominant pedagogy. The authors argue that AEINS incorporates appropriate game design principles and successfully manages the interaction between the narrative level and the tutoring level to maximize student learning. Moreover, it is able to convey the moral skills to its users, as shown in the evaluation.

DOI: 10.4018/978-1-60960-120-1.ch014

INTRODUCTION

"A moral is a message conveyed or a lesson to be learned from a story or event" (Dianne, 2001).

Mounting discipline problems, sometimes resulting in violence, shoplifting, drug abuse, and other criminal behaviors, raise the need to develop an awareness of social and moral responsibilities, a core component of character education. Character education implies the widely-shared, pivotally important, core ethical values, such as trustworthiness, caring, honesty, fairness, responsibility and respect for self and others along with supportive performance values that form the basis of good character, such as diligence, a strong work ethic, and perseverance (Lickona et al., 2007). Core ethical values are the basic principles that we consider when making decisions and judgments in our lives. Generally, character education aims to promote ethical, responsible, and caring young people. These values (virtues) are defined in terms of behaviors that can be observed in the life of the school.

One big challenge in character education is that *knowing* what is right does not guarantee *doing* what is right. As Watson (2003) illustrated: "getting high scores in an ethical course does not guarantee at all the actual behavior of that student." And more importantly, he added that the core issue lies in not only knowing what is right and good but also in building a love for the good and the worthwhile. Accordingly, and based on Watson's view, we should "identify what is good and what is bad behavior, instruct people as to what these are, and inspire people to behave in the right ways using examples for them to imitate." We argue that the development of moral virtues requires extensive practice in the same way as other skills such as reading or writing. Children need to practice enough independent thinking and develop their moral reasoning by being in different situations and to act according to their

beliefs. By presenting the effects of their actions on themselves and others as consequences, they can, eventually, begin to formulate their own conceptions of rights, values and principles.

Schools are trying to include moral teaching in every possible facet of school, such as core subjects (academic curriculum), sports teams and clubs (extracurricular programs), and more implicitly in the teacher-student relationship (hidden curriculum) (Lickona et al., 2007). In the classroom environment, Halverson (2004) had found that traditional teaching using terms and abstractions may not be the best way to help children connect to imagess or situations in their embodied experiences in the world. Therefore, efforts to develop moral reasoning skills are made by targeting elementary and middle school students through classroom activities such as role playing, which helps students to transfer their knowledge and beliefs into actions (McBrien & Brandt, 1997), brainstorming moral dilemmas (Bolton, 1999) and using interactive learning models (Shapiro, 1999). Such efforts aim to help students' cognitive development by allowing students to pursue moral actions and see how their decisions affect other people and themselves in relation to others. These trials have shown promising results demonstrating the effectiveness of learning by doing which helps students to draw analogies between what they experience in the classroom and that of real life, that is, to see the bigger picture. However, children differ in personalities and consequently in their strengths, weaknesses and needs, which raises the need for adaptive learning. Within the classroom environment this is very difficult to address because of time and curriculum constraints (Eiriksson, 1997). Halverson (2004) challenged teachers to provide the kind of teaching that creates a safe place for their students, allows them to move outside of their comfort level and also challenges them to think outside of their current level of experience. While it is challenging to create such an environment in classrooms, computers can act as a solution.

This chapter presents *AEINS*, Adaptive Educational Interactive Narrative System, a game environment inhabited with non-playing characters (NPCs), which aims to foster character education by allowing the student to practice various moral virtues through interacting with different moral dilemmas. Moral virtues are ethical values, such as trustworthiness, wisdom, courage, chastity and justice. Throughout the game, students can get involved in various moral dilemmas (teaching moments) that focus on virtues and provide moral exemplars. *AEINS* aims to involve the students in independent thinking processes, such as self-reflection and continuous self assessment. In addition, it promotes the acquisition of skills and knowledge through interactions in an authentic environment. This can mainly occur when the student is faced with unexpected reaction from the non-playing characters. In this case, he starts to think about the causes and effects and assesses the previous actions that lead to the current situation.

The main idea of the *AEINS* design is centered on the integration of two pieces, first, interactive narrative techniques that engage the student in a story where he is able to act and affect how the story unfolds. The generated narrative can be interleaved by structured moral dilemmas that use the Socratic method as the teaching pedagogy. Secondly, an intelligent tutoring technique that monitors, guides and evaluates the student's actions to provide a personalized learning process based on an existing student model.

The chapter begins with a background section that introduces the various methods and techniques used in this work, in addition to the learning theories that inspired the architecture. Next, we discuss issues, controversies and problems in previous work, followed by our work as a suggested solution. The chapter ends with results from *AEINS* evaluation.

BACKGROUND

"Stories are connections to the past and yet carry us into the future; they speak of relationships, of human connections, and to what gives quality to our lives" (Simpson, 1998).

In the last decade, there has been a significant growth in integrating narrative in education (Riedl & Stern, 2006; Thomas & Young, 2007; Vilhjalmsson et al., 2007; McQuiggan et al., 2008; Mckenzie& McCalla, 2009).). Interactive narrative brings students through a deep story experience, and has proven to be successful in creating enriching experiences for its users, sparking problem-solving skills and individual and group decision-making skills (Bayon, et al., 2003). More challenging is the combining of interactive narrative techniques with intelligent tutoring capabilities. In existing educational games, different techniques have been used such as story planning, graph structured plans, plots, and intelligent tutoring to achieve a platform that personalizes the learning experience and develops the student's knowledge and/ or skills in a motivating, engaging environment.

Story planning has been used in the *Mimesis* educational game (Thomas & Young, 2007) and the *IN-TALE* game (Riedl & Stern, 2006) where the learning tasks are represented in interactive narrative plans. In these systems the student's freedom is high and their actions affect how the story unfolds. Other games use a scripted approach to achieve greater control of the student's experiences, such as *StoryTeller* (Mott, et al., 1999) and *ELECT BILAT* (Lane, et al., 2007) or use separate subsequent plots or scenes as their teaching moments, such as *FearNot!* (Bayon et al. 2003, Aylett et al. 2007), *ISAT* (Magerko, 2006) and *Conundrum* (Mckenzie& McCalla, 2009).

In addition to interactive narrative, another important aspect in educational games is the tutoring aspect that aims to supply the educational process. Intelligent tutoring should possess one or more of the following: tutorial planning, student models, learning objectives, domain and pedagogical models. Despite the importance of each of these components, the student model is considered the key element in the adaptation process (Brusilovsky, 1994; Abraham & Yacef, 2002). It assists in providing a personalized learning process based on the student's strengths, his weaknesses and his needs. The *TLCTS* educational game (Vilhjalmsson et al., 2007) has a student model in its environment that is updated only based on the student's explicit actions and does not consider the student's intentions. *TLTS* (Johnson et al., 2004) is an interactive educational game that uses a student model to provide an adaptive learning process and simulates dialogues. However it does not take full advantage of the storytelling potential of games seen in interactive drama applications (Magerko et al., 2006). Other educational games that have been developed without considering the presence of a student model are: *TIME* (Harless, 1986), *TEATRIX* (Prada et al., 2000), *BAT ILE* (Waraich, 2004) and *Crystal Island* (Mott & Lester, 2006; McQuiggan et al., 2008).

As seen from the above review, educational games exhibit the presence of four features shown to individually increase effectiveness of educational games environments, yet not integrated together. These are: the presence of a student model; a dynamic generated narrative approach that aims to provide the student with high agency within the environment and generates a story according to the student's preferences; the use of scripted narrative that constrains the student agency at certain parts that supply education in order to allow tracking of the student's actions and assessment of them; and the presence of a continuous story that engages the user and allows the presence of believable, evolving non-player characters that support the educational process. To the best of our knowledge, no educational game has integrated these features in a single architecture before and this is the contribution of this work.

THE VISION

"To educate a person in mind and not in morals is to educate a menace to society" (President Theodore Roosevelt).

At this point, challenges in character education and the idea of using educational games to aid the education of character has been mentioned. The contribution in integrating individual components currently used in various educational games has been also justified. This section provides an overview of the ideas, learning theories and techniques that inspired the development of our educational game.

As the intention is to design and implement an educational game, both educational theories and game aspects should be considered. Educational theories such as Keller's ARCS model (Keller, 1987) and Gagné's nine events (Gagné et al., 2005) can help in designing the interface and the educational objects as part of the educational game world. Gee's game aspects can act as a benchmark in evaluating the game aspects in the developed educational game (Gee, 2004).

As mentioned earlier in this chapter, learning through practicing is one asset of an educational games environment. The environment can be enriched with interactive moral dilemmas (teaching moments), where the student can act and see the effect of their actions on themselves and others and the presence of evolving agents that can act as an emotional engaging hook. It can be seen that students of all ages use questions in their learning of topics; questions act as transition means between the observation and hypothesis stages. Discussions and involvement in moral dilemmas offer inspiring examples after which students can model their own behavior. They also provide authentic contexts that are considered an adequate framework to promote argumentation (Meacham & Emont, 1989). The Socratic method is one way of using questions in order to develop moral thinking and provides opportunities for personal discovery through problem solving.

In classroom environments, the Socratic method (Socratic dialogue) is dramatic and entertaining. It triggers lively classroom discussion and helps students make choices based on what is 'right' instead of what they can get away with. The evaluation of *AEINS* reflects the fact that most of the participants (around 86%) succeeded in recognizing what could be the 'right' thing to do after being involved in the Socratic Dialogue. According to this model, the teacher asks a series of questions that leads the students to examine the validity of an opinion or belief. This is a powerful teaching method because it actively engages the student and encourages critical thinking, which is just what is needed in examining ethics, values, and other character issues. It allows an appropriate amount of choice during ill-structured and authentic investigations that lead to the development of inquiry skills (Avner et al., 1980). In Lynch et al. (2008), it has been shown that even in domains where it is impossible to make sharp distinctions between good and bad solutions due to the lack of ideal solutions or a domain theory, solution differences are meaningful. In our opinion, the students' different answers to a Socratic Dialogue are also meaningful and reflect their own beliefs and thoughts. The Socratic method has been applied previously in the intelligent tutoring system, CIRCISM-TUTOR that teaches how the cardiovascular reflex system stabilizes blood pressure functions (Kim et al., 1989; Yang et al. 2000). It has been shown that applying the Socratic method positively influences the learning process.

An important aspect of moral dilemmas is that the ethical argument as a whole is ill-structured and it is hard to define the set of right answers or actions. Simon (1973) in his explanation of the architect's design process provides some insight about how to deal with these kinds of problems: "During any given short period of time, the architect will find himself working on a problem which, perhaps beginning in an ill structured state, soon converts itself through evocation from memory into a well structured problem." In other words, a problem that is ill-structured in the large can be well structured in the small. We therefore decided to make use of pre-analyzed moral dilemmas in a way that every analyzed part can act as a separate well-defined problem on its own. Moral dilemmas such as Kohlberg's moral dilemmas (Kohlberg, 1984) and other dilemmas designed specifically for school children can be used to construct so-called teaching moments. These dilemmas allow students to pursue different procedures for solving problems based on their perceptions and interpretations of the nature of the problem.

Every teaching moment can be imagined as non-interactive story presentations interleaved with user-decision points that allow the story to progress forward (see Figure 1). The teaching moments' representation allows them to become part of the main story as they have narrative prerequisites that allow its incorporation in the dynamic generated narrative and allows the use of an intelligent tutor system (ITS) that monitors the student and is able to evaluate his actions. The tutor aims to provide a student model that allows adaptive learning to occur. The purpose of the Student Model is to help students learn about moral situations and ethical actions by maintaining an accurate model of a student's current knowledge state which allows more intelligent and adaptive pedagogical decisions and actions to occur. The student's current knowledge state is expressed by the student profile within a rule-based representation. By the end of the whole experience, the student will have experienced some emotional and moral complexities. According to Freeman (2004), this kind of experience, especially when these complexities develop over the course of a game-like environment, can leave the player with a better and deeper understanding.

The presentation of the teaching moments should occur not as separate events, but as part of a continuous story. A planner should generate an interactive story that allows the student to act

Figure 1. A graph representation of a teaching moment (Adapted from Silva et al., 2003)

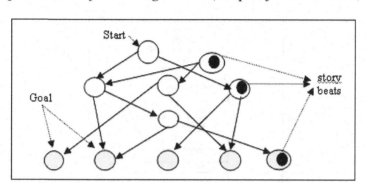

and affect how the story unfolds and at the same time targets to satisfy the goals (teaching moment preconditions). In this way, the story is generated for the sake of the educational targets and still preserves the dramatic pedagogy of interactive narrative. The continuous story allows the presence of agents that inhabit the story world and can participate in supplying the learning. The agents should be semiautonomous where this allows the story generator to dictate to them what to do at times when required. Autonomous agents can result in executing actions that can interfere with the educational aims. The agents characters should evolve as the story unfolds, for example, an agent who is a friend to the student can be an enemy based on certain actions of the student. If the teaching moment to be presented requires the presence of an enemy, this agent will be chosen for this role. We argue this should increase the believability of the environment. Having the agents as the student's friends offers a known environment to the student that facilitates the interaction and the virtual illusion.

For the purpose of evaluation, *AEINS* should be intrinsically evaluated to make sure that the design goals have been met, the levels of educational outcome can be measured according to Bloom's Taxonomy and an empirical evaluation should take place.

In the next section, we will present the educational game, *AEINS*, which aims to address the shortcomings encountered in the currently existed systems illustrated previously.

AEINS (ADAPTIVE EDUCATIONAL INTERACTIVE NARRATIVE SYSTEM)

The main idea of the proposed work is the integration of interactive narrative, evolving characters, and intelligent tutoring in a single architecture of an educational game called 'AEINS' in order to deliver basic moral virtues to young students. The ultimate advantage of AEINS lies in its ability to interact with every single student on a different basis according to the student model particularly built for that student. Before getting into the details of each module, it is worth to give the reader a general idea about how AEINS works. A model of the game can be seen in Figure 2.

The above image shows that the game starts by presenting the game world to the student. At the first two stages, the game gives a brief introduction about the world and allows the student to choose friends (each has different moral virtues) to initialize the student model. Then at the third stage, the pedagogical model chooses the next teaching moment (educational object) to present. At the fourth stage, the game generates the appropriate narrative that aims to achieve some narrative goals, the narrative preconditions of the teaching moments. In this stage, the student is

Figure 2. AEINS working model

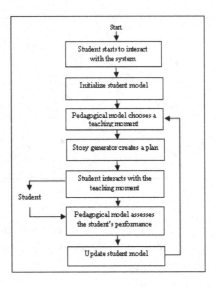

free to act and sometimes their actions can violate the generated plan, at which point the story generator has to alter the plan to accommodate the student's actions. Once the preconditions are satisfied, the teaching moment starts and the student interacts with it. In the sixth stage, the pedagogical model is tracing the student's action(s) and updates the student model accordingly. After finishing the teaching moment and based upon the current updated student model, the cycle continues as shown in Figure 2.

The Architecture of *AEINS*

The *AIENS* architecture is the main contribution of this work where it attempts to address the shortcomings of the existing systems. The architecture has been designed in a way that allows the generation of interactive narrative at run time. Such a design addresses the issue of tracking the student learning versus student's agency. In *AEINS*, agency is constrained when interacting with the teaching moments to preserve the educational targets. After finishing the teaching moment, the student resumes his high agency. This tactic is very similar to games design where

the player has many choices in the environment and, based upon a certain choice, he will be led to a specific path and then back to the main story after finishing the desired task.

The architecture consists of six models: four modules to serve the educational targets and two models for generating the story and storing information about the story world as shown in Figure 3. The following subsections introduce the *AEINS* working model and how the various architecture components are represented and utilized. In the next subsection, we will introduce the domain model and its representation.

Domain Model

The domain model was designed with the help of children's education expert. The model describes the various concepts (i.e. values) in the ethics domain and their relationships. One part of the model defines the principles of character education (Elkind & Sweet, 1997) and represents their relationships and dependencies. A frame-based representation has been used to demonstrate those relationships and dependencies as shown in Figure 4. Some values are considered main values such

Figure3. The AEINS architecture

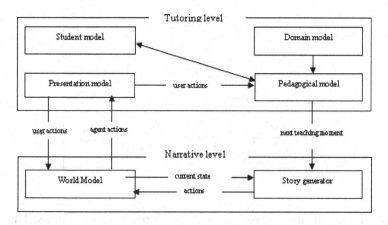

as *be honest*; this value composes of sub-values such as *do not lie*, *do not cheat* and *do not steal*. For the main value to be considered mastered, each of the sub-values has to be mastered. The other part of the domain model is a repertoire of moral dilemmas (teaching moments). Each sub-value is mapped to one or more teaching moment as visualized in Figure 5. The sub-values are the main focus of their corresponding teaching moments.

Teaching Moments

Keller (1987), in his paper, defined Attention, one condition of curiosity, as "capturing the interest of students and stimulating the motivation to learn." Teaching moments in *AEINS* are provided in a familiar context, for example, if the student fails to show that his beliefs toward a certain misconception (immoral value) have been not mastered yet then the next teaching moment will focus on the same immoral value. It has been shown that by providing a familiar context, students are able to better activate their prior knowledge (Anderson et al., 1977). When needed, during the interaction with a teaching moment, some questions are worded from the perspective of the student to facilitate the activation of prior knowledge (Anderson & Pichert 1978).

The story in *AEINS* is generated around the teaching moments. The teaching moments, as illustrated previously, are graph structured plans (see Figure 6). They allow the use of an intelligent

Figure 4. Part of the character education domain representation

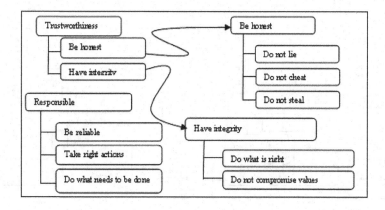

Figure 5. The relationship between principles and teaching moments

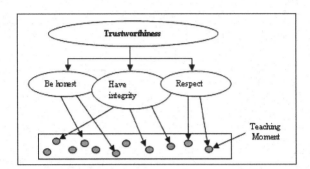

tutor to track the student's actions and assess them in the form of a step-by-step follow-up. Ideally, each teaching moment path describes an inquiry-based narrative, a story in which the protagonist is the user in the role of making moral decisions. The teaching moments allow students to pursue different procedures for solving the problem based on the student's perception and interpretation of the nature of the problem. The student's under-standing gained through this process is situated in their experience and can best be evaluated in terms relevant to this experience.

The Socratic method is used as the teaching pedagogy woven into the narrative in order to reinforce positive actions. The Socratic method is capable to force the student to face the contra-dictions present in any course of action that is not based on principles of justice or fairness. The voice of Socrates comes from the moral agent participating in the current teaching moment. When the student performs an incorrect choice, a text dialogue starts between the moral agent and the student that tries to emphasize the undesirable beliefs and encourage good actions. The dialogue continues until the story ends with either a nega-tive or positive reward based on the computation model of the student's actions.

Figure 6. Example of a teaching moment

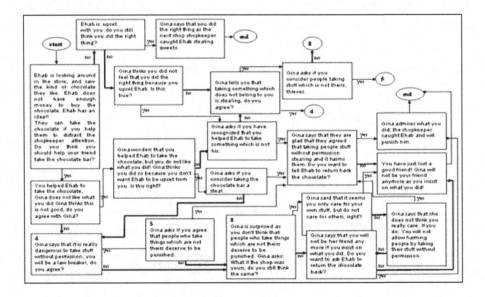

The pedagogical model runs the educational process effectively without interfering as a tutor; everything was blended together in the narrative experience: even feedback is tailored for the story context.

Although the different branches of every teaching moment are pre-defined, each teaching moment exhibits variability through allowing different characters and places to present the teaching moment depending on the story-world state. Each teaching moment represents a part of the whole story and focuses on teaching a specific concept (i.e., value) so that the concept mastery is established. Each teaching moment has certain prerequisites that must be fulfilled before the execution of the teaching moment takes place. Manipulating a teaching moment's priority is done via the represented rules as follows:

Trigger: teaching moment TM_1 has not been presented
and teaching moment TM_2 has not been presented
and value *"do not cheat"* is not held by the user
and value *"do not lie"* is held by the user
Action: set priority to teaching moment TM_2

The representation denotes that if (a) a specific pattern of teaching moments (TM_1 and TM_2) has not been presented to the student yet and (b) the student holds certain values (*do not cheat*) and does not hold others (*do not lie*), the action part of the rule executes (teaching moment TM_2 has priority over teaching moment TM_1). If several rules satisfy their premises, this results in having more than one teaching moment to present and any of them is suitable to be presented, next, to the student. In this case, one of these teaching moments is chosen randomly.

This section described the domain model and gave an example for the design of the graph structured teaching moments. In the next subsection, we will introduce the pedagogical model and its role in providing adaptation.

Pedagogical Model

The pedagogical model aims to adapt instruction by monitoring and evaluating the student's actions. The model is developed in the form of production rules. These rules are used to give the system specific cognitive operations to reason about the student and the teaching process. With ill-defined problems, development is a change in the way a person thinks and not merely a case of acquiring more knowledge. The idea is based on analyzing moral dilemmas and transforming them to a story graph structure, specifying the decision points that reflect the specified skills, and deciding what actions should be taken by the student in order to reflect these skills. The model specifies how a student would ideally use the system and how the system should assess the student's skills and update the student model accordingly. An example for a skill evaluation rule is as follows:

IF action ("student", "TM_1", "agreed to lie")
and IF action ("student", "TM_1", "insists to lie")
and IF action ("student", "TM_1", "lied for friend's sake")
and IF action ("student", "TM_1", "finally agrees that lying is bad")
THEN skill ("student", "do not lie", "acquired", 0.6)

The premises in the above rule are part of the student model constructed for each individual student. They represent the meaning of the actions taken by the student. The above rule evaluates the student actions in teaching moment TM_1 and assigns a confidence factor to the attempted skill. The confidence factor (CF) is a number between -1 and 1 indicating the strength of the belief in that fact. A CF of value equal to '1' represents total certainty of the truth of the fact, while a CF of value '- 1' represents certainty regarding the negation of the fact.

This section described how the pedagogical model's cognitive operations have been represented using the rules representation. In the next subsection we will introduce the main component that helps the pedagogical model to provide adaptation that is the student model.

Student Model

Student modeling aims to provide a personalized learning process based on the current student's skills. The student model in *AEINS* is currently a quite complex form of the overlay model represented in the form of rules, associated with certainty confidence, to allow access to sufficient data to permit reliable inferences about the student's beliefs. This can be solved using default assumptions which may later have to be withdrawn, or by initializing the student model through some preliminary actions that are designed specifically to help infer an initial model of the student as in *AEINS*. The model assumes that the student knowledge is a subset of the expert's knowledge. The model aims to expand the student knowledge until it matches the expert's. *AEINS* builds a model of the student's learning process by observing, analyzing, and recording the student's actions and choices from the generally accepted ethical views. Given the following representation, a model has been developed that infers the character stereotype:

IF skill ("student", "do not lie", "acquired", CF_1)
and IF skill ("student", "do not cheat", "acquired", CF_2)
and IF skill ("student", "responsible", "acquired", CF_3)
THEN concept-learned ("student", ``honest", "held", Z)

We are following the method used to calculate the confidence factor as that used in the Mycin system (Shortliffe, 1981). The above representation denotes that if the student acquires the skills *do not lie*, *do not cheat*, *do not steal*, and *responsible* with confidence factors CF_1, CF_2, CF_3 respec-

tively (CF_i values are obtained by the pedagogical model), then the rule confidence factor can be determined using the combination function. The rule confidence (Z) for the conjunctive premises is calculated using the following combination function: $Z = \min(CF_1, CF_2, CF_3)$

Story World

The world model contains all the information about the non-playing characters and the objects, such as their description, location, and their state in the game world. The story world consists mainly of the current world state, and its role is to track and save all the current actions of the student and the agents to be used later by the planner. The current world state is updated after every executed action either performed by the student or by one of the agents. The main advantage of having more than one non-playing character is the freedom to portray agents who do not share the student's goals, who can then be used to provide negative examples (Thomas & Young, 2007). On the other hand, they can also act according to the moral goals and can give positive examples or help the student to stay on the right track. The story is in effect a narrative describing the story world, the characters' actions, the actions the student is taking and the effect of these actions on the story world.

The presence of non-playing evolving characters helps in providing realism and believability to the environment and in supplying education to the student especially as a user of the Socratic method.

The story world houses the information about the non-playing characters and the objects. It also stores information about the current world state. In the next section, we will show how the story is generated in *AEINS* and how the non-playing characters can have direct reactions to the player student's ones.

Story Generation *in* AEINS

According to Riedl and Young (2006), planning is efficient and able to generate different narratives for different users; it can also generate different narratives for the single user on subsequent play turns. This technique enhances the user's sense of control in the narrative environment. The main story in *AEINS* is generated using a STRIPS-like planning algorithm, similar to the work of Barber and Kudenko (2007).

In a STRIPS-like representation planning algorithm, actions are instances of generic schemata called operators. An operator has preconditions and effects. The preconditions indicate the conditions that must be valid for the operator to be applicable. The effects indicate how the current situation changes as a result of applying the operator. Given a narrative goal (i.e., the preconditions of the next teaching moment) and the current world state, the story engine selects a story action to execute from the produced plan. Table 1 shows an example of two action operators represented with variable argument(s) for which different instances can be substituted. Currently for every possible way the student can violate the story plan, an alternative story plan is generated. However, alternative approaches need to be considered when scaling up the system to a very large story world.

As purely behavioral systems could not offer any guarantee that desired outcomes would be reached, combining planning with reactive execution can be seen as a solution (Aylett et al., 2008). The agent reactive action towards the student aims to provide a direct reaction to the last student's action instead of only basing the action choice on the whole past history of the narrative. Imagine the following situation, the planner picks 'be_friend_to' and 'move' actions to be executed. Luckily, the student follows the plan and chooses to 'be_friend' to one of the agents. In normal planning this will lead to the execution of the move action automatically. By the reactive planner, we aim to respond to the 'be_friend' action taken by the student before continuing to execute the original plan. We argue that this increases the believability of the agents' reactions.

The reactive planning selects an action to be executed from a set of pre-authored actions based on the associated value 'N', which is the suitability cost. The N value changes dynamically during runtime based on the student's actions. For example, if the student asked one of the agents to be his friend, the N value of 'reply_to_friendship' action will dominate the N value of 'respond_to_play' action according to a pre-defined relation matrix.

Table 1.

Action Name	Preconditions	Effects
move (Agent, $Place_1$, $Place_2$)	char(Agent) & place ($Place_1$) & char_at (Agent, $Place_1$)	char_at (Agent, $Place_2$)
be_friend_to ($Agent_1$, $Agent_2$)	char($Agent_1$) & char ($Agent_2$) & like ($Agent_1$, $Agent_2$)	friend ($Agent_1$, $Agent_2$)

Table 2.

Action Name	Preconditions	Effects
reply_to_friendship(Agent, student, N_1)	like(Agent, student)	agree_to_be_friend & friend(Agent, student)
respond_to_play(Agent, student, N_2)	not(current_TM(TM_2)) & friend(Agent, student)	accept_play_invitation

Table 2 shows an example of two action operators for the reactive planner.

After responding to the student's action, the STRIPS planner continues executing the previously generated plan, so for the above example the 'move' action will be executed. An example of a generated narrative is shown in Figure 7.

The first row represents the current story world and the last row represents the goals to be satisfied. The left column shows the first plan the story generator produces; the actions in italic are assumed student's actions. If the student's action does not satisfy the first plan, another plan is developed; the second plan in the middle column. Again if the student's action violates the plan, a third plan is developed; the plan in the right most column. This continues until the goals (teaching moment narrative preconditions) are satisfied. A full example run is attached as appendix.

As can be seen the story generation in *AEINS* is the learning medium that constitutes not only characters and objects participating in the generated story, but also it incorporates the learning objects wherein the evolving agents have a rec-ognized pedagogical role. In the next section, we will introduce the presentation model and how it makes use of Keller's ARCS model.

Presentation Model

The presentation model handles the flow of information and monitors the interactions between the user and the system. Keller's ARCS model provides four classes (Keller, 1987): Attention, Relevance, Confidence/Challenge, and Satisfaction/Success that has been considered while designing the educational game interface. This model mainly aims to gain and retain the student's attention and to understand implicitly how the activities relate to their current situations. In addition to making use of the surprise factor through the presence of unexpected problems or new situations, which helps capturing the student's attention (Mergel, 1998). At the awaken stage, the interface itself is designed in a way that captures the student's attention. The playing characters' personalities evolve over time, which make their reactions different every time with respect

Figure 7. Example of the generated plan

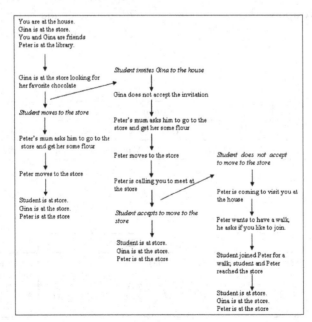

to their current personality. The variance of the narrative experience itself is engaging and helps to capture the attention of the student and create new experiences. At the explain stage, feedback and explanations are given to the student. This helps the student reflect on her own actions and their consequences. At the Reinforce and Transfer stages, the student has the freedom to see all the previous history of her actions and other playing characters' actions. The student is involved in the moral dilemmas and the consequences depending on her choices and actions. This forces the student to make a conscious choice in terms of ethics.

To interact with the story, a play screen is offered as shown in Figure 8 where the student is able to choose an action; actions include move, invite, persuade, etc. The student is then able to click on one of the characters and places pictures in the world. For example, the student can choose the *invite* action and then clicks on *Ziad's* and the *house's* pictures. The end result will be "*invite Ziad to my house.*" Ziad has the freedom to accept or reject the user's invitation according to a specific set of rules and constraints that determine the actions that the non player-characters can take.

The student is engaged in a text-based conversation that evolves depending on the student's actions. The aim is to enable students to test their own intuitions and thoughts about certain moral

values and experiments. In so doing, it is believed that students will better understand the nuances of the domain. In addition, the system presents the student with good models and examples, after which they, hopefully, will model their own behavior. *AEINS* allows the whole unfolding story to be recorded at run-time to allow the student to re-visit any part of it whenever he likes. This gives the student the chance for self-reflection and could lead him to re-evaluate the situation from a new perspective. This kind of situated learning helps the student learn not just the actions that are required, but also the perceptual conditions in which they apply.

The presentation model acts as the interaction window between the student and *AEINS* as it handles the flow of information in both directions. In the next section, we will elaborate on the educational theories that helped to shape this research.

EDUCATIONAL THEORIES

The importance of incorporating learning theories in the design of educational games has been discussed in previous sections. We talked about the three theories that appear to be most closely aligning with the generally accepted game design

Figure 8. A screenshot for the play window screen

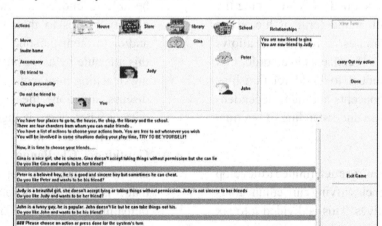

principles: Keller's ARCS Motivational Model, Gagné's Events of Instruction, and Bloom's Taxonomy. A failure to base serious game design on such well-established and practical instructional theories increases the risk of the game failing to meet its intended educational goals, yielding a participant who is entertained but has not acquired new skills or knowledge (Gunter, et al., 2006). In *AEINS*, the three principles Gagné considered essential for successful instruction have been considered as follows:

- Providing instruction on the set of component tasks that build toward a final task: This principle is tackled in designing the teaching moments, where coaching is realized using the Socratic method and by providing personalized feedback. Such teaching strategy contributes in the building of skills required to master the task.
- Ensuring that each component task is mastered: This principle has been attempted in *AEINS* using the pedagogical model that tracks the student's learning process and evaluate his moves. Accordingly if the component is still not mastered, the model chooses another educational object that attempts to address the misconceptions the student has.
- Sequencing the component tasks to ensure optimal transfer to the final task: This principle has been applied by representing the domain model in the form of hierarchal frames. The frames representation allows the sequencing of concepts in an order that allows the student to build relationships between the concepts and their dependency, leading to an understanding of the final task.

Bloom's taxonomy was determined to develop a practical means for classifying curriculum goals and learning objectives. This is divided into six levels; knowledge, comprehension, application,

analysis, synthesis, and evaluation. We argue that *AEINS* is capable of addressing the higher levels of Bloom's taxonomy. Through being involved and interacting in moral situations (teaching moments), the student is able to see the moral values (concepts) involved in the situation context, and the pattern they are framing of the situation. Accordingly, he is able to aggregate parts together, evaluate the situation and make judgments about the value of ideas. Based on the idea pictured, he can act to solve the problem encountered. These skills are part of the higher levels; analysis, evaluation and synthesis. Bloom's taxonomy has been used as an evaluation tool for the *AEINS*' educational outcome.

The last learning theory inspiring this work is Keller's ARCS model, which relies on four foundational categories that are to be applied when designing instructional activities. ARCS is an acronym that represents four classes: Attention, Relevance, Confidence/Challenge, and Satisfaction/Success. The details of how each has been applied are as follows:

- **Attention**: This aspect relates to gaining and keeping the student's attention. It aims to capture the student's attention by using a graphical user interface and inquiry arousal through enabling the student to affect how the story unfolds.
- **Relevance**: Simply put, students need to be able to understand implicitly how the activity relates to their current situation, and/or to them personally. *AEINS* tackles this attribute by designing and implementing teaching moments that contextually discuss situations the student is familiar with or where there is high probability the student will face one.
- **Confidence/Challenge**: This fundamentally paves the way for students to feel that it is worthwhile to put effort into participating in the activity. If students believe they are, somehow, incapable of achieving

the objectives or that they will be wasting their time because it will take too long, or, conversely, that the challenge is beneath them, their motivation will most assuredly decrease. *AEINS* uses various teaching moments that tackle different student knowledge levels to attempt this property.

- **Satisfaction/Success**: Students must attain some type of satisfaction or reward from the learning experience. *AEINS* provides positive and negative rewards as part of its teaching pedagogy. These rewards take the form of formative and summative feedback that is part of the teaching strategy within the teaching moments.

AEINS also considers other educational theories in its design and implementation, for example research suggested that students benefit from being encouraged to consider a collection of evidence and coordinate their theoretical ideas with supporting or contradictory evidence as they engage in argumentation (Koslowski, 1996; Bell & Linn, 2000). In addition, researchers suggest that students must have opportunities to choose among different options and to reason which criteria lead to the option chosen (Kuhn, 1993). *AEINS* follows these approaches and uses the Socratic method as it has been shown to be a highly effective approach (Elkind & Sweet, 1997) in helping children become ethical, respectful, responsible people.

AEINS uses misconception in favor of the learning process, where it has been shown that when students faced with evidence that they believe to be true is, in fact, false and a misconception, they are often interested in resolving the discrepancy (Bergin, 1999). *AEINS* also words the question from the perspective of the student to provide a meaningful context and facilitate the activation of prior knowledge; this technique has shown its usefulness in the learning process as demonstrated by Anderson & Pichert (1978). For example, if we would like students to investigate the effects of

stealing, we could pose the problem of shoplifting and the case when they are the owners themselves.

AEINS uses the Socratic method as its main teaching pedagogy. The Socratic method has been easily woven into the teaching moments' story lines. It displays its strengths when the students make a bad choice. Through discussion, students should then be forced to face the contradictions present in any course of action not based on principles of justice or fairness. This method requires a delicate balance between letting the students make decisions, and demonstrating the limits in their reasoning. Finally, "raising the ante," which is defined as raising the stakes and introducing consequences, is a tactic followed if a student sticks with the unethical choice. For example, if we would like students to investigate the effects of stealing, we could pose the problem of shoplifting and ask what they would do if they were the owners.

In the next section, we will present the game aspects in *AEINS* and how they have been evaluated against Gee's games criteria.

THE EVALUATION OF *AEINS* AGAINST THE GAMES' CRITERIA

In 2004, Gee published a condensed list of 13 principles of learning that should be built into good computer and video games. According to Gee (2004), the stronger any game is on more of the features on the list, the better its score for learning. Following the definitions provided in this list, this section describes the extent *AEINS* managed to achieve Gee's principles.

Empowering students is a principle that can be achieved through other principles, which are co-design, customize and giving students identities. Co-design is related to the players a feeling of control over the game by actively creating part of their experience and having an effect on the virtual world. In *AEINS*, this principle is applied. The student can take actions that influence how the story unfolds. In addition, the teaching moments' settings allow the student to act and apply his beliefs in various situations showing the impact of the student's actions in the short term and long term on the teaching moment story. Customize is the player's ability to influence the game play. *AEINS* partially supports customization through offering a personalized story and individualized learning process, but it does not offer different learning styles such as text, graphics, or audio; neither does it consider gender nor offer multiple interfaces for individual preference. Identity is an attribute that aims to foster motivation by allowing students to feel ownership by immersing players in an alternate reality where they take on a different identity. In *AEINS*, the player chooses a playing character to represent them in the virtual world and chooses friends from a group of non-playing characters (semi-autonomous agents). The player character has no history and the student can build it through his action choices that reflect his beliefs, in the game world. If the player succeeds in bridging the real identity and the virtual identity in the game, they should be motivated to learn the ethical values and skills to help that character succeed.

Manipulation and distributed knowledge is a principle that deals with actions and offering the player characters to move intricately, effectively and easily through the world. *AEINS* has partially achieved this aspect through the use of 2D interface and on-screen text to interact with the game. Knowledge distribution deals with knowledge split between the person playing the game and the virtual character. For example, the virtual character knows how to move in the environment and how to make friends, but the player knows when to do this and why. The *AEINS* design offers the virtual character that represents the student in the virtual environment. It helps the children to build a powerful bridge between their real identity and this virtual identity in order to progress in the game.

Problem solving and well-ordered problems are principles that are concerned by how skills gained in solving earlier problems help in solving further, more difficult, problems *AEINS* provides different levels of moral dilemmas that present various ethical concepts and reinforce desirable attitudes. The more the student practices and proceeds in the game the more complex conflicts will appear. Skills gained in solving simpler problems should help the student to solve more complicated conflicts. Pleasantly frustrating is a principle that deals with the appropriate challenge level that should be offered to the students. *AEINS* allows this through offering different level dilemmas that challenges the student at different knowledge levels.

Expertise is formed in any area by repetitive cycles of students practicing skills until they are nearly automatic, then having those skills fail in ways that cause the students to have to think again and learn anew. As mentioned throughout this chapter, in *AEINS*, each new dilemma (teaching moment) brings a new challenge that builds on previously-learned skills. Students advance between levels when a certain amount of proficiency is reached. Then they continue to practice those skills in the service of higher level goals. Practice helps the student to automate the new knowledge and feel pride in their growing expertise. As skills become automated, they serve as components in the higher level strategies that the students learn. This satisfies the cycles of expertise principle. Gee sees that humans are not efficiently capable of using verbal information (words). In *AEINS*, the player initially receives a brief introduction about the world and what should be done. Then the student is left to explore the environment by himself. *AEINS* is able to provide information on-demand and just-in-time.

Fish tanks are those simplified versions of the main game that allow tutoring and practicing in order to understand the game as a whole system. *AEINS* has not tackled this point. With regard to sand boxes, Gee defines the term as follows: students are put into a situation that feels like the real thing, but with risks and dangers greatly mitigated, they can learn well and still feel a sense of authenticity and accomplishment. In *AEINS*, this has been attempted in the design of teaching moments that provide realism in the game and social contexts. The game story elements are designed to motivate the student to learn ethical skills.

Gee found that people do not like practicing individual skills over and over in a meaningless context. However, they gladly practice a set of related skills as a strategy to accomplish designed goals. *AEINS* allows practicing individual skills as well as the applications of more than one skill through providing different interactive contexts and situations.

System thinking, understanding and meaning as action image are three further principles. People learn skills, strategies, and ideas best when they see and understand how they fit into an overall larger system to which they give meaning. The player learns most effectively when he understands his role within the system and can use that knowledge to set goals and determine actions (Hastings, 2009). The *AEINS* environment allows the student to picture himself in the virtual world and how he fits in, in addition to how his actions affect himself and others. Each *AEINS* story is generated in a way that gives the student this type of system within which to learn and practice ethical and moral skills. It was designed to provide the student with the conceptual connections required for learning with understanding. Moreover, humans do not usually think through general definitions and logical principles. Rather, they think through experiences they have had. It is the person's own experience that gives meaning to their words. Gee's opinion is that games can have marvelous effects if they succeed to tie words and concepts to actions in the world. In other words, by linking perception to action, the conceptual learning is strengthened and the student's experience is enriched. As we have discussed before, The *AEINS* design is all about situating the learning and use of ethical skills within a rich context that enables the player to learn with deep understanding.

In the next section, we will present the empirical study done to test *AEINS* on the technical side, the social effect and the educational outcomes.

EMPIRICAL STUDY

A study was done to test the developed educational game, *AEINS*. In designing this study, it was determined that the best way to approach it was to rely on a qualitative evaluation method to elicit users' thoughts. Since the participants were children, the use of in-depth, open-ended interviewing seemed the appropriate method to capture the interviewees' experiences and perspectives on the program being evaluated. It helped the participants to express their experiences and judgments in their own terms. The resulting data consists of quotations with sufficient context to be interpretable.

Twenty participants were randomly assigned to play with *AEINS* over a number of games. Their age was between 7 and 12 years old (15 male, 6 female, mean=9.6). The children were all an opportunistic sampling from schools in York who voluntarily agreed to use *AEINS* with their families' permission. The participants were of different origins and had different cultural backgrounds.

Prior to each experiment, demographic data was collected for each participant along with an informed consent form, signed by their parents. The participants were interviewed individually. The *AEINS* environment was briefly introduced to each participant. The participants were encouraged to explore the environment themselves and provided with the required privacy. Participants were explicitly told to be themselves while interacting with *AEINS*. The participants' reactions during their interaction with *AEINS* were watched and recorded. The participants worked at their own pace and all their actions were recorded by *AEINS* to be analyzed later. *AEINS* did not allow the participant to change their minds regarding their taken actions, as this is what could happen in real life, and thus the participant will experience the effects of his choices on himself and on others.

To evaluate *AEINS*, students' log files have been examined and post-participation interviews were conducted that focused on five different categories. The first category included questions related to the technical infrastructure and its functioning. The second category included questions related to the functions and features inherent in the system and its ability to support or enable a specific activity. The third category included questions related to the participant tasks. The fourth category included questions related to the capability for specific technology-based activities to generate predicted outcomes. And finally the fifth category included questions related to the re-playability and self reflection.

By looking at the student's log files and tracing the teaching moments' presentation, it has been found that the student model is able to identify the student's needs and present the teaching moments accordingly (address individual needs). By the end of the whole experience, the student will have truly experienced some emotional and moral complexities appropriate to their current moral understandings. This kind of experience, especially when complexities develop over the course of a game-like environment, can leave the player wiser (Freeman, 2004).

Results are organized around the main themes reflected by the data. These three themes are: *AEINS* architecture and implementation, social aspects in *AEINS*, and learning deployed in *AEINS* and educational achievements.

Results

The *AEINS* interface is a simple interface. However, some participants were slow to acquaint themselves with the game, but after a short time they became quicker and much more immersed. The interface uses check boxes to handle the

student's actions or choices. It allows more mouse clicks to interact with the game world and multiple-line text boxes to present the story, and stores every single action in the environment. This allows the student, at any time, to see past actions to solve a conflict or judge certain actions based on previous ones.

Interacting with *AEINS* has been shown to be an enjoyable experience for most of the participants, *AEINS* was described by one person as an environment where you can try wrong things and see what would happen. One participant said the following about *AEINS*: "…. very million times good." and added that "It tries to make you behave well in real life, this is your training to be good." Another participant, said: "I enjoyed finding new situations, meeting the characters and solving problems for them," and added "I like the idea of facing situations in different places."

Moreover, the story in *AEINS* has been described as connected, fun, defined and interesting. Another participant added: "the whole story is quite organized. It is good and simple…., it gives a variety of options and characters."

The evaluation shows that children appreciate the social characteristic in the system, as they were able to recognize the genuine social aspects and the realism represented in the game. The analytical questions confirm this recognition. For example, participants clearly cared about the outcome. For example, one participant said: "The best moment was when my parents and my teacher were proud of me because of what I had done." Another participant felt good when the teacher told the parents that he told the truth and he was rewarded by going on a nice summer holiday. This quote and others like "I was *upset* when my friend said that she will not be my friend anymore." shows emotional effect on the participants where they can feel good, bad, scared, surprised. Therefore, we can argue that emotional engagement is another positive point *AEINS* provides.

It seems that *AEINS* was able to make them feel that they are really involved in realistic situations and consequently they were acting accordingly. More evidence that the participants were recognizing the social situation and recognizing the non-playing characters as real friends have appeared in the following quotes: "I felt as if I am in a real world and these characters are really talking to me, they were very believable." Another participant said, "I did not mean to upset my friend, I felt as if it really happened and I had lost my friend who will not talk to me ever again. I think I will be careful next time."

Actually, what was most interesting is the way the participants personalize the non-playing characters in the game. They do not only interact with them as their friends in the game but also they gave them lives and they were picturing how these characters behave beyond these moments. For example one interviewee said, "I do not like Gina when she lies, I want to tell her that this is wrong and she has to stop lying." The interviewee added "If she keeps doing this now, no one will believe her in the future."

The participants also believe the non-playing characters personalities: they like some and dislike others. For example, one participant describes one of the non-playing characters as funny. Another participant said that the non-playing character 'Gina' is not a real friend as she always ask him to do something wrong, which is something real friends do not do.,

The realism present in *AEINS* allows the participants to think about the non-playing characters as real friends who can feel and expect certain actions from them. For example, one participant, explained, "If I choose to be on the side of one friend, the other one could become angry." Another participant, when asked about the non-playing characters said that, "They rely on me. They ask me to solve their problems. They need my help." However, when asked if any of them has behaved in a strange way, he replied. "They are trying to make me *cheat*; *real friends* do not do this." [Italics added]

This theme is very important as it tends to show that *AEINS* is an effective learning environment and is able to deliver effective learning, in other words develop the participant's reasoning process. The use of the Socratic method as the teaching pedagogy shows success. In every teaching moment, an agent who exhibits certain personality characteristics uses the Socratic Voice to raise the moral conflict. This pushes the student to think harder to solve the discrepancy inherent in these situations. For example, from one participant's log file, we found that the student followed this path in the shoplifting dilemma: agree to help his friend to take a chocolate bar without paying for it, and then undertake a discussion with the good moral character, who uses the Socratic Voice. The discussion ended by a change in the student behavior where he admitted he made a mistake and asked his friend to return the chocolate. In the post-participant interview with this participant, he mentioned that he made a mistake by helping Gina (the immoral character in the shoplifting dilemma) to take the chocolate. This corresponds well with the results obtained from the log file. Such changes in attitude reflect the power of the Socratic Method in forcing the student to face the contradictions present in any course of action not based on good moral principles.

One participant liked the fact that she can interact with the teaching moments and is able to see the effect of her decisions on herself and others. This interviewee asked to restart the game when she has been faced by negative consequences as a result of one of her choices. This shows that although the feedback was implicitly provided in the story, it manages to deliver the message (you did something wrong) which was not appropriate to be said explicitly as we discussed before. In the post-participant interview, it seems that the interviewee has an explicit representation about taking belongings. This appears in her final comment: "Taking other people's stuff is stealing and we should not take something without asking first."

We claim that the interactive teaching moments were able to provide the appropriate hints about various moral actions and situate the students in different mental and emotional states. Moreover they allow the student to attempt the high levels of Bloom's taxonomy such as Analysis. For example, the participants were analyzing the situations, where conflict exists, and trying to find a solution to the current dilemma as quoted by one participant: "It was difficult to take a decision as it can make my friend upset."

In the next section, we will discuss the main ideas presented in this chapter and the results obtained from the above evaluation.

DISCUSSION

This chapter presented the idea that integrating different educational game features has been shown to individually increase the effectiveness of various educational games, such as dynamic generated narrative, scripted narrative, student modeling and the presence of continuous story. The integration of dynamic generated and scripted narratives allows high user agency but also allows the educational game to track the learning process and assess it. The presence of a student model provides a personalized learning process. Finally, the continuous story allows the presence of evolving non-player characters that engage the student and increase the realism and believability of the environment. Although each individual attribute is not innovative in itself, their integration in one environment is.

Moreover, this chapter discussed problems encountered in classroom environments while teaching ill-defined domains such as ethics, and how computers can act as a solution. In the ethics domain, *AEINS* can act as an assistant tool in teaching the ethics curriculum, especially with its ability to provide summary reports, based on the student model, for individual students. Such reports help the teachers to identify the students'

weak points in a quick and easy way solving time constraints in the classrooms. The teachers can decide on upcoming educational materials which suit the majority of the class.

AEINS offers a compelling virtual world and virtual identity, at some level, where deep learning is able to occur. It can be noticed that the children were able to build a powerful bridge between their real identity and this virtual identity in the game. They did have emotional responses that transfer their real world responses to the game. This goes well with Gee's discussion about learning and identity and his illustration of the importance of children being able to build these bridges (Gee, 2004b).

AEINS has been designed as an endogenous game, not an exogenous one. In exogenous games, the learning content is often added into a general game framework like a quiz show or a shooter game. Researchers prefer endogenous games where the content material is intimately tied in with the game play, because of their theoretical advantage in learning effectiveness (Hastings, 2009). From the very beginning, we were aware of the importance of having the educational tasks weaved into the games directly and progress in the game should depend only on acquiring the required skills. We created multiple stories which are connected to the main story in which the player is put into a position where he must use the skills that we are trying to reinforce. Inability to perform the skills will bring feedback and extra practice. Mastery of the skills will bring success and progress within the game

Children became engaged in the game, all participants agreed on how interesting it was solving conflict situations especially between their friends and how this can be difficult sometimes. We believe that the interactive dilemmas in *AEINS* succeeded to induce moral interpretations. What is happening here fits well with Gee (2004b) and his theory about "what video games have to teach us" and how students can be unwilling to put in the effort and practice demanded for mastering a domain if this compelling component is missing. The fun provided by *AEINS* and the associated curiosity exists from the presence of various unexpected ends for the same teaching moments (learning objects) helped the participants to get immersed in the game and put the effort into solving the required tasks. In addition to the appropriate challenge level provided in the learning tasks as a result of the presence of an individualized student model built for every particular participant

To be able to assert that deep learning has occurred in an ill-defined domain like ethics requires some kind of transformation in the way a person thinks. Through the children's experiences with *AEINS*, it has been found, that they were using their real identities. They were applying their own beliefs and experiences from their lives in the game. For example, one of the participants did not like the homework scene presented to him when he was interacting with *AEINS* and when asked why? He answered that he does not like doing homework in real life.

However, this does not mean that every child has only one identity: it is actually a combination of various real identities mixed up together. Some of these identities appear in certain situations or under certain circumstances. With their ability to build this bridge between their real identities and the virtual one, the real identities are enriched with this new identity that can also appear in real situations. Gee (2004b) discusses this kind of unity, mentioning that if children are learning deeply, they will learn through their projective identities, new values and new ways of being in the world based on the powerful combination of their real world identities and the virtual identity at stake in the learning.

The post-participant interviews showed they had been inspired by the system. Some of them commented that they would be happy to take the system home and spend time with it. This provides evidence that they do have a pleasant experience. Among this group, the students gave the software a subjective evaluation and generally had a number of constructive suggestions about how to make the software better. The delivery platform was subsequently improved based on feedback from these evaluations.

Overall, we believe this research provides students with a practical means of exploring abstract issues in concrete settings, allows students to practice making ethical decisions in a realistic context and enables them to see various consequences in a safe environment.

RECOMMENDATIONS SUMMARY

Based on the experience of developing and testing *AEINS,* we developed a set of recommendations and considerations for creating games that support character education.

1. **First player perspective.** Allow the player to join the game as a first player to maximize the opportunity of situated learning and self reflection on their own experiences.
2. **Use various challenging levels.** Make sure that the players can explore the world in different ways and the game provides the appropriate level of challenge where the difficulty level increases gradually.
3. **Variable experience.** Make sure that the player is faced by different experiences over multiple play times. This can be achieved through the presence of a student model.
4. **Incorporate multiple perspectives.** Integrate diverse views on the same topic or situation, and place different types of people into the world so that players can interact with many types of ideas and beliefs, which can lead to deliberation with others, as well as reflection on one's own views.
5. **Presence of synthetic characters.** Show the emotional impact of actions on the non-playing characters to increase the world believability, allow the players to build

relations with them, to care about them and be committed to them.

6. **Provide feedback.** Make sure that players relate the feedback to their choices and actions. And that they understand how their choice led to a consequence.

7. **Positive and negative rewards.** Make sure the game provides positive as well as negative rewards that help the player to evaluate how his actions led to a certain kind of reward.

FUTURE RESEARCH DIRECTIONS

In this chapter, we have proposed an Adaptive Educational Interactive Narrative System (*AEINS*) that helps to teach ethics. While *AEINS* has been successful in many aspects, there is still room for further development. Specifically, the following aspects of the system could be improved:

- Enhance the graphical user interface to be 3D; this kind of interface offers visual appearances that attract human attention, especially children. The 3D interface will allow the presence of animated pedagogical agents that positively serve the educational process.
- Develop an authoring tool to help teachers with no or weak programming skills to author teaching moments in an easy way.
- Create a bigger story world to allow the presence of larger sets of actions the student can take. In turn this would increase the student's freedom and agency within the environment.
- Enhance the student-system interaction by using a full natural language engine; this would facilitate human computer interaction and allow free expressions, which in turn could cause more difficulties in analyzing the student's knowledge and intentions.

REFERENCES

Abraham, D., & Yacef, K. (2002). Adaptation in the Web-based Logic-ITA. In *Adaptive Hypermedia and Adaptive Web-Based Systems* ([]. Berlin: Springer.]. *Lecture Notes in Computer Science, 2347*, 456–461. doi:10.1007/3-540-47952-X_60

Anderson, R. C., & Pichert, J. W. (1978). Recall of previously unrecallable information following a shift in perspective. *Journal of Verbal Learning and Verbal Behavior, 17*, 1–12. doi:10.1016/S0022-5371(78)90485-1

Anderson, R. C., Reynolds, R. E., Schallert, D. L., & Goetz, E. T. (1977). Frameworks for comprehending discourse. *American Educational Research Journal, 14*, 367–381.

Avner, A., Moore, C., & Smith, S. (1980). Active external control: A basis for superiority of CBI. *Journal of Computer-Based Instruction, 6*(4), 115–118.

Aylett, R., Louchart, S., Tychsen, A., Hitchens, M., Figueiredo, R., & Mata, C. D. (2008). Managing emergent character-based narrative. In *Proceedings of the 2nd international conference on INtelligent TEchnologies for interactive entertainment (INTETAIN '08)*, Cancun, Mexico (pp. 1-8). Berlin: Springer.

Aylett, R., Vala, M., Sequeira, P., & Paiva, A. (2007). FearNot! - An emergent narrative approach to virtual dramas for anti-bullying education. In *Virtual storytelling: Using virtual reality technologies for storytelling, International Conference on Virtual Storytelling, Saint Malo, France* ([]. Berlin: Springer.]. *Lecture Notes in Computer Science, 4871*, 202–205. doi:10.1007/978-3-540-77039-8_19

Barber, H., & Kudenko, D. (2007). A user model for the generation of dilemma-based interactive narratives. Paper presented at *Workshop on Optimising Player Satisfaction (AIIDE' 07)*, Stanford, CA.

Bayon, V., Wilson, J. R., Stanton, D., & Boltman A. (2003). Mixed reality storytelling environments. *Virtual Reality Journal, 7*(1).

Bell, P., & Linn, M. C. (2000). Scientific arguments as learning artifacts: Designing for learning from the web with KIE. *International Journal of Science Education, 22*(8), 797–817. doi:10.1080/095006900412284

Bergin, D. A. (1999). Influences on classroom interest. *Educational Psychologist Journal, 34*(2), 87–98. doi:10.1207/s15326985ep3402_2

Bolton, G. (1999). *Acting in classroom drama: A critical analysis*. Birmingham, AL: Trentham Books.

Brusilovsky, P. (1994). Student model centered architecture for intelligent learning environments. In Proceedings of Fourth international conference on User Modeling, Hyannis, MA (pp. 31-36).

Daeg de Mott, D. K. (2001, April 6). Kohlberg's theory of moral reasoning. In *Encyclopedia of Childhood and Adolescence*. Retrieved from FindArticles.com.

Eiriksson, S. (1997). Preservice teachers' perceived constraints of teaching science in the elementary classroom. *Journal of Elementary Science Education, 9*(2), 18–27. doi:10.1007/BF03173774

Elkind, D. H., & Sweet, F. (1997). How to do character education. Retrieved from http://www.goodcharacter.com

Freeman, D. (2004). *Creating emotions in games: The craft and art of engineering* (p. 157). Berkeley, CA: New Riders Publishing.

Gagné, R. M., Wager, W. W., Golas, K. G., & Keller, J. M. (2005). *Principles of instructional design*. Toronto, ON: Thomson Wadsworth.

Gee, J. P. (2004a). *Situated language and learning: A critique of traditional schooling*. London: Routledge.

Gee, J. P. (2004b). *What video games have to teach us about learning and literacy*. New York: Palgrave Macmillan.

Gunter, G. A., Kenny, R. F., & Vick, E. H. (2006). A case for a formal design paradigm for serious games. *Journal of the International Digital Media and Arts Association, 3*(1), 93–105.

Halverson, S. (2004). Teaching ethics: The role of the classroom teacher. Association for Childhood Education International (ACEI) Subscriptions. Retrieved from http://www.acei.org

Harless, W. G. (1986). An interactive videodisc drama: The case of Frank Hall. *Journal of Computer-Based Instruction, 13*(4), 113–116.

Hastings, P., Britt, A., Sagarin, B., Durik, A., & Kopp, K. (2009). Designing a game for teaching argumentation skills. In *Proceedings of workshop on intelligent educational games, at the 14th International Conference on Artificial Intelligence in Education (AIED09)*, Brighton, UK.

Hodhod, R., Kudenko, D., & Cairns, P. (2009, April). Serious games to teach ethics. In *Proceedings of AISB'09: Artificial and Ambient Intelligence*, Edinburgh, Scotland, UK.

Johnson, W., & Marsella, L. S., & Vilhjálmsson, H. (2004). The DARWARS tactical language training system. In *Proceedings of the 26th Interservice/Industry Training, Simulation, and Education Conference* (I/ITSEC), Orlando, FL.

Keller, J. M. (1987). Development and use of the ARCS model of instructional design. *Journal of Instructional Development, 10*(3), 2–10. doi:10.1007/BF02905780

Kim, N. (1989). Circsim-tutor: An intelligent tutoring system for circulatory physiology. Unpublished doctoral dissertation, Illinois Institute of Technology, Chicago, IL.

Kohlberg, L. (1984). *The philosophy of moral development: Moral stages and the idea of justice. Essays on moral development* (*Vol. 1*). New York: Harper and Row.

Koslowski, B. (1996). *Theory and evidence: The development of scientific reasoning.* Cambridge, MA: MIT Press.

Kuhn, D. (1993). Science as argument: Implications for teaching and learning scientific thinking. *Scientific and Educational Journal, 77*(3), 319–337. doi:10.1002/sce.3730770306

Lane, H. C., Core, M. G., Gomboc, D., Karnavat, A., & Rosenberg, M. (2007). Intelligent tutoring for interpersonal and intercultural skills. In *Proceedings of Interservice/Industry Training, Simulation and Education Conference (I/ITSEC)* (pp. 1–11).

Lickona, T., Schaps, E., & Lewis, C. (2007). *Eleven principles of effective character education.* Washington, DC: Character Education Partnership.

Lynch, C., Pinkwart, N., Ashley, K., & Aleven, V. (2008, June). What do argument diagrams tell us about students' aptitude or experience? A statistical analysis in an ill-defined domain. In proceedings of a workshop held during *The 9th international Conference on Intelligent Tutoring Systems (ITS-2008),* Montreal, Canada.

Magerko, B. S. (2006). *Player modeling in the interactive drama architecture.* Unpublished dissertation, University of Michigan, Ann Arbor, MI.

Magerko, B. S., & Stensrud, B. S. (2006). Bringing the schoolhouse inside the box-a tool for engaging, individualized training. In *Proceedings of the 25th Army Science Conference,* Orlando, FL.

McBrien, J. L., & Brandt, R. S. (1997). *The language of learning: A guide to education terms* (pp. 17–18). Alexandria, VA: Association for Supervision and Curriculum Development.

Mckenzie, A., & Mccalla, G. (2009). Serious games for professional ethics: An architecture to support personalization. In *Proceedings of Workshop on Intelligent Educational Games (AIED 2009),* Brighton, UK.

Meacham, J. A., & Emont, N. M. (1989). Everyday problem solving: Theory and applications. In Sinnott, J. D. (Ed.), *The interpersonal basis of everyday problem solving* (pp. 7–23). New York: Praeger.

Mergel, B. (1998). Instructional design & learning theory. Retrieved from http://www.usask.ca/education/coursework/802papers/mergel/brenda.htm

Prada, R., Machado, I., & Paiva, A. (2000). Teatrix: A virtual environment for story creation. In *Proceedings of the 5th International Conference on Intelligent Tutoring Systems* (pp. 464-473). Berlin: Springer Verlag.

Riedl, M., & Stern, A. (2006). Believable agents and intelligent story adaptation for interactive storytelling. In *Proceedings of 3rd International Conference on Technologies for Interactive Digital Storytelling and Entertainment,* Darmstadt, Germany (Lecture Notes in Computer Science Vol. 4326). Berlin: Springer.

Shapiro, D. A. (1999). Teaching ethics from the inside-out: Some strategies for developing moral reasoning skills in middle school students. Paper presented at Seattle Pacific University conference on the social and moral fabric of school life, Edmonds, WA.

Shortliffe, E. H. (1981). Consultation systems for physicians: The role of artificial intelligence techniques. In Webber, B. L., & Nilsson, N. J. (Eds.), *Readings in artificial intelligence* (pp. 323–333). Palo Alto, CA: Tioga Publishing Company.

Silva, A., Raimundo, G., & Paiva, A. (2003). Tell me that bit again: Bringing interactivity to a virtual storyteller. In *Proceedings of the 2nd International Conference on Virtual Storytelling.* Berlin: Springer.

Simon, H. A. (1973). The structure of ill-structured problems. *AI, 4,* 181–201.

Simpson, D. (1998). Dilemmas in palliative care education. *Palliative Medicine, 1*(2).

Thomas, J. M., & Young, M. (2007). Becoming scientists: Employing adaptive interactive narrative to guide discovery learning. In *Proceedings of AIED-07 Workshop on Narrative Learning Environments*, Marina Del Rey, CA.

Vilhjalmsson, H., Merchant, C., & Samtani, P. (2007, August). Social puppets: Towards modular social animation for agents and avatars. *Lecture Notes in Computer Science* (pp. 192–201). Berlin: Springer.

Waraich, A. (2004). Using narrative as a motivating device to teach binary arithmetic and logic gates. *ACM SIGCSE Bulletin, 36*(3), 97–101. doi:10.1145/1026487.1008024

Watson, C. E. (2003, May). Using stories to teach business ethics – Developing character through examples of admirable actions. *Journal of Teaching Business Ethics, 7*(2), 93–105. doi:10.1023/A:1022660405619

Yang, F., Kim, J. H., Glass, M., & Evens, M. W. (2000). Turn planning in CIRCSIM-Tutor. In *Proceedings of the Thirteenth International Florida Artificial Intelligence Research Society Conference* (pp. 60-64).

Chapter 15

Leveraging Digital Games for Moral Development in Education:
A Practitioner's Reflection

Ross FitzGerald
Shady Hill School, USA

Jennifer Groff
Futurelab, UK

ABSTRACT

Ethical and moral development is a result of cognitive structures generated through experience in the pivotal stage of adolescence, during which formal education plays a critical role. Recent advancements in cognitive psychology have explored the very nature of moral development, as well as the critical role education plays in that development. Digital games are potentially powerful learning environments to shape moral development for students. This chapter describes two case studies of digital games used in a middle school classroom to enhance moral development. Finally, it reflects upon and analyzes these cases using the developmental theories of Robert Selman and others as a framework.

INTRODUCTION

Recent advancements in cognitive psychology have demonstrated that education plays a powerful role in ethical and moral development (more than age alone), influencing one's ability to make sophisticated judgments using moral reasoning (Fischer, Yan & Stewart, 2003). Specifically, adolescence is seen as a critical period where one's development in these areas is framed for

adulthood: "These are the years not only for learning specific social skills and strategies but also for the growth of our capacities for social understanding and empathy" (Selman, 2003). As a result, in our experience, many teachers concerned with student moral development seek tools and methodologies that help them positively shape this with their students

As digital gaming is increasing in acceptance for use in education, practitioners have begun exploring their potential to develop a classroom environment that will facilitate experiences to

DOI: 10.4018/978-1-60960-120-1.ch015

support healthy community and interpersonally oriented moral development—developmentally appropriate progression as "children become socially wise" (Selman, 1980, p. 311)New and emerging web-, computer- and console-based games and simulations can provide further support to the ethical development that pushes early adolescents to coordinate social perspectives, a key foundation for moral development. Within a classroom setting, games can provide both a tangible experience and a structure for intellectual exploration. Certain computer games, while not specifically created for an educational purpose, could potentially be a powerful platform for exploring and guiding the complex relationship that exists in an individual and in groups between thought and action—ultimately helping to shape ethical development at this opportune stage of development.

This chapter describes a case study on the application of such technologies to promote positive community and interpersonally focused moral development, combined with an analysis of the literature on human development of ethics. We argue, through our observations and reflections on the use of computer games in the classroom, that some games have the potential to be a powerful platform for promoting ethical development during the critical stage of adolescence.

Ethical Development

What are ethics and how do they develop? The fields of psychology and cognitive development have much to offer our understanding of ethical development, and therefore we will define *ethics* from a psychological perspective:

A set of principles derived from personal experience and informed by cultural mandates informs ethical behavior; contextual variables challenge these principles, and a highly ethical person will integrate awareness of himself and of others, to recognize how different contexts affect his thinking

and action, and then act from consistent principles despite diverse contexts.

In essence, "ethics" is one's "operating system" for navigating interpersonal and intercultural relationships and behavior. The field of cognitive psychology has made incredible advancements in the last several decades, with an increasing focus on understanding the nature of moral development. Researchers have found that this area of human development in particular is considerably influenced by the individual's surrounding environment—in particular education, where the environment has a structured purpose and focus (see Colby, Kohlberg, Gibbs, & Lieberman, 1983; Dawson, 2002; and King & Kitchener, 1994). Critically, leaders in this field note that a "stimulating environment *must* catalyze the development of the highest stages of moral and reflective judgment, and it may be essential for other domains of adult development as well" (Fischer, et al., 2003). Therefore, not only must moral development not be left to chance, but education has a powerful position in affecting the nature of that development for students.

This literature suggests three central components that build an "operating system" for ethical behavior. Developmental psychologist Lawrence Kohlberg was a pioneer in this area through the 1960s and 1970s, and concluded that human psychosocial competence (including ethical development) lies in the ability to see another's perspective (Kohlberg, 1969). Therefore, *social perspective-taking* "is critical for the growth of moral reasoning" (Selman, 2003). Selman, building on Kohlberg's work, saw that in addition to perspective-taking, "…a second key assumption was that *positive peer relationships* are an essential environmental or social condition for this growth" (Selman, 2003). In other words, how one negotiates interpersonal actions affects the positive outcome of peer relationships directly. Finally, Selman suggests a third key component of psychosocial competence: *Personal Meaning Awareness*, which addresses the question: how insightful is an individual at reflecting on emotions, actions and relationships for given social interactions or experiences? This is a higher level of development, where the individual is able not only to view herself from an outside observer's perspective, he uses this knowledge to construct understandings of his behavior that shapes future interactions.

Before examining each of these components more critically in the next three sections, it is useful to talk practically about what we are discussing. Every day, each of us behaves and interacts in the world, and with others. In any given context, one decides how he or she will respond in that context depending on her ability to take another's perspective, to sustain positive peer relationships, and the sense one makes of that given situation or context (which puts together numerous variables about the world and others). One's developmental level in each of these three domains (described further below), as well as how those converge, determines the nature and extent of one's behavior to be ethical. To support this, we explore each of these domains more fully below.

Social Perspective-Taking

As a child grows up, she moves from being able to understand herself from her own perspective to being able to understand and coordinate the perspective of others. Very young children are egocentric and most often do not understand that others view the world differently than they do (Selman, 1990). As a child grows, he begins to understand that others have a perspective different from his (Selman, 1990). Next a child begins to understand that another person has a perspective on whom he is, while also knowing that his perspective on another may be different than how that person views him or herself (Selman, 1990). Finally, a child will come to view the perspectives of one relationship within the context of multiple relationships; it is this developing ability to understand perspective that informs how children act interpersonally and within a community (Selman, 2003).

Peer Relationships & Negotiation Strategies

Interpersonal actions are based in part on a child's ability to coordinate their social perspective-taking. A child will connect to others on an emotional level, or relate to them, in varying degrees (see first column in Table 1). The child will also assert herself, or act within the relationship, in varying levels as well (see Autonomy Aspect, the third column in Table 1). As a child develops, he or she will progress in these areas from a very one-way, egocentric perspective, to being able to share vulnerabilities and self-identities inter-

Table 1. Repertoire of negotiation strategies. (Adapted from Selman, R., (2003)

Shared Experience: Relatedness Aspect	Social Perspective Coordination Levels	Interpersonal Negotiation Strategies: Autonomy Aspect
Unreflective Imitation or enmeshment; lack of differentiation	Level 0: Undifferentiated, egocentric	Physical force: impulsive fight or flight or freeze
Unreflective sharing of expressive enthusiasm	Level 1: Differentiated, subjective	One-way, unilateral power: orders or obedience
Reflective sharing of similar perceptions and experiences	Level 2: Reciprocal, self-reflective	Cooperative exchange reciprocity: persuasion or deference
Empathic sharing of beliefs and values	Level 3: third-person; Mutual	Mutual compromise
Interdependent sharing of vulnerabilities and self-identities	Level 4: Intimate, in-depth; Societal	Collaborative integration of relationship dynamics (commitment)

dependently. As autonomy develops, a child will move from impulsive fight or flight actions to using the commitment of a relationship to grow the relationship itself (Selman, 1990).

Personal Meaning Awareness

Personal meaning, like interpersonal negotiation strategies, also develops along a core of social perspective coordination. Meaning is created in a way that is oriented toward the self (autonomy) or toward a relationship (intimacy) (Selman, 2003). It can contain either positive or negative judgment, and it develops in parallel to perspective-taking. At basic levels, an individual's personal meaning is dismissive. It develops first through rule-based awareness, then to need-based awareness and finally, to an insightful awareness that integrates orientation and judgment (Selman, 2003). Understanding how a child connects her personal meaning with her ability to coordinate perspectives is key to understanding her social interactions. Selman explains,

"At any given moment in time–or in any given place–the personal meaning that an individual makes of the risks involved in a social interaction, incident or relationship provides an important key to understanding whether there will be a gap between the individual's level of interpersonal understanding and his or her level of actual social action" (2003, p.45).

Personal meaning, then, is the bridge between thought and action. As one's ability to negotiate relationships develops, and as one coordinates perspectives with greater complexity, an individual is likely to have increased positive interpersonal behavior as these two components are then integrated with personal meaning to create overall psychosocial competency (see Table 2). As each psychosocial component develops in balance with the other two, a person develops overall psychosocial competency.

Depending on the context, a more developed sophistication of personal meaning will lead to contextually successful outcomes. As an indi-

Table 2. Personal meaning awareness of behavior: "Fighting." (Adapted from Selman, R., (2003)

Level	Orientation to Self (Autonomy)		Orientation to Relationship (Relatedness)	
	(Pro) Positive	(Anti) Negative	(Pro) Positive	(Anti) Negative
0: Dismissive	It's fun beating up on people.	Fighting is stupid.	Fighting is cool.	Only jerks fight.
1: Rule-based Impersonal	You have to fight to survive.	Fighting only gets you suspended.	Everyone looks up to those who can fight; they're tough.	Fighting makes you unpopular.
2: Rule-based Personal	I'm a good fighter.	I promised myself never to get into a fight.	Our family is good at fighting: my cousin taught me how.	My girlfriend won't have anything to do with me if I get into a fight.
3: Need-based Personal	I fight when I'm tense. Anything will set me off.	I don't fight because I wouldn't respect myself.	If anyone insults my family, I'll fight to defend them.	I worry what others think of me if I fight.
4: Need-based Integrated	Part of what allows me to keep calm under pressure is the awareness that I will respond if provoked, but sometimes I may have to fight back or may even just lose my temper.	Violence is not a part of me, but I might use it as a last resort, rather than sitting on my hostility and having it expressed elsewhere.	I live in a violent neighborhood, and I have to adapt whether I like it or not, but I don't believe in fighting to solve problems, and it goes against my nature.	I seem to need to keep proving to people that they can't push me around, but I wish there were a better way.
Integrated	I used to tell myself that I needed to fight to survive in this neighborhood, but I took a real good look at myself and realized I need to look cool to cover up.			

vidual's personal meaning awareness becomes more insightful, he/she is able to understand variables within interpersonal and intrapersonal constructs that affect one's actions in any context. This insight underlies a set of principles that guides ethical behavior.

To summarize, the collective work of Kohlberg and Selman frames ethical and moral behavior as the result of three components of psychosocial growth (see Figure 1):

- The ability to see and coordinate others' perspectives (Social Awareness)
- The ability to form positive relationships with peers (Repertoire of Negotiation Skills)
- The Awareness of Personal Meaning

If we seek an ethical society, then we must support moral development at the opportunistic stage of development that is puberty. Educational endeavors to achieve such goals must work to develop the three aforementioned components in all students. By addressing three areas of psychosocial competence – Social Awareness (perspective taking), Repertoire of Negotiation Skills, and Awareness of Personal Meaning – a teacher can promote the growth of Social Perspective Coordination that is the heart of a system of ethics and moral reasoning. Teachers can guide students to actions that are ethically grounded for

any given context. Through the active promotion of self-exploration and interpersonal awareness in the classroom, students grow to understand the interplay between who they are in any context, who others might be, and how the interplay can be molded by ethical reasoning rather than by "a multiplicity of tendencies inside, which are activated by this or that context" (Brooks, 2009). Students who are socially competent will become persons who know themselves and act ethically in all the contexts of life.

In the complex dynamic of the structured classroom, it cannot just be assumed or left to chance that along the way students will begin to build the foundation of ethical behavior, including the accommodation of others' perspectives, the formation of positive peer relationships, and the creation of personal meaning. With this framework in mind, what classrooms activities, peer experiences, and tools can help students develop these skills and become ethical citizens in the classroom and beyond?

Developing Ethical Behavior in the Classroom

Even within the most structured classroom, social interaction is dynamic and complex. The nuance of body language, eye-contact, feelings left over from recess, daydreams of after school plans, or how to manage this weekend's first date at the cinema feeds this complexity. For some students who feel awkward in their relationships and who may not understand the social cues of others, a classroom's dynamic may dampen social interaction: the teacher is in charge and the task is to learn the lesson; the complexity of social interaction may be avoided by those who so desire. Therefore, in a structured classroom, students may not have much opportunity to practice the two key foundations for a system of ethics and morals: perspective-taking and positive peer relationships. An experiential educational tool can provide the needed platform from which first to

Figure 1. Framework for ethical development

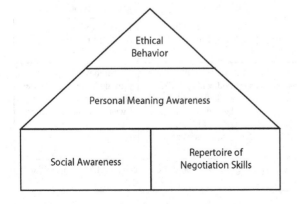

build relationships and perspective, and then to foster the growth of ethics from this foundation.

A suitable experiential tool must consider Selman's model: through shared experiences, children develop a repertoire of negotiation strategies that allow them to exercise autonomy in a relationship (Selman, 1990). At the same time, the shared experience itself creates a sense of intimacy with others (Selman, 1990). A balance between relatedness and autonomy is foundational to a relationship. In addition, as students integrate their negotiations and experiences, their success prompts them to progress from understanding their perspective alone to being able to see the world from another's view point and perhaps even to understanding the interplay of community and the individual (Selman, 2003)..

We argue that all gaming platforms can potentially support moral development within a classroom dynamic. They are a pedagogical tool that bridges the gap between the traditional structure of a teacher-led classroom and the potential chaos that may ensue when adults are completely absent. They allow for the practice of interpersonal negotiation strategies through chat functions or through cooperative problem-solving. They provide a space that scaffolds relationships and consequently fosters the growth of perspective-taking. Finally, it is through a computer game's capacity for detailed record keeping and management of logistics, that a teacher is allowed behavioral management time and class refelction time to promote self-understanding or personal meaning that informs the connection between thought and action (Selman, 2003). In our experience, since the computer manages the structure of the experience (the rules and the logistics of the game) the teacher is free to facilitate student thinking and development, whereas with non-digital games, a teacher can be quickly overwhelmed with game management and logistics.

In the next section, we describe two case studies of digital gaming in the classroom, using the digital games *Diplomacy* and *Civilization*

IV:Colonization, in an effort to promote positive moral development. These cases include examples of changes in student social perspective taking and negotiating strategies, as well as demonstration of pedagogies used to facilitate this growth at the Shady Hill School.

GAMING IN THE CLASSROOM: A CASE STUDY OF ETHICS DEVELOPMENT

With these beliefs about the potential of digital game-based learning for ethics development in the classroom, we set out to structure to classroom experiences that leveraged these technologies at the end of the academic year. Prior to beginning these activities, observations were made by the classroom teacher in regards to the students' current levels of Personal Meaning Awareness, as well as many of the common negotiation strategies demonstrated in and outside the classroom. We then collected qualitative and anecdotal evidence of changes in these during and following the game-based learning experiences.

Curricular Setting

Shady Hill is an independent Pre-K through 8 coeducational school in Cambridge, Massachusetts. Many of its students come from middle and upper income families where a thoughtful education is valued above one that is standard driven. The school teaches content through the interdisciplinary approach of Central Subject. The Central Subject method integrates literature, art, history, geography, and music to provide a year of study that emphasizes depth of learning, mastery of content and understanding of theme. Throughout their career at Shady Hill, students explore both academic content and also what it means to be a member of a community.

For any teacher, the choice of what materials to use in the classroom starts with how well it fits the program of the school. Given the academic rigor of the Central Subject method at Shady Hill, teachers develop their own lessons to revolve around a set of through-lines or themes that form the background conceptual knowledge for the year. The result is a program that uses content to develop a flexible process of learning and acquisition of ideas for Shady Hill students, who are then guided by their own thinking. Throughout Shady Hill there is emphasis on developing the ability to understand issues and events from another's perspective.

The School:

> Challenges prejudice, respects difference, and recognizes that multiple perspectives inform human experience
>
> Encourages children to be independent thinkers who can transform ideas into meaningful action
>
> Advocates learning through cooperation and collaboration

– Shady Hill School Mission, 2010

A teacher at Shady Hill (as well as all other middle schools we have encountered) must then provide academic content while also exploring morality and ethics. To be clear, we are not researchers, but practitioners, and we have structured our own reflections based on experience with the work of Selman et al, as well as familiarity with experiential education programs like Outward Bound Expeditionary learning or Project Zero where students learn social interaction and group dynamics through active gaming. As with many teachers, our methodology arises from the demands of the moment, a need for a tool that will provide academic content, promote social interaction and allow us to teach rather than to manage. We made daily observations of our students, collected their work and used it to assess their progress. In thinking about how to teach ethical behavior better, we returned to these classroom observations and assessments and applied our understanding of Selman's theories to the interactions we had observed. We want to make social behavior more teachable, and we want students to be aware both of themselves and of others. We assume that, throughout the school day, there are many opportunities to foster moral growth, but we want to discover a more intentional approach. At the heart of morality, we believe, are the day-to-day interactions that occur between us all. Our job as teachers is to promote the development of an ethical system that supports community oriented morality.

In the seventh and eighth grade we chose to play two games in particular, *Diplomacy* and *Civilization IV:Colonization*. The seventh grade curriculum centers on the colonial period of American history, hence our choice of *Civilization IV:Colonization*. In the eighth grade, the computer-based version of *Diplomacy* helps students understand the complexity of interdependence among European countries prior to World War I. Players face limited room for expansion, the need to gain resources and, most centrally, the dilemma of creating temporary alliances for one team to win. Initially, the decision to play these games was based solely in academic goals. Nevertheless, observations of students while they played sparked our interest in exploring their impact on affective learning, particularly their impact on the personal and interpersonal growth that we believe form the basis of a system of personal ethics.

About *Diplomacy & Colonization*

Diplomacy is a strategy game that simulates pre-WWI Europe where players vie to win the war by controlling a predetermined number of key places in Europe. Similarly, *Civilization IV:Colonization* is a strategy game where the goal is to build a colony strong enough and with enough political power to declare independence from its European mother country. This classroom implementation consisted of one computer running the game by projecting the display on the wall screen for the entire class. Eighth grade students worked in teams of two to develop their game strategy. In *Diplomacy*, there are only four available moves; winning the game depends on successfully negotiating with rival teams to gain territory in Europe. Without successful negotiations—or diplomacy—a team cannot win. Thus, students must work within their teams as well as with members of rival teams to become successful. The game provides the structure to these interactions allowing the teacher to become a facilitator, advisor, referee, and guide. For a class of adolescents, this game is very challenging interpersonally as it requires high levels of negotiation not only to win the game, but also to cooperate with team members while playing.

Originally, *Diplomacy* was published as a board game, however this format can be a bit cumbersome for classroom play. The electronic version makes classroom game play feasible because it facilitates game play quickly and manages logistics. Time and logistical management always challenge teaching, both academic and social.

Played with teams of two, *Diplomacy* becomes much more open-ended and the game dictates success through interaction with other teams. It is this interaction that necessitates the engagement of more sophisticated psychosocial development. At its fundamental level, *Diplomacy* relies on the successful negotiation of conflict to achieve success by controlling most of Europe. Whereas success at *Civilization IV:Colonization* can be found with relatively low levels of interpersonal skill and self-awareness, *Diplomacy* requires sophistication in both these areas. Additionally, *Diplomacy* demands greater capacity for the individual to compartmentalize the experience as a game, a serious challenge for adults as well as children. With this in mind, seventh grade students play *Civilization IV:Colonization* and it is only at the end of the eighth grade year and then only with a class that has demonstrated psychosocial sophistication do students play *Diplomacy*.

The Link between Shady Hill and Selman's Developmental Theory

The basis for our reflection on ethical development using *Diplomacy* and *Colonization* lies in elements of the aforementioned framework of ethical development—which provides a lens to observe and consider how well students develop and maintain relationships to meet the mission of Shady Hill to create "ethical citizens." *Diplomacy* and *Civilization IV:Colonization* are the tools to structure learning that not only meets curricular goals but also affective goals.

Game play potentially provides an environment to experiment with interpersonal negotiation strategies that foster autonomy. It also provides shared experiences that build intimacy (Relatedness), or "...interpersonal maturity represents an integration of the developmental lines of intimacy and autonomy" (Selman, 1990). The classroom structure of game play provides the environment for this integration. Our assumption, then, is that the ability to form solid relationships with others, where one is able to integrate relatedness and autonomy functions, is one of the most important pieces in the overall ethical development of the individual. Successfully generating this in the classroom requires a certain disposition and approach by the teacher, which is described in the next section.

Teacher's Role in Gaming

The teacher's role and desirable pedagogies with games have been noted considerably elsewhere (see Sandford, Ulicsak, Facer & Rudd, 2006; Sandford & Williamson, 2005; Clark, 2005; and Kirriemuir & McFarlane, 2002). Yet it is worth underscoring that gaming involves complex relationships between players. And, especially for middle school students (who focus on rules and fairness), the digital game provides the parameters for the social area in which relationships occur. As a result, students can focus on playing the game, or, possibly, they can practice their negotiation strategies, ability to see multiple perspectives, and capacity for personal meaning. By the teacher creating the opportunity for reflection on the game experience builds both an appreciation for different perspectives and an integration of the experience into a system of personal meaning. The result for students is greater social awareness around how actions affect others. Students come to integrate social understanding, awareness of personal meaning and their repertoire of negotiation strategies so that they are more psychosocially competent and, consequently, ethical—as demonstrated by student behavior described later in this case study.

When leveraging games for moral development, the most important consideration for the teacher is to seek games that provide a structured and safe environment for peer interaction. This is especially important given the complex overall dynamic of middle school student development. Negotiation strategies, ability to see multiple perspectives and sophistication of personal meaning, even at higher developmental levels, are especially fragile given the new social demands and the physical growth of the typical middle school student (Erickson, 1950; Selman, 2003). Successfully leveraging digital games to promote moral development requires the establishment of a safe educational environment that is perceived as a 'safe' space—where individual and different viewpoints are welcomed—for all participating students. The safer the child feels, the more he can be supported in his moral development (Brion-Meisels, 1978). In creating the initially safe environment, the teacher's role is to decide when to intervene intentionally to promote development and when to let events run their course.

Playing *Diplomacy* in the Middle School

While *Diplomacy* has the capacity to be an extremely powerful pedagogical tool for developing psychosocial competence, it also presents the greatest challenge for implementation and facilitation for the teacher. It is a challenge to maintain a constructive level of comfort within a classroom for the duration of the game, because students must function across a variety of interpersonal negotiation strategies while maintaining a societal level of perspective coordination. Simply, students must work the problem of the game through their interactions with peers without becoming angry at their actions.. The affective educational goal is to create an intentional experience that allows students to develop social perspective coordination and, therefore, familiarity with the game is essential. Within the context of the game, the teacher can then observe and facilitate the ensuing social interactions using Selman's work as a guide. For example, attacking an opponent is a relatively low-level interpersonal negotiation strategy where cooperating to expand is higher. *Diplomacy* rewards those students who are able to integrate their understanding of others with their own needs within the context of the game. Further intervention by the teacher prompts students to explore how they might transfer their successes in the game to other contexts. In this sense, as the teacher promotes reflection, students can think about how to apply their social knowledge and skills to other contexts. In this way, through game play, the teacher fosters a set of principles for social interaction that can be accessed across contexts. This is the basis of ethical action.

Games, by their nature, often promote a winner and a loser—they hinge on conflict. This is true of *Diplomacy* as well. In terms of safety, lower level strategies tend to lower the comfort level within the classroom and challenge the opportunity for positive shared experiences. Although students may build their sense of autonomy through unilateral action, the fact that these actions often challenge relatedness functions leads to poor overall psychosocial integration. To introduce a game that often requires unilateral victory threatens the safety of individuals in the classroom and therefore puts psychosocial growth at risk. The role of the teacher is to guide students through games as simulations of life experiences so that they can develop the successful integration of interpersonal and intrapersonal skills with self-understanding. Again, we view this integration as the basis for an ethical citizen and nowhere are a system of ethics more challenged than when there is conflict.

The idea of conflict even in a game situation disquiets many students while others dive into the challenge with gusto. Most important in the initial stages of the game is that the teacher has already created a mechanism for discussing conflict. In one class, students were required to keep journals of their actions and to report from their journals as a way to reflect on the experience. Shady Hill provides a comfort area in each of its classrooms consisting of plush chairs, couches, and rugs. Regular meetings to discuss classroom issues and conflicts occur in this area throughout the year. Thus, a space and format for discussion have become routine and moving discussion and reflection of the game to this space is natural. In addition, creating teams that balance outgoing students with more introspective students as well as matching students with computer experience (especially gaming) to those who have less can add intentionality to the experience that fosters a positive experience. For example, one pair consisted of a quiet student who had strong technology skills and another student who was particularly outgoing and well-liked. This complementary pair not only interacted with other teams, it also developed as its own team. The quiet student became more outspoken while the more outspoken student developed a greater appreciation for technological skill.

Outcomes and Discussion

Students advanced on levels of personal meaning awareness behavior.

On the broader classroom level, the class ultimately agreed that each country could maintain a set number of key centers and that, since this had been achieved, the game would end with everyone winning. In this game there was a core group of students who had a sophisticated knowledge of the game and there were those who could operate across both the autonomy and relatedness levels of interpersonal negotiation comfortably in other contexts. This core group, through teacher facilitation and reflection, created an experience where nearly all students were able to engage personal meaning awareness at the need-based, integrated level in many contexts (see Table 2). As students did become frustrated, members of this core group would work to bring those frustrated back into the game through interpersonal negotiation. The effectiveness of these negotiations depended on the facility with which these students could integrate their ability to see the perspective of others and then base their persuasion on corresponding strategies:

"I hate this game."
"But you have to play because it's part of the class."

The response to the Dismissive reaction to the game is to approach the negotiation from Level 2: Rule-Based and Impersonal. Instinctively by the student, the persuasion is aimed one level higher on the Personal Meaning Awareness scale (see Table 2).

"I don't want to play this game because Bob will hate me if I attack him"
"We're playing this game to learn about history and it's only a game anyway. You can make it up to him at recess."

The game play fails when students are not able to integrate psychosocial functions such that a response to "I hate this game" becomes "yeah, it's stupid." At this point neither student is able to engage in the game and both are mired at the Dismissive stage of Personal Meaning Awareness (see Table 2), that is, they are so frustrated that they cannot continue with the game. The teacher may then step in to assess where and if the integration of psychosocial functions has broken down, or if the game is just too complicated to understand.

Many Students Advanced in Their Capacity for Negotiation and Using Negotiation Strategies

Although the game began as a unilateral contest to acquire segments of the board, the nature of this class soon moved many students (but not all) to realize the power of cooperation and, ultimately, to integrate the needs of everyone to redefine how to win the game in order to maintain the positive cohesion of the class.

Discarding *Diplomacy's* traditional goals for winning in favor of a more community oriented set of conditions appeared to result from a core group of students successfully integrating the 3 domains discussed in the introduction to this chapter—their Personal Meaning Awareness, their repertoire of Negotiation Strategies, and Social Awareness or perspective-taking. They were cooperative and empathic within the awareness that they would continue to be classmates even when the game ended and would need to maintain positive relationships. Their negotiations considered both the goals of the game and of maintaining peace and comfort in the classroom. They were able to assess their own comfort and that of their classmates and integrate these self and other perspectives to arrive at a mutually successful goal...

Generally, however, *Diplomacy* does not elicit such high level outcomes. Simply, it demands a level of psychosocial integration that is above most students. The most common issue involves students who disengage. Often those to disengage first are either those who do not buy into the game, or those who are less able to engage in successful interpersonal negotiations. In failing games of *Diplomacy*, either students do not possess sufficient levels of psychosocial integration or they do not apply their sophistication to the context. For example, the post-game comment of student #3 suggests that he just wanted to win and that he is not satisfied with the mutually beneficial outcome developed by his classmates. *Diplomacy* as a classroom tool fails when too many students become angry or frustrated with the game and their classmate's play. Intervention by the teacher can then target interactions among students to promote higher functioning first for in-game relationships and self-awareness and then during post game debriefing and reflection sessions. Teacher prompts during reflection have ranged from addressing specific situations to reminding students that the game is a class requirement.

As already mentioned, one set of students was able to change the rules of the game to redefine success on their own terms. By not wanting "to leave anyone out," this group was considering a broader social context for the game. This allowed for discussion around the larger experience of the eighth grade at Shady Hill. Eighth grade is the last year at Shady Hill School and some students are involved in an application process to independent high schools. This process necessarily involves a degree of competition with classmates as they apply to many of the same schools and there are limited places available. Students explained during discussion that, in a sense, this application

Table 3. Player quotations pre-game versus post-game

Student	Pre-game	Post-game
Student #1 *Player #2* *Player #3*	"Let's take all of Russia from player # 4" "We'll need to work with player #6 and player #5 to take Italy" "Awesome! Let's take out all of Europe."	"We can't just take the places we want because we needed help." "We realized that we didn't need to get all the supply bases to have a successful game. We wanted to make sure that no one got left out. It's just a game." "Yeah, but no one won…"

process mirrors the game of *Diplomacy,* in that, Shady Hill students must work together during the school day, but they recognize that the independent schools to which they apply are judging them against one another. In *Diplomacy*, students explained, they must work together, but ultimately the game determines a winner by who gains the most supply centers.

Student 1: *"Why did you attack Galicia? I thought we were allies?"*

Student 2: *"Well we were, but someone has to win."*

Teacher: *"How is this like life?"*

Another student: *"What do you mean?"*

Teacher: *"Well... often we have to compete to win and at the same time maintain our friendships... or at least try not to fight with one another."*

Another Student: *"Yeah... kinda like the 'next schools' process... I mean we are all Shady Hillers but we have to get into high school and they can't take us all. So even though we're classmates, we're still in competition."*

The teacher in this case has moved the experience across contexts. Game play has become more relevant from a personal meaning standpoint. Personal Meaning Awareness is moved from Need-Based Self-oriented (autonomy) through a more Relationship Orientation (Relatedness) to Insightful [Level 3 through to Level 5 on Table 2].

The experience had a larger impact on students at more advanced levels of Personal Meaning Awareness and negotiation strategies.

Those students who were better able to integrate autonomy and relatedness functions in their negotiations and develop more insightful personal meaning proved more successful during the Diplomacy game play. The abridged conversation recounted above went on for some time before the cross context realization appeared

and depended on the already high level of social awareness integration of the students. Successful intervention by the teacher or by classmates, however, can promote more highly developed social perspective coordination which, in turn, leads to a more complex, better informed and more easily contextually diverse set of ethical principles. It is not enough for a teacher to tell a student to do the 'right thing'. Experiences and guidance must be in place to teach how to do this. These tools must also be mindful of students' psychosocial development. *Diplomacy* provides an affective learning experience for those students who are relatively highly developed. It is also an excellent assessment of high levels of psychosocial integration and the consequent set of ethical principles.

From this application, *Diplomacy* proved its capacity to provide a safe learning environment while also presenting conflict that provoked development of the three domains we include in moral and ethical development. Effects of this were seen across the class, with the largest impact demonstrated in students with more advanced levels of social perspective taking, personal meaning awareness, and negotiation strategies. Future work would include building more direct strategies to engage students at less advanced levels in these domains.

In the next section, we will describe the use of use of *Civilization IV: Colonization*, and how it compared to the outcomes of the use of *Diplomacy*.

Playing *Civilization IV:Colonization* in the Middle School

Students in a seventh-grade middle school class played *Civilization IV:Colonization*—a strategic level, multiplayer game—over a LAN system. Working in pairs, they would play one of several teams available in the game with the goal of becoming the first to gain independence from the mother country. Students' interactions with other teams are fixed within the parameters of the game. They can trade, negotiate land acquisition, declare war with one another, but their actions are restricted to the game's parameters. Within the team pair of course, the interactions are unlimited and potentially challenge the psychosocial level of comfort of the players. Nevertheless, because the game provides a focus, partners can retreat, or be redirected by the teacher, to the context of the game.

Strategic level games in a multiplayer format remove students from the need for direct interpersonal negotiation (it should be noted that this observation may not apply to games where an avatar represents a player.) The computer network limits interpersonal negotiation opportunities thereby reducing the dynamics of a live relationship. Interaction is confined to text over a chat function or the moves of the game. This potentially eliminates body language, eye contact and distractions from bystanders. This makes interpersonal negotiation simpler, but it also tempts lower functioning in some cases. In addition, the local area network game limits the promotion of Social Perspective Coordination to the confines of the game system. Unlike *Diplomacy* where the focus of the game becomes playing the interaction of relationships to win the game, a multiplayer LAN game's focus lies in playing the game to win. Potential interaction with others exists, but this interaction is not always necessary to play or to win. A strategic multiplayer LAN game is more suited to most middle-school students' developmental levels. The job of the teacher remains to promote growth and help apply the affective lessons of the game to other contexts.

Outcomes and Discussion

The game tools and dynamics provided opportunities for advancement of negotiation strategies and social perspective coordination.

Interpersonal negotiation can take place directly between students in real time, or they can communicate via the game's chat system, but their negotiations are tempered both by a more complex set of game rules and by the fact that they are focused on their own computer (although they work in pairs at a computer for some sessions). As with instant messaging and email, this allows students to communicate in a less direct, anonymous fashion. As a result, in certain cases more passive students become more active in their interpersonal negotiations and vice versa. Because of the parameters of the game, the challenge of creating a comfortable environment is lessened somewhat relative to playing *Diplomacy*; however, the teacher must deal with additional experimentation in communications that result from anonymity.

Below is an example of discourse in a chat window in the game between two students:

"You're stupid."
"Shut up."
"What is your problem? Why are you always so stupid?"

At this point the second student turns away from his computer.

"You're stupid!" the second student announces across the room.

The teacher then intervenes by reminding the students that they are to play a game.

Although a tame example of student interaction through the chat system, this interchange provides a window into the relatively low level functioning the anonymity of chatting can create. The intervention ends negotiation at a Differentiated level [Level 1 from Table 1] with no attempt to move the interaction higher.

Later in the debrief session, the teacher asks about the incident:

Student 1: *"I was joking!"*
Teacher: *"Would you joke like that in person?"*

Student 1: *"What do you mean? Like would I tell Jake that he's stupid? Probably, but just as a joke."*

Teacher: *"Do you think it makes a difference whether you tell him in person or via chat?"*

Student 1: *"Not really."*

Teacher: *"Do you mind telling us if there was a difference, [student 2]?"*

Student 2: *"There wasn't really a difference 'cause like I knew he was joking but it was still kind of distracting."*

Teacher: *"Which—when he chatted with you or."*

Student 2: *"I couldn't play the game because he was distracting me."*

Teacher: *"So does what happened in the game happen in class too?"*

Here the teacher begins to shift thinking to other contexts. "…But just as a joke" reveals that there is an understanding that lower levels of negotiation are not acceptable" Rather than guide the negotiation to higher levels, the teacher uses reflection to promote Awareness of Personal Meaning to Need-Based Personal [Level 3 from Table 2] with an orientation toward relationships. The teacher also moved this awareness across contexts pushing awareness toward more Integration and Insight [Level 5 from Table 2]. Interestingly, the students initially do not identify any difference between typing 'you're stupid' and saying it in person. No set of ethical principles exists to frame the behavior in different contexts. But later in the conversation, this exchange occurs.

Student 2: *"I know you're joking when you are in person, but the message made me angry."*

Teacher: *"Why do you think it is easier to know he's joking when he's in person?"*

Student 2: *"I don't know…"*

There is the beginning of awareness that communication is different in person than it is over the network. The teacher then seizes this dawning realization to steer the debriefing session to explore how communication can change depending on the context. Personal Meaning Awareness grows toward more Integrated and Insightful levels (see Table 2) as a result of the teacher's efforts to move the reflection across contexts. This growing awareness prompts the discovery that similar behavior produces similar results across contexts. A set of ethical principles rests on this discovery.

There was a high level of engagement in the activity.

Of course the holy grail of any teacher, particularly at the middle school level, is to engage learners more deeply and more consistently in the activity. In *Diplomacy*, some students tend to withdraw, an Undifferentiated [Level 0 from Table 1] negotiation strategy, especially from interactions with their peers, but in *Civilization IV:Colonization*, nearly every student continues to play with varying degrees of focus on the game. While some are focused on the goal of winning, others use the chat system for more personal conversations while the game runs in the background. Although they are playing the game, the primary focus for some becomes a personal conversation via chat. Interestingly this difference in focus is very gender specific. The boys tended to send short messages about the game whereas the girls more likely send messages about clothing, celebrities, or social life. We could speculate that the Personal Meaning of girls is more Integrated and Insightful because they are able to bring their Social Awareness to the gaming context. On the other hand, they may simply be multi-tasking and view game interaction and social interaction as discrete. Despite the social nature of the girls' chat session, they knew the dynamics of the game and appeared equally invested in winning, but perhaps for different motives.

Jill (while making her moves during the game, she types): *"Who's coming this afternoon?"*

Anne (looking up from her computer and over at Jill, then types): *"Aren't you? What would look good with the scarf Jane made? Would John look good in it?"*

Both girls turn from their computers to look at John and they giggle. John notices and smiles self-consciously but keeps his eyes on the computer.

Jill (speaking across the room): *"Let's declare war on John."*

John: *"What did I do?"*

The girls giggle and make their moves.

John: *"Hey! You're attacking my city!"* He smiles and makes his moves, which destroy the girls' attack.

Later in the debriefing session the teacher asks, "what made you girls decide to attack John?"

Jill: *"I dunno."*

Anne: *"Yes you do…"*

Teacher: *"Ok. How did the fact that you could have a chat session about your upcoming fashion show change your feelings about playing the game?"*

Previously, the girls had not known about the chat feature and had not really enjoyed the game. They had also not been able to follow the rules until a third student, Melissa, had shown them during recess.

Anne: *"Well we could talk about stuff while we were playing. It made it more fun."*

Teacher: *"What was fun? The game or the chatting?"*

Anne: *"The Chatting."*

Teacher: *"So what distracted you from the chat session back to the game?"*

Jill: *"John was all proud of winning and so we attacked him for fun."*

The teacher in this instance is crafting a conversation that skirts the issue of flirtation, but still attempts to get the students to explore their motivations, or self-awareness, and how these motivations affect their actions across contexts. In a sense, the game has allowed an interaction between the girls and John that might not have occurred in reality. The potential flirtation drives down the level of Interpersonal Negotiation and challenges the ability of students to use a set of ethical principles across contexts. The teacher might explore in further conversation why the girls chose to attack John rather than become his ally, although this conversation would be fraught with the perils of exploring flirting. This approach, nevertheless, might build Personal Meaning Awareness around the incident.

The social aspect of the game play providing equally fruitful opportunities for student growth.

Since moral and ethical development, by definition, involves interpersonal behavior, the social nature of the game play is certainly critical. However, the 'safe conflict' nature of the game play provides a unique opportunity not often otherwise generated in the classroom. One specific situation involved a student, Robert, who continued to be very aggressive while playing on his own against several others who were both in teams and working as individuals. As other students realized Robert's attitude, they began to take action that followed a progression of techniques. Initially, they tried to work within the game to limit his aggression. Tools here were limited to military operations against Robert [Differentiated and Subjective strategies]. When these did not work, some of his opponents suggested a treaty or an alliance on the chat system [Reciprocal and Self-Reflective strategies]. These strategies were refereed by the game system.

At the same time there began a conversation with Robert in the room: "What are you doing? Why do you keep attacking us? Hey, that isn't fair." Robert's response was, "I'm just playing the game."

Students appealed to him outside the game system to work more cooperatively at the game and to let others have a chance to succeed as well, especially given that several teams could meet the victory conditions. Curiously, Robert was unable to pull himself from a very Rule-Based, Personal awareness of the game. Ultimately, during a reflection period, the class decided to restart this game as well, although Robert did not appear to understand all the reasoning. Did the parameters of the game system inhibit the development of Personal Meaning Awareness for Robert and consequently his ability to apply a set of ethical principles across contexts?

In summary, this preliminary use of *Civilization IV: Colonization* has demonstrated similar outcomes as the use of *Diplomacy*, with an increased level of engagement by students.

CONCLUSION

Through our case studies, we have provided a narrow yet rich slice of classroom dynamics, which demonstrate the potential of digital gaming for assisting in the development of ethical behavior. In these classrooms, students challenged and pushed their ability to see another's perspective, to cultivate and negotiate improved peer relationships, and to heighten their awareness of personal behavior in interpersonal relations, all through motivated engagement in a digital medium that is akin to activities they are doing outside of school. For the teacher, it opens up opportunities for coaching and facilitation of such critical skills in a student-centered environment, allowing for more robust dialogue and collaboration between the students and her. While there are of course more options for games than just Civilization and *Diplomacy*, only certain games will create the environment and dynamics that set the stage for this work. These games produce dynamics where one player's actions affect another, and the dialogue and collaboration that ensues in the

classroom during game play help expose thinking and perspective of peers. Thus certain digital games, when properly facilitated in the classroom, can be powerful catalysts for students developing the critical components that congeal to form an operating system for ethical behavior.

A significant challenge in playing a game in the classroom is that it reaches across social environments. Robert, the student described previously who had a difficult time acclimating to the situation, could operate in the game at low levels and aggressively advance his colony. At the same time he had difficulty integrating his understanding of the strategies to win the game with real life strategies in being a kind and ethical member of the classroom. Creating and facilitating these connections for students is a key piece to developing ethical systems through game play. Further teacher intervention in the game Robert was playing might have revolved around how Robert could have succeeded better at the game with more cooperative strategies. Consideration of the real classroom dynamic might become the ultimate goal. At the root of the classroom gaming experience lies the necessity of resolving conflicts and building shared experiences so that students are more facile in coordinating social perspectives and integrating this understanding within their systems of personal meaning. In this sense, they build a system of ethical principles that are more robust and transfer more consistently across contexts.

In debriefing both games, a useful tool became the ability of the teacher to move student focus from the dynamics of game play to the context of history. Because games involve winning and losing, the emotion of the class can run high. By intervening with historical perspective, such emotional tension can be diffused. The teacher provides the third person, mutual perspective (see Table 1), provided by an historical perspective that allows everyone to step beyond the self. In one case, a student had been nearly eliminated early in a game. Of course, he was not happy, and during the debrief many students consoled him while others explained it was only a game: Rule- or Need-Based Personal and Rule-Based Impersonal Awareness responses respectively. What seemed to improve the situation further was a discussion of historical colonization and what happened when French control of North America was virtually eliminated by the English. In this sense, the role of the teacher was to bring the perspective of the students to a broader, more "Mutual," "Societal" perspective. On reflection, the students also decided to restart the game and not gang up on the other student.

Recommendations Summary for Optimal Classroom Dynamics:

1. **Emotional and Physical Safety**: Before playing any game, create a safe environment that values both the individual and the group
2. **Creating Teams**: Consider how best to create teams based on student personality and skills – for example, pair quiet students with more outgoing students.
3. **Reflection**: Build in time and tools for reflection on the gaming process
4. **Teacher Intervention during game play**: The goal is not always for students to function at the highest level for any given component but to have achieved an understanding that lets him act in ways that are best suited to the situation.
5. **Game as classroom manager**: Use the game to provide the structure for interaction and facilitate both action and reflection. ROSS

Cultivating moral development can be considerably more challenging than attempting to develop conceptual understanding in a discipline area with students. Employing games to do so can offer a vehicle to help educators explore and discuss the methodology and pedagogy for accessing moral development in the classroom.

The key to success with all games and simulations lies in the teacher's ability to become comfortable in the role of a facilitator. At Shady Hill, students already have years of student-led, teacher-facilitated learning experiences by the time they reach the middle school years, and they are used to reflecting on their academic and social development. These are significant advantages in using and reflecting on games and simulations in a classroom. Yet learning environments that are less strong in these areas should not be discouraged from using digital games for moral development. Rather, they should seek to identify the differences and likely challenges as a result of the variance in the contexts and apply the frameworks and approaches described in this case study where they align with your learning environment. In seeking to develop in students the central components that ultimately lead to ethical behavior, understanding the taxonomies and frameworks presented by Selman and others serves as a powerful tool for the educator. Eventually one can become well-versed in identifying the level or stage of development a student is at in each of the components based on their comments and work in the classroom. In turn, this assessment ultimately can help them strategically guide each student toward advancement in their own personal development.

Further work would include a broader scope in case studies—in terms of games used, age of students, varying learning environments, etc. It is our hope that more practitioners will engage in action research (research conducting in real-time by the practicing professional), which produces analyses of games for moral development in varying contexts. Assessing the impact of these pedagogies on student development is one critical need area: this might include developing assessments that focus on the experience of a student within a program that targets developing social perspective coordination across contexts. Subsequently, this could then broaden to explore the way in which a student understands how a situation informs his choice of what level at which to function. In essence, seeking to understand how the meaning she makes of a situation creates her thinking and acting around that situation. Finally, assessment and evaluation would need to connect how students develop in a gaming situation to how they bring this development to real world situations. Our observations suggest that these next steps are worth exploring. The very students we have worked with have demonstrated that digital games provide a structure in which to explore the socially interactive foundations of developing ethical men and women.

REFERENCES

Brion-Meisels, S. (1978). *Reasoning with troubled children: Classroom meetings as a forum for social thought*. New York: Moral Education Forum.

Brooks, D. (2009). Where the wild things are. *The New York Times*. October 20, 2009.

Clark, A. (2005). Learning by doing: A comprehensive guide to simulation, computer games, and pedagogy in e-Learning and other educational experiences.

Colby, A., Kohlberg, L., Gibbs, J., & Lieberman, M. (1983). A longitudinal study of moral judgment. *Monographs of the Society for Research in Child Development, 48*(1-2), Serial No. 200.

Dawson, T. (2002). New tools, new insights: Kohlberg's moral reasoning stages revisited. *International Journal of Behavioral Development, 26*, 154–166. doi:10.1080/01650250042000645

Erikson, E. (1950). *Childhood and society*. New York: Norton.

Fischer, K., Yan, Z., & Stewart, J. (2003). Adult cognitive development: Dynamics in the developmental web. In Valsiner, J., & Connelly, K. (Eds.), *Handbook of developmental psychology*. London: Sage Publications.

King, P., & Kitchener, K. (1994). *Developing reflective judgment: Understanding and promoting intellectual growth and critical thinking in adolescents and adults*. San Francisco, CA: Jossey-Bass.

Kirriemuir, J., & McFarlane, A. (2002). *Literature review in games and learning*. Bristol, UK: Futurelab.

Kohlberg, L. (1969). Stage and sequence: The cognitive developmental approach to socialization. In Goslin, D. A. (Ed.), *Handbook of socialization theory and research*. Chicago, IL: Rand-McNally.

Sandford, R., Ulicsak, M., Facer, K., & Rudd, T. (2006). *Teaching with games: Using commercial off-the-shelf computer games in formal education*. Bristol, UK: Futurelab.

Sandford, R., & Williamson, B. (2005). *Games and learning*. Bristol, UK: Futurelab.

Selman, R. (1980). *The growth of interpersonal understanding*. New York: Academic Press.

Selman, R. (2003). *The promotion of social awareness: Powerful lessons from the partnership of developmental theory and classroom practice*. New York: Russell Sage Foundation.

Selman, R., & Schultz, L. (1990). *Making a friend in youth: Developmental theory and pair therapy*. Chicago, IL: University of Chicago Press.

Section 5
Designing for Social Change and Civic Engagement

Chapter 16
Power to the People:
Anti–Oppressive Game Design

Andrea Gunraj
The Metropolitan Action Committee on Violence Against Women and Children, Canada

Susana Ruiz
University of Southern California & Take Action Games, USA

Ashley York
University of Southern California & Take Action Games, USA

With contributions from Mary Flanagan, Barry Joseph, Wendy Komiotis & Paolo Pedercini

ABSTRACT

This chapter defines basic principles of anti-oppression and its ethical implications. Anti-oppression is a framework used in social work and community organizing that broadly challenges power imbalances between different groups of people in society. This chapter positions these principles in the realm of game creation and argue for their use—particularly in the development of social issue games that in one way or another seek to spotlight and challenge social power imbalances. While the chapter outlines some essential theory, it ultimately takes a practice-based perspective to make a case for and support the incorporation of anti-oppressive principles in game design and development. It features the work of five organizations from around the world about their strategies for implementing equity in game/interactive design and development, and closes with broad guidelines to support integration of anti-oppression principles in game creation.

DOI: 10.4018/978-1-60960-120-1.ch016

INTRODUCTION

In 2009, a Danish advocacy group that initiates public awareness and education campaigns released an online game entitled *Hit the Bitch*. Produced by Børn og Unge i Voldsramte Familier (Children Exposed to Violence at Home), the game allows the player to enter the experience from the perspective of a man's hand, which can be swung to strike a woman's face by proxy using a mouse or webcam. A slider appears at the top of the screen. As the blows multiply, the slider creeps from one end, labeled "100% pussy," to the other, "100% gangsta." The woman in the game becomes increasingly upset, bruised, and bloodied. She eventually falls to the ground in tears, and a caption, "100% IDIOT!," concludes the playing experience. Following the end of the game play, players hear the voice of a woman issuing scolding words in Danish and on-screen statistics, presumably about the prevalence of violence against women in Danish communities.

Unsurprisingly, the release of *Hit the Bitch* evoked a flurry of commentary beyond borders, given its content and the group behind its development. In fact, traffic to the website was so heavy that access to it was limited to users from Denmark. A surface examination of online reactions reveals a common underlying question: is *Hit the Bitch*'s approach successful in denouncing, challenging or preventing violence against women? Amelia Thomson-DeVeaux writes that, despite noble intentions, "the method it uses is so offensive, misguided and disgusting that the message gets completely lost within sexualized violence and abuse" (2009). A blogger on *Feministe* says that the game "is supposed to convey to everyone that hitting women is bad. After you've played a game that rewards you for hitting a woman. Color me unconvinced" (Jill, 2009). *Hit the Bitch* "seems like the end result of some people sitting around a table trying to figure out how to make domestic violence edgy and attention-grabbing," another blogger writes, although she goes on to say, "then again, no one in mainstream media talks about domestic violence unless it happens to a good-looking famous person … are they on the right track by trying to be aggressively controversial?" (Ganeva, 2009).

Like other games on social issues, *Hit the Bitch* incorporates controversial messaging open to a wide range of interpretations. Just how the game fulfills presumed advocacy, awareness and/or educational goals concerning violence at home is difficult to determine. Players may struggle with those goals as much as critics have, given that the game places them in an abusing role and the game play does not delve into complexities inherent to violence against women. While a number of reviewers explore the controversy that surrounds *Hit the Bitch*, most of them do not comment on the game's use of "pussy" and "gangsta" or its use of background hip hop music. Besides a note that the music is "sad rap" and that the word "gangsta" is "an offensive stereotype of a black man," incorporation of "urban" artifacts into the game and their inescapable race and class implications seem to have gone unnoticed (Ganeva, 2009).

While satirical in its approach to violence, *Hit the Bitch*'s ambiguity does not sit comfortably in the context of anti-oppression. A game on gender-based violence designed with anti-oppressive principles in mind would open space for players to rethink the commonness of this violence—most often perpetrated by men against women they know and trust—with the goal of challenging, reducing and/or preventing it. *Hit the Bitch*'s uncritical inclusion of stereotypical "urban black" culture, whether intentioned or not, is at odds with an anti-oppressive approach. In the process of designing an anti-oppressive game, developers would be conscious of inserting any uncritiqued stereotypes into the game's look, feel, and play. They would resist associating gender-based violence with any single group of people, for example, challenging the Western tendency to blame violence against women on communities of color (Jiwani, 1997).

In this chapter, we argue that applying anti-oppressive principles in game design and development results in more purposeful, directive and transparent messaging and game play. Anti-oppressive practice, typically associated with social work and community activism, openly challenges discrimination and promotes rights and voice of those groups on the margins of society. It is grounded in specific understandings of equity and incorporates a sense of ethics that requires an individual to reflect upon their own behavior and assumptions, as well as society's norms. It encourages an individual to work toward closing the "power gap" between those who experience oppression and those who hold greater social privileges (Clifford & Burke, 2008, p. 16-23; Global Exchange, 2006, p. 2; Strier, 2007, p. 858).

This chapter introduces the application of anti-oppression principles to game creation, first defining basics of anti-oppression and touching upon various implications for individuals who use it. We discuss anti-oppressive principles in the context of video game design and development, particularly games that in one way or another spotlight social issues and seek to promote social change. Next, we share insights and examples of game partnerships and collectives, including those of Take Action Games (TAG) and the Metropolitan Action Committee on Violence Against Women and Children (METRAC), who partnered to develop *RePlay: Finding Zoe/ReJouer: Où est Zoé?* The contributors to this chapter speak to how they implement anti-oppressive practice and equity principles in their development and design processes. Finally, we conclude with broad guidelines to support integration of anti-oppression principles in game creation.

We outline essential concepts of anti-oppression as a starting point. However, a comprehensive overview of anti-oppressive theory is beyond the scope of this chapter. We take a practice-based perspective to support incorporation of anti-oppressive principles in game design and development. Despite some critiques of the mainstream game industry, our intent is not to disparage dominant practices of game design and development. Instead, we wish to encourage alternatives that ultimately support transformative social change and build the voices and access of marginalized communities.

BASICS OF ANTI-OPPRESSION

As already noted, the fields of social work, grassroots activism, and community development typically use an anti-oppression framework. It is broadly defined as efforts and actions to end social injustices and inequalities, particularly those based on factors like race, gender, sexuality, age, class, ability, and religion (Dumbrill, 2003, pp. 102-104). We can view the term and practice of "anti-oppression" as an umbrella concept with a great deal of variability. It encompasses ideas found in a number of theories, frameworks, and perspectives, including: feminism, critical race analysis and anti-racism, disability analysis and postmodernism. Theorists and practitioners often distinguish anti-oppression by contrast and by what it works against. Therefore, the concept of oppression deserves analysis. In the next section, we define oppression and its corollary, privilege. We then move to a definition of personal "reflexivity," an important concept in anti-oppressive practice, and touch upon anti-oppressive ethics.

Oppression and Privilege

Clifford and Burke (2008) define oppression as "the exploitative exercise of power by individuals and groups over others" and "the structuring of marginalization and inequality into everyday routines and rules, through the continuing acquisition and maintenance of economic, political and cultural capital by dominant social groups over long periods of time, reflecting the existence of major social differences" (p. 16). Oppression entails a great deal of "baggage." Individuals who face it often experience exploitation, marginalization, powerlessness, cultural imperialism, and outright violence (Young, 1990, pp. 48-63). Mullaly (1997) also pulls oppression out of the individual experience, describing it as domination of subordinate groups by a group or groups more powerful in the realms of politics, economics and culture (pp. 104, 145-146). To understand how oppression works, we have to recognize how groups interact with each other (Frye, 1983, pp. 8-10).

Groups that hold more money, political clout and sway over mainstream culture tend to become more powerful. By virtue of their power, the world they live in suits their needs, ideas and interests, undoubtedly undermining the needs, ideas and interests of groups with less power (Young, 1990, pp. 56-58; Chater, 1994, p. 102). Quite simply, "power is the ability to act" and "the more access to resources one has, the more options one has." Power is unequally distributed and impacts how people interact as individuals and groups (Adair & Howell, 1993). Clifford and Burke (2008) note that unequal distribution of power leads to the experience of everyday oppressions against groups with less power, and this oppression further exasperates social divisions between those with less and more power. They show that the experience of oppression is both constant and in flux, impacted by the changing circumstances of different groups. Usually resilient over long periods of time, the divisions between groups can vary quickly in intense periods of social change (p. 16). Young (1990) says that oppression is "a central category of political discourse" (p. 39) for contemporary social movements and activist organizing, even if many in the Western world hesitate to apply the term to injustices they perceive around them.

Anti-oppression activists and thinkers have identified different forms that oppression takes—racism, sexism, classism, heterosexism, ageism and ableism, to name the most common. Despite the heady analysis, we can view oppression more simply. Some groups of people are considered less worthy of power, rights and respect than

others. Those "less worthy" of power, rights and respect in today's society are racialized, women or transgendered, living in poverty, physically or mentally disabled, lesbian, gay, bisexual, or queer, elderly, and/or young (Young, 1990, p. 40). Other social divisions factor into a person's experience of oppression, such as their immigration status, their HIV status, and the social isolation or connectedness of the region where they live (Clifford & Burke, 2008, p. 19).

Since oppression is based on "unquestioned norms, habits, symbols, in the assumptions underlying institutional rules and the collective consequences of following those rules," it occurs on both a personal and systemic level (Young, 1990, p. 41). It impacts how individuals and communities view and treat themselves and others; how they behave and communicate; and how they envisage their position, worth, entitlement to resources, and validity in the world. Women, for example, share a collective experience of discrimination where they tend to be paid less for doing the same jobs as men (Johnson, 2009). Women are also statistically more likely to be murdered by male intimate partners or family members—the violence is a manifestation of systemic sexism women face in society, reproduced in their individual lives and most intimate experiences (Bureau of Justice Statistics, 2005; Porter, 2006, pp. 25-27).

People who employ anti-oppression principles name, dissect and challenge society's mainstream systems and structures, that is, the "normal" way of life or the "way things are", making visible the invisible. They acknowledge that what most people view as normal is determined by the perspectives, interests and desires of powerful and dominant groups. Dichotomies are often used to define groups and assign characteristics to them—white and black, man and woman, gay and straight, and rich and poor. This is how individuals and groups who are less powerful are placed on the far end of the spectrum of normalcy (Collins, 1986, p. S20). Those who are less powerful may be labeled exotic, special, fringe or different, but in dominant thinking, they tend to be marked as "Other" (Young, 1990, pp. 58-59). Individuals who face oppression can internalize this otherness and develop negative understandings about themselves, taking them in even if they logically know them to be untrue. In a similar way, people who belong to dominant groups learn favorable messages about themselves. They internalize their own dominance and privilege (Sinclair, 2003, p. 127). Anti-oppression, on the other hand, argues for multiplicity of voices, opinions and ways of thinking and being of marginalized groups in order to counter the narrow dichotomies. Dalrymple and Burke (2006) explain that "different perspectives on the truth" are necessary because "no one group or individual possesses the theory or methodology that allows it to discover the absolute truth about other people's experiences" (p. 11).

Personal "Reflexivity" and Anti-Oppressive Ethics

Employing anti-oppression as an individual requires reflection about the power one holds and oppression one faces. It requires sensitivity to the reality that anyone can unintentionally oppress other people and experience oppression at the same time (Clifford & Burke, 2008, p. 18). It encourages an individual to examine personal values, internalized dominance and oppression, and deeply held stereotypes, biases, and prejudices—the same ones so often reproduced in systems like the media, government, law and education.

Making reference to social workers, Kondrat (1999) says that self-awareness involves understanding one's own "social location"—that is, where a person's membership in various groups places them in society's matrix of power, privileges, oppressions and access to respect and resources. It is an examination of personal values and behaviors, how they may reproduce oppression or challenge it (p. 464). Those in grassroots, community, and activist circles have stressed that anti-oppressive self-reflection, or

"reflexivity," cannot be left to theory. It must penetrate the very core of who one is and how one thinks of themselves and their place in the world. Barbara Findlay reveals that scrutinizing her own social location "in the world as a white person" was "painful and shameful" and that "the work of looking at internalized dominance is very difficult" (1992, p. 47).

Anti-oppression practice is often referred to as a conscious decision, an individual choice to be challenged in order to promote values like equity, justice, inclusion, and a shared quality of life. Clifford and Burke (2008) note, "the aim of anti-oppressive ethics is to provide guidance to oppose, minimize and/or overcome those aspects of human relationships that express and consolidate oppression" (p. 16). While they do not assume that a fully articulated position on anti-oppression ethics exists, they speak to a useful approach to ethics using anti-oppressive concepts that incorporates a critical analysis of power, social differences and divisions, the impact of social systems and relationships, and the histories of individuals and groups.

In general, then, anti-oppression involves an analysis of power imbalances between groups and involves thinking and action, where individuals understand their place in groups and the broader society. Anti-oppression is deeply personal. People must consider the privileges they hold and oppressions they perpetuate in order to act ethically, based on reflection and critical thinking.

ANTI-OPPRESSION AND GAMES

Anti-oppression's encompassing analysis can extend beyond the realm of activism and social work. "Practitioners" of anti-oppression argue that the areas of governance, education and policy development should implement anti-oppressive principles. And while a range of opinions may exist about how to implement anti-oppression into life and society, practitioners have noted that anti-oppressive principles support equity, justice and inclusion to the benefit of marginalized groups. We assert that game makers may apply the principles of anti-oppression to the design of games and their development, particularly games that in some way call attention to and/or seek to challenge unequal power dynamics and inspire players to contribute to equitable social change.

Theorists have spoken to how oppression tends to get reproduced in the media and entertainment industry, in those dominant ideologies reproduced and disseminated by it. Stuart Hall (2003) argues that the media is "part of the dominant means of ideological production" and that it produces "representations of the social world, images, descriptions, explanations and frames for understanding how the world is and why it works as it is said and shown to work" (p. 90). Popular media, including popular digital games, tend to mirror the power imbalances of society, privileging the interests and perspectives of those in power.

Paolo Pedercini, the designer behind the Molleindustria game collective that develops online games that seek to express alternatives to dominant forms of gameplay, explains that the game industry "relies on a highly trained workforce, which is produced by universities." The industry's "[technologies and processes] are inaccessible to most people" and democratizing the system proves difficult because its structure lacks personal connection and original contribution by most participants (2010). Unequal power dynamics infuse the mainstream game industry's development practices and human resource processes and norms, as well as its most familiar perspectives.

Yet digital games, particularly those designed outside of the industry, are ripe for the incorporation of anti-oppressive principles. Ian Bogost (2007) explores how video games embody a "procedural rhetoric" that shifts opinion or motivates action of players (pp. 28-29). Video games make arguments about a social system's structure that can help support or challenge it. In the words of Clay Shirky (2005), games "offer the opportunity for players to change their worldview rather than to impart mere information."

Because video games have the ability to persuade or inspire people to critically examine mainstream norms and behaviors, we embrace the implementation of anti-oppressive principles, practices and ethics. Game makers can design their work to identify and challenge society's everyday dynamics of oppression and privilege. They can inspire players to act in new ways to break down those dynamics and divides. They can illustrate what players can do to affect anti-oppressive change in the real world, allowing them to practice and share their strategies for change with each other. By applying anti-oppressive principles in the process of building games, game makers can consciously provide a frame to alter the mainstream's typical *modus operandi*, where a small set of experts determine content and methodology. An anti-oppression-inspired process can seek out and incorporate the ideas and perspectives of players and non-players who do not usually have voice in game creation in order to challenge assumptions, stereotypes and norms that inform the look, story, arguments and rule sets of games.

In the next section, we move out of the realm of theory to explore insights of game collectives and partners. Their goals, thoughts and design processes enlighten how anti-oppression principles have been and can be applied in game design and development.

INSIGHTS AND EXAMPLES FROM GAME COLLECTIVES AND PARTNERSHIPS

To build an applied understanding of anti-oppression in game design and development, we interviewed individuals from game collectives and game development partnerships. This section includes contributions from Susana Ruiz and Ashley York of Take Action Games, Wendy Komiotis of the Metropolitan Action Committee on Violence Against Women and Children, Mary Flanagan of Values at Play, Barry Joseph of Global Kids, and Paolo Pedercini of Molleindustria. Their insights and examples enrich this chapter's practical application and inform the anti-oppressive guidelines outlined at the end. Given the novelty of anti-oppression language in the field of game creation, we asked each contributor to answer general questions about "equity" in game and interactive design and development. An important concept in anti-oppression theory, Lopes and Thomas (2006) define equity as "equal access to goods, services and opportunities in society" (p. 267). We asked game collective and partnership representatives how they implement equity in their design process, challenges and lessons they have encountered in the process, and advice they would share with other developers to increase the inclusion of equity in game creation. In this section, we highlight these game makers and explicate some examples of their games.

Take Action Games

Take Action Games (TAG) specializes in casual games for change. It uses games to address topics of social and political significance, employing design and content that traverses computational art, narrative, documentary, activism, and ethics. Susana Ruiz, Huy Truong, and Ashley York co-founded TAG in 2006 and launched their first game that year, *Darfur is Dying,* an activist game they developed as an MFA graduate thesis project (with the support of a number of students and colleagues) at the University of Southern California. Its development was sponsored by mtvU in partnership with The Reebok Human Rights Foundation, The International Crisis Group, and interFUEL.

They designed *Darfur is Dying* as an informational entryway to the humanitarian crisis in the Darfur region of western Sudan and the initial development resulted from a call by mtvU to mobilize university communities to raise awareness

about genocide through digital games. Stephen Friedman, general manager of MTV, explains that they wanted to extend awareness of the crisis beyond a relatively closed circle of experts, activists, and non-governmental organizations. Says Friedman,

It was an attempt to expand a campaign that already existed and to create a game that would spark a conversation and raise awareness beyond what our other programming was doing. We went in not knowing what we would get and with the goal to create something that would linger and would have more of an impact than a PSA or TV show. (2010)

Responding to the request, Ruiz and York sought to use "uncomplicated, immediate mechanisms" in *Darfur is Dying*'s gameplay. They wanted to inspire players to effect real world change by taking part in letter-writing campaigns and learning how to initiate divestment strategies in their college campuses. More than 700,000 people played it in the first month after the game's release on April 30th, 2006—the day of the Save Darfur Rally in Washington, D.C. That number grew to more than two million. Tens of thousands of players utilized "activist tools" that TAG wove into the game's reward structure. This includes the ability to write letters to the President and petition Congress to enact legislation to support the people of Darfur. Says Ruiz,

We were guided by a three-step design methodology. First, we wanted to construct an experience in which the player could become emotionally invested via personal narratives and testimonials. Secondly, we wanted to pull back and be able to offer her a broader context of the extremely complicated issue. Thirdly, we wanted to ensure that she had an immediate and simple means to make a difference in the real world in some small way, especially given the government and media's stark silence on the genocide in Darfur at the

Figure 1. Darfur is Dying game screenshot of the internally displaced persons camp. (© 2006, MTV, Take Action Games. Used with permission)

time. In this case, playing through a portrayal of genocide would be entirely disheartening were it not for a chance to spread awareness about the crisis, learn about divestment, sign a petition, or write a letter with the goal of evoking decision-makers to respond. (2010)

Ruiz presented the game to members of Congress and Pulitzer Prize winning *New York Times* columnist Nicholas Kristof (2006), who has worked extensively in the region, says it is "one of the best presentations of life in Darfur" (p. 12). In contrast, immediately after mtvU posted an early prototype of *Darfur is Dying,* Julian Dibbell wrote an article for the *Village Voice* entitled, "Game From Hell." Dibbell writes,

Folks, I've seen some sick and twisted video games in my day, but I hereby award the cake to a dark little perversion of the human imagination entitled Fetching Water, a finalist in the MTV/ Reebok Darfur Digital Activist contest... Currently playable in demo form at MTV's new college-targeted broadband site, mtvU, Fetching Water

casts the player as a cute Darfuri child dodging heavily armed militia gangs through the five kilometers of desert between home and the nearest well. Fail to outrun the militiamen and the game ends, with "kidnap, rape, and murder" listed as your likeliest fates; make it to the well and back, and maybe your family survives another day of drought. Is there even a rating for something this f***ed-up. (2006)

Ruiz and York were mindful of their position in addressing issues in Darfur and anticipated the potential for negative reactions. They noted that Dibbell's response was to a work-in-progress version of the game that was put online with little context. "We were leading a group of privileged college students from a private university to develop a game about something so far from our own daily realities. It's understandable that people would react viscerally to that," says Ruiz (2010).

The team consulted with various individuals and groups, including those with expertise on the genocide and those who spent time in the region. Paul Freedman, a Peabody Award Winning documentary filmmaker who was directing *Sand and Sorrow*, a film on Darfur at the time, provided invaluable consultation about the logistics of the camps inside Darfur, as well as imagery for the game's aesthetic modeling. Ruiz and York also consulted with activists and scholars such as Donald Miller, Executive Director of the USC Center for Religion and Civic Culture; and Brian Steidle, a former U.S. Marine, unarmed military observer and U.S. representative to the African Union. Additionally, the International Crisis Group and International Rescue Committee provided the team with information, perspective and imagery that proved critical to an understanding of the situation. Ruiz says,

These were incredibly helpful to game development but we didn't get the opportunity to speak with Sudanese experts who may have witnessed what was happening. It was an element that didn't quite match up with our understandings of equity in game design. More people from outside of the situation were contributing to content than those internal to it. There's no doubt that the game would have benefited greatly from the perspective of Sudanese experts who were much closer to the politics and history of the region. (2010)

Following the production of *Darfur is Dying*, TAG co-produced *RePlay: Finding Zoe/ReJouer: Où est Zoé?* along with the Metropolitan Action Committee on Violence Against Women and Children (METRAC), a Canadian non-profit organization that prevents violence against diverse women, youth, and children. METRAC approached TAG to develop an online game on healthy relationships amongst children and youth aged eight to fourteen with the goal of challenging gender stereotypes and gender-based violence. Ruiz says that the partnership with METRAC was TAG's first opportunity to work so closely with those engaged in community development work on the issues. Ruiz says that METRAC brought

invaluable knowledge about the topic and the target audience that the design team would not have had on its own as game developers (2010). *RePlay/ReJouer* tells the story of two friends searching for their friend, Zoe. After hearing sexist and stereotyping rumors about her, they conclude she is caught in an abusive relationship. During their search for Zoe, her friends navigate through their neighborhood and are challenged by situations that encourage them to work together and be respectful, confident communicators. Success in these situations equips them to find Zoe and cheer for her. The game includes information on the warning signs of violence and community services relevant to Ontario youth.

Funded by the Government of Ontario, METRAC assembled an Interdisciplinary Advisory Committee for the project that included educators and school board members, experts in technology and communications, violence prevention organizations, and people who work with youth. The committee provided guidance for all stages of the project. METRAC also completed a literature review on best practices for video game design and conducted focus groups with more than 250 diverse young people in the province of Ontario. Youth were asked about their game playing behaviors, ideas and preferences, information directly utilized in the game's design. Wendy Komiotis, METRAC's Executive Director, comments on the importance of focus groups:

As an organization that operates from an anti-oppressive framework and values equity so much, we knew we needed to find out what youth wanted in this game. Instead of settling on the advice of literature and adult experts, we thought it was important to listen to youth themselves. Not just the ones who could afford their own game consoles at homes. We made sure to ask what they liked in a game, digital or not, whether played at home or a friend's house, whether played every day or not. (2010)

Figure 2. RePlay: Finding Zoe/ReJouer: Où est Zoé? game screenshot of title page. (© 2007, METRAC, Take Action Games. Used with permission.)

Komiotis explains that METRAC discovered new things about the way young people play games:

They told us that it was action, not violence so much, that they looked for in a good game. This was interesting because we were totally new to the world of social issue games and had heard all the hype about how games promote and teach violence. The youth also shared that they wanted a lot of control, even in the process of playing a simple online Flash game like RePlay/ReJourer. They wanted to control the look of their characters. They wanted to play with characters that looked like them and looked nothing like them. Choice is important. In contrast to all the research on media violence we had read, these youth were not playing like mindless sponges. They applied a lot of their own agency in the process. (2010)

The ideas and preferences of the youth who participated in focus groups directly informed *RePlay/ReJourer*'s design. For example, a feature was included where players choose their character, and conscious effort was dedicated to representing characters in non-normative ways. Ruiz says

that METRAC and TAG worked hard to reflect the youth they had met in their focus groups, their "many skin and hair colors and types, their different physical abilities and body shapes, their dress and styles… The game does not place gendered limitations on characters, which was important in creating a game that challenges mainstream gender roles and stereotypes." (2010) In addition, a feature was included where players answer questions about issues of abuse and gender before and after they play the game and through an abstract graphic representation, they can view how other players answered as well. Komiotis explains the significance of this feature:

It helps us collect data about players' opinions. But, perhaps more importantly, it helps players contextualize themselves with other players. They get the opportunity to see that, for example, most players answer the question of whether or not girls can do anything boys can do in the affirmative. They understand that most people do have some positive ideas about gender and ending abuse. Even if it doesn't always translate to peoples' actions in relationships, seeing that most of us don't believe abuse is okay is a start to support positive attitudes in youth and help them form healthier behaviors in their relationships. (2010)

Since its release in 2007, more than 10,000 people have played *RePlay/ReJouer.* It won three awards for its design, two from Ashoka Changemakers and one from Adobe. Of the 353 players who chose to answer the post-game survey, 45 percent identified learning "something new." Additionally, *RePlay/ReJouer* was translated into French and updated for Francophone cultural competency in 2008 through a partnership with Centre ontarien de prévention des agressions (COPA), given the bilingual nature of Ontario. Komiotis explains,

It was important for us not to do a word-for-word French translation, because it would not be culturally competent. We partnered with COPA, who used their peer networks across the province to connect with Francophone youth and make sure the game's language reflected how they communicate. (2010)

Komiotis says that the incorporation of youth voices in the game's content and its diverse imagery are two of its greatest strengths. "If youth

were the ones who developed the game" Komiotis notes, "if they had learned the skills to make the games and actually did it, equity in the design process would have been even stronger" (2010).

TAG's current work, *In The Balance,* consists of a documentary film and a game. *In The Balance* explores the story of six Kentucky teenagers who were incarcerated for murder more than a decade ago. The game began as an experiment in computational documentary and evolved into an investigation of broader dynamics and personal stories embedded in America's criminal justice system and prison industrial complex. Some of the questions *In The Balance* provokes relate to the issue of ethics and documentary filmmaking and to one of the form's longstanding ethical concerns – the burden of responsibility documentarians have as they seek to represent, model and simulate real lives and situations.

In The Balance's core team engaged in five years of research. They visited prisons in Tennessee and immersed themselves in research on issues such as capital punishment, life sentencing of juveniles and the over-incarceration of America's poorest citizens. York, a trained journalist, notes that "objectivity is always a constant struggle" in the process of developing the documentary and

Figure 3. In The Balance game screenshot of a prison modeled after the Tennessee Prison for Women in Nashville. (© 2008, Take Action Games. Used with permission.)

game and "the range of opinions on it is something we were cognizant of and were always negotiating" (2010). In referencing Brian Winston's essay, "The Documentary Film as Scientific Inscription," York notes documentary filmmaker Frederick Wiseman's assertion:

[Films] have a point of view that allows you—or, hopefully, asks you—to think, to figure out what you think about what's happening. I don't know how to make an objective film. I think my films are a fair reflection of the experience making them. My subjective view is that they are fair films. (as cited in Winston, 1993, p. 49)

In contrast, documentary scholar Bill Nichols' believes that a subjective approach can help an audience examine their preconceived notions and assumptions. "Subjectivity itself compels belief: instead of an aura of detached truthfulness we have the honest admission of a partial but highly significant, situated and impassioned view." (2001, p. 51)

Adopting Nichols' "documentary modes," York says,

Our discomfort with calling In The Balance 'objective' will be reflected in the game's rules and the game's design. It mirrors the idea that there is no one 'true' perspective and the fabrication inherent to a documentary is purposefully and self-conscientiously exposed. One of the most challenging and problematic aspects of the project is discerning what the goals for the player should be. James P. Gee's [2007] concept of projective identity requires that we think clearly through the structure of identification for the player. This is challenging because ultimately, we don't feel we're making a project about either one "truth" or about what other outcomes may have been possible. Rather, it's about how multiple voices tell their versions of the story—from individuals directly involved and affected, to scholars that speak of broader systemic elements. (2010)

Values at Play

Values at Play (VAP) is a National Science Foundation research project whose principle investigator Mary Flanagan believes that technology has the power to transform human behavior, shift culture, and shape institutions. Flanagan directs the Tiltfactor game research lab at Hunter College, which harnesses video games in the service of humanistic principles, with the recognition that games hold great potential to educate and inspire. VAP investigates how designers can be more intentional about integrating human values into game systems. VAP seeks to assist designers to create games that further the understanding and appreciation of equality and diversity.

In the 1990s, VAP's principle investigator Mary Flanagan focused on gender equity, creating software for female players and initiating afterschool programs to build the technology skills of girls. She says that equity and inclusion have been essential to her work as a woman designer. The work of her game laboratory, Tiltfactor, emphasizes how white, male, and heterosexual participants dominate the world of software development and game design. Flanagan explains:

As a consequence, those who are not white/male/ heterosexual often feel like they have to conform to the mores of the dominant culture. A core principle in the laboratory is to create a space that celebrates and legitimates difference and diversity, rather than conformity. A corollary of this approach is that our games tend to fall outside of the mainstream (which is where we like them to be!)—they spotlight voices and perspectives that are usually found only at the margins. (2010)

VAP develops games as well as game creation tools. For example, the *Grow-A-Game* Cards is a simple and engaging tool that broadens access to game design by helping people brainstorm game ideas on social issues and societal values. Non-designers can also use the cards to create

Figure 4. Screenshot of Tiltfactor's Grow-A-Game Cards web page. (© 2010, Tiltfactor. Used with permission.)

powerful, expressive ideas. More importantly, Flanagan notes, *Grow-A-Game* Cards help non-developers view game design as an interesting, accessible and fun medium for personal, political, and artistic expression. She believes that increasing contributions of non-programmers and other non-experts will ultimately contribute to a more inclusive game development community. Says Flanagan,

It is relatively easy to see the benefits to a given design when enhanced by new ways of thinking due to the diverse voices of the design team and the player group. These arguments for innovation are often stronger to those in the industry than arguing for diversity's sake, just to be inclusive. In the end, the principle is served, and hopefully, new ideas, perspectives, technologies, rewards, points of view, and the like are actively developed. (2010)

Molleindustria

Molleindustria, founded by Paolo Pedercini, aims to "reappropriate" video games as a popular form of mass communication. It investigates the persuasive potentials of the medium by subverting mainstream video gaming cliché. Mollindustria produced a number of online games that explore issues such as abuse perpetrated by clergy, corporate food production and sexual and gender fluidity. With respect to incorporating equity in games, Pedercini says there is a risk in viewing it as a mere implementation issue, which can lead developers to creating little more than a series of guidelines for "politically-correct design practice" (2010).

For instance, he notes that *The Sims* allows players to design characters from every conceivable race and allows characters to form same-sex relationships with each other. However, gender, skin color, and sexual orientation are cosmetic options as the "family" portrayed in the game always conforms to the same parameters and is always contextualized into a North American suburban environment. He says that the game reinforces the "narrative of the American Dream" by depicting equal career and opportunities despite race and gender differences in characters. In this way,

Pedercini questions if *The Sims* actually reflects progressive design or just cultural mystification:

Certainly I prefer the highly politically incorrect world of Grand Theft Auto: San Andreas to the utopian suburbia of The Sims ... at least it provides a complex representation of the urban environment. The city of San Andreas, modeled after Los Angeles, is a space characterized by inequalities. Social and racial tensions inform the overarching plot, the player is continuously confronted with moral dilemmas that arise from being disempowered as citizen. (2010)

Pedercini refers to the "posturing of equity" in games when power and access to resources is so skewed (2010). Pedercini cites the recent alternate reality game, *EVOKE*, and how many of the problems the game purports to solve are directly or indirectly created by two decades of Washington consensus. Says Pedercini,

At first sight it appears a great initiative, the comic that introduces the online game is full of empowered men and women from developing countries and the promoters are actively trying to recruit a diverse player population. Except you notice that the game is sponsored by the World Bank, the infamous super-national institution controlled by the richest countries. The same institution that, together with the World Trade Organization and International Monetary Fund, imposed free-market policies to a number of developing countries with catastrophic consequences. (2010)

While the developers of *EVOKE* may be well-intentioned and there may be positive outcomes to the game, Pedercini warns about the "photoshopped diversity" found in the marketing of universities and corporations (2010). He notes that, when there is a large disconnection between the object of inquiry and the subject producing the text, misrepresentations and mystifications are difficult to avoid.

Pedercini explains that Molleindustria's *Oiligarchy* game exemplifies radical game design by allowing players to be the "protagonist of the petroleum era," where they fuel the world's oil addiction with the goal of successfully exploring, drilling, bribing and halting green energies as they run their oil company with limited resources. As an "oiligarch," the player manages the extraction business in the homeland and overseas and lobbies the government to keep the carbon-fossil based economy as profitable as possible. *Oiligarchy* illustrates what Pedercini believes to be the main potential of game systems. Pedercini says,

Their main potential lays in their ability to easily represent complex systems such as the economic and the political ones. Observing and interacting with a system "from above" allows the player to abstract from her everyday experience and think about the invisible threads that connect our globalized economy. In order to create an "ethical" game you just have to set up a system of rewards and punishments that force the player to be "good." I wish it was that easy! I believe players are smarter than lab rats in a Skinner box. If we dismiss the simplistic relation violent games = violent behavior, we also have to acknowledge that we need more than good scout simulations to foster critical thinking. (2010)

Global Kids

Global Kids in New York City reaches out to marginalized youth, primarily young people of color, in low-income neighborhoods. Barry Joseph, director of the organization's Online Leadership Program, stresses that Global Kids identifies the potential of young people to learn and view themselves as global citizens and community leaders. The Online Leadership Program builds on youths' existing strengths and assets, at the same time that it does not underestimate the impact of internalized oppressions they may

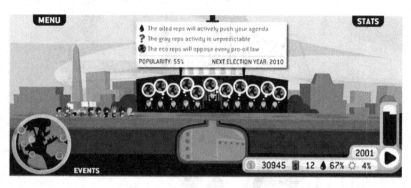

Figure 5. Oiligarchy game screenshot. (Public Domain)

face. "We look to the youth whenever we can to shape the content of the games—they pick the issues, they work out the core mechanics ... but we never leave them to do so on their own and provide more guidance with some groups than others" (2010).

Educators and professional game designers partner with youth throughout the game design process. While Global Kids cannot expect youth to have design skills that take experts years to develop, Joseph notes that youth bring unique and valuable assets and insights. For instance, a team of first and second-generation youth Caribbean immigrants developed *Ayiti: The Cost of Life*. The partnering gaming company, GameLab, wanted to locate the game in China, but the youth team wanted the game to reflect issues with which they were more familiar. Joseph explains that the youth were not shy in contributing their ideas, opinions and knowledge at key points in *Ayiti*'s development. For example, during the first play test, the youth team noticed how game characters that fell into debt immediately died. They pointed out that positive elements should be worked into *Ayiti* to more accurately reflect real life in Haiti, that it was not as stark as the game suggested. The team advocated for changes to game play, including an opportunity for players to build things in their communities. When the question arose about including cheat codes in the game to get out of debt, a team member aptly noted: "In Haiti, they don't have a cheat code" (2010).

Joseph speaks to challenges Global Kids faces as they seek to incorporate equity in collaborative digital media and game projects. He notes that time is often a limiting factor, which hinders the depth of game design skills they are able to develop. "This pressure means at times we need to move forward on the project and get youth buy-in after the fact," he says, a less-than-ideal process for equitable game development (2010). Time constraints can also limit learning opportunities for the young people as well. He offers an example from the design process of another Global Kids' game, *Hurricane Katrina: Tempest in Crescent City*, noting that the majority of youth on the design team originally shied away from giving the game's main character a name that they felt would be "too black" (2010). Joseph felt that the team did not get to explore or dissect this issue fully due to scheduling concerns in the development process.

GUIDELINES FOR ANTI-OPPRESSION IN GAME DESIGN AND DEVELOPMENT

An overview of anti-oppression principles, as well as insights provided by collectives and partners on equity issues and games, informed the guidelines we suggest in this section. These guidelines serve as a starting point to understand practicalities in building anti-oppressive games.

Figure 6. Ayiti: The Cost of Life game screenshot of title page. (© 2006 Global Kids. Used with permission.)

Figure 7. Hurricane Katrina: Tempest in Crescent City screenshot of gameplay (left) and main character (right). (© 2008, Global Kids. Used with permission.)

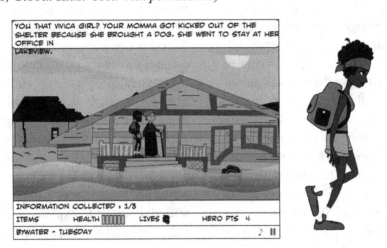

1. Disrupt Stereotypes

On a preliminary level, anti-oppression in game development and design entails making conscious efforts to disrupt the reproduction of oppressive assumptions in the look, feel, and play of a game. Makers must avoid uncritical stereotypes and "othering" depictions, especially of groups that are most marginalized in media and society. Richard Dyer (1996) draws connections between stereotypes and unequal power relationships be-

tween groups. He writes that "stereotypes express particular definitions of reality, with concomitant evaluations, which in turn relate to the disposition of power within society" (p. 248). In questioning "who proposes the stereotype" and "who has the power to enforce it," Dyer demonstrates how stereotypes tend to reinforce the worldviews and position of dominant groups (p. 248). While stereotypes of dominant individuals and groups certainly exist, the full harm of stereotypes play out against those who have less power to define reality, to deem who and what is "normal" and "abnormal."

For example, in creating *RePlay: Finding Zoe/ ReJouer: Où est Zoé*, mainstream understandings about gender—how girls and boys are "supposed" to look—the designers provide players with a wide range of options in choosing the look of their character. Given the invisibility and vilification of dark skin in media and negative connotations having dark skin carries in mainstream society, the game makers made a conscious decision to provide players with the option to choose a dark brown skin color for characters. However, as alluded to by Pedercini above, diversity that appears "photoshopped" can be problematic where it is tokenizing or exists on a purely surface level. When consciously representing groups of people typically underrepresented, game creators should not simply use a window dressing approach.

Game makers must adopt intentionality and conscientiousness when broadening diversity and challenging mainstream stereotypes in games. The *Diner Dash* franchise provides an interesting example. Many incarnations of the game have a young female character as the diner's server, Flo. While some may consider this a stereotyping depiction, deeper complexity is embodied in the character and her role. Flo is a former stockbroker who quit her job to run the diner. She is an entrepreneur who must utilize a variety of strategies and skills to successfully manage and expand her business. In many ways, Flo's portrayal moves beyond a one-dimensional understanding of women's role and qualities even if she engages in service and nurturing work in the game. Dyer (1996) distinguishes "social types" from stereotypes in media. "Although constructed iconographically similarly to the way stereotypes are constructed," he writes, "social types can be used in a much more open and flexible way" (p. 248-249). They can "figure in almost any kind of plot and can have a wide range of roles" while stereotypes "always carry within their very representation an implicit narrative" (p. 248-249). Inclusion of social type characters

like *Diner Dash*'s Flo is a helpful way to disrupt stereotypes in game representations.

2. Consider Players and Communicate with Them

Careful consideration of a game's target players and their unique experiences—power they may hold and oppressions they face—is critical to anti-oppression in game creation. It entails moving away from the assumption that only one type of player exists or that all players use games the same way. Game designers and developers must think reflectively about assumptions they make about target players' ideas, preferences, and needs. Before creating *Darfur is Dying*, for example, Take Action Games sought out information about mtvU's audience and network, as well as the evidence that pointed to their lack of knowledge about the situation in Darfur. Only then did the team feel equipped to start designing a game to expose these complex issues to American college-aged youth, with the intent of provoking and inspiring those players to take real-world action.

Communication with target players must have real implications for the shape a game takes; it cannot consist merely of testing pre-formed ideas. For the development of *RePlay/ReJourer*, focus groups with diverse Anglophone and Francophone young people were essential to conceptualizing a game targeted to youth aged 8 to 14. METRAC dedicated a segment of the development budget to travel across the province of Ontario and meet with children in schools and community settings. METRAC incorporated principles of community-based participatory research when it directed focus groups (Israel et al., 2005). Among other features, community-based participatory research "facilitates a collaborative, equitable partnership … [It involves] an empowering and power-sharing process that attends to social inequities" (p. 7). Community-based participatory research computes with anti-oppression and proves useful in the design process for anti-oppressive games.

3. Attend to Multiple and Hidden Perspectives

An essential element to anti-oppressive practice involves multiplicity, and game makers should open space for marginalized communities to share their ideas, opinions, and perspectives. Developers cannot assume that their own perspective is definitive and need time in the development process to proactively search out and reflect upon other perspectives, particularly those hidden in mainstream discussions. Through an anti-oppressive lens, it is clear that academics and professionals are not the sole experts on a subject. In the case of *Darfur is Dying*, they do not only consist of Westerners with particular perspectives on the crisis.

Game makers should converse with a diverse body of experts and witnesses. Chris Swain (2010) advises game developers to conduct needs analyses with the support of experts, to yield a list of pertinent concepts. These concepts contribute to the learning objectives of value-based or ethical games.

Game makers face a challenging and time-consuming task of identifying and opening space for hidden and marginal perspectives, which can require significant resources. *In the Balance*'s developer, Take Action Games, experienced a long and costly research phase because of the difficultly the creators faced in accessing criminalized people, especially those implicated in serious and highly newsworthy crimes. Beyond that, the process of building trust and comfort between criminalized youth and the game's developers presented its own difficulties and implications for project timelines.

Interestingly, hidden perspectives do not only lie with marginalized groups and can be found among those who have a great deal of socio-political power, whose perspectives, understandings and actions may be clouded by anything from propaganda and mainstream mythology to the sheer complexity of what they do. Molleindustria's *Oiligarchy* highlights oppressive practices of the oil industry by exploring a dominant perspective not often addressed in media, government, or policy development. Some may accuse the game of exaggerating the predatory intentions of the industry, but *Oiligarchy*'s depiction of the oppression and degradation that arise from oil addiction provokes players to reflect on a complicated and mystifying system, one with far-reaching but often hidden impacts on most peoples' daily lives.

4. Marginalized Groups Guide Design and Development

Applied to games, anti-oppression entails looking to marginalized groups to guide the process of design and development. Mary Flanagan speaks to how the Tiltfactor Laboratory has created opportunities for marginalized students, designers, and collaborators to participate in game design and build games that better reflect their ideas and play preferences. Since anti-oppression is a power-sharing perspective, one that seeks to decrease the divide between those considered experts and those viewed as non-experts, it is essential that game makers provide opportunities for laypeople to contribute to a game's development. The *Grow-a-Game* Cards make the specialized process of game development accessible and meaningful to people without game expertise. Global Kids' community-based initiatives exemplify how game makers can engage marginalized people to lead the game design process. Some Global Kids initiatives transfer programming skills to young people who may not otherwise have access to them, allowing them to plan and build their own digital games and interactive experiences.

Of course, sharing programming skills cannot be undertaken lightly or quickly. It may require significant resources and time, and unexpected issues that directly relate to oppressions marginalized people face may arise. A telling example comes from Joseph, who says they did not have adequate time to support a young development team who wanted to find a less "black" name for a game character. The harms, pains, and internalized concerns that oppression creates in the lives of marginalized people reveal themselves in many ways. For people who do not experience the same oppressions, it can prove difficult to anticipate these concerns in the planning process. As a result, allowing for flexibility in time and resources to process these concerns proves essential to anti-oppressive game design.

Game makers can establish balanced partnerships with non-governmental organizations and groups who work to support and learn from diverse communities as a means to get guidance from marginalized people. The partnership between Take Action Games and METRAC was not only instrumental in accessing funding for *RePlay/ ReJourer*, it also supported information-sharing between game developers, Ontario youth and violence prevention advocates.

CONCLUSION

Anti-oppressive principles are amenable to games with social issue content as well as commercial games. Henry Jenkins suggests:

The issues are complex because oppressive assumptions may be more deeply encoded into the genre norms of commercial games, while serious games may start from a pro-social agenda. But all the more reason why you want commercial designers to start reflecting on these concerns. (2010)

Beyond challenging "taken-for-granted" ideals and ideas about groups with lesser and more access to power, anti-oppression explores the structure of the world and how it functions to maintain social power imbalances between people. Root causes of society's contemporary dynamics are sought out and exposed through, among other things, the very mechanisms explained above—disruption of stereotypes, connecting with target communities, listening to multiple and hidden perspectives, and

opening space for the guidance and direction of marginalized groups.

For all of its heady theoretical underpinnings, anti-oppression is designed for practical application in building societal equity and flattening hierarchies. It requires reflectivity and holds strong ethical implications for those who practice it. It also holds a sense of urgency that changes must happen and that people on the margins as well as people with higher access to power and resources must be involved. A core goal of anti-oppressive games, then, is to inspire players to contribute to equitable social change.

Game collective members and partners interviewed for this chapter provided key starting points to support equitable principles in game and interactive design and development. These guidelines only scratch the surface of the potential anti-oppression principles hold to transform game design and development, especially games that seek to expose unequal power dynamics in society. Anti-oppression can support the process of giving players space to re-envision a more equitable world, where, as Flanagan says, working and fighting for equity, justice, and inclusion is learned and practiced, where players are agents of change who can create and share tools for social change.

REFERENCES: LITERATURE

Adair, M., & Howell, S. (1993). Creating an atmosphere where everyone participates. In *Anti-Oppression Reader* (pp. 11-12). San Francisco, CA: Global Exchange. Retrieved from http://www. globalexchange.org/about/AO_Reader_2007.pdf

Bogost, I. (2007). *Persuasive games: The expressive power of videogames.* Cambridge, MA: The MIT Press.

Bureau of Justice Statistics. (n.d.). Homicide trends in the U.S. Retrieved from http://bjs.ojp. usdoj.gov/content/homicide/gender.cfm

Chater, N. (1994). Biting the hand that feeds me: Notes on privilege from a white-anti-racist feminist. *Canadian Women's Studies Journal, 14*(2), 100–103.

Clifford, D., & Burke, B. (2008). *Anti-oppressive ethics and values in social work*. Basingstoke, UK: Palgrave Macmillan.

Collins, P. H. (1986). Learning from the outsider within: The sociological significance of black feminist thought. *Social Problems, 33*(6), S14–S32. doi:10.1525/sp.1986.33.6.03a00020

Dalrymple, J., & Burke, B. (2006). *Anti-oppressive practice: Social care and the law*. Buckingham, UK: Open University Press.

Dibbell, J. (2006, February 7). Game from hell: Latest plan to save Sudan: Make a

Dumbrill, G. C. (2003). Child welfare: AOP's nemesis? In W. Shera (Ed.), *Emerging perspectives on anti-oppressive practice* (pp. 101-119). Toronto: Canadian Scholars' Press.

Dyer, R. (1996). The role of stereotypes. In Morris, P., & Thornham, S. (Eds.), *Media studies: A reader* (pp. 245–251). New York: New York University Press.

Exchange, G. (2006). Anti-oppression reader. Retrieved from http://www.globalexchange.org/about/AO_Reader_2007.pdf

Findlay, B. (1992). Breaking the colour code: A white woman un-learns racism. *Our Times, 11*(4-5), 47–48.

Flanagan, M. personal communication, February 25, 2010

Friedman, S. personal communication, March 1, 2010

Frye, M. (1983). *The politics of reality: Essays in feminist theory*. Freedom, CA: The Crossing Press.

Ganeva, T. (2009, November 17). 'Hit the bitch': Domestic violence PSA goes very, very wrong. *AlterNet*. Retrieved from http://www.alternet.org/blogs/reproductivejustice/144018/%27hit_the_bitch%27%3A_domestic_violence_psa_goes_very%2C_very_wrong/

Gee, J. P. (2007). Pleasure, learning, video games, and life: The projective stance. In Knobel, M., & Lankshear, C. (Eds.), *A new literacies sampler* (pp. 95–114). Bern, Switzerland: Peter Lang Publishing.

Hall, S. (2003). The whites of their eyes: Racist ideologies and the media. In Dines, G., & Humez, J. M. (Eds.), *Gender, race, and class in media* (pp. 89–93). Thousand Oaks, CA: Sage Publications, Inc.

http://www.villagevoice.com/2006-02-07/screens/game-from-hell/

Israel, B. A., Eng, E., Schulz, A., & Parker, E. A. (2005). *Methods in community-based participatory research for health*. San Francisco, CA: Jossey-Bass.

Jenkins, H. personal communication, May 10, 2010

Jill. (2009, November 17). "Hit the Bitch"? *Feministe*. Retrieved from http://www.feministe.us/blog/archives/2009/11/17/hit-the-bitch/

Jiwani, Y. (1997, March). Culture, violence, and inequality [Keynote speech]. FREDA workshop, Violence against women: Meeting the cross-cultural challenge, Vancouver, Canada. Retrieved from http://www.harbour.sfu.ca/freda/articles/culture.htm

Johnson, D. S. (2009). Webinar on 2008 income, poverty and health insurances estimates from the current population survey. Retrieved from http://www.census.gov/Press-Release/www/2009/djohnson_remarks09iph_revised.html

Joseph, B. personal communication, February 1, 2010

Komiotis, W. personal communication, March 1, 2010

Kondrat, M. E. (1999). Who is the "self" in self-aware: Professional self-awareness from a critical theory perspective. In *Social Service Review* (pp. 451–475). Chicago, IL: University of Chicago Press.

Kristof, N. D. (2006, May 7). Heroes of Darfur. *The New York Times*, p. 4.12.

Lopes, T., & Thomas, B. (2006). *Dancing on live embers: Challenging racism in organizations.* Toronto, CA: Between the Lines Press.

Mullaly, B. (1997). *Structural social work: Ideology, theory and practices.* New York: Oxford University Press.

Nichols, B. (2001). *Introduction to documentary.* Bloomington, IN: Indiana University Press.

Pedercini, P. personal communication, February 24, 2010

Porter, A. (2006). *Well meaning men ... Breaking out of the "Man Box".* New York: A Call to Men.

Ruiz, S. personal communication, March 1, 2010

Shirky, C. (2005, October 21). Keynote. Presented at the Games for Change conference, New York.

Sinclair, D. (2003). *Overcoming the backlash: Telling the truth about power, privilege, and oppression: Exploring gender-based analysis in the context of violence against women: A resource kit for community agencies.* Durham Region, Ontario: The Violence Prevention Coordinating Council.

Strier, R. (2007). Anti-oppressive research in social work: A preliminary discussion. *British Journal of Social Work, 37*(5), 857–871. doi:10.1093/bjsw/bcl062

Swain, C. (2010). The mechanics is the message: How to communicate through the mechanics of user action and system response. In Shrier, K., & Gibson, D. (Eds.), *Ethics and game design: Teaching values through play.* Hershey, PA: Information Science Reference.

Thomson-DeVeaux, A. (2009). 'Hit the bitch' game is supposed to deter domestic violence? *Care2.* Retrieved from http://www.care2.com/causes/womens-rights/blog/hit-the-bitch-game-is-supposed-to-deter-domestic-violence/www.hitthebitch.dk/

video game dramatizing Darfur. *Village Voice.* Retrieved from

Winston, B. (1993). The documentary film as scientific inscription. In Renov, M. (Ed.), *Theorizing documentary.* New York: Routledge.

York, A. personal communication, March 1, 2010

Young, I. M. (1990). *Justice and the politics of difference.* Princeton, NJ: Princeton University Press.

REFERENCES: GAMES AND GAMES INITIATIVES

ArtsElectronic. (2002). *The Sims.*

Børn og Unge i Voldsramte Familier. (2009). *Hit the bitch.* Retrieved from http://www.hitthebitch.dk/

Rockstar Games. (2004). *Grand Theft Auto: San Andreas*

Global Kids & Gamelab. (2006). *Ayiti: The cost of life.* Retrieved from http://ayiti.newzcrew.org/globalkids/

Kids, G. *Creating leaders through experience.* Retrieved from http://www.globalkids.org/

Kids, G., & Creations, D. (2009). *Hurricane Katrina: Tempest in Crescent City.* Retrieved from http://tempestincrescentcity.ning.com/game

La Molleindustria. Retrieved from http://www.molleindustria.org/en/home

Metropolitan Action Committee on Violence Against Women and Children. Retrieved from http://www.metrac.org/

Metropolitan Action Committee on Violence Against Women and Children, & Take Action Games. (2007). *RePlay: Finding Zoe/ReJouer: Où est Zoé?* Retrieved from http://www.metrac.org/replay/index.html

Mollindustria. (2008). *Oiligarchy.* Retrieved from http://www.molleindustria.org/en/oiligarchy

mtvU, Susana Ruiz, Huy Truong, & Ashley York [collaboratively with colleagues from the University of Southern California, & InterFUEL]. (2006). *Darfur is Dying.* Retrieved from http://darfurisdying.com/

PlayFirst. (2003). *Diner Dash.*

Take Action Games. (forthcoming). *Balance (Alexandria, Va.).* Retrieved from http://www.takeactiongames.com/tag/criminal_justice.html.

Take Action Games. Retrieved from http://www.takeactiongames.com/TAG/HOME.html

Values at Play. *Designing social values in computer games.* Retrieved from http://www.valuesatplay.org/

World Bank Institute (Producer). (2010). *EVOKE.* Retrieved from http://www.urgentevoke.com/

Chapter 17
The Doctor Will Be You Now:
A Case Study on Medical Ethics and Role–Play

Nahil Sharkasi
University of Southern California, USA

ABSTRACT

In the field of fertility medicine, technology has vastly outpaced our ethical, legal, and social frameworks leaving us in a quagmire of gray morality. Seeds is a role-playing game and ethics simulation about Assisted Reproductive Technology and its effect on 21st century medical decisions. Players play the role of a fertility doctor and must make difficult ethical decisions through courses of treatment while balancing economic, emotional, and scientific concerns. With Seeds, the goal is to foster meaningful decision-making that may transfer from the game world into the real world through stimulating role-play and by creating a safe space for exploration of ethical issues. This chapter offers critical reflection on the design choices made in the process of creating this ethical exploration space on the subject of Assisted Reproductive Technology.

INTRODUCTION

Babies are in. Between the Octomom, Jon and Kate, and the Jolie-Pitt brood, baby stories are leading media sales (Washington, 2009). Often missing from these stories, however, is the ever-increasing use of Assisted Reproductive Technology (ART) and the ethical complexities that come with it. With new technological approaches to reproduction, such as in-vitro fertilization, pre-implantation genetic diagnosis, and the use of sperm donors, egg donors, surrogates and gestational carriers, come emergent ethical situations. Ethics, as a socially accepted notion of right and wrong, have not yet been defined in the United States as it pertains to ART. The field of fertility medicine is one area among many in the modern world where technology has vastly outpaced our ethical, legal, and social systems leaving us in a snarl of gray morality. We are becoming increasingly aware of the physical risks that come with the luxury to control the specific circumstances

DOI: 10.4018/978-1-60960-120-1.ch017

of the process of birth— chief among them multiple births and pre-maturity (Mundy, 2007). The rapidly growing population of parents and caretakers of premature children, and children conceived using ART, face unique challenges and may benefit from a game experience that allows them to explore these ethical issues.

At the core of each ethical conflict surrounding ART is the essential question of life and death that resonates intimately with each individual. Regardless of whether players have specifically considered this topic before, everyone has an opinion. The conflicts that arise from the availability of new reproductive technologies are receiving more and more coverage in popular media. While the drama unfolds—how many embryos to implant, or which donor to choose, this project, *Seeds*, specifically explores what it would mean to more actively engage with these ethical situations.

Ethics simulations are a niche in the field of interactive media, and are becoming an increasingly necessary tool to navigate the murky waters left in the wake of speeding technological advancement. Ethics simulation software is currently available for training in corporate ethics, financial ethics, biomedical ethics, and many other fields. Last year, the United States Office of Government Ethics developed their own ethical training software CD-Rom based on their established ethical training protocol (USOGE, 2009). Laws often represent a society's commonly agreed upon ethical standards, though legal codes cannot always be equated to ethical codes. Like most ethics simulation software, this CD-Rom uses some multimedia and limited interactivity to teach users a pre-determined code of ethical behavior, which is already established by law. For example, in a sexual harassment training simulation, the goal of the experience is to clarify the established right and wrong codes of behavior, even within socially ambiguous situations.

In areas of emerging technology, however, there are many ethical questions to which a right

or wrong has not yet been commonly agreed upon and codified by law. Whereas the goal of many current ethics simulations for established fields is to direct audiences to a so-called correct answer, role-playing games can provide alternative ways of understanding and evaluating ethics (Simkins, 2010). There is an increasing need for a virtual space for ethical exploration that lets the user understand their own ethical decision-making process and the implications of the choices they make to help navigate areas like ART where new technology yields emergent ethical conflict. Further, the model for ethical exploration outlined in this chapter may also be useful in revisiting areas of established ethical codes, as well as with emergent ethical codes.

In the next section, I will discuss my approach to creating a virtual space for ethical exploration in a role-playing game about fertility medicine called *Seeds*. I will describe the game and my design process, as well as my results and observations. Finally, I will discuss challenges I faced and outline directions for future research.

SEEDS OVERVIEW

The challenge of using role-playing game mechanics in an ethics simulation emerged from my graduate thesis project at The University of Southern California's Interactive Media Division with a game called *Seeds*. *Seeds* is a thought-provoking, interactive experience that positions players at the center of bio-ethical debate. Part serialized medical drama, part online role-playing game, *Seeds* prompts players to assess their own beliefs to determine an ethical treatment solution using Assisted Reproductive Technology. Through engaging role-play in which players treat and diagnose infertility using controversial technologies, players learn how each decision shapes their world and the fate of the characters in it. By illuminating some of the consequences of using ART, this game could prove instructive for people facing some of the real challenges these technologies give rise to (Levitt, 2010). The goal of *Seeds* is to provide a compelling narrative environment that facilitates reflection and safe exploration of ethical issues.

I developed Seeds over the course of one year with a team of graduate and undergraduate students, and with fellowship funding from Fox Interactive. *Seeds* was developed using Adobe Flash and Flex and can be run as a stand-alone Adobe Air application or in a web browser.

Where *Seeds* differs from other ethical simulation software is in the fact that the ethical code for the field of fertility medicine is emergent. In other, more established disciplines, where the ethical standards are widely known and agreed upon, the purpose of ethical training and simulation is simply to educate the users on those established ethical standards. In the United States, within the field of ART, a sharp distinction between right and wrong has not yet been fully established and codified by law. The primary need is to better understand the implications and consequences of ART, rather than to train an audience on a code of ethical behavior. Thus, *Seeds* is designed more as a space for safe exploration of ethical issues than a simulation that drives players to arrive at a pre-determined conclusion. The goal of *Seeds* is to spark an "Aha!" moment that lets the user under-

stand their own ethical decision-making process and the implications of the choices they make.

Seeds utilizes standard role-playing game structures: multiple characters (patients), quests (treatments), resources (money) and inventory (eggs, sperm, embryos). An embodied first-person experience puts the player in the decision maker's shoes for them to face making personal, gut-level decision. *Seeds* begins with the premise that the player is a new doctor at a top fertility clinic. The player is asked by "The Board of Directors" to take a survey as part of the new-employee paperwork. The results of the survey cast the player as one of three profile types, described in detail below. Next, the game starts, and the player consults with patients, treats them and follows-up with the results, making critical ethical decisions at each step of the way. Meanwhile the game system tracks each decision the player makes and evaluates it to see whether the player's behavior is consistent with his or her beliefs as declared in the introductory survey.

GOALS AND MEASURES FOR SUCCESS

When the goal of an interactive experience or game is more than to entertain, game designers

Figure 1. A screenshot from Seeds

often invoke the notion of meaningful play. As described by Katie Salen and Eric Zimmerman, meaningful play "occurs when the relationships between actions and outcomes in a game are both discernable and integrated into the larger context of the game" (2003). The communicative and persuasive power of a game lies in the game's mechanics, or procedures (Bogost, 2007). While the in-game procedures of *Seeds* are not faithful representations of what a doctor does, they are a comment on the mechanization of reproduction, and are prompts for ethical reflection on conflicts that are representative of conflicts outside the game world. Miguel Sicart defines players of computer games as ethical beings interested in the actions and goals defined by a game's design and therefore implicitly interested in "how that design can affect our moral fabric as ethical players" (2009). Whereas meaningful play is contextualized within the "magic circle" of the game, meaningful decision-making is about connecting the player as an ethical being to the game world's actions and consequences.

The goal of *Seeds* is to evoke not only meaningful play, but also meaningful decision-making that may suggest parallels between the game world and the real world. The strategy employed in the service of this goal draws parallels between the fiction and actions of the game world that exist within the magic circle to the conflicts and actions of the real world that the player inhabits. Meaningful decision-making is a necessary element of ethical reflection, and both meaningful play and meaningful decision-making are best fostered when contextualized within a rich and immersive narrative world.

To address this objective, *Seeds* uses role-play that involves the player's own personal beliefs. The game system challenges those beliefs through traditional role-playing game mechanics. The decisions the player makes are then evaluated within an ethical framework that is constructed according to real ethical situations from the scholarly literature in this field of medicine. The result is an immersive narrative-driven game experience that both educates and provokes thought without leading players to a predetermined resolution.

There are several user cues and behaviors used to evaluate whether or not each design decision serves the goals of the project. The first is the experience of the "yuck" factor.. The "yuck" factor is described in this field of medicine as the gut reaction against a particular decision, case, or procedure, and is a key factor used to determine the ethical soundness of treatment decisions (Kohl, 2007). Doctors rely on an elusive gut reaction to inform their ethical choices, and if the player experiences the same reaction, this indicates that they are engaged with the content and the connection to the doctor role is successfully established. The second cue is the "aha!" moment; an emotional response that would indicate a revelation or surprise where the game compels the player to understand an ethical issue in a different way, or change their mind. An "aha!" moment could also result when the consequences in the game reinforce the decisions made and strengthen a player's convictions. The key in either case is an emotional response that confirms that the player is engaged and is somehow connected into the network of responsibility in the game world.

In the next section, I will describe in detail my approach to designing a way for players to arrive at a point of ethical reflection created by an emotional response to the content and game play.

METHODOLOGY FOR PROVOKING ETHICAL DECISION-MAKING

The methodology used in *Seeds* to elicit emotional response and ethical reflection has four parts. First, the game assesses the user's ethical point of view; second, it challenges that stance through rich media; third, it solicits a response to that challenge; and fourth, it compares that response to the initially declared ethical point of view.

Table 1. Phases of play in Seeds

	Introduction	Consultation Phase (Act I)	Treatment Phase (Act 2)	Results Phase (Act 3)
4-part Methodology	Survey	Challenge	Response	Evaluation
Game Interface	Player completes introductory survey.	Player watches consultation scene.	Player responds to prompts and makes decisions about treatment.	Player receives results and feedback on his or her actions.
Internal Mechanics	System assigns player a profile type based on survey answers.	System delivers patient cases that specifically challenge the player's profile.	System collects data on each response.	System compares player's pattern of decisions against his or her profile type.

Survey

Three opposing forces frame the ethical issues surrounding Assisted Reproductive Technology: scientific advancement, economic constraints, and patients' desires (Hull, 2005). These three vectors shape the exploration space of the game. Upon starting the game, the player is asked by "The Board of Directors" to take a survey assesses the player's general point of view on some key ethical issues surrounding Assisted Reproductive Technology. Each of the choices to the multiple-choice questions in the survey represents one of these three opposing forces. Based on the survey results, the player is assigned one of three player profiles: The Entrepreneur, The Mad Scientist, The Miracle Worker-as well as a mission statement appropriate to that profile.

- The Entrepreneur believes fertility medicine is a service industry where the customer is always right.
- The Mad Scientist supports the advancement of science, experimental technologies, and research.
- The Miracle Worker favors strong familial relationships.

These profile types, as coarse as they are, provide necessary boundaries for the exploration of ethical conflict. The main function of this survey is to calibrate the player's ethical position to evaluate the decisions he or she makes, and to determine whether they are indeed consistent with their declared mission statement. This also allows the system to track whether the player has changed their mind over the course of play. The tertiary function of the survey is to prime the player to own the role and decisions he or she makes, supporting the player's embodiment of the role.

The survey contains 8 questions that each correspond to the ethical decisions the player will have to make in the game. These questions touch on the key areas of controversy in the field of Assisted Reproductive Technology as outlined in *Ethical Issues in the New Reproductive Technologies*, and other literature.

These topics include:

- Right to treatment—Is reproduction an inherent right? Should treatment be covered by insurance? Who sets the price for treatment?
- Risky technologies—Should ART be regulated?
- Donor anonymity—Does a donor's right to anonymity trump a child's right to know his or her biological origins?
- Third party parents (donors, surrogates, gestational carriers)—what is the legal and social status of these individuals? Does a social, legal, or biological relationship take precedent?
- How many embryos should be created in a course of treatment? How many should be implanted with each transfer?

- When is the best time implant the embryos? An early, three day transfer is riskier. Waiting until blastocyst stage (five days) is safer but could ultimately lead to more disappointment.
- Selective reduction— is this practice ethical? Can you risk the life of one to save many, or many to save few? On what basis can we selectively reduce a pregnancy (gender, health, ease of access)?
- What to do with leftover embryos? Can they be used for scientific research? Should they be destroyed or kept frozen in perpetuity? (Hull, 2005)

Challenge

Once the player's profile is established, the system delivers custom content to challenge their particular stance. For example, if a player in the intro survey states that donor anonymity should be outlawed, once the game starts that player will receive a patient case with a compelling request for an anonymous donor. These cases are presented as integral stories told in three acts: 1) consultation, 2) treatment, 3) follow up, and presented using a variety of media. The first act of each patient case is told in a brief Consultation scene with actors playing the patients. The second act, Treatment, consists of interactive game play, and the third act, Follow Up, is told in images and text with mild interactivity.

Response

Once the player's ethical stance has been assessed and challenged, the final step is to codify and systematize their reactions, and the risks and rewards associated with each decision. In upholding the design goal of creating a safe space for ethical exploration, it is vitally important that the game's reward system not reflect the designer's own personal ethical stance. Rather than simply rewarding morality points for some actions over others, the system is entirely context specific, ensuring that ethical decisions can be evaluated differently depending on what the player's mission statement is. The player's pattern of behavior is tracked and each decision is tallied into the score.

One conceit of the game is that the player, as the doctor, is the sole decision maker. In reality, the critical decisions featured in the game are made by doctors, patients, sperm and donors, and a variety of other stakeholders. For the purpose of maintaining a compelling single-player experience that exposes the player to a range of ethical decisions, the game assumes that the doctor has the final say, and the patients will always agree with the doctor's recommendations.

Evaluation

An essential part of the player feedback system is meaningful consequences for each action taken in the game. Each action deserves a substantial reaction from the game system, however all actions are not weighted equally. The game's evaluation system is based on ethical and legal frameworks currently in use in this field, such as the guidelines issued by the UK's Human Fertilization and Embryology Authority (Deech and Smajdor, 2007). Each decision in the game is evaluated by the game system for both its magnitude, such as how many people it affects, and directionality, such as which profile type the decision favors. For example, a decision to support the donation of leftover embryos to scientific research involves a group of people, such as the family, doctors, and researchers, and favors the Mad Scientist player profile, while a choice of an open donorship involves only the family and favors the Miracle Worker profile. These decisions are then aggregated and compared to the profile type chosen by the player.

The game becomes more complex when players make choices counter to their declared profile and mission statement. Once the system satisfactorily tracks and evaluates each ethical decision, the next challenge is to provide feedback and consequences so that the player feels the weight of their actions in the world. Players receive feedback in the form of letters from the Board of Directors, which either congratulate them for upholding the mission statement or reprimand them for diverging from it. When a player's decision pattern skews too far in one direction, the player is presented with consequences in the form of news events or correspondence from non-player characters, for example, a headline related to recent game actions that may have positive or negative implications for the player. Again, it is important that the game not steer the player to make one decision over another, but provide an engaging environment to make different decisions and see the repercussions for those decisions in world.

In the next section, I will describe the internal logic of the system for weighting and evaluating ethical decisions made in the game.

MECHANICS OF ETHICAL EVALUATION

The treatment phase of the game, also the second act in each patient case, is where the player practices his or her ethical decision-making. The game's evaluation system is influenced by the ethical and legal frameworks currently in use in this field, such as the guidelines issued by the UK's Human Fertilization and Embryology Authority (Deech and Smajdor, 2007). Ethical decisions are classified as having consequences in personal, professional, group, and government arenas (Hull, 2005). Each decision in the game is weighted based on sphere of influence, and how many people it affects (See Table 2).

Each ethical decision in the game is tracked with three indices for each of the three profile types. Each decision is evaluated on which profile type it favors as well as by how many people it affects. The treatment phase of game play introduces the use of an ethical decision-making

Table 2. Weighting decisions for level of impact

Level of decision's impact		Point value weight
Decision For	Government	+4
	Group	+3
	Professional	+2
	Personal	+1
	Neutral	0
Decision Against	Personal	-1
	Professional	-2
	Group	-3
	Government	-4

weighting matrix (Table 3). The matrix assigns point values to each decision in the game according to level of impact of the decision, and which profile type it favors. For example, a decision in favor of the Mad Scientist profile that only has impact on a personal level is valued at +1 (a decision that just passes the Yuck test), while a decision that impacts governmental policy, such as a life-defining policy decision, is valued at +4. Conversely a decision that hinders the cause of the Mad Scientist on the Government level would receive a -4, and a decision that doesn't pass the Yuck test is given a -1.

The first decision the player makes in consulting with a new patient is the decision to accept or reject the patient for treatment. The only information the player is given at that point is narrative information about the patient. The game is soliciting a pure gut-reaction, and this decision should be made purely based on the player's personal feelings. Since financial information does not factor into this decision, it can be classified as a decision that only affects the personal sphere. In applying the above-mentioned ethical framework as a weighting system, a personal decision has less weight than a professional, group or government decision. The "accept/reject" decision is weighted as either a positive or negative 1, given which profile type the case naturally favors.

Table 3. Ethical decision making weighting matrix

	Decision	Entrepreneur	Mad Scientist	Miracle Worker
1	Accepting a patient**	-1/+1	-1/+1	-1/+1
	Rejecting a patient*	-1/+1	-1/+1	-1/+1
2	Prescribing experimental technology	0	+2	-2
	Prescribing more expensive treatment	+2	0	-2
3	Choosing Donor Anonymity	3	3	-3
	Choosing Open Donorship	-3	3	3
	Choosing Delayed Disclosure	0	0	3
4	Harvesting the maximum number of gametes	3	3	-3
	Harvesting the minimum Number of gametes	-3	-3	0
5	Fertilizing the maximum number of eggs	-3	3	-3
	Fertilizing the minimum number of eggs	3	-3	3
6	Choosing 3 day transfer	3	-3	-3
	Choosing blastocyst-stage transfer	0	3	3
7	Choosing to selectively reduce a multiple pregnancy	4	0	4
	Choosing not to selectively reduce a multiple pregnancy	0	0	-4
	Reducing a multiple pregnancy to a single	4	0	4
	Reducing a high-order (quadruplets +) multiple pregnancy to low order multiples (twins, triplets)	4	0	4
8	Keep Leftovers Frozen	4	0	4
	Donate to Science	-4	4	-4
	Donate to Adoptive Family	-4	-4	4
	Destroy	0	-4	-4

* The specific value of these decisions depends on the nature of the patient case, and which profile would favor it.

The second decision the player impacts on a professional level. After accepting a patient, the player must then prescribe a treatment. The player is given two options for treatment. Each is described in terms of how much revenue it will generate for the clinic and what the likelihood of success is. This decision is about balancing economic concerns and professional concerns, while still not violating a player's personal gut choice that made them accept the patient in the first place. The choice of treatment is weighted at a positive or negative 2.

Once a course of treatment is prescribed, the next set of decisions is about considering the family as a group. This is called the Check List phase, and is where the player verifies that the patient

has all the right components in order to proceed with treatment. The ethical decision presents itself if the patient requires the use of a sperm or egg donor, surrogate, or gestational carrier. When third parties are involved in the reproductive process, the consequences can often be unpredictable for the doctor who may, in some cases, be held responsible for facilitating the relationship. In the Check List phase of the game, the patient has two ethical choices to consider: the donor agreement and the choice of donor.

The donor agreement is the contract that details the relationship the donor is to have with his or her offspring. In the real world brokers, or agencies outside the medical establishment often negotiate this contract, but for the purposes of including this important ethical choice in the game, the player is asked to advise his or her patient on a donor agreement. The three choices are 1) anonymity, 2) open donorship, and 3) delayed disclosure. In choosing anonymity, the player is effectively placing the rights of the customers, the parents, above the rights of the child. This decision is weighted positively for the Entrepreneur and Mad Scientist profiles, because studies show that anonymity encourages donation (Mundy, 2008). In choosing open donorship, the player is supporting a child's right to know his or her biological parent. This decision is weighted positively for the Miracle Worker profile and negatively for the Entrepreneur. Choosing delayed disclosure is somewhat of a middle ground, it is considerate of a donor's privacy for a limited time, but ultimately favors a child's right to know his or her genetic origins. This third choice is weighted as a neutral for the Entrepreneur and Mad Scientist and positively for Miracle Worker. Regardless of the choice, the decision is based on a consideration of another person or small group, and is thus weighted with a positive or negative 3.

Similarly, the decision of how many eggs to retrieve and fertilize, how many embryos to transfer, and when to transfer them is most relevant to the patient family as a group, so this decision is also weighted as a positive or negative 3.

The decisions in the remaining portion of the treatment cycle, through the Conception and Results phases, are weighted the highest, with a positive or negative 4 because of their relevance to an ongoing national dialogue on the nature of life and death, and have implications for policy decisions in those areas. These decisions are weighted much more heavily because of legal precedents that link fertility medicine to the abortion and end-of life debates.

One of the most common risks of Assisted Reproductive Treatment is the possibility of multiple pregnancy. When a patient has multiple embryos implanted successfully or an implanted embryo unexpectedly splits (as becomes increasingly common with age) (Mundy, 2008), the doctor and patient are faced with the difficult decision of selective reduction. They must consider, especially in the case of high order multiples, reducing the pregnancy to ensure the health of the mother and the remaining embryos. In the game, if a patient has a multiple pregnancy, the player has the choice to reduce or not, and is also asked on what basis to choose the fetuses that will be reduced—gender, health, or location in the uterus.

The final ethical decision in the treatment cycle comes up after a positive result is achieved from IVF treatment. As multiple embryos are often created in the process, the player must advise his or her patients on what to do with left-over embryos. There are four choices: keep them frozen, donate them to science, donate them to adoptive families, or destroy them. Each choice has advantages and disadvantages for each profile type. For example, donating leftover embryos to adoptive families is favorable to the Miracle Worker but not to the Mad Scientist who would rather use the excess embryos for research. Destroying leftover embryos seems like a waste to the Mad Scientist and the Miracle Worker, but to the Entrepreneur it's seen as the elimination of a liability.

In the next section, I will describe how the above described ethical evaluation system is employed to issue consequences to the player for his or her actions.

ETHICS AND CONSEQUENCES

Ethical game play arises when the game world responds to the player's values, and the player is positioned within the "network of responsibility of the game" (Sicart, 2009). Consequences tie the player to the game world and the network of responsibility. The evaluation process described above is hidden from the interface, and feedback on the player's ethical choices and behaviors is presented in terms of consequences. Periodically throughout the game, when a pattern of behavior emerges (i.e., behavior favoring one profile be-comes dominant), the player is given feedback about the decisions he or she has been making.

There are two tiers of consequences in *Seeds*: the player level and the level of the game world. On the player level, the system tracks the ethical decisions made in the game, and periodically as-sesses whether or not they are consistent with the player's profile. If the two scores are consistent, and the player indeed is acting according to his or her stated beliefs, he or she is awarded a finan-cial bonus from the clinic's Board of Directors. If, however, the player's pattern of decisions is inconsistent with his or her stated profile—if the self-declared Miracle Worker is behaving more like an Entrepreneur, for instance—the player takes a financial penalty accompanied by an ad-monition from the Board of Directors. This penalty or bonus is small and serves less to encourage or discourage specific choices, but rather to point out to the player what their beliefs and choices might look like if manifested in real scenarios.

The second tier of consequences is in the game world. News Events arise periodically from the game world indicating what the world would be like if the decisions the player has supported were proliferated throughout society. For example, if a player consistently decides against anonymous donorship, he or she might get a News Event that anonymous donorship has been outlawed.

An advantage of playing through different ethical decisions in a virtual space is the abil-ity to compress time, and explore the diverse consequences of different choices. In *Seeds*, the consequence of making one ethical choice over another is framed as pushing the game world's ethical position towards the worldview of one of the profile types. I wanted to be careful not to impose my own opinions on the content, but to allow the player to use the game system to see what would happen if everyone in the world made the same decisions they had made in the game. Consequences in this game are not inherently

positive or negative, but are relative to the player's profile and the choices he or she has made.

As a formal game element, consequences ap-pear like chance cards in *Monopoly*. Every so often, the player is dealt a consequence event that carries a financial penalty or bonus, or other rule change. As a narrative element, it appears in the player's in-game inbox as a news article, message from a colleague, or other correspondence. If a player consistently chooses an open donor agreement for his or her patients, he or she might receive a consequence event with a headline declaring that anonymous donorship has been abolished and sub-sequently the inventory of donors has decreased. The system tracks which profile type the player is most closely following, and issues consequence events related to the worldview that each profile represents. For example, the Entrepreneur favors a world with an unregulated fertility industry; the Mad Scientist favors a world with government funding for human embryo research; the Miracle Worker favors a world with laws that support and protect children and families.

In the next section, I will discuss the challenges, as well as the positive and negative results of the design decisions described above.

ENHANCING A POSITIVE PLAY EXPERIENCE

Many designers who create games whose goal is to educate or inform (sometimes called Serious Games) face the challenge of reconciling these goals with player's expectations of having an entertainment experience when playing a game. Though it may not be appropriate for this type of game to be "fun" in the same way many enter-tainment games are fun, the experience must be engaging, and the reward structures must encour-age continued engagement with the system.

By the time of the second round of playtests, all the ethical content points had been incorpo-rated, but balancing the content with compelling game play remained a challenge. In the initial playtests of the paper prototype, the probability of successful treatment in each patient case had been set at 60% to 90%. In reality IVF usually has a 30% probability of success per cycle. As much as ART has become a game of skill and resources, conception still holds an undeniable random element that needed to be represented in the system. The question presented itself: can a game still be engaging if there's only a 30% chance of success? Paper-prototyping was re-introduced at this stage to try to reach a design that would simulate a 30% success rate and avoid frustrating game play. First a statistical 30% for each round over multiple rounds was tested without much improvement on the original design. In the next attempt, the probability of success was increased slightly each round, so that by the fourth round, the player had a 75% chance of achieving a positive result. This solution was a little more satisfying to the player but still lacked a strong enough sense of agency.

In the next iteration of tests, a more nuanced approach to calculating success rate included the specifics of the patient case factored in with the user's inventory (power ups) and experience (the player's success rate). The quality of the sperm, egg, and womb each comprise 30% of this score; 5% was given to power-up inventory items such as fertility drugs, new equipment, etc.; and 5% was given to the player's own success rate indicating the doctor's experience in the game. This became known as the Check List Score in the game. The science on infertility supported this breakdown, but it still did not give the player much agency.

To address the problem of user agency, I decided to introduce a series of skill-based minigames that simulate the various reproductive technologies featured in the game: In Vitro Fertilization (IVF), Intra-uterine Insemination (IUI), and Intracytoplasmic Sperm Injection (ICSI). Each game presents a variation on a targeting or shooting mechanic, whether the player are targeting eggs in petri dishes, sperm cells under a microscope, or an egg traveling down a fallopian tube. The simple mechanic is a rhetorical comment on the mechanization of reproduction and makes players

Figure 2. A screenshot from Seeds related to IVF

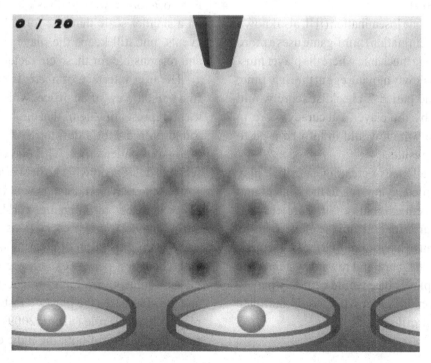

aware of the doctor's hand in the reproductive process where ART is used.

The results of treatment would be decided by a combination of statistical data and performance, giving the player much more of a sense of agency than would a simple dice roll. The mini-games also provide a break from the rhythm of the game, creating a more dynamic and varied experience. The success or failure of a patient's treatment would be calculated by multiplying the mini-game score by the Check List Score mentioned above. The Check List Score was turned into a percent value that is used as a multiplier for the mini-game scores.

The scoring system for each mini-game is slightly different depending on the mechanic. The IVF mini-game is an inverted shooting gallery where the player must inseminate eggs in Petri dishes as they move along a conveyor belt. In this case, the final results would be calculated as follows: if the patient's checklist score is 85%, each of the Petri dishes that the player successfully targets would be given an 85% chance of survival. The system would generate random numbers for each, and calculate how many embryos were successfully created.

The Intrauterine Insemination (IUI, also known as Artificial Insemination) mini-game uses a more standard shooting mechanic where the player must target a single, slowly moving egg at the right time. Once again, the patient's checklist score would be multiplied by the player's accuracy score in the mini-game, which would in turn be used to calculate final results.

Another challenge of creating a positive play experience while staying true to the content and balancing the ethics goals of the project was providing rewards for each unique player profile. Was it sufficient to have money be the key scoring mechanism in the game and reward system? The Entrepreneur player type would certainly play to earn the most money, but what would motivate the other two profile types?

To address this, other achievements and narrative awards were incorporated that would appeal to other player types. To appeal to the Mad Scientist profile, the content of the game inventory was adapted into reward badges and achievements so this player profile could be rewarded with new equipment, technologies, and scientific honors. A Mad-Scientist player who would be motivated by these rewards, rather than focusing on earning money to purchase these items and thereby behaving out of character, could focus on the aspects of game play that he or she finds compelling and subsequently be rewarded for that.

Similarly, to appeal to the Miracle Worker player, narrative rewards in the "Baby Wall" feature. Almost all fertility clinics display photographs of patients who have been successfully treated along with their new children. In the game, when a patient is successfully treated, their photos go up on the Baby Wall. Players can visit the Wall at any time and review their achievements. Clicking on the photos in the wall also reveals a flash-forward-style follow-up that tells the final chapter in the patient's story, so players can continue to visit with patients as time passes. This is also another way to illustrate consequences on a smaller scale than the formal consequence events, but still keeps the player involved with and responsible for these characters.

The user interface of *Seeds* is presented as a first person view of an office, with interface elements representing items that might be commonly found on a doctor's desktop such as and email inbox and patient files. The player is meant to feel like doctor and what he or she sees on screen is what the player character would see seated at his or her desk in the game world. In addition, during playtests and presentations, players have been given the option of wearing lab coats. The embodied first-person experience increases the player's subjectivization as the agent in the game, and thus increases the player's installation in the player character role (Sicart, 2009). This subjectivization is key for both the ludic experience of the game, but also for the player to own his or her actions as an ethical player.

DEVELOPMENT PROCESS

The project has been through three phases of development. The first stage of development consisted of paper prototype. The second phase of development saw the implementation of the system developed with the paper prototype in a digital form. The integration of the ethics methodology also happened in the second phase. The third phase of development was about refining the digital prototype and testing the methodology.

Paper Prototypes

The first iteration of *Seeds* was developed as a paper prototype that was played by teams with an emphasis on discussion and cooperative decision-making. The goal was to see if the narratives based on research with fertility specialists and patients were compelling enough to sustain engagement in the system. The focus was on the potential for episodic narrative and dramatic suspense to motivate game play.

In the first playtest, three teams of two people each played. They first agreed on a name for their clinic and a mission statement. Asking players to first agree on something helped established a core game mechanic and inviting them to customize their clinic added a sense of ownership that adds to the weight of the choices.

Each team was asked to keep track of their revenue and success rate. On each turn a folded slip of paper was distributed to each team. The first paper revealed the first act of each patient story, the Consultation. It also indicated a dollar amount for revenue and a percentage for the probability of success. The teams were asked to read the consultation and decide whether or not to take the case. If they decided not to take the case, it was thrown into the center for another

team to pick up. After they made their decision, they were dealt another patient. The turn lasted five minutes, and scores were tallied at the end. At the end of the turn, each team calculated the revenue they had received from each patient, and then began "treatment."

In this early paper prototype, treatment consisted of a random draw of a coin out of a bag, given the statistical probability for success for that patient. The treatment phase introduced a branching narrative, where the next act of the story was revealed and would be different depending on positive or negative results. After all the patients in the round were treated, teams were assessed based on which had earned the most money, and which team had the highest success rate. Winning teams were rewarded with 'follow up' points, limited resources they could use in subsequent rounds to reveal the final act of each patient arc. The goal was that players would seek the follow up points so that they could learn the final act of each story.

The results of this early play test provided a proof of concept for player engagement in ethical decision-making. In deciding whether to accept or reject patients, players were considering the mission statement they had declared during game set up, and basing their decision on those criteria. This was an important moment that informed the use of mission statement and the design for the decision evaluation system in the final digital game. Players were indeed engaging in social discussion within the team. Players also found the narratives compelling, and were successfully motivated by the desire to reveal each successive act of the patient's story.

One unanticipated mode of play emerged out of the discussion of patient stories. Players began to discuss other similar stories that they had heard in the news. They were asked to write down the stories in the same format as the patient profiles and those were added to the deck for the next round of play testers. As a result, the addition of user generated content feature was subsequently incorporated into the final design.

Digital Prototypes

The first playtests confirmed that the content was compelling, and it did map well onto a game system. The system that emerged began to seem more and more like a role-playing game system. More elements from the role-playing game genre were added, including an inventory of machines, drugs, and technologies that could improve the probability of successful treatment. Inventory items could then be purchased with the money earned. The three specific aforementioned player roles were defined, each with their own mission statement, and unique ability.

This increased detail and specificity made for more interesting game play, but it did not address issues of player agency, and ethical choice. The random assignment of positive or negative results of treatment left players feeling unsatisfied. After researching the subject further, the simplicity of basing the success/failure outcome of treatment on one statistic was both unsatisfying and untrue to the sophistication of the science and system being modeled. To avoid creating a management simulation about running a fertility clinic, ethical decisions and consequences need to be incorporated into the game's core mechanic. The complexity of the treatment phase of the game was increased to match the content, specifically by including all the key ethical decisions that a doctor and patient would have to consider in the course of fertility treatment.

Testing

Seeds was developed using an iterative process, with informal testing integrated at each stage of development. In the ongoing formal testing of the methodology for ethical game play, behavioral cues from the players supported what the research suggested—that role-play and emotional engagement with rich content is a sound strategy for encouraging ethical reflection. If, upon responding to the ethical challenges each patient posed, players developed a play pattern that was inconsistent with their profile type, and the players recognized their behavior in the new play pattern, the system is working.

Proof of concept for this project came early on during the paper prototyping phase. During a playtest, a player self-identified as an Entrepreneur, believing solidly that, like any other medical service, fertility medicine was primarily a business. She began by accepting all lucrative patients regardless of their low probability of success. By the fifth patient, her behavior suddenly changed, and she began rejecting patients with low probabilities of success, stating that she was "feeling like slime" for taking advantage of patients and giving them false hope. The player confessed to changing her mind about one aspect of Assisted Reproductive Technology.

Players often voiced a conflict between their own beliefs and the beliefs of the character role as they understood it. Though the performance of the Entrepreneur, Mad-Scientist, or Miracle-Worker role sometimes influenced how players made decisions during the game, this also provided an experience to explore a point of view that was not their own. During a later playtests of the digital prototype, one player exhibited a struggle with the introduction survey. With each question, she vocalized what she thought the "correct" answer was, though her personal opinion differed. This illustrates recognition of an ethical debate with multiple valid points of view. This player was profiled as a Mad Scientist upon starting the game. After losing money early in the game, she began to consistently prescribe the more expensive treatments. Her play pattern cast her as the Entrepreneur profile type. Similarly, another play tester who was profiled as a Miracle Worker type at the start of the game, found herself playing more like the Mad Scientist, when she wanted to her patient to donate her leftover embryos to science, rather than have them adopted.

As players are confronted with more developed characters, rendered in video and images, as well as text, players were less inclined to reject patients casually illustrating an emotional connection to the characters and the ethical struggles they present. Where players do consistently reject patients, it is because of a clearly stated moral objection. This at least proves that players are ethically engaged in the content.

FUTURE RESEARCH DIRECTIONS

As testing continues, it has become apparent that the project would benefit from a more sophisticated method for assessing player's ethical point of view at the start of the game. A method that captures the nuance of each ethical conflict and all the gray areas in between the three major vectors outlined in this iteration of seeds may provide for a more credible and stimulating experience. The three profile types currently featured in the game represent the primary archetypes and viewpoints in this field of medicine. Expanding upon these three roles and increasing the level of detail and nuance would enrich the experience.

Future possibilities for expanding on *Seeds* also include further developing the narratives featured in the game. Further, developing the patient characters and their narrative could also increase empathy for the characters and enrich the experience. Similarly, the addition of rich non-player characters, or a return to the social play model tested in the early phases of development may also increase the level of engagement

Further, as the methodology for ethics evaluation continues to be rigorously tested, it may prove useful to apply this methodology to other fields of study with emergent ethical conflict, such as financial ethics or military ethics, to better understand where the strengths and weaknesses of this methodology lie, and if it indeed is an

improvement on ethical simulation software as it stands today.

CONCLUSION

Assisted Reproductive Technology allows us to create life in ways that have never before been possible, however the long-term risks involved in using this technology are not fully understood. The fertility industry is largely privatized and un-regulated. Profit motives lead to rapid growth and sometimes irresponsible and reckless treatment of patients. Also, as a consumer industry, doctors are often compelled to honor patients' requests, even where they conflict with the patients' best interest. These three forces map very clearly onto traditional role-playing game elements. Players earn money by treating (or cheating) patients. Doctors advance science by taking risks, and putting your patient first may help or hurt you. Each patient the player treats presents a unique ethical conflict, and within each treatment cycle the player must make an array of decisions ranging from choosing donors to what to do with left over embryos. Regardless of what a player's ethical stance is upon entering the game, there is enough provocative material to challenge a wide range of beliefs. Also, knowing the player's profile allows us to customize the experience so that that we can challenge their specific beliefs.

Further, few of the currently available ethics simulation software products take advantage of the natural affordances of interactive digital media and the game literacy of modern audiences. Role-playing games, for instance, focus on developing characters through experience, accumulating wealth and status, and managing resources or inventory (Fullerton, 2008). Map the real world concerns of growing a business and personal character growth to this type of framework and you have a natural fit for an ethics simulation game. In this case, however, rather than leveling-up the status of your player character, you would be developing your own moral character. Digital games, virtual spaces, and interactive media are commonly used to place the user in another character's shoes, to experience his or her world and conflicts from a designed point of view. As a passive spectator it is easy to pass judgment on the right or wrong choice, or the obvious ethical choice given a particular narrative. Actions, however, speak louder than words. Ethical choices are simply easier said than done.

As the ethical complexity of our world increases, so does the need for our instructive and entertainment media to engage that complexity. For centuries people have used drama to engage and discuss ethical struggle. Interactive media has the capacity to not only involve us directly in the drama, but more deeply into the ethical conflict. By feeling, rather than watching, the dramatic tension over these ethical questions, we may better prepare ourselves to answer these questions when we come to face them in our own lives.

ACKNOWLEDGMENT

The author would like to thank her thesis advisors Professors Tracy Fullerton, Steve Anderson, and Topper Lilien of The Univeristy of Southern California's School of Cinematic Arts, as well as Laird Malamed, Senior Vice President of Production, Activision. This project was funded by a fellowship from Fox Interactive.

REFERENCES

Bogost, I. (2007). *Persuasive games: The expressive power of video games*. Cambridge, MA: The MIT Press.

Deech, R., & Smajdor, A. (2007). *From IVF to immortality: Controversy in the era of reproductive technology*. Oxford, UK: Oxford University Press. doi:10.1093/acprof:oso/9780199219780.001.0001

Fullerton, T. (2008). *Game design workshop*. Burlington, MA: Morgan Kaufmann Publishers.

Hull, R. T. (2005). *Ethical issues in the new reproductive technologies* (2nd ed.). Amherst, NY: Prometheus Books.

Kohl, B. (2007). *Embryo culture: Making babies in the 21st century*. New York: Farrar, Straus and Giroux.

Levitt, P. (2010). USC Zilkha Neurogenetic Institute. Interview taken on February 3, 2010.

Mundy, L. (2007). *Everything Conceivable: How assisted reproduction is changing our World*. New York, NY: Anchor Books.

Salen, K., & Zimmerman, E. (2003). *Rules of play: Game design fundamentals*. Cambridge, MA: The MIT Press.

Sicart, M. (2009). *Ethics of computer games*. Cambridge, MA: The MIT Press.

Simkins, D. (2010). Playing with ethics: Experiencing new ways of being in RPGs. In Schrier, K., & Gibson, D. (Eds.), *Ethics and game design: Teaching values through play*. Hershey, PA: Information Science Reference.

United States Office of Government Ethics. (2009). *Technology saves time and money in ethics training*. Retrieved December 10, 2009, from http://www.usoge.gov/ethics_docs/agency_model_prac/tech_saves.aspx

Washington, A. T. (2009, February 18). Babies, pregnancy, grab media's glare. *Washington Times*.

Chapter 18

Games, Ethics and Engagement:
Potential Consequences of Civic-Minded Game Design and Gameplay

Sharman Siebenthal Adams
University of Michigan-Flint, USA

Jeremiah Holden
InGlobal, USA

ABSTRACT

This chapter examines ethical ambiguities confronted by the design and play of serious games focused on civic engagement. Our findings derive from our examination of two educational simulation games that focus on contemporary issues related to social and political conflict. We believe game simulations are complex in nature and offer particularly rich environments for cognitive learning. Within the following chapter we examine the relationship between games and learning, specific approaches to game design, and the ability of games to encourage civic engagement. While we found that game participants gained knowledge of curricular content and practiced democratic skills during their experiences with the online simulations, there also occurred unintended consequences. In turn, we believe it is critical to analyze deeper ethical ambiguities related to the consequences of civic-minded game design and gameplay and support research efforts to further recognize and expand upon the development and research of serious games involving civic-minded educational online simulations.

INTRODUCTION

Within the following chapter we use two simulation games to focus on better understanding ethical ambiguities that arise from the design and play of games whose themes and content relate to contemporary social and political conflict. Building upon Shaffer, Squire, Halverson and

Gee's (2005) argument that games are "...most powerful when they are personally meaningful, experiential, social, and epistemological all at the same time" (Shaffer, Squire, Halverson & Gee, 2005, p. 3), we believe a specific subset of games—simulations—offer particularly rich and textured opportunities to explore the ethical ambiguities of design and play. As game designers and researchers, we borrow our definitions of simulations from Aldrich (2006, 2004), de Freitas (2006), and Frasca

DOI: 10.4018/978-1-60960-120-1.ch018

Copyright © 2011, IGI Global. Copying or distributing in print or electronic forms without written permission of IGI Global is prohibited.

(2003), noting that participants in these types of games adopt and interact through defined roles, often work collaboratively, solve problems based upon real-world dilemmas, and are immersed in virtual and in-person experiences with outcomes not easily categorized by wins and losses. Having created and studied games and simulations, we believe that when the dynamics of design and play intersect, the opportunities for learning are as rich as the possible ethical conflicts are complex. As a result, we argue that the importance of games to learning is deepened when the ethical ambiguities associated with design and play are studied and better theorized. In particular, it is our hope that the present research contributes to a growing discussion about the importance of learning, games, and ethics as applied to serious games involving civic-minded simulations.

In this chapter, we first exam and substantiate our position on the type of game 'play' found within our case studies. In doing so we delve into the role of serious games and the triad that exists between ludology, narratology, and affect. Examination of this triad sets up analysis of our work further by first pulling apart the importance of the third component of the triad, that of affect. In turn, we examine important aspects of affect related to game design and gameplay to further substantiate our research work on civic-minded game design and gameplay. These include; (1) the relationship between games and learning, (2) specific approaches to game design, and (3) the ability of games to encourage civic engagement. Following these sections, our research describes and analyzes two case studies involving educational online simulations that focus learning on civic engagement through participants' exposure to simulations that place individuals in ethically challenging contexts. These case studies are *The Arab Israeli Conflict* (AIC) and *First Wind* (FW).

Findings from these two case studies are then presented in the form of intended and unintended consequences that affect both game designers and players. Following summation of our findings, we

offer important avenues for scholars to consider in terms of potential future research involving serious games and the inclusion of civic content and action. Finally we provide concluding remarks in the form of ethical concerns that we believe should be considered by game designers, players, and individuals who use serious games for learning purposes.

Defining Gameplay

Once thought of as simply opportunities for "play," games have proven to be far more complex than initially given credit. As Malaby (2007) points out, it is often our misinterpretation about the power of games that impedes our greater understanding of these resources. One salient entrance into our examination of ethical ambiguities and game simulations begins with Frasca (2003) and her discussion of ludology, the formal discipline of game studies. While primarily concerned with introducing ludology within contexts of game authorship and narrative, Frasca differentiates between the design of games and the design of simulations as experiences for "experimentation where user action is not only allowed but also required" (Frasca, 2003, p. 229). Building upon a discussion of ludology, Simkins and Steinkuehler further posit that working in combination, "... the triad of ludology, narratology, and affect can help us understand how story, play, and feeling intertwine to create effective gameplay" (Simkins & Steinkuehler, 2008, p. 19).

As we move to examine the second aspect of the triad, we see that narratology within the role of game design and gameplay is described by the differences between "narrauthors" and "simauthors" (Frasca, 2003). Within contextual settings where "winning" a game is seen as a primary objective, and threat of loss is a motivation for rigidly defined success, games are designed by narrauthors who base their narratives upon fixed sequences of cause and effect events. Alternatively, games that allow for different degrees of fate, or possibilities of outcomes, are akin to simulations and are designed by simauthors. Importantly, simauthors "'educate' their simulations: they teach them some rules and may have an idea of how they might behave in the future, but they can never be sure of the exact final sequence of events and result" (Frasca, 2003, p. 229). The ambiguity surrounding unknown events and results derives from a key characteristic of simulations–the role of rules. As Frasca notes, "Rules... can be manipulated, accepted, rejected and even contested" (2003, p.229). Consequently, simauthors become similar to legislators who "craft laws," as "they do take more authorial risks than narrauthors because they give away part of their control over their work" (Frasca, 2003, p. 229). We agree with Frasca and believe that simulations, the simauthors who design them, and the events of play all have complex relationships related to rules, control, and outcome. Indeed, we propose it is because simulations invite rule negotiation and the relinquishing of control that they become ripe locations for the study of learning, games, and ethics involving civic engagement.

The third portion of Simkins and Steinkuehler's triad, affect, guides game designers and players in their ability to further effect the game itself. It is this aspect of the triad we feel most greatly impacts the following two case studies. Simkins and Steinkuehler (2008) note that the "...ability to make choices that affect the game world is one of the most basic in creating opportunities for ethical decision making" (Simkins & Steinkuehler, 2008, p. 16). As a result they argue that their "... first criteria for fostering ethical decision making within the context of a game is fairly simple: Player choices must have the potential to effect change in the world of which they are a part" (ibid, p. 16). Within the case study portion of this chapter, we describe and analyze two cases of educational online simulations that illustrate a variety of ethical conflicts associated with affect, and most notably the effects of game design and play. In critically examining this area of research, it

is necessary to first review three important aspects of affect related to game design and gameplay: (1) the relationship between games and learning, (2) specific approaches to game design, and (3) the ability of games to encourage civic engagement.

Games and Learning

During the past few decades researchers have seen increased scholarship related to the educational value of games; from who plays games and what is played, to how games are played and designed, to where games are played (including within school environments) to myriad connections between games as social media and their role in digital literacy. Games can now be defined as "… applications using the characteristics of video and computer games to create engaging and immersive learning experiences for delivering specified learning goals, outcomes and experiences" (de Freitas, 2006, p. 9). As a result, games are now recognized as "…more than a multibillion-dollar industry, more than a compelling toy for both children and adults, more than a route to computer literacy, videogames are important because they let people participate in new worlds" (Shaffer, Squire, Halverson & Gee, 2005, p. 105).

While we do not concentrate on proving whether games should in fact reside within social or educational contexts, or a mix of both, it is worth citing Gee's argument that the "...theory of learning in good videogames is close to...best theories of learning in cognitive science" (Gee, 2007, p. 4). As a result, we argue that this analogy also applies to simulation games and while many would acknowledge that there are in fact both "good" games and "good" school learning environments, the opposite of both is also possible. Further, it is not only possible, but probable, that one could envision a poorly designed and/or underutilized game as much as a poorly planned and/or under-implemented classroom curriculum; one or both of these scenarios may not in fact support strong learning practices. Gee argues that "...good videogames build into their very designs good learning principles and that we should use these principles, with or without games, in schools, workplaces, and other learning sites" (2007, p. 214).

Because games allow players to think, talk, and act in new ways (Shaffer et al, 2005), educational videogames and simulations are frequently being utilized in school settings as "...learning happens best when learners are engaged in learning by making, creating, programming, and communicating" (Bers, 2008, p. 145). Bers (2008), Kafai (2006), and Peppler and Kafai (2007) have built upon Papert's (1981, 1980) long argued stance about the differences between "constructionist models of learning" and "instructionist models of learning," with the former placing learning more in the hands of the learner. Games and role-playing simulations allow for constructionist learning, providing students as players with strong identities, the opportunity to see the world in new ways, and "a real sense of agency, ownership, and control" (Gee, 2005, para 7). Additionally, game cultures feature participation in a collective intelligence, are designed to foster knowledge through creative productive acts (Squire, 2008), emphasize expertise rather than status, and promote international and cross-cultural media and communities (Squire & Steinkuehler, 2005). The educational benefit of constructionist games and simulations as learning experiences is well documented (de Freitas, 2006; Gee, 2008, 2005, 2004; Squire, 2006; Games for Change (n.d.); Papert 1981, 1980).

Since Clark C. Abt's *Serious Games* (1970), game studies researchers have increasingly examined the intentionally designed educational purposes of games in contrast to more traditional understandings of games as activities played primarily for amusement. Bogost's *Persuasive Games: The Expressive Power of VideoGames* (2007) defines serious games as "videogames created to support the existing and established interests of political, corporate, and social institutions" (Bogost, 2007, p. 57). In turn, serious games engage learners, keep motivation for gameplay high (de Freitas & Griffiths, 2007), and have led to the emergence of communities of practice that share practical knowledge in pursuit of social change.

Despite growing acceptance that videogames and simulations proactively contribute to learning, some scholars have contested the ability of educational videogames to produce concrete learning outcomes and suggest that if the impact of computer games is to shift from malign to benign, issues of learning versus play, transference of game knowledge to other contexts, and the surrounding social environment must be concretely addressed (Egenfeldt-Nielsen, 2005).

With respect to ongoing discussions about the relationships between games and learning, this chapter examines the ethical ambiguities resulting from games designed to support civic content and action while generating constructionist learning experiences.

Approaches to Game Design

The overall importance of game design is evidenced by the fact that serious games have become rigorously "designed experiences," capable of achieving a variety of educational objectives, including recruiting diverse interests, promoting creative problem solving, creating productive acts such as game modification and modeling, and establishing digital literacies that produce meaning and tangible artifacts (Squire, 2008). If serious games are to serve a purpose greater than play and amusement, effective design elements must guide players' specific behaviors and attitudes, as well as influence the substantial relationship between players and game knowledge.

Squire (2006) argues that a game's learning objectives, whether perspective-taking or creative problem solving, are dependent upon a game designed and sustained by "powerful constraints" that promote engagement and foster learning (Squire, 2006). Such powerful constraints acknowledge the thoughtful approach taken to serious game design, an approach aptly summarized by Squire and Jenkins (2003); "Ultimately, educational game design is not just about creating rules or writing computer codes; it is a form of social engineering, as one tries to map out situations that will encourage learners to collaborate to solve compelling problems" (p. 30).

Collins and Halverson (2009) cite Squire's research on the game *Civilization*, noting that students who played strategy games based upon history began to "...check out books on ancient cultures and earn better grades in middle school" (2009, p. 132). Gee argues that gamers are required to "...draw on resources that reside in other gamers and their associate websites, and social interactions, resources such as strategy guides ('faqs'), cheats, boards, game modifications, magazines, review sites, Local Area Network (LAN) parties, and even schoolyard trading of Pokemon secrets" (Gee, 2007, p. 8). Effective and intentional game design can encourage a variety of learning activities, from reading broadly across a range of related fields (Squire & Jenkins, 2003), to the self-initiated research gamers are motivated to engage so as to improve game performance (Gee, 2007).

While some have noted that "we are a long way from having tapped the full pedagogical potentials of existing game hardware and design practices" (Squire & Jenkins, 2003, p. 30), designers and researchers have begun to proactively address the question; "How do good game designers manage to get new players to learn long, complex, and difficult games?" (Gee, 2004, p. 15). One possible answer to Gee's query is to approach game design through a framework sensitive to and supportive of specific values. Both simulation case studies examined within this chapter were significantly influenced by the role of values as an influence upon the design process. In terms of design, the creation of certain serious games can be analyzed using the Value Sensitive Design (VSD) framework, a methodology that examines the relationship between human values and computer systems.

Historically, the VSD framework emerged from an interest concerning the inclusion of human values in the design of computer systems such as digital media. VSD primarily focuses upon "enduring human values" (Friedman, Kahn & Borning, 2006, 2001), values such as autonomy, welfare, and accountability–and how these personal orientations are incorporated into the technical development and design of interactive technologies. Accounting for human values in the design process by integrating ethical considerations in development, for example, is accomplished through the VSD approach (Friedman, 1997). The methodological approach to game design offered by VSD is useful for examining various elements and dynamics central to serious games as educational technologies, and aligns well with the two simulations examined within this paper.

In addition to gameplay that encourages competitiveness and perseverance, a game's content or play might be designed to promote a set of values aligned with equality, conflict resolution, and advocacy–values directly associated with the ideals and practices of an engaged citizen. Game creators and researchers Flanagan and Nissenbaum (2007) argue in favor of such a complementary relationship between game design, values, and civic-mindfulness, demonstrating how game design may inherently incorporate certain social and civic values. Educational technologies such as serious games can promote values and engagement "to which the surrounding societies and cultures subscribe. These values might include liberty, justice, inclusion, equality, privacy, security, creativity, trust, and personal autonomy" (Flanagan & Nissenbaum, 2007, p. 2). In turn, serious games can be designed to offer play experiences promoting distinct sets of values, and as such value orientations may directly encourage role-play and democratic skill building in support of civic engagement.

Videogames and Civic Engagement

As game designers and players, we are encouraged by the opinions of individuals such as Michael Mino, director of the Education Connection's Center for 21st Century Skills, who believes that "if we have any hope of saving the real world from real problems, we must embrace teaching students through computer games and virtual simulations" (Libby, 2009, p. 2). As games studies researchers, however, we must critically examine such hopes by further investigating the possibility of games that may lead students towards "saving the real world from real problems." Scholars such as Bennett (2008) have examined the relationship between digital media and civic engagement, noting the emergence of new paradigms such as "Actualizing Citizens" who demonstrate a higher sense of individual purpose, personally define meaning associated with civic acts such as consumerism and volunteering, and favor loose networks of community action maintained by interactive technologies.

Critics, however, have questioned how traditional or novel conceptions of civic engagement may be related to or supported by games. Given such concerns, our research draws upon current interest regarding videogames and civic engagement. In addition to designing games to promote democratic and civic values (Flanagan & Nissenbaum, 2007; Flanagan, Howe & Nissenbaum, 2008), games may be designed to include content that is political in nature–such as the activities and tasks characterized by the two simulations within this chapter. Importantly, research has now confirmed that the processes of gameplay, regardless of whether game content is specifically political, can promote dispositions towards civic engagement (Lenhart et al., 2008). In regards to our present research, we define civic engagement gameplay as play that is based upon civic content such as politics, economics, and society; play that encourages democratically oriented skills such as communication, negotiation, and problem solv-

ing; play that fosters responsibility to co-create the game; and play that provides advocacy opportunities.

Research by Jenkins (2007a) and Jenkins, Clinton, Purushotma, Robison and Weigel (2006) has documented how digital, internet-based games and other media represent one concrete means to facilitate and engage in interactive participatory cultures that support artistic expression, informal mentorship, collaboration and sharing, social connections, and civic engagement. More specifically, virtual environments and games may be designed to provide "access to a wide range of information and resources, communication mechanisms for engaging in critical debates, and tools for supporting collaboration and for enabling new expressions of social life, [and] they can serve as powerful platforms for developing educational programs to promote civic education" (Bers, 2008, p. 141). The process of playing digital videogames, especially those games whose content explicitly relates to political and social issues, parallels the dynamic and complex nature of the real world and real problems, and "understanding [these social and political problems] involves analyzing cause and effect, multiple viewpoints, and rapidly shifting scenarios. Games easily mirror this fluidity" (Platoni, 2009, p. 1). Indeed, the growing relationship between games and civic engagement is further inspired by the belief that our society can "reimagine the relationship between participatory culture and participatory democracy, embracing new political language and images that mobilize us as fans as well as citizens" (Jenkins, 2007b, p. 1).

The ability of digital videogames to mobilize players as citizens invested in civic engagement is highlighted in the recent *Teens, Videogames and Civics* (Lenhart et al., 2008) study. This study offers a mixed assessment related to specific civic engagement indicators such as following politics, persuading others how to vote, contributing to charities, volunteering, or staying informed about politics and current events, and reveals some encouraging signs related to the relationship between videogames and teenage civic engagement. Some critics noted that the study found no positive correlation between the frequency of gameplay or amount of time spent playing games and a significant increase in civic and political outcomes. However, findings did confirm that:

Certain kinds of gameplay do appear to foster higher levels of civic engagement. The social context of gaming offers opportunities for "civic gaming experiences," in which players have opportunities to help or guide other players; learn about problems in society; think about moral or ethical issues; help make decisions about how a simulated community, city, or nation should be run; and organize game groups or guilds. (Perkins-Gough, 2009, p. 94)

Perhaps the most significant finding of the *Teens, Videogames and Civics* study relates to these "civic gaming experiences." Study participants who identified themselves as encountering these types of gaming experiences "sometimes" while also having several experiences "frequently"–a full 25 percent of all respondents–reported "much higher levels of civic and political engagement than teens who have not had these kinds of experiences" (Lenhart et al., 2008, p. 75). Specifically, these game players were "more likely to go online to get information about politics or current events, to raise money for charity, to say they are committed to civic participation, to express an interest in politics, to stay informed about current events, and to participate in protests, marches, or demonstrations" (Perkins-Gough, 2009, p. 94). Findings related to civic gaming experiences were statistically significant for all eight of the civic outcomes considered (Lenhart et al., 2008), and have been further supported by additional studies confirming that videogame play can lead towards civic engagement (Library Technology Reports, 2009a, 2009b). Similar to the constructionist education tradition helping to establish meaningful relationships between learning and videogame play, so too has research begun to prove a positive relationship between games and civic engagement.

CIVIC ENGAGEMENT THROUGH GAMEPLAY: TWO CASE STUDIES

Overview of Cases

We believe games are more than playful distractions or theoretical exercises in narrative construction; rather, they can be designed to introduce players to real world problems through content and play processes that are serious, a benefit to learning, and a means to engage in civic action and discourse. To design and study games as experiences central to constructionist learning processes, we draw upon Malaby's (2007) analysis of the relationship between games and society. Writing about games as social artifacts characterized by process, Malaby notes, "Ironically, it is how we have sought to account for what is remarkable about games by setting them apart (as play-spaces, as stories) that is the largest roadblock to understanding what is powerful about them" (Malaby, 2007, p. 96). We wish to remove that roadblock and place games front and center in a discussion concerning learning, play, ethics and real world civic engagement. The following two case studies aim to demonstrate how power and meaning are generated as games promote civic engagement and create ethically ambiguous consequences related to principles of design and practices of play.

As game designers and researchers, we investigate simulations that draw upon a tradition of constructionist education, invest players in solving problems based upon real world social and political conflict, and—we hope and believe—encourage civic engagement and mindfulness. Simulations, unlike some games, allow players to "replay" history (Collins & Halverson, 2009; Squire 2008, 2006), and this "replay" factor is of particular importance as it can repeatedly expose students to content about political and social conflict, and allow for repetitive participation in play processes and game activities that encourage civic engagement and discourse. Additionally, the play of simulations—which we believe is both powerful and valuable for learning–is, as noted earlier when discussing Frasca's (2003) distinctions between narrauthors and simauthors, textured with dynamics of control and negotiation. Consequently, gameplay of these interactive, educational experiences is inherently ethically ambiguous.

Just as the simulations we describe offer players opportunities to adopt and interact through various roles, the authors have themselves "played" many roles in the creation, implementation, and study of each simulation. These roles included game player, mentor to other players, administrator and designer, developer and programmer, professor, research supervisor and finally research assistant. Following the presentation of these two case studies, we offer a comparative analysis related to learning, civic engagement, and the ethical conflicts and consequences that arose from design and play processes.

Case Study One: *The Arab Israeli Conflict* (AIC)

The Arab Israeli Conflict (AIC) is a web-based game that simulates geopolitical crises and negotiations associated with various Middle East conflicts. Hosted for nearly two decades by the University of Michigan Department of Education's Interactive Communications and Simulations (ICS) group, teams of students are assigned roles as politicians and other influential government and cultural leaders who work together in country and organization-specific teams to role-play a variety of political, economic, and social scenarios through online interactions. For example, three students may play a team representing the Israeli government, with students role-playing the prime minister, foreign minister, and chief military commander, while another team of students represents the United Nations and various officials within that organization. Nearly two-dozen teams, comprised of students at K-12 schools in numerous countries around the world, play the

various countries, international organizations, and political entities critical to the negotiation of conflict throughout the Middle East. Amongst its goals, AIC exposes players to civic-minded social studies content such as history, politics, and culture while simultaneously managing the use of this content in simulated teamwork and communication challenges that facilitate processes of conflict resolution and non-resolution.

Before the play of AIC begins, participating students prepare for gameplay by conducting research about the political figures whom they will be role-playing, the countries they are representing, historical events critical to understanding tensions within the region, and policies that currently shape society and governance in the Middle East. After preparation concludes, play begins for a period lasting approximately ten weeks. While AIC is based upon real world circumstances, once gameplay begins only decisions and events internal to the game change the course of action. For example, were a real world Syrian politician to be wrested from office due to scandal a week after play commenced, the role of the politician within AIC would remain unchanged. As students communicate and propose actions in the best interest of their countries, organizations, or political entities, various groups of adults support and facilitate the progress of play. Classroom teachers provide immediate assistance with both content and decision-making, and an additional group of advisors comprised of faculty and students at the University of Michigan provide technical assistance, guidance in strategy, and determine final actions within the game.

When looking specifically at the interactions between players, AIC is characterized by a variety of play patterns. These forms of interaction occur both in-character, as students play various politicians and government officials, as well as out-of-character, as students make decisions based upon their own ideas or motivations when working with their country teams. In-character communication most frequently occurs online as students commu-

Figure 1. A screenshot from AIC that shows an example of the game

nicate with other teams by sending communiqués between characters (a simplified form of email), write and publish press releases to a game-wide audience in order to report on events or comment upon policy proposals (similar to blog posts), and submit action forms (a plan outlining a team's proposed action), which, upon approval from a game mentor, determine actions related to various game scenarios. Out-of-character communication most frequently occurs offline between players on the same country team, and is often related to decisions about the game content and future interactions with other characters and teams.

Case Study Two: *First Wind*

First Wind, also a web-based game, simulates the economic supply chain of product creation and consumption as these processes relate to fair labor and globalization. *First Wind* was developed in

partnership between the University of Michigan-Flint's Masters Level Global Program: Technology in Education, and the Fair Labor Organization (FLA), an international nongovernmental organization dedicated to ending sweatshop conditions (Fair Labor Association, 2008). The game was named after the real world Chen Feng silk factory outside Shanghai, China, a factory itself in partnership with the FLA. *First Wind* was piloted for a single semester in the spring of 2008 between four teams of high school and college students in five different locations throughout the United States. Teams of players were assigned to various roles in the supply chain, including factory workers and managers, business executives, code compliance officers from the Fair Labor Association, and American consumers. The goal of *First Wind* was to provide players with opportunities to construct understandings of economic and political issues, negotiate the complexities of globalization and

Figure 2. A screenshot from FW that shows an example of the game

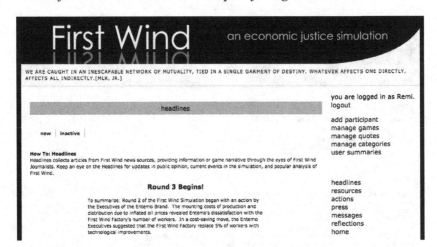

fair labor, and encourage the translation of learning experiences into advocacy for social change.

Like AIC, *First Wind* began with weeks of preparation as players researched issues and statistics related to labor, production and consumption, learned about the political and economic history of China, and researched the history and policies of fair labor practice. Players also all learned about the Fair Labor Association and its role as arbiter of compliance code, policy, and business partnership related to international fair labor standards. Play in *First Wind* was structured around successive rounds of interaction, with each of the four role-groups leading a weeklong round. Rounds began with a specific action initiated via interactive tools based upon a design structure similar to that of AIC, where action forms proposed a single event or a series of events to alter game-play within a round, and press releases reported on actions or policies to the entire game community. Once one role-group began a round with an action, the three other groups reacted to the initial action, establishing cause and effect interactions between players and teams. Actions and their related communications and press releases began, sustained, and concluded weeklong rounds of play, all of which were guided by classroom teachers serving as simulation facilitators. After completion of four rounds of play, players re-

flected on lessons learned and created a fair labor best practices document suitable for submission to the FLA and real world businesses as a form of political and economic fair labor advocacy.

Online player interactions and communication in *First Wind* were distinguishable between those that were distinctly in character versus those that were considered out-of-character. In character communication was facilitated online through messages using a simplified email system much like that of the aforementioned AIC communiqués. Such messages allowed players to communicate with other teams in order to discuss events and send messages to fellow role-group members to help in decision-making processes. In character communication also occurred off-line as players worked as a team to make decisions about game-play, such as submitting action forms or writing press releases. Out-of-character communication also occurred both online and offline. Online, out-of-character communication took place within a reflection forum (modeled after typical blog posts) that allowed players to comment on the progress of the game throughout the four rounds of play. Semi-structured reflection questions facilitated this out-of-character communication within the reflection forum. Offline out-of-character communication occurred as players commented on the progress of the game and reflected upon consequences of action and patterns of interaction that emerged over the four rounds of play.

Similarities of Games Encouraging Civic Engagement

We define civic engagement as play based upon content related to politics, economics, and society; play that allows for the practice of democratic skills such as communication, negotiation, and problem-solving; play that encourages a sense of responsibility to co-create the game; and play that provides game-based and real-world opportunities for advocacy. The following chart outlines similarities of game-based civic engagement that exists across AIC and FW. Similarities of civic content and action included play with civic content, democratic skill building, co-creation of gameplay, and civic engagement opportunities.

Case Study Methodology: Game-Based Civic Engagement

Our case study methodology draws upon the qualitative research work of Miles and Huberman (1994), as well as a variety of narrative analysis devices that constitute what Lincoln and Guba (1985) call an "audit trail." Constructing audit trails for both AIC and FW occurred over many months, and in one case over many years, and included field notes, participants interviews, digital audio recordings, digital video recordings, and reflection and process notes. The following examples of game-based civic engagement draw from this primary research, with information about play and patterns of interaction in AIC from Kupperman (2002) and in FW from Chao and Holden (2008). Each are salient instances of engagement with civic content and action, and

Table 1. Comparing characteristics of AIC and FW

Characteristic/ Game	Playing with Civic Content	Democratic Skill-Building Through Play	Responsibility to Co-Create the Game	Opportunities for Civic Engagement
The Arab Israeli Conflict	Players wrote proposals and actions with best interests in mind, selectively analyzed data and history to support political agendas, manipulated allegiances and international governance organizations, and introduced facts or reports to create bias and/or support of play actions.	Players debated actions, proposed solutions, and solved problems while working as a team. They also communicated, negotiated, and resolved conflicts with those who disagreed, both on-line and off-line and between their own teammates and across other teams.	Players actively introduced content, made decisions based upon interpretations of content, and produced strategies in order to win. Winning required the responsibility of creating innovative strategies. Also, players initiated advocacy and introduced negotiation to manage content and game interactions.	Players advocated for policy positions and specific action plans, argued in support of agendas and policies with both team members and with members of other country teams. Advocacy was seen as an essential component of successful strategy.
First Wind	Players manipulated civic content to fit the "world view" of specific group role. Players both disregarded and promoted the importance of selective content and background information. Players and teams relied upon hierarchical systems of economic, social, and political power, whether real or imagined.	The action and reaction, cause and effect, structure of the four-round game provided unique engagement with the democratic practices of negotiation and communication. This trial and error approach to problem solving and conflict resolution paralleled democratic processes of decision-making used in a variety of simulated and real world contexts.	Players had a responsibility to test and implement effective strategies as the four-round structure of play allowed players to reflect upon the successes and failures of actions. This provided repetitious "replay" opportunities to advocate for policies and actions, and further enforced cyclical learning processes that players created, owned, and controlled.	Participants were provided with formal advocacy opportunities post game play after having developed fair labor best practices. These best practices were presented to the Fair Labor Association and, in turn, real world businesses invested in practicing and promoting fair labor as one aspect of a commitment to greater corporate social responsibility.

are indicative of similar play experiences that occurred throughout both games.

The four characteristics and similarities of simulations encouraging civic engagement from Table 1 are each highlighted with an example from either AIC or FW. Given predominant similarities in design and play between the two simulations, the following examples note instances of play that were particularly salient to a characteristic of civic engagement.

Playing with Civic Content in *First Wind*

Participants in FW engaged, manipulated, and reflected upon play with civic content. A scenario established before gameplay was referenced as a starting point for action and exposed players to the impact of economic policy and instability through a fictitious crisis involving the Organization of Petroleum Exporting Countries (OPEC). Summaries of four rounds of FW play reveal an influence on team choices and decision-making. The first round was characterized by unilateral decision-making regarding regulations for product consumption and distribution, with the factory and brand each creating new independent business partnerships to increase sales. Round two focused upon the impact of economic and health care policies on factory workers and consumers, ultimately resulting in decreased sales and a new brand-initiated company partnership. The third round centered upon negotiations concerning product volume, commitments towards the use of alternative energy and increased health care benefits, and greater consumer confidence. The fourth and final round revealed fair labor code compliance violations, resulting in corporate social responsibility proposals and charges of manipulation and fabrication.

Reflections made by FW participants, after each round, further support the engagement individual players had with civic content and realistic and constructed notions of economic, political, and social power. Data from participant transcripts illustrate interaction patterns revealing how decisions were made as students continued to play with civic content. A reflection after the fourth round by a player of the brand team emphasized how playing with civic content involved selective use of data and manipulation of strategy within fluctuating hierarchies, resulting in decisions intentionally aligned to an ideal win state:

Player 3: "When I'm trying to manipulate or figure out how to win, I'm thinking about how to get over the factory workers, and how to slip by the FLA and I guess I should also want to please my consumers but I feel like I don't think about that unless I feel threatened by them. I assume they'll always be there ready to buy from me unless they're like, 'Amazon,' and then I'm like, 'Oh no no no, wait, wait, wait."

Democratic Skill-Building through Play in *The Arab Israeli Conflict* (AIC)

By playing with civic content, participants in AIC developed a fluency in the practice of certain democratic skills. Democratic skill-building occurred as participants debated actions within team groups, chose courses of action, made recommendations or demands to other teams, negotiated solutions, and engaged processes of conflict resolution and non-resolution. By developing and experimenting with certain democratic skills, players' actions aligned to civic values such as equality and independence reflected by their broader society and culture. Throughout the course of the simulation, players and teams in AIC refined the use of democratic skills, established more effective interaction and win strategies, and increased investment in play based upon civic content.

The prevalence of democratic skill building through play is illustrated by a post-simulation reflection by a player concerning the effectiveness of negotiation. The following example demonstrates a player, and that player's team's, struggles with various dynamics associated with negotiation processes, including effective communication, goal development, and resolution:

As Ehud Barak, Israeli prime minister, it was imperitive [sic] that the Israeli team constantly negotiate with many teams in order to accomplish any of our goals. Despite numerous attempts to negotiate with many teams, we had trouble negotiating. There was one main reason for this. Many countries could not specifically state their demands or goals, and this made it very difficult to negotiate. Although Israel was willing to negotiate with many countries, we were unable to since the countries we wanted to talk to would not provide us with specific goals which we could work from. If countries did provide specific goals, they usually addressed a separate topic, not the one currently being discussed. In the one case where a country provided very specific and tangible goals, they did not represent the aims of there own country, but that of three others. Therefore, it was impossible to work with that country.

Co-Creation of Gameplay in *The Arab Israeli Conflict* (AIC)

It is worthwhile returning to Frasca (2003) to emphasize that the nature of simulations given their design is one in which it impossible to "be sure of the exact final sequence of events and result" (Frasca, 2003, p. 229); simulations, by definition, require students to take responsibility in co-creating the game. Participants in AIC did so actively, co-creating the events and outcomes of gameplay based upon their knowledge and interpretation of geopolitics and history, experiences with conflict and negotiation, and individual creativity. Through individual communications sent between players and actions initiated by teams, the simulation's design afforded those participating in AIC unique opportunities to determine the direction of gameplay, raise and debate policy,

and create an environment within which to make their own decisions.

A communication sent by a student role-playing Israeli Prime Minister Ehud Barak to Syrian Foreign Minister Farouk al-Sharaa is illustrative of game co-creation. In this example, the broad issue of security in the Golan Heights is discussed in relation to five specific measures. The decision to include and emphasize these measures, however, was initiated through student-centered research and decision-making, just as the broader focus on negotiating Golan Heights security was an issue co-created by participants through play. The communiqué reads in part:

I believe we need to first focus on small details, and not on solving the entire Golan Heights problem. Israel would first like to discuss the issue of security. We believe that before anything can be done in the heights the issue of security needs to be resolved. Therefore, Israel would like to provide some of the security measures that we would like to see in the area, and that we can talk about in our negotiations.

1. *Israel would like to keep our early warning station in the region.*
2. *Israel would like a peace keeping force occupy the area after Israel has left, UN or otherwise.*
3. *Israel would like a new demilitarized zone in the Golan Heights.*
4. *Cooperation from Israel and Syria to control terrorist and militant groups from travelling through the area into either of the countries.*
5. *All citizens living in the Golan Heights to comply to strict security measures.*

I believe that by negotiating on these measures can lead to further negotiations dealing with the entire Golan problem. Lets us negotiate about security, and let us meet soon.

Civic Engagement Opportunities in *First Wind*

Following gameplay, participants in each FW team created a role-specific best practices document for use in real world civic engagement activities. For example, students who role-played the Entemo brand executives reflected upon their gameplay and then created a document highlighting corporate social responsibility and the protection of fair labor. Students concluded that, "A company that values corporate social responsibility will integrate visionary executive leadership and collaborative corporate governance into its business practice." Similarly, students who role-played Fair Labor Association code compliance officers stated, "A successful relationship between a factory and the Fair Labor Association (FLA) should demonstrate effective communication, stakeholder involvement, and transparency." These best practices documents extrapolated game-based experiences to real-world dynamics of a globalized economy. Significantly, these documents were then shared with real-world business owners and representatives from the Fair Labor Association, providing participating students with an opportunity to share lesson learned while advocating for economic, business, and social policy in an authentic civic engagement activity.

AIC and FW offer the field of game studies important findings related to game design, gameplay, gaming as civic engagement, and ethics. AIC and FW successfully demonstrate how to incorporate content related to political and social conflict in game design. The games also encourage sustained civic engagement and advocacy through accessible, user-friendly platforms and play experiences. These characteristics, however, also present ethical concerns evidenced by various intended and unintended consequences associated with game design and gameplay.

ETHICAL ISSUES, CONTROVERSIES, AND PROBLEMS: INTENDED AND UNINTENDED CONSEQUENCES

The following section is divided into two subsections; the intended consequences found across both gameplay and game design, and the unintended consequences that researchers found analyzing participant use of *The Arab Israeli Conflict* (AIC) and *First Wind* (FW).

Intended Consequences

The intended consequences of gameplay and design may result in ethical conflict as students engaged real world problems and realistic scenarios constructed and facilitated by the game.

1. Game design characteristics promoted the practice of democratic skills as participants played each game. The games forced players to practice a "messy" process of decision-making that included interacting with other players and teams, in turn requiring communication skills, negotiation tactics, and engagement in simulated civic processes. The design of both games dictated that participants become part of democratic process through their practice of what Swain (2007) describes as "wicked problems." This process of play was neither easy nor "clean," and encompassed a complex set of ongoing and to-be-determined outcomes that arose from complex interactions and that could frequently conflict or become ethically challenging.

2. Engagement with civic content and action occurred, though participants may not have intended, or volunteered, to play a game where civic engagement was a norm. From a design perspective, however, engagement with civic issues and processes was an expected outcome of both AIC and FW. While

the practice of civic engagement happened by default within these gaming environments, the nature of this engagement is of ethical importance and may be a concern for the design and play of similar games.

3. AIC and FW gameplay encouraged connections between what players wanted to learn and what educators believed they should know. Students may have desired to learn a topic dichotomous to the intentions of the instructor, however these gaming environments were designed to blend the act of play with comprehension of critical content issues. The relationship between expectations of gameplay and content delivery may have led to further ethical ambiguity associated with civic content and action.

4. Constructionist learning principles guided gameplay and encouraged students to make connections between school-based learning and broader engagement with real world political and social issues. Gameplay sought to promote civic engagement activities as a way of learning and as a realistic real world activity, rather than only as a school-based topic or assignment. While some players did internalize game roles and transfer knowledge and skills to broader civic engagement issues, this concept of transference may raise ethical concerns related to game design.

5. Gameplay exposed controversial content and scenarios without discrete or "right" answers. The interactive nature of role-play ensured that no single player could anticipate future scenarios or outcomes. Also similar to Swain's (2007) embrace of "wicked problems," difficult and controversial scenarios developed unexpectedly and players were required to work within the game parameters to collaboratively find solutions. As topics and action did not correlate to one single right answer, players were forced to learn from one another and experiment with interventions. In working with one

another, ethically complex, and sometimes conflicting, solutions were devised based upon negotiated strategies and interactions.

Unintended Consequences

Unintended consequences related to the implementation games promoting civic content and action also present ethical conflicts and concerns. The following unintended consequences resulted from this research.

1. Play strategies were driven by a desire to win, leading democratic processes within the game to conform to win strategies. For example, as players negotiated policy proposals the quality of content and the democratic action of negotiation frequently deteriorated in favor of quicker, easier, less-equitable solutions. This often led to one constituency emerging more dominant and in a position with a greater likelihood of winning. As players sought to win games they pursued less ethical means of achieving victory rather than concentrating on civic engagement issues or game practices. In turn, the practice of resolving conflicts could become a vulnerability that jeopardized prospects of winning, and was therefore often pirated by players trying to win. Researchers found that some gaming practices were not ethically "clean;" instead, they were based on individual desires to win. In the end, some players' interest lay more solidly in the basic premise of a game to be won rather than a civic-minded activity requiring cycles of practice and negotiation. Our research found that gaming practices can be ethically ambiguous concerning the motivation and practice of participant gameplay.

2. Alternatively, AIC and FW allowed for civic engagement in meaningful ways not previously considered. Some students sought resources external to the game in order to

enhance the efficacy of their play. In some instances this taught players to meaningfully participate as citizens of both the game and the world at large. One such example included a student who began reading the newspaper each morning as part of his participation with AIC. In conjunction with his experiences in gameplay and in relation to life outside the game, this former student carried a new awareness about social justice, advocacy, and civic engagement into his adult life and now seeks out such news on a daily basis.

3. In both games, researchers found that promoting civic engagement required complex political, economic, and social issues to be simplified. While useful as a mechanism for clarifying content comprehension and implementing gameplay, this process may have caused participants to believe that civic engagement is, likewise, a simple process. In practice, civic engagement and political advocacy are as intricate and nuanced processes as are the complex real world issues they seek to address.

4. The curricular content and civic focus of AIC and FW placed the central issues of these games (for example, Middle East peace and fair labor) on a pedestal that may have caused participants to believe these issues were of primary importance in the realm of real world politics and civic engagement. Whether these social and political issues are of a greater importance is not the issue. Rather, designers must consider that the real world beliefs of players may become intertwined with the designed focus of a game based upon a simulated reality. The priorities and social values of game designers can become the real world priorities of game players. As a result, possible misrepresentation of the importance of political and social issues can occur, with game designers emphasizing a priority that may, or may not, be either realistic or ethically appropriate.

5. Participants may perceive their individual agency, as it relates to civic engagement, as dependent upon the construct of a game and the medium of gameplay. It is important that games promote civic engagement and knowledge of political and social issues as games have the opportunity to become vehicles for broad civic engagement. However, games should not train participants to believe that this medium is the only mode of individual agency leading towards civic engagement, or that civic engagement is a form of "play" with little to no real world consequence.

FUTURE RESEARCH DIRECTIONS: ANALYSIS OF ETHICAL CONSEQUENCES

In addition to the previously documented intended and unintended consequences related to the design of games supporting civic engagement through civic content and action, researchers were pleased to discover that game participants gained knowledge of curricular social studies content and practiced democratic skills during their experiences with the simulations. Researchers also noted that many players developed new understandings of issues related to social justice, ethics and civic engagement. Furthermore, this body of research caused designers and researchers to reflect upon the idea of what is most important to both gameplay and game design. As a result, researchers found that games could act as vehicles for civic engagement by connecting players to important global issues through civic content and action. When games serve as vehicles for civic engagement we found that players were exposed to controversial content and scenarios without discrete answers. As such, players were encouraged to pursue civic engagement activities more as a way of life rather than only as a topic or assignment. Findings related to conflict and ambiguity, as outlined in the previous section, illustrate the intended and unintended ethical consequences of gameplay and design, and also reveal the following four significant ethical concerns that should be considered by those interested in the relationship between educational gaming and civic engagement.

Forced Civic Engagement and Gameplay

The design of civic-minded games intends for players, whether or not they are interested or aware, to engage in highly structured ethical scenarios and civic engagement activities. In turn, researchers must examine these experiences perhaps more closely than that of players' perceptions towards more traditional games. In other words, an ethical challenge exists related to game design due to the fact that players may not have agreed to engage in gameplay with civic engagement processes in mind; rather, they may have assumed play was to be of a more traditional process. As a result, participants' experiences can and do have an impact on their perception of the world around them and future game design and research on civics-focused gameplay must take the ethical implications of forced civic engagement into consideration.

Corruption of Democratic Practices

Because the setting of these civic-minded activities is located within the context of a game, winning can threaten to overtake goals of civic engagement and democratic processes. Separate from an analysis of value associated with winning, the emphasis of a win-strategy can corrupt the practice of democratic processes such as conflict resolution, negotiation, and communication. This distortion leads to ethically dubious outcomes as players pursue a strategy to win rather than an ethic of play based upon values aligned with egalitarian ideals. For one player, such as the student who sought out a daily newspaper, this quest for external resources made him more knowledgeable and engaged with

game content. Conversely, another player could potentially use similar or alternative strategies to manipulate gameplay. As such, participants may learn that they can manipulate group practices, teamwork norms, and communication patterns so as to win or even 'position' certain other players to win. There are severe ethical implications related to players using civic engagement practices within games as a means for mastery or for winning the overall game. This in turn reveals the potential for further dubious action and the need for extended future research.

Changing Perspectives of Gameplay and Game Design

In examining our findings we realized that one might view many of the intended and unintended ethical consequences from multiple perspectives–namely, from either the perspective of game design or gameplay. This change in perspective sometimes alters whether or not the ethical conflict becomes itself an intended or unintended consequence. This ambiguity, in itself, is an ethical dilemma. While one participant may in fact see an outcome as an intended consequence, another participant may contradict this perspective by taking an inverse approach. In reexamining this body of work, we realize that certain design elements may themselves be ethically ambiguous conflicts related to the relationships between game design and gameplay, and between game designers and game players.

Ethical Assumptions of Civic Engagement Game Designers

Civic engagement game designers have inherent biases about the importance of civic engagement, political advocacy, and social justice issues presented within games. Values are intentional components of game design, are built into the intended consequences of gameplay, and are revealed in the unintended ethical consequences.

In revisiting the issue of exposing players to controversial and civic-minded scenarios, we further realize the potential for manipulation on behalf of game designers and note this ethical assumption and potential conflict of interest as an important direction for future scholarship and research.

CONCLUSION

We believe that assumptions made by game developers about civic engagement and specific values orientations must be further examined as central to the process of creating and implementing serious games. Questions must be asked: What qualifies as an acceptable social justice game scenario? How can developers design ethical civic engagement gaming practices? And, how are important social justice, advocacy and civic engagement issues realistically incorporated into game design so they are both relevant to constructionist learning while also limited in ethical ambiguity? As we attempt to accurately portray social and civic causes, do we, as game developers, researchers, and players, do justice to the causes? We support Gee's (2007) arguments concerning the importance of recognizing and developing strong cognitive learning opportunities that not only enhance gaming experiences but also learning experiences inside schools. Given the potential for games to influence students in various educational environments, such as school, we support future research efforts that focus not only on the design of serious games and the implementation of these games, but also on the ethical conflicts resulting from the consequences of that design and play.

In examining our work we believe that game designers and researchers of AIC and FW had good intentions, and valued important educational foundations related to constructionist learning, civic engagement, and game studies. However, our findings indicate this is but one perspective, and perhaps an idealistic one, when considering alternate scenarios. Reflecting upon the broader theoretical frameworks of designing and researching games that encourage civic engagement, we believe ethical considerations related to the consequences of gameplay must be taken into consideration. Our findings have implications for game designers creating games and also researchers observing players interacting with games that promote civic engagement values and processes. Additionally, we find that it is not enough to only examine whether events and actions within games are successful or not, lead or do not lead towards winning outcomes, support learning, or encourage civic engagement. Rather, we believe it is critical to analyze deeper ethical ambiguities related to the consequences of game design and gameplay. In turn, we support research efforts to further recognize and expand upon the development and research of serious games that provide all participants, at levels of both design and play, with strong cognitive learning opportunities.

REFERENCES

Abt, C. A. (1970). *Serious games*. New York: Viking.

Aldrich, C. (2004). *Simulations and the future of learning*. San Francisco, CA: John Wiley and Sons.

Aldrich, C. (2005). *Learning by doing*. San Francisco, CA: Pfeiffer.

Bennett, W. L. (2008). Changing citizenship in the digital age. In Bennet, W. L. (Ed.), *Civic life online: Learning how digital media can engage youth* (pp. 1–24). Cambridge, MA: The MIT Press.

Bers, M. (2008). Civic identities, online technologies: From designing civic curriculum to supporting civic experiences. In Bennett, W. L. (Ed.), *Civic life online: Learning how digital media can engage youth* (pp. 139–160). Cambridge, MA: The MIT Press.

Bogost, I. (2007). *Persuasive games: The expressive power of videogames*. Cambridge, MA: The MIT Press.

Chao, J., & Holden, J. (2008). One game and two stories: First Wind, Our Second Simulation Thematic Dialogues Concerning a Simulation-Game. Unpublished master's thesis, University of Michigan-Flint, Flint, MI.

Collins, A., & Halverson, R. (2009). *Rethinking education in the age of technology: The digital revolution and schooling in America*. New York: Teachers College Press.

De Freitas, S. (2006). *Learning in immersive worlds*. Bristol, UK: Bristol Joint Information Systems Committee. Retrieved December 17, 2009, from http://www.jisc.ac.uk/eli_outcomes.html

De Freitas, S., & Griffths, M. (2007). Online gaming as an educational tool in learning and training. *British Journal of Educational Technology, 38*(3), 535–537. doi:10.1111/j.1467-8535.2007.00720.x

Egeneldt-Nielsen, S. (2005). *Beyond edutainment: Exploring the educational potential of computer games*. Unpublished doctoral dissertation. Retrieved December 15, 2009 from http://www.itu.dk/people/sen/egenfeldt.pdf

Fair Labor Association. (2008). Nonprofit organization dedicated to ending sweatshop conditions. Retrieved December 22, 2009, from http://www.fairlabor.org/

Flanagan, M., Howe, D., & Nissenbaum, H. (2008). Embodying values in design: Theory and practice. In van den Hoven, J., & Weckert, J. (Eds.), *Information technology and moral philosophy* (pp. 322–353). Cambridge, UK: Cambridge University Press. doi:10.1017/CBO9780511498725.017

Flanagan, M., & Nissenbaum, H. (2007, September). A method for discovering values in digital games. Paper presented at the Proceedings of DiGRA 2007 Conference, Tokyo, Japan.

Frasca, G. (2003). Simulation versus narrative: Introduction to ludology. In Wolf, M. J. P., & Perron, B. (Eds.), *The videogame theory reader* (pp. 221–236). New York: Routledge.

Friedman, B. (1997). *Human values and the design of computer technology*. New York: Cambridge University Press.

Friedman, B., Kahn, P. H. Jr, & Borning, A. (2001). *Value sensitive design: Theory and methods*. Seattle, WA: University of Washington Technical Report.

Friedman, B., Kahn, P. H. Jr, & Borning, A. (2006). Value sensitive design and information systems. In Zhang, P., & Galetta, D. (Eds.), *Human-computer interaction in management information systems: Foundations* (pp. 348–372). Armonk, NY: M.E. Sharpe.

Gee, J. P. (2004). Learning by design: Games as learning machines. *Interactive Educational Multimedia, 8*, 15–23.

Gee, J. P. (2005). The classroom of popular culture. *The Harvard Educational Letter, 21*(6), 8. Retrieved December 23, 2009, from http://www.hepg.org/hel/article/296

Gee, J. P. (2007). *What videogames have to teach us about learning and literacy*. New York: Pelgrave MacMillan.

Gee, J. P. (2008). Learning and games. In Salen, K. (Ed.), *The ecology of games: Connecting youth, games, and learning* (pp. 21–40). Cambridge, MA: The MIT Press.

Jenkins, H. (2007a). From participatory culture to participatory democracy (part 2). *Confessions of an aca-fan: The official weblog of Henry Jenkins*. Retrieved December 20, 2009, from http://www.henryjenkins.org/2007/03/from_participatatory_culture_t_1.html

Jenkins, H. (2007b). From participatory culture to participatory democracy (part 1). *Confessions of an aca-fan: The official weblog of Henry Jenkins*. Retrieved December 20, 2009, from http://henryjenkins.org/2007/03/from_participatory_culture_t.html

Jenkins, H., Clinton, K., Purushotma, R., Robison, A. J., & Weigel, M. (2006). *Confronting the challenges of participatory culture: Media education for the twenty-first century*. Chicago, IL: MacArthur Foundation.

Kafai, Y. B. (2006). Playing and making games for learning: Instructionist and constructionist perspectives for game studies. *Games and Culture*, *1*(1), 36–40. doi:10.1177/1555412005281767

Kupperman, J. (2002). *Making meaningful experiences through an on-line character-playing simulation*. Unpublished doctoral dissertation, University of Michigan, Ann Arbor, MI.

Lave, J., & Wenger, E. (1991). *Situated learning: Legitimate peripheral participation*. Cambridge, MA: Cambridge University Press.

Lenhart, A., Kahne, J., Middaugh, E., Macgill, A., Evans, C., & Vitak, J. (2008). *Teens, videogames, and civics*. Washington, DC: Pew Internet & American Life Project.

Levine, J. (2009a). Lessons we've learned from society. *Library Technology Reports*, *45*(5), 7–10.

Levine, J. (2009b). Libraries, videogames, and civic engagement. *Library Technology Reports*, *45*(5), 11–18.

Libby, B. (2009, January 28). *Sustainability themed computer games come to the classroom*. Retrieved December 22, 2009, from http://www.edutopia.org/environment-sustainability-computer-games# Lincoln, Y. S., & Guba, E. G. (1985). *Naturalistic inquiry*. Beverly Hills, CA: Sage Publications.

Löwgren, J., & Stolterman, E. (1998). Developing IT design ability through repertoires and contextual product semantics. *Digital Creativity*, *9*(4), 223–237. doi:10.1080/14626269808567130

Malaby, T. (2007). Beyond play: A new approach to games. *Games and Culture*, *2*(2), 95–113. doi:10.1177/1555412007299434

Miles, M. B., & Huberman, A. M. (1984). *Qualitative data analysis: A sourcebook of new methods*. Newbury Park, CA: Sage Publications.

Papert, S. (1980). *Mindstorms: Children, computers, and powerful ideas*. New York: Basic Books.

Papert, S. (1981). Society will balk, but the future may demand a computer for each child. In Hass, G. (Ed.), *Curriculum planning: A new approach* (pp. 99–101). Boston: Allyn & Bacon.

Peace, C. (1997). *The interactive book: A guide to the interactive revolution*. Indianapolis, IN: Macmillan Technical Publishing.

Peppler, K. A., & Kafai, Y. (2007). What videogame making can teach us about literacy and learning: Alternative pathways into participatory culture. Paper presented at Digital Games Research Association, Tokyo.

Perkins-Gough, D. (2009). Videogames and civic engagement. *Educational Leadership*, *66*(6), 94.

Platoni, K. (2009). *Computer games explore social issues*. Retrieved December 22, 2009, from http://www.edutopia.org/serious-games-computer-simulations

Shaffer, D., Squire, K., Halverson, R., & Gee, J. P. (2005). Videogames and the future of learning. *Phi Delta Kappan*, *87*(2), 105–111.

Simkins, D. W., & Steinkuehler, C. (2008). Critical ethical reasoning in role play. *Games and Culture*, *3*(3-4), 333–355. doi:10.1177/1555412008317313

Squire, K. (2006). From content to context: Videogames as designed experiences. *Educational Researcher*, *35*(8), 19–29. doi:10.3102/0013189X035008019

Squire, K. (2008). Open-ended videogames: A model for developing learning for the interactive age. In Salen, K. (Ed.), *The ecology of games: Connecting youth, games, and learning* (pp. 167–198). Cambridge, MA: The MIT Press.

Squire, K., & Jenkins, H. (2003). Harnessing the power of games in education. *Insight (American Society of Ophthalmic Registered Nurses)*, *3*(1), 5–33.

Squire, K., & Steinkuehler, C.A. (2005, April 15). Meet the gamers. *Library Journal*.

Stokes, B., Seggerman, S., & Rejeski, D. (n.d.). For a better world: Digital games and the social change sector. New York. *Games for Change*.

Thomas, P., & Macredie, R. (1994). Games and the design of human-computer interfaces. *Educational Technology*, *31*(2), 134–142.

Trotter, A. (2008). Teens and videogames. *Education Week*, *28*(5), 4–5.

Chapter 19

Uganda's Road to Peace May Run through the River of Forgiveness:
Designing Playable Fictions to Teach Complex Values

Sasha Barab
Indiana University, USA

Tyler Dodge
Indiana University, USA

Edward Gentry
Indiana University, USA

Asmalina Saleh
Indiana University, USA

Patrick Pettyjohn
Indiana University, USA

ABSTRACT

While gaming technologies are typically leveraged for entertainment purposes, our experience and aspiration is to use them to encourage engagement with global, politically-sensitive issues. This chapter focuses on our game design concerning the struggle of Uganda, a design that allows players to experience the atrocities and inhumane conditions and, by illuminating such values as peace and justice, helps them more generally to appreciate the moral complexity of a humane intervention. Rather than theoretical constructs to be debated in the abstract, the ethical struggles involved in determining a humane intervention in the game setting are grounded in different Non-Player Characters' perspectives and operationalized within the underlying game dynamics. Beyond reporting on the designed game, the chapter draws the reader into the struggles of designing such an ethically contentious game.

DOI: 10.4018/978-1-60960-120-1.ch019

INTRODUCTION

One of the most persistent problems of this period is how to reconcile conflicting goals in the aftermath of severe criminality.... The regime responsible for crimes against humanity or genocidal behaviors [remains] as part of a bargain by which its impunity was "purchased" in exchange for its voluntarily relinquishment of power (Falk, 2000, pp. 24–25).

The violence committed by the Lord's Resistance Army (LRA) for over 20 years on the Acholi people of northern Uganda has resulted in the death and displacement of millions, and left countless others mutilated, raped, or enslaved as child soldiers (Eichstaedt, 2009). Reports suggest that torture continues to be practiced among security organizations, including the arrest and beating of opposition members of Parliament (Central Intelligence Agency, 2008). In 2007, the President of Uganda, Yoweri Museveni, requested support from the International Criminal Court (ICC), which then issued arrest warrants for top LRA leaders. However, a year after the warrants were issued, Museveni offered the LRA amnesty in exchange for an initial ceasefire and eventual comprehensive peace agreement—despite the fact that the warrants were issued at Museveni's request. This example highlights the tension between seeking peace and attaining justice. Ugandan human rights lawyer Barney Afako argued that seeking justice through the courts will prolong violence, stating: "Justice needs to be justified in terms of lives," adding that "the [international] criminal justice system is isolated from the moral consequences of its intervention" (Legalbrief Today, 2006). Others, however, maintain that peace is dependent on justice, as only through attaining justice can there be reconciliation and rehabilitation (Falk, 2000).

A core question illuminated in this chapter is how these particular dilemmas and the underlying universal struggles that they involve might be translated into game play. More generally, we are interested in how to leverage videogames to engage citizens in challenging situations so that they can appreciate the ethical and moral complexities of social issues while experiencing the problem in a personally-relevant way. This challenge—to structure engagement with issues in ways that both address their complexity and bear relevance beyond the specific context—is what we regard as central to our work as designers of games. To tease out these challenges, we use the complex case of Uganda. Solutions to Uganda's situation that are prominently advocated by the international community and in human rights statements have emphasized the need for justice to achieve peace, as if this were a universal truth. Such a perspective, that peace is dependent on justice being enforced, is regularly adopted regarding global justice more generally (Falk, 2000). However, as one inquires deeper into the local phenomena, which in this case is the Ugandan story of justice, the accepted disciplinary "truths" become complexified (Hannum, 2006). Indeed, as our design work advanced, we examined more perspectives and even talked with local Ugandans, and such lofty statements became less useful, compelling us to question whether peace in Uganda is necessarily dependent on justice being enforced.

Such grounded engagement with any theoretical claim, shifting from general platitudes to specific instances, is necessary not only for the struggles of Uganda and the tension between peace and justice but for other concerns as well. The hesitation to accept such a ready-made solution as the correlation between justice and peace and, instead, the patience to discern an emergent solution, synthesized from alternative perspectives, represents a sophisticated and adaptable approach to a wide range of important problems. It reveals aspects of Uganda's struggles not previously appreciated and offers, if not a path to their resolution, then at least a step toward that path. And to consider the Ugandan context from this perspective equips one with the experience of engaging complex issues in a manner bearing relevance to all walks of life. Our work is predicated on the belief that contemporary videogames can afford such forms of engagement: they constitute complex, ideological worlds in which players can work individually and in large groups to engage and overcome sophisticated challenges (Barab, Dodge, Ingram-Goble et al., 2010; Squire, 2006). Being narratively elaborate yet capacious, thus inviting players' own elaborations, they allow the player to take on roles that might not be accessible in their everyday life, and in the context of these roles, players make decisions and experience the consequences as they unfold in the designed world of the game (Barab, Gresalfi, Dodge, & Ingram-Goble, 2010).

This chapter focuses on our game, The River of Justice, which centers on the struggles of Uganda by embedding the player in the fictional, virtual world referred to as Bunala. The game was designed to help players to experience the atrocities and inhumane conditions of that country and, by illuminating such values as peace and justice, help them more generally to appreciate the moral complexity of a humane intervention. Game play begins in the briefing room of a company that has been commissioned to advance a recommendation regarding how to proceed with the Bunala situation, specifically the Liberation Resistance Move-

ment or LRM (a fictionalized LRA). The player's character, a freelance investigator, represented in the three-dimensional world as an avatar, is required to travel to in-game villages where they talk to local Bunalians and determine which response to the LRM is most appropriate: amnesty, justice, or forgiveness (see Figure 1 for an illustration of the virtual world, the dialogue of a game character, and the player game meter). Using their keyboard, the player moves their in-game avatar around a three-dimensional world, unlocking different villagers and talking to different types of people in the fictional world by clicking on them, listening to what they have to say, and choosing responses from a menu of choices. The implicit objective of the game is to raise the Satisfaction level of most Victims (unless they are resentful, desiring Justice), and to lower the Satisfaction level of most Perpetrators (unless they can be redeemed through Forgiveness). The explicit outcome is to recommend a decision to the fictional ICC, with the player's in-game boss judging the alignment between the recommendation and particular game play interactions and choices.

Beyond offering a simulation of the conditions and struggles, which might draw upon arrays of factual data to show and speculate the outcomes of a user's actions, our goal with the game is to

Figure 1. Screen shot depicting the virtual world in the left, the dialogue of a game character Teresa on the right, and the player game meter above the dialogue

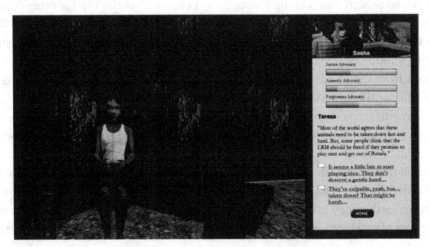

situate the player as a decision-maker immersed in the dramatic setting, enmeshed in its tangle of possibilities and consequences. To illustrate, at one point in the game discussed further below, the player meets a member of the rebel army and must decide whether the member's actions were born of necessity, thus warranting their forgiveness and rehabilitation, or of choice and desire, thus demanding justice to achieve long-term peace—in short, demanding their death. More than a theoretical question, the game forces the player to commit to a decision and, in the subsequent scene, directly witness the consequences of their choice, thus making salient the player's own beliefs and biases instantiated as irrevocable outcomes.

Given our emphasis on dramatic agency (Murray, 1997) in which the player actions in part determine how the game story unfolds, we refer to our game designs as playable fictions. Playable fictions are interactive stories in which one is positioned as a protagonist who makes game choices that have consequence in the fictional world. The design of any playable fiction involves defining a storyline as well as the game dynamics that make game play challenging and enjoyable. For a playable fiction concerning an actual and politically-sensitive event, the design challenges involve choosing which aspects of the narrative to fictionalize, and doing so in such a way that the design affords an experience that is pedagogically-illuminative yet narratively coherent. Additionally, for the designers to operationalize their own beliefs and biases into a narrative rule set (i.e., decision X causes outcome Y) requires a defensible commitment. That is, because the actual game choices serve to reify the designers' beliefs, those beliefs must be scrutinized and found to provide a valid platform upon which to base the gameplay. For example, it is one thing to argue that ends justify means, yet quite another to force the player to sacrifice a Ugandan child if she is to save a larger number of people and possibly bring an end to the atrocities.

In this chapter, we discuss The River of Justice so that others can consider the process and problems we faced in reifying the Ugandan situation into representative characters, proxy variables, interactive rule sets, unfolding plotlines, and other design decisions. First we discuss our design methodology, including outlining the affordances of fictionalization and of playability. Next, we analyze the game design, providing details that illuminate the design problems, decisions, and solutions. Finally, we explicate the lessons that we learned through the design work and that want to share with others.

THE EDUCATIONAL AFFORDANCES OF PLAYABLE FICTIONS

While considered by some as mere amusement, videogames are becoming critically recognized as sophisticated vehicles for participation, including academic and civic engagement (Jenkins, 2008; Lenhart, Kahne, Middaugh, Macgill, Evans, & Vitak, 2008). In many contemporary videogames, players do not simply click buttons without thinking, but instead engage rich narrative storylines and employ complex discursive practices and problem solving strategies as they come to master and appreciate the underlying game dynamics (Barab & Dede, 2007; Gee, 2003; Shaffer, 2007). In fact, scholars have been documenting the discursive richness, depth of collaborative inquiry, complexity of game play, opportunities for consequentiality, rich perception-action cycles, exploration of situated identities, and sophisticated forms of learning and participation that can occur during game play (Barab, Gresalfi, & Arici, 2009; Gee, 2003; Shaffer, 2006; Squire, 2006; Squire & Jan, 2007). Videogames can stimulate rich forms of participation that enlist membership and identity in ways that often occur only in advanced curricular designs, story books, or other media (Murray, 1997).

Central to our work is the conviction that through game play, one can be experientially situated within a space that entwines real with fictional details, and authentic with playful activities, to embed the player and the subject matter within an engaging and dynamic context (Barab, Gresalfi, Dodge, & Ingram-Goble, 2010). An important component, and one highlighted in this chapter, is their power as playable fictions, that is, a story to be realized or completed through the act of making choices and solving play tasks that co-determine with the designer how the game narrative will unfold for a particular player. In this way, playable fictions can position the learner in a consequential role that personalizes the narrative challenges, affording players an investment in the situation and responsibility for the direction of the narrative. Gee (2003) hypothesized that while playing a videogame the player develops a hybrid identity that is part real player making decisions, and part in-game character executing those decisions and part player-character as the real player reflects on themselves as people who make decisions that cause particular game character and world outcomes. This dynamic, in which the player and the context co-define each other and evolve together through meaningful inquiry, epitomizes Dewey's (1938) notion of transactivity, or how "every experience enacted and undergone modifies the one who acts and undergoes…for it is a somewhat different person who enters into them" (pp. 35). As Vygotsky (1978) argued, through play one can act a head above oneself, with play providing an effective scaffold for expanding one's zone of proximal development, that is, for understanding more than one could understand by oneself.

As Gadamar (1976, p. 112) argued, when playing a game, one is "playing out oneself" or, at least, an extension of one possible self. Play invites us into an experience that plays us, affording particular actions and at the same time leaving us as one who has realized these opportunities in a particular way. By being playable,

our pedagogical designs contextually bind the learner and content affording a sense of intentionality, legitimacy, agency, consequentiality, accountability, and reflexivity (Barab, Dodge, Ingram-Goble, & Gresalfi, 2010; Barab, Gresalfi, & Arici, 2009). This is in part because the designs position the learner as a first-person protagonist doing epistemological work on the context by allowing the player a sense of dramatic agency in terms of the underlying narrative (Murray, 1997). Such a design involves a curricular context that is less a set of information to be acquired and more a world to be played. Learning in such dynamic environments becomes a way of seeing the world or of being in the world (Thomas & Brown, 2006), one that requires enlisting general concepts and understandings (e.g., justice, amnesty, and forgiveness) as tools for considering, determining, and ultimately transforming particular storylines, and this, in turn, can foster deep understanding of complex and value-rich domains.

Videogames can enable players, even if they are novices in a subject area, to recognize its complexity through engaging with it in a personally meaningful way. The player's regular life largely precludes such engagement for a host of reasons: for instance, the object of inquiry may be abstruse or precious; the procedures may be uncommon, complicated, or objectionable; the outcomes may be offensive or dangerous; and so forth (Frasca, 2000). In contrast, videogames can be structured around an issue to, in essence, constitute an ideological world that establishes a rich context for participation and learning (Squire, 2006), including learning of ethics, and invites the player to adopt hybrid roles in that world neither limited to nor divorced from the player's natural sense of self (cf. Gee, 2003). Leveraging the power of videogames, we have been designing pedagogical worlds that deliberately foster a sense of agency and explicitly present educational tasks, pedagogical scaffolds, social interactions, and reflective moments to support meaningful learning about significant issues (Barab, Jackson,

& Arici, 2004; Barab, Thomas, Dodge, Carteaux, & Tuzun, 2005; Barab, Sadler, Heiselt, Hickey, & Zuiker, 2007).

Such work combines literary techniques, game principles, and academic pedagogy to achieve narrative cohesion, immersive experience, academic utility, and meaningful play. The types of virtual worlds we create are educationally valuable and socially meaningful because they are designed such that the solving the embedded problems require that players enlist conceptual understandings to make effective choices (Barab, Gresalfi, and Arici, 2009; Barab, Zuiker et al, 2007). In our design work, the most important pedagogical utility derives not from the hard affordances of videogame technology such as multisensory immersion or instantaneous interactivity, but from the soft ones like hybrid roles, emergent challenges, and unfolding storylines. These affordances can be conceptually organized in a way that, while not suited to all domains, helps to guide designs for teaching values. As *playable fictions,* videogames entail two families of affordances conducive to scaffolding experience with values: *fictionalization* and *playability.*

Both the technology and the culture of contemporary videogames allow for designs that afford one the opportunity to play through fictions in a way that does not necessarily place game play and storyline in conflict. By fictionalization, we mean the process of turning particular content into a story that, while sometimes featuring veridical elements, involves imaginative or even fantastical ones across the domain of the story, including its setting, characters, and dramatic conflicts. The fiction in a game responds to the player's directions yet must be designed to retain integrity and cohesion; it accommodates the player's projection yet bears specificity and nuance; it resonates with the player's experience yet suggests widespread and enduring wisdom (Calvino, 1999; Gee, 2003; Murray, 1997). Fiction and play each serve to shelter the experience as a space with specifica-

tions that structure both the fiction and the game play. Through fictionalization, we are able to design with pedagogical liberty about issues that have political sensitivity, ethical subjectivity, and interpretive contestation while still ensuring intrinsic fidelity and projective capacity.

The context entwines real and fictional elements designed to embed the learner and the curricular content within a complex and credible situation. This embedding occurs, in part, because of the player being positioned with dramatic agency in making choices that influence the direction of the story and that make apparent to the player his or her own biases. However, the field of game design has not established best practices and we have limited powerful exemplars regarding how to illuminate political events and contested histories, foster appreciation of what transpired, and position the player to struggle with the underlying ethical decisions that arise during these moments. In using games to complex ethical struggles without simplistic answers, the game designers must confront both pragmatic confounds and theoretical tensions and accordingly must pose many design decisions as conjectures to be tested through actual game play. Choices regarding how to fictionalize the history or operationalize the values reveal as much about the designer's biases as about the phenomena being illuminated.

In the next section, we show how our ethical biases became reified as we made choices on what aspects to include in our virtual world, in terms of what tasks the player would be expected to engage, and in deciding what outcomes would result from particular actions. Toward this end, we describe our designed game (see a multimedia presentation at http://ijlm.net/knowinganddoing/10.1162/ijlm.2009.0023; Barab et al., 2009), occasionally inserting meta-reflections to illuminate the struggles we went through in building this game and the power of playable fictions for teaching ethics.

RIVER OF JUSTICE OVERVIEW

Setting the Stage

The player, after choosing his or her gender's avatar and other features, begins in the lobby of a company named A Just World, which has been commissioned by the ICC to advance a recommendation regarding how to proceed with the situation in Bunala, a country wrought with civil strife and violence. Here, she takes on the role of a freelance investigator and is briefed on the assignment by Timothy Deckard, an experienced field agent who is also the boss:

Glad to hear it! Let's get you through this thing. First, have a look at some documents. There's some general information about the situation here, as well as some letters from some Bunalan citizens. More importantly, you'll see how the Bunalan government cried for help but then tried to call it off. That's a no-no. You're required to read them, but you and I both know the real information is on the ground.

Examining the company documents, the player learns about the severity of the crimes occurring in Bunala (a fictionalized version of Uganda) and gains additional background that justifies the ICC arresting a number of members of the Liberation Resistance Movement (LRM, a fictionalized version of the LRA). For example, the player reads a newspaper article on the discovery of a mass grave that was attributed to the LRM and another article asserting that the LRM is responsible for killing thousands of citizens and for kidnapping children and raping women, with estimates of 1.4 million internally displaced persons (see Figure 2 for an example of the fictional newspaper they engage). Likewise, the player reads a letter from an ex-LRM member who was forced to kill his family to preserve his own life. Statements from Bunalan citizens, official letters, and other docu-ments all help the player understand the current assignment.

To help the player understand his assignment, Timothy recounts stories from other engagements in which A Just World failed to deliver swift justice, resulting in genocide. Thus, he emphasizes the importance of company policy and impresses upon the player, as a company representative, to consistently advocate justice. Timothy explains that one's field reputation reflects how legitimate the player's philosophy is, based on one's consistency of advocacy. For example, if in the end of the game the player recommends amnesty but has been consistently advocating and making choices in dialogues with game characters that reflect justice, Timothy comments on the apparent disconnect. The player's Advocacy is a game score comprised of several values and displayed in a meter in the sidebar beside the virtual space. Timothy also urges the player to quickly pass the company exam so that the player can enter the field and collect the interviews necessary to justify bringing in the military and securing the arrests. Soon after the player starts the first mission, he and his colleague, Teresa Teresa (a non-player character, NPC) are sitting in the back of a truck driving to where they can interview locals, but is attacked by the guerilla army.

They are captured by the LRM, and the player begins to experience first-hand the cruelty and complexity of the situation. This is initially done through a series of dialogue bubbles with cut-scenes, presented as hazy memories, informing the player that he is regaining consciousness. While previous game play usually took place in the virtual window where the player had some agency of what they focused on in the scene, in this moment and a few other occasions, player-driven game play is interrupted with the presentation of cut-scenes, or sequences of still images based on actual photographs germane to the game narrative. Commonly used in videogames, cut-scenes can

Figure 2. Screenshot showing one of the fictional news documents that the player interrogates in the game

02 March 2010

The Bunala Daily

MASS GRAVE DISCOVERED

Northern Bunala – Bodies were discovered in a mass grave after Bunalan forces took siege of an Liberation Resistance Movement (LRM) camp in the northern Kaberamaido region. It has been long suspected that Richard Yeona, leader of the LRM, has committed war crimes, including attacks against unarmed Bunalan civilians, abducting children and sexual enslavement.

Bunalan officials examined the grave and found women and children amongst the dead. Susan Balogun, a veteran Bunalan official explained to reporters, "I have witnessed some of the worst things humans can do to each

other. But never have I witnessed such a disregard for life. My God, I counted over 45 boys and girls no more than age 4 in that grave. This

Bones of women and children found in Northern Bunala

man Yeona needs to be stopped!"
After identifying the body of her 3 year old girl, Ester Okurut told reporters, "I can't imagine why anyone would do these things to children.

They're just children! They NEVER hurt anybody. At least now I can give my little Dalila a proper burial where she can rest with her other family members."

President Kulani traveled to the grave site and offered a passionate speech promising justice and peace. "This is a great tragedy for our country and our people. We will never forget these people whose lives were taken from them against their will. Their lives and their legacy will not be forgotten. As your president, I will shout their stories to the corners of the earth, that we might find help from our international friends to stop Yeona and his

INSIDE THIS ISSUE:

History of the LRM	2
Negotiation of Peace Bill	2
Refugees from Northern	2
Regional news	3
Economics	4
Commentary	5

MUDSLIDES BURY VILLAGES

Jekat, Bunala — Heavy rain caused a series of mudslides in Eastern Bunala, burying as many as 120 houses. This has caused at least several hundred families to be displaced and they are in need of dire aid.

Due to the mudslides however, it has been impossible to reach the affected areas. The govern-

ment has plans to airlift aid to the affected areas but has yet to gain approval from Senate.

Criticisms have already been expressed over the government's delay in response. There are currently 94 people reported missing and efforts to rescue trapped victims have been delayed by lack of tools. Citizens

have had to volunteer and dig out affected victims to rescue them.

A Red Cross volunteer expressed her frustration over the situation. "There needs to be better tools for us to save people. The government needs to act quicker. You cannot wait to save these people."

provide plot or character development or backstory information, and they are used in this way in *River of Justice*. Here, the cut-scene conveys the physicality of the wreckage and the extent, in terms of both distance and time, of the abduction, all in a manner that might be less manageable and effective if transpiring in the virtual space as part of a playable scene. Further, by divorcing the scene from the space and flow of game play, cut-scenes shift the player from an active to a reflective stance and by thus positioning the player once again as a witness, cut-scenes can reclaim the reality and poignancy of the story content that may be neglected during game play.

As the cut-scenes stop, the player experiences being held captive in a roughly-built shack, bare, apart from an interrogation chair and other prisoners (see Figure 3). Teresa, also in the room, informs the player that they have been prisoners for three days. Appearing bruised and with ripped clothes, she hints at the harrowing experiences that she underwent while the player's character was unconscious, including physical and sexual abuse. She becomes quiet when a teenage boy, Mukasa, enters the detention room.

Mukasa is an LRM guard, and he approaches the player's character, stating, "I have brought you some food, my friend." The player is given

Figure 3. Screenshot depicting NPCs in a prison cell

a list of choices that reflect choices of how to respond:

a)   *Please, please let me go. I just want to go home.*

b)   *Thank you. [Take food.]*

c)   *[Say nothing and refuse food.]*

As a non-player character (NPC) programmed by the design team, Mukasa responds in one of three ways, depending on what the player chooses above:

a)   *This is your home now. You are with the LRM. Your life is their life. You come with me now, we have much work to do. You must pay us back for this delicious food and the warm shelter.*

b)   *You are most welcome! Food is the least of the many benefits of being in the LRM. Please, bring your food and come with me. There is much to do! If you do good, you will get more good stuff.*

c)   *You do not want our hard work to make your food and give you shelter? That is not good, my friend. Come with me. There is work to*

do. Maybe if you do good, I will not tell the Captain that you were rude.

The Captain hates rude people. If you keep that attitude, he might not let you join us.

In this way, the NPCs treat the player's character in differing ways, depending on the player's choices. Similarly, in a later scene, the captive player wakes to witness a young boy who has his hands and feet bound by tight rope. Mukasa tells the player, "You meet this boy. His name is Bale. We caught him stealing food from our stores." The player has two available responses:

What are you going to do to him? Just leave him alone!

He's just a child. Let him go or…!

If the player chooses option (b), the Justice value of the Advocacy meter increases. Mukasa's programmed response follows:

a)   *Oh, but no. To let him go would not be good for us. In Bunala, if you do not show your strength, people will take from you. No. We cannot let that happen. You will help us teach him a lesson today.*

The player could reject Mukasa by replying, (a) "I won't help you! If you hurt him, I'll make sure you die when they rescue me!" But, with the goal of self-preservation and with hopes to avoid further bloodshed, the player can inst ead choose to respond, (b) "I understand. Just don't hurt me. What do you want me to do?" Upon choosing this response, a meter is then revealed to the player and he or she may notice the Amnesty value of the Advocacy meter increase. Mukasa then responds with the second of the two programmed responses:

b) *You will shoot this thief with my own gun. If you do not, we will do it anyway. But we will do more, too. We will shoot two other prisoners. Maybe you will pick them for us. Then we cut off this girl's hand. You will watch us do this. After that I will offer you my gun again. If you still do not shoot her, then we start over with two more people and the other hand. Or, you can punish her like I say. We maybe even spare another prisoner that you choose who has done us wrong.*

Here, again, a cut-scene is used, as the virtual world is replaced with a series of images depicting the player shooting the boy. We chose to use a cut-scene here to prompt a reflective moment, to make the player stop and reflect on the decision not simply in terms of the videogame, but by divorcing the scene from the flow and by using more realistic images the consequences of the in-game decision are given enhanced significance. In an interview with one player, she stated:

The feeling of helpless rage which that scene engendered in me completely changed the way I view my personal values... you might say it transformed my sense of self and the world... I am no longer so smug in my feeling of moral superiority... and I will never forget that in the end

my values didn't protect me from being forced to take an intolerable action.

Such uses of cut-scenes serve to deliver particular content with an authenticity not easily afforded by immersion in the virtual space. While this scene might seem extreme, it is in fact consistent with the horror of the events being fictionalized.

However, and quite germane to this chapter, it is not simply the horror that our game is designed to illuminate. Rather, our goal is to embed the player in the complicated ethical struggles that the rest of the world has undergone in deciding whether to take action on the nation's behalf. Reflecting on the Uganda situation and on political violence more generally, one might argue that unless justice is served, countries like Uganda will never have peace. In fact, as one reads about the atrocities or witnesses the thousands of dead bodies and vacant eyes of kidnapped children, it is hard not to desire justice. As educators and game designers, it was this message that we initially wished to share, but it was also our commitment to help the reader appreciate the complications of such a simplistic conception in practice. Consider, for example, this interaction between the player and an NPC, Bacia, midway through the game. Bacia is the mother of a Bunalan family; her husband was killed by the LRM, her nephew was kidnapped, and her son is bitter with vengeance. She is angry but also weary of the suffering, and she simply wants to salvage what is left of her family. Bacia says,

You think I want it this way? I am so tired, stranger. Tired of sleeping through the sounds of guns. Tired of wondering where my nephew disappeared to in the middle of the night. Tired of watching my son get so bitter that he wants to kill people. He has not even experienced any of the joys of life yet!

She beseeches the player to recommend amnesty to the ICC so that the soldiers can leave and the villagers can be safe (see Figure 4). The player can then respond with a choice:

a) *What about the crimes they've committed? Shouldn't they have to face punishment? What about justice?*

b) *I understand, Bacia. With the LRM gone, you could be safe...*

In this instance, Bacia believes that Justice would prolong her troubles, while Amnesty would help solve them. Therefore, if the player chooses response (a) above, the Justice level of his Advocacy increases, but Bacia's Satisfaction level decreases. Conversely, if the player chooses (b), his Amnesty level increases, as does Bacia's level of Satisfaction. These visibly impact the player's Advocacy meter, as the levels change based on the bias of her choices. Not displayed, but nonetheless affecting the ensuing game dynamics, are an array of variables reflecting each character's level of Satisfaction with regard to the value being advocated by the player. They understand this through the language of game characters and, in some places, the actions required of the player. These game mechanics are further elaborated below.

Revealing the Mechanics

The game design underlying the player experience requires of designers a deep appreciation of their own ethical biases and social commitments. Such self-understanding informs, and becomes evident in, not simply their writing the storyline and developing selected backstory elements but further in their scripting of the options, determining the consequences, and engineering the game dynamics driving the meters and other outcomes. To explain the game design using loosely the language of mathematics, the ethical values like amnesty and justice become variables in a narrative expression, wherein player choices serve as operations on the variables toward the resulting solution. By developing awareness of and experience with the values as they function in specific contexts, the player develops personal understandings both of the dynamics related to these particular values and, more broadly, of how to work with disparate values in complex ways to integrate seemingly incommensurate perspectives into a systemic and nuanced conception.

Specifically, each choice presented to a player is associated with the value that it implicitly serves

Figure 4. Screen shot depicting Kihini, a village Elder, with another NPC. She is prompting the player to consider forgiveness as an option

to advocate (initially either Amnesty or Justice and later they unlock forgiveness). The level of each value is persistently displayed to the player in a meter that he may consult to gauge his reputation acquired through his fieldwork thus far, though the association between his choices and the variable levels is never explicated. Two fundamental roles in the conflict (Perpetrator and Victim) are each differentiated into various stances toward the dilemma (Perpetrators: for Evil, or by Necessity; Victims: Resentful, Tired, or Forgiving), defining five character types for the NPCs. Each NPC is associated with a particular character type (their "bias") and individuated with a unique name, narrative function, and baseline Satisfaction level, which is not displayed but which figures into the game dynamics. However, each character type (and thus all NPCs with that bias) responds uniquely to the possible value statements advocated by any player choice. The player enacts his choice by selecting one of the multiple choice response options, and in response to that choice, the Satisfaction level of each character is adjusted either up or down, depending on the valence of the choice in relation to their bias (see Table 1). As an example of these causal relationships between player choices and Satisfaction levels, a Resentful Victim (V_R), intent on vengeance, is satisfied by a choice advocating Justice, but a Tired Victim (V_T), weary of the struggle, is dissatisfied.

Table 1 describes player Advocacy choices along the rows and NPC Satisfaction levels along the columns, with the intersecting cells indicating the effect of a particular Advocacy represented in a choice. Again, some decisions increase and some decrease the Satisfaction levels, depending on the bias of the NPC type. Though this operation chiefly corresponds to their role in the conflict (i.e., Perpetrator or Victim), for some NPCs, the response to an advocacy runs counter to the general rule. For example, a Resentful Victim (V_R) is satisfied only if the player adopts their particular agenda for justice. To illustrate these mechanics in terms of game play dynamics, consider Ochen (V_R), a young Ugandan boy whom the player meets when rescued by Ochen's family. Ochen is bitter and resentful of the LRM, due largely to the murder of his father. The player has just met the boy's mother, who expressed her desire for amnesty for the LRM to clear them out quickly. Ochen, on the other hand, tries to recruit the player to fight the LRM, to which the player refuses. Ochen retorts,

Do you believe that I like to kill? That I am good at soldiering? Maybe I like this life? You are foolish if you think so. I like to run around and act silly. I like to play games with my friends. But do you know why I cannot? Because my friends are dead or captured. I have no choice. Now that you are here…you have no choice, too.

Ochen believes that soldiers of the LRM should be killed, but the player can choose to respond with one of the following:

Table 1. Data operations on NPC satisfaction as a function of player advocacy

Satisfaction by Character Type					
	Perpetrator		Victim		
Advocacy	Evil (P_E)	Necessity (P_N)	Resentful (V_R)	Tired (V_T)	Forgiving (V_F)
Justice	-	-	+	-	-
Amnesty	+	+	-	+	+
Forgiveness	-	+	-	-	+

a)   *Won't that just piss them off? They'll just send more soldiers...*

b)   *I agree that they should be punished...but what about trials?*

If the player selects choice (a), then the level for Amnesty increases in the player's Advocacy meter, and Ochen's Satisfaction level decreases. Alternately, if the player chooses (b), then the player's Justice level increases, Ochen's Satisfaction level rises slightly, but that of his mother drops slightly.

In this way, player choices serve to advocate ethical values, and both the momentary and cumulative Advocacy for each value is dynamically reflected in the responses made by each NPC according to their bias toward the player choices. These choices bear differential effects on each of the main NPCs—the six victims, three perpetrators, and three stakeholders (see Table 2) —and

they are also sometimes referred to by NPCs, who may respond to the ethics inherent in a choice. In one instance, if the player advocates justice, an NPC who had lost her husband to the LRM expresses frustration with the choice, stating that the player does not understand the extent of torment that the people have experienced and what a blessing even amnesty would be for the country. As a broader example, the player can choose to either escape or cooperate with the LRM soldiers, thus changing the sequence and details of the subsequent acts of the unfolding drama. Finally, in the most sweeping example, one's closing recommendation for the ICC transforms the experience of the ending such that some players might return jobless to Bunala, where they implement forgiveness, while other players espousing the company line enjoy the comforts of their new position. In this way, based on both individual and cumulative

Table 2. Backstory details for NPCs

	Name	Gender	Role	Bias
Victims				
	Bacia	F	Mother of Amebe Family	V_T
	Miremba	F	Eldest Sister of Amebe Family	V_F
	Acanit	F	Middle Sister of Amebe Family	V_T
	Ochen	M	Youngest Brother of Amebe Family	V_R
	Akello	M	Villager nearby Family	V_T
	Jendyose	F	Villager nearby Family	V_R
	Kaikara	F	Mother of slain boy, Bale	All three possible
Perpetrators				
	Mukasa	M	LRM Recruiter	P_E
	Dembe	F	LRM Soldier; Sister of Sahnde	P_E
Stakeholders				
	Timothy	M	Senior Worker	Justice
	Sahnde	F	Government Soldier; Brother of Dembe	Amnesty
	Kihini	F	Council Elder of Village	Forgiveness
Others				
	Theresa	F	Colleague at A Just World	–
	Bale	M	Tortured boy accused of theft	–
	Sandra	F	Ambassador	–

choices, the player directs the unfolding dialogue and, in other cases, broader storyline.

Forgiveness is not initially represented along with Amnesty and Justice in the Advocacy options; rather, it becomes available as an option after the player has engaged with certain characters, chiefly Kihini, the Council Elder of the village (see Figure 5). Further, because of the record that his choices will have left, unless the player practices a particular value, he will not, in the end, be able to convincingly advocate that value as a solution. The game design accommodates any of the three final recommendations, but the importance of forgiveness is reflected in all of the endgame feedback, such as this response to the player in a final letter from Kihini:

Our people have suffered at the hands of the LRM for many years. I believe it would take over 100 years of restitution to begin repaying us for what they took…. In the end, the oppressed develop into oppressors, new prejudices form, and the cycle of violence will rear its ugly head and devour us again…. I hope that you will personally choose to free yourself from your oppressors and seek forgiveness.

This statement, combined with the other forms of endgame feedback (discussed below), sug-gests recommendations for how the player might improve his score if he replays the game, and it also articulates important lessons about broader ethical struggles and the role of the game values in relation to those struggles.

Note that, as for the player, forgiveness was not among the initial choices considered by the design team; rather, it emerged through a grounding experience during the design phases. As we worked to implement the conception that peace requires justice, the first author was given the opportunity to visit Uganda and South Africa, where meetings with individuals there began to complexify the choices being made available in the game. More than idiosyncratic encounters, our team member travelled through South Africa, experienced Gibbon Island, the holding place for Nelson Mandela, and spent time at a local orphanage in Uganda. These experiences revealed that our previous studies had resulted in an inadequate set of response options for the player. As South Africans and Ugandans shared their stories, we learned that for many of them, acts of forgiveness are much more important than are notions of justice. They explained that, unlike justice or amnesty, only forgiveness gave them, as victims, power. By granting themselves the ability to de-

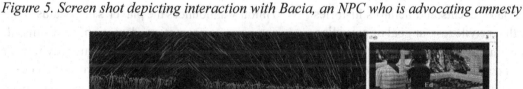

Figure 5. Screen shot depicting interaction with Bacia, an NPC who is advocating amnesty

termine how they viewed their plight and to forgive their transgressors, they could control some portion of the situation. The other solutions did not allow them that control. As a result, we began to wonder if the international conception that peace demands justice is a theoretical sentiment that problematically belies real-world experience, and we questioned whether the international community should enforce its perspective on those who must live out the consequences.

It was a turning point in our work, as we endeavored to explicate a satisfactory offering of in-game options, when we realized the power of this game narrative and why some consider videogames as becoming a dominant storytelling medium in the 21st Century (Herz, 1997). Thinking through the Ugandan dilemma as game designers, we were forced to consider the actions a player might take, the potential consequences of those actions, and the sufficiency of those consequences as compared to the real world. This involved, in our work, examining our own biases and determining how best to fictionalize the narrative in terms of the setting and backstory, the character types, and the unfolding plotline, as well how best to operationalize our moral and ethical biases into a playable game grammar. In practice, these all emerge dialectically, and this account while attempting to illuminate that trajectory, opportunistically relates events and delimits histories in a manner that privileges our goal of providing the reader an illuminative account of our work without them necessarily playing the game itself.

Bringing Closure

Central to the purpose of *River of Justice* is its bearing on real-world issues and on players' engagement with these issues, both particular to the tragedy of Uganda and more broadly on players' ethical stances in their daily lives. To scaffold this engagement, the connection between players' game participation and their daily lives is established at the beginning and made increas-

ingly explicit during the game. To illustrate, in the introductory briefing, players complete a personality profile in which they reveal certain attitudes and beliefs, some of which later impact the course of the narrative. For instance, if one expresses support of corporal punishment, then their in-game colleague Teresa is later killed, instead of being merely beaten and abandoned, and the guard responsible states that his decision was in response to the profile, discovered when the player was taken prisoner. Likewise, in the ending, the player receives a letter from Teresa's fiancé lamenting her murder. Such customization of game play serves to prompt players to reconsider the attitudes and beliefs that they harbored before playing the game.

The game also prompts reflection on the alignment between one's beliefs and actions, evident especially in the ending. After the lengthy ordeal in the field, the player submits a final recommendation regarding how the company should direct the ICC. Notably, if the player's decision is inconsistent with their record of advocacy throughout the game as favoring Amnesty, Justice, or Forgiveness, then Timothy, the company boss, balks at the discrepancy. Further, depending on the player's recommendation and its alignment with not only the company policy of advocating justice but also the player's Advocacy scores, Timothy announces the player's new status at the company as promotion, demotion, or dismissal, thus consolidating the span of game play into an opportunity for reflection. Then, as a final occasion of grounding for the player the challenges of realizing ethical bias in their own game decisions, the player is bedridden after falling ill. The player is visited by Mukasa, the young guard who had previously held her hostage and forced her to shoot a young boy; Mukasa had fled the LRM and is trying to leave Bunala. Confronted by the situation at hand, the player must make a decision: (a) to seek justice on Mukasa by notifying the nearby guard of his past actions, (b) to express forgiveness toward his former captor, or (c) to show amnesty by not alerting the guard but not forgiving the boy either. Just as the player had advanced a recommendation affecting the fate of Bunala, she now must decide the fate of this boy—and, like the boy, accept the decision as one she must bear henceforth.

Our interviews with players indicate that this particular scene was quite challenging for some, inviting them to reflect on and question their own ethical biases. As one player recounted her experience, "I started believing in forgiveness" after earlier scenes, but said, "… that sense of forgiveness was shaken to its core when I was handed a gun and given that impossible choice. How can you forgive someone who has forced you to take an action that you find intolerable?" Another player stated, "Just having a decision like that that feels so embodied… it feels so real… it makes it more than an academic question in ways that talking about it just doesn't do. Because he's not a real boy—I'm stunned that it mattered so much."

It is our conviction that the reason it mattered so much is because, in part, of the player's history with the narrative and the fact that she has dramatic agency on how the story unfolds. For, in a game, the decision has not been determined. Instead, in a game, it is our choices that move the narrative forward. In this instance, the player likely struggles with resentment she has towards the fictional character who previously forced the player to kill a helpless boy or accept responsibility for additional deaths. At some level, choosing not to forgive the guard is a personal accusation

that one's own crimes in the game were also not justified, but forgiveness brings an additional set of ethical conflicts in that it could be construed as vindicating the guard of his responsibility, potentially establishing an ethical dilemma for the player.

Completing the game play story, the player once recovered at the hospital either returns to the office or, if fired from the company job, returns to Bunala, where, reunited with Kihini as support, they help advocate and disseminate the power of forgiveness. In either case, the player undergoes a final debriefing that facilitates a closing reflection on the issues addressed by the game. Now neither actively in role-play nor withdrawn from the narrative, the player reviews a series of artifacts or representations describing the outcomes for various characters and for the country of Bunala as a whole (see Table 3 for a listing of the artifacts). These forms of feedback serve not only to illuminate for players the broader consequences of their choices but also to motivate them to replay the game, perhaps with different choices in the hopes of different outcomes. The first is a reminder of the player's changed status at the company, and the second is the letter pertaining to Teresa, who had been either harmed or murdered. Another is a letter from Kihini, with insight about the implications of the player's recommendation as it affects the people of Bunala. The last is a newspaper clipping that speculates and outlines the broader impact of the player's recommendation.

Once the game is complete, the player may access the game Codex, a review of the player's

Table 3. Relationship between player recommendation and endgame representations

| | Endgame Representation | | | |
| | | | Newspaper | |
Recommendation	Job Status	Village Elder	Short Term	Long Term
Justice	Promotion	Accusatory	Violence	Peace
Amnesty	Demotion	Advisory	Peace	Violence
Forgiveness	Dismissal	Grateful	Isolated Violence	Peace

game choices and outcomes (see Figure 6). First, it includes summary scores of the Advocacy choices that the player made as they relate to the three ethical biases, showing how many times the player chose each of the values, Justice, Amnesty, and Forgiveness. It also presents a report of the player's final recommendation as well as its implications in terms of the game artifacts already encountered but presented again in the context of review. The benefit of the Codex for teaching values is that it demonstrates the relationships among values, decisions, and consequences, thus explicating the agenda embedded in the game design and scaffolding reflection on the multiplicity of perspectives and the need to consider value-based solutions within a systemic context. Its benefit for the field of game design is that it invites conversation with players about how, through their game play, they take up our designs to become lived-through stories. Such an understanding will help to establish best practices in designing games that serve to narrate problematic issues and foster appreciation of the underlying values.

LESSONS LEARNED AND IMPLICATIONS

Although there have long existed technologies for engaging learners in understanding ethical struggles, we regard videogames as especially efficacious in that they can foster a state of engagement that involves projection into the role of a character who, enmeshed in a partly fictional problem context, must develop and apply particular understandings to make sense of and, ultimately, transform the context (Barab, Gresalfi, & Ingram-Goble, 2009). While typically gaming technologies are leveraged for entertainment purposes, our experience and aspiration is to use them to afford engagement with complex and sensitive issues transpiring around the world. Significantly, designers of such games must attend not simply to

the database of facts and probabilities of outcomes, but also to the implications of players' decisions and to the in-game and user-created narratives that give meaning to such decisions. To curtail the creation of pedagogically imperialistic games, that is, ones presuming the legitimacy of a hegemonic perspective, socially responsible game designers must remain cognizant of important questions: How do we represent the various perspectives on an issue, especially issues as complex and volatile as those discussed above, and do this in the context of a game design? How do we decide which choices to make available to the player and determine which consequences should be linked to particular player actions? How do we advance an agenda and do so in a way that doesn't simply promote the biases of the designers or of one political perspective at the exclusion of others?

Figure 6. Screenshot depicting the Codex review of in-game statistics

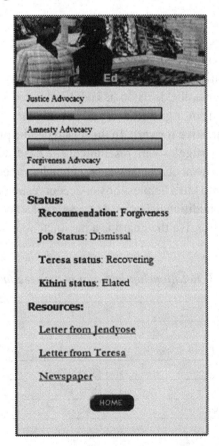

The following is a list of lessons that other designers may derive from the experience that we have recounted above. In particular, we briefly reflect on issues of cultural sensitivity, empirical legitimacy, pedagogical lesson, player reflection, and identity transformation. Each of these are expanded on below, grounded in our experience but discussed in relation to concerns of others as they reflect on their own work and that of others.

Cultural Sensitivity

This work can be considered an example of what Barab, Dodge et al. (2005) described as critical design work, referring to design work that calls in to question and even prompts users to critique commonly held beliefs or practices. Similarly, Thomas, Mitchell, and Joseph (2002, p. 44) wrote that designers need to bear an "ethical commitment to creating culturally sensitive products." Indeed, through advancing such a design, we have developed a richer appreciation of why critical curriculum scholars are so impassioned against claims of "truth." In critical work, one begins to question whether idealized notions are useful or, instead, problematic in that they communicate an extraneous, locally immaterial, and potentially hegemonic perspective on the world (Apple, 1976; Freire, 1970/2000; Giroux, 1991). When designing a game, one must not only develop a particular story about the core ideas, but also position players such that they experience outcomes associated with particular choices. This can be challenging in practice because, in choosing which outcomes to associate with given actions, the designer must necessarily privilege particular perspectives over others. In the case of designing an educational game about Uganda, the "win" condition is that which achieves enduring peace, but should this condition be dependent on retributive justice? Or should the game tell a more locally contextualized story, even if such a claim may violate what is more generally argued, namely that justice is prerequisite for peace? We chose to allow for all three choices as possibly bringing about a satisfying closure to the game, but with forgiveness producing the optimal outcome in terms of citizen satisfaction although the player is fired as a result.

Empirical Legitimacy

This design challenge requires intimacy with the situation, the underlying struggles experienced by people who have actually lived the story and it demands recognition of one's own biases. As anthropologists and historians have argued, cultures and histories are human constructions, but their constructed nature should not suggest unconstrained liberty for the designer. Rather, due to both what these works represent and what they will engender, the designer bears a responsibility to ground the work in empirical storylines and locally-felt experiences (Geertz, 1978; Marcus, 1981). It is our experience—and a fundamental argument of this chapter—that it is in the particulars that meanings are engaged and transformation occurs. For us, the Uganda story remains a compelling one, albeit tragic, but not our own story. Though we could have translated a textbook-style articulation of a resolution strategy into a game design (i.e., necessarily advocating justice over amnesty), and though this resolution would still represent an experiential articulation, through more deeply engaging with those whose experiences brought the story to life, we began to understand the limitations of such a simplistic resolution. Through fictionalization, we are able to design with pedagogical liberty about issues that have political sensitivity, ethical subjectivity, and interpretive contestation while still ensuring intrinsic fidelity and projective capacity. The context entwines real and fictional elements designed to embed the learner and the curricular content within a complex and credible situation, establishing what Riffarterre (1990) and Walton (1990, p. 21) referred to as "fictional truths." Clearly, the explicit details and even the unfolding trajectories of our game are fictional, but it s based in very real events and is designed to foster a real experiential state within the player. In fact, it is this freedom to fictionalize that, we believe, makes playable fictions so pedagogically powerful.

Pedagogical Lesson

A core question raised by this project is how best to illuminate particular situations as well as the universal struggles that they manifest. In response to this question, the challenge becomes how to scaffold players in a balanced sense of engagement, neither remaining as mere witnesses, nor interacting with such simplistic rules that the ethical struggle feels trite, nor performing within such a complex game system that the lessons become obscure. In this case, the Ugandan struggles reflect universal tensions and enduring concerns that arise in diverse forms in diverse contexts but still demonstrate underlying aspirations and disappointments. Such honoring of the particular, simultaneous with appreciation of commonality, is a challenge likewise embraced in the field of historical empathy. These practitioners engage in cognitive empathy characterized by informed perspective taking, not projection, sympathy, or personal distress (Foster, 2001; Polman, 2006). They retain their cultural and individual character *in order to* understand another context, and this paradox bears implications for the present purpose. Specifically, our designs seek to bridge between local happenings and enduring issues in a way that does not disperse their local meanings but, rather, positions them within the conversation and, at the same time, engages them in a universal debate (Geertz, 1976). As designers, we strive to recognize not only the commonality of the issues but the shared responsibility for their consideration and, hopefully, solution: our players are implicated in the history of Uganda and invested in its resolution toward peace. It is in the player's reflection on the deeper meaning of these struggles that the pedagogical value of these spaces is realized.

Player Reflection

Intricate game design can not only instantiate such dynamics as these but also foster player reflection about them, and ideally these reflections can involve not only self-reflection in relation to the game space but, more toward our objectives, reflection on the dynamics of the content, that is, the themes and issues of the game. Such reflection, however, is not an affordance directly borne by videogame technology. Media affording precise depiction serve learning that sort of content, such as the visual features of a botanical species, just as media affording fluid motion serve learning content like the principles of physics. Pictures, films, and even videogames may be suited to these ends. For learning less concrete, objective, or instrumental content like values, media affording narrative, interaction, and inquiry are advantageous because such media afford reflection on dynamics of interrelation and mutuality. A player engaged in fictional play is ideally situated to consider multiple perspectives and to integrate them in novel, tentative, productive ways, exhibiting deep learning of values and their meaning. However, if the game does not provide experiences that afford or even necessitate reflection, then the player might not engage deeply with the underlying messages even if he potential to do so exists.

Identity Transformation

A game space like this one serving to illuminate such complex values as peace and justice does not merely portray for players the shocking atrocities and inhumane conditions. In our game, the player inhabits the role of a representative of the ICC who enters Bunala (i.e., Uganda) expecting to implement a plan for rehabilitation—a workable path to peace. As players engage the Bunalan situation, the game context, characters, and dynamics scaffold their progress from initially comparing justice and amnesty to eventually conceiving an alternative solution based on forgiveness. This synthesis emerges through reflection on the game dynamics and, ideally, the player's own transactive identity, and such reflection fosters deep understanding of the dynamics of values and their function in the player's own life. Generalizing from this experience, education might be broadly conceived as a process of transformation (Engeström, 1987). Understanding what conditions lead to true transformation is part of the larger agenda of the work, but minimally we are arguing for embedding learners in situations where they must adapt general concepts to appreciate and transform virtual worlds and, ultimately, reflect on what their critical choices say about themselves. As designers as well as players, not despite but because we retain our identity when engaging with these issues, do we recognize our role in their unfolding and resolution (Clifford & Marcus, 1986).

In closing, it is our belief that through the power of gaming technologies and specifically the affordances of play and fiction, designers are able to invite others to engage in the experience of *their own* story. Such opportunity and responsibility can be daunting. While we created a game, the play dynamics were about real people and real happenings. We had to continually ask ourselves, are the in-game solutions respectful and empowering or naively problematic? Are we helping players to better understand both Uganda and themselves, or might offering our perspective do them a disservice? Asking such questions is essential to a reflexive design process. In answer, we believe that history is less likely to be repeated if these stories are understood. More importantly, despite the disheartening stories that we tell through this work, we continue to believe in people's capacity to reflect on their experiences and to develop their own perspectives: perspectives that may or may not align with those we have designed but that nonetheless allow one to better engage and embrace the stories that our designs illuminate. It is for this reason that we are committed to the design of these stories, even as biased and problematic as they are when designed and played.

We further view games and the dramatic agency they support as providing a powerful medium for establishing fictional spaces that through player actions in relation to the virtual world can help to foster a more ethically sophisticated society in the real world.

ACKNOWLEDGMENT

The work reported in this manuscript was supported by the National Science Foundation (Grant # 9980081 and 0092831) and by the John D. and Catherine T. MacArthur Foundation (Grant # 06-88658-000-HCD). Also, thanks to Eric Hamilton for all his support in helping us come to terms with the ideas included in this manuscript.

REFERENCES

Apple, M. W. (1976). Curriculum as ideological selection. *Comparative Education Review*, *20*(2), 209–215. doi:10.1086/445883

Barab, S., & Dede, C. (2007). Games and immersive participatory simulations for science education: An emerging type of curricula. *Journal of Science Education and Technology*, *16*(1), 1–3. doi:10.1007/s10956-007-9043-9

Barab, S., Dodge, T., & Ingram-Goble, A. (2008). Reflexive play spaces: A 21st century pedagogy. In Steinkuehler, C., Squire, K., & Barab, S. A. (Eds.), *Games, learning, and society: Learning and meaning in the digital age*. Cambridge, MA: Cambridge University Press. [Volume in preparation.]

Barab, S., Dodge, T., Tuzun, H., Job-Sluder, K., Jackson, C., & Arici, A. (2007). The Quest Atlantis Project: A socially-responsive play space for learning. In Shelton, B. E., & Wiley, D. A. (Eds.), *The educational design and use of simulation computer games* (pp. 159–186). Rotterdam, The Netherlands: Sense Publishers.

Barab, S. A., Arici, A., & Jackson, C. (2005). Eat your vegetables and do your homework: A design-based investigation of enjoyment and meaning in learning. *Educational Technology, 65*(1), 15–21.

Barab, S. A., Dodge, T., Ingram-Goble, A., Peppler, K., Pettyjohn, P., Volk, C., & Solomou, M. (2010). Pedagogical dramas and transformational play: Narratively-rich games for learning. *Mind, Culture, and Activity, 17*, 235–264. doi:10.1080/10749030903437228

Barab, S. A., Dodge, T., Thomas, M., Jackson, C., & Tuzun, H. (2007). Our designs and the social agendas they carry. *Journal of the Learning Sciences, 16*(2), 263–305.

Barab, S. A., Gresalfi, M., & Arici, A. (2009). Why educators should care about games. *Educational Leadership, 67*(1), 76–80.

Barab, S. A., Gresalfi, M., Ingram-Goble, A., Jameson, E., Hickey, D., Akram, S., & Kizer, S. (2009). Transformational play and virtual worlds: Worked examples from the Quest Atlantis project. *International Journal of Learning and Media, 1*(2). Retrieved from http://ijlm.net/knowing-anddoing/10.1162/ijlm.2009.0023. doi:10.1162/ijlm.2009.0023

Barab, S. A., Gresalfi, M. S., Dodge, T., & Ingram-Goble, A. (2010). Narratizing disciplines and disciplizing narratives: Games as 21st century curriculum. *Journal for Gaming and Computer Mediated Simulations, 2*(1), 17–30.

Barab, S. A., Sadler, T., Heiselt, C., Hickey, D., & Zuiker, S. (2007). Relating narrative, inquiry, and inscriptions: A framework for socio-scientific inquiry. *Journal of Science Education and Technology, 16*(1), 59–82. doi:10.1007/s10956-006-9033-3

Barab, S. A., Thomas, M., Dodge, T., Carteaux, R., & Tuzun, H. (2005). Making learning fun: Quest Atlantis, a game without guns. *Educational Technology Research and Development, 53*(1), 86–108. doi:10.1007/BF02504859

Barab, S. A., Thomas, M. K., Dodge, T., Newell, M., & Squire, K. (2004). Critical design ethnography: Designing for change. *Anthropology & Education Quarterly, 35*(2), 254–268. doi:10.1525/aeq.2004.35.2.254

Barab, S. A., Zuiker, S., Warren, S., Hickey, D., Ingram-Goble, A., & Kwon, E. J. (2007). Situationally embodied curriculum: Relating formalisms and contexts. *Science Education, 91*(5), 750–782. doi:10.1002/sce.20217

Bruner, J. (2002). *Making stories: Law, literature, life*. New York: Farrar, Straus and Giroux.

Calvino, I. (1999). Why read the classics? In *I. Calvino & M. McLaughlin (Trans.), Why read the classics?* (pp. 3–9). New York: Vintage/Random House.

Central Intelligence Agency. (2008). *The world factbook*. Available from https://www.cia.gov/library/publications/the-world-factbook/

Dewey, J. (1938). *Experience and education*. New York: Macmillan.

Dibbell, J. (1988). A rape in cyberspace (Or TINYSOCIETY, and how to make one). In *My tiny life: Crime and passion in a virtual world*. New York: Holt. Retrieved May 18, 2001, from http://www.levity.com/julian/bungle.html

Eichstaedt, P. (2009). *First kill your family: Child soldiers of Uganda and the Lord's Resistance Army*. Chicago, IL: Lawrence Hill Books.

Engeström, Y. (1987). *Learning by expanding*. Helsinki: Orienta-konsultit.

Falk, R. A. (2000). *Human rights horizons: The pursuit of justice in a globalizing world*. New York: Routledge/Taylor & Francis.

Freire, P. (1970/2000). *Pedagogy of the oppressed*. New York: Continuum.

Gadamer, H. G. (1975). *Truth and method*. New York: The Seabury Press.

Gee, J. P. (2003). *What videogames have to teach us about learning and literacy*. New York: Palgrave Macmillan.

Geertz, C. (1976). From the native's point of view: On the nature of anthropological understanding. In Basso, K., & Selby, H. A. (Eds.), *Meaning in anthropology* (pp. 33–72). Albuquerque, NM: University of New Mexico Press.

Geertz, C. (1983/2002). *Local knowledge* (3rd ed.). New York: Basic Books.

Giroux, H. (1991). Schooling as a form of cultural politics: Toward a pedagogy of difference. In Giroux, H., & McLaren, P. (Eds.), *Critical pedagogy, the state and cultural struggle*. New York: Routledge.

Hannum, H. (2006). Peace versus justice: Creating rights as well as order out of chaos. *International Peacekeeping*, *13*(4), 582–595. doi:10.1080/13533310600988895

Herz, J. C. (1997). *Joystick nation: How videogames ate our quarters, won our hearts, and rewired our minds*. Boston: Little, Brown and Company.

Jenkins, H. (2005). Game design as narrative architecture. In Salen, K., & Zimmerman, E. (Eds.), *Game design reader: A rules of play anthology* (pp. 670–689). Cambridge, MA: MIT Press.

Jenkins, H. (2006). *Convergence culture: Where old and new media collide*. New York: New York University Press.

Legalbrief Today. (2006, October 16). Quotes of the Week. *Legalbrief Africa* (Issue 202). Retrieved from http://www.legalbrief.co.za/article.php?story=2006101612490881

Lenhart, A., Kahne, J., Middaugh, E., Macgill, A. R., Evans, C., & Vitak, J. (2008). *Pew Internet Report: Teens, video games, and civics*. Washington, DC: Pew Internet & American Life Projects.

Marcus, G. E., & Fischer, M. M. J. (1986). *Anthropology as cultural critique: An experimental moment in the human sciences*. Chicago, IL: University of Chicago Press.

Murray, J. (1997). *Hamlet on the Holodeck: The future of narrative in cyberspace*. New York: The Free Press.

Polman, J. (2006). Mastery and appropriation as means to understand the interplay of history learning and identity trajectories. *Journal of the Learning Sciences*, *15*(2), 221–259. doi:10.1207/s15327809jls1502_3

Shaffer, D. W. (2006). *How computer games help children learn*. New York: Palgrave Macmillan. doi:10.1057/9780230601994

Squire, K. (2006). From content to context: Videogames as designed experiences. *Educational Researcher*, *35*(8), 19–29. doi:10.3102/0013189X035008019

Squire, K. D., & Jan, M. (2007). Mad City Mystery: Developing scientific argumentation skills with a place-based augmented reality game on handheld computers. *Journal of Science Education and Technology*, *16*(1), 5–29. doi:10.1007/s10956-006-9037-z

Thomas, D., & Brown, J. S. (2006). *The play of imagination: Beyond the literary mind*. Unpublished manuscript, University of Southern California.

Thomas, M., Mitchell, M., & Joseph, R. (2002). The third dimension of ADDIE: A cultural embrace. *TechTrends*, *46*(2), 40–45. doi:10.1007/BF02772075

Vygotsky, L. (1978). *Mind in society. (Trans. M. Cole)*. Cambridge, MA: Harvard University Press.

(1986). Writing culture. In Clifford, J., & Marcus, G. (Eds.), *The poetics and politics of ethnography*. Berkeley, CA: University of California Press.

Compilation of References

Abbott, A. (1843). *The mansion of happiness: An instructive moral and entertaining amusement* [Board game]. Salem, MA: W. & S. B. Ives.

Abondonware Ring. (2002). Abandonware: The official ring. Retrieved February 22, 2010, from http://www.abandonwarering.com

Abraham, D., & Yacef, K. (2002). Adaptation in the Web-based Logic-ITA. In *Adaptive Hypermedia and Adaptive Web-Based Systems* ([). Berlin: Springer.]. *Lecture Notes in Computer Science*, 2347, 456–461. doi:10.1007/3-540-47952-X_60

Abt, C. A. (1970). *Serious games*. New York: Viking.

Adams, E. (2006). The designer's notebook: Asymmetric peacefare. *Gamasutra*. Retrieved from http://www.gamasutra.com/features/20070131/adams_01.shtml

Addams, S. (1990). *The official book of Ultima*. Radnor, PA: COMPUTE! Books.

Aion Source. (2010). Spam Filter–Block Goldspam. Retrieved February 22, 2010, from http://www.aionsource.com/forum/aion-discussion/73017-spam-filter-block-goldspam.html.

Ajar. (2007). *BioShock spoiler thread* [Online posting]. The Escapist Forums, Gaming Discussion. Retrieved June 1, 2010 from http://www.escapistmagazine.com/forums/read/9.48000-BioShock-Spoiler-Thread#318863

Aldrich, C. (2004). *Simulations and the future of learning*. San Francisco, CA: John Wiley and Sons.

Aldrich, C. (2005). *Learning by doing*. San Francisco, CA: Pfeiffer.

Ali, M. R. (2005). Why teach reverse engineering? *ACM SIGSOFT Software Engineering Notes*, 30(4), 1–4. doi:10.1145/1082983.1083004

Allport, G. W. (1954). *The nature of prejudice*. Cambridge, MA: Perseus Books.

Amichai-Hamburger, Y., & McKenna, K. Y. A. (2006). The contact hypothesis reconsidered: Interacting via the Internet. *Journal of Computer-Mediated Communication*, 11(3), article 7. Retrieved from http://jcmc.indiana.edu/vol11/issue3/amichai-hamburger.html

Amir, Y. (1969). Contact hypothesis in ethnic relations. *Psychological Bulletin*, 71(5), 319–342. doi:10.1037/h0027352

Anderson, C. A., & Bushman, B. J. (2001). Effects of violent video games on aggressive behavior, aggressive cognition, aggressive affect, physiological arousal, and prosocial behavior: A meta-analytic review of the scientific literature. *Psychological Science*, 12(5), 353–359. doi:10.1111/1467-9280.00366

Anderson, R. C., & Pichert, J. W. (1978). Recall of previously unrecallable information following a shift in perspective. *Journal of Verbal Learning and Verbal Behavior*, 17, 1–12. doi:10.1016/S0022-5371(78)90485-1

Anderson, R. C., Reynolds, R. E., Schallert, D. L., & Goetz, E. T. (1977). Frameworks for comprehending discourse. *American Educational Research Journal*, 14, 367–381.

Andrejevic, M. (2004). *Reality TV: The work of being watched*. Lanham, MD: Rowman & Littlefield Publishers.

AP2. (n.d.) Poppy game insult to our war dead. *The Complete AP2*. Retrieved from http://dspace.dial.pipex.com/ap2/dissent/poppy.html

Apperley, T. (2007). Citizenship and consumption: Convergence culture, transmedia narratives and the digital divide. In *Proceedings of the 4th Australasian conference on Interactive entertainment*. New York: ACM.

Appiah, K. A. (2005). *The ethics of identity*. Princeton, NJ: Princeton University Press.

Apple, M. W. (1976). Curriculum as ideological selection. *Comparative Education Review, 20*(2), 209–215. doi:10.1086/445883

Apple Inc. (2009). *Version 2.1.2 (80.3) Apple Inc. dictionary*. Cupertino, CA: Apple Inc.

Arneson, D., & Gygax, G. (1974). *Dungeons & Dragons* [Role-playing game]. Lake Geneva, WI: TSR.

Atari, (2004, June). Driv3R [Xbox].

Au, W. (2000, June 20). Game over. *Salon*. Retrieved from http://www.salon.com/technology/feature/2000/06/20/dark_glass

Avellone, C. (Lead Designer). (1999). *Planescape: Torment* [Computer game]. Beverly Hills, CA: Interplay Entertainment.

Avner, A., Moore, C., & Smith, S. (1980). Active external control: A basis for superiority of CBI. *Journal of Computer-Based Instruction, 6*(4), 115–118.

Axelrod, R. (1984). *The evolution of cooperation*. New York: Basic Books.

Aylett, R., Vala, M., Sequeira, P., & Paiva, A. (2007). Fear-Not! - An emergent narrative approach to virtual dramas for anti-bullying education. In *Virtual storytelling: Using virtual reality technologies for storytelling, International Conference on Virtual Storytelling, Saint Malo, France*. Berlin: Springer. *Lecture Notes in Computer Science, 4871*, 202–205. doi:10.1007/978-3-540-77039-8_19

Aylett, R., Louchart, S., Tychsen, A., Hitchens, M., Figueiredo, R., & Mata, C. D. (2008). Managing emergent character-based narrative. In *Proceedings of the 2nd international conference on INtelligent TEchnologies for interactive entertainment (INTETAIN '08)*, Cancun, Mexico (pp. 1-8). Berlin: Springer.

Bailey, R. (2006). Morality on the brain: Cerebral scans for right and wrong. *Reason Magazine*. Retrieved April 14, 2010, from http://reason.com/news/show/35014.html

Baldwin, J. M. (1973). *Social and ethical interpretations in mental development*. New York: Arno. (Original work published 1899)

Bamby, E. (2007, April 17). Violent video games – recent research. *Psychology and Crime News*. Retrieved April 30, 2009 from http://crimepsychblog.com/?p=1453

Barab, S., & Dede, C. (2007). Games and immersive participatory simulations for science education: An emerging type of curricula. *Journal of Science Education and Technology, 16*(1), 1–3. doi:10.1007/s10956-007-9043-9

Barab, S. A., Arici, A., & Jackson, C. (2005). Eat your vegetables and do your homework: A design-based investigation of enjoyment and meaning in learning. *Educational Technology, 65*(1), 15–21.

Barab, S. A., Dodge, T., Ingram-Goble, A., Peppler, K., Pettyjohn, P., Volk, C., & Solomou, M. (2010). Pedagogical dramas and transformational play: Narratively-rich games for learning. *Mind, Culture, and Activity, 17*, 235–264. doi:10.1080/10749030903437228

Barab, S. A., Dodge, T., Thomas, M., Jackson, C., & Tuzun, H. (2007). Our designs and the social agendas they carry. *Journal of the Learning Sciences, 16*(2), 263–305.

Barab, S. A., Gresalfi, M., & Arici, A. (2009). Why educators should care about games. *Educational Leadership, 67*(1), 76–80.

Barab, S. A., Gresalfi, M., Ingram-Goble, A., Jameson, E., Hickey, D., Akram, S., & Kizer, S. (2009). Transformational play and virtual worlds: Worked examples from the Quest Atlantis project. *International Journal of Learning and Media, 1*(2). Retrieved from http://ijlm.net/knowinganddoing/10.1162/ijlm.2009.0023. doi:10.1162/ijlm.2009.0023

Barab, S. A., Gresalfi, M. S., Dodge, T., & Ingram-Goble, A. (2010). Narratizing disciplines and disciplizing narratives: Games as 21st century curriculum. *Journal for Gaming and Computer Mediated Simulations, 2*(1), 17–30.

Barab, S. A., Sadler, T., Heiselt, C., Hickey, D., & Zuiker, S. (2007). Relating narrative, inquiry, and inscriptions: A framework for socio-scientific inquiry. *Journal of Science Education and Technology, 16*(1), 59–82. doi:10.1007/s10956-006-9033-3

Barab, S. A., Thomas, M., Dodge, T., Carteaux, R., & Tuzun, H. (2005). Making learning fun: Quest Atlantis, a game without guns. *Educational Technology Research and Development, 53*(1), 86–108. doi:10.1007/BF02504859

Barab, S. A., Thomas, M. K., Dodge, T., Newell, M., & Squire, K. (2004). Critical design ethnography: Designing for change. *Anthropology & Education Quarterly, 35*(2), 254–268. doi:10.1525/aeq.2004.35.2.254

Barab, S. A., Zuiker, S., Warren, S., Hickey, D., Ingram-Goble, A., & Kwon, E. J. (2007). Situationally embodied curriculum: Relating formalisms and contexts. *Science Education, 91*(5), 750–782. doi:10.1002/sce.20217

Barab, S., Dodge, T., Tuzun, H., Job-Sluder, K., Jackson, C., & Arici, A. (2007). The Quest Atlantis Project: A socially-responsive play space for learning. In Shelton, B. E., & Wiley, D. A. (Eds.), *The educational design and use of simulation computer games* (pp. 159–186). Rotterdam, The Netherlands: Sense Publishers.

Barab, S., Dodge, T., & Ingram-Goble, A. (2008). Reflexive play spaces: A 21st century pedagogy. In Steinkuehler, C., Squire, K., & Barab, S. A. (Eds.), *Games, learning, and society: Learning and meaning in the digital age*. Cambridge, MA: Cambridge University Press. [Volume in preparation.]

Barber, H., & Kudenko, D. (2007). A user model for the generation of dilemma-based interactive narratives. Paper presented at *Workshop on Optimising Player Satisfaction (AIIDE'07)*, Stanford, CA.

Barkley, R. (2005). *Attention-deficit hyperactivity disorder: A handbook for diagnosis and treatment* (3rd ed.). New York: Guilford Press.

Barr, P., Noble, J., & Biddle, R. (2007). *Video game values: Human–computer interaction and games* (pp. 180–195). HCI Issues in Computer Games.

Barton, M. (2008). *Dungeons and desktops*. Wellesley, MA: A K Peters.

Barton, M. D. (2004, March 17). Gay characters in videogames. *Armchair arcade*. Retrieved April 1, 2006, from http://www.armchairarcade.com/aamain/content.php?article.27

Bateson, C. D., Early, S., & Salvarani, G. (1997). Perspective taking: Imagining how another feels versus imagining how you would feel. *Personality and Social Psychology Bulletin, 23*(7), 751–758. doi:10.1177/0146167297237008

Baudrillard, J. (2003). The Hyper-realism of simulation. In Harrison, C., & Wood, P. (Eds.), *Art in theory 1900-2000: An anthology of changing ideas* (pp. 1018–1020). Malden, MA: Blackwell.

Baudrillard, J. (1988). Simulacra and simulations. In Poster, M. (Ed.), *Selected writings* (pp. 166–184). Stanford, CA: Stanford University Press.

Bayon, V., Wilson, J. R., Stanton, D., & Boltman A. (2003). Mixed reality storytelling environments. *Virtual Reality Journal, 7*(1).

Beasley, B., & Collins Standley, T. (2002). Shirts vs skins: Clothing as an indicator of gender role stereotyping in videogames. *Mass Communication & Society, 5*(3), 279–293. doi:10.1207/S15327825MCS0503_3

Beattie, S. (2007). *Sam Fischer versus Immanuel Kant: The ethics of interactive media*. Paper presented at the 4th Australasian conference on Interactive entertainment, Melbourne, Australia.

Becker, R. (2006). *Gay TV and straight America*. New Brunswick, NJ: Rutgers University Press.

Bell, P., & Linn, M. C. (2000). Scientific arguments as learning artifacts: Designing for learning from the web with KIE. *International Journal of Science Education, 22*(8), 797–817. doi:10.1080/095006900412284

Bell, V. (2009). Experimental philosophy of others' intentions. *Mind Hacks*. Retrieved April 14, 2010, from http://www.mindhacks.com/blog/2009/02/experimental_philoso.html

Bennett, W. L. (2008). Changing citizenship in the digital age. In Bennet, W. L. (Ed.), *Civic life online: Learning how digital media can engage youth* (pp. 1–24). Cambridge, MA: The MIT Press.

Bergin, D. A. (1999). Influences on classroom interest. *Educational Psychologist Journal, 34*(2), 87–98. doi:10.1207/s15326985ep3402_2

Bers, M. (2008). Civic identities, online technologies: From designing civic curriculum to supporting civic experiences. In Bennett, W. L. (Ed.), *Civic life online: Learning how digital media can engage youth* (pp. 139–160). Cambridge, MA: The MIT Press.

Biocca, F. (1997). The cyborg's dilemma: Progressive embodiment in virtual environments. *Journal of Computer-Mediated Communication, 3*(2).

Blow, J. (2006). *Game design rant 2006: "There's not enough innovation in games!"*. Retrieved May 1, 2009, from http://number-none.com/blow/slides/rant_2006.html

Bogost, I. (2006). *Unit operations*. Cambridge, MA: The MIT Press.

Bogost, I. (2007). *Persuasive games: The expressive power of videogames*. Cambridge, MA: The MIT Press.

Bogost, I. (2009). Persuasive games: Gestures as meaning. *Gamasutra*. Retrieved from http://www.gamasutra.com/view/feature/4064/persuasive_games_gestures_as_.php

Bolton, G. (1999). *Acting in classroom drama: A critical analysis*. Birmingham, AL: Trentham Books.

Brenton, S., & Cohen, R. (2003). *Shooting people: Adventures in reality TV*. New York: Verso.

Brey, P. (1999). The ethics of representation and action in virutal reality. *Ethics and Information Technology, 1*(1), 5–14. doi:10.1023/A:1010069907461

Brion-Meisels, S. (1978). *Reasoning with troubled children: Classroom meetings as a forum for social thought*. New York: Moral Education Forum.

Brooks, D. (2009). Where the wild things are. *The New York Times*. October 20, 2009.

Brown, J. S., Collins, A., & Duguid, P. (1989). Situated cognition and the culture of learning. *Educational Researcher, 18*(1), 32–34.

Brown, S., & Vaughan, C. (2009). *Play: How it shapes the brain, opens the imagination, and invigorates the soul*. New York: Penguin Group.

Brown, T. (2006). *Attention deficit disorder: The unfocused mind in children and adults*. New Haven, CT: Yale University Press.

Brown, T. (2009, September). Tim Brown urges designers to think big. *TED: Ideas worth spreading*. Retrieved January 15, 2010, from http://www.ted.com/talks/tim_brown_urges_designers_to_think_big.html

Bruner, J. (2002). *Making stories: Law, literature, life*. New York: Farrar, Straus and Giroux.

Brusilovsky, P. (1994). Student model centered architecture for intelligent learning environments. In Proceedings of Fourth international conference on User Modeling, Hyannis, MA (pp. 31-36).

Bullough, E. (1912). *Psychical distance' as a factor in art and as an aesthetic principle*.

Burch, A. (2008). *Indie nation #19: Execution*. Retrieved April 15, 2010, from http://www.destructoid.com/indie-nation-19-execution-87257.phtml

Butler, J. (2004). *Precarious life: The powers of mourning and violence*. New York: Verso.

Cage, D. (Designer). (2005). *Fahrenheit* [Computer game]. New York: Atari.

Caillois, R. (1961). *Man, play, and games* (Barash, M., Trans.). New York, NY: Free Press of Glencoe.

Caillois, R. (2006). The classification of games. In Salen, K., & Zimmerman, E. (Eds.), *The game design reader: A rules of play anthology* (pp. 129–147). Cambridge, MA: MIT Press.

Cain, T. (Producer). (1997). *Fallout* [Computer game]. Beverly Hills, CA: Interplay Entertainment.

Calhammer, A. (1959). *Diplomacy*. Boston: Games Research, Inc.

Calvino, I. (1999). Why read the classics? In *I. Calvino & M. McLaughlin (Trans.), Why read the classics?* (pp. 3–9). New York: Vintage/Random House.

Carless, S. (2004). *Gaming hacks: 100 industrial-strength tips & tools*. Boston: O'Reilly.

Carless, S. (2009). In-depth: Peter Molyneux on the importance of choice. Retrieved February 12, 2010, from http://www.gamesetwatch.com/2009/08/indepth_peter_molyneux_on_the.php

Carless, S. (2009, April 2). Interview: Screen digest on subscription MMO growth, Blizzard's next. *Gamasutra*. Retrieved from http://www.gamasutra.com/view/news/23003/Interview_Screen_Digest_On_Subscription_MMO_Growth_Blizzards_Next.php

Cassell, J., & Jenkins, H. (2000). *From Barbie to Mortal Kombat: Gender and computer games*. Cambridge, MA: The MIT Press.

Cassell, J. (2002). "We have these rules inside": The effects of exercising voice in a children's online forum. In *Children in the Digital Age: Influences of Electronic Media on Development*. Westport, CT: Praeger.

Castillo, J. J. (2010) Sherif's Robbers Cave experiment: Realistic conflict theory. *The scientific method, science, research and experiments.* Retrieved June 13, 2010 from http://www.experiment-resources.com/robbers-cave-experiment.html

Castle, L. (Executive Producer). (1997). *Blade Runner* [Computer game]. London, United Kingdom: Virgin Interactive Entertainment.

Castronova, E. (2005). *Synthetic worlds: The business and culture of online games*. Chicago, IL: University of Chicago Press.

Central Intelligence Agency. (2008). *The world factbook*. Available from https://www.cia.gov/library/publications/the-world-factbook/

CGW. (1996). *150 best games of all time* (pp. 64–80). Computer Gaming World.

Chan, D. (2005). Playing with race: The ethics of racialized representations in e-games. *IRIE, 4*, 24–30.

Chandler, M. J. (1973). Egocentrism and antisocial behavior: The assessment and training of social perspective-taking skills. *Developmental Psychology, 9*(3), 326–332. doi:10.1037/h0034974

Chao, J., & Holden, J. (2008). One game and two stories: First Wind, Our Second Simulation Thematic Dialogues Concerning a Simulation-Game. Unpublished master's thesis, University of Michigan-Flint, Flint, MI.

Chappel, L. (2008). The vintage game preservation society. *The Escapist*. Retrieved February 22, 2010, from http://www.escapistmagazine.com/articles/view/issues/issue_177/5502-The-Vintage-Game-Preservation-Society

Charles, A. (2009). Playing with one's self: Notions of subjectivity and agency in digital games. *Eludamos, 3*(2), 281–294.

Chilling Effects Clearinghouse. (2010). Chilling effects. Retrieved February 22, 2010, from http://www.chillingeffects.org

Christians, C. G., Ferrâe, J. P., & Fackler, M. (1993). *Good news: Social ethics and the press*. New York: Oxford University Press.

Citizen Science Projects. (2010). Citizen science projects. Retrieved February 22, 2010, from http://citizensci.com

Clarfield, J., & Stoner, G. (2005). Research brief: The effects of computerized reading instruction on the academic performance of students identified with ADHD. *School Psychology Review, 34*(2), 246–254.

Clark, A. (2005). Learning by doing: A comprehensive guide to simulation, computer games, and pedagogy in e-Learning and other educational experiences.

Colby, A., Kohlberg, L., Gibbs, J., & Lieberman, M. (1983). A longitudinal study of moral judgment. *Monographs of the Society for Research in Child Development, 48*(1-2), Serial No. 200.

Collins, A., & Halverson, R. (2009). *Rethinking education in the age of technology: The digital revolution and schooling in America*. New York: Teachers College Press.

Computer Gaming World. (1986). *Inside Ultima IV*. Anaheim, CA: Golden Empire Publications.

Consalvo, M. (2007). *Cheating: Gaining advantage in videogames*. Cambridge, MA: The MIT Press.

Consalvo, M. (2003b). *It's a queer world after all: Studying the Sims and sexuality*. New York: GLAAD Center for the Study of Media & Society.

Consalvo, M. (2009). There is no magic circle. *Games and Culture, 4*(4), 408–417. doi:10.1177/1555412009343575

Consalvo, M. (2003a). Hot dates and fairy-tale romances: Studying sexuality in videogames. In Wolf, M. J. P., & Perron, B. (Eds.), *The videogame theory reader* (pp. 171–194). New York: Routledge.

Consalvo, M. (2005, December). Rule sets, cheating, and magic circles: Studying games and ethics. *International Review of Information Ethics*, pp. 11-12.

Coppola, F. F. (Producer) & Coppola, F. F. (Director). (1979). *Apocalypse now* [Motion picture]. United States: United Artists.

Costa-Soria, C., Llavador, M., & Penadés, M. D. C. (2009). An approach for teaching software engineering through reverse engineering. In *European Association for Education in Electrical and Information Engineering Council Annual Conference Proceedings* (pp. 1-6). Valencia, Spain: European Association for Education in Electrical and Information Engineering Council.

Costikyan, G. (2001). *Where stories end and games begin*. Retrieved from http://www.costik.com/gamnstry.html

Costikyan, G. (2002). I have no words and I must design: Towards a critical vocabulary for games. Retrieved from http://www.costik.com/nowords2002.pdf

Couldry, N. (2006). *Listening beyond the echoes: Media, ethics, and agency in an uncertain world*. Boulder, CO: Paradigm Publishers.

Couldry, N. (2005, March 4-5). Media and the ethics of 'reality' construction. *Media and Belief*. Retrieved from http://www.lse.ac.uk/collections/media@lse/Word%20docs/media_and_ethics_of_reality_construction.doc

Cowan, D. (2009). American Council on Exercise charts 'underwhelming' health benefits. *Gamasutra*. Retrieved from http://www.gamasutra.com/php-bin/news_index.php?story=26016

Crampton, J. (1994). Cartography's defining moment: The Peters projection controversy, 1974–1990. *Cartographica: The International Journal for Geographic Information and Geovisualization, 31*(4), 13–32. doi:10.3138/1821-6811-L372-345P

Crawford, C. (1984). *The art of computer game design*. Berkley, CA: McGraw Hill.

Crawford, C. (1985). *Balance of Power* [Computer game]. Novato, CA: Mindscape.

Crawford, C. (2003). *Chris Crawford on game design*. Boston, MA: New Riders.

Csikszentmihalyi, M. (1991). *Flow: The psychology of optimal experience*. New York: Harper Collins.

Curran, S. (Producer), Curran, S. (Writer), & Susan, G. (Director). (2010). *Global game jam keynote* [Video]. Global Game Jam.

Curtis, A. (2002). *The Thing* [Computer game]. Los Angeles, CA: Vivendi Games.

D'Acci, J. (1994). *Defining women: Television and the case of Cagney & Lacey*. Chapel Hill, NC: The University of North Carolina Press.

Daeg de Mott, D. K. (2001, April 6). Kohlberg's theory of moral reasoning. In *Encyclopedia of Childhood and Adolescence*. Retrieved from FindArticles.com.

Damasio, A. (1994). *Descartes' error: Emotion, reason, and the human brain*. New York: G.P. Putnam.

Davidson, D. (2009). *Well played 1.0: Video games, value and meaning*. Pittsburgh, PA: ETC Press.

Dawson, P., & Guare, R. (2004). *Executive skills in children and adolescents*. New York: The Guilford Press.

Dawson, P., & Guare, R. (2009). *Smart but scattered: The revolutionary "executive skills" approach to helping kids reach their potential*. New York: The Guilford Press.

Dawson, T. (2002). New tools, new insights: Kohlberg's moral reasoning stages revisited. *International Journal of Behavioral Development*, *26*, 154–166. doi:10.1080/01650250042000645

De Freitas, S. (2008). Emerging trends in serious games and virtual worlds. In *Emerging technologies for learning* (*Vol. 3*). Coventry, UK: Becta. [Research report]

De Freitas, S., & Griffths, M. (2007). Online gaming as an educational tool in learning and training. *British Journal of Educational Technology*, *38*(3), 535–537. doi:10.1111/j.1467-8535.2007.00720.x

De Freitas, S. (2006). *Learning in immersive worlds*. Bristol, UK: Bristol Joint Information Systems Committee. Retrieved December 17, 2009, from http://www.jisc.ac.uk/eli_outcomes.html

Deech, R., & Smajdor, A. (2007). *From IVF to immortality: Controversy in the era of reproductive technology*. Oxford, UK: Oxford University Press. doi:10.1093/acprof:oso/9780199219780.001.0001

Delp, C. A. (1997). *Boy toys: The construction of gendered and racialized identities in videogames*. Greenville, NC: East Carolina University.

Delwiche, A. (2006). Massively multiplayer online games (MMOs) in the new media classroom. *Journal of Educational Technology & Society*, *9*(3), 160–172.

Delwiche, A. (2007). From the Green Berets to America's Army: Video games as a vehicle for political propaganda. In Williams, J. P., & Heide Smith, J. (Eds.), *The players' realm* (pp. 91–107). London: McFarland and Company.

Dempere, L. A. (2009). Reverse engineering as an educational tool for sustainability. In *International Symposium on Sustainable Systems and Technology* (pp. 1-3). Washington, DC: IEEE.

Denham, S. (1986). Social cognition, prosocial behavior, and emotion in preschoolers: Contextual validation. *Child Development*, *57*(1), 194–201. doi:10.2307/1130651

Deuze, M. (2009). Media industries, work and life. *European Journal of Communication*, *24*(4), 467–480. doi:10.1177/0267323109345523

DeVane, B., & Squire, K. D. (2008). The meaning of race and violence in Grand Theft Auto: San Andreas. *Games and Culture*, *3*(3-4), 264–285. doi:10.1177/1555412008317308

Dewey, J. (1938). *Experience and education*. New York: Macmillan.

Dibbell, J. (1988). A rape in cyberspace (Or TINYSOCIETY, and how to make one). In *My tiny life: Crime and passion in a virtual world*. New York: Holt. Retrieved May 18, 2001, from http://www.levity.com/julian/bungle.html

Dietz, T. L. (1998). An examination of violence and gender role portrayals in videogames: Implications for gender socialization and aggressive behavior. *Sex Roles*, *38*(5-6), 425–442. doi:10.1023/A:1018709905920

Doctorow, C. (2009). *Makers*. New York: Tor Books.

Doctorow, C. (2009). Homebrew banjo game-controller by RIT students. Retrieved February 22, 2010, from http://boingboing.net/2009/03/26/homebrew-banjo-gamec.html

Dodig-Crnkovic, G. (2006). On the importance of teaching professional ethics to computer science and engineering students. In Magnani, L. (Ed.), *Computing and Philosophy*. Pavia, Italy: Associated International Academic Publishers.

Dourish, P. (2001). *Where the action is: The foundations of embodied interaction*. Cambridge, MA: The MIT Press.

Dow, S. (2009, June). Damn it Jim, I'm a gamer not a therapist. *Ambidextrous*.

Dow, S., MacIntyre, B., & Mateas, M. (2008). *Styles of play in immersive and interactive story: Case studies from a gallery installation of AR Façade.* Paper presented at the ACM SIGCHI Conference on Advances in Computer Entertainment (ACE'08).

Dubner, S. (2009). The 'Guitar Hero' answers your questions. *The New York Times.* Retrieved from http://freakonomics.blogs.nytimes.com/2009/01/13/the-guitar-hero-answers-your-questions/

Dulin, R. (1997). Jedi Knight: Dark Forces II: Review. Retrieved March 17, 2009, from http://uk.gamespot.com/pc/action/jediknightdarkforces2/review.html

Dunne, A., & Raby, F. (2001). *Design noir: The secret life of electronic objects.* Basel, Switzerland: Birkhäuser.

Dunne, A., & Raby, F. (2005). Projects. *Dunne and Raby.* Retrieved January 15, 2009, from http://www.dunneandraby.co.uk/content/projects/

DuPaul, G., & Stoner, G. (2003). *ADHD in the school: Assessment and intervention strategies* (2nd ed.). New York: Guilford Press.

Dyer, R. (2002). *The matter of images: Essays on representation* (2nd ed.). New York: Routledge.

Dyer, R. (1999). Stereotyping. In Gross, L., & Woods, J. D. (Eds.), *The Columbia reader on lesbians & gay men in media, society & politics.* New York: Columbia University Press.

ECE238Spr08. (2008). Assembly language programming. Retrieved February 22, 2010, from http://cratel.wichita.edu/cratel/ECE238Spr08

Edge. (2007). Final Frontiers. *Edge Magazine, 177,* 72-79.

Egeneldt-Nielsen, S. (2005). *Beyond edutainment: Exploring the educational potential of computer games.* Unpublished doctoral dissertation. Retrieved December 15, 2009 from http://www.itu.dk/people/sen/egenfeldt.pdf

Eichstaedt, P. (2009). *First kill your family: Child soldiers of Uganda and the Lord's Resistance Army.* Chicago, IL: Lawrence Hill Books.

Eiriksson, S. (1997). Preservice teachers' perceived constraints of teaching science in the elementary classroom. *Journal of Elementary Science Education, 9*(2), 18–27. doi:10.1007/BF03173774

Electonic Freedom Foundation. (2010). Blizzard v. BNETD. Retrieved February 22, 2010, from http://www.eff.org/cases/blizzard-v-bnetd

Elkind, D. (2007). *The power of play: How spontaneous imaginative activities lead to happier, healthier children.* Cambridge, MA: Da Capo Press.

Elkind, D. H., & Sweet, F. (1997). How to do character education. Retrieved from http://www.goodcharacter.com

Encyclopædia Britannica. (2010). Aesthetic distance. *Encyclopædia Britannica Online.* Retrieved June 10, 2010, from http://www.britannica.com/EBchecked/topic/7465/aesthetic-distance

Engeström, Y. (1987). *Learning by expanding.* Helsinki: Orienta-konsultit.

Erikson, E. (1950). *Childhood and society.* New York: Norton.

Ermi, L., & Mayra, F. (2005). *Challenges for pervasive mobile game design: Examining players' emotional responses.* Paper presented at the Proceedings of the 2005 ACM SIGCHI International Conference on Advances in computer entertainment technology.

ESA v. Blagojevich. (2006). 469 F.3d 641 (7th Cir.).

Fair Labor Association. (2008). Nonprofit organization dedicated to ending sweatshop conditions. Retrieved December 22, 2009, from http://www.fairlabor.org/

Falk, R. A. (2000). *Human rights horizons: The pursuit of justice in a globalizing world.* New York: Routledge/Taylor & Francis.

Falstein, N. (2004, November 10). Natural funativity. Retrieved from http://www.gamasutra.com/features/20041110/falstein_01.shtml

Favaro, P. J. (1986). *Alter Ego* [Computer game]. Santa Monica, CA: Activision.

Fear, E. (2008, January 3). Jade Raymond interviews Hideo Kojima. *Develop*. Retrieved from http://www.develop-online.net/news/29006/Jade-Raymond-interviews-Hideo-Kojima

Fein, G. (1981, December). Pretend play in childhood: An integrative review. *Child Development, 52*(4), 1095–1118. doi:10.2307/1129497

Ferland, M. (Producer). (2006). *Splinter Cell: Double Agent* [Computer game]. Montreuil-sous-Bois, France: Ubisoft.

Filiciak, M. (2003). Hyperidentities: Postmodern identity patterns in massively multiplayer online role-playing games. In Wolf, M. J. P., & Perron, B. (Eds.), *The videogame theory reader*. New York: Routledge.

Fischer, K., Yan, Z., & Stewart, J. (2003). Adult cognitive development: Dynamics in the developmental web. In Valsiner, J., & Connelly, K. (Eds.), *Handbook of developmental psychology*. London: Sage Publications.

Flanagan, M., Howe, D., & Nissenbaum, H. (2008). Embodying values in design: Theory and practice. In van den Hoven, J., & Weckert, J. (Eds.), *Information technology and moral philosophy* (pp. 322–353). Cambridge, UK: Cambridge University Press. doi:10.1017/CBO9780511498725.017

Flanagan, M., & Nissenbaum, H. (2007, September). A method for discovering values in digital games. Paper presented at the Proceedings of DiGRA 2007 Conference, Tokyo, Japan.

Flood, M. M. (1952). *Some experimental games. Research memorandum RM-789*. Santa Monica, CA: RAND Corporation.

Flowers, S. (2006). Harnessing the hackers: The emergence and exploitation of outlaw innovation. Retrieved February 22, 2010, from www.sussex.ac.uk/spru/documents/flowers-paper.pdf

Foo, C. Y., & Koivisto, E. M. I. (2004). Defining grief play in MMORPGs: Player and developer perceptions. In *Proceedings of the 2004 ACM SIGCHI International Conference on Advances in Computer Entertainment Technology.* (pp. 245-250). New York: ACM.

Foot, P. (1967). The problem of abortion and the doctrine of the double effect. *Oxford Review, 5*, 5–15.

Fox, N. (Director). (2009). *inFAMOUS* [Computer game]. Tokyo, Japan: Sony Computer Entertainment.

Frasca, G. (2004). Videogames of the oppressed: Critical thinking, education, tolerance, and other trivial issues. In Wardrip-Fruin, N., & Harrigan, P. (Eds.), *First person: New media as story, performance, and game* (pp. 85–94). Cambridge, MA: MIT Press.

Frasca, G. (2003). Simulation versus narrative: Introduction to ludology. In Wolf, M. J. P., & Perron, B. (Eds.), *The video game theory reader* (pp. 221–235). New York: Routledge.

Frasca, G. (2000). Ephemeral games: Is it barbaric to design a game after Auschwitz? *Ludology.org.* Retrieved from http://www.ludology.org/articles/ephemeralFRASCA.pdf

Frasca, G. (2001). *Kabul Kaboom* [Videogame, Flash software]. United States: Ludology.org.

Frasca, G. (2001). *Videogames of the oppressed: Videogames as a means for critical thinking and debate.* Retrieved May 1, 2009, from http://www.ludology.org/articles/thesis/

Fraser, N. (2005). Rethinking recognition. In Leistyna, P. (Ed.), *Cultural studies: From theory to action*. Malden, MA: Blackwell.

Free Radical Design. (2008). *Haze* [PlayStation 3 software]. Montreal, Quebec: Ubisoft, Inc.

Freeman, M. (1991). Rewriting the self: Development as moral practice. *New Directions for Child and Adolescent Development, 54*, 83–102. doi:10.1002/cd.23219915407

Freeman, D. (2004). *Creating emotions in games: The craft and art of engineering* (p. 157). Berkeley, CA: New Riders Publishing.

Freier, N. G. (2009). Accounting for the child in the design of technological environments: A review of constructivist theory. *Children, Youth and Environments, 19*(1). To be available online from http://www.colorado.edu/journals/cye

Freier, N. G., & Kahn, P. H., Jr. (2009). The fast-paced change of children's technological environments. *Children, Youth and Environments, 19*(1). To be available online from http://www.colorado.edu/journals/cye

Freire, P. (1970/2000). *Pedagogy of the oppressed*. New York: Continuum.

Friedman, B. (1997). *Human values and the design of computer technology*. New York: Cambridge University Press.

Friedman, B., Kahn, P. H. Jr, & Borning, A. (2001). *Value sensitive design: Theory and methods*. Seattle, WA: University of Washington Technical Report.

Friedman, B. (1997). Introduction. In Friedman, B. (Ed.), *Human values and the design of computer technology* (pp. 1–18). New York: CSLI Publications.

Friedman, B., & Nissenbaum, H. (1997). Bias in Computer Systems. In Friedman, B. (Ed.), *Human values and the design of computer technology* (pp. 21–40). New York: CSLI Publications.

Friedman, B., Kahn, P. H. Jr, & Borning, A. (2006). Value sensitive design and information systems. In Zhang, P., & Galetta, D. (Eds.), *Human-computer interaction in management information systems: Foundations* (pp. 348–372). Armonk, NY: M.E. Sharpe.

Fructus, N. (Original designer). (1999). *Seven Games of the Soul* [Computer game]. Paris, France: Cryo Interactive Entertainment.

Fuller, M. (2008). *Software studies: A lexicon*. Boston: MIT Press.

Fullerton, T. (2008). *Game design workshop: A play-centric approach to creating innovative games*. Oxford, UK: Elsevier.

Gadamer, H. G. (1975). *Truth and method*. New York: The Seabury Press.

Gagné, R. M., Wager, W. W., Golas, K. G., & Keller, J. M. (2005). *Principles of instructional design*. Toronto, ON: Thomson Wadsworth.

Galinsky, A. D., & Moskowitz, G. B. (2000). Perspective-taking: Decreasing stereotype expression, stereotype accessibility, and in-group favoritism. *Journal of Personality and Social Psychology, 78*(4), 708–724. doi:10.1037/0022-3514.78.4.708

Garriott, R. (Designer). (1985). *Ultima IV: Quest of the Avatar* [Computer game]. Austin, TX: Origin Systems.

Gasperini, J. (1988). *Hidden Agenda* [Computer game]. Minneapolis, MN: Springboard Software.

Gaynor, S. (2008). *The immersion model of meaning*. Retrieved April 15, 2010, from http://fullbright.blogspot.com/2008/11/immersion-model-of-meaning.html

Gee, J. P. (2005). *Why videogames are good for your soul: Pleasure and learning*. Melbourne, Australia: Common Ground.

Gee, J. P. (2004a). *Situated language and learning: A critique of traditional schooling*. London: Routledge.

Gee, J. P. (2004). Learning by design: Games as learning machines. *Interactive Educational Multimedia, 8*, 15–23.

Gee, J. P. (2007). *What videogames have to teach us about learning and literacy*. New York: Pelgrave MacMillan.

Gee, J. P. (2008). Learning and games. In Salen, K. (Ed.), *The ecology of games: Connecting youth, games, and learning* (pp. 21–40). Cambridge, MA: The MIT Press.

Gee, J. P. (2004). *Game-like learning: An example of situated learning and implications for opportunity to learn*. Retrieved from http://www.academiccolab.org/resources/documents/Game-Like%20Learning.rev.pdf

Gee, J. P. (2005). The classroom of popular culture. *The Harvard Educational Letter, 21*(6), 8. Retrieved December 23, 2009, from http://www.hepg.org/hel/article/296

Geertz, C. (1983/2002). *Local knowledge* (3rd ed.). New York: Basic Books.

Geertz, C. (1976). From the native's point of view: On the nature of anthropological understanding. In Basso, K., & Selby, H. A. (Eds.), *Meaning in anthropology* (pp. 33–72). Albuquerque, NM: University of New Mexico Press.

Genov, E. (2008). Designing robust copy protection for software products. In *International Conference on Computer Systems and Technologies* (pp. IIIB 14.1-14.6). New York: ACM.

Gert, B. (1998). *Morality: Its nature and justification.* Oxford: Oxford University Press.

Gert, B. (1999). Common morality and computing. *Ethics and Information Technology, 1*(1), 53–60. doi:10.1023/A:1010026827934

Gibson, J. P. (2009). Software use and plagiarism: A code of practice. In *Proceedings of the 14th annual ACM SIGCSE conference on Innovation and technology in computer science education* (pp. 55-99). New York: ACM.

Gijsbers, V. (2006). *The Baron* [Computer game].

Giroux, H. (1991). Schooling as a form of cultural politics: Toward a pedagogy of difference. In Giroux, H., & McLaren, P. (Eds.), *Critical pedagogy, the state and cultural struggle.* New York: Routledge.

Glaubke, C. R., & Children Now. (2002). *Fair play?: Violence, gender and race in videogames.* Oakland, CA: Children Now.

Goldberg, E. (2001). *The executive brain: Frontal lobes and the civilized mind.* New York: The Oxford University Press.

Gotterbarn, D. (2008). Video game ethics: Mayhem, death, and the training of the next generation. In *Proceedings of Ethicomp.* Mantova, Italy: Tipografia Commerciale.

Gotterbarn, D., & Moor, J. (2008). Virtual decisions: Just consequentialism, video game ethics, and ethics on the fly. *ACM SIGCAS Computers and Society, 39*(3).

Grace, L. (2009). Critical gameplay. Unpublsihed MFA thesis, University of Illinois, Chicago. Retrieved from http://www.evl.uic.edu/files/events/Critical_Gameplay_Thesis.pdf

Grace, L. (2010, April 10). The games. *Critical gameplay.* Retrieved April 10, 2010, from http://www.CriticalGameplay.com

Grace, L. (Designer). (2009). *Bang! You're Dead* [Windows software]. United States: L. Grace.

Graner Ray, S. (2004). *Gender inclusive game design: Expanding the market.* Hingham, MA: Charles River Media.

Green, C. S., & Bavelier, D. (2003). Action videogame modifies visual selective attention. *Letters to Nature, 42*(3), 534–537. doi:10.1038/nature01647

Greene, J. D., Sommerville, R. B., Nystrom, L. E., Darley, J. M., & Cohen, J. (2001). An fMRI investigation of emotional engagement in moral judgment. *Science, 293*(5537), 2105–2108. doi:10.1126/science.1062872

Gregersen, A., & Grodal, T. (2009). Embodiment and interface. In Perron, B., & Wolf, M. J. P. (Eds.), *The video game theory reader 2* (pp. 65–83). New York: Routledge.

Gross, L. P. (2001). *Up from invisibility: Lesbians, gay men, and the media in America.* New York: Columbia University Press.

Gross, L. P., & Woods, J. D. (1999). *The Columbia reader on lesbians and gay men in media, society, and politics.* New York: Columbia University Press.

Gross, L. (1988). The ethics of (mis)representation. In Gross, L., Katz, J. S., & Ruby, J. (Eds.), *Image ethics: The moral rights of subjects in photographs, film and television.* New York: Oxford University Press.

Gunter, G. A., Kenny, R. F., & Vick, E. H. (2006). A case for a formal design paradigm for serious games. *Journal of the International Digital Media and Arts Association, 3*(1), 93–105.

Haggin, T. (2009). Blackless fantasy: The disapperance of race in massively multiplayer online role-playing games. *Games and Culture*, *4*(3), 3–26.

Halford, N., & Halford, J. (2001). *Swords and circuitry: A designer's guide to computer role-playing games*. Roseville, CA: Prima Publishing.

Halter, E. (2006). *For Sun Tzu to Xbox: War and video games*. New York: Thunder's Mouth Press.

Halverson, S. (2004). Teaching ethics: The role of the classroom teacher. Association for Childhood Education International (ACEI) Subscriptions. Retrieved from http://www.acei.org

Hannum, H. (2006). Peace versus justice: Creating rights as well as order out of chaos. *International Peacekeeping*, *13*(4), 582–595. doi:10.1080/13533310600988895

Harding-Rolls, P. (2007). Western world MMOG market: 2006 review and forecasts to 2011. *Screen Digest* [London]. RetrievedA pril 13, 2009, from http://www.screendigest.com/reports/07westworldmmog/NSMH-6ZFF9N/sample.pdf

Harless, W. G. (1986). An interactive videodisc drama: The case of Frank Hall. *Journal of Computer-Based Instruction*, *13*(4), 113–116.

Hastings, P., Britt, A., Sagarin, B., Durik, A., & Kopp, K. (2009). Designing a game for teaching argumentation skills. In *Proceedings of workshop on intelligent educational games, at the 14ᵗʰ International Conference on Artificial Intelligence in Education (AIED09)*, Brighton, UK.

Hayes, E. (2007). Gendered identities at play: Case studies of two women playing Morrowind. *Games and Culture*, *2*(1), 23–48. doi:10.1177/1555412006294768

Heir, M. (2010). *Designing ethical dilemmas*. Paper presented at Games+Learning+Society conference, Madison, WI.

Henderson, L. (1999). Storyline and the multicultural middlebrow: Reading women's culture on National Public Radio. *Critical Studies in Mass Communication*, *16*(3), 329–346. doi:10.1080/15295039909367099

Hermes, J. (2005). *Re-reading popular culture*. Malden, MA: Blackwell Publishing. doi:10.1002/9780470776568

Herz, J. C. (1997). *Joystick nation: How videogames ate our quarters, won our hearts, and rewired our minds*. Boston: Little, Brown and Company.

Higgin, T. (2010). 'Turn the game console off right now!': War, subjectivity, and control in *Metal Gear Solid 2*. In Huntemann, N. B., & Payne, M. T. (Eds.), *Joystick soldiers* (pp. 252–271). New York: Routledge.

Hocking, C. (2004, September). *Ethical decision making in Splinter Cell*. Paper presented at IGDA Chapter meetingMontreal, Canada.

Hodhod, R., Kudenko, D., & Cairns, P. (2009, April). Serious games to teach ethics. In *Proceedings of AISB'09: Artificial and Ambient Intelligence*, Edinburgh, Scotland, UK.

Hofer, M. (2003). *The games we played: The golden age of board and table games*. Princeton, NJ: Princeton Architectural Press.

Hofmeyr, B. (2009). *Radical passivity: Rethinking ethical agency in Levinas*. London: Springer.

Hollingsworth, J. (2006, March 19). Serenity Now bombs a World of Warcraft funeral. Retrieved from http://www.youtube.com/watch?v=IHJVolaC8pw

Holmberg, K., & Huvila, I. (2008). Learning together apart: Distance education in a virtual world. *First Monday*, *13*(10). Retrieved from http://firstmonday.org/htbin/cgiwrap/bin/ojs/index.php/fm/article/viewArticle/2178/2033.

Honneth, A. (2007). *Disrespect: The normative foundations of critical theory*. Cambridge: Polity Press.

Huang, A. (2003). *Hacking the Xbox: An introduction to reverse engineering*. San Francisco, CA: No Starch Press.

Hudson, C. (Director). (2007). *Mass Effect* [Computer game]. Redmond, WA: Microsoft Game Studios.

Hudson, C. (Producer). (2003). *Star Wars: Knights of the Old Republic* [Computer game]. San Francisco, CA: LucasArts.

Huijboom, S. (2009). Fallout 3: Broken Steel: Broken Steel Walkthrough version 1.01. Retrieved February 12, 2010, from http://www.gamefaqs.com/console/xbox360/file/959299/56480

Huizinga, J. (1955). *Homo ludens: A study of the play-element in culture*. Boston, MA: Beacon Press.

Hull, R. T. (2005). *Ethical issues in the new reproductive technologies* (2nd ed.). Amherst, NY: Prometheus Books.

Humphreys, S. (2008). The challenges of intellectual property for users of social networking sites: A case study of *Ravelry*. In *Proceedings of the 12th international conference on Entertainment and media in the ubiquitous era* (pp. 125-130). New York: ACM.

Huntemann, N., & Media Education Foundation. (2002). *Game over: Gender, race & violence in videogames*. Northhampton, MA: Media Education Foundation.

Ibrahim, M. (2010). Analysis: Reverse engineering and you. *Gamasutra*. Retrieved February 22, 2010, from http://www.gamasutra.com/view/news/26845/Analysis_Reverse_Engineering_and_You.php

IGDA. (2010). Game preservation SIG. Retrieved February 22, 2010, from http://wiki.igda.org/Game_Preservation_SIG.

Igoe, T., & O'Sullivan, D. (2004). *Physical computing: Sensing and controlling the physical world with computers*. Florence, KY: Course Technology PTR.

ImpactGames. (2007). *PeaceMaker* [Windows software]. Pittsburgh, PA: ImpactGames.

Instructables. (2009). Instructables. Retrieved February 22, 2010, from http://www.instructables.com

Intelligent Systems. (2007). *Fire Emblem: Radiant Dawn*. Redmond, WA: Nintendo.

Jarvinen, A. (2009). Understanding video games as emotional experiences. In Perron, B., & Wolf, M. J. P. (Eds.), *The video game theory reader 2*. Cambridge, MA: MIT Press.

Jenkins, H. (2008). *Convergence culture: Where old and new media collide* (revised ed.). New York: NYU Press.

Jenkins, H., Clinton, K., Purushotma, R., Robison, A. J., & Weigel, M. (2006). *Confronting the challenges of participatory culture: Media education for the twenty-first century*. Chicago, IL: MacArthur Foundation.

Jenkins, H. (2005). Game design as narrative architecture. In Salen, K., & Zimmerman, E. (Eds.), *Game design reader: A rules of play anthology* (pp. 670–689). Cambridge, MA: MIT Press.

Jenkins, H. (2007a). From participatory culture to participatory democracy (part 2). *Confessions of an aca-fan: The official weblog of Henry Jenkins*. Retrieved December 20, 2009, from http://www.henryjenkins.org/2007/03/from_participatatory_culture_t_1.html

Jenkins, H. (2007b). From participatory culture to participatory democracy (part 1). *Confessions of an aca-fan: The official weblog of Henry Jenkins*. Retrieved December 20, 2009, from http://henryjenkins.org/2007/03/from_participatatory_culture_t.html

Jeppesen, L. B., & Molin, M. (2003). Consumers as co-developers: Learning and innovation outside the firm. *Technology Analysis and Strategic Management, 15*(3), 363–383. doi:10.1080/09537320310001601531

Johnson, D. (2001). *Computer ethics* (3rd ed.). Upper Saddle River, NJ: Prentice Hall.

Johnson, S. (2005). *Everything bad is good for you: How today's popular culture is actually making us smarter*. New York: Penguin Group.

Johnson, W., & Marsella, L. S., & Vilhjálmsson, H. (2004). The DARWARS tactical language training system. In *Proceedings of the 26th Interservice/Industry Training, Simulation, and Education Conference* (I/ITSEC), Orlando, FL.

Jones, C. (Designer). (1996). *The Pandora Directive* [Computer game]. Salt Lake City, UT: Access Software.

Jones, D. (2008). The emerging moral psychology. *Prospect Magazine*. Retrieved April 14, 2010, from http://www.prospect-magazine.co.uk/article_details.php?id=10126

Juul, J. (2005). *Half-real: Video games between real rules and fictional worlds*. Cambridge, MA: The MIT Press.

Kafai, Y. B., Heeter, C., Denner, J., & Sun, J. Y. (Eds.). (2008). *Beyond Barbie and Mortal Kombat: New perspectives on gender and gaming.* Cambridge, MA: The MIT Press.

Kafai, Y. B. (2006). Playing and making games for learning: Instructionist and constructionist perspectives for game studies. *Games and Culture, 1*(1), 36–40. doi:10.1177/1555412005281767

Kaptelinin, V., & Nardi, B. (2006). *Acting with technology: Activity theory and interaction design.* Cambridge: MIT Press.

Kawano, J. (Producer). (2001). *Shadow of Memories* [Computer game]. Tokyo, Japan: Konami.

Kayany, J. M. (1998). Contexts of uninhibited online behavior: Flaming in social newsgroups on Usenet. *Journal of the American Society for Information Science American Society for Information Science, 49*(12), 1135–1141. doi:10.1002/(SICI)1097-4571(1998)49:12<1135::AID-ASI8>3.0.CO;2-W

Keane, S. (2002). From hardware to fleshware: Plugging into David Cronenberg's eXistenZ. In King, G., & Krzywinska, T. (Eds.), *ScreenPlay: Cinema, videogames, interfaces* (pp. 154–165). London, New York: Wallflower Press.

Keller, J. M. (1987). Development and use of the ARCS model of instructional design. *Journal of Instructional Development, 10*(3), 2–10. doi:10.1007/BF02905780

Kiciński, M. (Game Vision). (2007). *The Witcher* [Computer game]. Warsaw, Poland: CD Projekt.

Kiesler, S., Siegel, J., & McGuire, T. W. (1988). Social psychological aspects of computer-mediated communication. In Greif, I. (Ed.), *Computer support cooperative work: A book of readings* (pp. 657–682). San Mateo, CA: Morgan-Kaufmann.

Kim, N. (1989). Circsim-tutor: An intelligent tutoring system for circulatory physiology. Unpublished doctoral dissertation, Illinois Institute of Technology, Chicago, IL.

Kinder, M. (2000). An interview with Marsha Kinder. In Jenkins, H., & Cassell, J. (Eds.), *From Barbie to Mortal Kombat: Gender and computer games* (pp. 214–228). Cambridge, MA: MIT Press.

King, G., & Krzywinska, T. (2002). *Introduction. Screenplay: Cinema/videogames/interfaces* (pp. 1–32). London: Wallflower.

King, G., & Krzywinska, T. (2006). *Tomb Raiders & Space Invaders: Videogame forms & contexts.* New York: I.B. Tauris.

King, P., & Kitchener, K. (1994). *Developing reflective judgment: Understanding and promoting intellectual growth and critical thinking in adolescents and adults.* San Francisco, CA: Jossey-Bass.

King, C., & Leonard, D. (2010). Wargames as a new frontier—Securing American empire in virtual space. In Huntemann, N. B., & Payne, M. T. (Eds.), *Joystick soldiers* (pp. 91–105). New York: Routledge.

Kirriemuir, J., & McFarlane, A. (2002). *Literature review in games and learning.* Bristol, UK: Futurelab.

Klemmer, S. R., Hartmann, B., & Takayama, L. (2006). How bodies matter: Five themes for interaction design. Paper presented at the 6th conference on Designing Interactive Systems, University Park, PA.

Klepek, P. (2008). Peter Molyneux believes 'Fable II' solves the 'Han Solo Problem'. *MTV Multiplayer.* Retrieved April 14, 2010, from http://multiplayerblog.mtv.com/2008/09/16/molyneux-fable-ii-han-solo/

Klingberg, T. (2009). *The overflowing brain.* New York: Oxford University Press.

Klingberg, T., Fernell, E., Olesen, P., Johnson, M., Gustafsson, P., & Dahlström, K. (2005). Computerized training of working memory in children with ADHD – A randomized, controlled, trial. *Journal of the American Academy of Child and Adolescent Psychiatry, 44*(2), 177–186. doi:10.1097/00004583-200502000-00010

Kohl, B. (2007). *Embryo culture: Making babies in the 21st century.* New York: Farrar, Straus and Giroux.

Kohlberg, L. (1984). *The philosophy of moral development: Moral stages and the idea of justice. Essays on moral development* (*Vol. 1*). New York: Harper and Row.

Kohlberg, L. (1969). Stage and sequence: The cognitive-developmental approach to socialization. In Goslin, D. A. (Ed.), *Handbook of socialization: Theory in research* (pp. 347–480). Boston: Houghton-Mifflin.

Kohlberg, L. (1980). High school democracy and educating for a just society. In Mosher, R. L. (Ed.), *Moral education: A first generation of research* (pp. 20–57). New York: Praeger.

Kohler, C. (2008, August 28). Captain Rainbow: Birdo's gender crisis. *Game Life* Retrieved May 5, 2009, from http://www.wired.com/gamelife/2008/08/captain-rainb-1/

Kojima, H. (Designer). (2004). *Metal Gear Solid 3: Snake Eater* [Computer game]. Tokyo, Japan: Konami.

Kolko, B., Nakamura, L., & Rodman, G. B. (2000). *Race in cyberspace*. New York: Routledge.

Konami Computer Entertainment Japan, Inc. (1998). *Metal gear solid* [PlayStation software]. El Segundo, CA: Konami Digital Entertainment, Inc.

Konami Computer Entertainment Japan, Inc. (2004). *Metal gear solid 3: Snake eater* [PlayStation 2 software]. El Segundo, CA: Konami Digital Entertainment, Inc.

Konami. (2001). *Metal Gear Solid 2: Sons of Liberty* [Playstation 2].

Koslowski, B. (1996). *Theory and evidence: The development of scientific reasoning*. Cambridge, MA: MIT Press.

Koster, R. (2005). *A theory of fun for game design*. Scottsdale, AZ: Paraglyph Press.

Kreimeier, B. (2000). *Puzzled at GDC 2000: A peek into game design*. Retrieved May 1, 2009, from http://www.gamasutra.com/features/20000413/kreimeier_01.htm

Kuhn, D., Goh, W., Iordanou, K., & Shaenfield, D. (2008). Arguing on the computer: A microgenetic study of developing argument skills in a computer-supported environment. *Child Development*, *79*(5), 1311–1329. doi:10.1111/j.1467-8624.2008.01190.x

Kuhn, D. (1993). Science as argument: Implications for teaching and learning scientific thinking. *Scientific and Educational Journal*, *77*(3), 319–337. doi:10.1002/sce.3730770306

Kupperman, J. (2002). *Making meaningful experiences through an on-line character-playing simulation*. Unpublished doctoral dissertation, University of Michigan, Ann Arbor, MI.

Kutner, L., & Olson, C. K. (2008). *Grand Theft Childhood: The surprising truth about violent video games and what parents can do*. New York: Simon & Schuster.

Landers, A. (1995). Heaven and hell – The real difference. In Canfield, J., & Hansen, M. V. (Eds.), *A 2nd helping of chicken soup for the soul: 101 more stories to open the heart and rekindle the spirit* (p. 55). Deerfield Beach, FL: Health Communications.

Lane, H. C., Core, M. G., Gomboc, D., Karnavat, A., & Rosenberg, M. (2007). Intelligent tutoring for interpersonal and intercultural skills. In *Proceedings of Interservice/Industry Training, Simulation and Education Conference (I/ITSEC)* (pp. 1–11).

Lanning, L. (Director). (2001). *Oddworld: Munch's Oddysee* [Computer game]. Redmond, WA: Microsoft Game Studios.

Laurel, B. (1991). *Computers as theatre*. Reading, MA: Addison-Wesley Publishing.

Lave, J., & Wenger, E. (1991). *Situated learning: Legitimate peripheral participation*. Cambridge, MA: Cambridge University Press.

Lavelle, S. (2009). *Opera Omnia* [Computer game]. UK: increpare games.

Lawrence, V., Houghton, S., Tannock, R., Douglas, G., Durkin, K., & Whiting, K. (2002). ADHD outside the laboratory: Boys' executive function performance on tasks in videogame play and on a visit to the zoo. *Journal of Abnormal Child Psychology, 30*, 447–462. doi:10.1023/A:1019812829706

Le Guin, U. K. (1975). *The wind's twelve quarters: Short stories*. New York: Harper & Row.

Leary, T. (1985). *Timothy Leary's Mind Mirror* [Computer game]. Redwood City, CA: Electronic Arts.

Lee, S. (2003). 'I lose, therefore I think': A search for contemplation amid wars of push-button glare. *Game Studies, 3*(2). Retrieved from http://gamestudies.org/0302/lee/

Legalbrief Today. (2006, October 16). Quotes of the Week. *Legalbrief Africa* (Issue 202). Retrieved from http://www.legalbrief.co.za/article.php?story=2006101612490881

Lenhart, A., Kahne, J., Middaugh, E., Macgill, A., Evans, C., & Vitak, J. (2008). *Teens, videogames, and civics*. Washington, DC: Pew Internet & American Life Project.

Lenhart, A., Kahne, J., Middaugh, E., Macgill, A. R., Evans, C., & Vitak, J. (2008). *Pew Internet Report: Teens, video games, and civics*. Washington, DC: Pew Internet & American Life Projects.

Leonard, D. J. (2006a). Not a hater, just keepin' it real: The importance of race- and gender-based game studies. *Games and Culture, 1*(1), 83–88. doi:10.1177/1555412005281910

Leonard, D. J. (2006b). Virtual gangstas, coming to a suburban house near you: Demonization, commodification, and policing blackness. In Garrelts, N. (Ed.), *The meaning and culture of Grand Theft Auto*. Jefferson, NC: McFarland and Company.

Leonard, D. J. (2004). High tech blackface: Race, sports, videogames and becoming the other [Electronic version]. *Intelligent Agent, 4*(4). Retrieved from http://www.intelligentagent.com/archive/IA4_4gamingleonard.pdf

Lepore, J. (2007, May 21). The meaning of life. *The New Yorker*.

Levinas, E. (1996). *Emmanuel Levinas: Basic philosophical writings*. Bloomington, IN: Indiana University Press.

Levinas, E., & Poirie, F. (2001). Interview with Francois Poirie. In Robbins, J. (Ed.), *Is it righteous to be? Interviews with Emmanuel Levinas* (pp. 23–83). Stanford, CA: Stanford University Press.

Levine, J. (2009a). Lessons we've learned from society. *Library Technology Reports, 45*(5), 7–10.

Levine, J. (2009b). Libraries, videogames, and civic engagement. *Library Technology Reports, 45*(5), 11–18.

Levine, K. (Writer). (2007). *BioShock* [Computer game]. Novato, CA: 2K Games.

Levitt, P. (2010). USC Zilkha Neurogenetic Institute. Interview taken on February 3, 2010.

Libby, B. (2009, January 28). *Sustainability themed computer games come to the classroom*. Retrieved December 22, 2009, from http://www.edutopia.org/environment-sustainability-computer-games# Lincoln, Y. S., & Guba, E. G. (1985). *Naturalistic inquiry*. Beverly Hills, CA: Sage Publications.

Lickona, T., Schaps, E., & Lewis, C. (2007). *Eleven principles of effective character education*. Washington, DC: Character Education Partnership.

Lopez, M., & Theobald, P. (2004). Case file 28: Is Square Enix milking the Final Fantasy VII franchise? Retrieved March 12, 2009, from http://www.gamespy.com/articles/551/551742p2.html

Löwgren, J., & Stolterman, E. (1998). Developing IT design ability through repertoires and contextual product semantics. *Digital Creativity, 9*(4), 223–237. doi:10.1080/14626269808567130

Lucas, K., & Sherry, J. L. (2004). Sex differences in videogame play: A communication-based explanation. *Communication Research, 31*(5), 499–523. doi:10.1177/0093650204267930

LucasArts. (1997). *Star Wars Jedi Knight: Dark Forces II*. San Francisco, CA: LucasArts.

349

Lynch, C., Pinkwart, N., Ashley, K., & Aleven, V. (2008, June). What do argument diagrams tell us about students' aptitude or experience? A statistical analysis in an ill-defined domain. In proceedings of a workshop held during *The 9th international Conference on Intelligent Tutoring Systems (ITS-2008),* Montreal, Canada.

Macgill, A. (2007). *Is video gaming becoming the next family bonding activity?* Retrieved from http://www. pewinternet.org/Commentary/2007/November/Is-video-gaming-becoming-the-next-family-bonding-activity.aspx

Machin, D., & Suleiman, U. (2006). Arab and American computer war games: The influence of global technology on discourse. *Critical Discourse Studies, 3*(1), 1–22. doi:10.1080/17405900600591362

Magerko, B. S. (2006). *Player modeling in the interactive drama architecture.* Unpublished dissertation, University of Michigan, Ann Arbor, MI.

Magerko, B. S., & Stensrud, B. S. (2006). Bringing the schoolhouse inside the box-a tool for engaging, individualized training. In *Proceedings of the 25th Army Science Conference,* Orlando, FL.

Main, D. (1975). *Drop Zone 4* [Arcade software]. United States: Meadows Games.

Makow, H. (1984). *Scruples: The game of moral dilemmas* [Board game]. Winnipeg, Canada: High Game Enterprises.

Malaby, T. (2007). Beyond play: A new approach to games. *Games and Culture, 2*(2), 95–113. doi:10.1177/1555412007299434

Malewicki, D. (Designer). (1965). *Nuclear war* [Card game]. Scottsdale, AZ: Flying Buffalo.

Manovic, L. (2008). *Software takes command.* San Diego, CA: UCSD Software Studies Initiative. Retrieved from http://softwarestudies.com/softbook/manovich_softbook_11_20_2008.pdf

Manovich, L. (2001). *The language of new media.* Cambridge, MA: The MIT Press.

Marcus, G. E., & Fischer, M. M. J. (1986). *Anthropology as cultural critique: An experimental moment in the human sciences.* Chicago, IL: University of Chicago Press.

Mary, F., & Anna, L. (2009). *Anxiety, openness, and activist games: A case study for critical play. Breaking new ground: Innovation in games, play, practice and theory.* London: Digital Games Research Association.

Massey, D. (2007). Richard Garriott Interview, Part 2. Retrieved March 2, 2009, from http://www.warcry. com/articles/view/interviews/1436-Richard-Garriott-Interview-Part-2

Mateas, M., & Stern, A. (2005). *Façade* [Computer game]. Procedural Arts.

Mateas, M., & Stern, A. (2003). *Facade: An experiment in building a fully-realized interactive drama.* Paper presented at the Game Developer's Conference, Game Design Track, San Jose, CA.

Matsuno, Y. (Designer). (1993). *Ogre Battle: The March of the Black Queen* [Computer game]. Tokyo, Japan: Quest Corporation.

Mäyrä, F. (2008). *An introduction to game studies: Games in culture.* London: SAGE.

McBrien, J. L., & Brandt, R. S. (1997). *The language of learning: A guide to education terms* (pp. 17–18). Alexandria, VA: Association for Supervision and Curriculum Development.

McConnell, T. (2006). *Moral dilemmas.* Retrieved June 1, 2010, from http://plato.stanford.edu/entries/moral-dilemmas/

Mckenzie, A., & Mccalla, G. (2009). Serious games for professional ethics: An architecture to support personalization. In *Proceedings of Workshop on Intelligent Educational Games (AIED 2009),* Brighton, UK.

McLoughlin, I. (2008). Secure embedded systems: The threat of reverse engineering. In *14th IEEE International Conference on Parallel and Distributed Systems* (pp. 729-736). Washington, DC: IEEE.

Meacham, J. A., & Emont, N. M. (1989). Everyday problem solving: Theory and applications. In Sinnott, J. D. (Ed.), *The interpersonal basis of everyday problem solving* (pp. 7–23). New York: Praeger.

Meadows, M. (2002). *Pause & effect: The art of interactive narrative*. New York: New Riders.

Meltzer, L. (Ed.). (2007). *Executive function in education: From theory to practice*. New York: Guilford Press.

Mendes, S. (Director), Wick, D., & Fisher, L. (Producers). (2006). *Jarhead* [Motion picture]. United States: Universal Studios.

Mergel, B. (1998). Instructional design & learning theory. Retrieved from http://www.usask.ca/education/coursework/802papers/mergel/brenda.htm

Midway. (2005). *Mortal Kombat: Shaolin Monks* [Playstation 2].

Miles, M. B., & Huberman, A. M. (1984). *Qualitative data analysis: A sourcebook of new methods*. Newbury Park, CA: Sage Publications.

Miller, E., & Almon, J. (2009). *Crisis in the kindergarten: Why children need to play in school*. College Park, MD: Alliance for Childhood.

Miller, P. (2006). You got your race in my videogame [Electronic version]. *Escapist, 56*. Retrieved from http://www.escapistmagazine.com/issue/56

Miyamoto, S. (Designer). (1985). *Super Mario Bros.* [Computer game]. Kyoto, Japan: Nintendo.

Miyamoto, S. (Designer). (1986). *The Legend of Zelda* [Computer game]. Kyoto, Japan: Nintendo.

Molyneux, P. (Designer). (2001). *Black & White* [Computer game]. Redwood City, CA: Electronic Arts.

Molyneux, P. (Designer). (2004). *Fable* [Computer game]. Redmond, WA: Microsoft Game Studios.

Monnens, D. (2008b). *Giant tank* [Scratch software]. Denver, CO: Desert Hat.

Monnens, D. (2008a, April 12). An 'interview' with David Main. Message posted to http://deserthat.wordpress.com/2008/04/12/an-interview-with-david-main/

Monnens, D. (2008c). *War and play: Insensitivity and humanity in the realm of pushbutton warfare*. Unpublished master's thesis, University of Denver, CO. Retrieved from http://www.deserthat.com/media/critical_game_theory/game_studies/WarAndPlay.pdf

Moor, J. (1985). What is computer ethics. *Metaphilosophy*, *16*, 266–275. doi:10.1111/j.1467-9973.1985.tb00173.x

Moor, J. (1998, March). Reason, relativity, and responsibility in computer ethics. *ACM SIGCAS Computers and Society*, *28*(1), 14–21. doi:10.1145/277351.277355

Moor, J. (1999). Just consequentialism and computing. *Ethics and Information Technology*, *1*, 65–69.

Moore, M. (2009, February 13). Rapelay virtual rape game banned by Amazon. *The Telegraph*. Retrieved from http://www.telegraph.co.uk/technology/4611161/Rapelay-virtual-rape-game-banned-by-Amazon.html

Morley, D., & Robins, K. (1995). *Spaces of identity: Global media, electronic landscapes and cultural boundaries*. New York: Routledge. doi:10.4324/9780203422977

Mosberg Iversen, S. (2010). Between regulation and improvisation: Playing and analyzing games in the middle. Unpublished doctoral dissertation, IT-University Copenhagen. Retrieved from http://ncom.nordicom.gu.se/ncom/research/between_regulation_and_improvisation%28186467%29/

Mundy, L. (2007). *Everything Conceivable: How assisted reproduction is changing our World*. New York, NY: Anchor Books.

Murray, J. (1997). *Hamlet on the Holodeck: The future of narrative in cyberspace*. New York: The Free Press.

Myers, D. (2009). The video game aesthetic. In Perron, B., & Wolf, M. J. P. (Eds.), *The video game theory reader 2*. New York: Routledge.

Nakanishi, K. (Director). (2002). *Way of the Samurai* [Computer game]. Tokyo, Japan: Spike.

Nasaki, K. (2007). *I Wanna be the guy* [Game]. Retrieved December 23, 2009, from http://kayin.pyoko.org/iwbtg/downloads.php

NCSoft Corporation. (2009). Aion user agreement. Retrieved February 22, 2010, from http://us.ncsoft.com/en/legal/user-agreements/aion-user-agreement.html

Newman, J. (2002). The myth of the ergodic videogame: Some thoughts on player-character relationships in videogames. *Game Studies, 2*(1).

Newsgaming. (2003). *September 12th, A toy world: Political videogame about the war on terror.* Retrieved from http://www.newsgaming.com/press092903.htm

Newsgaming. (2004). *Madrid* [Flash Software]. Uruguay: Newsgaming.

Nichols, S., & Mallon, R. (2005). Moral dilemmas and moral rules. *Cognition, 100*(3), 530–542. doi:10.1016/j.cognition.2005.07.005

Niebuhr, R. (1960). *Moral man and immoral society.* New York: Scribner's.

Nietzsche, F. (2000/1886) *Beyond good and evil.* In *Basic writings of Nietzsche* (W. Kaufman, Trans., pp. 179-436). New York: Modern Library. (Original work published 1886)

Nietzsche, F. (2000/1887) *On the genealogy of morals.* In *Basic writings of Nietzsche* (W. Kaufman, Trans., pp. 437-600). New York: Modern Library. (Original work published 1887)

Nintendo. (2010). Legal information (copyrights, emulators, ROMs, etc.). Retrieved February 22, 2010, from http://www.nintendo.com/corp/legal.jsp

Nucci, L. (2001). *Education in the moral domain.* New York: Cambridge University Press. doi:10.1017/CBO9780511605987

Ochalla, B. (2006, December 8). Boy on boy action: Is gay content on the rise? *Gamasutra.* Retrieved from http://www.gamasutra.com/features/20061208/ochalla_01.shtml

Ohlen, J. (1998). *(Lead Designer). Baldur's Gate* [Computer game]. Beverly Hills, CA: Interplay Entertainment.

Osborne, J. W. (2007). Linking stereotype threat and anxiety. *Educational Psychology, 27*(1), 135–154. doi:10.1080/01443410601069929

Palmer, G. (Producer). (2004). *The video game revolution* [Television program]. Seattle, WA: KCTS Television.

Paoletta, N. D. (2007). *Carry. A game about war.* Carol Stream, IL: Hamsterprophet Productions.

Paoletta, N. D. (2006, July 21). Literacy. *Hamsterprophecy: Prevision.* Message posted to http://hamsterprophet.wordpress.com/2006/07/21/literacy/

Paoletta, N. D. (2010). Personal correspondence. January 29, 2010.

Papert, S. (1980). *Mindstorms: Children, computers, and powerful ideas.* New York: Basic Books.

Papert, S. (1981). Society will balk, but the future may demand a computer for each child. In Hass, G. (Ed.), *Curriculum planning: A new approach* (pp. 99–101). Boston: Allyn & Bacon.

Parker, R. (1984). Blame, punishment, and the role of result. In Feinberg, J., & Gross, H. (Eds.), *Philosophy of law* (4th ed.). Belmont, CA: Wadsworth Publishing Company.

Parkin, S. (2008). Opinion: 'Fallout 3—I kill children'. *Gamasutra.* Retrieved April 14, 2010, from http://www.gamasutra.com/php-bin/news_index.php?story=20908

Peace, C. (1997). *The interactive book: A guide to the interactive revolution.* Indianapolis, IN: Macmillan Technical Publishing.

Penn, G., & Root Associates. (1993). Cannon Fodder instruction manual (p. 18). Retrieved from http://files.the-underdogs.info//games/c/cannon/files/cannon.pdf

Peppler, K. A., & Kafai, Y. (2007). What videogame making can teach us about literacy and learning: Alternative pathways into participatory culture. Paper presented at Digital Games Research Association, Tokyo.

Perkins-Gough, D. (2009). Videogames and civic engagement. *Educational Leadership, 66*(6), 94.

Perron, B., & Wolf, M. J. P. (Eds.). (2009). *The video game theory reader 2*. New York: Routledge.

Piaget, J. (1932/1969). *The moral judgment of the child*. Glencoe, IL: Free Press.

Piaget, J. (1985). *The equilibration of cognitive structures: The central problem of intellectual development*. Chicago, IL: University of Chicago Press.

Pinchevski, A. (2005). *By way of interruption: Levinas and the ethics of communication*. Pittsburgh, PA: Duquesne University Press.

Pinckard. (2003). Gender play: Successes and failures in character designs for videogames. Retrieved April 16, 2005, from http://www.gamegirladvance.com/archives/2003/04/16/genderplay_successes_and_failures_in_character_designs_for_videogames.html

Planet Fallout Wiki. (2009). *Fallout 3 Karma*. Retrieved June 10, 2010, from http://planetfallout.gamespy.com/wiki/Fallout_3_Karma

Platoni, K. (2009). *Computer games explore social issues*. Retrieved December 22, 2009, from http://www.edutopia.org/serious-games-computer-simulations

Pohl, K. (2008). Ethical reflection and involvement in computer games. In S. Günzel, M. Liebe & D. Mersch (Eds.), *Conference proceedings of the philosophy of computer games 2008* (pp. 92-107). Potsdam, Germany: Potsdam University Press.

Polman, J. (2006). Mastery and appropriation as means to understand the interplay of history learning and identity trajectories. *Journal of the Learning Sciences, 15*(2), 221–259. doi:10.1207/s15327809jls1502_3

Poole, S. (2000). *Trigger happy: The inner life of videogames*. London: Fourth Estate.

Portnow, J. (2008). *The ethics of persuasive games*. Retrieved May 1, 2009 from http://www.edge-online.com/blogs/the-ethics-persuasive-games

Prada, R., Machado, I., & Paiva, A. (2000). Teatrix: A virtual environment for story creation. In *Proceedings of the 5th International Conference on Intelligent Tutoring Systems* (pp. 464-473). Berlin: Springer Verlag.

Prensky, M. (2007). *Digital game-based learning*. New York: Paragon House Publishers.

Preserving Virtual Worlds. (2010). Preserving virtual worlds. Retrieved February 22, 2010, from http://pvw.illinois.edu/pvw

Rachels, J. (1999). *The elements of moral society: The elements of moral philosophy* (3rd ed., pp. 70–95). Boston: McGraw Hill.

Raja, V., & Fernandes, K. J. (2008). *Reverse engineering: An industrial perspective*. New York: Springer.

Rauch, P. (2007). Playing with good and evil: Videogames and moral philosophy. Unpublished master's thesis, Massachusetts Institute of Technology. Retrieved from http://cms.mit.edu/research/theses/PeterRauch2007.pdf

Rauch, P. (2008, March 23). Guns, germs and steel: Ethics and genre shift." In *Undisciplined*. Retrieved from http://undisciplinedtheory.blogspot.com/2008/03/guns-germs-and-steel-ethics-and-genre.html

Ravaja, N., Saari, T., Laarni, J., Kallinen, K., & Salminen, M. (2005). *The psychophysiology of video gaming: Phasic emotional responses to game events*. Paper presented at the Changing Views: Worlds in Play, DIGRA.

Ravaja, N., Salminen, M., Holopainen, J., Saari, T., Laarni, J., & Jarvinen, A. (2004). *Emotional response patterns and sense of presence during video games: potential criterion variables for game design*. Paper presented at the Proceedings of the third Nordic conference on Human-computer interaction.

Rawls, J. (1971). *A theory of justice*. Cambridge, MA: Harvard University Press.

Reign-Hagen, M. (Designer). (1991). *Vampire: The masquerade* [Role-playing game]. Stone Mountain, GA: White Wolf.

Rejects Video Game Manhunt, B. B. F. C. 2. (2007). Retrieved March, 2009, from http://www.bbfc.co.uk/news/press/20070619.html

Remedy Entertainment. (2001). *Max Payne*. Espoo, Finland: Gathering of Developers.

Reynolds, B. (Lead Designer). (1998). *Sid Meier's Alpha Centauri* [Computer game]. Redwood City, CA: Electronic Arts.

Ricoeur, P. (2007). *Reflections on the just*. Chicago, IL: University of Chicago Press.

Rideout, V. J., Foehr, U. G., & Roberts, D. F. (2010). *Generation M2 media in the lives of 8- to 18-year-olds*. Retrieved from http://www.kff.org/entmedia/mh012010pkg.cfm

Rideout, V. J., Foehr, U. G., & Roberts, D. F. (2010). *Daily media use among children and teens up dramatically from five years ago*. Retrieved from http://www.kff.org/entmedia/entmedia012010nr.cfm

Riedl, M., & Stern, A. (2006). Believable agents and intelligent story adaptation for interactive storytelling. In *Proceedings of 3rd International Conference on Technologies for Interactive Digital Storytelling and Entertainment*, Darmstadt, Germany (Lecture Notes in Computer Science Vol. 4326). Berlin: Springer.

Rockstar North. (2003). *Manhunt*. New York: Rockstar Games.

Rockstar North. (2002, May). Grand Theft Auto III [Playstation 2].

Rodoy, D. (2003). Manhunt: Hardcore 5-Star Level FAQ. Retrieved April 2, 2009, from http://www.gamefaqs.com/console/ps2/file/915100/27381

Rollings, A., & Morris, D. (2000). *Game architecture and design*. Scottsdale, AZ: Coriolis Group Books.

Rose, N. S. (1999). *Powers of freedom: Reframing political thought*. New York: Cambridge University Press. doi:10.1017/CBO9780511488856

Rouse, R., III. (Writer). (2004). *The Suffering* [Computer game]. Chicago, IL: Midway Games.

Ruberg, B. (2007). *Clint Hocking speaks out on the virtues of exploration*. Retrieved May 1, 2009, from http://www.gamasutra.com/features/20070514/ruberg_01.shtml

Rueda, M. R., Rothbart, M. K., McCandliss, B. D., Saccomanno, L., & Posner, M. L. (2005). Training, maturation, and genetic influences on the development of executive attention. *Proceedings of the National Academy of Sciences of the United States of America*, *102*(41), 14931–14936. doi:10.1073/pnas.0506897102

Runyan, B. (Designer). (2010). *Real Lives* [Computer game]. Marysville, CA: Educational Simulations.

Ryan, M. L. (2001). *Narrative as virtual reality*. Baltimore, MD: Johns Hopkins University Press.

Salen, K., & Zimmerman, E. (2004). *Rules of play: Game design fundamentals*. Cambridge, MA: The MIT Press.

Sandford, R., Ulicsak, M., Facer, K., & Rudd, T. (2006). *Teaching with games: Using commercial off-the-shelf computer games in formal education*. Bristol, UK: Futurelab.

Sandford, R., & Williamson, B. (2005). *Games and learning*. Bristol, UK: Futurelab.

Sartre, J. P. (1957). Existentialism is a humanism. In Kaufmann, W. (Ed.), *Existentialism from Dostoevsky to Sartre* (Mairet, P., Trans.). New York: Meridian.

SCEA. (2005). *God of war* [Playstation 2].

Schank, R. (1995). *Tell me a story*. Chicago, IL: Northwestern University Press.

Scharrer, E. (2004). Virtual violence: Gender aggression in videogame advertisements. *Mass Communication & Society*, *7*(4), 393–412. doi:10.1207/s15327825mcs0704_2

Scheer, K. (Director). (2007). *Karma Tycoon* [Computer game]. New York: DoSomething.org.

Schell, J. (2008). *The art of game design: A book of lenses*. Burlington, MA: Morgan Kaufmann.

Schreiber, I., Seifert, C., Pineda, C., Preston, J., Hughes, L., Cash, B., & Robertson, T. (2009). *Choosing between right and right: Creating meaningful ethical dilemmas in games.* Paper presented at Project Horseshoe conference, San Antonio, TX. Retrieved June 1, 2010, from http://www.projecthorseshoe.com/ph09/ph09r3.htm

Schulz, C., & Wagner, S. (2008). Outlaw community innovations. Retrieved February 22, 2010, from http://epub.ub.uni-muenchen.de

Scorpia. (1986, Jan-Feb). Ultima IV: Quest of the Avatar. *Computer Gaming World,* pp. 12-14.

Sellers, M. (2008). Otello: A next-generation reputation system for humans and NPCs. In C. Darken & M. Mateas (Eds.), *Proceedings of the Fourth Artificial Intelligence and Interactive Digital Entertainment Conference,* Stanford, CA (pp. 149-154). Menlo Park, CA: AAAI Press.

Selman, R. L. (1971). Taking another's perspective: Role-taking development in early childhood. *Child Development, 42,* 1721–1734. doi:10.2307/1127580

Selman, R. (1980). *The growth of interpersonal understanding.* New York: Academic Press.

Selman, R. (2003). *The promotion of social awareness: Powerful lessons from the partnership of developmental theory and classroom practice.* New York: Russell Sage Foundation.

Selman, R., & Schultz, L. (1990). *Making a friend in youth: Developmental theory and pair therapy.* Chicago, IL: University of Chicago Press.

Sensible Software. (1993). *Cannon fodder* [Amiga software]. London: Virgin Interactive Entertainment (Europe) Ltd.

Shaenfield, D. (In review). Arguing with peers: Examining two kinds of discourse and their cognitive benefits. *Discourse Processes.*

Shaffer, D. W. (2006). *How computer games help children learn.* New York: Palgrave Macmillan. doi:10.1057/9780230601994

Shaffer, D., Squire, K., Halverson, R., & Gee, J. P. (2005). Videogames and the future of learning. *Phi Delta Kappan, 87*(2), 105–111.

Shakespeare, W. (1975). *King Henry IV*—First Part. In *The Complete Works of William Shakespeare* (pp. 424-454). New York: Avenel Books.

Shapiro, D. A. (1999). Teaching ethics from the inside-out: Some strategies for developing moral reasoning skills in middle school students. Paper presented at Seattle Pacific University conference on the social and moral fabric of school life, Edmonds, WA.

Shaviro, S. (2003). *Connected, or, what it means to live in the network society.* Minneapolis, MN: University of Minnesota Press.

Shaw, A. (2009b). Putting the gay in game: Cultural roduction and GLBT content in videogames. *Games and Culture, 4,* 228–253. doi:10.1177/1555412009339729

Shaw, A. (2007, September 15-18). *In-gayme representation?* Paper presented at the The 7th International Digital Arts and Culture Conference: The Future of Digital Media Culture, Perth, Australia.

Shaw, A. (2009a, June). Peliharrastaja, or what gaming in Finland can tell us about gaming in general. Paper presented at Under the Mask: Perspectives on the Gamer, University of Bedfordshire, Luton, UK.

Shaw, A. (2010a). Beyond Comparison: Reframing analysis of videogames produced in the Middle East. *Global Media Journal, 9*(16). Retrieved from http://lass.calumet.purdue.edu/cca/gmj/sp10/graduate/gmj-sp10-grad-article-shaw.htm

Shaw, A. (2010b, April). "Nice when it happens": An audience-based approach to the representation of marginalized groups in videogames. Paper presented at Now Conference, Madrid.

Shaw, P., Ward, J. G., & Weber, R. (2005). *Player types and game qualities: A model to predict video game playing.* Paper presented at FuturePlay conference, Ann Arbor, MI.

Sheff, D. (1993). *Game over: Nintendo's battle to dominate an industry.* London: Hodder & Stoughton.

Short, E. (2009). Homer in Silicon: Communicating character. Retrieved February 1, 2010, from http://www.gamesetwatch.com/2009/10/column_homer_in_silicon_commun.php

Shortliffe, E. H. (1981). Consultation systems for physicians: The role of artificial intelligence techniques. In Webber, B. L., & Nilsson, N. J. (Eds.), *Readings in artificial intelligence* (pp. 323–333). Palo Alto, CA: Tioga Publishing Company.

Sicart, M. (2009). *The ethics of computer games*. Cambridge, MA: The MIT Press.

Sicart, M. (2005). The ethics of computer game design. Paper presented at the Digital Games Research Association, Vancouver, Canada.

Sicart, M. (2008). *The banality of simulated evil*. Paper presented at the iEnter.

Sieberg, D. (2000). The world according to Will. Retrieved May 25, 2010, from http://www.salon.com/technology/feature/2000/02/17/wright/print.html

Siegler, R. (2006). Microgenetic studies of learning. In W. Damon & R. Lerner (Series Eds.), D. Kuhn & R. Siegler (Vol. Eds.), *Handbook of child psychology*: *Cognition, perception, and language* (Vol. 2, 6th ed.). Hoboken, NJ: Wiley.

Silva, A., Raimundo, G., & Paiva, A. (2003). Tell me that bit again: Bringing interactivity to a virtual storyteller. In *Proceedings of the 2nd International Conference on Virtual Storytelling*. Berlin: Springer.

Silverstone, R. (2007). *Media and morality: On the rise of the mediapolis*. Malden, MA: Polity Press.

Simkins, D. W., & Steinkuehler, C. (2008). Critical ethical reasoning in role play. *Games and Culture*, *3*(3-4), 333–355. doi:10.1177/1555412008317313

Simkins, D. (2010). Playing with ethics: Experiencing new ways of being in RPGs. In Schrier, D. K., & Gibson, D. (Eds.), *Ethics and game design: Teaching values through play* (pp. 69–85). Hershey, PA: IGI Global.

Simon, H. A. (1973). The structure of ill-structured problems. *AI, 4*, 181–201.

Simpson, D. (1998). Dilemmas in palliative care education. *Palliative Medicine, 1*(2).

Sirlin, D. (2007). *Can games teach ethics?* Retrieved April 15, 2010, from http://web.archive.org/web/20080525080934/http://www.sirlin.net/archive/can-games-teach-ethics/

Sisler, V. (2006). Representation and self-representation: Arabs and Muslims in digital games. In Santoineous, M., & Dimitriadi, N. (Eds.), *Gaming realities: A challenge for digital culture* (pp. 85–92). Athens: Fournos.

Siy, S. (2008). MDY v. Blizzard: Cheating at WoW may be bad, but it's not copyright infringement. *Public Knowledge*. Retrieved February 22, 2010, from http://www.publicknowledge.org/node/1546

Slater, M., & Usoh, M. (1994). Body centered interaction in immersive virtual environments. In Magnenat Thalmann, N., & Thalmann, D. (Eds.), *Artificial life and virtual reality* (pp. 125–148). Chichester, UK: John Wiley and Sons.

Slaughter at the magic funeral [Video]. (2006, May 4). Blog post on *Inane Asylum: Feeds of sound and fury signifying nothing*. Retrieved April 13, 2009, from http://www.hiphopmusic.com/inane/archives/2006/05/slaughter_at_th.html

Slim, H. (2008). *Killing civilians: Method, madness, and morality in war*. New York: Columbia University Press.

Smetana, J. (2006). Social-cognitive domain theory: Consistencies and variations in children's moral judgments. In Killen, M., & Smetana, J. (Eds.), *Handbook of moral development* (pp. 119–154). Mahwah, NJ: Lawrence Erlbaum Associates.

Smith, H. (2010). Jean Baudrillard. Retrieved from http://www.witchboy.net/2010/02/20/jean-baudrillard/

Smith, H., & Spector, W. (Designers). (2000). *Deus Ex* [Computer game]. London, United Kingdom: Eidos Interactive.

Sniderman, S. (1999). Unwritten rules. *The Life of Games 1*. Retrieved from http://www.gamepuzzles.com/tlog/tlog2.htm

Solid States. (2007)... *Edge, 173*, 54–61.

Spears, R., & Haslam, S. A. (1997). Stereotyping and the burden of cognitive load. In Spears, R., Ellemers, N., Oakes, P. J., & Haslam, S. A. (Eds.), *The social psychology of stereotyping and group life* (pp. 171–207). Oxford, UK: Wiley.

Spector, C., & Tyler, M. (1999). Interview with Richard Garriott. In McCubbin, C., & Ladyman, D. (Eds.), *Ultima IX Ascension: Prima's official strategy guide* (pp. 246–297). Rocklin, CA: Prima Publishing.

Spencer, S. J., Steele, C. M., & Quinn, D. M. (1999). Stereotype threat and women's math performance. *Journal of Experimental Social Psychology, 35*(1), 4–28. doi:10.1006/jesp.1998.1373

Square. (1997). *Final Fantasy VII*. Foster City, CA: Sony.

Squire, K. (2003). Video games in education. *International Journal of Intelligent Simulations, 2*(1), 49–62.

Squire, K., & Jenkins, H. (2003). Harnessing the power of games in education. *Insight (American Society of Ophthalmic Registered Nurses), 3*(1), 5–33.

Squire, K. (2006). From content to context: Videogames as designed experiences. *Educational Researcher, 35*(8), 19–29. doi:10.3102/0013189X035008019

Squire, K. D., & Jan, M. (2007). Mad City Mystery: Developing scientific argumentation skills with a place-based augmented reality game on handheld computers. *Journal of Science Education and Technology, 16*(1), 5–29. doi:10.1007/s10956-006-9037-z

Squire, K. (2008). Open-ended videogames: A model for developing learning for the interactive age. In Salen, K. (Ed.), *The ecology of games: Connecting youth, games, and learning* (pp. 167–198). Cambridge, MA: The MIT Press.

Squire, K., & Steinkuehler, C. A. (2005, April 15). Meet the gamers. *Library Journal*.

Staff, E. (2006, October). The lurking deep. *Edge, 169*, 44–49.

Staines, D. (2010). Videogames and moral pedagogy: A neo-Kohlbergian approach. In Schrier, D. K., & Gibson, D. (Eds.), *Ethics and game design: Teaching values through play* (pp. 35–51). Hershey, PA: IGI Global.

Steele, C. M. (1997). A threat in the air: How stereotypes shape intellectual identity and performance. *The American Psychologist, 52*(6), 613–629. doi:10.1037/0003-066X.52.6.613

Stemmle, M. (Designer). (1996). *Afterlife* [Computer game]. San Francisco, CA: LucasArts.

Stern, R. H. (2008). Quanta Computer Inc v LGE Electronics Inc: Comments on the reaffirmation of the exhaustion doctrine in the United States. Retrieved February 22, 2010, from http://docs.law.gwu.edu/facweb/claw/EIPR%27Quanta.pdf

Stewart, N. (2009). *Ethics: An introduction to moral philosophy*. Cambridge: Polity Press.

Stokes, B., Seggerman, S., & Rejeski, D. (n.d.). For a better world: Digital games and the social change sector. New York. *Games for Change*.

Stone, J., Lynch, C. I., Sjomeling, M., & Darley, J. M. (1999). Stereotype threat effects on black and white athletic performance. *Journal of Personality and Social Psychology, 77*(6), 1213–1227. doi:10.1037/0022-3514.77.6.1213

Sutton-Smith, B. (1997). *The ambiguity of play*. Cambridge, MA: Harvard University Press.

Švelch, J. (2010). The good, the bad, and the player: The challenges to moral engagement in single-player avatar-based video games. In Schrier, D. K., & Gibson, D. (Eds.), *Ethics and game design: Teaching values through play* (pp. 52–68). Hershey, PA: IGI Global.

Swink, S. (2009). *Game feel*. Cambridge, MA: MIT Press.

Tangney, J. P., Miller, R. S., Flicker, L., & Barlow, D. H. (1996). Are shame, guilt, and embarrassment distinct emotions? *Journal of Personality and Social Psychology, 70*(6), 1256–1269. doi:10.1037/0022-3514.70.6.1256

Tapper, J. (2007). *Hillary and Manhunt 2*. Retrieved from http://blogs.abcnews.com/politicalpunch/2007/11/hillary-and-man.html

Tapscott, D. (2009). *Grown up digital: How the next generation is changing your world*. New York: McGraw Hill.

Tavinor, G. (2007). Towards an ethics of video gaming. Paper presented at FuturePlay, Toronto, Canada.

Taylor, C. (1994). *Multiculturalism: Examining the politics of recognition*. Princeton, NJ: Princeton University Press.

Taylor, T. L. (2006). *Play between worlds: Exploring online game culture*. Cambridge, MA: MIT Press.

Taylor, L. N. (2008). Gaming ethics, rules, etiquette and learning. In Ferdig, R. E. (Ed.), *Handbook of research on effective electronic gaming in education*. Hersheyp, PA: Information Science Reference.

Team, H. J. (2009). Group report: Choosing between right and right: Creating meaningful ethical dilemmas in games. The Fourth Annual Game Design Think Tank, Project Horseshoe. Retrieved from http://www.projecthorseshoe.com/ph09/ph09r3.htm

Thomas, P., & Macredie, R. (1994). Games and the design of human-computer interfaces. *Educational Technology*, *31*(2), 134–142.

Thomas, M., Mitchell, M., & Joseph, R. (2002). The third dimension of ADDIE: A cultural embrace. *TechTrends*, *46*(2), 40–45. doi:10.1007/BF02772075

Thomas, D. (2004). Jedi Knight: Dark Forces II FAQ. Retrieved March 17, 2009, from http://www.gamefaqs.com/computer/doswin/file/24354/18837

Thomas, D., & Brown, J. S. (2006). *The play of imagination: Beyond the literary mind*. Unpublished manuscript, University of Southern California.

Thomas, J. M., & Young, M. (2007). Becoming scientists: Employing adaptive interactive narrative to guide discovery learning. In *Proceedings of AIED-07 Workshop on Narrative Learning Environments*, Marina Del Rey, CA.

Thompson, J. J. (1976). Killing, letting die, and the trolley problem. *The Monist*, *59*, 204–217.

Thompson, J. J. (1985). The trolley problem. *The Yale Law Journal*, *94*, 1395–1415. doi:10.2307/796133

Thompson, C. (2004, April 7). The game of wife. *Slate*. Retrieved April 1, 2006, from http://www.slate.com/id/2098406/

Totilo, S. (2008). 'Fallout 3' developer tackles, fails to conquer Han Solo problem. *MTV Multiplayer*. Retrieved April 14, 2010, from http://multiplayerblog.mtv.com/2008/07/28/fallout-3-and-the-han-solo-problem/

Totilo, S. (2008). An ethical dilemma like I've never played before — "Fire Emblem" beats "BioShock" at its own game? Retrieved March 19, 2009, from http://multiplayerblog.mtv.com/2008/02/05/an-ethical-dilemma-like-ive-never-played-before-fire-emblem-beats-bioshock-at-its-own-game/

Trotter, A. (2008). Teens and videogames. *Education Week*, *28*(5), 4–5.

Trumbo, D. (1971). *Johnny got his gun*. New York: Bantam Books.

Turiel, E. (1983). *The development of social knowledge*. Cambridge: Cambridge University Press.

Turiel, E., Killen, M., & Helwig, C. C. (1987). Morality: Its structure, functions and vagaries. In Kagan, J., & Lamb, S. (Eds.), *The emergence of morality in young children* (pp. 155–244). Chicago, IL: University of Chicago Press.

Turiel, E., & Davidson, P. (1986). Heterogeneity, inconsistency, and asynchrony in the development of cognitive structures. In Levin, I. (Ed.), *Stage and structure: Reopening the debate* (pp. 106–143). Norwood, NJ: Ablex.

Turkle, S. (1995). *Life on the screen: Iidentity in the age of the Internet*. New York: Simon & Schuster.

U. S. Copyright Office. (2010). Copyright: Fair use. Retrieved February 22, 2010, from http://www.copyright.gov/fls/fl102.html

U. S. Patent and Trademark Office. (2010). Glossary. Retrieved February 22, 2010, from http://www.uspto.gov/main/glossary/index.html

Ueda, F. (Director). (2005). *Shadow of the Colossus* [Computer game]. Tokyo, Japan: Sony Computer Entertainment.

Ulmer, G. (1989). *Teletheory*. New York: Routledge.

Underwood, B., & Moore, B. (1982). Perspective-taking and altruism. *Psychological Bulletin*, *91*(1), 143–173. doi:10.1037/0033-2909.91.1.143

United States Office of Government Ethics. (2009). *Technology saves time and money in ethics training*. Retrieved December 10, 2009, from http://www.usoge.gov/ethics_docs/agency_model_prac/tech_saves.aspx

Valdivia, A. N. (2002). bell hooks: Ethics from the margins. *Qualitative Inquiry*, *8*(4), 429–447. doi:10.1177/10778004008004003

Van Deusen, A., & Burd, E. (2005). Software reverse engineering. *Journal of Systems and Software*, *77*(3), 209–211. doi:10.1016/j.jss.2004.03.031

Van Zelfden, N. (2008). Inside David Jaffe's Heartland. *The Escapist, 146.*Retrieved from http://www.escapistmagazine.com/articles/view/issues/issue_146/4817-Inside-David-Jaffes-Heartland

Venbrux, J. (2008). *Execution, a postmortem (heh)*. Retrieved April 15, 2010, from http://www.venbrux.com/blog/?p=23

Vilhjalmsson, H., Merchant, C., & Samtani, P. (2007, August). Social puppets: Towards modular social animation for agents and avatars. *Lecture Notes in Computer Science* (pp. 192–201). Berlin: Springer.

Von Lohmann, F. (2007). You bought it, you own it: Quanta v. LG Electronics. *Electronic Freedom Foundation*. Retrieved February 22, 2010, from http://www.eff.org/deeplinks/2007/11/ you-bought-it-you-own-it-part-iv-quanta-v-lg-electronics

Vygotsky, L. S. (1967). Play and its role in the mental development of the child. *Social Psychology*, *5*(3), 6–18.

Vygotsky, L. S. (1980). *Mind in society: The development of higher psychological processes*. Cambridge, MA: Harvard University Press.

Waddington, D. (2007). Locating the wrongness in ultra-violent video games. *Ethics and Information Technology*, *9*, 121–128. doi:10.1007/s10676-006-9126-y

Waraich, A. (2004). Using narrative as a motivating device to teach binary arithmetic and logic gates. *ACM SIGCSE Bulletin*, *36*(3), 97–101. doi:10.1145/1026487.1008024

Ward, S. (2009). Journalism ethics. In Wahl-Jorgensen, K., & Hanitzch, T. (Eds.), *The handbook of journalism studies* (pp. 295–309). New York: Routledge.

Wardell, B. (Designer). (2003). *Galactic Civilizations* [Computer game]. Montreal, Canada: Strategy First.

Washington, A. T. (2009, February 18). Babies, pregnancy, grab media's glare. *Washington Times*.

Watson, C. E. (2003, May). Using stories to teach business ethics – Developing character through examples of admirable actions. *Journal of Teaching Business Ethics*, *7*(2), 93–105. doi:10.1023/A:1022660405619

Wegerif, R. (2002). *Thinking skills, technology and learning*. Retrieved from http://futurelab.org.uk/resources/publications-reports-articles/literature-reviews/Literature-Review394

Weizenbaum, J. (1986). *Computer power and human reason: From judgment to calculation*. San Francisco, CA: WH Freeman & Co.

Westecott, E. (2008). *Bringing the body back into play*. Paper presented at the [player] conference, IT University of Copenhagen.

Westell, G. (2006). *War cinema: Hollywood on the front line*. London: Wallflower.

Williams, B. A. O. (2002). *Truth & truthfulness: An essay in genealogy*. Princeton, NJ: Princeton University Press.

Williams, D., Martins, N., Consalvo, M., & Ivory, J. D. (2009). The virtual census: Representations of gender, race and age in videogames. *New Media & Society*, *11*(5), 815–834. doi:10.1177/1461444809105354

Winograd, T. (1997). Categories, disciplines, and social coordination. In Friedman, B. (Ed.), *Human values and the design of computer technology* (pp. 107–113). New York: CSLI Publications.

Woo, J. (Director), & Woo, J., Chang, T., & Sanping, H. (Producers). (2008). *Red cliff* [Motion picture]. United States: Summit Entertainment.

Woods, S. J. (2009). (Play) ground rules: The social contract and the magic circle. *Observatorio (OBS*). Journal, 3*(1), 204–222.

World Emulators, R. O. M. (2009). Retrieved February 22, 2010, from http://www.rom-world.com/emulators.php

World Intellectual Property Organization. (2010). What is intellectual property? Retrieved February 22, 2010, from http://www.wipo.int/about-ip/en

Wright, P. (2009). Trainee teachers' e-learning experiences of computer play. *Innovate, 5*(4). Retrieved from http://www.innovateonline.info/pdf/vol5_issue4/Trainee_Teachers'_e-Learning_Experiences_of_Computer_Play.pdf

Wright, W. (Designer). (1989). *SimCity* [Computer game]. Emeryville, CA: Maxis.

Wu, C. (2008). Some disassembly required. *PRISM October 2008*. New York: ASEE. Retrieved February 22, 2010, from http://www.prism-magazine.org/oct08/tt_01.cfm

Yang, F., Kim, J. H., Glass, M., & Evens, M. W. (2000). Turn planning in CIRCSIM-Tutor. In *Proceedings of the Thirteenth International Florida Artificial Intelligence Research Society Conference* (pp. 60-64).

Yee, N., & Bailenson, J. (2006). Walk a mile in digital shoes: The impact of embodied perspective-taking on the reduction of negative stereotyping in immersive virtual environments. In *Proceedings of PRESENCE* (pp. 24-26).

Zagal, J. (2009, September). Ethically notable videogames: Moral dilemmas and gameplay. Paper presented at the *Breaking new ground: Innovation in games, play practice and theory* conference of the Digital Gameresearch Association, London, UK.

Zanna, M. P., & Olson, J. M. (1993). *The psychology of prejudice: The Ontario symposium* (*Vol. 7*). Hillsdale, NJ: Lawrence Erlbaum.

Zieminski, C. (2008). Game over for reverse engineering?: How the DMCA and contracts have affected innovation. *Journal of Technology Law & Policy, 13*(2), 289–339.

About the Contributors

Karen Schrier is a doctoral student at Columbia University, where she is finishing her dissertation on ethics and games. She also currently works full-time as the Director of Interactive Media at ESI Design, an experience design firm in New York City. Previously, she worked as a portfolio manager and executive producer at Scholastic, where she spearheaded digital initiatives for the Corporate and International divisions. She has also worked at Nickelodeon, BrainPOP and Barnes & Noble's SparkNotes. Karen was the Games Program co-chair of the ACM SIGGRAPH Conference in 2008 and 2009, currently serves on the advisory boards of the Computer Game Education Review (CGER), and is an adjunct professor at Parsons The New School. Karen has spoken on games and learning at numerous conferences, including GDC, SIGGRAPH, AERA, Games for Change, NECC, and SITE. She also helped develop numerous games and digital properties, such as Mission U.S.: For Crown or Colony?; Scholastic Summer Reading Challenge, and Scholastic.com; and Nickelodeon's ParentsConnect. Her digital and non-digital games have been featured in festivals such as Come Out and Play. Karen holds a master's degree from MIT and a bachelor's degree from Amherst College.

David Gibson conducts research at the Equity Alliance at Arizona State University (http://www.equityallianceatasu.org/), the Region IX assistance center of the U.S. Department of Education, and serves as Executive Director of The Global Challenge Award (www.globalchallengeaward.org), a team and project-based learning and scholarship program for high school students that engages small teams in studying science, technology, engineering and mathematics in order to solve global problems. His research and publications include work on complex systems analysis and modeling of education, Web applications and the future of learning, the use of technology to personalize education, and the potential for games and simulation-based learning. He is creator of simSchool (www.simschool.org), a classroom flight simulator for training teachers, currently funded by the US Department of Education FIPSE program and eFolio, an online performance assessment system. His business, CURVESHIFT, is an educational technology company (www.curveshift.com) that assists in the acquisition, implementation and continuing design of games and simulations, e-portfolio systems, data-driven decision making tools, and emerging technologies.

* * *

Sharman Siebenthal Adams is an Assistant Professor of Education at the University of Michigan Flint, where she specializes in technology, literacy, international education, and program development. Much of her work has concentrated on putting technology in the hands of school age learners through the use of digital video and web development production. In addition to being one of the Founding Directors of the Global Program in Educational Technology-Geneva, Switzerland, she also partners with various non-profit organizations, schools, teachers, and students around the world to develop media literacy, game simulations, and other technology related projects. Much of this work concentrates on raising awareness about the importance of community-school partnerships and fostering learning across all age groups.

Sasha Barab is a Professor in Learning Sciences and Cognitive Science at Indiana University. He holds the Barbara Jacobs Chair of Education and Technology, and is the Director of the Center for Research on Learning and Technology. His research has resulted in numerous grants, dozens of academic articles, and multiple chapters in edited books, which investigate knowing and learning in its material, social, and cultural context. The intent of this research is to develop rigorous claims about how people learn that have significant practical, pedagogical, and theoretical implications. His current work involves the research and development of rich learning environments, frequently with the aid of technology, that are designed to assist children and adults in developing their sense of purpose as individuals, as members of their communities, and as knowledgeable citizens of the world.

Jessica D. Bayliss received her Ph.D. in Computer Science from the University of Rochester in 2001. Her background is in Artificial Intelligence, where she has done research on the design and implementation of brain-computer interfaces as well as hyperspectral data analysis for the NASA Goddard Space Flight Center. She joined the faculty of Computer Science at the Rochester Institute of Technology in 2001. Jessica's research interests focus around using technology to help people and in 2005 she received a grant from Microsoft Research for using games as a context in order to teach computer programming concepts. Games turned out to be a very strong motivator for learning computing and in 2009 Jessica became a founding member of the Department of Interactive Games and Media at the Rochester Institute of Technology.

Paul Cairns is a Senior Lecturer in Human Computer Interaction at the University of York. He is a Program Leader for the MSc in Human-Centered Interactive Technologies. His interests are in Human Computer Interaction generally but, with a background in mathematics, he is interested in statistical methods for understanding user behaviour and mathematical knowledge management. He has more recently developed an interest in understanding the positive experience of using interactive systems, in particular, understanding what it means to be immersed in videogames. Dr. Cairns is also very interested in research methods and with Anna Cox wrote: Cairns, P. and Cox, A.L. (2008) Research Methods for Human-Computer Interaction, Cambridge University Press.

Bryan Cash has worked in the game industry for four years now. He studied computer science and theatre at Rice University. Wanting to somehow combine the two, he pursued a Masters degree in Entertainment Technology from Carnegie Mellon University. While there, he was part of the team that designed and installed an interactive tour of the submarine USS Requin for the Carnegie Science Center and worked on a Flash multiplayer game called Skyrates (sky-pirate) that experimented with the idea of sporadic play. Currently he does design and programming work at the Austin, TX branch of Schell Games where he worked on Pixie Hollow (an MMOG of the Disney Fairies universe) and is currently working on an unannounced Nintendo DSi title. Making games is his bliss.

Alice Wen-jui Cheng, MS, is a graduate student in the psychology department at the University of Rhode Island. Alice has been a major contributor to research projects developing assessment tools for measuring executive skills in children and has assisted in the development of a video game-based curriculum for teaching executive functions in the classroom.

Mia Consalvo is Visiting Associate Professor in the Comparative Media Studies program at MIT. She is the author of Cheating: Gaining Advantage in Videogames from MIT Press, and is co-editor of the forthcoming Blackwell Handbook of Internet Studies with Charles Ess. She is President of the Association of Internet Researchers, and she is on the steering committee of Women in Games International. Her current research examines several topics, including the role of Japan in the formation of the videogame industry, the culture and players of casual games, and women's gameplay. Her work has been published in Journal of Communication, Cinema Journal, Critical Studies in Media Communication, Game Studies, and Games and Culture, among others.

Greg Costikyan has designed more than 30 commercially published games—tabletop, PC, online, mobile, and social network—been a game industry entrepreneur, and written extensively about games, game design, and game industry business issues for publications as diverse as the New York Times, Salon, The Escapist, and Verbatim: The Language Quarterly. He has consulted on game industry business issues to clients including Motorola, Nokia, Intel, IBM, British Telecom, France Telecom and Sarnoff Corporation. He designed one of the earliest online games, one of the earliest web games, and one of the earliest mobile games. Some of his writings are extensively used in game studies courses across the globe. He's received the Maverick Award (for "tireless promotion of independent games"), the Gamer's Choice Award, five Origins Awards, and is an inductee into the Adventure Gaming Hall of Fame. At present, he is working as a freelance game designer and game industry business consultant.

Cathy N. Davidson is the Ruth F. DeVarney Professor of English and the John Hope Franklin Humanities Institute Professor of Interdisciplinary Studies at Duke University. Her work for the last decade has focused on the role of technology in the twenty-first century. In 1999 she helped create ISIS (the program in Information Science + Information Studies) at Duke University and, in 2002, co-founded HASTAC (Humanities, Arts, Science, and Technology Advanced Collaboratory, pronounced "haystack"), an international network of networks with now over 4500 members. Her MacArthur research (with HASTAC co-founder David Theo Goldberg) was hosted on the interactive Institute for the Future of the Book website and then published as MacArthur report, The Future of Learning Institutions in a Digital Age (MIT Press). From 1998 until 2006, Davidson served as Vice Provost for Interdisciplinary Studies at Duke and she was a founding co-director of the John Hope Franklin Humanities Institute. Davidson is the author or editor of some twenty books on wide-ranging topics including technology, the history of reading and writing, literary studies, travel, Japan, Native American writing, electronic publishing, and the future of learning in a digital age. Her forthcoming book is Now You See It: The Science of Attention in the Classroom, at Work, and Everywhere Else (forthcoming, Viking Press, 2011). Davidson blogs regularly on new media and learning as Cat in the Stack at www.hastac.org.

Drew Davidson is a professor, producer and player of interactive media. His background spans academic, industry and professional worlds and he is interested in stories across texts, comics, games and other media. He is the Director of the Entertainment Technology Center – Pittsburgh at Carnegie Mellon University and the Editor of ETC Press. http://waxebb.com/

Tyler Dodge holds a doctorate in Instructional Systems Technology and Telecommunications from Indiana University, Bloomington. His work in the research and development of narrative media reflects a concern with media literacies and aesthetics and a commitment to empower youth and to advance design knowledge. More specifically, his research concentrates on empathy as a multi-dimensional, multi-stage construct related to a range of outcomes important in education, from immediate ones like perspective taking to distal ones like citizenship. Professionally, he has co-authored articles and book chapters, presented at conferences and workshops, and taught at the college and high school levels. His community service includes working with youth as a mentor and tutor and participating in theater and poetry events.

Amanda Dyl is a graduate student in the psychology department at the University of Rhode Island. Amanda has been a major contributor to research projects examining parent-child communication about digital media and has assisted in the development of a video game-based curriculum for teaching executive functions in the classroom.

Nick Fortugno is a game designer and entrepreneur of digital and real-world games based in New York City, and a founder of Playmatics, a NYC game development company. Before Playmatics, Fortugno was the Director of Game Design at gameLab, where he served as lead designer on the blockbuster Diner Dash and the award-winning Ayiti: The Cost of Life. Nick teaches game design and interactive narrative design at Parsons The New School of Design and is also a co-founder of the Come Out and Play street games festival.

Ross FitzGerald has been a middle school educator for 22 years. He began his career as a Latin teacher outside of Philadelphia, Pennsylvania and then moved to the Boston, Massachusetts area to engage in counseling work with students at risk for dropping out and for substance abuse. From this background, he moved to independent school administration where he created a curriculum for a newly located school outside Philadelphia. This work included the establishment of an experiential program to complement academic curricula as well as integration of early computer technologies into the curriculum. He currently works as the Eighth-Grade Gradehead at the Shady Hill independent school outside of Boston, where he has developed a curriculum on immigration and served on the Board of Trustees and developed a Service Learning program.

Nathan G. Freier is an Assistant Professor of Human-Computer Interaction in the Department of Language, Literature, and Communication at Rensselaer Polytechnic Institute. He received his Ph.D. in Information Science from the Information School at the University of Washington in 2007. His publications have appeared in such journals as the International Journal of Human-Computer Studies, Journal of Environmental Psychology, Interaction Studies, and Networks and Spatial Economics. His research focuses on children's social and moral relationships to personified technologies, including graphical avatars and social robots. Email: freien@rpi.edu; Web: http://www.rpi.edu/~freien

Edward L. Gentry is a published fiction writer and game designer for both electronic and paper media. His writings include fantasy, science fiction and modern drama. His work in the field of video games focuses on player-centric narrative, agency and innovation in game mechanics. His main game design interests lie in player immersion and perceived morality with a concentration on character development and consequentiality that drives participation. He is the Lead Writer and Designer for Quest Atlantis, an educational video game, as well as an original member of Playable Fictions Studios.

Lindsay Grace is a teacher, software developer and designer. He earned the Masters of Science in Computer Information Systems and the Bachelor of Arts in English, both from Northwestern University. He also completed the Master of Fine Arts at the University of Illinois' Electronic Visualization Laboratory. He has served industry as an independent consultant, web designer, software developer, entrepreneur, business analyst and writer. Lindsay has a joint position between Miami University's Armstrong Institute for Interactive Media Studies and the School of Fine Arts. His research areas include human-computer interaction, creative and critical gameplay, and web design. He writes regularly about interactive media design and education.

Jennifer Groff is a visiting Fulbright Scholar at Futurelab in Bristol, United Kingdom. Her research focuses on innovation and systems design for education. She is also a collaborating researcher on the OECD project Innovative Learning Environment. Formerly an elementary Instructional Support teacher and a middle school teacher of Gifted Learners, Jennifer most recently served as the Resident Academic Technologist at the Shady Hill School in Cambridge, Massachusetts where she led a school-wide technology & innovation transformation initiative that spanned two years. She has also served in various educational research roles at the Annenberg Institute for School Reform at Brown University and the Education Arcade and Teacher Education Program at MIT. Jennifer holds a master's degree in Educational Technology and in Specialized Studies in education, and she is a Microsoft Innovative Teacher Leader and a Google Certified Teacher.

Andrea Gunraj has a decade of experience in youth and community development, gender-based violence prevention, anti-racism/anti-oppressive practice, and sexual and reproductive health. She is currently Outreach Director at the Toronto-based Metropolitan Action Committee on Violence Against Women and Children (METRAC), an organization that seeks to prevent violence against diverse women, youth, and children. An avid writer, Andrea's first novel "The Sudden Disappearance of Seetha" was published by Random House of Canada in January 2009.

Rania Hodhod is a Ph.D. student and a member of the Artificial Intelligence Research Group in the Computer Science Department at the University of York, with Departmental Overseas Research Studentship (DORS). Her aim is to create an adaptive educational interactive narrative drama by integrating intelligent tutoring systems main components to the interactive narrative environments. Rania got her Masters degree in computer and information sciences from Ain Shams University, Egypt. She also obtained a diploma on Tutoring in on-line learning environment from the E-Learning lab, Aalborg University, Denmark. Her research interests include e-learning, intelligent tutoring systems, educational games and user modeling. Within these areas, Rania has several publications in international conferences that have gained general interest. Rania was also responsible of developing and designing an online course in computer science during her participation in the European funded project, The Mediterranean Virtual University.

Jeremiah Holden received his M.Ed. from the University of Michigan-Flint's Technology in Education: Global Program. He began his career as an educator by founding the Voice is Power Academy at

Middle School 22 in New York City, is a former mathematics and English teacher, and is an alumnus of Teach For America. He also directed civic engagement programs for high school students through YouthAction NYC at the Citizens' Committee for Children of New York. He will begin his doctoral research with the Games, Learning, and Society Research Group at the University of Wisconsin's School of Education in the fall of 2010.

Link Hughes is a Game Designer at CCP with a background in programming, ritual studies, and theater. He has previously shipped two young adult titles for the Nintendo DS and now works at CCP North America in Atlanta, GA where he is hard at work on an unannounced MMO.

Mitu Khandaker is currently a Ph.D. candidate at the University of Portsmouth, UK, where she is a member of the Advanced Games Research Group at the School of Creative Technologies. She holds a Master of Engineering degree in Computer Engineering, also from the University of Portsmouth. Her research interests are based around embodiment in video games. She was also a Kauffman Global Scholar, during which time she was an intern at the Education Arcade at MIT.

Daniel Kudenko is a lecturer in Computer Science at the University of York, UK. His research areas are AI for interactive entertainment, machine learning (specifically reinforcement learning), user modeling, and multi-agent systems. In many of these areas he has collaborated with industrial partners in the entertainment and military sector, and has been involved in projects for Eidos, QinetiQ, as well as the Ministry of Defense. Dr. Kudenko has been heading a research group in York on AI for games and interactive entertainment, which works on topics ranging from interactive drama for entertainment and education to football commentary generation. Dr. Kudenko received a Ph.D. in machine learning in 1998 at Rutgers University, NJ. He has participated in several research projects at the University of York, Rutgers University, AT&T Laboratories, and the German Research Center for AI (DFKI) on various topics in artificial intelligence. Dr. Kudenko's work has been published in more than 70 peer-reviewed papers. He has served on multiple program committees and has been chairing a number of workshops, as well as co-edited three Springer LNCS volumes.

Randy Kulman, Ph.D., is the Founder and President of LearningWorks for Kids, an educational technology firm that specializes in the use of video games for teaching executive-functioning and academic skills. He has been the Clinical Director of South County Child and Family Consultants, a multidisciplinary group of private practitioners that specialize in assessment and interventions for children with learning and attention difficulties. He is the author of numerous essays on the use of digital technologies for improving executive functioning skills in children and has developed concepts such as "play diets," and "engamement" to help parents and teachers understand the impact of digital technologies on children. His current research projects include the development of a parent and teacher scale for assessing executive functioning skills in children and phase two of a multi-school based study of using popular video games to teach problem solving skills.

Stephanie Marshall, MA is a graduate student in the psychology department at the University of Rhode Island. Stephanie has been a major contributor to research projects examining parent-child communication about digital media and has assisted in the development of a video game-based curriculum for teaching executive functions in the classroom.

Jonathan Melenson was first smitten with a love of video games upon encountering the arcade game Kangaroo as a small child. Mesmerized by the flashing lights, he begged his father for a quarter and ever since has been fascinated by the medium and its capacity to express ideas. More recently, he has worked as an instructional designer, creating educational software and training simulations for Fortune 500 companies, non-profit organizations, and the United States Armed Forces. His design work has won awards at the Utah Multimedia Arts Festival, the Chief Learning Officer Provider Awards, and the 2008 Davey Awards. He holds a B.A. in philosophy from Brandeis University and currently resides in Arlington, VA.

Devin Monnens is an independent scholar and game designer working with socially conscious games, game history, and preservation. He holds an MFA in Electronic Media Arts Design with a focus on antiwar games from the University of Denver, after which he taught Introduction to Game Design at the University of Colorado, Colorado Springs. He is an active member of the International Game Developers Association (IGDA), working with the IGDA Game Preservation Special Interest Group (SIG) on preservation projects and memorials to deceased game developers. In 2009, he helped author the SIG's paper Before It's Too Late: A Digital Game Preservation White Paper, published in American Journal of Play 2 (2). Currently, he is working on several projects in game criticism, history, and preservation, including an in-depth survey of videogames designed prior to 1973.

Patrick Pettyjohn is a Learning Science Ph.D. student at Indiana University. He is interested in developing a means of understanding how people perceive opportunities for action, which he seeks to apply to areas of education, leadership development, and philanthropies. His current work involves designing and researching how multi-user virtual learning environments can be used as reflective tools that communicate one's academic understanding while simultaneously allowing the player to experience the consequences of their choices and ethical beliefs. His research interests have been strongly influenced by domestic and cross-cultural roles with various nonprofit organizations and as a personal and team consultant.

Peter Rauch is a graduate of MIT's Comparative Media Studies graduate program, and studies the intersections between fiction, morality, and rule sets in videogames and other media. He has previously published work in the Journal of Social Science Education, as well as the pop-philosophy anthology The Legend of Zelda and Philosophy. He resides in Cambridge, Massachusetts, from whence he haphazardly maintains a blog at http://undisciplinedtheory.blogspot.com.

Louis Ruffolo, Ph.D. is a licensed psychologist and certified school psychologist who specializes in the assessment of ADHD. He has been a major contributor to research projects examining brain-training games, parent-child communication about digital media and has assisted in the development of a video game-based curriculum for teaching executive functions in the classroom.

Susana Ruiz is a media artist and scholar working in the intersections between art, game design, documentary and activism. In partnership with mtvU and a team of USC colleagues, Susana developed the game Darfur is Dying, which won several awards, was said to be one of the best representations of life in Darfur by Pulitzer Prize winner New York Times columnist Nicholas Kristof, and was presented in Capitol Hill to members of Congress. The game RePlay: Finding Zoe—a collaboration with the Metropolitan Action Committee on Violence Against Women and Children—addresses gender stereotyping and teen dating abuse, and is also a multiple award winner. She received a BFA from The Cooper Union and an MFA from the University of Southern California, where she is currently a doctoral student. She is the co-founder of the game design collective Take Action Games, which seeks to address critical social issues via innovative gameplay.

Asmalina Saleh is a Ph.D. student in Indiana University's Learning Sciences program. Her work includes designing casual games for an independent game design company and the implementation of educational games in classrooms. Her current research interests include learning and design for classrooms, with a focus on how cultural and social histories impact implementation. In particular, she is interested in the trajectory and emergence of youth owned spaces. Her current work involves designing game based curriculum for informal and formal learning environments by introducing advanced academic concepts to younger children. These designs are predicated on the belief that immersive learning environments provide rich contexts for children of all ages to learn and create empowering and transformative identities of their own.

Emilie T. ("Tobi") Saulnier is the Founder and CEO of 1st Playable Productions, a video game development studio with a focus on handheld games for children. She received her PhD in Electrical Engineering from Rensselaer Polytechnic Institute in 1994. Before joining the game industry, Tobi spent 12 years at General Electric Research and Development in research and management positions in R&D in embedded and distributed systems, where she earned 16 patents and wrote articles appearing in over 25 professional publications. As a former President of the Montessori School of Albany, and mother of two, she is particularly interested in how the virtual world and games can have a positive impact on children, whether for education or for play. Email: tobi@1stplayable.com; Web: http://www.1stplayable.com.

Ian Schreiber has worked in the game industry as a programmer and game designer since the year 2000, and has been teaching game design and development since 2006. He is currently a freelancer and adjunct faculty based in Columbus, Ohio.

David I. Schwartz, PhD, published two textbooks while completing his dissertation in civil engineering, which sparked Cornell University's interest. So, in 1999, Schwartz accepted a lecturer position in the Department of Computer Science to teach computer programming. Recognizing the academic potential of games, Schwartz founded the Game Design Initiative at Cornell (GDIAC) in 2001. By 2006 Cornell offered a Minor in Game Design, the first formal undergraduate Ivy League games program. In 2007, Schwartz joined the Rochester Institute of Technology's Game Design & Development program as an assistant professor. In 2009, he joined his new colleagues in founding RIT's Department of Interactive Games and Media, in which Schwartz's engineering and computer science experience paved the way for him to teach game programming, prototyping, design, and physical modeling. Dr. Schwartz currently researchers a range of applications: instructional design and sustainability ethics education, wargame design, and alternative interfaces.

David Shaenfield is an Adjunct Assistant Professor at Teachers College, Columbia University and Hunter College. His research focuses on the development of argumentative and collaborative skills across the lifespan focusing on the meta-level processes regulating these skills. He is excited to extend his work into the world of video games to investigate the potential of game play in developing metacognitive competencies. David has spoken at AERA, ICLS, The Piaget Society, and IES. He has a doctorate in Cognitive Studies of Education from Teachers College, Columbia University and a B.A. from the University of Texas at Austin.

Nahil Sharkasi is a recent graduate of the University of Southern California's Interactive Media Division within the School of Cinematic Arts. She spent her time at USC researching methods for designing games that illustrate complex real-life systems and communicate factual information. Through work in the Game Innovation Lab, she participated in game projects such as Participation Nation for the Corporation for Public Broadcasting, a game which teaches American constitutional history, as well as contributing to a study on inter-generational play patterns for The Joan Gantz Cooney Center and Sesame Workshop. Seeds was Sharkasi's M.F.A. graduate thesis project at USC. She also holds a B.A. in Broadcast Journalism from the University of Maryland.

Adrienne Shaw is a Ph.D. Candidate at the University of Pennsylvania's Annenberg School for Communication. Her research focuses on popular culture, the politics of representation, cultural production and qualitative audience research. Her primary areas of interest are video games, gaming culture, representations of gender and sexuality, and the construction of identity and communities in relation to media consumption.

Jennifer Slater has worked for five years with LearningWorks for Kids, and has studied the relationship between executive functioning and academic skills, as well as worked to develop recommendations for parents and teachers to help children in specific skill areas. Jen is a current graduate student at the University of Rhode Island, pursuing a Master's degree in Education.

Jamey Stevenson is a writer, programmer, and game designer who hails from Albany, NY, but currently resides in Dundee, Scotland. After earning a degree in Game Design and Development from Full Sail University in Orlando, FL, he cut his teeth developing handheld and mobile games at 1st Playable Productions in Troy, NY. He is currently toiling away on some top secret AI-related projects at Realtime Worlds in Dundee; projects which almost certainly do not entail the imminent subjugation of the human race. While you wait for all of the startling details to be unveiled, please feel free to pass the time by visiting Jamey's blog at http://jameystevenson.com, where you will discover absolutely no evidence to support any erroneous claims regarding an alleged production fleet of sinister robotic henchmen.

Gary Stoner, Ph.D., is Professor and Director of the School Psychology Program, Psychology Department, University of Rhode Island. Dr. Stoner is currently the Chair of the American Psychological Association Interdivisional Coalition for Psychology in Schools and Education. He served as the President of Division 16 (School Psychology) of the American Psychological Association from January 2005 through December 2007. Gary is the co-author of the best-selling book, ADHD in the Schools. He has written dozens of articles and books about Attention Deficit Hyperactivity Disorders and is currently involved in research examining the impact of video games and digital technologies on children with attention and learning problems. Gary's recent research has explored the use of computerized reading programs with children with ADHD. He is also involved in a set of studies that examines parent-child communication about the use of video games and other digital technologies.

Chris Weaver is the Founder of Bethesda Softworks, a software entertainment company that has won every major national and international industry award, including over two hundred "Best Game of the Year" awards, the Codie, IGDA and ADC awards, two Clios and the Golden Cyber Lion at Cannes. Bethesda is credited with the creation of physics-based sports simulation and built the original John Madden Football, which has become the top-selling sports game of all time. Bethesda has also created over 75 other hit titles, including Gridiron; Wayne Gretzky Hockey; The Terminator, Burnout Drag Racing, NCAA Basketball, and The Elder Scrolls — one of the best-selling role-playing series in the history of computer games. Last year the company released Fallout 3 and earlier this year acquired id Software. Chris received his SM in Engineering from MIT and was the initial Daltry Scholar at Wesleyan University, where he earned dual Masters Degrees in Japanese and Computer Science and a dual CAS Doctoral Degree in Japanese and Physics. An author and advisor to government and industry, he holds patents in interactive media, system security and broadband communications. A former member of the Architecture Machine Group and Fellow of the MIT Communications and Policy Program, Weaver was a Fellow of the Robotics Simulation Laboratory at Carnegie Mellon and currently teaches at MIT in the Comparative Media Studies program and as a Senior Fellow in Engineering. He is a Board Member of the MIT Communications Technology Roadmap group and a Visiting Scientist in the Microphotonics Center. In 2005, he was inducted into the Cosmos Club for excellence in engineering.

Pete Vigeant is an Interaction Designer for ESI Design, a camp activities expert, experiential educator and gaming enthusiast. He worked on the live-action version of Pacman in New York City called PacManhattan while getting his Masters at NYU as well as a live-action version of Kaboom! for the 2010 Come Out and Play festival. Pete has designed many outdoor games that are played at summer camps around the country.

Ashley York is a mediamaker whose research interests include journalism, socially conscious media and digital activism. She has worked on Academy Award® nominated teams and served as a producer on documentary projects that have premiered at international film festivals as well as on HBO, Discovery International and the Sundance Channel. She has worked with award-winning filmmakers, including Mark Jonathan Harris, Fenton Bailey, Randy Barbato and Kirby Dick. Ashley holds a Master of Fine Arts from the University of Southern California's School of Cinematic Arts and a journalism degree from the University of Kentucky. She was a filmmaker in residence at the 2009 Working Film's Content + Intent Documentary Institute at MASS MoCA as well as an artist in residence at the 2008 Bay Area Video Coalition's Producer's Institute for New Media Technologies. She is presently adjunct faculty for the School of Cinematic Art's Institute for Multimedia Literacy.

José P. Zagal is an Assistant Professor at the College of Computing and Digital Media (CDM) at DePaul University. His research explores the development of frameworks for describing, analyzing, and understanding games from a critical perspective. He is also interested in supporting games literacy through the use of collaborative learning environments. His book on this topic, Ludoliteracy: Defining, Understanding, and Supporting Games Education, was published by ETC Press in 2010. Dr. Zagal is on the editorial boards of the International Journal of Gaming and Computer-Mediated Simulations and the Journal of the Canadian Gaming Studies Organization. He is also a member of the executive board of the Digital Games Research Association (DiGRA). José received his PhD in computer science from Georgia Institute of Technology in 2008, his M.Sc. in engineering sciences and a B.S. in industrial engineering from Pontificia Universidad Católica de Chile in 1999 and 1997.

Index

A

abandonware 110, 115, 116, 120
ableism 256
academic pedagogy 317
A Clockwork Orange 151, 152
activist games 253
adaptive 36, 37, 38, 40, 41, 43, 45, 46, 50, 52
Adaptive Educational Interactive Narrative
 System (AEINS) 208, 210, 212, 213,
 214, 215, 218, 219, 220, 221, 222, 223,
 224, 225, 226, 227, 228, 229, 230
add-on 110, 119
aesthetic distance 142, 143, 145, 146, 147,
 148, 149, 150, 155, 156
ageism 256
alternative play 128, 129
ambiguity 83, 89, 90, 93, 95
America's Army 83
Animal Crossing 203
anti-oppression 253, 254, 255, 256, 257, 258,
 259, 267, 268, 269, 270, 271
anti-oppression theory 259
anti-oppressive approach 254
anti-oppressive ethics 255, 257
anti-oppressive games 267, 269, 271
anti-oppressive principles 253, 254, 255, 257,
 258
anti-oppressive self-reflection 257
anti-racism 255
antiwar game 83, 84, 85, 86, 87, 89, 90, 91, 92,
 93, 94, 95
antiwar rhetoric 83, 84, 86, 89, 90
Artificial Insemination 286
Assisted Reproductive Technology (ART) 275,
 276, 277, 279, 285, 286, 288, 289

Atari Games v. Nintendo 112, 113
Attention Deficit Hyperactivity Disorder
 (ADHD) 193, 194, 199, 201, 206
Attention, Relevance, Confidence/Challenge,
 and Satisfaction/Success (ARCS) 211,
 220, 222, 231
avatar 98, 100, 101, 102, 103, 104, 107, 185,
 186
Ayiti: The Cost of Life 267, 268

B

BAT ILE 211
Batman 197
bio-ethical debate 276
bio-ethics 275
BioShock 39, 50, 54, 76, 79, 81
BioWare 72, 78, 79, 82
Black & White 41, 54
Blade Runner 40, 52
Blizzard v. BnetD 114
Blizzard v. Glider 119
Blizzard v. MDY 113
Boom Blox 148
Brain Age 200, 201
brain-training games 200
British Board of Film Classification (BBFC)
 142
Bully 161, 165

C

Calculations x 20 200
Call of Duty 84, 85
Cannon Fodder 83, 88, 89, 97
case study 19, 25